Unity in the Church
or
The Principle of Catholicism

Unity in the Church
or
The Principle of Catholicism

Presented
in the Spirit of the Church Fathers
of the First Three Centuries

by
Johann Adam Möhler

edited and translated with an introduction by
Peter C. Erb

The Catholic University of America Press
Washington, D.C.

The paper used in this publication meets the minimum requirements of American National Standards for Information Science—Permanence of Paper for Printed Library materials, ANSI Z39.48-1984.

Library of Congress Cataloging-in-Publication Data

Möhler, Johann Adam, 1796-1838.
    [Einheit in der Kirche. English]
    Unity in the church, or, The principle of Catholicism: presented in the spirit of the Church Fathers of the first three centuries / by Johann Adam Möhler ; edited and translated, with an introduction by Peter C. Erb.
       p. cm.
    Includes bibliographical references and index.
    1. Church—Unity. 2. Church—Catholicity. 3. Catholic Church—Doctrines. I. Erb, Peter C., 1943- . II. Title.
    BX1746.M6313
    1995 262'.72—dc20
    95-7264
    ISBN 0-8132-0621-9

To

Betty, Catharine, and Suzanne

Contents

Introduction

In September 1825 Johann Adam Möhler (1796-1838), a twenty-nine-year-old lecturer in Church history, patristics, and canon law at the Catholic seminary in Tübingen, completed his first major publication, *Unity in the Church, or, the Principle of Catholicism Presented in the Spirit of the Church Fathers of the First Three Centuries*,[a] and sent a copy of the volume to his close friend, Joseph Lipp. His cover letter indicates how much significance the publication had for him. The volume reflected, he insisted, not only the thought and practice of the early Church, but his personal theological position:

> It has been long since you received anything from me; I now give you myself: the image of my most interior and characteristic being—the true portrayal of my view regarding Christianity, Christ, and our Church. You will find that I have changed much. Earlier you noted that there were many points over which I hesitated and others that I commented on without assurance. But if you could look into my innermost being, you would find my religio-Christian view completely changed. Earlier I had only the word, only the concept of Christ. I now have something quite different in me and an inner witness tells me that it is true, or at least that it will be true. A careful study of the Fathers has stirred up much in me. While undertaking it I discovered for the first time a living, fresh, full Christianity, and Christ desires that I do not leave fruitless that which he gave life to and awakened for his full defense.[b]

a. Johann Adam Möhler, *Die Einheit in der Kirche Oder das Prinzip des Katholizismus dargestellt im Geiste der Kirchenväter der ersten drei Jahrhunderte* (Tübingen: Heinrich Laupp, 1825).

b. For the text of this letter, see Stephan Lösch (hrsg.), *Johann Adam Möhler. Bd. 1: Gesammelte Aktenstücke und Briefe* (Munich: Josef Kösel & Friedrich Pustet, 1928), 251-52; The letter is reprinted in the anthology edited by Paul-Werner Scheele, *Johann Adam Möhler* (Graz: Styria, 1969), 85-86. Lipp (1795-1869) first met Möhler in 1813; after serving in various capacities in teaching positions and the pastorate he became bishop of Rottenburg in 1848 (see Lösch, 249).

1. The *Unity* as a Catholic Apologia

The excitement that Möhler exhibited on the appearance of the *Unity* had marked every stage of its composition. He wrote the book in two years, during which time he completely reconstructed a first and a second draft and then thrice revised his final version. The change in his "religio-Christian view, "as he described it to Lipp, may, in large part, have initially stimulated his writing, but, as is evident from the extensive revisions in each successive reworking and the sketchiness of the second section, this change was still ongoing when the piece went to press. Even in its final version the *Unity* remained a book in process. Möhler's discovery of "a living, fresh, full Christianity" continued, so much so in fact—so much did he wish not to "leave [it] fruitless" and to sustain a firm Christian apologetic—that the speed and change evident in this first of his many works extended throughout the few years that remained to him, such that at the close of his life he no longer considered this first work significant. In 1837, a mere twelve years after the *Unity*'s publication, and the year before he died, Möhler was visited by Johann (Beda) Weber (1798-1858), a Benedictine, who noted:

> When asked to give a full listing of his writings, he passed by his first work, *Unity in the Church*, in silence, and when reminded of it, he said: "I am not really eager to be reminded of this work. It is the work of an enthusiastic youth that proposes to speak about God, the Church, and the world. Much that is in it I can no longer hold to; it is not all properly digested or convincingly presented."[a]

Möhler's disparaging comments on the *Unity* are supported elsewhere, and those who protested its illicit second printing in 1843[b] were properly reflecting Möhler's mature view of the matter.[c] But to characterize Möhler's later position as his "mature" view is to misrepresent the situation. Möhler completed his *Unity* as he was

a. Beda Weber, "Möhler in Meran (1837)," in *Charakterbilder* (Frankfurt am Main, 1853), 3-18; quoted in Lösch, 511.

b. Johann Adam Möhler, *Die Einheit in der Kirche Oder das Prinzip des Katholizismus dargestellt im Geiste der Kirchenväter der ersten drei Jahrhunderte* (Tübingen, Vienna, and Prague: Heinrich Laupp, Braunmüller and Seidel, C. Gerold, and Haase Söhne, 1843).

c. For details, see Lösch, 498-500, 539-40.

facing his thirtieth year. He died at forty-two, and although he produced a mass of significant work in these years, the description of his *Unity* as an "early" composition is somewhat of a misnomer, considering the short length of his career. Certainly, by 1827 it no longer represented his developed theological position fully (indeed, he expressed reservations regarding it just a few months after its publication[d]), but all his work is best described as "occasional" and reflects his consideration of changing contemporary concerns. Nevertheless, the *Unity* deserves careful study both in itself and for its importance as a notable example of the early-nineteenth-century Catholic Awakening. It was the initial work out of which Möhler's concern with the theme of the unity of the Church, which remained strong throughout his life,[e] arose. In its two German editions and in its French translations,[f] moreover, the *Unity* continued to have an impact on Catholic authors well into the twentieth century,[g] and on

d. Möhler to Lipp, in Lösch, 254-55.

e. On the significance of the theme for Möhler, see Paul-Werner Scheele, *Einheit und Glaube: Johann Adam Möhlers Lehre von der Einheit der Kirche und ihre Bedeutung für die Glaubensbegründung* (Munich: Ferdinand Schöningh, 1964).

f. *De l'unité de l'église; Ou, Du principe du Catholicisme d'après l'esprit des Pères des trois premiers siècles*, trans. Ph[ilippe] Bernard (Tournai: Castermann, 1835). The translation was reprinted in Brussels by H. Remy in 1839 and again in the same year in Paris by Sagnier et Bray. Important for twentieth-century studies of Möhler (particularly since no English translation was ever done) was *L'unité dans l'église; Ou, Le principe du Catholicisme d'après l'esprit des Pères des trois premiers siècles de l'église*, trans. André de Lilienfeld, with an introduction by Pierre Chaillet (Paris: Les Éditions du Cerf, 1938), vol. 2 in the series *Unam Sanctam*. The Italian translation *Dell'unità della chiesa ossia principio del cattolicismo secondo lo spirito del padri dei primi tre secoli della chiesa* (Milan: Pirotta, 1841; 2d ed., 1858) also served in popularising Möhler's thought. The only other translation of the work has been into Flemish (*De eenheid in de kerk of hat principe van het katholicisme in den geest van de kerkvaders uit de eerste drie eeuwen*, trans. A.T.W. Bellemans, with an introduction by G[ustave] Thiels [Antwerp: Paul Brand Bussum, 1947]).

g. Perhaps the most direct impact on modern theology has been through the work of Karl Adam, Yves Congar, and members of the Tübingen School. Note also Renée Bedarida, "Le pere Pierre Chaillet: De la théologie de Moehler à la résistance," in P. Bolle and J. Godel, eds., *Spiritualité, théologie et résistance* (Grenoble: Presses universitaires, 1987), 49-61; the numerous articles in Hermann Tüchle, ed., *Die Eine Kirche: Zum Gedenken J.A. Möhlers, 1838-1938* (Paderborn: Ferdinand Schöningh, 1939); and Harald Wagner, "Johann Adam Möhler: Fakten und Überlegungen zu seiner Wirkungsgeschichte," *Catholica* 43 (1989): 195-208. Note as well Pablo Sicouly, "Yves Congar und Johann Adam Möhler: Ein theologisches Gespräch zwischen den Zeiten," *Catholica* 45 (1991): 36-43, and compare Walter Kasper, "Verständnis der Theologie damals und heute," in his *Glaube im Wandel der Geschichte* (Mainz: Matthias Grüne-

Catholics and Protestants alike who have been concerned with dialogue between the two communities following the publication of the author's *Symbolik oder Darstellung der dogmatischen Gegensätze der Katholiken und Protestanten nach ihren öffentlichen Bekenntnisschriften* in 1832.[h]

Primarily an apologist for Catholic principles, Möhler carried out a careful analysis of Protestant confessional statements, and in this sense he may be classed among the precursors of modern ecumenical discussions.[i] As Reinhold Rieger has pointed out, however, there are serious problems with describing Möhler as principally interested in reconciling differences between Protestants and Catholics.[j] That he was concerned to maintain close dialogue with Protestants cannot be questioned. In 1822, while at Göttingen on a study visit, he wrote:

---

wald, 1973), 9-38. Note also Möhler's importance for the nineteenth-century painter Lindner (Rudolf Reinhardt, "Johann Adam Möhler und die Konversion der Malerin Emilie Lindner: Ein unbekannter Brief aus Möhlers Münchener Zeit," *Theologische Quartalschrift* 151 [1971]: 264-68) and the modern convert Albert von Ruville (*Back to Holy Church: Experiences and Knowledge acquired by a Convert*, trans. G. Schoetensack [London: Longmans, Green, 1911], 28. General essays of interest include Philipp Funk, "Die geistige Gestalt Johann Adam Möhlers," *Hochland* 27 (1929): 96-110; Bernhard Hanssler, "Johann Adam Möhler—Theologe der Kirche," *Hochland* 35 (1938): 17-26, and Yves Congar, "Johann Adam Möhler, 1796-1838," *Theologische Quartalschrift* 150 (1970): 47-51. An interesting broader discussion of the theme of unity is taken up by Serge Bolshakoff, in *The Doctrine of the Unity of the Church in the Works of Khomyakov and Möhler* (London: SPCK, 1946).

h. The work went through a number of editions in Möhler's lifetime. See the critical edition *Symbolik oder Darstellung der dogmatischen Gegensätze der Katholiken und Protestanten nach ihren öffentlichen Bekenntnisschriften*, eingeleitet und kommentiert von Josef Rupert Geiselmann (Cologne and Olten: Hegner, 1958). See also John Adam Moehler, *Symbolism; Or, Exposition of the Doctrinal Differences between Catholics and Protestants, as Evidenced by Their Symbolical Writings*, 2 vols., trans. James Burton Robertson (London: Charles Dolman, 1843). The English translation went through seven editions prior to 1900.

i. In this regard, see Harald Wagner, "Das Amt vor dem Hintergrund der Diskussion um eine evangelisch-katholische Grunddifferenz" with a "Vorbemerkung J. A. Möhlers Darstellung der Ordination in 'Einheit,' 65," *Catholica* 40 (1986): 39-58; Heinrich Petri, "Katholizität in der Sicht Johann Adam Möhlers und ihre Bedeutung für den ökumenischen Dialog," *Catholica* 42 (1988): 92-107; and Hans Friedrich Geisser, "Die methodischen Prinzipien des Symbolikers Johann Adam Möhler: Ihre Brauchbarkeit im ökumenischen Dialog," *Theologische Quartalschrift* 168 (1988): 83-97. On the broader ecumenism, note the section originally written by Möhler for inclusion in the *Unity*, "On the Salvation of the Pagans," translated in Appendix 4.

j. Reinhold Rieger, "Johann Adam Möhler—Wegbereiter der Ökumene? Ein Topos im Licht neuer Texte," *Zeitschrift für Kirchengeschichte* 101 (1990): 267-86.

Twenty years ago there was little religious contention, but this, it seems to me, was the result of indifference. Consequently, I must interpret the present strife that has flared up between Catholics and Protestants as a result of the renewal of the religious life. However, those with whom one differs on matters of doctrine and against whom one defends oneself (since difference should be based on conviction), one ought to bear in love throughout life: this, it seems to me, is the behavior worthy of a Christian. That the Protestants bestir themselves is a proximation to Catholicism since it is a distancing from indifference. That Catholics answer is a proximation to Protestantism, a departure from spiritual slumber and religious-ecclesiastical death. When two opponents begin to talk together once again . . . a good step is taken toward reconciliation.[k]

Talk of reconciliation and love, however, does not negate frank discussion. Differences exist "on matters of doctrine" and one must "defend oneself (since difference should be based on conviction)." Möhler is an apologist from the beginning. Thus shortly after his visit to Göttingen, he moved on to Berlin, where he was deeply impressed by the work of Johann August Wilhelm Neander (1789-1850) and of Friedrich Schleiermacher (1768-1834), both of whom used organic images of the body to describe the Church.[l] The latter's appropriation of romanticism Möhler could never accept, but he was impressed and influenced by Schleiermacher's willingness to develop a defense of Christianity against its "cultured despisers" in their own language.[m]

Möhler was convinced that this new, dynamic, and no longer indifferent Protestantism, needed answering on its own terms, and immediately on his return to Tübingen in April 1823 he began to develop that answer. All his work at the time—his insistence that Catholic writers take up the new "scientific" historiography, his patristic studies, and his romantic concerns—is consistently directed

k. Möhler to Herbst (?) at Tübingen, October or November 1822, in Lösch, 72.

l. Note, as well, his comment on Neander: "In Berlin he knows no streets except those which lead to the university, and no person except his colleagues. But Origen, Tertullian, Augustine, Chrysostom, St. Bernard, the letters of Boniface, and many others, he knows by heart" (Möhler at Berlin to Messner at Rottenburg, January 30, 1823, in Lösch, 83-84).

m. Friedrich Schleiermacher, *On Religion: Speeches to Its Cultured Despisers*, trans. John Oman (New York: Harper and Row, 1958).

by his interest in supporting Catholic theology against Protestantism and its secular romantic compeers, and two years later resulted in *Unity in the Church*. Therefore, it is not surprising that in his letter to Lipp when his book was published he noted that in his study of the early Church he had "discovered for the first time a living, fresh, full Christianity, and Christ desires that I do not leave fruitless that which he gave life to and awakened *for his full defense*" (italics mine). This interest in defense, in developing a consistent Catholic apologetic in the context of modern values, lies at the heart of his work. Because of his concern with reconciliation, ecumenical dimensions are present in his work, but they arise not so much out of that concern as in his vigorous defense of central Catholic values. It was the way in which Möhler formulated these values, not his evaluation of Protestant confessional statements, that attracted his most significant Protestant defenders.[n]

2. Personal Faith and the Historical Faith of the Church

Möhler's blending of his own religious stance and his reading of early Church history as outlined in the letter to Lipp was deliberate. Early, in his lectures on Church history of 1823, he had raised the issue of the relationship between historical study and faith,[a] and only a short time before his *Unity* appeared, in an unpublished draft preface, he described his initial motivations for writing the book.[b] In it he noted three issues that particularly troubled him: the "contradictory explanations" given to the history of the Church, the resulting inevitability he felt of arriving at anything other than a "subjective view" of history, and the impossibility of arriving at a "historical [*historische*] construction." The latter issue he struggled with from two perspectives, that of gaining an underlying "higher idea that would contain and penetrate the whole of history," an understanding of "what is firm and enduring," and thereby of attaining a historical point from which to begin and on which to interpret developments.

n. See below, Introduction, section 10.

a. See below, "Purpose of the Study of Church History" in Appendix 2, "Selections from Lectures on Church History [1823]."

b. For the Preface and the quotations cited from it which follow, see "Endnotes to Preface and Part 1, Chapter 1," note 2.

To resolve his difficulties, Möhler tells his reader, he turned to a study of the early Church for a "firm historical center" "out of which everything developed," and he studied the primary materials related to it on his own, thereby avoiding "contradictory explanations" as exhibited in secondary studies. He admits, however, that he could not avoid his own "subjective view of the matter." According to Goethe's *Faust*, any historian such as Möhler who tries to describe the spirit of the Ante-Nicene Church describes his "own spirit, in which the times mirror themselves" (1:577-79). Because of this problem, Möhler contends, he has cited sources extensively, but he does not deny the charge: "The times treated by a historian must reflect themselves in that historian." Christianity is life, not opinion, and as life it is integrated over the whole of its history. As life, as well, it can only be understood through living:

> The person who now lives in the Church and truly lives in her will also live in her earliest era and understand her, and the person who does not live in the Church of the present will not live in the earliest Church and will not understand her because both are one and the same. Above all, it must be one's own spirit in which the times not only mirror themselves but live.

"[W]ill we not thus carry ourselves into the history of Church?" Möhler asks rhetorically. Without any doubt this will occur, but for Möhler the result is not problematic:

> The person who has come from the Church carries nothing foreign back into her. The Church has nursed such a person and placed an image of her being and essence in that person. She first set herself in the individual, and it is this that the individual sets forth again. Thus the true image of the Church must be given again. It is she who writes about herself, who describes her essence. Who can know it better than she?

The danger of "reading oneself" into the text is therefore overcome. Believer and community are of the same life and of the same spirit, reflecting the common bounty in one another. Any proposal for a "scientific" description of a historical era from a point outside the historical process is therefore rejected:

One can easily see that I do not think much of the proposition that to write a history one must be without religion, native land, and the like. Insofar as this means that a historian must be unbiased, I agree, but one can be unbiased only if one has religion, and this must be a specific religion since there are no unspecific ones.

Persons from outside the Church cannot describe her any more than persons who have not grasped the spirit of the ancient Greeks can describe Greek culture. Nor, Möhler goes on to say in a clear attack on Protestantism, can those describe an earlier era of the Church properly who suppose that the Church does not contain an integrated life and spirit, or that her original state was for a time lost and then had to be discovered again. "A Catholic will thus write history as a Catholic and a Protestant as a Protestant. The Protestant will everywhere discover self, that is, the party that arose in the sixteenth century, or will cast aside everything that is not of this party."

The hermeneutical problems that result from an approach such as Möhler's are immense if one presupposes that he is studying the early Church to write a scientifically accurate account of the period he has chosen to investigate and thus to establish a historically defensible position on which to build an apologetics. Möhler's approach to apologetics lies in a different direction; in the human sciences (if I may anachronistically so describe his position) "truth" is to be sought through self-reflection on the historical tradition living in the individual believer and not in the dead letters of the past. As a search for clarification, as the life of faith ever seeking a deeper understanding of its own existence, such self-reflection will, since it is imperfect, regularly result in imperfect descriptions of itself, of the life in the individual historian, and of the institution and individuals who shared the same life in the past as described by that historian:

> Anyone who argues that the study of the early Church was useless for my purpose, that what I first was to clarify, I must have already clarified so as to write what I wrote, is correct in a certain sense. But through this history I first brought to consciousness what I already carried in me without clear consciousness—therefore, the indecision and the possibility of self-contradiction.

One need not fear, however, that indecision and self-contradiction will be the end result. As the title of the work indicates, the *Unity* is, in the first place, not properly speaking a historical study. It is rather a theological treatise on the unity of the Church, a theme that in itself is the principle of Catholicism. Möhler was led to a direct living experience of this principle residing in himself by his study of the early Church, but, as he noted in his earlier comment, although the study of history brings to consciousness what the historian has within in concept, there remains "indecision and the possibility of self-contradiction" in the process. Nevertheless, the inner witness of the Spirit testifies to the inner person that what has been discovered is true "or at least that *it will be* true," since the life of the Church continues to develop to the fulfillment of the Kingdom of God at the close of time.[c]

3. The Argument of the Unity and the Nature of Romanticism

Church history, viewed in this manner, is a primary source for faith as it seeks understanding. Accordingly, believer-historians will find themselves, not only providing material for dogmatic and moral theologians, but also offering directives for growth in holiness to fellow believers. Not surprisingly, therefore, Möhler begins his *Unity* with the third person of the Trinity, the Spirit, rather than with the second or the first person. Thus posited on an image of the Church as an organic life form, the work is divided into two parts, the first section describing the inner life or spirit of the Church, the second more briefly depicting the external visible form of the Church's body.

The first section is the largest and most significant. The unity of the exterior Church is the direct result of the interior mystical unity of the Church, communicated and maintained by the Holy Spirit present in each individual Christian and in the Christian community as a whole. From humanity's point of view, the Spirit is first in the process of salvation. It leads the individual to the Son, and the Son then leads the individual to the Father. The Holy Spirit's communication is, then, the basis of an individual's acceptance of Christianity. Faith has its source in the Holy Spirit and unity follows. The Spirit

c. In his 1826 and 1827 lectures on Church history, Möhler works out the implications of his position in greater detail. See, Appendix 5, first three sections.

unites all believers into a spiritual community, the body of Christ, a community that is prior to any individual and extends beyond that individual in time and space.

Through the Christian community the Spirit communicates itself to those who are not yet believers. Previous to the Christian era this Spirit was present, but only sporadically so. Thereafter, through the love that is engendered in believers in the Church, Christ is given, and believers are fed and nourished. The Church thus continues through history from the apostles in a visible form. Only in the life reigning in the Church, in the love of the community, does one become conscious of Christ, first as a concept and then increasingly as a living power in the believer's life.

In his initial discussion of the individual's consciousness of Christ Möhler links a number of theological topics together. In faith the believer receives a direct imprint of "the holy life extended forth in the Church," the love of Christ. By contemplation of this love the individual appropriates that communal experience as his or her own, develops Christian knowledge, and expresses himself or herself in acts of holiness. The love of Christ, the life and spirit of the community, the life of the individual in faith accepting that larger life, and trust, building upon and through it, are in this way all united as tightly as the visible and invisible aspects of the Church are.

Having outlined the nature of this mystical unity in general, Möhler goes on to treat intellectual unity. Just as life precedes structure and community, Christian doctrine is the external conceptual expression of the Christian Spirit; the Spirit and the life communicated by the Spirit precede doctrine. Christianity extends itself by the living word that communicates itself as a living tradition through external tradition. As a result, external tradition, the written word, cannot be understood without the Spirit, which provides each believer with a center from which to interpret the whole of history, the key with which to unlock "catholic" history, and without which historical facts remain merely broken pieces of a supposed whole.

Tradition and Scripture, internal and external, belong together and are not to be separated. The letters of Scripture did not come before their inspiration, and the Spirit from which they do come is thus necessary to interpret them. Since that Spirit is a communal Spirit, to discover what true doctrine is the individual is directed to the totality of believers and to the developing tradition among them as a whole. Any individual premise must always be directed back to this whole and to the doctrine preserved through time and the succession of bishops.

Although Möhler uses the term "development" with regularity in his *Unity*, he does not treat the concept in detail in this study. For him all tradition is firmly bound to the initial revelation, but he offers no clear analysis of the exact nature of the unity between earlier and later traditions.[a] The principle of unity here too serves as a base for his explanation of development, as is well exemplified in his pun on *Überzeugen*, which in the first instance in which it appears[b] is hyphenated after the "Über" to link together "conviction," the primary meaning of the term, with "witness" (*bezeugen*). It may also be that in his use of *Überzeugen* he is playing or expects his reader to play with a false root in the word, *erzeugen* ("beget"), the biological term that he uses extensively throughout the book.

---

a. On Möhler's later views on the development of doctrine, see Josef Rupert Geiselmann, *Lebendiger Glaube aus geheiligter Überlieferung: Der Grundgedanke der Theologie Johann Adam Möhlers und der Katholischen Tübinger Schule* (2. Aufl.; Freiburg: Herder, 1966), 299-408; Hans Geisser, *Glaubenseinheit und Lehrentwicklung bei Johann Adam Möhler* (Göttingen: Vandenhoeck & Ruprecht, 1971); Stephan Lösch, "Möhler und die Lehre von der Entwicklung des Dogmas," *Theologische Quartalschrift* 99 (1917-1918): 28-59, 129-52; A. Minon, "L'attitude de Jean Adam Möhler dans la question du dévelopement du dogma," *Ephemerides Louvanienses* 16 (1939): 328-84; and G. Voss, "Johann Adam Möhler and the Development of Dogma," *Theological Studies* 4 (1943): 420-44. A summary of Möhler's treatment of tradition is found in Josef Rupert Geiselmann, *The Meaning of Tradition*, trans. W.J. O'Hara (New York: Herder and Herder, 1966), 52-72, Yves M.-J. Congar, *Tradition and Traditions: A Historical and Theological Survey*, trans. Michael Naseby and Thomas Rainborough (London: Burns & Oates, 1966), 189-96; Henry Raphael Nienaltowski, *Johann Adam Möhler's Theory of Doctrinal Development: Its Genesis and Formulation* (S.T.D. dissertation, The Catholic University of America, 1959 [A lengthy abstract was published in "The Catholic University of America Studies in Sacred Theology," no. 113 (Washington: The Catholic University of America Press, 1959)]); and Martin Gritz, "Kirchengeschichte als Geschichte des Christenthums: Anmerkungen zur Konzeption eines christlichen Geschichtsbildes bei Johann Adam Möhler," *Zeitschrift für Kirchengeschichte* 101 (1990): 249-65. Also note Walter Kasper, *Die Lehre von der Tradition in der Römischen Schule* (Freiburg: Herder, 1962), passim; Josef Rupert Geiselmann, *Die Lebendige Überlieferung als Norm des christlichen Glaubens: Die apostolische Tradition in der Form der kirchlichen Verkündigung—der Formalprinzip des Katholizismus dargestellt im Geiste der Traditionslehre von Joh. E. Kuhn* (Freiburg: Herder, 1959); and Herbert Hammans, *Die neuen Katholischen Erklärungen der Dogmenentwicklung* (Essen: Ludgerus-Verlag Hubert Wingen, 1965), 30ff. A brief general treatment of the question of development is available in Aidan Nichols, *From Newman to Congar: The Idea of Doctrinal Development from the Victorians to the Second Vatican Council* (Edinburgh: T.&T. Clark, 1990).

b. *Unity*, section 3.

Conviction, then, is directly related to tradition; it is "begotten" when an earlier "witness" (*bezeugen*) is passed "over" (*über*) to a later one in a unity established between them. Scripture is thus the first member of the written tradition and is at the same time created out of that tradition.[c]

Such an approach is opposed, Möhler holds, by heretics who are primarily egoistic in their orientation. For them the individual precedes the community, and unity is set aside. For heretics, the individual must seek truth according to the pattern that the individual alone establishes and must therefore be free from all faith commitments in that seeking. Centered as they are on the external, heretics make the biblical text the basic principle of their schools and develop rationalistic hermeneutical principles. Their program thus induces division in and separation from the main body, and splinters the unity of the Church.

Diversity need not always lead to disunity, however. In the final chapter of the Part I, Möhler takes up this theme, insisting that the unity of all believers in a whole does not necessitate loss of individual identity and a monolithic structure. Certainly, no knowledge of God comes through individual human understanding left to itself; such knowledge rests on revelation that is given in the community, but it is received by and in the many differing forms of ethnic and national culture as embraced within the community. As a result of this process, Christian customs are widely diverse, but the Church remains unified, since all true knowledge of God is rooted in a living faith that is the same for all. In the early Church, according to Möhler, speculations were allowed to develop in their own ways, provided that they did not do so beyond the constraint of the admonitions of fellow believers. In such circumstances antitheses necessarily arise, but these are not detrimental to a community. They function just as the male and female voices do in a harmonious choir. "Contradictions," however, a term Möhler chose late in his composition of the *Unity* to describe heresies, destroy the harmony.

Möhler's extensive attention to heretical schools in the later sections of Part I leads him directly in Part II of his *Unity* to examine the unity of the visible body of the Church. As the Catholic prin-

---

c. On Möhler's treatment of the topic of tradition and of Church history as a whole in the period immediately following his writing of the *Unity*, see Appendices 5 and 6, "Introduction to the Lectures on Church History" and "Outline of the Lectures on Church History."

ciple, the principle of unity requires that the invisible life power of the Church be united to its visible form. The Church is the external living structure of the power of love that manifests itself externally. Heretical doctrines concerning an invisible Church as the true one must therefore be rejected. Such an invisible Church is a mere concept, not a reality, and persons who hold to it are not united in reality (in life) but only in thought.

To understand this visible unity, one must look first to the bishop. Gifts of the Spirit are distributed among clerics and laity and in this sense there is a general priesthood of Christians, but the communal centre is the bishop, the personal, concrete image of the community's love. Just as the love of the community within the diocese is expressed in the bishop, so neighboring dioceses are joined, and their bishops form a harmonious whole that in turn begets a center in the metropolitan. The individual bishop cannot undertake anything aside from this whole, and for this reason synods are held. In synodal unions the unity of the total Church is made manifest. That unity that was expressed in the apostles was continued in the bishops who were appointed by them. The total episcopate expresses its unity in the metropolitanate. The development of individual churches that cannot be independent of the unity of all, if unity is to be upheld.

The question remains whether full unity exists in the metropolitanates as a whole or whether the principle of unity requires that one move to a further point of contact, a primacy. In his final chapter, Möhler indicates that he once doubted the need to teach the doctrine of a primacy as a characteristic of the Catholic Church. As he reflected on the issue, however, he tells his readers, he came to understand that the principle of unity as expresses itself from the interior outward, and therefore must continue until it reaches it fullest form. The Church is visible and the unity of the episcopate and all believers must represent itself in one church and one bishop. This is the keystone of the system. A single bishop, the primate, is the center of the living unity of the whole Church.

Möhler was of course well aware of the many tensions that had existed throughout history and continued to exist in his own day between the hierarchy he had described in Part II of the *Unity* and the laity. Because he was particularly aware of the results of such tensions in the early sixteenth century, he turned in the concluding section of the book directly to the apologetic concerns that began his initial reflections and would be the primary focus of his scholarship thereafter.

There is no question, he notes, that in time the hierarchy found itself separated from the believers of which it was to be a reflection. A dialectical relationship was expected to exist between the two: in the first instance, the hierarchy was simply to reflect the common faith and love of all believers and to consider its actions in that context, but, at times when the larger body of believers drifted from their central goal, the hierarchy directed them to their proper end. In the fifteenth century, however, the hierarchy did not properly understand its role and function, and tragic division resulted. The Protestant Reformation that desired to correct the situation under- took its work externally, from outside the Church, and separated from it, although the greater part of the Church held firmly to Catholic views, developed and meant to be applied in very different times. In summation of the argument, Möhler, in what would be his characteristic fashion, remained firm in his opposition to any denial of *the* Catholic principle, that of the unity of the Church, and to all forms of separatism, while admitting the misconceptions that had existed within the Church, but that in his day, he perhaps over optimistically reflects, are all but overcome:

> The forming principle, the inner character of the constitution of the Church, was unclear to both parties, although much more *greatly* in the separated group than in the stiffly medieval group, which of course in Germany has now hardly any followers who think that that earlier condition is necessary for all times.[d]

As is immediately evident, Möhler's apologetic in the *Unity* at large and his uniting of the life of the believer-historian with that of the life spirit of the Church as a whole as a base for historical knowledge implies a romantic reader; his vocabulary and mode of argument follow accordingly. But one must take great care when speaking of Möhler's "romanticism" or even of the influence of romanticism on him.[e] Certainly, he represents a countermovement to eighteenth-century rationalism; as Carl Schmitt puts it, however,

---

d. *Unity*, section 71.

e. Note, for example, the way T.M. Schoof applies the term to Möhler and others in his *A Survey of Catholic Theology, 1800-1970* (Paramus, N.J.: Paulist Newman Press, 1970), 25ff.

"[T]here were many such countermovements. They were quite diverse, and it would be superficial to call romantic everything which does not qualify as modern rationalism."[f]

His organicistic hermeneutics, for example, appears initially to reflect a strictly romantic subjectivism. But Möhler is not a subjectivist. To define him as such is to emphasize his understanding of the life of the Spirit in the believer-historian without reading it fully within that believer's obedient life within the inclusive Spirit of the Church and to ignore Möhler's insistence on the unity of that Spirit with visible, historical, theological, and ecclesiastical structures. The individual is formed by the community, which is greater than the sum of its parts. The study of Church history, Möhler states in his 1823 lectures,[g] "cannot be used as a means to something else," particularly to serve individual constructions of truth. "We reiterate the events of this history ideally," he continues, "so as to tell of the temporal works of Christ and his Spirit with pure joy and to have an overview of these and to learn to know how he is the one in whom human beings are awakened." For the believer, history is "a school of piety and virtue," and for the theologian it provides "a historical consciousness of the basis and consciousness of the Church whose spiritual potential the theologian particularly represents."

In his lectures on Church history of 1826 and 1827 the concrete, external forms of the Spirit are once again considered primary. There he initially reviews Church history objectively ("Objectively considered, history is the spiritual life of humanity developing and establishing itself in time under the direction of Providence"[h]) and subjectively ("Subjectively it is the ideal reconstruction, the knowledge concerning the development of that spiritual life of humanity"). As objective it is realization; as subjective it is knowledge concerning that realization. In both cases the humanity that is spoken of ("the human person") is a single unity of humanity as a totality, not an autonomous individual subjective will, responsible to nothing but its own possibility, treating, as Schmitt describes the romantic spirit,[i] each passing moment as an occasion for ironic displacement[j] under

---

f. Carl Schmitt, *Political Romanticism*, trans. Guy Oakes (Cambridge, Mass.: MIT Press, 1986), 53.

g. See Appendix 2.

h. See Appendix 5.

i. Schmitt, 161.

j. On the romantic use of irony, see Jack Forstman, *A Romantic Triangle: Schleier-*

its own directive and never passing beyond that directive. For Möhler, such a spirit, whether romantic, rational, or Protestant, was best summarized under the generic term "Gnostic."[k] And as Gnostic, he opposed it, since in every Gnostic, in every heretic, as

> [i]n every Romantic, we can find examples of anarchistic self-confidence as well as an excessive need for sociability. . . . An emotion that does not transcend the limits of the subjective cannot be the foundation of a community. The intoxication of sociability is not a basis of a lasting association. Irony and intrigue are not points of social crystallization; and no societal order can be established on the basis of the need not to be alone but rather to be suspended in the dynamic of an animated conversation. This is because no society can discover an order without a concept of what is normal and what is right.[l]

4. Möhler's Early Life and Study

Möhler was born on May 6, 1796, at Ingersheim on the Tauber, into an innkeeper's family, and at age twelve he was sent to the Latin school in the nearby town of Mergentheim.[a] In spite of working as

---

macher and Early German Romanticism (Missoula, Mont.: Scholars Press, 1977), 1-33.

k. Cf. the similar use of the term by Möhler's later Protestant opponent at Tübingen, Ferdinand Christian Baur (*Die christliche Gnosis, oder die Religionsphilosophie in ihrer geschichtlichen Entwicklung* [Tübingen: C.F. Osiander, 1835]), and in the work of contemporary writers, above all Eric Voegelin (see, for example, his *Science, Politics, and Gnosticism* [Chicago: Henry Regnery, 1968]).

l. Schmitt, 161.

a. For biographical studies of Möhler, see, in addition to the extensive materials gathered in Lösch, Hervé Savon, *Johann Adam Möhler: The Father of Modern Theology*, trans. Charles McGrath (Glenn Rock, N.J.: Paulist Press, 1966); Paul-Werner Scheele, "Johann Adam Moehler," in Heinrich Fries and Georg Schwaiger, eds., *Katholische Theologen Deutschlands im 19. Jahrhundert*, 3 vols. (Munich: Kösel, 1975), 2: 70-98; Edmond Vermeil, *Jean-Adam Möhler et l'école catholique de Tubingue (1815-1840): Étude sur la théologie romantique en Wurtemberg et les origenes germaniques du modernisme* (Paris: Librairie Armand Colin, 1913); the introduction by Chaillet in the Lilienfeld French translation of *L'unité*; and the memoir in Moehler, *Symbolism*, translated with a memoir of the author by Robertson, 1:xxvii-cxxiv. A full bibliography of Möhler's work is available in *Verzeichnis der gedruckten Arbeiten Johann Adam Möhler's (1796-1838)* Aus dem Nachlass Stefan Lösch (*1966) Unter Mitarbeit von Jochen Köhler und Carola Zimmermann . . . herausgegeben von Rudolf Reinhardt. The bibliography is printed as an addendum to Georg Schwaiger, ed., *Kirche und Theologie im 19. Jahrhundert*

a baker each morning before classes, he did well in the local school, and in 1813 entered the Lyceum at Ellwangen in philosophy. Two years later he began his study of theology in the university in the same city, and in 1817 he moved with it to Tübingen where a Catholic faculty was established at the Wilhelmstift.[b] On November 8, 1818, he entered the seminary at Rottenburg and the following September 18th he was ordained.[c]

Following a year's work in a pastorate in Weilderstadt and Riedlingen, he returned to the Wilhelmstift in the fall of 1820 as a teacher in the hostel and early in 1821 was appointed as a tutor in Church history, teaching metaphysics in the winter semester,[d] and continuing his interest in canon law.[e] Möhler took up his responsibilities with dedication and zeal and, as was required, compiled

---

(Göttingen: Vandenhoeck und Ruprecht, 1975). R. W. Franklin, *Nineteenth-Century Churches: The History of a New Catholicism in Württemberg, England, and France* (New York: Garland, 1987); and Donald J. Dietrich, *The Goethezeit and the Metamorphosis of Catholic Theology in the Age of Idealism* (Bern: Peter D. Lang, 1979), place Möhler in a more general framework.

b. An overview of the early history of the Catholic faculty at Tübingen and Möhler's role in it is found in Rudolf Reinhardt, "Die katholisch-theologische Fakultät Tübingen im 19. Jahrhundert. Faktoren und Phasen ihrer Entwicklung," in Georg Schwaiger, ed., *Kirche und Theologie im 19. Jahrhundert*, 55-87, his *Tübinger Theologen und ihre Theologie: Quellen und Forschungen zur Geschichte der Katholisch-theologischen Fakultät Tübingen* (Tübingen: J.C.B. Mohr, 1977), and Werner Gross, *Das Wilhelmstift Tübingen, 1817-1869* (Tübingen: J.C.B. Mohr, 1978). Note as well the discussions in Karl Werner, *Geschichte der katholischen Theologie, seit dem Trienter Concil bis zur Gegenwart* (Munich: J.G. Cotta, 1866), 342-642; and in Edgar Hocedez, *Histoire de la théologie au XIXe siècle*, 3 vols. (Brussels and Paris: L'Edition Universelle et Desclée de Brouwer, 1948), 1:131-250. Martin Grabmann, *Die Geschichte der katholischen Theologie seit dem Ausgang der Väterzeit* (Freiburg im Breisgau, 1933), 227ff., is of limited use. See also Max Müller, "Die Tübinger Kath.-theologische Fakultät und die württembergische Regierung vom Weggang J.A. Möhlers (1835) bis zur Pensionierung J.S. Drey (1846)...." *Theologische Quartalschrift* 132 (1952): 22-45; 213-33. On the term, see Abraham Peter Kustermann, "'Katholische Tübinger Schule'. Beobachtungen zur Frühzeit eines theologiegeschichtlichen Begriffs," *Catholica* 36 (1982): 65-82.

c. The records of Möhler's early studies at Mergentheim and Ellwangen, as well as those related to his work in the seminary, are available in Lösch, 8-22. Brief reflections on his background are made in Helene Gollowitzer, "Drei Bäckerjungen," *Catholica* 23 (1969): 147-53.

d. Johann Adam Möhler, *Nachgelassene Schriften Nach den stenographischen Kopien von Stefan Lösch (1881-1966)*, Herausgegeben von Rudolf Reinhardt. Band I. *Vorlesungen, Entwürfe, Fragmente*, Übertragen, bearbeitet und eingeleitet von Reinhold Rieger (Paderborn: Bonifatius Druck, 1989), 54-60.

e. Correspondence relating to the appointment can be found in Lösch, 23-27.

thesis topics for the quarterly debates. Of these, two were on metaphysics (January 10, 1821; February 28, 1822), one on Church history (January 25, 1821), and one on canon law (June 28, 1821).[f] In the spring of 1822, following extensive discussions about the establishment of another chair in the Catholic theological faculty, he was offered the position in Church history "and related disciplines," among which, on the requirements of the State office, was canon law.[g]

At the Wilhelmstift, as at Ellwangen earlier, Möhler was heir to the wide-ranging Catholic renewal in Germany that had followed the French Revolution and the secularization of the Napoleonic era.[h] In 1803 the political map of continental Europe was restructured:

f. Lösch, 31-34. In accordance with legal stipulations, the theses were submitted to the General Vicariate; the first one on metaphysics resulted in a reprimand (Lösch, 35).

g. See Lösch, 35-47, 48-64, 99ff., for the continuing discussion over the chair. The relationship between the various governmental offices and the Tübingen Stift are outlined in Rudolf Reinhardt, "Quellen zur Geschichte der Katholisch-Theologischen Fakultät Tübingen," *Theologische Quartalschrift* 149 (1969): 369-91.

h. For an overview of this renewal, see Roger Aubert, "Die ekklesiologische Geographie im 19. Jahrhundert," in Jean Daniélou and Herbert Vorgrimler, eds., *Sentire Ecclesiam: Das Bewusstsein von der Kirche als gestaltende Kraft der Frömmigkeit* (Freiburg: Herder, 1961), 430-73; Josef Rupert Geiselmann, "Kirche und Frömmigkeit in den geistigen Bewegungen der ersten Hälfte des 19. Jahrhunderts, " in ibid., 474-530; and Roger Aubert and Rudolf Lill, "The Awakening of Catholic Vitality," in Roger Aubert et al., *The Church between Revolution and Restoration*, trans. Peter Becker (New York: Crossroad, 1989), 206-57. A more general historical overview is E.E.Y. Hales, *Revolution and Papacy* (Notre Dame, Ind.: University of Notre Dame Press, 1966). On the state of the Church prior to the Catholic Awakening, see Owen Chadwick, *The Popes and the European Revolution* (Oxford: Clarendon Press, 1981). Jonathan Sperber's *Popular Catholicism in Nineteenth-Century Germany* (Princeton: Princeton University Press, 1984) is more concerned with the latter half of the century, but his first chapter, "Popular Religious Life during the *Vormärz*," is useful.

For general histories of the period, see Roger Aubert et. al., *The Church in the Age of Liberalism*, trans. Peter Becker (New York: Crossroad, 1989) and Franz Schnabel, *Deutsche Geschichte im neunzehnten Jahrhundert*, 8 vols., (Freiburg im Breisgau: Herder, 1965), particularly the volumes entitled *Die Katholische Kirche in Deutschland, Die protestantischen Kirchen in Deutschland*, and *Die Erfahrungswissenschaft*. More directly concerned with the intellectual and religious background is Gerald McCool, *Catholic Theology in the Nineteenth Century* (New York: Seabury, 1977), the collection *Theologie in Aufbruch und Widerstreit: Die deutsche katholische Theologie im 19. Jahrhundert*, introduced and edited by Leo Scheffczyk (Bremen: Carl Schünemann, 1965), and Ninian Smart et al., eds., *Nineteenth-Century Religious Thought in the West*, 3 vols. (Cambridge: Cambridge University Press, 1985)—the latter publication includes a useful survey of Tübingen theologians by James Turstead Burtchell, "Drey, Möhler and the Catholic School of Tübingen" (2:111-40).

Church states were integrated into larger political (and for the most part Protestant) units; many cloisters, monasteries, and Catholic universities were suppressed; much Catholic property was destroyed or expropriated; and the earlier bases for Catholic political power in Germany were diminished accordingly. The situation facing German Catholics required them to give up their traditional views regarding the linkage between Church and state, and to develop new practices and theories to survive in "parity" with Protestant and nonaligned fellow citizens.

The new political reality and its subsequent social impact was only one aspect of the changed environment, however. In the last half of the eighteenth century, Catholic thinkers were adjusting to many Enlightenment doctrines, adopting attitudes, in varying degrees, either of opposition or appropriation, as they struggled with new views of rationality, authority, the human person, knowledge, the natural world, jurisprudence, social and political structures, and ethical theory.

The eighteenth-century inheritance lasted well into the nineteenth century in spite of the opposition to it by romantics and Idealistic philosophers, all of whom in turn required a response from Catholics.[i] Thus writers like Möhler continued a dialogue with other writers who held Deistic and naturalistic views of nature and revelation and developed their ideas in the context of both Enlightenment and romantic concerns. That the *Unity* can be read as a conversation with the Protestant theologian Friedrich Schleiermacher,[j] and is at many points influenced by Idealist philosophers

i. For general background, see Bernard M.G. Reardon, *Religion in the Age of Romanticism* (Cambridge: Cambridge University Press, 1985). Leonard Swidler in *Aufklärung Catholicism 1780-1850: Liturgical and Other Reforms in the Catholic Aufklärung* (Missoula, Mont.: Scholars Press, 1978), treats the period in a somewhat broad perspective. Note as well Alexander Dru, *The Contribution of German Catholicism* (New York: Hawthorn Books, 1963), 1-85. For a guide to Protestant thinkers during the period, see Claude Welch, *Protestant Thought in the Nineteenth Century*, 2 vols. (New Haven, Conn.: Yale University Press, 1972-1985).

j. Möhler was early acquainted with Schleiermacher. In its first issue the *Theologische Quartalschrift* reviewed the Protestant theologian's work ("Ueber die Schriften des Lukas. Ein kritischer Versuch von Dr. Fr. Schleiermacher. . . . Erster Theil. Berlin 1817," *Theologische Quartalschrift* 1 [1819]: 218-33) and the following year it published an analysis of the first volume of the journal, *Theologische Zeitschrift*, with which Schleiermacher was associated ("Theologische Zeitschrift. Herausgegeben von Dr. Friedr. Schleiermacher, Dr. W.M.L. de Wette, und Dr. Friedr. Lücke. Erstes Heft. Berlin 1819. . .," *Theologische Quartalschrift* 2 [1920]: 278-90).

such as F.W.J. Schelling (1775-1854)[k] is obvious, but it is equally true that Möhler's book was not written aside from his knowledge of such earlier Catholic ecclesiologists as Engelbert Klüpfel (1733-1811) and Patriz Benedict Zimmer (1752-1820),[l] the latter whom he quotes directly,[m] and the ongoing discussions around the career of Ignaz Heinrich von Wessenberg (1774-1860)[n] who with his mentor Karl Theodor von Dalberg (1744-1817), represented a Catholicism that fully appropriated Enlightenment ideals.

It would be false, however, to suggest that Catholicism merely responded to a changed situation. From 1780 to 1830 Catholicism in Germany was undergoing an internal renewal. At Münster a circle was early established around Princess Amalie Gallitzin (1748-1806), to which belonged the educators Bernard Overberg (1754-1826) and Franz von Fürstenberg (1729-1810), the Lutheran Pietist Count Friedrich Leopold zu Stohlberg (1750-1819) who was received into the Catholic Church in 1800, and the scholar Johann Theodor Katerkamp (1764-1834), who with Stohlberg did much to direct attention to the history of the early Church.

At Vienna, Clemens Maria Hofbauer (1751-1820) attended to historical, political, and other cultural questions of the day. Catholic political theory was of particular interest for a number of members of this circle, especially the widely known converts Friedrich Schlegel (1772-1829) and Adam Müller (1779-1829).[o] Müller's work may well have influenced Möhler's, particularly his theory of antithesis (Müller's *Die Lehre von Gegensatz* appeared in 1804) and its application in political theory. Political positions similar to those of Schlegel and Müller were held by the conservative Bern political scientist Karl Ludwig von Haller (1768-1854), another convert whose work was used by Möhler.

Political and institutional issues were at the forefront of Catholic renewal in Mainz, too. Elsewhere Catholic theology was being

---

k. Schelling's impact on Catholicism is well treated in Thomas F. O'Meara, *Romantic Idealism and Roman Catholicism: Schelling and the Theologians* (Notre Dame, Ind.: University of Notre Dame Press, 1982).

l. On Klüpfel and Zimmer, see Fries and Schwaiger, 1:35ff. and 94ff., respectively.

m. On Klüpfel's and Zimmer's ecclesiology and that of their contemporaries, see Philipp Schäfer, *Kirche und Vernunft: Die Kirche in der katholischen Theologie der Aufklärungszeit* (Munich: Max Hueber, 1974).

n. On Wessenberg, see Fries and Schwaiger, 1:189-204.

o. For a stimulating study of the political theories of Schlegel and Müller, see Carl Schmitt, *Political Romanticism*, passim.

revived by New Testament scholarship such as that of Johann Leonard Hug (1765-1846)[p] and the apologetics and general studies of men such as the legal scholar Ferdinand Walter (1794-1879), the theologians Franz Joseph Seber[q] and Johann Baptist Kastner,[r] and the biblical scholar Peter Gratz (1769-1849). At Munich, where Möhler would pass the final years of his life, historical and broader cultural studies shaped the direction of Catholic thought under such scholars as Ignaz von Döllinger (1799-1890), an avid supporter and editor of Möhler's work,[s] Franz von Baader (1765-1841),[t] and Joseph Görres (1776-1848), among others.[u]

Perhaps the most important figure in the Catholic Awakening, however, was Johann Michael Sailer (1751-1832).[v] Especially interested in moral and pastoral theology, Sailer was a popular and effective teacher at Dillingen, Ingolstadt, and Landshut before becoming bishop of Regensburg. Rejecting traditional Scholasticism, he directed his attention to the Bible, early Christianity, and mystical materials as the source of religious doctrine; emphasized "living Christianity" rather than the Church as an institution; was concerned with developing "inwardness" and piety; and opened discussions with Protestants (particularly Pietists). Sailer's influence was great at

---

p. On Hug, see Fries and Schwaiger, 1:253-73. Hug's study of the New Testament ("*Einleitung in die Schriften des neuen Testament* von Dr. Joh. Leonard Hug, Professor der Theol. an der Universität zu Freiburg in Breisgau, Groszherzogl. Badischen Geistl. Rath und des Königl. Würtembergischen Verdienstordens Ritter. Zweite verbesserte und vermehrte Auflage. i Th. 503 S. Stuttgart und Tübingen in der J. G. Cotta'schen Buchhandlung, 1821") which Möhler used while writing the *Unity*, was reviewed in *Theologische Quartalschrift* 4 (1822): 276ff., 461ff.

q. "*Ueber Religion und Theologie*. Eine allgemeine Grundlage der christlichen Theologie von Franz Joseph Seber, Doctor der Philosophie und Theologie, und öffentl. ordentl. Professor der Dogmatik und Moral and der katholisch-theologischen Facultät der Königl. Preussischen Universität Bonn. Köln, 1823. b. M. Du Mont-Schauberg. VIII. und 306 S. in 8," *Theologische Quartalschrift* 6 (1824): 452ff.

r. For a brief comment on Kastner and Möhler see Harald Wagner, "Möhler auf dem Weg zur 'Symbolik,'" *Catholica* 36 (1982): 15-30.

s. On Döllinger, see Fries and Schwaiger, 3:9-43. Note particularly his edition, *Dr. J. A. Möhler's . . . gesammelte Schriften und Aufsätze*, 2 vols. (Regensburg: G. Joseph Manz, 1839-1840).

t. On Baader, see Fries and Schwaiger, 1:274-302.

u. Note also the association of the Englishman Lord Acton with the Munich School. On Acton, see Gertrude Himmelfarb, *Lord Acton: A Study in Conscience and Politics* (Chicago: University of Chicago Press, 1962).

v. On Sailer, see Fries and Schwaiger, 1:55-93.

Lucern under Alois Gügler (1782-1827),[w] and Josef Widmer, one of Sailer's students who supported his master's supernaturalism against Enlightenment naturalism.

Of all the centers of renewal at the time, however, Tübingen has attracted the most attention.[x] Although never reflecting a single system of thought, members of the "Tübingen School" in the first thirty years of the nineteenth century nevertheless did share a number of similar approaches, best exhibited in the pages of their journal, the *Theologische Quartalschrift*, initiated in 1819. Like Sailer, Tübingen theologians maintained dialogue with the secular and Protestant intellectual movements of their day, took particular interest in the moral and pastoral renewal of the Church, emphasized living Christianity, and viewed the Church in organic terms rather than according to its structural and hierarchical aspects. Almost all took a special interest in liturgical reform, including the vernacularization of the liturgy. Some, like Johann Baptist Hirscher (1788-1865,)[y] directed attention to pastoral training and catechetical matters. Many were involved in the contemporary debates over mixed marriages, issues of Church and State, and struggles over the relationship between faith and reason sparked by the work of George Hermes (1775-1831).[z] Members of the school approached theology historically rather than philosophically; when they did take up philosophical questions, they tended to oppose Enlightenment rationalism and appropriate the work of Idealist philosophers, in particular Schelling.

Of first importance among the Tübingen group was Johann Sebastian von Drey (1777-1853), cofounder of the *Theologische*

w. On Gügler, see Fries and Schwaiger, 1:205-226.

x. The fullest study of the Tübingen School in the nineteenth century is Josef Rupert Geiselmann, *Die Katholische Tübinger Schule: Ihre theologische Eigenart* (Freiburg: Herder, 1964). Among the most significant members of the school in the generation immediately following Möhler, note the work of Franz Anton Staudenmaier (1800-1856), Johannes Evangelist von Kuhn (1806-1887), Karl Josef von Hefele (1809-1893), and Martin Joseph Mack (1805-1885). On the first three, see biographies in Fries and Schwaiger, 2:99-211. For a list of Tübingen theologians, see Josef Rief and Max Seckler, "Eine Liste der Tübinger," *Theologische Quartalschrift* 150 (1970): 177-86.

y. On Hirscher, see Fries and Schwaiger, 2:40-69.

z. On Hermes, see Fries and Schwaiger, 1:303-22. A useful brief introduction with a collection of texts, including works by Möhler, is available in Joseph Fitzer, *Romance and the Rock: Nineteenth-Century Catholics on Faith and Reason* (Minneapolis, Minn.: Fortress Press, 1989).

Quartalschrift and a formative force in the school as a whole.[aa] Following theological studies at Augsburg and Pfaffenhausen, Drey was ordained in 1801 and taught for a decade in a secondary school before his appointment as professor of apologetics and dogma at Ellwangen in 1812. Making use of the philosophy of Schelling, Drey interpreted Creation as the first revelation, and thereby was able to develop an organic view of history centered on the idea of the Kingdom of God as developing throughout human history and reaching its fullest expression in the history of the Christian Church. Any turn from accepting the revelatory activity of God was, according to Drey, a rejection of the Kingdom and of a share in its development: "The earliest period of Christianity remains its primary form according to which the exterior form for the Church and ecclesiastical forms can only slowly advance."[bb] But advance they do, and Drey was primarily concerned with the whole Church throughout the whole of time. Placing full emphasis on the historical life of the Church and not merely its dogmatic interests, Drey directed attention to the sacramental and liturgical life of the Church, and understood theology as serving the whole community of believers. It was Drey, perhaps more than any other Tübingen theologian of the day, who stimulated the young Möhler's work at the time he was writing the *Unity*.

5. The Study Trip of 1822-1823

Möhler was designated Privatdozent in Church history at Tübingen on September 10, 1822, and, as was then the custom, he was directed to prepare himself for the position by undertaking a "literary journey to acquaint himself with the primary aids for the study of history and Church history in particular, the most useful methods for its study, and the chief scholars in the area."[a] On September 21 Hirscher, dean of the faculty, outlined a suggested travel plan that

aa. On Drey, see Fries and Schwaiger, 2:9-39, Wayne L. Fehr, *The Birth of the Catholic Tübingen School: The Dogmatics of Johann Sebastian Drey* (Chico, Calif.: Scholars Press, 1981), and Bradford E. Hinze, *Narrating History, Developing Doctrine* (Atlanta, Ga.: Scholars Press, 1993).

bb. Drey, quoted in Geiselmann, *Geist*, 126.

a. For full details, see Lösch, 67-68. Additional letters related to the matter are available in Lösch, 52ff. A review of the study tour is available in Rudolf Padberg, "Johann Adam Möhlers 'Literarische' Reise 1822/23," *Catholica* 42 (1988): 108-18.

he submitted to the Royal Council on the following day. In particular the faculty wished Möhler to visit Göttingen and Breslau to investigate the libraries in those areas and to attend the lectures of the historian Gottlieb Jacob Planck (1751-1833), who had studied and taught at the Protestant Seminary in Tübingen before taking up a position at Stuttgart and then at Göttingen in 1784,[b] K.F. Stäudlin (1761-1826),[c] and A. Heeren (1760-1842),[d] to acquaint himself above all with the Catholic theological faculties. There appears to have been no expectation that he undertake any detailed study since his directives were that, whenever possible, he visit other institutions of higher learning, including: Würzburg, Giessen, Halle, Leipzig, Prague, Landshut, the Collegium Carolinum in Braunschweig, the Francke institutions in Halle, the "Saxon schools," and philological seminars. He was to undertake the journey as soon as possible and to report back "from time to time" to the faculty.

Möhler's "literary journey" established the direction his later work would follow. In the few months in which he traveled, he contacted directly and came to appreciate the revived Protestant theology, then aggressively confronting the cultural and philosophical theories that followed the publication of Kant's *Critique of Pure Reason* and the work of Fichte, Schelling, and Hegel, and which was at the same time developing and appropriating the new spirit of German scientific scholarship for its own ends, particularly in the study of Church history.

The first of Möhler's reports was sent from Göttingen on October 30, where he had arrived ten days earlier.[e] By that time he had

b. See Lösch, 271-75. On Planck's work, see Michael A. Lipps, *Dogmengeschichte als Dogmenkritik: Die Anfänge der Dogmensgeschichtsschreibung in der Zeit der Spätaufklärung* (Bern: Peter Lang, 1983), 42-65, and passim.

c. Stäudlin had been professor of theology at Göttingen since 1790 and was particularly interested in history. With H.G. Tschirner of Leipzig and J.S. Vater of Halle, Stäudlin began publication of *Kirchenhistorisches Archiv* in 1823 (Halle, 1823-1826), discussed by Möhler in *Theologische Quartalschrift* 11 (1829): 325ff.

d. Heeren had held the position of professor of world history at Göttingen since 1787.

e. Lösch, 68-70. Only one additional report came to the faculty, dated February 20, 1823 (Lösch, 85-90). Information regarding Möhler's trip comes to us through letters he wrote to his uncle, Philipp Joseph von Messner (1763-1835), the general counsellor for the vicariate in Rottenburg from 1817 to 1828 and who in large part paid the costs of the study tour (see Möhler in Munich to his brother, Adam, in Munich, June 24, 1835, in Lösch, 395-96). In a letter to Messner from Berlin on January 30, 1823, Möhler refers specifically to the travel plan as Messner's ("according to your plan"; Lösch, 83).

already visited Würzburg, where he remained only briefly since he was already well acquainted with the professors; had gone to Bamberg (where he met Friedrich Brenner [1784-1848], professor of dogmatics in the lyceum[f]); to Jena;[g] and finally to Leipzig, where he arrived in the midst of the Michaelmas celebrations.[h] At Halle, unfortunately, school was not in session, and he could not see the education program in action at firsthand, but he did speak with a number of individuals, including the well-known Hebraist W. Genesius (1786-1842).[i]

When he reached Göttingen, Möhler was able to direct closer attention to his study. The weather was excellent and he had access to the university library,[j] where, he notes, the theological collection, "particularly patristics," was excellent.[k] What impressed him even more was the energy with which the librarians sought out works he wanted that the library did not possess, even those of Catholic theologians.

There were some initial frustrations at Göttingen: Möhler had wished to attend Hugo's[l] lectures on institutions but the jurist

f. See Gerhard Förch, *Theologie als Darstellung der Geschichte in der Idee: Zum Theologiebegriff Friedrich Brenners, 1784-1848* (Würzburg: Echter Verlag, 1980).

g. Here he consulted with Baumgarten-Crusius, Luden, Gabler, and others. A professor of dogmatics and the history of dogma, L. Fr. O. Baumgarten Crusius (1788-1843) had been at Jena since 1812. Heinrich Luden (1780-1847) is the only professor of history whom Möhler mentions to this point. J. Ph. Gabler (1753-1826) was professor of exegesis.

h. First among these was H.G. Tschirner (1778-1828), a professor of theology. At Leipzig Möhler also met with the prolific philosopher W. Tr. Krug (1770-1842) whose work he would later review (see *Theologische Quartalschrift* 9 [1827]: 77). Tschirner and Krug had left Leipzig before Möhler's arrival since, rumor had it, they feared Catholic attacks on them during Michaelmas celebration (Lösch, 71), but they returned before he left. In addition he consulted with a student of Semitic languages, E.F.K. Rosenmüller (1763-1835) and the classical philologist and rhetorician G. Hermann (1772-1848).

i. Genesius was professor of theology at Halle. Möhler also met with A. H. Niemeier (1754-1828), professor of theology, inspector of the Francke Paedagogium, and chancellor of the university; E. Bernhardt (1782-1831), a teacher at the school; and the theologians G. Ch. Knapp (1758-1825), J.A.L. Wegschneider (1771-1849), and J.S. Vater (1771-1826), who was also a Semiticist.

j. The librarian Jeremias David Reuss (1774-1837) had been at the Universitätsbibliothek in Tübingen until 1782, after which he became the chief librarian at Göttingen.

k. Lösch, 73.

l. G. Hugo (1764-1844) had been professor of law at Göttingen since 1788 and had a particular interest in legal history.

canceled them in order to devote more energy to publication. In other cases there were conflicts in the schedule, forcing Möhler to take up the tedious but not difficult task of studying legal matters on his own. But Planck's lectures on church history more than compensated for the disappointment. Möhler reported:

> I attend [the lectures] regularly . . . and sit in amazement before Planck: his great learning, striking collection of the best data, and splendid assembling and ordering of facts along with a practical development of his subject often leads me to reflection and stimulates an uncommon seriousness in me. His lectures teach me what it is properly to teach Church history; I count this as the greatest victory. He brings in highly significant material of which I had never or only briefly heard, and he treats it in the nonpartisan manner and with the discretion for which he is especially noted. Private discussions with him are especially instructive.[m]

Stäudlin was less impressive. Narrower in scope and more pragmatically treated, the lectures nevertheless shared with Planck's a nonpartisan approach. Neither was a pleasing lecturer: Stäudlin spoke in a tedious monotone, and Planck had an especially annoying habit of gurgling when he reached for a breath; "Both read their notebooks word for word."[n] Möhler also attended Heeren's lectures, but he makes no comment on them.[o] He was especially struck by the jurist K. Friedrich Eichhorn (1781-1854),[p] a friendly person who attracted over three hundred students to each of his lectures,[q] offered two lecture series each term, and thus drew an addition to

m. Möhler to Messner at Rottenburg, November 1822, in Lösch, 74.

n. Möhler to Messner at Rottenburg, November 1822, in Lösch, 75.

o. In addition he attended the exegetical lectures of J.G. Eichhorn (1752-1827), professor of Semitic languages since 1788, and those of D.J. Pott (1760-1738), professor of New Testament exegesis since 1810. Möhler also attended philological lectures and seminars given by Christoph Wilhelm Mitscherlich (1760-1854), Ludolf Dissen (1784-1837), and Karl Ottfried Müller (1797-1840)—all professors of classics (see Lösch, 85-86).

p. Eichhorn had been a professor of law at Göttingen from 1810 to 1832, when he took up the same position in Berlin. Möhler attended Eichhorn's lectures, as he had hoped to attend Hugo's, since he was designated to teach canon law at Tübingen on his return (cf. Möhler to Messner at Rottenburg, November 1822, in Lösch, 77).

q. Möhler attended those on the history of law and on German state history and similar lectures by Friedrich Saalfeld (1785-1834), professor of history (Lösch, 85).

his salary, since the custom was for each person attending a lecture series to offer the lecturer a gratuity.

It may be that Eichhorn needed the additional money to finance his social life. It was the custom at Göttingen to invite guests continually and to serve them elaborate meals. Möhler regularly received invitations and had to buy new clothes to keep with local customs; the Göttingen theologians were certainly much gayer than the Tübingen Protestants: even dull Stäudlin gave *thées dansants* every winter.[r] At the time Möhler was also associating with several former schoolmates and others from Tübingen who were then at Göttingen.[s] Nevertheless, his academic interests remained foremost: inspired by the scholarship around him, he started a monograph on the beginnings of Christianity in south Germany, a project that he asked his Tübingen correspondent to keep secret and which he never completed.[t]

Remaining at Göttingen over the Christmas vacation, he left on the twenty-four-hour trip to Braunschweig in the bitter cold of January 1, 1823. There he was introduced to the program of the Collegium Carolinum by Julius Levin Ulrich Dedekind (1795-1872), syndicus of the Collegium and instructor in jurisprudence,[u] with whom he had a particularly pleasant time, spending evenings over tea and tobacco and together laughing over the motto on the St. Martin's Church ("In 1528 papal idolatry was completely eradicated from the churches of this city") and over the historical explanation of it by the local sacristan. Möhler did not find it necessary, he writes, to indicate to every person he met that he was a Catholic priest.[v]

By January 11 Möhler had arrived, in spite of the cold, at Magdeburg where, as in Braunschweig, he endeavored to learn as much as possible about trade schools and trade-school instruction.

---

r. Möhler to Messner at Rottenburg, November 1822, in Lösch, 75.

s. Chief among these was Hermann Autenrieth (1799-1874), later professor of medicine at Tübingen, and Robert von Mohl (1799-1875), later professor of politics at Tübingen and Heidelberg.

t. Möhler to Messner at Rottenburg, November 1822, in Lösch, 76. The remaining fragments of the work are edited by Reinhold Rieger in *Nachgelassene Schriften*, 1:61-85.

u. Dedekind's appointment at the Carolinum had been made in April 1822. The faculty at the Wilhelmstift appears to have been especially interested in the program at the Carolinum. In Möhler's February 20, 1823, report to them, he devotes the greater part of his discussion to a full description of the collegium (see Lösch, 86-89).

v. Möhler in Braunschweig to Messner in Rottenburg, January 4, 1823, in Lösch, 79.

Here, too, he was impressed with the conviviality. He was invited to both public and private gatherings of the learned, and complained about the requirement that one smoke a pipe or drink the very poor beer almost immediately after being introduced to someone.

The high point of the whole journey came with Möhler's arrival in Berlin. After his initial shock on entering the city (brought on by extremely high costs for food and lodging, his fear of being robbed, the continuing cold, and his trepidation before the police), he settled into a routine relatively quickly for the three brief weeks he was to spend there. On January 30, at the end of his stay, he summed up his time in the intellectual center of Germany. First among all the scholars stood the historian Johann August Wilhelm Neander:[w]

> In fact my journey would have been near to worthless had I not . . . visited Berlin. One need only hear the names of the theological professors here, Schleiermacher, Marheinecke, Neander, Strauss (the author of the *Glockentöne*) and know what he has awaited. Here there is a surging, inner, deep, and genuine scientific life and drive. Scholarship here reflects its characteristic essence: it embraces thought and life. I was amazed at Planck, but what is Planck beside Neander? Planck swims upon the surface; Neander grasps everything in the deepest depths! What a study of the sources, what judgment, what deep religiosity, what earnestness, what clarity and conciseness in description; how full of life, how clear is the image of the historical period that Neander paints! How masterly he describes the men who were the Coryphaers of their time. With what undisturbed justification does he allow each to live again! He stands high above Planck. I will never forget Neander's lectures. They will have a decisive influence on my studies of Church history. In addition his private life is penetrated by illuminating religiosity, simple like the bearing of a local school-teacher. His character is worthy of love and unpretentious in the highest degree. In Berlin he knows no streets except those that lead to the university, and no person except his colleagues. But Origen, Tertullian, Augustine, Chrysostom, St. Bernard, the letters of Boniface, and many others, he

w. Review of *Denkwürdigkeiten* in *Theologische Quartalschrift* 4 (1823): 727ff.: "*Denkwürdigkeiten aus der Geschichte des Christenthums und des christlichen Lebens.* Herausgegeben von Dr. A. Neander. Erster Band. Berlin, bei Ferdinand Dümmler. 1823. . . ."

knows by heart. Because of his ignorance [of the normal patterns of life] his bearing is often comic in its tone and pattern, but no one laughs at him. The honor and love that his students have for him, the attention that his colleagues give him, and the respect that the government offers him knows no bounds. I have often met with him both in public and alone. I have spoken with him concerning the most significant historical matters and works that I was considering: on the time of the fall of the papacy, namely, from the time it gave up Rome and established itself at Avignon to the councils of Constance and Basel. He said that there was a greater subject *if one did not merely, as is often the case, raise up the negative.*[x]

Möhler then continues, noting that he intends to take up this "greater subject," but asks that it not be made public since it will take many years to complete.

On February 1, at ten in the morning, he left for Breslau where his experience was radically different: "The only value of the Catholic faculty for me is that one can learn by such an institution what ought not to be."[y] Anton Dereser (1757-1827) stood alone against the "hyperorthodox" and alone attracted Möhler's attention.[z] Some claimed to be liberals, but their comments quickly dissuaded Möhler that they were; the majority considered his south German extraction to be the equivalent of "liberal, Wessenberger, no Romanist, no obscurant." Many were old men, living in a world that they no longer understood. What was particularly disturbing to Möhler was that the student body showed signs of great promise but had little respect for most of the faculty members. His circumstances were mitigated to some extent by the "Schnellpost" which could cover the distance between Breslau and Berlin in 36 hours.[aa]

---

x. Möhler at Berlin to Messner at Rottenburg, January 30, 1823, in Lösch, 83-84. A much briefer, but no less enthusiastic, description of his time at Berlin is given in his official report to the faculty of February 20, 1823 (Lösch, 89). In it he emphasizes the energy the professors direct to their lectures, the love they have for their students, and their special interest in the students' formation and spiritual welfare.

y. Möhler in Breslau to Herbst in Tübingen, February 1823, in Lösch, 90.

z. Dereser had wide experience in teaching philosophy and exegesis at Heidelberg, Bonn, Strasbourg, Paris (where he fell afoul of the revolutionaries, was condemned to death, but eventually freed after the fall of Robespierre), Freiburg, and elsewhere.

aa. Möhler in Tübingen to Anton Möhler in Ingersheim, April 18, 1823 (Lösch, 95).

Following three weeks' stay in Breslau (enduring the continuing extreme cold), he traveled through deep snow past Glatz and over the Riesengebirge to Prague and Vienna (where he stayed for a month but noted little academic contact), and then through St. Pölten, Linz, Landshut, Munich, Augsburg, and Ulm back to Tübingen. On April 18 he wrote his father from Tübingen, informing him of his return and briefly outlining the last section of his journey.[bb]

6. Initial Teaching and Reviews (1823-1825)

On Möhler's return further discussions were held with von Schmidlin, the Württemberg minister responsible for religious matters,[a] and by May the "additional disciplines" for which Möhler was to be responsible were being described as patristics,[b] although correspondence continued for some time concerning his obligation to teach law, an obligation he fulfilled in the summers of 1823-1825.[c] In August 1823 he suggested three lecture series for the following winter semester, one on Church history generally, a second introducing the Fathers of the first three centuries, and a third on Clement of Alexandria's *Miscellanies*,[d] on which he was to depend heavily in his *Unity*. From then on his work on the early Church continued apace. In the winter semester of 1824, for example, he was teaching Church history, patristics, and a seminar on Chrysostom's *On the Priesthood*,[e] and in the summer of 1825 Church history, Augustine's *Confessions*, a continuation of the Chrysostom study, and a seminar on Theodoret's commentary on Romans.[f]

It was not only to the early Church that Möhler directed attention at the time. His teaching of canon law also reflects the kind of

bb. Möhler in Tübingen to Anton Möhler in Ingersheim, April 18, 1823 (Lösch, 94-96).

a. For details, see Lösch, 99-103.

b. Lösch, 103.

c. Cf. discussions in March 1824 (Lösch, 107), March 1825 (Lösch, 109-13, 116), and April of the same year (Lösch, 120), for example. Note as well a letter to Schmidlin on September 6, 1825, in which the unknown writer pleads that a historian of Möhler's reputation be released from the requirement of teaching canon law (Lösch, 122-23).

d. Lösch, 104.

e. Lösch, 108.

f. See Lösch, 116, 120-21.

questions foremost in his thought and appears to have been done primarily in a historical context that focused on tradition. In his lectures on canon law, for example, he took up a theme that would be central to his *Unity*, commenting at length on the role of the Holy Spirit in the life of the Church and its importance for understanding tradition.

Until their destruction in World War II, the lectures were preserved with other Möhler manuscripts in the Gregorianum in Munich, where they were studied by Alois von Schmid and Josef Rupert Geiselmann, a scholar whose dedication to the study of the Tübingen School generally and to Möhler in particular preserved much material that would have otherwise been lost.[g] The Geiselmann selections taken from a single sheet included among the lectures were published in 1940.[h] In his 1897 study of Möhler's theory of development, Schmid, too, quoted from them extensively.[i] As Geiselmann demonstrated, however, Schmid's use of the lectures was uncritical; the latter tended to consider them all of a piece with Möhler's later work and did not indicate where revisions occurred, thus leading readers to false impressions regarding his initial stance on the nature of the Church.[j] In his earliest lectures he held to an eighteenth-century view of the Church as a religious institution, maintaining a specific doctrine, system of worship, and constitution, and characterized by its universality, holiness, infallibility, and unity in truth.[k]

g. On the significance of Geiselmann's work, see Leo Scheffczyk, "Josef Rupert Geiselmann—Weg und Werk," *Theologische Quartalschrift* 150 (1970): 385-95. Geiselmann's fullest study of Möhler is his *Lebendiger Glaube aus geheiligter Überlieferung: Der Grundgedanke der Theologie Johann Adam Möhlers und der Katholischen Tübinger Schule* (Freiburg: Herder, 1966).

h. See Appendix 3 and Geiselmann, *Die Katholische Tübinger Schule*, 605.

i. See Alois von Schmid, "Der geistige Entwicklungsgedanke Johann Adam Möhlers," *Historisches Jahrbuch* 18 (1897): 322-56, 572-99.

j. See Geiselmann, "Der Wandel des Kirchenbewusstseins und der Kirchlichkeit in der Theologie Johann Adam Möhlers," in Daniélou and Vorgrimler, eds., *Sentire Ecclesiam*, 531-675. On Möhler's students' notes see Geiselmann, "Wandel," 533-58.

k. For a succinct review of Möhler's early position, see Hermann Josef Pottmeyer, *Unfehlbarkeit und Souveränität: Die päpstliche Unfehlbarkeit im System der ultramontanen Ekklesiologie des 19. Jahrhunderts* (Mainz: Matthias Grünewald, 1975), 134-42, and the extensive treatment in Geiselmann, "Wandel." Möhler's treatment of the characteristics of the Church as outlined in his lectures on canon law are discussed in Geiselmann, *Johann Adam Möhler: Die Einheit in der Kirche und die Wiedervereinigung der Konfessionen. Ein Beitrag zum Gespräch zwischen den Konfessionen* (Wien: Verlag Friedrich Beck

Möhler's work on law also resulted in a number of reviews during his first years at Tübingen, and reflected his particular interest in three matters: marriage,[l] Protestantism and Church-State issues (particularly the Prussian agenda for Church union),[m] and liturgy.[n] In most cases the book he was reviewing focused attention on several of these themes. His first review, published in 1823, was

---

[Schöningh & Haindrich], 1940), 12-24. Möhler's developing view of the Church is outlined in Yves M.-J. Congar, "Sur l'évolution et l'interprétation de la pensée de Moehler," *Revue des sciences philosophiques et théologiques* 27 (1938): 204-12. Compare Peter Riga, "The Ecclesiology of Johann Adam Möhler," *Theological Studies* 22 (1961): 563-87, and the more general study by Donald J. Dietrich, "German Historicism and the Changing Image of the Church, 1780-1820," *Theological Studies* 42 (1981): 46-73.

l. "*De iuris austriaci et communis canonici circa matrimonii impedimenta discrimine aTheologische Quartalschriftue hodierna in impedimentorum causis praxi austriaca, dissertatio. Additis duobus ad historiam juris circa matrimonia utilibus monumentis.* Scripsit Dr. Clem. Aug. de Droste-Hülshoff. Bonnae, prostat apud E. Weber, 1822," *Theologische Quartalschrift* 6 (1824): 280-83; "*Vergleichung des gemeinen Kirchenrechts mit dem preuss. Allgem. Landrecht, in Ansehung der Ehehindernisse. Ein notwendiges Hülfsbuch für Rechts-Gelehrte und Pfarr-Geistliche besonders in Provinzen gemischten Glaubens-Bekenntnisses.* Von Dr. Daniel. . . . Berlin, 1823. . .," *Theologische Quartalschrift* 6 (1824): 283-85; and "*Variae doctorum Catholicorum opiniones de iure statuendi impedimenta matrimonii dirimentia. Dissertatio canonica.* Scripsit Joannes Antonius Theiner. . . . Wratislaviae, apud Jos. Max et Socium, 1825," *Theologische Quartalschrift* 7 (1825): 462-86.

m. "*Handbuch des katholischen und protestantischen Kirchenrechts(,) mit geschichtlichen Erläuterungen und steter Rücksicht auf die neusten kirchlichen Verhältnisse in den deutschen Bundesstaaten, und namentlich im Königreich Baiern.* Von Dr. Sebald Brendel. . . . Bamberg, 1823. . .," *Theologische Quartalschrift* 6 (1824): 84-113; "*Ideen zur Beurtheilung der Einführung der preuszischen Hofkirchenagende aus dem sittlichen Standpunckte.* . . . Leipzig bey Johann Friedrich Hartknoch, 1824," *Theologische Quartalschrift* 7 (1825): 278-85; "*Die Kirchenagenden-Sache in dem preuszischen Staate. Eine geschichtliche Mittheilung zur bessern Einsicht in die stetigen Umstände.* Von Ludwig Schaaf. . . . Leipzig, bey C.H.F. Hartmann. 1824," *Theologische Quartalschrift* 7 (1825): 285-92; "*Theologisches Votum für die neuen Hofkirchenagende und deren weitere Einführung,* abgesehen von D. Carl Imanuel Nitzsch, ordentl. Prof. der Theol. und Evangel. Universitäts Prediger an der Königl. Preuss. Rheinuniversität. Bonn, bey Eduard Weber 1824," *Theologische Quartalschrift* 7 (1825): 292-98; and "*Einführung der Berliner Hofkirchenagende, geschichtlich und kirchlich beleuchtet* von D. Christoph Friedrich von Ammon, Königl. Sächs. Oberhofprediger und Kirchenrathe. Dresden, 1825. . . ," *Theologische Quartalschrift* 7 (1825): 298-302.

n. "*Ueber das liturgische Recht evangelischer Landesfürsten. Ein theologisches Votum* von Pacificus Sincerus. Göttingen bei Vandehoeck und Ruprecht. 1824," *Theologische Quartalschrift* 7 (1825): 244-61, and "*Ueber die wahre Stelle des liturgischen Rechts im evangelischen Kirchen-Regiment. Prüfung der Schrift: Ueber das liturgische Recht des evangelischen Landesfürsten.* Von D. Philipp Marheineke. Berlin, 1825. . . ," *Theologische Quartalschrift* 7 (1825): 261-77.

a discussion of Walter's *Lehrbuch des Kirchenrechts*,[o] a work that he had made extensive use of in his lectures. The review's opening paragraph strikes a keynote, not only for the review itself, but for much of Möhler's work at the time. Continually changing political circumstances shape the thoughts and opinions of human beings, Möhler states; there are some who believe that by changing their interpretation of things, things themselves will inevitably change:

> But this is not the case: a higher being directs the path of things. Individuals and their individual knowledge for the most part follow after circumstances, seldom travel along with them, and almost never go before. Anyone who does not so much as follow or change finds himself immediately in another world. Its sounds are heard only by that individual; others catch from it only a distant, unintelligible murmur.[p]

Möhler then continues in a carefully worded piece to press for the invigoration of an episcopal model of Church government, a recognition of freedom of conscience on the part of the Church, and the use of the vernacular in the liturgy.

As important as canon law was for him in his first two years as a teacher, Möhler's central focus at the time was on Church history, and what remains of his early history lectures along with his book reviews of historical studies and his own articles on aspects of Church history provide us with valuable insights into the development of his thought during the period in which he was writing the *Unity*.[q] Thus, in the 1823 form of his lectures on Church history, he described the Church as an institution much in the same way as his eighteenth-century predecessors did:[r]

---

o. "*Lehrbuch des Kirchenrechts mit Berücksichtigung der neuesten Verhältnisse*. Von D. Ferd. Walter, ord. Professor der Recht auf der rheinischen Universität zu Bonn. (440 S. 8) Bonn, bey Adolph Markus, 1822," *Theologische Quartalschrift* 5 (1823): 263-99.

p. Ibid., 263-64.

q. For the historiographic context see Gustav Adolf Benrath, "Evangelische und katholische Kirchenhistorie im Zeichen der Aufklärung und der Romantik," *Zeitschrift für Kirchengeschichte* 82 (1971): 203-17. See also Karl Bihlmeyer, "Möhler und die Kirchengeschichte," in Tüchle, 87-108, and Martin Gritz, "Kirchengeschichte als Geschichte des Christentums. Anmerkungen zur Konzeption eines christlichen Geschichtsbildes bei Johann Adam Möhler," *Zeitschrift für Kirchengeschichte* 101 (1990): 249-66, although the latter is primarily concerned with Möhler's post-*Unity* studies.

r. See Appendices 3 and 5 for details.

In general, a Church is a union of human beings who acknowledge the same religion so as to broaden and maintain among
themselves a specific religiosity and ethic of this religion. Since
this institution unites itself on the basis of a sure doctrine of faith,
a history of the Church must tell the character and fate of the
Church. . . . As a religious union it has religious practices
directed to the external adoration of God. . . . As an institution
the union of these individuals has a constitution which history
treats in its various changes. . . . [I]n a word it is the narration of
the events in and with a religio-moral union.

But Möhler did not keep to such a structural definition; his
consideration of the Church as an organic body is also quite clear:

[H]istory . . . is an *experiential* science. The question concerning
the principle of Church history is nothing other than: What forms
unity in the endless diversity of things that drew themselves
together in the course of the Christian centuries? What is the
direction of the chaos of events? What is the goal of the swirl of
phenomena? History begins its path according to the eternal
plans of Providence and follows, in spite of many obvious
disturbances, one given direction. The point toward which this
direction moves must be the principle of Church history. What is
the direction of the Church? Or rather, what should the Church
be? The idea of the Church herself is the realization of the
Kingdom of God on earth. Therefore the history of the Church in
the objective sense can be nothing other than the history of the
realization of the Kingdom of God on earth. The principle of
Church history is thus the Kingdom of God or that which under
the special leading of the Providence of the Holy Spirit in faith in
Jesus brings into realization the Kingdom of Love. This is the
principle that preserves unity in diversity for us. This is the point
toward which the course of events takes its direction, toward
which the historian must thus continually look and never be in
error.[s]

In Möhler's articles and his reviews of historical monographs one
notes a similar development. In 1823, in his first term at Tübingen,

---

s. See Appendix 3.

he published a lengthy and detailed review of Theodor Katerkamp's *Das erste Zeitalter der Kirchengeschichte*, in which he regrets the lack of historical scholarship among German Catholics.[t] In Germany bishops and other clerical authorities, Möhler claims, are commonly called from the nobility and are for the most part unlearned and despise both scholars and the lower clergy. He complains that "the lower clergy dare not think, the higher cannot; the lower are curtailed by circumstances, the higher by themselves."[u] But times have changed, as the work of the learned Katerkamp demonstrates.

For Möhler, Katerkamp's erudition is not without problems. The writer of Church history must take care that individual facts themselves are not separated from the whole. Details on feast days and liturgy are not to be separated from the history of dogma,

> for it [Church history] forms all into *one* whole and a part, torn from its relationship, from its context, loses its meaning. . . . We are first given to understand the true meaning of the whole external worship when we view it in light of the powerful inner life, the deep religiosity of the earliest Christian period. . . . The establishment of both together leads us to the striking comment that the external religious life stands in an immediate unchangeable relationship with the inner.[v]

In passages such as this and the discussion that follows the Möhler of the *Unity* is already present. What must be studied, he writes, is the whole of Church history, the unity of its inner and outer life and its unity throughout time. The development that occurs in the history of the Church is properly speaking organic growth in which changes occur, but do so in continuity with past forms. Thus Peter first saw the distinction between the Jewish

---

t. "*Des ersten Zeitalters der Kirchengeschichte erste Abtheilung: Die Zeit der Verfolgungen.* Von Dr. Theod. Katerkamp, ordentlichem Professor an der theologischen Fakultät zu Münster. Münster, 1823. . . ," *Theologische Quartalschrift* 5 (1823): 484-532. In 1825 Möhler reviewed the second part of the Katerkamp work, but for the most part merely outlined the argument with extensive quotations. See "*Des ersten Zeitalters der Kirchengeschichte zweite Abtheilung: Streitfragen über Dreieinigkeit und über die Heilsanstalt in der Kirche.* Von D. Theodor Katerkamp, Domkapitular und Professor und der theol. Facultät zu Münster. Münster, 1825. . . ," *Theologische Quartalschrift* 7 (1825): 486-500.
u. Ibid., 485.
v. Ibid., 487.

tradition and Christianity, a distinction that is continued in the work of Paul.

The debate between Peter and Paul over the place of the Gentiles was of special interest to Möhler. He took it up again in an expository article less than a year later on the Jerome-Augustine struggle over a proper interpretation of Galatians 2:14. In it Möhler describes the nature of early Christian contentions (pointing a parallel between Jerome-Augustine and Peter-Paul), drawing from them directives for theological conflicts in general. Debates will arise, he states, but they must be solved in a spirit of humility and in the context of what is best for the *whole* Church. In spite of the misunderstandings that could have led to even further contention, Jerome remained open to Augustine, writing: "I have no doubt that you as well as I wish that truth might be the final victor in our debate; for you seek Christ not your own glory, and if you are victorious, I too am a victor in that I will see my own error."[w] And in this article, as well, Möhler has an eye on heresy, which he will describe more fully in the *Unity* as separation on the part of arrogant one-sided individuals: "Great men can begin battles, but only great men can bring them to a close; the first separate from every other person; the second from themselves."[x] Paul was the image of great candor, but Peter was even greater in his "holy humility."[y]

Möhler's interest in early Christian theological debate in the Katerkamp review leads him to a discussion of the controversy between Cyprian and Stephen over the baptism of heretics. Both agreed that "in baptism, sins are forgiven, and through divine grace a disposition to further sanctification is shared; both these things could occur only through the Holy Spirit and the Spirit is only in the *one* Church."[z] Cyprian could not accept the idea that the Spirit was present in a heretical community and therefore could not accept heretical baptism; Stephen held to the tradition. For Augustine, according to Möhler, the problem could be solved only by understanding that the heretics received external baptism, but could not have the power of the Holy Spirit until they returned to the *whole*

---

w. "Hieronymus und Augustinus im Streit über Gal. 2, 14," *Theologische Quartalschrift* 6 (1824): 195-219; citation from 206 [Jerome, Letter 75]; reprinted in *GS*, 1:1-18.

x. Ibid., 217.

y. Ibid., 219.

z. Möhler, "Katerkamp," 492.

Catholic Church where the Spirit resided. Their fault lay in their willingness to remain separate from the unity of the Church.[aa]

The question of that unity's foundation Möhler took up in a discussion of the hierarchy. Katerkamp maintained that the hierarchy "was the center" of the Church and "the leading principle of all of history."[bb] Against this belief Möhler contended with an argument, almost exactly that of the later *Unity*:

> [For Katerkamp] God created the hierarchy and the Church is more than enough cared for until the end of the world. But according to a higher, more authentic Christian view, which is especially preeminent in Catholicism, the Spirit of God is ever continuing and rules in the Church; its purpose is to be the Church's leading principle. All else is the organ of this Spirit, the means, and so on, and anyone who chooses anything other than the Spirit as a center of history grasps the Spirit externally.[cc]

Tradition cannot be explained as an unbroken hierarchical succession.[dd] One can demonstrate that there were times, in the twelfth century, for example, when children were elected to hierarchical positions; if one holds Katerkamp's position, the tradition must then have been broken. But this was not the case:

> The true center, the true leading principle of the Church, the Spirit of God, had already introduced the means by which these times would not be lost. In the best years of the Church, Christian traditions were incorporated in the Creeds. The basic doctrines of Christianity were, if one may so say it, *lived*; they were in the feasts, in the whole liturgy and *presented with physical necessity* and preserved for Christians.[ee]

It was not Latin that preserved Christianity; Christianity preserved Latin. It was not the hierarchy that brought monasticism to the West: "The hierarchy often deserted the Church, but the Spirit never did."[ff]

---

aa. Ibid., 494.
bb. Ibid., 496-97.
cc. Ibid., 497.
dd. Ibid., 498.
ee. Ibid., 500.
ff. Ibid., 501-2.

In taking up the question of the foundation of the hierarchy Möhler enters more closely into a treatment of tradition and of Christian historical writing itself. Katerkamp based his concept of the hierarchy on the idea of the Kingdom of God, a theme widely discussed in Germany at the time, particularly in Tübingen where Drey and Hirscher were among the foremost proponents of the idea albeit not in the way in which it was developed by Katerkamp. In 1824, for example, Möhler wrote a long review of Franz Theremin's study of the doctrine, unfortunately devoting most of his attention to introducing the reader to its content.[gg] The Kingdom-of-God principle did not attract Möhler, however, in the way it did Drey and Hirscher, and certainly not in the form in which it was expressed by Katerkamp.[hh] On the basis of a purely historical analysis, Möhler writes, it is not possible to demonstrate what Katerkamp is attempting. Katerkamp has failed both the secular historian and the Catholic:

> As a historian he will not convince anyone who has not already been convinced. The charge will be laid before him: *He carries his preconceived conviction into history; he explains history from his own point of view.* And the Catholic will say: *We want ideas created from Tradition, not a tradition formed according to an idea.*[ii]

The hermeneutical implications of this Catholic concern Möhler worked out later in his second (unpublished) preface to the *Unity*, discussed above. In this review he merely hints at their direction. For him it would have been better had Katerkamp stuck firmly to historical facts, but this does not mean that interpretation is set aside. As to the treatment of the early Church, for example, "The historian should take it as a personal duty to warm the reader with a living portrait of the beautiful relationship that existed at that time between clergy and people."[jj] A historian should seek to inspire readers since

---

gg. "*Die Lehre vom göttlichen Reiche*, dargestellt von Franz Theremin, Berlin. Im Verlage von Dunker und Humblot. 1823," *Theologische Quartalschrift* 6 (1824): 622-42.

hh. For details on the development of the idea of the Kingdom of God in Drey, Hirscher, and earlier Protestant and Catholic thought, see Josef Rief, *Reich Gottes und Gesellschaft nach Johann Sebastian Drey und Johann Baptist Hirscher* (Paderborn: Ferdinand Schöningh, 1965). Rief, 204-13, devotes a small section to Möhler's limited use of the idea and the way in which he relates it to the concept of the *Universum*.

ii. "Katerkamp," 503.

jj. Ibid., 506.

the period that follows the earliest age of the Church is so sorrowful. At the same time one must take care not to emphasize the negative continually: "There was a time when the proclamation was: 'If anyone denies this, let that person be anathema,' and this period must be described. But this does not mean that one is hindered from reminding readers of the time when such a statement was not necessary, and therefore to hold forward the hope that the time may again come, when it will not be necessary."[kk]

Möhler devoted the final section of the Katerkamp review to a treatment of two patristic texts that relate to the primacy of Rome. The first is the description of the Roman church as "preeminent in love" in the greeting of Ignatius of Antioch's letter to the Romans. Möhler will not accept the phrase as meaning "head of the bond of love" but as "Rome, which has distinguished itself through love," thus limiting its use as a proof for papal primacy,[ll] while insisting that the term "catholic" is as old as Christianity itself and only came "into full consciousness through its antithesis, the heresies."[mm]

In his discussion of Katerkamp's interpretation of Cyprian in the last twenty pages of his review, Möhler is also concerned with Petrine and papal authority. After quoting the crux text in Cyprian's *On the Unity of the Church*, 4, and Katerkamp's translation of it, Möhler notes in detail the interpolations (supportive of papal primacy) that must be removed and then sets the piece in its historical context. For Cyprian, Möhler writes, the central cause of all schism rests in this: that "we do not return to the source of truth (*veritatis origio*), nor seek the head (*caput*), nor keep the teaching of the heavenly master" (*On the Unity of the Church*, 3).[nn] He goes on:

> This *origio veritatis* and *caput* is the unity of the whole episcopate. Yet a bishop is not catholic in that he agrees with this or that bishop, but if he stands in union with *all*, with *the one and general Church*. One who is in this unity has truth; one who is outside it does not. Anyone who wishes to find truth should go to *the one* Church, that is, back to the unity of the whole episcopate.[oo]

---

kk. Ibid., 506-7.

ll. Ibid., 507-9.

mm. Ibid., 508. Cf. Möhler's use of the term "antithesis" (*Gegensatz*) here and in the *Unity*, section 46.

nn. Ibid., 514.

oo. Ibid., 516.

Nor will Möhler accept the principle that for Cyprian the Roman Church is the *matrix* and *radix* of the whole Catholic Church; these terms must be applied to all the apostolic principal churches.[pp] The reference to Peter as the foundation of the Church is intended symbolically ("it indicates that the Church must be one and manifest a unity") and mystically ("that the episcopate is one and that this unity is an essential character of the Christian Church").[qq]

But Möhler's interpretation of Cyprian in this episcopal sense in no way leads him to a rejection of the visible Church. He has already insisted that the "idea" directs the believer (the believer does not make the "idea"); at this point he again emphasizes the objective nature of the Church: the unity of the episcopate manifests itself in practical ways,[rr] and he presses the point in articles of the next year,[ss] including his generally laudatory review of Neander's work on Chrysostom.[tt]

7. Early Versions of the *Unity*

Having dropped his initial idea to write a book on the history of Christianity in south Germany shortly after his research trip in 1823,[a] Möhler gathered his thoughts on the nature of heresy in the

---

pp. Ibid., 519-20.

qq. Ibid., 523-24.

rr. Ibid., 525, 529.

ss. See "Brendel," 86-87, where he quotes his author positively as opposing the notion of an invisible Church, and his "Karl der Grosze und seine Bischöfe. Die Synode von Maynz im Jahre 813," *Theologische Quartalschrift* 6 (1824): 367-427, in which he supports the need at times for the secular authorities to direct reform programs. Compare, as well, his "*Geschichte der christlichen Religion und Kirche*, von Johann Nepomuk Locherer, Pfarrer zu Jechtingen am Rhein, im Groszherzogthum Baden. Erster Theil, Ravensburg in der Grandmannschen Buchhandlung 1824. . . ," *Theologische Quartalschrift* 7 (1825): 99-108, 665-92.

tt. "*Der heilige Johannes Chrysostomus und die Kirche, besonders des Orients, in dessen Zeitalter*. Von A. Neander, Dr. ordentl. Prof. an der königl. Universität zu Berlin und Consistorialrath. Berlin, bei Ferdinand Dümmler. Erster Band. 1821. Zweiter Band 1822," *Theologische Quartalschrift* 6 (1824): 262-80. While he was completing the *Unity*, Möhler was reading Neander's *Antignostikus*, a review of which appeared shortly thereafter ("*Antignostikus(.) Geist des Tertullianus und Einleitung in dessen Schriften, mit archäologischen und dogmen-historischen Untersuchungen*, von Dr. August Neander. . . . Berlin, bei Ferdinand Dümmler 1825," *Theologische Quartalschrift* 7 (1825): 646-64.

a. It is likely that in his draft preface for the *Unity* where he speaks of an early intention to write a history of medieval Christianity Möhler is not referring to this but

fall of that year or at the latest in the spring of 1824. Entitled "Pragmatic Glimpses," the piece indicates how much his travels forced upon him the need to come to grips with Protestantism in the context of the patristic studies to which he had been directed primarily by Protestants such as Planck and Neander, and by his colleague Drey, whose review of J.G. Ratze's *Das Suchen nach Wahrheit, oder Vergleichung der katholischen und protestantischen Kirche mit der apostolischen der ersten Jahrhunderte* appeared in the *Theologische Quartalschrift* in 1823 along with Möhler's own review of Katerkamp.[b] Thus, the Protestant fact was there from the beginning of his life and would remain to its end. Throughout his life he remained an apologist for the Catholic faith.

The first section of the "Glimpses"[c] links heresy and the Protestant "sola scriptura" principle, the second treats heresy in the period following the sixth century. But "Scripture alone" is not the only issue in the "Glimpses" that is continued into the earlier drafts and the final version of the *Unity*: There is also an insistence on heresy as separation from a central universal body, as the manifestation of a single individual's will, and as an egotistic self-centered theology that upholds seeking above finding and, with its principle of freedom of study, human reason above faith.

Positive notes regarding the Catholic faith are also present in the work. What is particularly noteworthy is his emphasis on the role of the "living Spirit" in the Church, which he argues was there from the time of Christ and the apostles and has since continually directed the Catholic Christian in his or her understanding of externals such as the letter of the Scriptures. Indeed, in the "Glimpses" Möhler explicitly questions the definition of the Church as "an institution or an association" and speaks of it as "a begetting of the love, living in the believer in the Holy Spirit" in a section that he takes up later in

---

to the proposal he made to Neander that he write a book on the papacy in Avignon. See "Endnotes to Preface," below.

b. [Johann Sebastian von Drey,] *Das Suchen nach Wahrheit, oder Vergleichung der katholischen und protestantischen Kirche mit der apostolischen der ersten Jahrhunderte. Von J.G. Rätze. Leipzig, 1803. . . ,*" *Theologische Quartalschrift* 3 (1823): 450-84.

c. For a translation of the full text of the "Pragmatic Glimpses" as edited by Reinhold Rieger in Möhler, *Nachgelassene Schriften*, see Appendix 1. See, as well, Reinhold Rieger, "Unbekannte Texte von Johann Adam Möhler: Bericht über eine Edition," *Theologische Quartalschrift* 168 (1988): 153-58, and Rudolf Reinhardt, "Bekannte und unbekannte Texte aus dem Nachlass Johann Adam Möhlers. Eine kritische Sichtung," *Catholica* 36 (1982): 49-64.

his *Unity*. Such passages suggest that an interpretation of Möhler's view of the Church as one that moved from an eighteenth-century to a romantic and then back again to a modified eighteenth-century view are too rigid.[d] The teaching of canon law required certain modifications to his organic definition of the Church for pedagogical purposes, just as his emphasis in the *Unity* was more directly shaped by his implied romantic audience. Thus when one takes into consideration the occasion of Möhler's early teaching and composition, one need not insist on a radical shift in his thought, which was in any event developing over a very brief period of time, nor need one interpret his work as inconsistent because it supported two mutually exclusive definitions.[e]

The speed with which Möhler's thought was developing is reflected in the similar speed with which he reworked and revised his writing. Early in 1824, for example, he shifted his attention from the "Glimpses" and began another study specifically directed to a description of faith and love in the life and thought of the early Church. This initial untitled study, which I will refer to as "Faith and Love," borrowed heavily from the "Glimpses" and formed the base for his *Unity* as published in 1825. The manuscripts of "Faith and Love," as well as those of the revisions Möhler made to it, were destroyed in World War II. For our knowledge of this work and the revisions it underwent, we are indebted primarily to Geiselmann, who prepared transcriptions for a critical edition in 1932 and was finally able to publish that edition in 1957.[f]

The theme of "faith and love" as a basic principle of the early Church may have been inspired by the work of Drey whose "Reflections on the Relationship between Catholicism and the Basic Principles of Christianity" contain a number of suggestive similarities with Möhler's work.[g] "Faith and Love"[h] was divided into three

---

d. Cf. Geiselmann, "Wandel," 535-38.

e. Cf. Geiselmann, *Wiedervereinigung*, 27-28, and his emphasis on the dual motifs of classicism and romanticism in Möhler's ecclesiology as outlined in the introduction to his edition.

f. Earlier the manuscripts were transcribed and printed in part in Johann Adam Möhler, *Die Einheit in der Kirche*, ed. E.J. Vierneisel (Mainz: Matthias-Grünewald Verlag, 1925).

g. Drey's text is printed in Geiselmann, *Geist*, 203-12.

h. In its original form of twenty sheets, "Faith and Love" included sections from the *Unity* in whole or part in the following order: Sheet 1: *Unity* sections 1, 32, 34; Sheet 2: *Unity* sections 2, 3, 6, 2; Sheet 3: *Unity* sections 4, 6, 5, 4; Sheet 4: *Unity* sections 4,

sections, a first untitled general introduction, a second treating the nature of heresy, and a third on the relationship between the community and the individual. The author's prefatory remarks establish the central matter that Möhler wished to use throughout the piece. The Church, Möhler tells his readers in strikingly Schellingesque language, is understood according to the analogy of the reflective and the active powers, the first seen in faith, the second in love. These two powers are bound together as one in the Church and cannot be simply divided:

> The Church as a moral person presents herself in a twofold mode after the analogy of the physical being in its reflective and productive powers—the first, which contains the characteristic of her contemplation, or faith; the second, which expresses her productive activities, the foundation of which is love. The principle of a Church will therefore need to penetrate both its modes. These are characteristically only different structures of one and the same thing, if there is to be *one* principle, and reflection only divides what in its life and essence is indivisible into apprehension and description. If the principle of the Church in her productive and contemplative activities as in her unfoldings is one thing, these two aspects are often not separated when they are described, and the one demands light from the other and crosses over into the other's territory.
>
> Our work is thus divided into the following sections: (1) into the history of the Catholic principle in relation to faith and (2) into the history of the Catholic principle in relation to love.
>
> The basis for the division of our subject as well as the justification of the formulae in which it is conceived devolves on the description of this subject itself.[i]

Following the preface, the first section opens with what would appear as *Unity*, section 1, by directing the reader to consider the

---

27, 28; Sheet 5: *Unity* sections 7, 8, 18; Sheet 6: *Unity* sections 18, 19; Sheet 7: *Unity* sections 20, 21, 22; Sheet 8: *Unity* sections 23, 24, 25; Sheet 9: *Unity* sections 26, 27, 29; Sheet 10: *Unity* sections 29, 8, 9, 10; Sheet 11: *Unity* sections 11, 12, 34; Sheet 12: *Unity* sections 34, 12, 14, 15; Sheet 13: *Unity* sections 16, 17; Sheet 14: *Unity* sections 27, 28, 32; Sheet 15: *Unity* sections 33, 34; Sheet 16: *Unity* Addendum 12; Sheet 17: *Unity* sections 35, 36, 37; Sheet 18: *Unity* sections 36, 37, 38, 39; Sheet 19: *Unity* sections 39, 40, 41; Sheet 20: *Unity* sections 42, 43.

  i. See "Endnotes to Preface and Chapter 1," note 2, below.

role of the Holy Spirit in the life and thought of the early Church. It was the conviction of the early Church, the argument continues, that faith in Christ and all things relating to it had their source in the Spirit. Just as the Holy Spirit is one, so are its acts if they are allowed to flow freely and are not curtailed. Such a Spirit must bring all the individuals whom it penetrates together into a unity of faith and love (cf. *Unity*, 32, 34). A number of early Fathers provide proof for this reading (cf. *Unity*, 2). Before the time of Christ the Spirit manifested itself only sporadically, but thereafter it was present continually (cf. *Unity*, 3). The apostles received the Spirit directly; a new life principle was directly communicated to them to enable them to communicate it to others. After it was once given, it was to flow forth from those to whom it was given. A separatistic life was a false one. The life-power that continues the Church is tradition (cf. *Unity*, 6). Just as Original Sin is passed on from generation to generation, so is the life principle of the Church, tying together all Christian generations back to Christ (cf. *Unity*, 2).

The Church as the totality of believers is filled by the Spirit and is the treasure of this life principle (cf. *Unity*, 4). Individuals are to take up the common experience of the Church as their own and to bring it forth in their thought and deeds (cf. *Unity*, 6). Paganism has its roots in the fall of humanity, but the holy life in the Church (cf. *Unity*, 5, 4) drew them to itself (cf. *Unity*, 27, 28). The early Church opposed all separatistic life, as numerous Fathers made clear (cf. *Unity*, 7). In sum, Christianity is grounded in the Spirit and not in concept, and faith is taken up in life (cf. *Unity*, 8). On the basis of this the relationship between the Catholic principle and the Scriptures can be made clear. In the mind of the Lord and of the Apostles, Christianity was first filled with the Holy Spirit before it was a letter.

At this point (end of Sheet 5, beginning with what would become *Unity*, 18) Möhler begins his second chapter, "The Catholic Principle in Conflict with the Heretics or with Ecclesiastical Egoism, and External Tradition as the Dismissal of Heretics from the Domain of Christianity" (cf. *Unity*, 18). Christianity wished to build a new system of thought on a new life. This was much different from earlier attempts made in the ancient world which built new thought systems on the old life. Christianity was too simple and too unpretentious for them. It did not satisfy their curiosity.

In the Greek and Eastern religions there were possibilities for arrogant fantasy and speculation. These made use of Christianity, which they accepted not to learn anything from it, but as if to first learn what it was (cf. *Unity*, 19). Such heretics insisted on freedom of study. Human consciousness is twofold: a contemplating reflective consciousness and a living consciousness; the second is the basis of the first both in human life generally and in Christianity. The Christian first lives and then reflects on the lived experience. A Christian first takes up Christianity before reflecting on it, whereas a heretic insists that Christianity must be discovered before it can be accepted, and that such discovery can take place only if one is free of preconceptions (cf. *Unity*, 20).

As a result, there is great disagreement between heretics and Catholics as to the interpretation of the Scriptures. The Church recognizes the genuine Scriptures on the basis of her own oral tradition (cf. *Unity*, 21), whereas the heretics often create fictional gospels, acts, or letters (cf. *Unity*, 22), or corrupt genuine texts to support their own false doctrines (cf. *Unity*, 23). Against Catholic caution, accuracy, and exegetical precision, the heretics put forward a secret tradition (cf. *Unity*, 24). Initially the Church had no need for hermeneutical principles; these were developed only after the heretics began to attack it with their own (cf. *Unity*, 25). The first of these principles that it applied was historical and grammatical, but by itself, aside from the Spirit that is given to the Church, even this method is problematic (cf. *Unity*, 26, 27, 29). Separatistic heresy rejects the live-giving Spirit and replaces it with its own lesser spirit, but heretics nevertheless see themselves as the knowledgeable ones and designate Catholics as simplistic (cf. *Unity*, 8).

As soon as the divine Spirit is present it presses outward and expresses itself as a living word. Christ bore the divine in his consciousness and then expressed it. The same is true of Peter (cf. *Unity*, 9) and of the other apostles, who proclaimed in living speech what they had heard (cf. *Unity*, 10), and who shared their experiences and ideas regarding particular matters with each other (cf. *Unity*, 11). Egotistical developments were opposed by reference to the apostolic succession, as is made clear from the works of Tertullian and Irenaeus (cf. *Unity*, 12, 34). Such a use of tradition did not prove the truth of the matter, but it did disprove novel interpretations. Catholicism does not know of a past or a future; it rests in an eternal present (cf. *Unity*, 12).

Not only is tradition maintained externally, it is also preserved internally. The consciousness of each individual member or generation can be identified with the consciousness of the whole Church (cf. *Unity*, 14). Because the proclaimed living-word tradition was first an oral teaching (cf. *Unity*, 15), the Scriptures were not thought of as separate from that oral teaching. The oral tradition was not considered a different source, and because of it the Scriptures were highly venerated (cf. *Unity*, 16). The external tradition such as the Scripture is thus the ever-present expression of the Holy Spirit, embodied at all times in the whole Christian life. It is on this point that both sixteenth-century and contemporary Protestants are mistaken in maintaining a "Scripture alone" principle.

Möhler's third chapter treats "The Relationship of the Catholic Principle to the Individuality of Believers" (end of sheet 13, *Unity*, 17), and opens by questioning why Christianity was not originally spread by Scripture. According to Möhler, had Christianity been so propagated, individual interpretations of individual texts would have arisen and the communal nature of the Christian life (which was maintained by the ties between those who passed on the tradition and those who received it) would have been broken (cf. *Unity*, 27). Likewise, the early Church maintained that it was united over time (cf. *Unity*, 28); it is sin that brings forth disunity (cf. *Unity*, 32).

Heresy in this way was evil in its root. From Christianity's beginning, unity is a central image: the unity of the divine and the human in Jesus, the union of Christ with his disciples, and the unity of Christians with one another (cf. *Unity*, 33). Heresy is denial, and can therefore be understood in analogy with the privation theory of evil as the absence of the good, as division, contradiction, disharmony (cf. *Unity*, 34), even though heresy takes elements from the true Christian faith (cf. *Unity*, Addendum 12). Heresy is always in ignorance, since the first thing that Christianity grasps is the mind (cf. *Unity*, 35).

In spite of the Church's strong emphasis on the unity of believers, the individuality of each is not set aside. Each individual reveals his or her own specific characteristics. This was already clear in the apostolic period in which the Johannine group was more concerned with interior and mystical aspects of the Christian life, whereas the Pauline group directed attention to the speculative aspect. The links between these two groups reflects the linkage that exists between faith and knowledge (cf. *Unity*, 36). Early Christian theologians such as Clement of Alexandria and Origen who were interested in speculation all insisted that knowledge was based on faith (cf. *Unity*, 37, 38, 39). In all human beings there is a power of faith, according to early Church teaching, a desire for the divine, an anticipation, but there is no knowledge of God by faith, which is not tied to revelation (cf. *Unity*, 40). Since faith penetrates the whole being of a person, philosophy too must be penetrated by faith. Mystical theology (cf. *Unity*, 41, 42) and speculative thought are linked together; both are needed within the whole body (cf. *Unity*, 43). Some final comments then follow on Christian morals.

8. The New Form of *Unity in the Church*

8.1 Initial Restructuring

The closing comments of the "Faith and Love" manuscript (the first autograph, referred to in the Endnotes as A1) may have been intended as introductory to a fourth chapter but, as appears more likely, mark a point at which Möhler was convinced that the direction of his book had to be completely revised, and restructured into the first draft of the *Unity* proper (A2).[a] To form A2 Möhler took the pages of A1 and cut them up and placed them where they served best in the new order.

A2 was far from a final draft, however. When Möhler completed it, he had a calligraphic copy (K) made, which included further deletions and additions, and when K was completed he hastened to make extensive corrections once more (referred to as A3). Once the text finally reached the printer, it is clear that Möhler continued to make changes since some of the changes in the earlier drafts were not taken up and that others were added in the final printed form of the *Unity* (T).

The new structure of A2, maintained throughout all the later revisions, divided the work into two parts as follows:

Part I: Unity of the Spirit of the Church
    Chapter 1: The Mystical Unity of the Church
    Chapter 2: The Unity of Doctrine
    Chapter 3: The Attempt to Destroy Unity
    Chapter 4: Relation of the Unity of Believers to the
        Individuality of Each Person

Part II: The Visible Church
    Chapter 1: The Bishop and the Diocese

---

a. For details on the manuscripts, see Geiselmann edition, "Introduction," 87ff. and 319ff.

Chapter 2: The Metropolitan and His Area
Chapter 3: The Visible Unity of All Individual Churches
Chapter 4: The Primate

In 1940 Geiselmann published a study of Möhler's use of the term
"antithesis" (*Gegensatz*) and suggested that the outline of the *Unity*
was shaped by Hegelian notions: the first two chapters of each
section are descriptions of a thesis, the third of an antithesis, and the
fourth of a synthesis.[b] Certainly, as Geiselmann proves, Möhler did
rethink his position on heresy as an antithesis to the Church,[c] did
redefine heretical teaching as "contradiction" while he was working
on the *Unity*, and did rework chapter titles in the final printed
edition (particularly in Part I) to emphasise a dialectic of unity and
diversity in the early Church. Thus, in Part I he changed the chapter
titles to emphasize the unity-disunity theme as follows:

Chapter 1: Mystical Unity
Chapter 2: Intellectual Unity
Chapter 3: Diversity without Unity
Chapter 4: Unity in Diversity

But Geiselmann's suggestion in its particulars seems unlikely. In
Part II Möhler stresses unity, but he does it in an hierarchical order,
not in a clearly dialectical one:

Chapter 1: Unity in the Bishop
Chapter 2: Unity in the Metropolitan
Chapter 3: Unity of the Total Episcopate
Chapter 4: Unity in the Primate

Moreover, dialectical interests were common at the time; Möhler
makes no direct reference to Hegel; and when his vocabulary does
reflect philosophic reading, it points the reader to Schelling. This is
particularly the case, of course, in his early reference to the Ideal and
the Real in the "Pragmatic Glimpses," in the draft introduction to A1,
and in his contrast of "antithesis" and "contradiction" in section 46 of

b. Geiselmann, *Wiedervereinigung*, 148-49. See also the Geiselmann edition, 398.
Geiselmann's broader discussion of Drey and Möhler on "antithesis" is in ibid., 147-65.
c. Note his reference to schismatic communities as antithesis to the universal Church
in the Katerkamp review of 1823, 523n.

the *Unity* which has clear parallels with Schelling's *Bruno*.[d] The shift to a contrast of "antithesis" and "contradiction" on Möhler's part, moreover, need not be interpreted as shaped by any particular philosopher. Indeed, most of Möhler's vocabulary shares a common romantic source, and throughout the *Unity* he is much more interested in revising the positions of and opposing Protestants such as Schleiermacher than of addressing contemporary philosophers.

The "Pragmatic Glimpses" are explicitly directed against Protestant points of view and the same "polemic" (although the term is perhaps too strong) is evident in the "Faith and Love" study. From the A2 draft of the *Unity* and the revisions thereafter, however, this aspect is consistently made less obvious (references to Schleiermacher in the final version, for example, are for the most part positive), but the general parallel that is drawn between pre-Nicene heresy and Protestantism remains, particularly in the emphasis on individualism, freedom of study, the Bible as a single source of revelation, and the invisible Church.

When Möhler undertook the initial restructuring of A1 into A2 is not known. In 1824 Hermann Joseph Schmitt's *Harmonie der morgenländischen und abendländischen Kirche* appeared. Möhler wrote a review on it in the *Theologische Quartalschrift* later in the year.[e] The Schmitt volume makes significant use of the theme "Spirit and Love," a theme emphasized in A2, and may mark a transition point in Möhler's thought regarding his draft on "Faith and Love." Although it is difficult to date the "Pragmatic Glimpses" for certain, the piece cannot be earlier than the autumn of 1823 and may even have been drafted early in 1824. "Faith and Love" was written after the "Glimpses," and thus probably in the early part of 1824 because of annotations in the latter work referring to sections of the former.

---

d. See Harald Wagner, *Die eine Kirche und die vielen Kirchen: Ekklesiologie und Symbolik beim jungen Möhler* (Munich: Ferdinand Schöningh, 1977), 177-81, and Schelling's 1802 *Bruno oder über das göttliche und natürliche Princip der Dinge. Ein Gespräch* in *Schellings Werke*, ed. Manfred Schröter, 6 vols. (München: C.H. Beck and R. Oldenbourg, 1927), 3:109-228. Note as well Wagner's discussion of parallels between Möhler and Johann August Starck's (1741-1816) 1809 *Theoduls Gastmahl oder über der Vereinigung der verschiedenen christlichen Religions-Societäten* on this section and others (ibid., 182-90).

e. "*Harmonie der morgenländischen und abendländischen Kirche. Ein Entwurf zur Vereinigung beider Kirchen.* Von Hermann Joseph Schmitt, Kaplan in Lohr bei Aschaffenburg. Nebst einem Anhange über die anerkannten Rechte des Primats in den ersten acht Jahrhunderten. Mit einer Vorrede von Friedrich Schlegel. Wien, im Verlage bei Franz Wimmer. 1824," *Theologische Quartalschrift* 6 (1824): 642-56.

At the very earliest the *Unity* was begun in the spring of 1824. By February of the following year Möhler was confident enough about its final form that he wrote his preface; although the volume did not appear until September or October of 1825,[f] Möhler left the February date on his preface,[g] indicating that the *Unity* was complete by that time, less than a year after A2 was undertaken, and perhaps only a year from the time A1 was assembled. The speed with which he worked may explain some of the repetitiveness of the piece, the brevity of all the chapters in Part II, the tendency in them to take up arguments on Church polity as discussed by Peter De Marca (1594-1662), Louis du Pin (1657-1719), and Claude de Saumaise (1588-1653), among others, rather than developing the discussion on patristic texts, and a number of errors and inconsistencies in the citations.

8.2 The Shape and Themes of the *Unity*

One of the reasons Möhler may have ceased work on "Faith and Love" was that the issues that he was attempting to treat broke through the work's somewhat simple structure. In both the "Pragmatic Glimpses" and "Faith and Love" he wished to write an apologetic for Catholic Christianity against Protestantism in the context of a study of early Christianity, and he wished to do this with an eye to the "modern" world, particularly to the new political situation within which German Catholicism found itself. To deal with Protestantism he was required to treat the problem of Scripture and tradition, the nature of revelation, the interpretation of that revelation by individuals and community, and the authority of the visible Church; because of Protestant and Enlightenment concerns, as well as debates within Catholicism itself, he was directed to the faith-reason dichotomy; and to help Catholicism deal with the new political situation he needed to discuss Church-State relationships.

In the "Glimpses" he endeavored to take up these concerns by focusing his study on the essence of heresy. In "Faith and Love" he moved to a more romantic mode of argumentation, initiating his

---

f. Cf. Stephan Lösch, "Der Geist der Ecclesia und das Werden ihrer sichtbaren Form: Der Weg von 'Einheit' zu 'Athanasius,' in Tüchle, 241.

g. Of the two extant prefaces, the first appears to have been written in February 1825 but was redrafted, according to the manuscript annotation in August 1825. See Friedrich, 7, and "Endnotes to Preface," below.

discussion with the overarching organic image of the Holy Spirit as the life force of the Church and the relationship of that life to each individual. At no point in his discussion did he accept the positions of Schleiermacher and Wilhelm Martin de Wette (1780-1849), whom Möhler understood as defining the Holy Spirit as the common feeling of Christians. As he developed his theology of the Spirit in the *Unity*, he came to see heresy as separation from this life force of the Spirit and noted the heretical insistence on the letter of Scripture alone, on private judgment, and the resulting disunity, a topic that led him further in the work to discuss the unified nature of the Spirit's life in the Church as a whole and in each individual.

The unity topic was widespread in the romantic climate of Möhler's day. Both Schleiermacher and Friedrich Schlegel had special interests in it,[h] as did many others who integrated biological and organic metaphors into their descriptions of the life of individual peoples (*Völker*).[i] It is not surprising as a result that in the *Unity* this theme was explored as foundational in his treatment of all the theological and practical issues with which he was faced. Moreover, it allowed him a way to overcome the polemical tones of the early drafts: in the *Unity* he critiqued Protestantism by suggesting analogies between earlier heretical and Protestant positions and was thus able to delete more and more of the explicit anti-Protestant language in each successive revision.

8.3 The *Unity* and Earlier Scholarship

The speed with which Möhler wrote the *Unity* left its mark on the book in a number of ways. There are a number of slips in transcriptions of Greek and Latin sources, for example, and, as I already noted, Part II which was intended to balance Part I by stressing the exterior visible nature of the Church where Part I had stressed the Spirit and the interior nature, is cursory and shows a tendency to take up post-Tridentine debates on the matter rather than offering a close description of the early Church's view.

h. For background information on the theme, see Harald Wagner, *Die eine Kirche*, 56ff.

i. See F.W. Coker, *Organismic Theories of the State* (New York: Columbia University Press, 1910).

Indeed, in neither of the two parts can the reader gain assurance that what is presented is properly speaking a full "portrayal" of the position of the Fathers of the first three centuries as promised in the title. Möhler clearly did a great deal of reading in patristic sources while he was writing the work, but his reading was selective, and highly dependent on what he was teaching at the time. As a result, he makes heavy use of Clement of Alexandria's *Miscellanies* and Origen's works. His attraction to Tertullian's *On the Prescription of Heretics* and Irenaeus's *Against the Heresies* was shaped by his initial interest in the nature of heresy. Cyprian's writing on the unity of the Church seems to have attracted Möhler secondarily; his primary approach to that author, already indicated in his early reviews on Katerkamp and Neander, was raised by issues related to contemporary concerns over the primacy of Rome.

In whatever way Möhler came to the pre-Nicene texts, however selective his reading was, it remains nevertheless true that he worked through his sources extensively and with care. His early study of the *Letter to Diognetus*, as well as his detailed criticism of historical studies such as that of Katerkamp, proves that he had not drunk at the well of the new "scientific history" in vain, even though his work is far from the kind of "social history" that he praises in his reviews of Neander and other works and consistently calls for in his early reviews. The *Unity* does not offer a description of the pre-Nicene era, for example, in the way in which the works of Möhler's Protestant forebears William Cave (1637-1713) and Gottfried Arnold (1666-1714) do.[j]

Like anyone writing on a specific historical era, Möhler had read much of the secondary literature and some of his primary reading was directed by it. Quite regularly he cites earlier editorial notes from patristic editions he was using to support his particular reading of a text, and he made use of handbooks on Church history such as those written by Claude Fleury (1640-1723)[k] and the Protestants Johann Matthias Schröckh (1733-1808), Heinrich Philipp Henke (1752-

j. On Arnold, see my *Pietists, Protestants, and Mysticism: The Use of Late Medieval Spiritual Texts in the Work of Gottfried Arnold* (Metuchen, N.J.: Scarecrow Press, 1989), which includes discussion and a bibliography on earlier Protestant historiography. The parallels between Möhler and Arnold are especially interesting, particularly in their similar emphasis on the Spirit and their hermeneutical theories. On Arnold and Möhler, see Wagner, *Die eine Kirche*, 45ff., 48ff., 160ff.

k. See his reference to Fleury in "Pragmatic Glimpses" and compare the reference in *Theologische Quartalschrift* 5 (1823): 266.

1809), and Johann Carl Ludwig Gieseler (1792-1854), but there is no immediate proof that his choice of texts was largely dependent on these or other authors. Dionysius Petavius's (1583-1652) *Opus de theologicis dogmatibus*, for example, was very popular in Möhler's day for both Catholics and Protestants; indeed, there is evidence that Staudenmeier took patristic citations directly from him.[l] However, a similar charge should not be laid against Möhler simply because in several instances in the *Unity* he cites Petavius.[m] Thus, in the First Addendum to the *Unity*, Möhler directs his readers to Petavius 8:7 and 7:4 for further information on his subject and the citation appears to be genuinely intended *for further direction*; only one of the major texts that he quotes also appears in the Petavius's sections, and in two cases where an A3 addition contains a citation that is in Petavius,[n] these are overscored.

There are places in the *Unity* where Möhler uses his secondary sources in very close ways, but not so closely that one might define the dependency as plagiarism.[o] In one case in a note on Irenaeus's *Against the Heresies*, 4:33,8 (*Unity*, Part I, Chapter 1, section 15) he refers to four scholars—Grabe, Massuet, Goetze, and Lessing—who discuss the relationship between Scripture and tradition in differing ways. His comment appears to indicate that he has read each of them on the subject, but it is far more likely that he has simply taken the names from Massuet's own note in the latter's edition of

l. See Bernhard Casper, "Erkenntnisse aus der kritischen Beschäftigung mit den frühen Aufsätzen und Rezensionen F.A. Staudenmaiers (1828-1834)," *Theologische Quartalschrift* 150 (1970): 262-68.

m. See Rudolf Reinhardt, "Dionysius Petavius (1583-1652) in der Tübinger Schule: Ein Bericht aus dem Nachlass von Stefan Lösch," *Theologische Quartalschrift* 151 (1971): 160-62. Note as well Peter Stockmeier, "Der Kirchenväter in der Theologie der Tübinger Schule," in *Theologie im Wandel: Festschrift zum 150jährigen Bestehung der Katholisch-theologischen Fakultät an der Universität Tübingen, 1817-1967*, ed. J. Moeller et al. (Munich, 1967), 131-54, and Abraham Peter Kustermann, "Pseudepigraphie und literarische Anleihen in der Tübinger Theologie des 19. Jahrhunderts: Ein Plädoyer für den kritischen Umgang mit Texten," *Zeitschrift für Kirchengeschichte* 101 (1990): 287-300 (see esp. 290-91).

n. One is to Cyril, *Thesaurus*, 34 (Petavius, 8:7) and one to Demetrius Cydones (Petavius, 7:4, 15-16).

o. For example, in his inaugural address as *ordinarius* in church history, presented in 1829, Möhler made extensive use of earlier work by L. Thomassin. See Joachim Köhler, "War Johann Adam Möhler (1796-1838) ein Plagiator? Beobachtungen zur Arbeitstechnik und zu den literarischen Abhängigkeiten in der Katholischen 'Tübinger Schule' des 19. Jahrhunderts," *Zeitschrift für Kirchengeschichte* 86 (1975): 186-207.

Irenaeus. A second instance shows much greater dependency. In *Unity*, Part II, Chapter 4, section 69, he discussed the crux text on Roman preeminence in Irenaeus, *Against the Heresies*, 3:3,2:

> The hypothesis that Rome's political greatness established the influence of the Roman Church, . . . was already markedly opposed by Irenaeus in the famous passage: "It would take too long to explain the succession of all churches in this work. It is therefore enough to embarrass all who form false churches to cite the tradition set down by the apostles of the greatest, oldest, and best-known church founded by the glorious apostles Peter and Paul. . . . With this church because of its greater preeminence [*potiorem principalitatem*] all churches necessarily [*necesse est*] agreed [*convenire*], that is, all believers everywhere, for the apostolic tradition is preserved [*conservata est*] in it [*in qua*] always by those who are everywhere."

In his note he quoted the source and then continued:

> That *convenire* can mean *symbainein* [come together] cannot be doubted; *potior*, or *potentior*, as it is often read, is not "more powerful" but is equivalent to *hikanōteros* [most competent]; for this word earlier translators often used *potens*. Thus, the letter of Clement to the Corinthians is called *potentissimas litteras*, whereas the original text preserved by Eusebius, *Ecclesiastical History*, 5:6, reads *hikanōtatēn graphēn*, that is, "a preeminent, remarkable letter." *Principalitas* is not merely *archē*, "origin" (as in Gieseler [section 51, 150-51] and Böhmer in de Marca, 1: 1, section 9) which the translator would not have mistaken since he renders it properly elsewhere. Nor can it properly be linked with *in qua* [in which], in which the basis of the principality is to be contained. It is equivalent to *kyros* [authority] which gains precedence in ecclesiastical language (Canon 4, Nicea on the metropolitan) and may easily be translated with *principalitas*. *Necesse est* is clearly *anankē* [constraint] not *dei* [it is to be], but *conservata est* [it is preserved] is not to be rendered with *sōzesthai* [to save] but with *diaphyllattesthai*, *thesaurizesthai* [to conserve, accumulate]; it is customary to render it with both together, indeed, with *aoristos* [indefinitely]. This accumulation of doctrine in Rome I understand from the letters of peace that were sent by bishops on their election to many others but especially and always to the bishop

of Rome so that it expresses what Optatus of Milevus said of the Roman Church: "with whom the whole commerce of forms of the earth are concordant in one society of communication."

With the reference to Johann Karl Ludwig Gieseler, whose *Textbook of Church History* was extremely popular throughout the nineteenth century,[p] even without reference to a specific page or section of the other historian's work, Möhler intended to make his debt in the footnote clear, and as a result feels no need to comment on how close some sections of his note are to Gieseler, who points out that Massuet was the first to change *potentiorem* to *potiorem* in the text under discussion and continues:

Irenaeus wishes to prove that the doctrine of the Catholic Church is apostolic, preserved by the successors of the bishops ordained by the apostles. Since it is too prolix to point out this connection of the apostles with all the churches, he wishes to limit his proof to the Church of Rome alone, and finally to represent the doctrine of the Roman Church as necessarily agreeing with that of the whole remaining Church. Necesse est (*anankē*) must not be confounded with oportet (*dei*); the former expresses a natural necessity, the latter an obligation, duty. Potentior is *hikanōteros* (cf. iii. 3.3: potentissimas litteras, *hikanōtatēn graphēn*). . . . A preeminence belonged to all apostolic churches, to the Roman Church a more important pre-eminence on account of its greatness, and its having been founded by the two most distinguished apostles.[q]

The note has other parallels as well. Möhler had obviously read the Massuet note on the passage (as had Gieseler) which might have directed Möhler's attention to the Eusebius section, and both were also acquainted with Massuet's *Dissertatio 3* which treats the Irenaeus

---

p. Gieseler's work first appeared in 1824 and went through four editions. The study was translated into English twice, first as *Textbook of Ecclesiastical History*, 3 vols., trans. F. Cunningham (Philadelphia: Carey, Lea, and Blanchard, 1836), and second as *A Compendium of Ecclesiastical History*, trans. Samuel Davidson (Edinburgh: T.&T. Clark, 1854). According to the second translation the first was highly problematic. Another of Gieseler's works was reviewed in the first issue of *Theologische Quartalschrift* ("*Historisch-kritischer Versuch über die Entstehung und die frühesten Schicksale der schriftlichen Evangelien. Von D. Johann Carl Ludwig Gieseler. Leipzig 1818. . .,*" *Theologische Quartalschrift* 1 (1819): 579ff.

q. Gieseler, 1854 translation, section 51, note 10, pp. 150-51.

passage.[r] But all other aspects of the discussion, including a lengthy addition made in A3, appear to be Möhler's own. The Böhmer reference in Möhler is to Iustus Henning Böhmer's *Observationes*, which has an extensive discussion of the term "episcopus."[s]

9. Möhler's Changing Perspective

No sooner had Möhler published his *Unity* than he was revising its premises to meet theological concerns arising out of it. Just as each of the various revisions of the *Unity* reflect his changing orientation, so do the reviews and studies he completed after its appearance. Two years later, in 1827, his large study *Athanasius der Grosze und die Kirche seiner Zeit* appeared,[a] in which once again he used patristic studies to confront the Protestantism of Schleiermacher and others and to comment by analogy on faith-reason, Church-State, and other issues of his day. At the same time he was completing a book-length study of Anselm,[b] writing articles,[c] and carrying on what would be his practice until 1834 of regularly reviewing works for the *Theologische Quartalschrift*.[d]

After the publication of *Athanasius* Möhler taught and wrote regularly on patristics, completing articles on the *Letter to Diogne-*

---

r. *PG* 7, Diss. 3, Art. 4, sections 30ff.

s. Böhmer's *Observationes* are printed in Peter de Marca, *Dissertationum de concordia sacerdotii et imperii. . . ,* 6 vols. (Bamberg: 1788), 1:98-176. The observation on 1, 1, section 9, is on p. 137.

a. *Athanasius der Grosze und die Kirche seiner Zeit, besonders im Kampfe mit dem Arianismus.* (Mainz: Florian Kupferberg, 1827). There were four nineteenth-century translations into French and two into Italian (see Reinhardt, *Verzeichnisz*, 40-42).

b. "Anselm, Erzbischof von Canterbury. Ein Beitrag zur Kenntnisz des religiös-sittlichen, öffentlich-kirchlichen und wissenschaftlichen Lebens im elften und zwölften Jahrhundert," *Theologische Quartalschrift* 9 (1827): 435-97, 585-664 and 10 (1828): 62-130; reprinted in *GS*, 1:32-176. The work was translated into English as J.A. Möhler, *The Life of St. Anselm, Archbishop of Canterbury; A Contribution to the Knowledge of the Moral, Ecclesiastical, and Literary Life of the Eleventh and Twelfth Centuries*, trans. Henry Rymer (London: T. Jones, 1842).

c. For a full list, see Reinhardt, *Verzeichnisz*, 17. Most of Möhler's articles were written before 1833, after which he devoted his attention to the revisions of his *Symbolik* and the debates arising out of it.

d. From 1826 to 1834 Möhler wrote thirty-eight reviews, all but two for *Theologische Quartalschrift*.

tus,[e] the Pseudo-Isidorian decretals,[f] the rise of Gnosticism,[g] and Justin Martyr.[h] His lectures on patrology—which he continued to give until the end of his life—were published posthumously.[i] But by 1828 his work exhibits a marked change. His publications take up contemporary concerns directly (clerical celibacy,[j] the relationship between the State and the universities,[k] Christian-Islamic dialogue following the Greek revolution[l]) and, as always, the Protestant fact.[m]

In 1832 his *Symbolism*, the central work on the Catholic-Protestant debate and the major work of his life, appeared. It was revised in a new edition every year for the next three years, and was reprinted in the year of his death and sixteen additional times before World War I. Its initial translation in English was reprinted five times.

---

e. "Über den Brief an Diognetus. Die Zeit seiner Herausgabe. Darstellung seines Inhalts," *Theologische Quartalschrift* 7 (1825): 444-61; reprinted in *GS*, 1:19-31.

f. Fragmente aus und über Pseudo-Isidor," *Theologische Quartalschrift* 11 (1829): 477-520, 14 (1832): 3-52; reprinted in *GS*, 1: 283-347.

g. "Versuch über den Ursprung des Gnosticismus," first published in *Beglückwünschung . . . Dr. Gottlieb Jacob Planck. . . .* (Tübingen: 1831), and reprinted in *GS*, 1: 403-35.

h. "Über Justin Apologie, I c. 6. Gegen die Auslegung dieser Stelle von Neander," *Theologische Quartalschrift* 15 (1833): 49-60.

i. *Johann Adam Möhlers Patrologie oder christliche Literärgeschichte. Aus dessen hinterlassenen Handschriften samt Ergänzungen. 1. Band: Die ersten drei Jahrhunderte.*, ed. Franz Xaver Reithmayr (Regensburg, Vienna, and Linz: Georg Joseph Manz, Gerold, Mechitaristen, von Mösle and Braunmüller, and F. Eurich and Son, von Fink and Q. Haslinger, 1840).

j. "Beleuchtung der Denkschrift für die Aufhebung des dem katholischen Geistlichen vorgeschriebenen Cölibates. . . ," *Katholik* 30 (1828): 1-32, 257-97; reprinted in *GS*, 1:177-267, and edited with an afterword by Dieter Hattrup, *Johann Adam Möhler, Vom Geist des Zölibates* (Paderborn: Bonifatius Verlag, 1992). Note, as well, his earlier article on the shortage of priests at the time: "Einige Gedanken über die zu unserer Zeit erfolgte Verminderung der Priester, und damit in Verbindung stehender Puncte," *Theologische Quartalschrift* 8 (1826): 414-51.

k. "Kurze Betrachtungen über das historische Verhältnis der Universitäten zum Staate," (1829), reprinted in *GS*, 1:268-82.

l. "Über das Verhältnis, in welchem nach dem Koran Jesus Christus zu Mohammed und das Evangelium zu Islam steht. Mit besonderer Berücksichtigungen der künftigen Schicksale des letzteren gegenüber dem Christenthum," *Theologische Quartalschrift* 12 (1830): 3-81, reprinted in *GS*, 1: 348-402. The work was translated into English as *On the Relation of Islam to the Gospel*, trans. J.P. Menge (Calcutta: Ostell and Lepage, British Library, 1847).

m. See "Betrachtungen über den Zustand der Kirche im 15. und zu Anfang des 16. Jahrhunderts, in Bezug auf die behauptete Nothwendigkeit einer die bestehenden Grundlagen der Kirche verletzenden Reformation," *Theologische Quartalschrift* 13 (1831): 589-633, reprinted in *GS*, 2:1-33.

There were four printings of the translation in French, six in Italian, one in Dutch, one in Swedish, and one in Polish. The *Symbolism* continued his early apologetic interest that he gave special attention to in the year the *Unity* appeared,[n] and its importance was immediately recognized by such Protestants as Philipp Konrad Marheinecke (1780-1846), Karl Immanuel Nitzsch (1797-1868),[o] and, above all, the Tübingen theologian Ferdinand Christian Baur (1792-1860). In 1834 the latter published his *Der Gegensatz des Catholicismus und Protestantismus*,[p] which Möhler answered in the same year with his *Neue Untersuchungen*.[q] Baur immediately printed an "Erwiderung,"[r] and Möhler a second enlarged edition of the *Neue Untersuchung* the following year which Baur took up in a second edition of the *Gegensatz* in 1836.

The change that marks Möhler's post-*Unity* period is not only in the direction of his research and publication, however. His theology also underwent a shift. Very soon after the *Unity*'s appearance Möhler came to realize that the theological structure of the earlier work restricted his ability to deal fully with the human and institutional limitations faced by the Church of his day and that it required a firmer foundation on which to structure arguments on the

---

n. For details, see Möhler, *Nachgelassene Schriften*, 86-189, and Abraham Peter Kustermann, "Der Name des Autors ist Drey: Eine unvermeidliche Vorbemerkung zum Apologet-Manuskript Johann Adam Möhlers," *Catholica* 43 (1989): 54-76.

o. Karl Immanuel Nitzsch, *Eine protestantische Beantwortung der Symbolik Möhler's* (Hamburg: F. Perthes, 1835).

p. F.C. Baur, *Der Gegensatz des Catholicismus und Protestantismus nach den Principien und Hauptdogmen der beiden Lehrbegriffe, mit besonderer Rücksicht auf Herrn Dr. Möhlers Symbolik* (Tübingen: Ludwig Friedrich Fues, 1834).

q. Johann Adam Möhler, *Neue Untersuchungen der Lehrgegensätze zwischen den Katholiken und Protestanten: Eine Vertheidigung meiner Symbolik gegen die Kritik des Herrn Professors Dr. Baur in Tübingen* (Mainz and Vienna: Florian Kupferberg und Karl Gerold, 1834). For a full discussion of the Möhler-Baur controversy, see Joseph Fitzer, *Moehler and Baur in Controversy, 1832-1838: Romantic Idealist Assessment of the Reformation and Counter-Reformation* (Tallahasee, Fla.: American Academy of Religion, 1974). Compare, as well, debate with the equally well-known Protestant Tübingen scholar David Friedrich Strauss, in Hans Friedrich Geisser, "Glück und Unglück eines Theologen mit seiner Kirche—am Beispiel der beiden Tübinger Johann Adam Möhler und David Friedrich Strauss," *Zeitschrift für Theologie und Kirche* 83 (1986): 85-110, and William Madges, *The Core of Christian Faith: D. F. Strauss and His Catholic Critics* (New York: Peter Lang, 1987).

r. "Erwiderung auf Herrn Dr. Möhler's neueste Polemik gegen die protestantische Lehre und Kirche in der Schrift: *Neue Untersuchungen*. . . ," *Tübinger Zeitschrift für Theologie* 8 (1834): 127-248.

relationship between faith and reason, the Church and individual states (both Protestant and Catholic) and theology and contemporary thought.

In a number of his works Geiselmann has succinctly outlined the theological turn Möhler made.[s] In the first place, following the *Unity*, Möhler shifted his emphasis from the activity of the Divine in the world to the nature of the human person, thereby overcoming the danger of pantheism in the use of romantics such as Schelling; of Sabellianism, which he saw manifested in Schleiermacher; of traditionalism and fideism, as upheld by a number of French writers, particularly Joseph de Maistre (1754-1821) and Louis Bautain (1796-1867);[t] and of Romantic organicism generally. There was a resulting shift in Möhler's anthropology from a total emphasis on the individual as rooted in the being of God in the *universum* and through the Holy Spirit to one that views the human creature as the image of God but stresses its fallen nature.[u]

Second, there is a shift from the pneumatic interpretation of the Church to a Christocentric one. Unity is now considered in light of the Incarnation, the unity of the person and work of Christ, in which a new beginning for humanity is offered, and the Church is now understood in analogy to the divine-human unity of Christ. According to Geiselmann's interpretation, this Christocentric focus does not negate, but rather reinforces, Möhler's interpretation of "the community of saints" in the *Unity*, by its emphasis on the *sanctorum communio* as a *communio* of holy things (*sancta*) rather than a social-moral union of individuals (*communio* of *sancti*).[v] Third, the inner-

s. Geiselmann, *Wiedervereinigung*, 56-68.

t. On this issue, see, above all, Möhler's "Sendschreiben an Herrn Bautain, Professor der philosophischen Facultät zu Strassburg," *Theologische Quartalschrift* 17 (1835): 421-53, reprinted in *GS*, 2:141-64, and the earlier review of Adam Gengler's *Über das Verhältnis der Theologie zu Philosophie* (Landshut, 1826), in *Theologische Quartalschrift* 9 (1827): 498-522. An overview of Möhler's developing position on faith and its foundation from the *Unity* to the close of his career is available in Paul-Werner Scheele, "Glaube und Glaubensbegründung in der Sicht Johann Adam Möhlers," *Catholica* 23 (1969): 91-111. From the earliest period Möhler is distinguished in his thought from individuals such as de Maistre, who was not a direct influence on him. See Geiselmann edition, Introduction, 15.

u. The implications of this shift for Möhler's anthropology are described in Josef Rupert Geiselmann, *Die theologische Anthropologie Johann Adam Möhlers: Ihr geschichtlicher Wandel* (Freiburg: Herder, 1955).

v. Ibid., 56-106. Compare Gerhard Ludwig Müller, "Vom Leben mit dem Toten zum Leben nach dem Tod. Die Bestimmung der Communio Sanctorum als Ort christlicher

outer dialectic of the *Unity* is set aside for one that speaks in images of above-below, and the theme of truth rises to a level equal with that of love.

The theological shift in Möhler's work does not negate his earlier study—Möhler always remains concerned with the unity of the Church[w]—and in his later work much of the earlier romantic language remains, but the radically different context in which that language is used immediately informs readers that they are to avoid interpreting his words in the context of the *Unity*. Thus, in the *Symbolism*, he speaks of the communication of the Spirit, but links it with Christ and Christ's directives:

> When the time appointed by Christ for the sending down of the Spirit was come, he communicated himself to the apostles and the other disciples, when gathered together in one place, and all of "one accord" they were longing for his coming.[x]

And when the activity of the Spirit as uniting believers in love is described, its visibility, its movement from above rather than from within, and the Christological analogy is emphasized:

> At last the Holy Spirit, that had been promised, appeared: he took an outward shape—the form of fiery tongues—an image of his power that cleansed hearts from all wickedness, and thereby united them in love. He wished not to come inwardly, as if he designed to uphold an invisible community; but in the same way as the Word was become flesh, so he came in a manner obvious to the senses, and amid violent sensible commotions, like to "a rushing mighty wind." If individuals were filled with power from above in such a way, that, only in as far as they constituted a unity, could they become participators of the same; and if the hallowing of the Spirit took place under sensible forms; so, according to the ordinance of the Lord for all times, the union of

---

Auferstehungsbotschaft in der "Symbolik" J.A. Möhlers," *Catholica*, 36 (1982): 31-48.

w. On Möhler's continuing concern with the question of unity in the context of the Protestant-Catholic division in the three years following the publication of his *Unity* see Harald Wagner, "Die Kirche und ihre Einheit in J.A. Möhlers 'Athanasius,'" in Peter Neuner and Franz Wolfinger, eds., *Auf Wegen der Versöhnung: Beiträge zum ökumenischen Gespräch* (Frankfurt am Main: Josef Knecht, 1982), 81-94.

x. This and the following quotations are from *Symbolism*, Part I, Chapter 5, sect. 37.

the interior person with Christ could take effect only under outward conditions, and in communion with his disciples. Under outward conditions: for independently of outward instruction, what are the sacraments but visible signs and testimonies of the invisible gifts connected with them?

Then, in words that with very slight editing might well have appeared in the *Unity* (the first sentence is almost a direct quotation from that work), he shapes his argument to stress his revised position on the nature of the Church in a section that, better than any other, reflects the way in which his *Unity in the Church* is of one piece with the work of his later years, and is yet the work of a "younger" scholar:

> In communion: for no one by the act of baptism sanctifies himself; each one is, on the contrary, referred to those who already belong to the community. Nor is any one but momentarily introduced into fellowship with the members of the Church—to remain only until, as one might imagine, the holy action should be consummated; for the fellowship is formed in order to be permanent, and the communion begun in order to be continued to the end of life. Baptism is the introduction into the Church—the reception into the community of the faithful, and involves the duty, as well as the right, of sharing forever in her joys and sorrows. Moreover, the administration of the sacraments, as well as the preaching of the word, was entrusted by the Lord to the Apostolic College and to those commissioned by it; so that all believers, by means of this Apostolic College, are linked to the community, and in a living manner connected with it. The fellowship with Christ is accordingly the fellowship with him in community—the internal union with him a communion with his Church. Both are inseparable, and Christ is in the Church, and the Church in him (Eph. v. 29-33).

10. The *Unity* and Möhler's Influence on English Readers

How extensive an influence the *Unity* had has not yet been fully studied. In spite of Möhler's reservations concerning the work later in his life, its impact was far-reaching, and his apologetic intentions succeeded more than he might have expected. Some sense of the

Unity's significance in this regard, for example, can be gained by
briefly reviewing the impact of the work on Protestantism in
Möhler's own day, particularly in the English-speaking world. In
1837 the Protestant Richard Rothe (1799-1897) published a volume on
the early Church, entitled *Die Anfänge der christlichen Kirche und ihrer
Verfassung,*[a] in the preface of which he described his study as a
Protestant parallel to that of Möhler's *Unity* (ix). Like Möhler, Rothe
emphasized the importance of the universality and visibility of the
Church. Rothe's work came in for particular praise in Philip Schaff's
Germany: Its Universities, Theology, and Religion.[b] Schaff (1819-1893)
himself was enthusiastic about Möhler's study and through him the
Tübingen Roman Catholic played a role in the development of the
nineteenth-century American High Church movement in the
Reformed Church known as the "Mercersburg Theology."[c]

In England, too, supporters of the Tractarian Movement at Oxford
found much in Möhler's work valuable for their position.[d] Thus in
1841 William George Ward (1812-1882) of Balliol College introduced

---

a. Richard Rothe, *Die Anfänge der christlichen Kirche und ihrer Verfassung: Beilage über
die Echtheit der Ignatianishen Briefe* (Wittenberg: Zimmermann, 1837).

b. Philip Schaff, *Germany: Its Universities, Theology, and Religion, with Sketches of
Distinguished German Divines of the Age* (Philadelphia: Lindsay and Blakiston, 1857).

c. For a general overview of the movement, see James Hastings Nichols, ed., *The
Mercersburg Theology* (New York: Oxford University Press, 1966).

d. For a general review of the Oxford Movement and other background for the
section that follows, see Owen Chadwick, *The Victorian Church*, 3rd. ed. (London:
Adam and Charles Black, 1971). Interest in Anglicanism, particularly in Tractarianism,
was also developing at Tübingen. See, for example, the early reviews "Ansichten und
Beobachtungen über Religion und Kirche in England. Von Karl Heinrich Sack . . .
Berlin, 1819. . .," 2 (1820): 105-17, and "Herbert Marshs . . . vergleichende Darstellung
der protestantisch-englischen und der römisch-katholischen Kirche. . . . Aus dem
Englischen übersetzt und mit Anmerkungen und Beylagen versehen, von Dr. Johann
Christoph Schreiter. . . . Sulzbach . . . 1821. . .," in *Theologische Quartalschrift* 4 (1822):
60-81. Note, as well, Möhler's "Anselm, Erzbischof von Canterbury. . .," his extensive
comments on the English Church in the *Symbolism*, and later publications in the 1840s
in *Theologische Quartalschrift*. Note especially von Drey, "Das Wesen der Puseyitischen
Doctrin," *Theologische Quartalschrift* 26 (1844): 417-57, and see "Vorträge über die in der
päpstlichen Kapelle übliche Liturgie der stillen Woche; von Dr. Nicolaus Wiseman. .
. . übersetzt durch Joseph Maria Axinger . . . 1840," *Theologische Quartalschrift* 22 (1840):
667ff.; "Reisen eines Irländers, um die wahre Religion zu suchen . . . von Thomas
Moore . . . übersetzt von Mortiz Lieber . . . 1840," *Theologische Quartalschrift* 23 (1841),
315-316, "Maria Ward's . . . Leben und Wirken. . . . 1840," *Theologische Quartalschrift* 23
(1841): 683-91; and "Irland's Zustände alter und neuer Zeit. Von Daniel O'Connell. .
. Aus dem Englischen von Dr. A. Willmann . . . 1843," *Theologische Quartalschrift* 25
(1843): 667-78.

readers of the *British Critic* to Möhler's *Unity*. The setting for Ward's remarks was a critical review of Thomas Arnold's sermons. Arnold's theological position, Ward contended, with its emphasis on practical duties "makes little account of the hidden life of a Christian."[e] He then went on:

> The French translation of Möhler's work, "On the Unity of the Church," . . . has just come to hand, as though for the very purpose of drawing out the full answer to such reasonings as Dr. Arnold's: we cannot too earnestly recommend for that purpose the first two chapters and part of the third. It is impossible of course by any extracts which we have room for to give an idea of the full scope of his argument, but the few which follow may show its general bearing."[f]

And in four aptly chosen passages Ward then provided the reader with the central premise of Möhler's book, the second and third of which sum up the study:

> The principle of the Church is this, that man cannot live a Christian life, and, by consequence know his religion, without the influence which is exerted upon him by the community of the faithful inspired by the Holy Ghost. . . .
> This doctrine (the Christian scheme) from the time of the Apostles downwards, was far from perfectly understood by each one of their hearers; for since at first it developed itself but slowly in each individual, before it was perfectly known to them it might well appear defective and obscure under more than one point of view. . . . None of them lived apart from the rest, but they considered each other as forming one whole, and they kept up the habit as long as possible of referring the solution to the whole community.[g]

Ward's reference did not arise in a vacuum. English readers were early aware of the German historian-theologian. As early as October 1834, T.D. Acland wrote to John Henry Newman (1801-1890), relaying a message from Nicholas Wiseman (1802-1865) that

---

e. [William George Ward,] "Arnold's Sermons," *British Critic* 30 (1841): 298-364, 311.
f. Ibid., 329.
g. Ibid. Ward's translation from French version of 1939.

Newman should consult Möhler's *Athanasius*.[h] It is not surprising, as a result, that in 1845 Newman should claim that Möhler's principles were parallel to his in the *Development of Christian Doctrine*.[i] How closely Newman knew Möhler is questionable, but a mark of the German author's popularity at the time can be seen in the work of the Anglican George Stanley Faber, who in an attack on Newman felt it necessary to devote equal time to a refutation of Newman's German "predecessor."[j]

Continuing interest in Möhler among British theologians was certainly sparked by James Burton Robertson's translation of Möhler's *Symbolism* in 1843,[k] and new concern with the *Unity* itself can be noted at midcentury. On September 5, 1850, Henry Edward Manning (1808-1892), deeply disturbed over occurrences in the Church of England, wrote to his friend William Ewart Gladstone (1809-1898)[l] with words directly influenced by Möhler:

It seems to me that indivisibleness of communion was held to be by a Divine necessity so that any person or portion falling off, or

h. Acland to Newman, May 11, 1834, in Anne Mozley, ed., *Letters and Correspondence of John Henry Newman during His Life in the English Church*, 2 vols. (London: Longmans, Green, and Co., 1898), 1:40.

i. John Henry Newman, *An Essay on the Development of Christian Doctrine: The Edition of 1845*, ed. J.M. Cameron (Harmondsworth: Penguin, 1974), 90. Note as well Newman's reference to Moehler on 'development,' later in his life in the same general way in his Theological Commonplace Book. (Birmingham Oratory Archives, p. 27)

j. George Stanley Faber, *Letters on Tractarian Secession to Popery: With Remarks on Dr. Newman's Principle of Development, Dr. Moehler's Symbolism. . . .* (London: W.H. Dalton, 1846), 142-94. Newman's linking of the German theologian with de Maistre in his *Development* leads one to question how fully he understood the former's work. Much study remains to be done on the links between Möhler and the English-speaking world. A good overview of the literature is available in Franklin, *Nineteenth-Century Churches: The History of a New Catholicism in Württemberg, England, and France*, 25ff. but Owen Chadwick, *From Bossuet to Newman: The Idea of Doctrinal Development* (Cambridge: Cambridge University Press, 1957), 114ff., and Henry Tristram, "J.A. Moehler et J.H. Newman; La pensée allemande et la renaissance catholique en Angleterre," *Revue des sciences philosophiques et theologiques* 27 (1938): 184-204, still remain important.

k. Note esp. "Romanism and Protestantism in Germany," *The English Review* 2 (1844): 1-35, which reviewed the sixth edition of the *Symbolik*, the *Neue Untersuchungen*, and critiques of Möhler by Baur and Nitzsch.

l. On the correspondence between Manning and Gladstone, see my forthcoming edition (Atlanta, Ga.: Pitts Theology Library); Perry Butler, *Gladstone: Church, State and Tractarianism. A Study of His Religious Ideas and Attitudes* (Oxford: Oxford University Press, 1982); and relevant sections in David Newsome, *The Convert Cardinals: Newman and Manning* (London: John Murray, 1993)

being in fact separate ceased to be of the Church; and yet the indivisible remainder was the Church as fully as before. Ephes.-IV.1-16. especially v.v.13 & 16 appear to me to be decisive, speaking popularly. In the whole passage I see that the Church is:—

1. One. v.4. A Body Visible.
2. Living by the Life of the Head.
3. Organised by unity of members.
4. Self edifying by Pastors of itself.
5. Successive in all time.
6. Self contained by harmony of parts.
7. Conscious of its own intelligence and charity.
8. Divinely guided for the sake of its members.
9. Perpetual and self edifying until its work shall be complete—the number and perfection of the elect—"the Christ Mystical."

All this appears to me to show *that indivisibleness is of the essence of indefectibility*—except so far as a living body may lose members. But they are no longer of the body. They *were*, but *are* not.

And also it shows *that indivisible unity is essential to the functions of life intelligence and love.*

I have no doubt that you know Möhler's book on the Unity of the Church. It is a small work written when he was young but very able.[m]

Only a few months earlier Manning had published his fourth volume of sermons in which his theology of the Church shows striking parallels to that of Möhler's *Unity.* Möhler's apologetic had its effect. One year later Manning joined Ward and Newman in the Roman Catholic communion, and would become before his death archbishop of Westminster and cardinal.

In 1850 Manning had no need to remind his friend Gladstone of Möhler's work. Gladstone was well acquainted with it through his friendships with the liberal Catholic Lord Acton and Döllinger, the German historian and editor of Möhler. In the mid-1840s he had not only read and carefully annotated Möhler's *Symbolik* and *Neue*

---

m. Pitts Theology Library, Emory University, Atlanta, Ga., MS 500905mg. See also Manning's comments to his friend James Hope on Dec. 11, 1850, in reference to Möhler's *Symbolism* (National Library of Scotland, Edinburgh, MS 3675, 98-101).

Untersuchungen, but also Nitzsch's and Baur's critiques.[n] At the same time Manning was writing to Gladstone on Möhler, both were corresponding with a mutual High Church friend, Robert Isaac Wilberforce (1802-1857), who was also much impressed by the German author's early work and passed on his enthusiasm to John Williamson Nevin (1803-1886), the colleague of Schaff at Mercersburg, for whom Möhler's early vision of the Church would remain a support in his own Reformed catholic opposition to the ultramontanism of his fellow countryman, Orestes Brownson (1803-1876).

Even so brief a discussion of only one aspect of Möhler's influence provides insight into its multifaceted nature. As an apology for Catholic faith his *Unity* was successful, beyond his expectations, but, in almost every case, the book's success reflected an underlying paradox, inherent perhaps in the very "principle of Catholicism" that he had described: like the bulk of his work, it supported both progressive and conservative forms of the catholic tradition. Thus within the Roman Catholic Church his writing was an important influence on liberals such as Acton and Döllinger as well on more conservative members of the Roman School such as Giovanni Perrone, for example.[o] Outside of the Catholic Church the *Unity* played a role in the conversion of the Englishmen Ward and Manning, who in their Catholic careers supported an institutional form of the faith that at times appeared to stifle the inner spirit of the Church Möhler had so forcefully supported in his earliest work. And his *Unity* at the same time inspired other Protestants, such as Rothe, Gladstone, Nevin, and Schaff, to reform their own traditions and thereby to develop a fuller and more effective Protestant apologetic as part of the diversity within the living tradition of catholic Christianity.

11. On Translation and Editorial Principles

The translation that follows is based on the 1825 Johann Adam Möhler edition, *Die Einheit in der Kirche Oder das Prinzip des Katholizis-*

---

n. Gladstone's annotated copies are preserved in St. Deiniol's Library, Hawarden, Wales.

o. See Kasper, *Die Lehre von der Tradition*, passim. Note as well Perrone's suggestion to Newman that the latter read Möhler (T. Lynch, "The Newman-Perrone Paper on Development," *Gregorianum* 16 (1935): 402-47; 405).

mus dargestellt im Geiste der Kirchenväter der ersten drei Jahrhunderte (Tübingen: Heinrich Laupp, 1825). The footnotes are Möhler's own, although I have used letters to distinguish them from numeral endnote references; in only two cases have I entered a footnote source that he omitted and I have indicated these and all other editorial insertions with square brackets.

As indicated in section 8, Möhler's final published version was the result of a number of rewritings, each of which added and deleted significant passages that provide insight into his own thought and that of contemporary questions facing him. An initial essay on the topic, "Pragmatic Glimpses," is translated in Appendix 1 with the permission of Bonifatius Druck, Paderborn from Johann Adam Möhler, *Nachgelassene Schriften Nach den stenographischen Kopien von Stefan Lösch (1881-1966)*, edited by Rudolf Reinhardt. *Band I. Vorlesungen, Entwürfe, Fragmente*, translated, edited and introduced by Reinhold Rieger (Paderborn: Bonifatius Druck, 1989), 36-53. Parts of his "Pragmatic Glimpses" were taken up in his inital draft of the *Unity*, "Faith and Love," which was then completely redrafted and revised three more times (including revisions made during the printing stage). Superscript numbers throughout the text direct the reader to the Endnotes, which include translations of all variants in earlier drafts except those which are simply stylistic.

Throughout the Endnotes I have used the following sigla to indicate references:

A1: "Faith and Love": Möhler's initial draft for the *Unity*.
A2: Möhler's reformulated draft of the *Unity*.
K: Calligraphic copy of the *Unity*.
A3: Möhler's annotations to K.
T: 1825 published form of the *Unity*.
+: indicates an addition made by the particular version noted.
Angle brackets < > indicate the placement of a footnote by Möhler
    in an Endnote; the text of the footnote follows the Endnote extract and is marked with << >>.

The Endnotes are translated from the critical edition by Josef Rupert Geiselmann, ed., *Johann Adam Möhler. Die Einheit in der Kirche Oder das Prinzip des Katholizismus Dargestellt im Geiste der Kirchenväter der ersten drei Jahrhunderte* (Cologne and Olten: Jakob Hegner, 1957), 398-553, and are translated and published with the permission of

Jakob Hegner Verlag of Cologne. We are dependent for most of our information on Geiselmann's edition, which was prepared prior to World War II, during which the manuscripts were in large part destroyed. In some cases reference is made to the edition of E.J. Vierneisel, ed., *Die Einheit in der Kirche* (Mainz: Matthias Grünewald Verlag, 1925 [Vol. 2. *Deutsche Klassiker der Katholischen Theologie aus neuer Zeit*. Edited by Heinrich Getzeny]) who also consulted the original manuscripts. A large section, seemingly written for inclusion in the *Unity*, "On the Salvation of the Pagans," is translated in Appendix 4 with the permission of the *Theologische Quartalschrift*, Tübingen, from the edition by Emil Joseph Vierneisel, "Aus Möhlers handschriftlichem Nachlass," *Theologische Quartalschrift* 119 (1938): 109-17.

When inconsistencies or problems occur in the Geiselmann edition, these have been noted. In some cases Geiselmann uses the term "early draft," but is unclear whether this is A1 or A2. Endnotes that indicate an addition to the text and follow a footnote number signify that the footnote is an addition as well, even though the endnote does not state this explicitly; when the footnote is not an addition, the endnote is placed before the footnote number. In some cases, however, since the addition of the majority of footnotes was the work of A2 and to a lesser extent of A3, I have not noted the addition when it was intended only to cite particular patristic sources and did not include interpretive material. For reasons of space I have omitted a full version of the A1 text, based on Geiselmann's reconstruction which required some revision after a close comparison of that reconstruction with Geiselmann's textual notes; the two are not fully consistent. All variants are to A2 unless otherwise noted.

I have included in the Appendices materials on which Möhler was working at the time he was writing the *Unity* and which cast light on his subject. Appendix 2, "Selections from the Lectures on Church History, 1823," is translated with the permission of Erich Wewel Verlag, Munich from Johann Adam Möhler, *Vorlesungen über die Kirchengeschichte*, ed. Reinhold Rieger, 2 vols. [Munich: Erich Wewel, 1992], 1:10-11, 29-42; Appendix 3, "Selections from the Lectures on Canon Law, 1823," with the permission of Matthias-Grünewald Verlag, Mainz from Josef Rupert Geiselmann, *Geist des Christenthums und des Katholizismus* (Mainz: Matthias-Grünewald, 1940), 399-403; respective sections in Appendix 5, "Introduction to the Lectures on Church History, 1826-1827," with the permission of

Matthias-Grünewald Verlag, Mainz, from Josef Rupert Geiselmann, *Geist des Christenthums und des Katholizismus* (Mainz: Matthias-Grünewald, 1940), 391-96, and with the permission of Erich Wewel Verlag, Munich, from Johann Adam Möhler, *Vorlesungen über die Kirchengeschichte*, ed. Reinhold Rieger, 2 vols. [Munich: Erich Wewel, 1992], 1:3-8, 9-10; and Appendix 6, "Outline of the Lectures on Church History," with the permission of Erich Wewel Verlag, Munich, from Johann Adam Möhler, *Vorlesungen über die Kirchengeschichte*, ed. Reinhold Rieger, 2 vols. [Munich: Erich Wewel, 1992], 1:xxi-xxiv.

If Möhler has translated a source in the body of the text and quoted it again in the original language in the footnote, I have not retranslated the passage in the footnote, but indicated it as '[source quoted].' Full bibliographic details to all citations in the *Unity* can be found in the second section of the Bibliography. Rather than append a series of additional editorial notes to the text, I have attempted to include in the Introduction all necessary information or bibliography on Möhler's contemporaries or earlier theologians whom he cites. Translations of patristic quotations that are in Greek or Latin in Möhler's footnotes or his Addenda are taken and revised as necessary from *Ante Nicene Fathers* and the *Nicene and Post Nicene Fathers* series.[a] In his text Möhler always translates his patristic sources, but in the footnotes he almost always quotes in Greek or Latin, whereas in the Addenda he appears to have no pattern for translating or quoting original sources; I have therefore noted when I have translated from Möhler's own German translation either in the footnotes or in the Addenda. All patristic citations are to Migne's *Patrologia*[b] which, for the most part, is based on the editions used by Möhler. When this is not the case the original edition has been cited. Readers who wish further information on specific texts are directed to handbooks such as Altaner and Quasten and to Reinhold Rieger's recent edition of the *Vorlesungen über die Kirchenhistorie* for details.[c]

---

a. *The Ante-Nicene Fathers. Translations of the Writings of the Fathers down to A.D. 325*, 10 vols., ed. J. Roberts and A. Donaldson (New York, 1884-1886), and *A Select Library of the Nicene and Post-Nicene Fathers of the Christian Church*, 28 vols., ed. Philip Schaff and H. Wace (New York, 1886-1900).

b. Jacques Paul Migne, *Patrologia cursus completus: Series graeca*, 161 vols. (Paris: Lutetiae, 1857-1866) and *Patrologia cursus completus: Series latina*, 221 vols. (Paris: Lutetiae, 1844-1855).

c. See Berthold Altaner and Alfred Stuiber, *Patrologie; Leben, Schriften und Lehre der Kirchenväter*, 9th ed. (Freiburg: Herder, 1980), and Johannes Quasten, *Patrology*, 4 vols.

All letters of Cyprian follow the Oxford edition. Parentheses within quotations are Möhler's own and indicate his commentary on the text.

The translation uses inclusive language wherever appropriate (*Männer* is used only in section 42 [once] and section 57 [once] and five times in the Addenda; in all cases except that in section 57 it is translated inclusively as well.) However, where reference is directly to a priest or bishop, I have used exclusive referents. In all cases I have avoided the practice of translating singular words as plurals for inclusive terms, since Möhler is quite consistent in his use of the singular to emphasize the individual in contrast to the community; moreover, when he refers to the actions of members of heretical groups he almost always uses the singular.

Möhler makes heavy use of romantic language. Thus the reader will note the regularity of words denoting and connoting life, source, begetting, development, formation, and preservation, almost all intended in a biological sense, and Möhler's regular use of *unmittelbar* to emphasize the direct relationship between the divine Spirit and the individual believer. For readers who are interested in considering his work in the context of writers such as Schleiermacher, Schelling, and Hegel, therefore, I have endeavored to be consistent in my translation of specific terms, although Möhler himself does not always seem to apply them so; only in the case of *Historie* have I found it necessary to add the German word in brackets in the translation to overcome ambiguity, but even in this case, as the reader will note, Möhler does not always distinguish between *Historie* and *Geschichte*. A brief listing of the most important terms is presented in the glossary.

In addition to the publishers who have kindly given permission to translate materials, I am especially indebted to the following persons and institutions: Catherine Huggins, administrative assistant to the Department of Religion and Culture, Wilfrid Laurier University, Waterloo, Ont.; Marcella Martin of the Inter-Library Loan Department, Wilfrid Laurier University Library; Arleen Greenwood

---

(Westminster, Md.: Christian Classics, 1950-1966) for references to the critical editions: *Die Griechischen christlichen Schriftsteller der ersten Jahrhunderte*, 41 Bde. (Berlin: Academie Verlag, 1897-1941), *Corpus scriptorum ecclesiasticorum latinorum*, 100 vols. (Vienna: apud C. Geroldi filium, 1866-1913), and *Corpus Christianorum* (Turnhout: Brepols, 1954-). See, as well, Reinhold Rieger, ed., *Johann Adam Möhler. Vorlesungen über die Kirchengeschichte* (Munich: Erich Wewel Verlag, 1992), xxxv-xli.

and Ellie Muir of Computing Services, Wilfrid Laurier University; David J. Reimer, Regent's Park College, Oxford; Donald F. Finlay and the staff at the University of St. Michael's College Library and the Pontifical Institute of Medieval Studies Library, Toronto, Ont.; Channing Jeschke and Patrick Graham of Pitts Theology Library, Emory University, Atlanta, Ga.; Deb Crispin, Paul Wagner, and Alice Croft, all of whom helped cross-check variants and patristic citations; Sally Gray, who worked on many bibliographic details; Silke Force, who compiled the preliminary index, and Heather Kelly, Lorraine D. VanderHoef, and Richard D. Mann, who helped with the compilation of the final version; Reinhold Rieger for his advice on a number of issues and his careful reading of the Introduction; and the Universitätsbibliothek, Tübingen, the Staatsbibliothek, Munich, the Bodleian Library, Oxford, Pusey House Library, Oxford, and the British Library, London, for the generous help they offered over a number of years. The study was made possible by a grant and a leave from Wilfrid Laurier University, Waterloo, Ont. I find it difficult to express my gratitude fully enough to The Catholic University of America Press, Washington, D.C.; to John T. Ford, who worked meticulously through the final draft and made many helpful suggestions for its improvement, to David J. McGonagle for his patient encouragement of the project, to Philip G. Holthaus for closely copyediting the manuscript, and to Susan Needham for reviewing the final text. To the Board of Schwenkfelder Library, Pennsburg, Pa., I owe continuing thanks for support in all aspects of my study.

Peter C. Erb
Waterloo, Ont.
October 7, 1995

Unity in the Church
or
The Principle of Catholicism

Presented
in the Spirit of the Church Fathers
of the First Three Centuries

by
Johann Adam Möhler

Hold fast to what you see to be true and attribute it to the Catholic Church; cast out what is false and pardon me, a mere human being.

—Augustine, *On True Religion*, 10.20

Table of Contents[1]

Preface[2]

Since this monograph in itself will demonstrate whether or not I had significant enough reasons for writing it, it seems unnecessary to clarify fully what induced me to compose the volume or my intention in so doing. A few comments regarding its general design will suffice. It begins with the Holy Spirit. That I did not begin with Christ, the center of our faith, may appear strange. Certainly, I could first have explained that Christ, the Son of God, was sent by the Father, that he became our redeemer and teacher, that he promised us the Holy Spirit, and that he fulfilled his promise. But I did not wish to discuss what might reasonably be assumed as already known; rather, I wished to begin with the topic that belonged fully to the matter at hand. The Father sent the Son, and the Son sent the Spirit: in this way God came to us. We come to him in the reverse way: the Holy Spirit guides us to the Son, and the Son to the Father. Therefore, I began with what is temporally first in our becoming Christians. The monograph will describe this in more detail.

As the title indicates, the subject of my small endeavor is not pursued beyond the third century. From this one might rightly expect that no facts, statements, or other matters from later centuries are noted. Such an expectation should not lead one to suggest, however, that the whole development of the Church was completed within this period. I have at times introduced quotations from later Fathers, but the reader will note that this occurs very seldom, and that when it does nothing new is added. When I have cited later Fathers in a reflection, I could have as easily introduced modern writers. More often, the incorporation of later authors occurs in the Addenda which I have added to explain specific points more clearly; in the Addenda I intended in no way to remain within the confines of the first three centuries.

I ask those who take the trouble to criticize my work publicly to have reasons for their judgments and not to reject it immediately. I have not rejected the judgments of others lightly, but have offered reasons for everything I have written. It would be most displeasing to me, however, if the central issue were set to the side and peripheral issues alone scrutinized, or if my descriptions, judgments, and opinions were interpreted solely by themselves and viewed aside from the work as a whole. If the latter approaches are taken, there are a few cases in which my words may appear rigid or vacuous. Every single thing is tightly bound to the whole; at least I believe this is so. Therefore, everything is to be seen and grasped only in its relation to the whole.

February, 1825
The Author

Part I

Unity of the Spirit of the Church

1. Mystical Unity

The communication of the Holy Spirit is the source of the acceptance of Christianity in us. The Spirit unites all believers into a spiritual community, through which it communicates itself to those who are not yet believers. Christ is given in the Church through love which is engendered in us as we accept the life reigning in her. Only in the community of believers do we become conscious of Christ.[3]

1

Jesus did not look upon the confession of Peter (Matt. 16:16-17) as the work of a person dependent solely upon his own human spirit,[4] but understood it as one of those divine actions that influence[5] his disciples. And Paul often describes faith in Christ as the activity[6] of the Holy Spirit.[a] Likewise, in the eras immediately following that of the apostles, there was a firm conviction that faith in Christ and all that was associated with it resulted from the influence of the Holy Spirit.[b/7] These activities of the Holy Spirit in us are most often

a. Origen, *Commentary on Matthew*, 12:10: "And Simon Peter answered immediately and said, 'You are the Christ, the Son of the living God' [Matt. 16:16]. If we say it as Peter, not by flesh and blood revealing it unto us but by the light from the Father in heaven shining in our hearts, we too become as Peter." Cf. Origen, *On First Principles*, 2:7, 4.

b. Ignatius of Antioch, "Letter to the Ephesians," 9: "Being, therefore, stones of the temple of the Father, prepared for the building of God the Father, and drawn up on high by the instrument of Jesus Christ, which is the cross, making use of the Holy Spirit as a rope." Cf. *The Shepherd* of Hermas, "Mandates," 3, 13 [*sic*; cf. "Similitudes," 9, 13]. Tertullian, *On the Soul*, 1: "For by whom has truth ever been discovered without God? By whom has God ever been found without Christ? By whom has Christ ever been explored without the Holy Spirit? By whom has the Holy Spirit ever been attained without the mysterious gift of faith?" Origen, *On First Principles*, 1:3, 5: "Nevertheless it seems proper to inquire what is the reason why one who is regenerated by God unto salvation has it by Father and Son and Holy Spirit, and does not obtain salvation except with the cooperation of the entire Trinity, and why it is described as the Spirit *essentially (ousiōdōs)*[8] *communicating* itself to believers (see Addendum 1).[c] This mysticism, grounded in the essence of Catholicism, stands in the closest relationship to Catholicism's characteristic mode of grasping the Eucharist.[9] The Spirit that penetrates and gives life to all believers must in this way unite them to a greater life of the whole, beget a spiritual community, and bring forth a unity of all. "Why," writes Clement of Rome in his letter to the Corinthians, "Why are there contention and wrath, discord, division, and war among you? Do we not have one God, one Christ, and one Holy Spirit poured out over us, one calling in Christ? Why do we divide and tear apart the members of Christ? Why do we stir ourselves up against our own body to such great madness that we forget that we are[10] members who belong together?"[d]

In this passage Clement expresses the spirit of his great teacher, the spirit of Paul, who designated the totality of believers as the body of Christ and who thus described Christ as the life-giving and life-forming principle to which his true disciples are related, as the spirit in a person is to the body,[11] its image, its impression and expression.[12] By this metaphor the Spirit's characteristic, which, as is obvious, is determined in a different manner than is the body, is not limited.[e] (The same conviction is at the basis of the metaphor that describes the relationship of Christ to the totality of believers, to the Church, as that of a bridegroom to a bride. In this case Christ is viewed as the begetting principle, the Church as the receptive one.[f])[13] All believers thus form the body of Christ, and among

---

impossible to become partaker of the Father or Son without the Holy Spirit."

c. Origen, *On First Principles*, 1:1, 2-3: "Inhabiting along with his Son . . . as is said, 'I and the Father shall come, and we shall make our abode with him' [John 14:23]. . . . And since many saints participate in the Holy Spirit . . . in which all are said to have a share who have deserved to be sanctified by his grace." Ibid., 1:6, 2: "And only then are they blessed, when they participate in holiness and wisdom, and in divinity itself."

d. Clement of Rome, "Letter to the Corinthians," 46

e. Justin Martyr, *First Apology*, 10: "For the coming into being at first was not in our own power; and in order that we may follow those things that please him, choosing them by means of the rational faculties he has himself endowed us with, he both persuades us and leads us to faith."

f. Cyprian, *On the Unity of the Church*, 6: "The spouse of Christ cannot be adulterous." Clement of Alexandria, *Miscellanies*, 3:4-5, and cf. 2. Augustine, *Confessions*, 8:27: "A fruitful mother of children, of joys, by you, O Lord, her husband." Augustine, *On the Unity of the Church against the Donatists*, 17: "We know the most sacred married persons from the Scriptures—bridegroom and bride, Christ and the Church. . . ." In

themselves are a spiritual unity, just as the higher principle from which that unity is begotten and formed is itself but one and the same.[14] The same ideas are found in the similitudes in which the Good Shepherd of Hermas presents a perceptive image of the Church. He describes her with the image of a tower to be built, well constructed, and resting upon a rock. In the erection of the tower all parts[15] that are useful and are not[16] to be cast aside as useless must be selected and prepared by the Holy Spirit. In the explanation of his images he says, "The rock and the door to the tower are the Son of God. . . . You thus see the whole tower *joined together with the rock* as if it were made with *one stone*. Those who believe in God through his Son, who have put on his Spirit, have such unity as well. *'There is one body and one Spirit'* [Eph. 4:4]."[g/17] This image, which Peter had used earlier (1 Peter 2:1), expresses very beautifully the fact that Christ gives life to believers through the Holy Spirit. Through the Spirit they are held and bound together as a whole[18] so that the *one* spirit of believers is the action of the *one* divine Spirit.[19] In a short and convincing statement [Firmilian in a letter to] Cyprian says: "Where one and the same Lord dwells in us, he binds and unites everywhere with the bonds of unity those who belong to him."[h] And Origen writes: "Out of the fullness of the Holy Spirit, the fullness of love is poured into the hearts of the saints so that through the gift of the Holy Spirit the word of the Lord will be fulfilled: 'That they may all be one; even as you, Father, are in me, and I in you, that they also may be in us' [John 17:21], namely, through the fullness of love that is given through the Holy Spirit."[i/20]

Optatus of Milevius's *Against the Donatists*, 2, allusion is made to the *dotes* [gifts] that Christ gave to his bride. These are the *sacramenta* [sacraments] in the broad sense of the word. Another meaning of this passage will be explained below. [See Part II, Chapter 4, section 69.]

g. *The Shepherd* of Hermas, "Similitudes," 9, 12-13: "'The rock and this gate are the Son of God. . . .' For this reason you see that the tower was of one stone with the rock. So also they who have believed in God through his Son are clothed with the Spirit. They shall become one spirit and one body."

h. [Firmilian of Caesarea, "Letter to] Cyprian," 74, 3: "For even as the Lord who dwells in us, is one and the same, he joins and couples everywhere his own people in the bond of unity."

i. Origen, *Commentary on Romans*, 4:9.

2

Before the time of Christ the Spirit that forms, quickens, and unites the totality of believers descended only haltingly and sporadically, here and there, on individuals. As a result no common, spiritual, or religious life could be established: everything was a special and peculiar case. Following the great and miraculous descent of the Spirit upon the apostles and the whole Christian congregation, which with this descent properly began in a true and living way at this time, the same divine Spirit would never again leave believers, would never come again but would *continually be present*. Because the Spirit fills her, the Church, the totality of believers that the Spirit forms, is the unconquerable treasure of the new life principle, ever renewing and rejuvenating herself, the uncreated source of nourishment for all.[21] Therefore Irenaeus writes: "We preserve the faith received from the Church, a gift of the Holy Spirit. It is to be compared to a costly treasure in a fine vessel that continually rejuvenates itself and the vessel in which it is preserved. The task entrusted to the Church is to communicate this Spirit to God's creatures so that all members who receive it are made alive. Union with Christ consists in this: the power of the Holy Spirit, the pledge of the continuation of our faith[22] and its strengthening, the way that leads to God. . . ."[23] Where the Church is, there is the Spirit of God, and where the Spirit of God is, there is the Church and the totality of grace. But the Spirit is truth. Therefore, none can have a part in the Spirit who have not been nourished to life at the breasts of the mother and who have not received the pure source streaming from the body of Christ (the Church)."[24/a] In the same manner Cyprian writes: "The Church penetrated by the light of the Lord extends its rays over the whole earth's circumference. It is one light, however, that pours itself forth on all sides, and the unity of the body will not be destroyed. Through its fullness of life its branches stretch forth over the whole earth. They pour out from themselves richly flowing fountains. It is a well, a source, a mother increased by an unbroken fruitfulness. She bears us, her milk nourishes us, her spirit quickens us."[b] The same conception is found in Origen: "We have lights, Christ and his Church, which are to enlighten us. He himself is the

a. Irenaeus, *Against the Heresies*, 3:24, 1.
b. Cyprian, *On the Unity of the Church*, 5: "From her womb we are born, by her milk we are nourished, by her spirit we are animated."

light of the world; he enlightens his Church with his light. . . . . Christ is thus the true light, through whose light the Church is enlightened and in herself also becomes a light to the world."[c/25]

3

The continual existence of the divine Spirit among human beings thus began with the apostles who received it directly. The Spirit grasped and penetrated those who had received it and were active in the reception,[26] communicating a new life principle to them. Where such reception was present, it was to be shared *outwardly by those who received it*, so that individuals no longer obtained it directly as the apostles did,[27] but engendered new lives in others similar to the new life that had begun in them. The life of the natural person comes directly from the Creator's hand only once. If there is to be any further natural life, it arises when one person already alive communicates the power of life to another. In the same way the new divine life is to flow out from those already made alive. Such begetting is to bring about further begetting. Only where the apostles lived and worked did the new life expand. In their day those geographically distant from one another could receive the Spirit only through those who, sent out by the Lord,[28] obtained the communication of life from the Spirit directly. In later times the Spirit could be received by others from those members who were partakers of the Spirit through the apostles. Thus all generations formed steps after them, but all, even the latest generations most distant from others, are quickened by one and the same Spirit, present *one community*, establish themselves as *one communal life*,[29] are to make up one Church.[a] If the direct communication of the Holy Spirit should

c. Origen, *Commentary on Genesis*, 1:5 [source cited]; cf. ibid., 1:7, and Lactantius, *Institutes*, 4:30.

a. Cyprian, *On the Unity of the Church*, 5: "The Church also is one, which is spread abroad far and wide into a multitude by an increase of fruitfulness. There are many rays of the sun, but one light; and many branches of a tree, but one strength based in its tenacious root. And since from one spring flow many streams although the multiplicity seems diffused in the liberality of an overflowing abundance, yet the unity is still preserved in the source." Cyprian writes elsewhere, "We gave the greatest thanks to the Lord because it happened that we who are separated from one another in body are thus united in spirit, as if we were not only occupying one country, but inhabiting together one and the self-same house" (Letter 75, 1. Cf. Letter 60).

reoccur and descend directly upon someone through raptures, it would have to be an intimate, indeed, the same Spirit; as a result the individual penetrated by it would feel irresistibly drawn to kindred spirits. Any such person would then walk in the community of the same spiritual life as Paul.[b] The formation of a separate life, however, the lack of a need to unite oneself or the impossibility to do so, would indicate how different the self-revealing spirit would be from the first Spirit and would prove the new one as a false and lying spirit. This spiritual power of life that perpetuates and transmits itself in the Church is tradition, the inner, mysterious aspect of the Church that draws back from all scrutiny.[c/30] No merely self-taught individual in any part of the world has so suddenly declared the Christian faith by himself or herself.[31] No one since the beginning of the Church has been self-baptized,[32] but the source[33] of the preserving power had always been bestowed and communicated through a member of the Church. No one has offered Communion to himself or herself alone in such a way that, separated and without knowing something about other believers,[34] he or she partook of the power of the sacrament; indeed, the possibility of such an act denies the very concept of the sacrament. No one has yet laid hands upon himself or herself in the conviction[35] that by this gesture something might be effected as was believed[36] in the Church from the time of the apostles to the present day.[d/37]

---

b. Tertullian, *On the Prescription of Heretics*, 23: "Now they [the apostles] certainly would not have been surprised at his [Paul] having become a preacher instead of a persecutor, if his preaching were of something contrary [to what was preached earlier]; nor, moreover, would they have 'glorified the Lord,' because Paul had presented himself as an adversary to him. Accordingly, they even gave him 'the right hand of fellowship' as a sign of their agreement with him, and arranged among themselves a distribution of office, not a diversity of gospel, so that they should each preach not a different gospel, but the same, to different persons."

c. Tertullian, *Scorpiace*, 9: "With the entire sacrament, with the shoot of the name, *with the root of the Holy Spirit*, the rule about enduring persecution also would have had respect to us too, *as to disciples by inheritance, and the fruits of the apostolic seed*."

d. Augustine, *Against Cresconius*, 2:14, 17: "When the Holy Spirit came upon them, it gave them this first miracle. When they received it, they began to speak in the tongues of all peoples. Thus the Spirit indicated that the Church is to embrace all peoples and that *no one is to receive the Holy Spirit except one who is coupled in unity with it*. Through the rich and invisible stream of this source God gives joy to his kingdom." Augustine, *On Baptism*, 3:2, 3, speaks to the Donatists who separated from the Church, holding it as something soiled through and through, and who wished to begin anew once more: "If the Church existed even then and had not perished through a breach of its continuity, but was, on the contrary, holding its ground and receiving increase

4

According to the teaching of the primitive Church, true faith, true Christian knowledge, has its beginning in the Holy Spirit and the communication of the Spirit through the bond with the Church. If we look closer to discover[38] how early Christians thought about this, we are answered as follows: *Each individual is to receive the holy life extended forth in the Church by a direct imprint in himself or herself.[39] By direct contemplation one is to make the experience of the Church one's own, to beget in oneself holy thought and action, and to develop Christian knowledge in the sanctified mind.* Clement of Rome impressed this deep truth on the Corinthians. After demanding a holy life of them,[40] he said, "[41]This is the way by which we find our Saviour, Jesus Christ. . . .[42] Through him let us look to the heights of the heavens. Through him let us contemplate God's holy exalted countenance. Through him the eyes of our hearts will be opened. Through him our ignorant darkened thought will look up to his miraculous light. Through him, according to God's will, we are to taste immortal knowledge."[a] Clement thus taught that empirical knowledge of Christ springs from a holy life and that empirical knowledge of Christ is the source of knowledge of the Father. The writer of the splendid letter to Diognetus, also a disciple of the apostles, likewise describes the life flowing from and taken up in the Church as the source of the knowledge of what is characteristic of Christianity. For after he described this, he continues, "Then, although you are on earth, you will see that God rules in heaven, you will begin to speak of the mysteries of God, you will both love and marvel at those who have suffered because they would not deny God (Christ), you will reject[43] the deception and error of the world, if you truly know how to live in heaven, if you despise what here appears to be death, and fear what is real death."[b/44] No one is more impressed with the topic, however, than[45] Ignatius. With deep insight this great disciple, the

---

in every nation, surely it is the safest plan to abide by this same custom. . . . If there was then no Church . . . whence has Donatus made his appearance? From what land did he spring? Or from what sea did he emerge or from what sky did he fall?"

a. Clement of Rome, "Letter to the Corinthians," 35, 36: "This is the way, beloved, in which we find our Saviour, even Jesus Christ. . . . By him our foolish and darkened understanding blossoms up anew towards his marvellous light. By him the Lord has willed that we should taste of immortal knowledge."

b. "Letter to Diognetus," 10. This letter is clearly not Justin's but was written much earlier.

true image of the apostle John, conceived of the essence of Christianity[46] and throughout his letters in so many of his turns of phrase that arose from a light-filled[47] heart, he describes one thing: only love arising out of the womb of the Church and embracing believers teaches[48] what Christ and Christianity is. One can sum up all his letters as follows: *Christ is love; by loving you will find Christ.*[49] Therefore he writes: "In the Church community Christ is to be praised" and portrayed. "In the community the heavenly Father recognizes who the members of his Son are and in it believers are made partakers in God."[c] Again he writes: "All evil will be destroyed in her,"[d/50] and "Faith and love (he always means that which forms the unity of believers) arise out of one another, grow with one another, and perfect themselves in their penetration into God and their unity in him."[e] The power begotten in the Church community and retained only in it[51] is thus for Ignatius the highest principle; in its flowering all other things are established. It is—where it is present in its purity—the destruction of all self-seeking, the greatest expansion of our individual lives, because all believers live in us and we in them.[52]

There is generally scarcely a Church father during this period who does not speak on many occasions of this foundation of the Christian Church, of the divine power that fills her, from which she directly receives life, and which is the source of Christian[53] knowledge. Clement of Alexandria already makes this clear:[54] "Only one reborn," he says, "as is evident in the designation 'reborn,'[55] is immediately freed from darkness.[56] After the new birth the one reborn receives the light,[57] . . . like those[58] who seek to clean their infected eyes. External light does not reach infected eyes; they do not

c. Ignatius of Antioch, "Letter to the Ephesians," 4: "Therefore in your concord and harmonious love, Jesus Christ is sung. And do you, person by person, become a choir, that being harmonious in love, and taking up the song of God in unison, you may with one voice sing to the Father through Jesus Christ, so that he may both hear you, and perceive by your works that you are indeed the members of his Son. It is profitable, therefore, that you should live in an unblamable unity, that thus you may always enjoy communion with God."

d. Ibid., 13: "The powers of Satan are destroyed, and the destruction at which he aims is prevented by the unity of your faith."

e. Ibid., 14: "None of these things is hid from you, if you perfectly possess that faith and love toward Christ Jesus which are the beginning and end of life. For the beginning is faith, and the end is love. Now these two, being inseparably connected together, are of God."

have it unless the hindrance is removed from their eyes and the power of sight is once again given free movement. In a similar way, we who have been baptized, after we left the dark cloud of sin by the power of the divine Spirit, have a free, unhindered, bright eye of God.[59] Only with it do we look upon the divinity, in that the divine Spirit flows in from above. Thus, the eye that can see the divine light is created eternally. Only like can rejoice in like; *the holy can only find joy in the source of the holy.*"[60/f] This great thought that lies at the base and is the mark of everything said to this point Clement explains clearly: Christianity is no mere concept but a matter to be understood as grasping the whole person and having rooted itself in that person's life. "We do not assert that knowledge consists merely in concepts, but that it is a *divine science and a light that has arisen* in the soul *through obedience to God; it reveals everything to humanity, teaching human beings to know themselves and God.*"[g] It will suffice to cite Origen here. Along with the other Fathers quoted, he understood the Holy Spirit communicated in the Church as the source of the salvation of human beings, but he also described this Spirit as the source of faith in Christ.[h] Thus he writes expressly: "*The Son of God who dwells in the midst of individuals is grasped in the community of believers.*"[i/61] In other places he construed this in a different way and said that the power of Christ that creates a new life is a proof of his divinity.[j/62]

f. Clement of Alexandria, *The Instructor*, 1:6 [source of italicized section quoted]. Clement particularly likes to quote Matthew 5:8: "Blessed are the pure of heart for they shall see God." Cf. *Miscellanies*, 1:19

g. Ibid., 3:5 [source quoted].

h. Origen, *On First Principles*, 1:3, 8: "On this account, therefore, is the grace of the Holy Ghost present, that those beings that are not holy in their essence may be rendered holy by participating in it." Ibid., 1:3, 7: "But a share in the Holy Spirit we find possessed only by the saints. And therefore it is said, 'No one can say that Jesus is Lord, but by the Holy Ghost.'" [1 Cor. 12:3].

i. Origen, *Commentary on Matthew*, 14, 1 [source quoted], after discussing divisions.

j. Origen, *Against Celsus*, 1:47: "of whose divinity so many churches are witnesses, composed of those who have been converted from a flood of sins, and who have joined themselves to the Creator, and who refer all their actions to his good pleasure."

5

Christianity's characteristic existence, the conception of it as a matter of communal life, further explains the facts of its growth and expansion in the pagan world. Justin says that he was won to Christianity by the life of Christians, by viewing their lives directly,[a] and he regularly makes the same point regarding others.[b] Gregory Thaumaturgus writes often in the same sense.[c/63] It was also this holy, divine life, spreading itself abroad in the Church and often flowing out from the Church, that grasped and drew non-Christians in a mysterious and irrepressible way.[d] As a result the apologists of Christianity said that it acted "by spirit and power" and not by scholarly demonstration that wishes to convince and win through mere concepts.[64] Against Celsus, who wrote of Jesus and his apostles in a mocking way, Origen noted in a striking passage: "For the person who can view the deeds of the apostles clearly and without prejudice, it must be obvious that they preached the Christian doctrine with divine power.[65] Their listeners did not charge them with a dialectical and rhetorical formation. It seems to me that if Jesus had chosen servants of his word who possessed what one

a. Justin Martyr, *Second Apology*, 12: "For I myself, too, when I . . . heard the Christians slandered, and saw them fearless of death and of all other things that are counted fearful, perceived that it was impossible that they could be living in wickedness and pleasure." Cf. Eusebius, *Ecclesiastical History*, 6:15.

b. Justin Martyr, *First Apology*, 16: "And this indeed is proved in the case of many who once were of your way of thinking, but have changed their violent and tyrannical disposition, being overcome either by the constancy that they have witnessed in their neighbors' lives, or by the extraordinary forbearance they have observed in their fellow travelers when defrauded, or by the honesty of those with whom they have transacted business." Cf. ibid., 15.

c. Gregory Thaumaturgus, *Panegyric on Origen*, 9: "Not thus, however, in mere word only did this teacher go over the truths concerning the virtues with us; but he incited us much more to the practice of virtue, and stimulated us by the deeds he did more than by the doctrines he taught." Cf. ibid., 6 and 11.

d. Origen, *Against Celsus*, 1:46: "Many have been converted to Christianity as if against their will, some sort of spirit having suddenly transformed their minds from a hatred of the doctrine to having a readiness to die in its defense, and having appeared to them either in a waking vision or a dream of the night." Although Origen adds, however, that the pagan Celsus and his Jewish battle companions find it laughable ("Even if Celsus or the Jews may treat with mockery what I am going to say"), he had no inclination that fifteen centuries after him people would similarly find it laughable—and among Christians no less. Cf. A. Neander, *Denkwürdigkeiten aus der Geschichte des Christenthums*, 9ff.

usually calls wisdom so as to win the masses by acuteness and eloquent speeches, one might justifiably have believed that he was like the philosophers who founded schools: his promises that his words were from God would not then have been fulfilled in that they would have rested on the persuasive power of a wisdom based on words or descriptions, and faith would have been similar to that which the wise of this world made with their doctrines. It would have been human wisdom, not divine power (1 Cor. 2:5). But if one saw a fisherman or a tax collector who had never learned any elements of science (as the Gospels state—and Celsus eagerly accepts the truth of their statements regarding the apostles' ignorance) but who not only spoke courageously to Jews about faith in Jesus and preached successfully about him to other people as well, would such a one not seek the source of the convincing power in which the fisherman or tax collector participated? Who would not wish to say that Jesus had with divine power fulfilled his words to his disciples: 'Follow me, and I will make you fishers of men' [Matt. 4:19]. . . . In this way, those who heard the disciples' sermon enunciated with power were in turn filled with power, and they revealed this power in their disposition, lives, and battle for truth to the death."[e/66]

The manner in which pagans were accepted into the Church corresponded very well to the basic perception of Christianity concerning its birth among human beings.[67] The early Christians were not satisfied in any way with a mere statement that Christian religious *concepts* were better than pagan ones. They did not want Christianity to be received after a mere comparison of concepts, or that it be chosen for this reason. The pagan had first to be proven in his or her association with Christians, and if the Christians were convinced that the individual pagan had taken on a Christian way of life, that *this* activity preserved the conviction that he or she was *inwardly fully conscious* that the teaching of Christ was from God,[68] the act of consecration followed. The Church expressed this convic-

---

e. Origen, *Against Celsus*, 1:62: "On this account they who hear the word powerfully proclaimed are filled with power, which they manifest both by their disposition and their lives, and by struggling even to death on behalf of the truth." Concerning this *theia dynamis* [divine power], note further, ibid., 3:68, where the power of the gospel rooting out the evil life is praised. Cf. Clement of Alexandria, *Miscellanies*, 1:20. In other places Origen understands by this term the miracle in the proclamation of it (*Against Celsus*, 8:48). Elsewhere the concept has its simple meaning (ibid., 3:2-5, et al.).

tion by calling rebaptized persons the *reborn*, the *illuminated*,[f] and *Christian life* she called the true and *divine philosophy*.[g/69]

6

It is a basic principle of the Church[70] that the individual's Christian life and through this life the individual's Christian knowledge has its source[71] in the influence of the Church community[72] enlivened by the Holy Spirit.[73] Closely related to this basic principle are the very striking concepts of the Fathers concerning the rise of paganism. By their opposition to paganism they fully clarify the circle of ideas developed here. Theophilus considered polytheism to be rooted in the practical moral fall[74] of humankind by which human consciousness of God was darkened. A thick cloud was drawn over the spiritual eye by the Fall. As a result, divinity could no longer be mirrored and taken up in it. Thereafter, the human person always directed his or her sight toward the earth, and since no one could live completely without God, the individual created gods according to *his or her disposition* as earthly gods.[a/75] Therefore, Theophilus also demanded, above all, practical moral purity for understanding Christianity.[76] Through the pagan community sin arose with all the influences stemming from it, among which were false conceptions of God and religious error above all. Through the life of the holy Christian Church, however, true knowledge was to be given; this knowledge was formed out of the life of the Church and each of the two—knowledge and life—in its own way drew closer to the other. In paganism ethical incapacity and moral death were *inherited* by each individual directly, as well as by whole generations, from the

---

f. Clement of Alexandria, *The Instructor*, 1:6.

g. Eusebius, *Ecclesiastical History*, 2:23: "They were unable to bear longer the testimony of the man who, on account of the excellence of ascetic virtue and of piety which he exhibited in his life, was esteemed by all as the most just of men, and consequently they slew him." Ibid., 3:37: "animated by the divine word with a more ardent love for philosophy"—concerning the first proclaimers of Christianity. Cf. ibid., 6:3, 4:7; Justin Martyr, *First Apology*, 7. Cf. Clement of Alexandria, *The Instructor*, 3:11; John Chrysostom, *On the Priesthood*, 1:1.

a. Theophilus of Antioch, *To Autolycus*, 1:2; Clement of Alexandria, *The Instructor*, 1:6. This is also the sense if idolatry is understood as begun by evil spirits. Augustine, *On Baptism*, 1:11, 16: "For sins are the darkness of the soul." Cf. Tholuck in A. Neander, *Denkwürdigkeiten*, 1:6, 1ff., and passim.

generations that went before.[77] Going back in time this incapacity and death were linked to the sin of the first human being. In a similar way, the reception of the Christian life principle in each specific individual generation has its source in its link to and spiritual root[78] with and from all earlier Christian generations, back to Christ.[b] In paganism[79] the person who could have avoided descent from previous generations would not have inherited spiritual ruin. Likewise, the person who is not now spiritually descended, whether consciously or unconsciously, from the unbroken Christian Church, has no spiritual rebirth and no adoption by God. Earlier, because of one's placement in the mass of sin, one took up in oneself as an individual a curtailment and denial of life. Such an individual, who is now placed in the life of the holy Church, participates in life of the fullest reality. As individuals earlier were placed in slavery to sin by physical birth, now, by spiritual birth in the Church, each person is placed in the freedom of the children of God.[80]

7

The chief result in determining the principle of the unity of the Christian Church can be seen from the previous discussion: *the Church exists through[81] a life[82] directly and continually moved by the divine Spirit, and is maintained and continued by the loving mutual exchange of believers.* Specifically, the following points are also evident:

b. Tertullian, *On the Soul*, 39-40: "The Apostle said that when either of the parents was sanctified, the children were holy [1 Cor. 7:14]; and this as much by the prerogative of the seed *as by the discipline of the institution.* . . . 'Except one be born of water and of the Spirit, one cannot enter into the Kingdom of God' [John 3:5]; in other words, one cannot be holy. Every soul, then, by reason of its birth, has its nature in Adam until it is born again in Christ; moreover, it is unclean all the while that it remains without this regeneration. *Because unclean, it is sinful, receiving shame by its conjunction with the flesh.*" Ibid., 41: "When the soul embraces the faith, being renewed in its second birth by water and power from above, the veil of its former corruption being taken away, it beholds the light in all its brightness. It is also taken up by the Holy Spirit, just as in its first birth it is embraced by the unholy spirit." Tertullian thus clearly sets in opposition the *tradux spiritus* (section 3) and the *tradux peccati*. These comparisons are more specifically raised by many Fathers in the following century and by modern authors (Schleiermacher, *The Christian Faith*, 109, 3). On the controversy over the manner of communicating the new mediating power, see Augustine, *Against Parmenian*, 2:23, 32, 35, *Against Cresconius*, 2:13-17, and elsewhere.

1. Faith or Christian knowledge and the love begotten in the community of believers are fully related to one another. Where faith has developed itself through the communication of the Holy Spirit, this same divine power reveals itself as uniting, and where such union is found, there this same faith is given. [See Addendum 2.]

2. In particular:[83] Just as we experience nothing historically [*historisch*] of Christ without the Church, we experience him in ourselves only from and in the Church. The more we take up into ourselves the divine life flowing in her, the more alive the community of believers will be in us. The more we *live* internally in her and she in us, so much the more alive is the conviction from Christ manifested in us and from it what he is and is to be for us. Through him the community was established, by him the wall of partition that stood between human beings was destroyed, by him the love in the Holy Spirit flowed forth into our hearts. How can we attain to consciousness of his power and attain worth more than by the conscious acceptance of the community of believers in us, *his characteristic work*?[84] Moreover, as Christ was given directly from life to the believers, he became their life and was indivisible from it.[a] Their Christian life, however, is one with the life of the Church out of which it flowed into them, and therefore is indivisible from them.

3. The predicates of the Church—one, holy, true—are one in their essence. The *Holy* Spirit is also the Spirit of *truth*, and holiness and love are the same,[b] or, love, the unifying principle of the faithful, is identical with holiness.[85] Love is the source of truth,[86] or the knowledge of a Christian is formed from the rays of *holy love*,[c] which

---

a. Ignatius of Antioch, "Letter to the Magnesians," 9: "Our life has sprung up again by him and by his death—whom some deny. . . . How shall we be able to live apart from him?" "To the Ephesians," 3: "Jesus Christ our inseparable life." "To the Magnesians," 1: "I commend the churches, in which I pray for a union both of the flesh and spirit of Jesus Christ, the constant source of our life." Clement of Alexandria, *Miscellanies*, 6:16.

b. Justin Martyr, *First Apology*, 14: "We who hated and destroyed one another, and on account of their different manners would not live with those of a different tribe, now, since the coming of Christ, live familiarly with them." Division brought sin; love and communion was given with holiness.

c. Origen, *Commentary on Matthew*, 12:14: "For I think that for every virtue of knowledge certain mysteries of wisdom, corresponding to the species of the virtue, are opened up to the person who has lived according to virtue. The Saviour gives to those who are not mastered by the gates of Hell as many keys as there are virtues, which open gates equal in number, which correspond to each virtue according to the revelation of the mysteries."

raising themselves from the mind are begun, gathered, and grasped as concepts by the understanding. The gifts of the Holy Spirit are unity, truth, and holiness;[87] thus it can be said: if the Spirit is always in the Church she cannot cease to be one, holy, and true.[88]

2. Intellectual Unity

Christian doctrine is the conceptual expression[1] of the Christian Spirit. The written word is not understood without the Spirit. Christianity extends itself by the living word, by external tradition. By discovering what true doctrine is, the believer is directed to the totality of believers. Scripture and tradition belong together and are not to be divided.

8

[2]As soon as it is present, the inner spiritual life of the Christian,[3] the work of the divine Spirit living in believers, must seek expression,[4] press outward, and express itself just as it earlier communicated itself by means of words, of the faith expressed by others (Rom. 10:17).[5] The internal was[6] thus described first, partly because inner faith is the root of the external, partly because, properly understood, it is given before the external, before doctrine.[a/7] Before he expressed himself, Christ bore his doctrine[8] in his consciousness. By divine inspiration Peter was first convinced of the majesty of Christ before he gave his answer to Jesus' question "But who do you say that I am?" [Matt. 16:16], even if we are here speaking of Peter's inspiration as preceding his confession by only a brief moment of time.[9] All the

---

a. To overcome any possible misunderstanding and so as not to associate myself with a false idealistic school, I must overemphasize the need for one to cling fully to the text. My point is: all truth is *originally* in Christ, since in him is the divinity in its total fullness. However, we have truth only insofar as we participate in his divine life and take truth from him. Again: we are only able to have it and proclaim it as living if that divine life is already established in us. As the divinity and, with it, the truth, is in Christ, so we only participate in his divine life and only *receive* the truth that must be, as such, *given* to us, and we are *not* able, if it is not given to us externally through the Church, *to develop it* from ourselves. Both come to us at the same time. The communication of the higher life expanding in the Church links itself to an acceptance of truth in the Church. Thus *hearing* precedes slightly, but *convinced possession and propagation* can only *follow* the new life already begotten in us.

apostles together obtained the Holy Spirit before they proclaimed their inner stirrings, their inner faith.[10] Like the apostles, we must say of ourselves in every case that we do not understand the doctrine, the intelligible expression of the new life communicated through the Holy Spirit, before we have received the life principle itself.[11] Without any further study we can now see, as the immediate result of the earlier discussion, that the Christian Church is not based on the Holy Scriptures.[12] If Christianity first lived in the mind of our Lord and in the minds of his apostles who were filled by the Holy Spirit before it was a concept, speech, or letter, we must assert: the Spirit was before the letter. Anyone who possesses the life-giving Spirit will understand the Spirit's expression, the letter. The same Spirit, however, that filled the apostles[13] is the Spirit that will eternally fill[14] the Church. The person who has this Spirit from the Church[15] will acknowledge and understand the Church's form: the Spirit only meets itself again.[16] Outside the Church the Holy Scriptures are therefore not understood, for if the Church is found where the Spirit is and the Spirit is where the Church is (section 2), the Spirit must be outside of itself if one understands the Holy Scriptures, the Spirit's work, outside of the Church. As a result there is the principle that the Church explains the Bible, that is, one needs the Spirit for the letter; the letter is not the Spirit itself[17] but is only[18] an expression of the Spirit, and if one has obtained this Spirit in the Church's life, one will understand the expression.[b] The apostles themselves only understood the words of Christ perfectly after the Holy Spirit taught those words to them.[c/19] The universal whole and history are revelations of God, but they do not teach one to know the true God if one does not already carry an internal consciousness of God. Likewise, the biblical words are revelations of the Holy Spirit,

b. Tertullian, *Scorpiace*, 12: "who, now, should know better the marrow of the Scriptures (the content and the spirit of the Scriptures) than the school of Christ itself—those whom the Lord adopted, . . . to be fully instructed in all points and appointed as masters to instruct us in all points."

c. Origen, *On First Principles*, 2:7,3: "The Gospel shows it (the Holy Spirit) to be of such power and majesty, that it says the apostles could not yet receive those things that the Savior wished to teach them until the advent of the Holy Spirit, who, pouring itself into their souls, might enlighten them regarding the nature and faith of the Trinity." Cf. ibid., 1:121-28. On the necessity of divine illumination for the understanding of the Holy Scripture there is one voice everywhere during this period. Cf. Justin Martyr, *Dialogue with Trypho*, 7:100, 109, and Clement of Alexandria and Origen, passim.

but they are only understandable to the person to whom the Spirit has already communicated itself. Only Spirit begets Spirit, and life, life; the letter never begets the Spirit, nor does death beget that which is living.[20] In vain have some endeavored to prove that what was passed on was a book written by human beings so as to find in it something of lesser significance, the product of a human spirit, *only* thoughts concerning *human* ways and customs. Thus the pagan Celsus often said that nothing good was found in the Bible that had not already been said by a multitude of philosophers and poets.[d/21] Origen opposed him with the argument that the letter kills but the Spirit is that power and life by which one must judge Christianity.[e] Celsus did not have this Spirit, and therefore he only found things in the Holy Scriptures that suited his low point of view.[22] As has been pointed out and demonstrated earlier, the custom of the Church is not grounded on letters and words, on the lofty conceptions of its adherents, or on the dignity of its believers.[23] The Church views a believer as a new creation, as a person completely changed by a new life principle, marked by a new spirit.[f] If one is to understand the speech of the new spirit, one must possess this new life principle.[24]

d. Origen, *Against Celsus*, 6:1, 7:41: "He refers us to divinely inspired poets, as he calls them, to wise men and philosophers, . . . promising to point out those who should guide us," etc.

e. *Ibid.*, 6.4-5, 7.3, 3.68: "The proof that followed the words of Jesus' apostles was given from God, and was accredited by the Spirit and by power. And therefore their word ran swiftly and speedily, or rather the word of God through their instrumentality, transformed numbers of persons who had been sinners both by nature and habit." Cf. ibid., 5.

f. Clement of Alexandria, *Miscellanies*, 2:4: "'Lo I make things new,' says the Word, 'which eye has not seen, nor ear heard, nor has it entered into the heart' [1 Cor. 2:9]. With a new eye, a new ear, a new heart, whatever can be seen and heard is to be apprehended by the faith and understanding of the Lord's disciples, who speak, hear, and act spiritually." Cf. ibid., 6:8. This high view of Christian dignity has its source in the teaching of many Church fathers that a person is divided into spirit, soul, and body, and that the spirit, the *pneuma*, lost through sin, was once again given to human beings for the first time in Christianity. Cf. Tatian, *Oration against the Greeks*, 13, 12, and Irenaeus, *Against the Heresies* 5:8, 2: "The union of flesh and spirit, receiving the Spirit of God, comprises the spiritual person." There is a beautiful thought of a great theologian of our day [Schleiermacher, *The Christian Faith*, section 74; trans., section 59] who states that by the communication of the Holy Spirit through Christianity the creation of humanity was first perfected, but the teaching of the Fathers is more correct. They teach that humanity was perfect in the beginning, but that it fell from perfection by sin; if this were not the case, one could not characteristically speak of the Fall and a redemption from the Fall, etc.

9

We have yet to discuss how all this was considered and more fully determined in the early Church.[25]

Inspired by *one* Spirit, the apostles proclaimed in living[26] speech and in all locations what they had received in living speech from the Lord. Wherever a congregation was founded, they established the same doctrine through the same Holy Spirit, because without this Spirit the foundation of a Christian Church is not possible.[27] Thus, in the whole Church, in all her expansion, one and the same doctrine must be sounded forth as the utterance of one inner religious life, as well as the expression of one and the same Spirit. So, too, it continued after the apostles had left the young congregations. Indeed, the apostles could be taken from these congregations, but the Spirit that was promised to their disciples and given to them could not be taken away. They installed teachers in each church as the continuation and organ of this Spirit, entrusting them to pass on faithfully what they themselves had been given in trust (2 Tim. 1:13-14; 2:1-2; cf. Titus 1:5). Thus, in the first and second generations and thereafter, Christian doctrine was planted in living word and in all places as the same doctrine. The churches that arose out of an apostolic church were the true impression of it, as their common mother. Thus Tertullian said: "The apostles first confessed faith in Jesus Christ in Judaea, founded churches, and then traveled into the whole world. They proclaimed this same doctrine of the same faith to all peoples. They continued to found churches in every city. From these churches, the other churches daily derived the roots of faith and the seeds of doctrine so that they became churches.[a] As a result they were themselves apostolic churches, because they were witnesses of the apostles. Every essence must be judged in every way according to its source; all these great and many churches are therefore *one*. These first churches out of which all stemmed were founded by the apostles. Thus all are the first (the original)[28] and all

---

a. "The root [*tradux*] of the faith and the seeds of doctrine" [Tertullian, *On the Prescription of Heretics*, 20]. Note the parallel between the living spirit, *traducem spiritus* (section 3), that perpetuates itself in the Church, and the *tradux* of faith and doctrine that perpetuates the expression of the spirit. On the word *tradux*, see Pamelius [208, note i, who quotes Quintilian on *traduces* as coming from one trunk and associates the meaning with Tertullian's usage].

are apostolic in that they are *one*. All proclaim unity."[b] As a result,
Irenaeus could also say: "This sermon, this doctrine, which the
Church, as we have said, received, is preserved by her with care.
Although it is scattered throughout the whole world, it is as if she
dwelt in one house. She believes it as if she were one soul and one
heart, preaches it with one voice, teaches and passes it on as if she
had one mouth. There are many languages in the world but the
power of transmission is but one and the same. And neither the
churches founded in Germany nor in Spain nor among the Celts
believe in or pass on something different. Neither do those founded
in the east, in Egypt, in Libya, or those found in the middle of the
world. But as the sun is one and the same in the whole world, so
also the sermon of truth gleams forth on all sides and illuminates all
who wish to gain knowledge of it."[c]

10

Just as the divine Spirit did not disappear with the apostles, but is
always present, so the apostolic doctrine never disappears but is
always present with the Spirit at all times. However, in apostolic
times this doctrine[29] was not fully grasped by every person who
heard it. As something that only gradually comes into the full
consciousness of each individual by outward formation,[30] the
doctrine[31] could only appear as faulty or unclear in many respects.
In earlier times questions were brought before the apostles. Each
handled them in and for himself insofar as he was capable because

---

b. Tertullian, *On the Prescription of Heretics*, 20.

c. Irenaeus, *Against the Heresies*, 1:10, 2. The assertion that only Tertullian and
Irenaeus cited tradition is completely unfounded. Cajus, or whoever the author of the
Little Labyrinths is, also demonstrated the divinity of Jesus from tradition. According
to Eusebius, *Ecclesiastical History*, 5:28, Hegesippus traveled everywhere in search of
the tradition that he found everywhere and received the same doctrine from them all" (ibid., 4:22). Finally in Justin Martyr,
Dialogue with Trypho, 63, it is stated: "Those who believe in him as being one soul, and
one synagogue, and one church. . . ." Cf. ibid., 116. This is clearly to be understood as
of the same traditional doctrine. That an unspecified general feeling is not referred to
in Justin is proven in his *First Apology*, 26, and in his *Dialogue*, 36, where he sets the
one Catholic doctrine against the heretical doctrine. No one who knows the history
of the canon and is acquainted with the present state of research concerning the
Gospels that Justin used would ever assert that this one doctrine could come from the
Holy Scripture. The thoughts of the Alexandrians will be explained below.

of his special[32] association with the Lord and by the special[33] gifts with which he had been endowed. Yet none formed a separated life.[34] They all saw themselves as a whole, and the solution [to a question], as long as it was possible, was given over to the totality (Acts 15). Moreover, there are still indications that one apostle often sought an explanation[35] or found one from another apostle or from all. At times one was pressed by his spirit to compare his opinion with that of the others since he could be at peace only if his opinion appeared to be harmonious with that of the whole.[36] Thus Paul, according to Galatians 1:16 and 17, could praise himself with having direct divine revelations, but according to Galatians 2:2 he laid his gospel before the apostles "so that he might not walk or have walked in vain."[a] Peter Judaized in Antioch; in Paul he found one who changed his weakness into power (Gal. 2:11-12).[b] How beautiful is the passage that Paul wrote to the Romans, "asking that somehow by God's will I may now at last succeed in coming to you. For I long to see you, that I may impart to you some spiritual gift to strengthen you, that is, that we may be mutually encouraged by each other's faith, both yours and mine" (Rom. 1:10-12).[c] This order is always to be observed. In apostolic times it raised concern about future doubts and contentions, but with these the model for their solution was also given.

By nature one is directed to the need to state and support one's intentions and judgments to one's fellows. One will only be at peace if one discovers them outside of oneself again, and one's subjectivity seems to be or becomes objective the more it multiplies itself externally. This is an indication as to how all persons form an integral whole. But this need is only an analogy by which to understand Christians; no Christian characteristic is without analogy in the general human world. In Christendom each individual must

---

a. Tertullian, *On the Prescription of Heretics*, 23: "Having been converted from a persecutor to a preacher he is introduced as one of the brethren to brethren, by brethren—to them, indeed, by men who had put on faith from the apostles' hands. Afterward, as he himself says, he 'went up to Jerusalem for the purpose of seeing Peter,' *because of his office, no doubt, and by right of preaching*" [Gal. 1:18].

b. See Augustine, Letters 40, 82. He often used this fact in his polemical writings.

c. Origen [*Commentary on Romans*, 1:12] has the proper explanation. It is not opposed to what I wish to say.

be completely determined in regard to doctrine by the totality of believers. It should be impossible for an individual to form doctrine by himself or herself. Each specific individual has the inner Christian life principle, the inner power of faith, only from the totality, and in this way the believers together form a unity from the apostles throughout all time. Likewise, the true expression of inner faith, true doctrine, can also be held and determined only by the totality; that is, with regard to the determination as to what true doctrine is, a Christian is directed to the totality of all contemporary believers and to all earlier believers as far back as the apostles. Just as Christian doctrine is the Christian Spirit expressing itself in concepts, so the manner and method by which one comes to doctrine is patterned on the manner and method by which one is a partaker of the Christian Spirit itself. The question "What is Christian doctrine?" is completely historical [*historisch*]. It asks, "What has always been taught in the Church from the time of the apostles? What does the *common, enduring* transmission say?"[37] In the early Church if anyone ever doubted what true Christian doctrine was, the doubter was not immediately directed to private study as to a human solution,[d] but to the doctrine passed down in that individual's church,[38/e] chiefly to those churches in which the apostles themselves taught,[f] and finally to the whole contemporary Church,[39] which again only made decisions according to the doctrine that the apostles taught, that is, what the generations before them taught or what they received directly from the apostles.[g/40] What resulted from this the believer

---

d. Tertullian, *On the Prescription of Heretics*, 6: "We, however, are not permitted to cherish any object after our own will, nor choose what another has introduced of private fancy. In the Lord's apostles we possess our authority; for even they did not of themselves choose to introduce anything, but faithfully delivered to the nations the doctrine that they had received from Christ. If, therefore, even 'an angel from heaven should preach any other gospel,' he would be called accursed by us" [Gal. 1:8].

e. Irenaeus, *Against the Heresies*, 3:3, 1: "It is within the power of all, therefore, in every church, who may wish to see the truth, to contemplate clearly the tradition of the apostles manifested throughout the whole world." Cf. Katerkamp, *Kirchengeschichte*, 1:49.

f. Tertullian, *On the Prescription of Heretics*, 36: "Achaia is very near you, in which you find Corinth. Since you are not far from Macedonia, you have Philippi; if you are able to cross to Asia, you find Ephesus. If, moreover, you are close upon Italy, you have Rome." Cf. Irenaeus, *Against the Heresies*, 3:4.

g. Augustine, *On Baptism against the Donatists*, 5:27, 38: "They observe most constantly the rule of faith that has been sought out with diligence; and if they stray from it in any way, they submit to speedy correction under Catholic authority,

accepted unconditionally even if that believer did not find in himself
or herself the inner basis for it. The believer did so in the firm and
reasonable assumption that just as the divine Spirit testified in the
whole Church, so it would testify in the believer too, if that believer
matured to greater perfection in the inner person.[h/41] If Christian
doctrine is the necessary complete expression of the Holy Spirit
living in the totality of believers, this totality cannot in any way ever
forget a doctrine or allow it to perish because the Spirit *active* in the
totality would thereby be proven *inactive*. No less can the totality
express the opposite of true doctrine because the Holy Spirit would
be seen as contradicting itself, that is, as invalidated and as not
present. The individual believer as an individual could err, but never
if that individual clung to the totality, to the Church. At the time of
the apostles the one who held to the Church must have received true
doctrine infallibly, not because the Church was filled by human
beings but because it was filled by the Holy Spirit. Likewise, the
individual who turns to the common teaching of the Church cannot
be in error, not because all or many people in the Church agree, but
because the totality of gifts of the Holy Spirit is in the totality of
believers. Doctrine cannot and must not be viewed as a human work,
but as the gift of the Holy Spirit. Thus all believers are seen as parts
integrating themselves on all sides and are directed back to the basic
insight that truth is in unity and love.[42]

---

although, in Cyprian's words, they be tossed about, by reason of their fleshly appetite, with the
various conflicts of fantasies." Cf. ibid., 6:1, 2: "For the spiritual person, keeping 'the end
of the commandment,' that is, 'charity out of a pure heart, and of a good conscience
and of faith unfeigned' [1 Tim. 1:5], can see some things less clearly out of a body that
is yet corruptible and presses down the soul, and is liable to be otherwise minded in
some things that God will reveal in his own good time if the person abides in the
same charity."

h. Tertullian, *On the Prescription of Heretics*, 28: "Grant, then, that all have erred; that
the apostle was mistaken in giving his testimony, that the Holy Spirit had no such
respect for any as to lead them into truth, although sent with this view by Christ, and
for this asked of the Father that he might be the teacher of truth. . . . Is it likely that
so many and great churches should have gone astray into one and the same faith? No
casualty distributed among many individuals issues in one and the same result. Error
of doctrine in the churches must necessarily have produced various results. When,
however, that which is deposited among many is found to be one and the same, it is
not the result of error, but of tradition. Can anyone, then, be reckless enough to say
that those who handed on the tradition were in error?"

11

If anyone initiated an egotistical development, its rejection was based finally on tradition that was nothing other than an agreement with the continuing faith of the Church and the resulting demonstration of the novelty of that development.[43] This demonstration occurred by means of the unbroken episcopal succession from the time of the apostles. Thereby it was proven that heresies first arose during the earliest periods and that these heretics did not receive their doctrine from the apostles since they did not live with the apostles nor were they taught by the apostles, that is, they taught themselves and they proclaimed a human doctrine[a/44] even if they cited a written Gospel. Thus Irenaeus said: "We can count those bishops who, with their followers up to our own day, were placed in the churches by the apostles. They do not teach the same as the heretics. They know nothing of what these heretics sowed."[45/b] And Tertullian says: "If any begin to link themselves to the apostolic era so as to indicate that their doctrines seemed to be handed down from the apostles because they were found among the apostles, we can say: Let them point to the origin of their churches; let them develop a list of their bishops who have come down from the beginning in an unbroken succession so that the first bishop had an apostle or one of the apostles' disciples as a teacher or predecessor; and let them prove that the bishop always remained faithful to those teachers. The apostolic churches descended in such a way. The church of Smyrna shows that John installed Polycarp, the Roman church that Clement was ordained by Peter, and likewise all the others point to persons whom the apostles installed as bishops so as to plant further the apostolic seed through them."[c] It is in no way to be said that each of the bishops always and in all times must find himself in possession of the true *apostolic* doctrine simply because he is placed in apostolic succession and that this quality flows magically through to him from the bishop before him. This would be a highly materialistic

---

a. Tertullian, *On the Prescription of Heretics*, 31: "From the actual order, therefore, it is clear that what was first delivered is of the Lord and is true, whereas what was later introduced was strange and false." Irenaeus, *Against the Heresies*, 3:2.1: "Every one of these, being altogether of a perverse disposition, depraving the system of truth, is not ashamed to preach *self*."

b. Ibid., 3:3.1.

c. Tertullian, *On the Prescription of Heretics*, 32.

point of view. Only the unbroken perpetuation of Christian doctrine in opposition to the new heretical doctrine should thus be demonstrated. Therefore, it was possible for Clement of Alexandria, setting aside a Church type, to make use of a political image, a succession of emperors, to demonstrate this truth. He writes: "The Savior carried forth his doctrine during the time of the Emperors Augustus and Tiberius. The apostles lived to the time of Nero. Between Hadrian, however, and the Antonines heresies arose (which, Clement believed, did not all arise in his own time)."[d/46] One can compare with this the manner in which, in another place, he demonstrates that Hebrew philosophy, as he expresses himself, is far older than Greek.[e]

One would not give a correct impression of the character of the period immediately following that of the apostles if one neglected to say that in the preservation and explication of received doctrine by far the greatest weight was laid upon the bishops who followed the apostles. This is already clear from the Pauline passages cited above (section 9; we will come to the inner basis of this later). Most of the Church fathers agree with this. Just as the apostles chose the most faithful and capable of their disciples as church leaders,[f] so immediately after their deaths only those were chosen who still belonged to their number or who, among their many disciples, followed them directly and had repeatedly taken up apostolic doctrine.[g/47]

In the middle of the second century Polycarp, the disciple of John, still lived, and toward the end of this century Irenaeus,

---

d. Clement of Alexandria, *Miscellanies*, 7:17: "That the human assemblies that they held were later than the Catholic Church, requires few words to demonstrate. For the teaching of our Lord at his advent, beginning with Augustus and Tiberius, was completed in the middle of the reign of Tiberius. And that of the apostles, embracing the ministry of Paul, ends with Nero. It was later, in the times of the Emperor Hadrian, that those who invented heresies arose."

e. Ibid., 1.21.

f. Irenaeus, *Against the Heresies*, 3:1: "If the apostles had known hidden mysteries, which they were in the habit of imparting to 'the perfect' apart and privily from the rest, they would have delivered them especially to those to whom they were also committing the churches themselves. For they were desirous that these individuals should be perfect and blameless in all things, whom they were leaving behind as their successors, delivering up their own place of government to them."

g. Ibid., 3:3, 3: "In the third place from the apostles, Clement was allotted the bishopric. Since he had seen the blessed apostles and had been conversant with them, he might be said to have the preaching of the apostles still echoing in his ears and their traditions before his eyes. Nor was he alone in this, for there were many still remaining who had received instructions from the apostles."

Polycarp's pupil, passed down evidence of his teacher's speeches
against many heretics, which, Eusebius remarked, Irenaeus still
received in the first generation after the apostles. Thus, in the middle
of the second century, many of the apostles' disciples could have
been bishops and toward the end of the century, disciples of their
disciples. Is one then not justified in calling on their doctrine, and
their *harmonious* doctrine, as of apostolic origin? At the end of the
second century there is such a rich flow of compositions by Christian
teachers, who had begun to work at the beginning of the century
with disciples who were directly connected to the apostolic period,
that the fullest witnesses of the common teaching of the time are
preserved. Irenaeus indicates, in the passage already noted, how
closely and securely the transmitted doctrine was held. They held
more firmly to oral statements because they had no or few apostolic
writings in the congregations, and the bishop was controlled from
silent arbitrary deviation by the congregation, many members of
which also had as their teachers apostles and other disciples directly
taught by the apostles. Even more was he controlled by the union
between all congregations (yet to be discussed).[48] There is a passage
in a letter of Irenaeus to Florinus, a Roman presbyter who joined the
Valentinian sect,[49] which reads as follows: "These conceptions,
Florinus, are, to express[50] myself economically, of little healthy
content. These doctrines do not agree with those of the Church. They
trip those who follow them into the greatest godlessness. The
heretics never once trusted themselves to carry these doctrines
outside the Church. The priests before our time who walked with the
apostles did not pass on these doctrines to you. For I, while still a
youth, saw you in Asia Minor when you lived in pride in the
emperor's court. You often endeavored to gain Polycarp's favor. I
would prefer to remember what has happened than what has
recently occurred. What is learned in youth grows with the soul and
unites itself with it. I can still point to the place where the holy
Polycarp sat and taught, his exits and his entrances, his manner of
life, the shape of his body. I still know the talks that he held with the
people. I remember how he spoke of his association with John and
of the others who had seen the Lord, how he mentioned their talks
and what he had always heard from them regarding the Lord, of his
miracles and his teaching. He, who had seen the life of the Lord with
his eyes, related everything in agreement with the Scriptures. What
I then heard came to me by the grace[51] of God. I do not write it
down on paper but in my heart, and I renew it with simplicity by

this same grace. Before God I can confess that if the apostolic priest (Polycarp) had heard something similar to this [Valentinian teaching], he would have stopped his ears and, as he often did, called out: 'Oh good God, have you preserved me in such a time that I must experience this?' He would have fled from the place where, either sitting or standing, he heard the doctrine. The same can be seen in his letters that he wrote to strengthen neighboring churches or to fellow believers to admonish and encourage them."[h]

12

Gathering together what we have said concerning transmission (see Addendum 3) or tradition the following points may be noted:

1. The gospel, proclaimed, complete, living, proceeding from the fullness of the sanctified mind from the time of the apostles, is that which is expressed in one part of believers as the work of the living Spirit in them and through which the faith is chiefly mediated to others. By it the Church's nurture is made known. It is self-evident that consequently tradition dare not be divided from life in the Church.

2. Among the apostles' disciples tradition was first the living word that went out from them and was received by others. In part this was still so among the disciples of those who were directly taught by disciples of the disciples. (We are not speaking here of the written gospels.) For the generations thereafter the tradition that began with the apostles was no longer *merely* oral, but is embodied in the confessions of the Church[52] and, in an unbroken succession, the writings of those who wrote from the time of the apostles to our time. However, tradition is also always the name for the word that was first spoken and is continually expounded in a living way in the Church;[53] it is then immediately embodied again for the future. A proof from tradition is not cited from a doctrine present in[54] a certain generation, but as disciples of the apostles and disciples of their disciples lead back to the first member, that is, to the apostles, so an example from tradition must go back to the apostolic period. Tradition is thus no unspecified past notion.

---

h. Eusebius, *Ecclesiastical History*, 5:20,4-8.

3. If tradition is the word of the divine Spirit moving through all centuries, then outside of the Church tradition is as little understood as Scripture itself.

4. Tradition can and should transmit no *proof* in the specific sense for any Christian doctrine. As Christ and the apostles did not prove their doctrines, so tradition is not to prove them. It sets forth its truth[55] of which each person *is to become inwardly conscious. Tradition is only to refute those who establish foreign developments in the territory of the Church and wish to describe these as Christian doctrine.* Therefore, the Church fathers say only that such phenomena are *novelties,* and Tertullian makes use of the expression "prescription," borrowed from the language of jurisprudence. By this expression he designates the well-founded possession of true doctrine transmitted from the apostles,[56] and he designates the *later* incursion of a sect that wishes to study so as to know Christianity as if it were something which did not exist earlier,[57] as an improper beginning, as a usurpation.[a] The proof from tradition is a call upon the Christian consciousness that always existed and existed among all. To others who do not have it, it is not yet given. Their statements are rightly rejected; no other action is possible against those who do not have this consciousness, who do not possess the faith.[58]

5. If this side of tradition is directed more toward the external,[59] another draws itself more toward the internal, *namely, to demonstrate the identity of the Christian consciousness of each individual member or of a specific generation with the consciousness of the whole Church.*[60] The divine power, active and forming itself in the Church from the Church's beginning, is the same throughout all time and binds in essence the latest generation with the generation of the first century. (The Church, then, to this degree, knows no past, and the past here with the future loses its meaning, and both are dissolved into an eternal present.)[61] As a result the belief of one specific generation and of each individual believer is only a new structure and form of this same divine power. Thus the whole Church is a type of each of her members. In a like manner each of the members is to become

---

a. Tertullian, *Against Marcion,* 1:1: "But another brief treatise will maintain this position against heretics, refuted even without consideration of their doctrine by a prescription of the novelty of their opinions." Therefore his book, *On the Prescription of Heretics.* Cf. Rigaltus [who comments] on Tertullian, *On the Prescription of Heretics,* 1:6 [and cites this passage in *Against Marcion* as referring to *On the Prescription of Heretics*].

conscious of his or her character as counterpoint and impression of the whole.[62] By an inner necessity the love in Christ, through the Holy Spirit, unites individual believers with the contemporary totality of believers. (The believer can ascertain this unity by contemplation and experience.) In a like manner this love binds the believer with all previous generations, and that individual believer is at peace only if he or she has gained clear consciousness of an identity with earlier generations.[63] As human beings are not aware of the harmony of their spirits as such, except by means of external actions given to them in some way or other, so external written[64] tradition is the means of understanding. By tradition, then, as soon as the life of the Church has developed in the believer,[65] that believer will be conscious that his or her Christian consciousness agrees with and is the same as the enduring consciousness of the Church, that the Church never lives through a moment in which she has seen herself different from the believer in essential designations, and thus that the believer is the true, same, faithful likeness of that which is ever the same and unchangeable.[66] It is self-evident that if developments that are not found ever again in the whole life of the Church present themselves to the individual or to a whole series of generations, the believer must either reject them or see them as mere appearances which, although they continued after the foundation, he or she cannot accept as apostolic or essential doctrines.

The believers of all times are thus present to us in tradition. They appear as integrating members of a whole: they teach, admonish, and direct us properly so that we accept nothing as apostolic doctrine unless accepted by all believers from the time of the apostles. By tradition we believe and see everything as the true expression of the Christian Spirit, which as far back as the apostles is found as apostolic doctrine.[67]

13

A Catholic of Cyprian's time did not believe any doctrine finally *because* it was believed in Irenaeus's day and was believed in the Church in his or her own day: *with such external faith, only a beginning was given*. Truth testified to itself by the power of the Holy Spirit in the believer. However, since this same Spirit, which gave life to the Church at the time in which those individuals lived, continued to give life to her, it testified to the later believer in the same way as it did to earlier Christians. The Catholic believed *what* all periods of Christianity earlier believed. *The Catholic's faith was not faith in authority, as the heretics' disciples charged in the second century, but the Catholic had all authority for himself or herself;*[a] *individual agreement with the faith of all times was a necessary consequence of the characteristic of Christianity.* The same foundation begets the same result. All the faithful have *one* consciousness, *one* faith, because *one* divine power forms them. Again, a doctrine is not false *because* it first arose in the third or the fourth century, but because it, if it is to be Christian, always had to be there, at least in seed. Christian consciousness formed by the Holy Spirit could not have arisen first in that generation, nor could it ever perish. Thus what first came at a later time is not Christian, since everything Christian was given at once with the divine Spirit that always had to express itself. Therefore, the basic principle: nothing except what is transmitted. Neither the Docetists nor the Nazareans, neither Artemon, Paul of Samosata, nor Praxeas had the correct Christology, because their conceptions did not exist before them and could not have perished with them [had they been the true ones]. The Holy Spirit did not teach what had not previously existed and could not be. It must have had a weak power if it could only manifest itself so correctly in Noetus and yet remain completely powerless in someone similarly minded several centuries later. *Refuted, egotistical explanations are opposed to the enduring consciousness of Christians as well as to each individual believer.* If a believer rejects any doctrine, the believer does so because it is opposed to his or her faithful consciousness. In that it is so opposed, it is necessarily also opposed to the general consciousness because the individual consciousness cannot be anything other than the general consciousness and an outflowing of it. A believer's rejection of heresy is not a refutation by mere authority, but by living faith. Nevertheless, authority is necessarily tied to individual faith. The *isolated* believer, however, cannot direct a refutation against false teachers because they pride themselves with direct enlightenment, or, as always, the same law could be used against that believer *if the unbroken consciousness of the whole Church did not stand on a historical*

---

a. Augustine, in *On the Remission of Sins*, 3:7, 14, after he was given a traditional proof of the doctrine of Original Sin, states: "I do not call this to memory as if we were supporting ourselves on the views of learned men with canonical authority, but I only wish to point out that from the beginning to the present whenever something new arose in the faith of the Church, the witness concerning Original Sin was maintained."

[historische] *basis at his or her side.* In such an isolated position are
those who do not assert a unity of all believers at all times, who
express no "prescription," and can point to no notion as unchristian.
If they inconsistently set down an unchangeable Christian faith, a
tradition, they make themselves guilty of presumption by their
inconsistency. Nor is tradition to be understood as treating only
various expressions of the same inner disposition (Henke 1:129, 154;
Gieseler 1, section 34). Christianity does not consist in expressions,
formulae, or figures of speech; it is an inner life, a holy power, and
all doctrinal concepts and dogmas have value only insofar as they
express the inner life that is present with them. Indeed, as a concept,
which is always confined, dogma does not embrace and create life,
the unspeakable, and it is always defective. However, as life, it is
also not communicable and cannot be fixed; this occurs through
explanations in concepts, through expressions. Since doctrinal
concepts, dogmas, and the like, are explanations of a *specific* inner
life and inner life is to be made firm by them, they are not matters
of indifference but highly necessary. One who *stands upon* expressions as did Noetus or Artemon, Mani, or Pelagius—in such a person
another spirit, another life, expresses itself (at least so the Church
must maintain). Such a person must be rejected not because of
different expressions, but because of a different spirit. Such a spirit
must be first of all viewed with dread in its form of speech. So it is
with Sabellius. His doctrine of the Trinity does not express Christian
consciousness. In his doctrine, the one who redeems is different from
the one who will redeem, the reconciler different from the one who
reconciles us with the Father. Sabellius's intention, very splendidly
stated, was first arrived at, like others that had been rejected, so as
to bring the faith of the Church more in harmony with the understanding. This it did not achieve. It established a different consciousness from that[68] which existed, declaring the latter irrational. Because
of this, Sabellianism was always rejected as in opposition to the
Church. The Church never built upon Sabellian Trinitarian doctrine,
and therefore will never build upon it.[69]

7. Since Christianity is seen as a new divine life given to people,
not as a dead concept,[70] it is capable of development and cultivation,
the promoting elements of which will be discussed later. The identity
of the consciousness of the Church in the various moments of its
existence thus in no way needs a mechanistic protection: *The inner
unity of life must be preserved or it will not always be the same Christian
Church; but the same consciousness develops, the same life unfolds itself*

ever more, is always more specific, makes itself always clearer. The Church attains to the humanity of Christ. These forms are the characteristic *developments of the life* of the Church, and tradition contains these successive unfoldings of the higher seed of life by protecting the inner unity of life itself. These developments of life are already evident in Paul, continue in John and in the first centuries, and appear in glorious bloom in the great synods.[71]

14

We explained earlier why the Christian Church could not be grounded on the Scriptures.[72] It now remains only to describe how tradition or the proclaimed living word, remaining continually in the Church, relates to Scripture, since early Christianity expressed itself very specifically on this point.

When the first individual Gospels were written, the gospel, the full doctrine of Christ, had already been proclaimed for a long time both within and outside of Palestine and, as Irenaeus said, was deposited in the hearts of believers. The Gospels, therefore, arose out of the living word as heard from Jesus and proclaimed once again.[73] That which lived was made by them into a permanent form insofar as they created it. However, the apostolic Epistles themselves indicate that they did not create the living gospel. In them we find much completed, more closely specified, more precisely presented and developed than is the case in the Gospels. Controversies developed in the congregations over the apostolic statement and the proclaimed gospel. The apostles who were still alive settled these and explained what seemed to be at points obscure to some individuals, or insufficiently dealt with earlier. Our apostolic Epistles, the source of which is to be sought and is clearly indicated for the most part in these circumstances, contain such explanations. Consequently, all these Epistles make reference to an earlier oral teaching. In his Epistles Paul refers to it (2 Thess. 2:15; 2 Tim. 2:2). The doubts that the Epistles themselves raised[74] could be removed by the authors themselves on a later visit to the congregations to whom the Epistles were addressed. Thus Paul went to the Corinthians after he had written Epistles to them; likewise he went to Rome, from where he sent Epistles to other congregations. The heretics point out how disunities arose at the very beginning of Christianity by citing passages in Paul's Epistles: "O foolish Galatians! Who has bewitched you" (Gal. 3:1), "I am astonished that you are so quickly deserting him who called you in the grace of Christ and turning to a different gospel" (Gal. 1:6-7), and in the Epistle to the Corinthians: "But I, fellow believers, could not address you as spiritual persons but as fleshly, as babes in Christ. I fed you with milk, not with solid food" (1 Cor. 3:1-2). The heretics cite these texts to make everything uncertain, to cast out the common doctrine of the Church, to make plain their own alleged calling, their awakening for the renewal and completion of Christianity, and to create an opening for their secret doctrine. The Church fathers can thus justifiably oppose them: if they present us with corrupted churches, they ought also to guarantee that they will be made better and acknowledge those churches for whose faith the apostle Paul thanked God (Rom. 1:6).[a]

All the writings of the New Testament were given in consequence of this to the persons addressed who were already believers, that is, to those who had already received the Spirit from the community of believers and with it the evangelical doctrine. One can never hold to the written word without having earlier known the Christianity in which the written word was received. Matthew did not write his Gospel to the Palestinian Jews but to the Christians in Palestine. Luke wrote his to Theophilus who was already a Christian. John did not write his for the Cerinthians but against them (if we wish to accept this as the reason for his writing) and to those who had long accepted in oral form what he now wrote. Thus, the living gospel always preceded the written gospel and went along with it, even after the authors of the Holy Scriptures had passed away. Irenaeus could say: "If the apostles left no writings, must one not follow the order of the oral transmission which they gave, which they entrusted to the Church?" And: "Many races of barbarians who believed in Christ assented to this living gospel in that without paper and ink

---

a. Tertullian, *On the Prescription of Heretics*, 27: "Since, therefore, it is incredible that the apostles were either ignorant of the whole scope of the message that they had to declare, or failed to make known to all the entire rule of faith, let us see whether, while the apostle proclaimed it, perhaps, simply and fully, the churches, through their own fault, set it forth otherwise than the apostles had done. All these suggestions of distrust you may find put forward by the heretics. They bear in mind how the churches were rebuked by the apostles: 'O foolish Galatians . . .' [Gal. 3:1]. When they raise the objection that the churches were rebuked, let them suppose that they were also corrected; let them also remember those (churches), concerning whose faith and knowledge and conversation the Apostle 'rejoices and gives thanks to God.'"

they had salvation written in their hearts by the Holy Spirit and carefully preserved the old tradition."[b] When these people later received the written Gospels and Epistles, and the like, it was the same with them as it was in the time of the apostles, that is, they too received in writing what they had already long received and preserved. So we also now believe in Christ before we understand that there is a written gospel in the world.

15

The Holy Scriptures are not thought of as something different from the living gospel, nor the living gospel, the oral tradition, as something different from the written Gospels, as a different source. As both were the word and doctrine[75] of the Holy Spirit and both were given by the apostles to the believers, so both forms of the word were viewed as belonging fully together and in no way separable. If the heretics who had turned from the living gospel of the Church cited the Holy Scriptures, they were refuted with the same Scriptures[76] which they did not understand, because the Scriptures, composed only in the Church and intended for the Church, are only understood in her and cannot be set in contradiction to the living gospel. Since the heretics had not taken their conceptions from the Church but from themselves and could not trace them back to the same source, to the apostles, they called upon the Holy Scriptures one might say, "falsely." "If it is the case," says Tertullian, "that the truth is on our side, according to whose[77] rule we walk, and that the Church received this truth from the apostles, the apostles from Christ, and Christ from God, then it is clear that the heretics cannot in any way be allowed to call upon the Holy Scriptures. Without Scripture we can demonstrate that the Scriptures do not belong to them. If they are heretics they cannot be Christians since they do not have from Christ what they took from themselves if they took the name of a heretic. If they are not Christians, they have no rights to the writings of the Christians. We can rightly say to them: Who are you? When and from where have you come? What do you want with my possessions since you do not belong to my people? With what right, Marcion, do you cut my forest? (do you

---

b. Irenaeus, *Against the Heretics*, 3:4, 2.

mutilate the gospel?)[78] With what right, Valentinus, do you twist my sources? By what power, Apelles, do you move my borders? It is my possession. And the rest of you, what do you sow and on what do you pasture your flocks according to your own capriciousness? It is my possession. I have possessed it from all time. I possessed it earlier. I have firmly established, original rights from the owner himself, whose own possession this was. I am an heir of the apostles. As they ordained it in their testaments, as they entrusted it, as they swore it, so I possess it. They have dispossessed you; they have cast you off as a stranger, as an enemy."[a] From this inner and essential bond, in which the Holy Scriptures stand with the unbroken living gospel, from the way in which they are constructed together, it follows that the Church never cast away one part of the Holy Scriptures, that she never corrupted a text,[b] but that she always honored the Scriptures with a pure, holy disposition as the most costly treasure entrusted to her, and that she must transmit them to future generations unspotted, unharmed as they came from the hands of the apostles. Because of the identity of the two the Church fathers often cited both together as one and the same. "One must note carefully and flee their (the heretics') doctrines," says Irenaeus, "so that one will not fall because of them. Rather, one must hold to the Church, *be brought up in her, and be nourished on the Holy Scriptures.*"[c]/[79] In another place he says: "True knowledge (Gnosis) is the apostolic doctrine, the ancient support of the Church in the whole world, the characteristic of the body of Christ according to the

a. Tertullian, *On the Prescription of Heretics*, 37.

b. Ibid., 38: "Where diversity of doctrine is found, the corruption both of the Scriptures and the expositions of them must be regarded as existing. On those whose purpose it was to teach differently lay the necessity of differently arranging the instruments of doctrine. As in their case, corruption in doctrine could not possibly have succeeded without a corruption also of its instruments, so to ourselves also the integrity of the doctrine could not have accrued, without integrity in those means by which doctrine is managed. Now, what is there in our Scriptures that is contrary to us? What of our own have we introduced, that we should have to take it away again, or else add to it, or alter it, in order to restore to its natural soundness anything that is contrary to it, and contained in the Scriptures? What we are ourselves, that also the Scriptures are from the beginning. Of them we have our being, before there was any other, before they were interpolated by you."

c. Irenaeus, *Against the Heresies*, 5:20, 2. He states the same in the letter written by him to Florinus saying that the oral speeches of Polycarp agreed completely with the Gospels, that is, with the Church's interpretation, not with that of Florinus.

apostolic succession, that which the apostles transmitted to the Church in every place it is found. This came to us in faithful preservation and with it the fullest use of the Holy Scriptures without addition or deletion."[d/80] This view is also found in Clement of Alexandria in whose writings "the rule of the Church," "the truth," "the ancient Church," "the divine Scripture," and "the Church's transmission" are all treated as identical. He says, for example, "The Gnostic (in Clement this means the perfect Christian) alone, who has matured in the *Holy Scriptures*, who preserves the *apostolic* and true faith *of the Church*, lives fully according to the gospel."[e] In Origen the same insight is found: "The doctrine of the Church" and to defend "the preaching of the gospel" are for him the same.[f] Along with this it is often stated that the doctrines of the heretics are "unevangelical" and opposed to "the doctrine of the Church." In like manner Origen sees "Church tradition" and "apostolic succession" as identical.[g]

From this come the expressions of honor and veneration for the Holy Scriptures that one finds in the Church.[81] "The Church," says Irenaeus, "has been sown throughout the whole earth. Her pillars

---

d. Ibid., 4:33, 8: Strife cannot be overcome by the nonobservance of the relationship between Scripture and tradition as Grabe and Massuet, Goetze and Lessing suggest against one another [as cited in Massuet's notes to Irenaeus 4:32]. Since Irenaeus (ibid., 2:28, 2) finally says, "The Scriptures are indeed perfect, since they were spoken by the Word of God and his Spirit," this is a censure of the heretics and their suppression of the Scripture. But he says that everything in them is perfect and good and he expressly adds that this is so even if we do not understand much of them. In modern times it is also believed that the essence of tradition must be found in the Scriptures, in that reference is made to the "few books and the uncertainty in reading" in the early Church [in Ferdinand Walter, *Lehrbuch des Kirchenrechts*, 22]. This remark implies that they are now superfluous. This situation, however, is not in the least related to the essence of tradition.

e. Clement of Alexandria, *Miscellanies*, 7:16. In this and the preceding chapter many such comparisons are found. "We use it (the New Testament) as a criterion in the discovery of things." Ibid., 8:16: "We have the source of the teaching of the Lord in the prophets, the Gospel, and the blessed apostles. . . . But if one should suppose that another origin was required, then no longer truly could an origin be preserved." However, a few sentences earlier he writes: "The person who has spurned the ecclesiastical tradition and darted off to the opinions of heretics, has ceased to be of God." And ibid., 15: "So also are we bound in no way to transgress the canon of the Church."

f. Origen, *Commentary of John*, 5:4: "the word of the Church," "the Gospel," and "the kerygma of the gospel."

g. Ibid., *Against Celsus*, 5:61; 8:16 [passage translated not cited in Origen]. Cf. Irenaeus, *Against the Heresies*, 1:3.6.

and foundations, however, are the gospel, the breath of life. The Church must thus have four pillars that oppose unreality and give life to her on all sides."[h] As a result the admonishment and command to read the Holy Scriptures is ever repeated and in the Church it is insisted that to deny Christian doctrine or to depart from the Holy Scriptures is one and the same thing.[82] The Christian calls both a denial of Christ. The Christian has always understood the Holy Scriptures in the spirit of Church doctrine.

16[83]

From what has been said above and in section 12 we are required to draw the following conclusions regarding the relationship between Scripture and tradition:

1. Tradition is the expression of the Holy Spirit giving life to the totality of believers. It extends throughout all periods, is alive at every moment, and is at the same time the embodiment of that totality.

2. Scripture is the expression of this same Holy Spirit embodied at the beginning of Christianity through specially graced apostles. To this degree Scripture is the first member in the written tradition.

3. Scripture was created out of the living tradition, not vice versa. Thus it cannot be demonstrated from Scripture that something dare not be preserved in tradition that is not preserved in Scripture. Scripture itself says the opposite (John 20:30-31; 21:24-25).[84] Much less can it be justifiably asserted that the apostles did not expound or preach as specifically in an oral fashion in the congregations as in their letters.[85]

4. If it is said that Scripture alone is enough for the Christian, one is justified in asking the meaning of this assertion. Scripture alone, apart from our apprehension, is nothing at all; it is a dead letter. Only the product, which comes into light by the direction of our spiritual activities from the Scripture, is something. In this matter it must be asserted that tradition is necessary in its twofold or given meaning (indeed, in its ground).[86] If it is understood as the living gospel, proclaimed in the Church with all that which belongs to its proclamation and which is called by Irenaeus "Church nurture," we

h. Ibid., 3.11.8.

understand tradition as given to believers without the Holy Scriptures, as little as we do the Scriptures without it. Our spiritual
activity must thus be penetrated by the Church spirit if a Christian
product is to come to light from our relationship to the Scripture.

If the living gospel proclaimed at all times had not also been
written down, if tradition had not thus been at the same time
embodied, no historical [*historisch*] consciousness would have been
possible, and we would have lived in a dreamlike state, without
knowing how we came to be, indeed not knowing what we are and
are to become. If the Church and its individual members could not
have demonstrated the identity of her Christian consciousness with
that of all ages, doubt would have come upon us, we would have
had no certainty if she was Christian, would have been cut off, and
as a result rootless. Indeed, there would have been no Church since
the Church is like the unity of inner life. Likewise, stability of
consciousness of this unity in all changing circumstances is absolutely necessary for its existence. This identity must be able to be
demonstrated in the same way as a moral person must demonstrate
morality through his or her thought. (Thus we can also designate the
embodied tradition.[87]) Since it can be shown through tradition how
the Christian spirit expressed itself at all times and that it always
expressed itself as the *same spirit*, it will be certain what the correct
apprehension of Christian doctrine is, namely, that which existed at
all times. If this is not correct, Christians might rightly doubt
whether they will ever experience what Christianity is; they might
rightly doubt if there is a holy, indeed a Christian, spirit, filling the
Church, and a specific Christian consciousness. Those who cast aside
tradition found themselves, as we shall see, in such a situation. In
this case one could not speak of an objective ecclesiastical Christianity. The apostles' disciples in direct contact with them, that is, with
the totality of Christians at the time, had an external proof of the
truth of their point of view. So too did those[88] who followed
throughout the centuries in ever the same character of the apostolic
doctrine. In other words, as we have already said repeatedly: all
Christians form *one* whole without separation in time.[89]

5. The question if tradition is coordinate with or subordinate to
Scripture is to be rejected as based on false principles.[90] There is no
antithesis between the two. Moreover, this question has at its base
the assumption that Scripture and tradition are transmitted together
in two parallel lines. As history indicates, this is not so. They
proceed in one another and live in one another. As little as one reads

the Scripture in the Church without the influence of the Church's nurture, so little could the Church's nurture in the second and third centuries be considered without the influence of the Scripture.[91]

6. The assertion that what is written is to be taken up in tradition is itself unclear.[92] This too arises from an antithesis: what tradition, *as we have developed a concept of it historically*, contains is never against Holy Scripture. Where Scripture is said to contradict tradition, it does not do so in itself, but is said to do so.

The following chapter will more closely describe the characteristic source of this assertion.[93]

7. Those who think that only *one thing* can be demonstrated from tradition and all other things from Scripture do not have proper insight into the matter. We have and hold everything through tradition. Those who did not accept it in the early Church have already cast out everything without it.[94] Does nurture in the community of believers and the Holy Spirit who holds us by it relate only to the one or the other? There is no such division.[95] Of such division the earliest Church knew nothing. In the first centuries everything was refuted[96] by the Holy Scripture, and the Church step by step had to hold fast by tradition to everything Christian. The doctrines of God in their total expansion, of the Son of God in all points, of the Holy Spirit, of freedom and grace, and so on, were already rejected at the beginning of the Church by those who called themselves Christians and who carried Bibles in their hands (that is, by their twisted use of them).[97] These doctrines and the transmission of these doctrines were preserved by the Spirit of the Church. How astonishing it is that some wish to give up and twist what lies so clearly before them in history.[98]

8. Without the Holy Scripture as the oldest embodiment of the gospel, Christian doctrine would not have been kept in its purity and simplicity.[99] It is certainly a great lack of praise for God to assert that this came about by chance since it *seems to us* to have been brought about by purely fortuitous circumstances. What a conception of the power of the Holy Spirit in the Church![100] Moreover, without the Scripture, the first member in the succession is lacking. Without the Holy Scripture, without a characteristic beginning, it would not be understood; it would be erratic and chaotic. But without continuing tradition the higher sense of the Scripture is lacking because without intermediary steps we would know no coherence of the later with the earlier. Without Scripture we can establish no complete image of the Redeemer because we lack reliable material, and for certain

everything turns into uncertain fables. Without continuing tradition the Spirit and the interest to establish such an image of it will be lacking. Indeed, without tradition, as we shall soon see, we would have no Scripture.[101] Without Scripture the characteristic form of the speeches of Jesus would have been kept from us. We would not know *how* the divine-human person spoke, and I think I would not wish to live any longer if I could not hear him speak. But without tradition we would not know *who* spoke and *what* he proclaimed, and the joy in knowing *how* he spoke would be lost![102] In brief, everything belongs together and it will be given to us indivisibly with divine wisdom and grace.[103]

17

The questions that are so often placed before us may also be answered from the position we have taken. Why was Christianity not originally spread by Scripture? Why did Christ not teach his disciples according to such a written record? Why were almost all establishments of these early centuries long satisfied with the living word? And why is Scripture itself open to so many meanings[104] (at least outside the Church)?[105]

The reason for this was that disciples held fast to teachers, individuals to the whole. Slowly and imperceptibly the necessity that each individual was nothing without the whole came to consciousness. Before the egotistical principle gained a solid source of food and cultivation through a general expansion of literacy, Christianity was established generally and bound everything so firmly into a whole that the letter could never be victorious over the Spirit, the concept[106] over life, or self-seeking[107] over the universal good. If it so happened, who can not be convinced that it had to so happen? The Spirit had shown that it could indeed dispense with the letter, but in no way could the letter dispense with the Spirit. Once the Spirit was thus spread about, it was to serve as confirmation of the Scripture, and in this organ the Spirit itself was to be clearer in individual believers. If Christ had written a book or given one to each of his apostles, each would have grasped it, locked himself up at a table with it, drawn concepts from it, and would have begotten no Church, no communal life (indeed, no Christian life because the concepts deduced would have preceded life).[108] Moreover, each written work must be written in the language of a specific people since we have no general language. It therefore carries a specific national character. But if one gives this work to another nation before that nation is acquainted with its content,[109] the nation cannot know how to separate the characteristically Christian from the national (Jewish), that is, it will not understand it. Living proclamation is freer from national characteristics. To desire to study in a foreign nation already indicates interest in Christianity, but to possess it one must already know Christianity. One is therefore required to know Christianity before one reads its books, even though one must learn to read it only through books. One must not compare our relationship to the Bible with a relationship in which a people totally unacquainted with the Bible stand. From youth we learn its language and are biblically raised.[110]

3. Diversity without Unity[1]

Heretical teachers and their schools; the principle of the masters and those associated with them (heretics, churchly egoists); freedom of study; they make the biblical text the basic principle of their schools; a rationalist exegetical principle. Heresy arises from evil.

18

The principle of the unity of the Church will be much clearer to us if we contrast it with the characteristic of heresy, the subject of this chapter.[2]

Christianity wished to build a new thought system concerning God, the world, and human beings on the basis of a new, holy, and therefore necessarily common life, in the same way as the pagan way of looking at things proceeded from the earlier pagan life. This was completely opposed to the pattern of all previous philosophical schools in which approaches and principles were set down on the so-called highest subjects. They endeavored to work on life by a system of concepts, but they remained in the old life even though they were distant from it in their concepts. This is a permanent proof that mere concepts possess no lasting power over life. The ancients could not bring forth new life, partly because the very idea that one must begin with a change of life was strange to them (Socrates was a prelude to Christianity),[3] but more because they had to pass on a better testimony than they themselves were.[4] Christianity, however, gave a creative power,[5] able to beget a new life to its adherents; it made individuals aware that they were nothing aside from a continual living relationship with God,[6] and it taught them that they must take up[7] their instruction with humility if they wished to know anything. Nevertheless, the example of the old philosophical schools, albeit withering beside flourishing Christianity, was still attractive. As a result, Christianity was also understood as a mere system of concepts by those who still did not know its Spirit deeply enough.[8] There were many pagan schools that held different ideas[9] and wished in an unholy sense to gain power over the Christian school. In paganism no unity was possible because human beings by themselves can only err, the ways of error are uncountable, and a higher unifying principle was still not available. Therefore, these pagans felt that there could be no unifying principle in Christianity because they believed that as individuals they were able to analyze and discover Christianity for themselves. Pagan division was to be planted in Christian territory; pagan egoism was to uplift itself there as well. But as there had been no conceptual framework in the pre-Christian period that was able to create new life, so there would be no conceptual framework that could push out the one that had been newly created in and with[10] the Church.[11]

Many heretics were in possession of numerous ideas, but despising what was for them the too narrow forms of positive Christianity, they lost all true power and vivacity. Others distinguished themselves by a religious interiority and depth, but not knowing the source from which this flowed to them, they rose up against the Church to which they were unconsciously indebted for all goodness and entered the saddest path of error. The majority united studies based on Oriental theosophy and Greek philosophy[12] with Christianity, which was opposed to them. However, because they viewed these studies as so essential, indeed as most essential, the basic doctrines of Christianity were removed from their weak sight and marred by the most foreign of patterns. In the majority of cases, the disciples were more unchristian then their teachers. They consequently used the basic principles more consistently. The teachers had brought much good with them from the Church without having discovered it by their basic principles. Their disciples continued this one-sidedness, followed the principles through completely, and in general lost everything.

The founders of such views of Christianity were named "heresiarchs," "masters," and the system as well as all their followers, "heresy" (see Addendum 4), "sects," and "schools." The designation of different philosophical schools, medical schools, and so on, was already used in pagan times. In general, heresy is the attempt to discover Christianity by mere thought (we are speaking here especially of the mystical separatists),[13] without consideration for the

common Christian life and that which arises from it.[14/a] As a result
it develops as a doctrine calling itself Christian, but separated from
the continuing common life of believers.[b] It is in opposition to the
unity that forms believers, which has been explained and will be
further explained. This unity is called "catholic," a designation that
was already used by Ignatius,[15] a contemporary disciple of the
apostles themselves[16] (see Addendum 5).[c]

According to this concept the following can be inferred:

1. The solution of the heretical masters, based on the first
principle of *freedom of study*, was that Christianity must be sought.[d]
They thus insisted that Christianity had been lost or that in time it
could pass away.[17] Because of this they saw their duty[18] as rediscov-
ering [true doctrine], in opposition to the Church which asserted that
true doctrine was always present with her and could never pass
away. Catholics asked, "What is proclaimed in the Church and what
is always proclaimed in her as the doctrine of Christ?" Heretics
asked, "What is to be *thought* of as Christianity?" They changed the
earlier historical [*historische*] direction of Catholicism in the determination of doctrine into a purely speculative one.

2. Heresy also taught that Christianity and Christ could be
grasped most certainly in a separatistic and egotistic manner[e] aside
from any Church community. According to the heretics, the
preservation of Christian doctrine must be viewed as a human work
because they believed that *they* were to call upon human beings to

a. Tertullian, *On the Prescription of Heretics*, 6: "called in Greek 'heresies,' a word
used in the sense of a 'choice' that one makes when one either teaches heresies (to
others) or accepts them. For this reason one calls the heretic self-condemned, because
that heretic has chosen that for which he or she is condemned."

b. Clement of Alexandria, *Miscellanies*, 1:19: "Such are the sects that deserted the
primitive Church." Cf. Irenaeus, *Against the Heresies*, 3:14, 4, 2.

c. Ignatius of Antioch, "Letter to the Smyrnaeans," 8, 2: "Wherever Jesus Christ is,
there is the Catholic Church."

d. Irenaeus, *Against the Heresics*, 3:14, 4: "Their excuse is always the search because
they are blind and not able to find anything." Ibid., 5:20, 2: "They shall deservedly fall
into the ditch of ignorance lying in their path, *ever seeking* and never finding out the
truth." Tertullian, *On the Prescription of Heretics*, 4: "They interpret his words in a
contrary manner to suit their own purpose, when he says in another passage, 'Prove
all things; hold fast that which is good' [1 Thess. 5:21] as if, after proving all things
amiss, one might not through error make a determined choice of some evil thing."
Ibid., 8: "Which will be the meaning of 'Seek and you shall find'" [Matt. 7:7].

e. Irenaeus, *Against the Heresies*, 3:2, 1: "Every one of these, being altogether of a
perverse disposition, depraving the system of truth, is not ashamed to preach *self*."

discover it again and they did not see it as existing before their time. It is obvious that one could not be speaking here of the Holy Spirit who continually preserves the Church, formed and enlivened by that Spirit.

3. The heretical masters held that faith and love, begotten in the Church community, were two completely separate things. They were of the opinion that one could possess *community* without *its* faith.[f] The Holy Spirit that begets love in us was seen as different from the spirit of truth. In this division of Christian knowledge from the love that creates the Church rests the possibility of heresy; the Catholic Church rests on the unity of the two (section 7, n3). Heretics must therefore hold that either love or truth is of purely human making since they divide the two. But since both are one, both are for human beings, and therefore every heretic is necessarily a Pelagian.[19] Heresy can therefore be called theoretical Pelagianism, and the Pelagianism that is commonly so called, practical Pelagianism. Practical Pelagianism declares that the natural inclination to good is given by God as sufficient in and for itself so that one can become holy. It does not acknowledge grace, the uncaused necessity of a continuing dynamic unity with God to arrive at the good. Theoretical Pelagianism gives a Christian the possibility of coming to Christian truth and remaining in it by means of a book. According to this doctrine, God gives a book, and then leaves. His continuing inflowing activity is thus immediately set aside as unnecessary. However, according to the Catholic view, truth and holy love are identical and both have their roots in the Holy Spirit. Thus every consistent heresy must leave both to human beings by human means. Theoretical and practical Pelagianism are thus the same; they find themselves divided only on inconsequential matters. I said above that most heresies lost everything Christian during their development. The common reason for this can be more closely specified from our present point of view. Although the founders of heresies unconsciously took much from the Church, they believed that they had found and known this by their own purely human activity. By their human activity their disciples in turn drew upon what was still held from the teachers. But the divine cannot be held firm by the human, for the human needs the

f. Tertullian, *On the Prescription of Heretics*, 5, where he refutes the complaint of the heretics that they were locked out of the Church community only because they had a different opinion, and that the apostles merely forbade schism.

divine itself working in it if the divine is to be held. Thus the divine and what was characteristically Christian was continually lost until, finally, all that remained was only the purely human. The apprehending power and what was apprehended by it functioned similarly, and thus moved on to the consequence of the system, to a fully internal nothingness. If a school, such as that of Heracleon, for example, taught that love and truth could be ours only through the activity of the Holy Spirit, it is inconceivable why it would not wish to acknowledge this same doctrine with the same community that held it and at least set forth unity of doctrine and of community as a basic principle since opposing actions cannot have their source in the *same* power. But what they wished from the Church community is not conceivable since they insisted at the beginning that they could be everything for themselves, isolated, without the community. What drew them on? It was the hidden active love that disciplined the understanding.[20]

4. Heretics were eventually drawn to Holy Scripture, and its letter was considered by them as the basic principle,[g] that is, as is clear from what has been said, Holy Scripture was separated from the Church for whom it was given and interpreted by a spirit found outside of her. Without this spirit, the heretical master would not have been able to begin a school and would not have separated.

5. Finally, the majority of heretics designated *primitive Christianity* as the point to which one must return. Marcion had already done this,[h/21] and in his day there lived disciples who had been taught directly by the apostles. Such a position was already established as a result of their principle that Christianity could be lost[22] and the

g. Tertullian, *On the Prescription of Heretics*, 14: "But they actually treat of the Scriptures and recommend (their opinions) out of the Scriptures! From what other source could they derive arguments concerning the things of the faith, except from the records of the faith?" Ibid., 15: "They put forward the Scriptures and by this insolence of theirs they at once influence some. In the encounter itself, however, they weary the strong, catch the weak, and dismiss waverers with a doubt." Their interpretations were false in every way, but they nevertheless made an impression. One sees how necessary it is to explain the Scriptures simply and to place them in the hands of the people. Mistrust arises from not having them.

h. Neander, *The Gnostic System*, 277ff. They thus make a distinction between the teaching of Christ and that of the apostles, and they try to build a contradiction between the two. Therefore, Irenaeus, for example, took proofs from the words of Jesus and each of the apostles in particular to demonstrate to anyone who wished to divide the two that the doctrines of the heretics could not be shown to have a source in any of these texts.

method by which they used the Scriptures; and according to the heretical *principle*, Christianity was viewed not as something living, but as a dead, conceptual matter that needed, and was capable of, no development, and could be returned to in a mechanistic way. Christianity was always seen as completed. With this teaching the deceptive doctrine arose that one still knew what biblical Christianity was even if stability of consciousness had been broken for a century or a millennium.[23] It is as if one lost one's mind for a number of years, but at times, having a glimmer of earlier life, viewed oneself as a child, accused others of degeneration, and counseled them to become children likewise.[24] *Those who had maintained consciousness could indeed direct the person, but that person could not direct them. And if such a person complained with self-made false changes about possession of goods, that person would always be in error, not having truly kept the account book of the congregation and the keys to it. Beginning a new book or changing the one that had been transmitted, or forgetting where the keys were, would be a false and arbitrary act in such a case, as would the desire to restore everything to the status quo (according to one's own individual way).*[25]

By this return to primitive Christianity there occurred a journey beyond Christianity to paganism[26] and Judaism. We now turn to a historical discussion of specific matters.[27]

19

The principle concerning freedom to study what Christianity is seems to deprive the word "catholic" of all sense and real meaning if one speaks of the principle as a *Christian, a Church principle.*[28] (See Addendum 6.) Our consciousness is in general double: an intuiting, reflecting consciousness and an intuited, living, working conscious-ness. The second provides material for the first. It is the same with Christian consciousness. A Christian must live as a Christian. A Christian must take up Christianity into his or her consciousness and will then have Christian material at hand to rule the reflecting consciousness before Christian study can begin.[29] If study comes first, what is to be studied? What is the material? How can a Christian product result when reflection is not on anything Christian because, as was said earlier, no Christian material is at hand that must first be studied?[30] Thus, if a heretic wishes to be consistent, the heretic must see Christianity not as something *living* and as present *within* a person, as the heretical principle itself states, but as a mere thought, as a dead concept, with which a heretic begins all operations[31] that the understanding is accustomed to propose for each chosen subject. The heretic is of the opinion that one must be truly able to study impartially, if one is a stranger to the material. The Church fathers very clearly noted that this principle characterizes Christians as non-Christians. If the heretic were a Christian, how could he or she first wish to study *what* Christianity is?[a] The heretic changes the situation that existed *before* Christianity to that following Christianity.[32] The heretic thus thinks of himself or herself as a Christian without Christianity, and because the heretic believes that the Church accepts the principle of "free study," the heretic demands that the Church, too, is to look upon Christianity as not yet known, that is, to view herself as not existing or to contradict herself. Could the Church do this as if she did not know what she knew? The Church knows herself as an unmediated power of God. Only as such can she establish or, much more, be established. She is positive throughout, in no way skeptical. The Catholic thus enters into study with a Christian consciousness, since the Catholic does not wish to cease to be a Christian during study, nor could a Catholic do so since the individual Christian consciousness so grows up with its essence that it would cease to be what is and is considered to be Catholic. But we think of it as Christian. The heretic views Christianity as an unknown greatness and yet wishes to be called a Christian.[33] The Catholic proceeds from certainty given by the Church.[34] Only before being a Christian was the Catholic in the position of the heretic.[35]

The Catholic was thus truly convinced that he or she could study freely, that is, no longer dared to choose between truth or error (the lower freedom to study is a step that a Catholic has fortunately risen above). As a Christian a Catholic decides only to be resolute against evil and to judge it.[b] Because a heretic has the so-called concept of

a. Tertullian, *On the Prescription of Heretics*, 14: "For since they are still seekers, they have no fixed tenets; and not being fixed in tenet, they have not yet believed; and not being believers, they are not Christians." Tertullian comments correctly concerning the biblical passage cited by the heretics in which Jesus or his apostles ordered the search for truth [Matt. 7:7]. This is said to those who first wish to be Christians, but who are not yet or were not completely decided. It was also said to the Jews concerning citations from the Old Testament.

b. Irenaeus, *Against the Heresies*, 4:33, 1-7: "A spiritual disciple of this sort truly receiving the Spirit of God that was from the beginning in all the dispensations of God

intellectual freedom, he or she must say that one is not free but will become free in concept and always first in concept, since a heretic must first seek Christianity, the truth, and of course only the truth makes one free, that is, the possession of the truth, not the seeking of it. For a heretic this is the same as saying: The heretic will be enslaved by a concept because a heretic can be grasped just as well by error and then certainly is enslaved. A heretic then finds himself or herself always on the point of indifference. However, if a heretic believes that he or she no longer seeks but has found—as heretics always in fact dogmatically and deceptively state[c]—then that heretic must acknowledge, according to the heretical position, that he or she no longer has freedom to study, that through freedom the heretic has become a slave, and that freedom always ends with servility since the goal of seeking is finding. If a heretic holds that what has been found can be cast aside, clearly he or she has not yet risen above being conceptually free. The heretic always desires freedom first, but wishing it to be first, it never is.[36/d] If we consider ourselves to be a church union of many people, a school that sees the principle of freedom of study as the highest principle, we will be able to view it

---

. . . does indeed 'judge all but is judged by no one' [1 Cor. 2:15]. For the disciple judges the Gentiles, . . . the Jews, . . . the doctrine of Marcion, . . . the followers of Valentinus . . . and all those who are beyond the pale of the truth, that is, who are outside the Church; but the disciple shall be judged by no one. For the disciple all things are consistent: . . . *a firm belief in the Spirit of God who furnishes us with a knowledge of the truth.*" Cf. ibid., 7.

c. Tertullian, *On the Prescription of Heretics*, 14: "But, for the sake of deceiving us, they pretend that they are still seeking, in order that they may palm their essays upon us by the suggestion of an anxious sympathy,—in short, after gaining access to us, *they proceed at once to insist on the necessity of our inquiring into such points as they were in the habit of advancing.*"

d. Ibid., 11: "Yet, if I have believed what I was bound to believe, and then afterward think that there is something new to be sought, I of course expect that there is something else to be found, although I should by no means entertain such expectation, unless it were because I either had not believed although I had apparently become a believer, or else have ceased to believe. If I thus desert my faith, I am found to be a denier of it. Once for all I would say, 'No one seeks, except the one who either never possessed or has lost what was sought.' The old woman lost one of her ten pieces of silver, and therefore she sought it; when, however, she found it, she ceased to look for it [Luke 15:8. . .]. The widow kept asking to be heard by the judge because she was not admitted; but when her suit was heard, she was silent [Luke 18:2]. Thus there is a limit both to seeking, and to knocking and to asking[. . . .] Away with the one who is ever seeking because such a person never finds; *for he or she seeks where nothing can be found.*"

in this form as a type of the individual, not as a Christian school but as one that is first to become Christian conceptually. The opinion that such a union is Christian because it refers itself in general to the Bible is a great external enslavement. It is the same case, as has already been said in part, with the assertion that such a union is grounded on the Bible. It is as if someone asking about the character of a specific nation received the answer: "Its basic foundation is natural law."

The basic foundation of the Church is the *living* Christ, the God who became human, not the search as to whom he might be.[37] The freedom of the Christian is living faith within, which cannot be changed since Christ is the same today and forever.[38]

Tertullian also rightly says that because Christianity has a specific and certain character,[39] it cannot be the subject of an ongoing search.[e] If the search is set forth as a basic principle, there is no possibility of ever coming to the faith that is the previously given[40] goal of the search,[f] nor is there reason ever to give up the search since the schools,[41] all of which must be studied (as is reasonable), are innumerable.[g] If this were the case, the greater part of Christians and Christianity itself in fact would be poorly provided for and would seldom provide a structure for the salvation of human beings. From what has been said earlier concerning the heretical principle, it follows that that principle must characteristically ever have doubts in determining with certainty[42] what Christianity is and that it makes

---

e. Tertullian, *On the Prescription of Heretics*, 9: "However, there can be no indefinite seeking for that which has been taught as one definite thing alone. You must 'seek' until you 'find,' and believe when you have found; nor have you anything further to do but keep what you believed, provided you believe this besides which nothing else is to be believed, and therefore nothing else is to be sought, after you have found and believed what has been taught by him who charges you to seek no other thing than that which he has taught."

f. Ibid., 10: "Your object, therefore, in seeking was to find; and your object in finding was to believe. All further delay for seeking and finding you have prevented by believing. The very fruit of your seeking has determined for you this limit. . . . If, however, because so many other things have been taught by one and another, we are on that account bound to go on seeking; so long as we are able to find anything, we must be ever seeking, and never believe anything at all."

g. Ibid., 10: "For where shall be the end of seeking? Where the end in believing? Where the completion in finding? with Marcion? But even Valentinus purposes: 'Seek and you shall find.' [Matt. 7:7] with Valentinus? But Apelles, too, will assail me with the same quotation; Hebion also, and Simon and, all in turn, have no other argument by which to entice me, and draw me over to their side."

real and objective Christianity into something merely subjective. Therefore, the charge is laid that heretics, if not teaching indifference, teach something close to it.[h] It now also follows that they place Christian freedom in absolute authority, always insisting that facts ought to be considered opinions, and yet they assert that they possess Christian truth or at least can possess it. The Catholics do not deny that anyone *can* do this,[i/43] but they argue against the opinion that on the basis of necessary Christian principles one is capable of doing it.[44]

20

In regard to the Holy Scriptures and their interpretation, moreover, there is great disagreement.[45] The first question that necessarily raises itself is "Which are the divine writings?" On this the greatest differences immediately arise. As we have already suggested, the Gospels and the apostolic writings that we still possess were in no way given to all Christians by their authors themselves, but for the most part, as mere occasional pieces, they were given directly only to their addressees and their neighbors. Only near the middle of the second century were they first circulated in a larger community so that from then on individual churches found themselves possessing a more or less complete collection of them.[46] While the Holy Scriptures were still scattered throughout the Church were faithfully preserved by the protection of the Holy Spirit and the veneration of the Church, a mass of Gospels, Acts of the apostles, Apocalypses, epistles, and so on, were fabricated and forwarded as the works of apostles so as to support of false doctrine. Thus Eusebius wrote after he had listed the genuine writings of the apostles and those of

---

h. *Apostolic Constitutions*, 6.10: "All these had one and the same design . . . [to reject every decision]." Tertullian, *On the Prescription of Heretics*, 41: "Peace also they muddle up with all comers; for it matters not to them, however different be their treatment of subjects, provided only they can conspire together to storm the citadel of the one only truth." Ibid., 42: "Hence it is that schisms seldom happen among heretics, because even when they exist, they are not obvious. Their very unity, however, is schism."

i. Cyprian, *On the Unity of the Church*, 10: "Hence heresies not only have frequently been originated, but continue to be so; while the perverted mind has no peace—while a discordant faithlessness does not maintain unity. But the Lord permits and suffers these things to be, while the choice of one's own liberty remains."

dubious authorship: "In this way we can more easily distinguish these writings from those that were brought forward under the names of the apostles by the heretics. Among these are the Gospels of Peter, Thomas, and others, the Acts of Andrew, of John, and of other apostles. But none among the writers of the Church has acknowledged any of these with as much as a word. Their language itself is different from that of the apostles; their basic principles and their ruling opinions are very distant from the true doctrine of the Church. As a result they must be heretical fictions and they are thus not even to be counted among the false compositions but among senseless and godless writings."[a] This passage may serve in place of the many we could cite concerning forgeries. It indicates the reasons for declaring a composition forged: the transmission did not speak for it, there was no agreement between its content and that of the composition accepted as genuine, and its content was opposed to the doctrine of the Church. For the reasons stated, one judges the Catholic Gospels and Epistles as genuine: The Church only recognizes in them what she already for long has come to experience through the oral instruction of the disciples and their followers; the Church discovers an agreement between their oral doctrine and what is written. The external testimonies of the individual churches speak for them. Both belong together. However, the Church does not allow a composition to be declared canonical by external witness alone, as is testified expressly in a passage from the *Apostolic Constitutions* in which it is said that one must be moved to declare a book as inspired by the nature of its content and the character of its doctrine, but in no way by the name of the apostle.[b] There was then a common saying that held both principles together: whatever composition was commonly acknowledged by the Church's tradition and was uncontested.[c/47] But even in this case the early Church was not anxious to consider a book canonical if the content alone was the chief reason for accepting its genuineness and external reasons did not fully support it.[d/48]

---

a. Eusebius, *Ecclesiastical History*, 3:25, 6-7 [source quoted].

b. *Apostolic Constitutions*, 6:16: "We have sent all these things to you, that you may know what our opinion is; and that you may not receive those books that are signed with our names but are written by the ungodly. For you are not to attend to the names of the apostles, but to the nature of the things, and their settled opinions." Particularly striking is Tertullian, *On Chastity*, 10.

c. Eusebius, *Ecclesiastical History*, 3:24

d. Ibid., 25. See Hug, *Introduction to the New Testament*, 2:605.

21

The fictional creation of Holy Scriptures was the most vulgar mode by which some individual heretics endeavored to form for themselves their own Christianity. Others did not create new gospels, but they cast aside one or another of the Catholic Gospels. The Ebionites retained only that of Matthew, the Marcionites that of Luke, many Docetists chose the Gospel of Mark, the Valentinians that of John.[a/49] The Ebionites felt that the Johannine Jesus was valued far too highly. Most Gnostics, who did not wish to accept the doctrine that Jesus was truly human, treated the other three Gospels with too little care. According to the writings of Irenaeus[b/50] and Eusebius,[c/51] almost everywhere the comment was made that many took offense that the descriptions of Jesus in the first three Gospels did not appear in that of John, and that, therefore, as their other conceptions concerning Christianity accordingly rooted themselves more or less deeply, they believed themselves justified in casting aside one or another of the Gospels. From the mystical observations of Irenaeus and the unexcelled reflections of Eusebius in explaining the major differences between the Gospels, it can be seen that the early Church found that element that imparted the unity of the gospels only in the Church's own enduring doctrine and not dependent on one or another of the Gospels. The Church accepted this as the unshakeable ground for a Gospel's authenticity.[d] The Epistles of the apostles had the same fate.[e/52]

22

It often happened that a heretical teacher acknowledged the same Gospels and Epistles as did the Catholic Church but corrupted the

---

a. Irenaeus, *Against the Heresies*, 3:11, 7.

b. Ibid., 11.8.

c. Eusebius, *Ecclesiastical History*, 3:24. (The idea is only briefly commented on.)

d. Origen, *Commentary on John*, 5:4: "But they fail to see that as he is one of whom all the evangelists write, so the Gospel, though written by several hands, is, in effect, one."

e. Eusebius, *Ecclesiastical History*, 4:29, 5: "They, indeed, use the Law, and Prophets, and Gospels, but interpret in their own way the utterances of the Sacred Scriptures. And they abuse Paul the apostle." This concerns the followers of Tatian.

text and expurgated those passages from it that contradicted the heretic's preconceived insights or, as he or she said,[53] the Holy Scripture. Thus Marcion shortened the Gospel of Luke, which he still accepted as genuine,[54] and did the same with the Pauline Epistles.[a/55] The call for such expurgation was known even among the pagans, and Celsus used it as a charge against Christianity.[b] The statement of an early Christian writer quoted by Eusebius may be repeated here: "At a very early period, they (the followers of Artemon) corrupted the Holy Scriptures. They cast out the rule of the original faith. They did not know Christ. They did not seek to discover what the Holy Scriptures taught but untiringly endeavored to find what sort of syllogism they would be able to twist to support their godlessness. If anyone placed a biblical passage before them, they sought to explain it as a hypothetical or disjunctive conclusion. . . . They used the arts of unbelievers to support the basic principles of their sect and they undermined the simple faith of the Holy Scriptures with the sophistry of the godless. What needs to be said other than that they were far from faith? As a result, they laid their hands shamelessly upon the Holy Scriptures and said they had improved the text. Each individual can know that I am not lying about them, for if one brings together their manuscripts and compares them, one will find them in disagreement. . . . Those of Asclepiades do not agree with those of Theodotus. One can find many manuscripts that their disciples zealously copied from the so-called corrected, that is, corrupted, text. With these the copies of Hermophilus do not agree. Those of Apollonius do not agree among themselves."[c] This was as little historical [*historische*] criticism as was the method of Marcion. Our position is certainly granted that, for example, Marcion had gained a high conception of Christianity and in it had known a revelation of divine grace that rose above all else,[d] but he could not possibly have created his true conviction from the Holy Scripture. If this were the case, how could he wish to teach his teacher and, as Tertullian said, cut the teacher down with

---

a. Tertullian, *On the Prescription of Heretics*, 38: "Marcion expressly and openly used the knife, not the pen, since he made such an excision of the Scriptures."

b. Origen, *Against Celsus*, 2:27.

c. Eusebius, *Ecclesiastical History*, 5:28, 13, 15-17. Hug[, *Introduction to the New Testament*, 1:44-53] expresses himself very well on the Marcionite critique.

d. Neander, *The Gnostic System*, 30ff.

the sword?[e] We must acknowledge that the life of the Church communicated this high idea to him unconsciously, but that he did not have enough humility to accept it fully and then rose up against the Church, his teacher, charged her with error, and truncated the Holy Scriptures, which he did not wish to allow to agree with Church doctrine.

23

For those parties who did accept the genuine New Testament compositions in their integrity, the chief problem to arise concerned the hermeneutical principles by which to approach them. But exegesis, like criticism, was then in its infancy, and the arbitrariness of which all parties were guilty knew no limits. If I were to give examples, I would be considered to be jesting rather than intending to offer a true picture of the practice in the period. Certainly, no one who has read and compared with care the interpretations of the heretics and those of the Church fathers has failed to note that the Fathers, when they were led to defend a dogmatic or moral doctrine against the heretics, developed an astonishing caution, accuracy, and exegetical precision. The Fathers thus made their opponents aware of their violation of those hermeneutical principles that presupposed a self-developing consciousness. From this they deduced that in the discussion of moral, dogmatic, or homiletic material, references to and citations of biblical passages on a known Christian truth were not disallowed even if the references and citations were not directly demanded by a strict consideration of the context. They practiced this since an individual *proof* ought not to be deduced in such a situation. But if any biblical passage was cited *against* a Church doctrine, they studied everything with the closest precision. Examples are to be found everywhere in Irenaeus, Tertullian, Clement of Alexandria, and Origen. Now the charges that the Church fathers brought against the heretics may be evaluated: that the heretics were poor interpreters of good speeches;[a/56] that they did not expound the Holy Scriptures but introduced into these their own preconceived

e. [Cf. Tertullian, *On the Prescription of Heretics*, 37.]
a. Irenaeus, *Against the Heresies*, preface: "evil interpreters of the good word."

opinions;[b] that without considering the context, the relation of ideas, or the nature of the materials, they looked only at the words in and for themselves, whereas the words had different meanings in different contexts;[c] that they put together individual words from different books so as to make up a full sentence and then used this as a proof text;[d] that, above all, they preferred to use obscure, ambiguous passages,[e] and that they did this to deceive simple people. If the Catholics pointed out the abuse of such interpretations and asserted that they had no validity, they were reduced to silence with the retort that they could not grasp their (the heretics') deep ideas. "The false doctrines, which they spread among the people," says Clement of Alexandria, "openly oppose all the Scriptures and are always refuted by us. The heretics continually defend the Scriptures, at times not accepting some of them, at other times asserting that we are of another nature altogether and are incapable of understanding their characteristic doctrines."[f] To indicate their pride we offer this more fitting example; in another way as well they sought to avoid the charges of the Catholics. They put forward a *secret* tradition according to which the Lord entrusted certain doctrines only to individual apostles who could understand him. These doctrines were set forth in parables, obscure in certain statements, so as to enlighten only those who were permitted and who had received the key to the secret doctrine.[g] Clement of

b. Ibid., 1:36.

c. Clement of Alexandria, *Miscellanies*, 7:16: "Selecting ambiguous expressions, they twist them to their own opinions." Irenaeus, *Against the Heresies*, 1:8, 1: "They disregard the order and the connection of the Scriptures, and as far as in them lies, dismember and destroy the truth."

d. Ibid., 9:4: "Collecting a set of expressions and names scattered here and there, they twist them, as we have already said, from a natural to a nonnatural sense." Cf. Clement of Alexandria, *Miscellanies*, 3:4.

e. Irenaeus, *Against the Heresies*, 2:10: "For by the fact that they thus endeavor to explain ambiguous passages of Scripture . . . they have constructed another god." This gives him opportunity to establish the rule: "For no question can be solved by means of another that itself awaits solution; nor, in the opinion of those possessed of sense, can an ambiguity be explained by means of another ambiguity, or enigmas by means of another greater enigma, but things of such character receive their solution from those that are manifest, consistent, and clear." Cf. ibid., 1:27; 1:16.

f. Clement of Alexandria, *Miscellanies*, 7:16.

g. Irenaeus, *Against the Heresies*, 2:27, 2: "That there is nothing whatever openly, expressly, and without controversy said in any part of Scripture respecting the Father conceived of by those who hold a contrary opinion they themselves testify when they maintain that the Saviour privately taught these same things not to all, but only to

Alexandria states that Basilides pointed to Glaucias, the interpreter of Peter, but Valentinus to Theodas, a disciple of Paul, as the person by whom the secrets came from the Lord.[h] For persons who had not been initiated into this secret doctrine, they cast aside the use of the Scriptures completely.[i/57] One can understand that Catholics would not allow this practice to stand unrefuted. When Catholics opposed this secret doctrine according to their method by the open tradition present in all churches, the heretics declared that *the apostles and the Lord had accommodated themselves*, that they had adapted themselves to Jewish conceptions that now must be rejected, and that they, the heretics, alone preached pure, unfalsified Christianity.[j] The last step they took was to raise their wisdom over that of the apostles, and they were satisfied to say not only that the wisdom of the apostles was marred by certain conceptions of an earlier period, but that the apostles themselves were still trapped and constrained by false Jewish conceptions, and even that the Lord himself had taught in a very questionable manner.[k] We might hesitate to find Irenaeus, Tertullian, and others trustworthy if our own times did not convince us of the possibility of their trustworthiness. It is now clear to us what Basilides and Valentinus must have thought of as the secret

---

certain of his disciples who understood them and who understand what was intended by him through means of arguments, enigmas, and parables."

h. Clement of Alexandria, *Miscellanies*, 7:17 [source, paraphrased in T, quoted].

i. Irenaeus, *Against the Heresies*, 3:2: "When, however, they are refuted from the Scriptures, they turn round and accuse these same Scriptures, as if they were not correct nor authoritarian, and assert that they are ambiguous, and that the truth cannot be extracted from them by those who are ignorant of tradition."

j. Ibid., 3:5, 1: "These most vain sophists affirm that the apostles framed their doctrine hypocritically according to the capacity of their hearers, and gave answers after the opinions (*suspiciones; hypolēpseis*, opinions according to Massuet)]. . . . so that the Lord and the apostles exercised the office of teacher not to further the cause of truth, but even hypocritically, and as each individual was able to receive it." Cf. ibid., 12.

k. Ibid., 1:2, 2; 3:2, 2: "When we refer them to that tradition that originates from the apostles . . . they object to tradition saying that they themselves are not merely wiser than the presbyters, but even wiser than the apostles because they have discovered the unadulterated truth. For they maintain that the apostles intermingled the things of the law with the words of the Saviour, and that not the apostles alone, but even the Lord himself spoke at one time from the Demiurge, at another time from the intermediate place, and yet again from the Pleroma, but that they themselves, indubitably, unsulliedly, and purely, have knowledge of the hidden mystery." Ibid., 3:12, 12: "The apostles preached the Gospel still somewhat under the influence of Jewish opinions."

doctrine. It is composed of pure rational ideas, empty husks, and manufactured veils of positive doctrine that are fitting for the mob. Thus without reason was Glaucias, the *brightly beaming one*, chosen as the protector.[l/58] It is now also made clearer what the traditional deviations of the heretical teachers reproved by the Catholics were and why one cannot engage in any kind of a refutation[m/59] (see section 12, n4.).[60]

24

What has been said is a clear demonstration of how dangerous it would have been for Christianity to be founded on Scripture alone, and thereby on critical and hermeneutical principles. The Christian religion blossomed for a long time before any sort of hermeneutical principles were established. Indeed, one can assert in addition that a hermeneutic was first formed from and by the Church's tradition. The Fathers of the Church were led and preserved by the Spirit of the Church in their exegesis that was correct in so far as they found nothing in the Bible that was not grounded in it *generally*, even though they uncovered allusions in *individual* passages that in no way were in them. In the battles with the heretics, in which they had to invalidate their sophistical and allegorical-mystical explanations or those that arose out of preconceived opinions against the common Christian consciousness,[61] it was necessary for them to develop the

l. *glaukos*, bright, gleaming. There can be no doubt that a secret tradition must be embraced in the manner indicated. But what Christian can believe that the apostles had such and passed on such a tradition? There are many examples in the Clementine writings. Without closer examination Church historians, out of a love for truth, must not set the tradition of the heretics in the same class with that of the Catholics or they make the Catholic tradition laughable.

m. Tertullian, *On the Prescription of Heretics*, 17: "Now this heresy of yours does not receive certain Scriptures. Whichever of them it does receive, it perverts by means of additions and diminutions for the accomplishment of its own purpose, and such as it does receive it receives not in their entirety. Even when it does receive any up to a certain point as entire, it nevertheless perverts even these by the contrivance of diverse interpretations. . . . Though most skilled in the Scriptures, do you progress, when everything which you maintain is denied on the other side, and whatever you deny is maintained by them? As for yourself, indeed, you will lose nothing but your breath." As a result the Church fathers often say that they do not so much wish by their writings to convince the heretics as to set forth faith for Catholics so that the latter will not fall into error.

reasons for their rejection. In this way rules were slowly formed, until Origen described with full consciousness the grammatical-historical interpretation as the basis for the use of the Scriptures. (See Addendum 7.) However, without any hermeneutic, indeed without Scripture, one still had the same doctrines of faith. They discovered first that the faith of the Church would only be directly made firm by a *correct* hermeneutic. The defense of the faith led them to this position. Thus life always preceded rules. If one has rules and wishes to separate life from them, they return again to nothing.

25

From these facts the following conclusions arise:

1. The concept of a positive religion was first confirmed by the Catholic Church and its practice.[62]

2. Holy Scripture was saved because in the Catholic Church a tradition stood in aid of the Scriptures before them and beside them. Both Scripture and tradition belonged fully together.

3. The Holy Scripture was misused by the heresies in their rejection, truncations, and false interpretations[63] of it. They did this out of obscure or clear feelings swimming before them that the Holy Scriptures and the heresies do not belong together.

4. The preservation of Christianity cannot rest only on the Scriptures alone,[64] for the Scriptures themselves are indeed saved by the fact that Christianity is not built on them.

5. Every heresy that refers itself to the written Catholic Gospel is not consistent with its own principles, since the heresy has nothing by which to be certain if the Gospel was written by the apostles or if the Church did not cast out the genuine Gospels. The Catholic Church moves in a circle if she trusts the Gospels only because *they* give her a testimony of credibility. She trusts *herself* and knows why. Should she trust the heretics more than herself? As the Church presents herself and her tradition, through which the written gospel was transmitted to us as divine, so also she presents the gospel. Church, gospel, and tradition always fall and stand together.

(Those who support a rationalistic principle of interpretation would be more honest if they, like the old heretical congregations, would write their own Gospels, that is, immediately commend their works as Gospels for themselves. Then everything would harmonize.

What purpose is there in citing the Gospel which is superseded in wisdom?)[65]

6. The person who always cites the letters of Holy Scripture must always take something other than them for help. Catholics have the Church's tradition, that is, the *open* doctrine set down in the Church from the time of the apostles and with it the Spirit ruling in the Church,[66] and the heretics have the *secret* tradition, that is, the doctrine not given by the apostles of the Church but from the heretics' own spirit.[67]

7. The Catholic Church and its characteristic first applied the historical-grammatical interpretation to the Bible. Aside from the Church one always necessarily comes back to the allegorical-mystical principle of interpretation through which first to determine the content of Christianity. The reason for this is that hermeneutics is a reversed logic. One can make no heuristic use of logic, nor has hermeneutics any criteria for the statements found through its rules.[68] It transmits only an aggregate of doctrines, opinions, and insights of a writer, *which are first to be communicated with our spirit*, that is, it seeks a third entity through which our spirit accepts them or does not. This third entity is, in all that is human, the principles of our reason. If one thus establishes historical-grammatical interpretation as the decisive norm and sets aside the Spirit given to the Church in her practice, *the keystone itself is lacking*. In modern times this keystone is [purportedly] given in that the content of Scripture, brought to light by the use of hermeneutical rules, is communicated to the interiority of human beings by those [interpretive] principles, that is, one receives that religion within the limits of reason.[69] The acts and characteristics of Christianity are then merely the husks of so-called rational ideas; they are, as it were,[70] only used by such rational ideas to give them objectivity. Thus, by a long way round, one finally comes to the point where the heretical schools of the early Church soon[71] began. The reverse danger, which one notes in both cases, arises in that the ancients wished to gain entrance into Christianity, whereas the moderns wish to leave it. The ancients initiated the dominion of rational ideas into Christianity; for the moderns Christianity is to end with rational religion. The difference in dress, however, and in the activity of both groups, lies in the different character of time and place.[72]

It is self-evident that not all heretical schools and teachers eventually arrived at establishing a rational principle of interpretation. Many only turned, as they said, toward a simple hermeneutic.

But, as follows from the essence of heresies' principles outlined above, since they did not develop consistently, special notice cannot be taken of them.

26

If arbitrary speculation characterized the heresy described to this point,[73] separatist mysticism was the basis for another heresy on which it built up its version of Christianity. The latter developed a form for[74] a speculative boldness, measuring what was divine and characteristically Christian by what was human, and doing so only if the human was incapable of taking up the divine into itself by its own power. But only when imprisoned in their self-seeking did heretics not acknowledge the divine Spirit, which, primarily[75] after Pentecost, had formed the Church, filled her, and never deserted her. They understood it rather as a miserable spirit, with no power, one that broke in here and there, enlightening single individuals[76] and then withdrawing again, or perhaps, remaining from the time of the earliest heretics. This spirit was in part to suppress and in part to complete the Spirit that had filled the Church from the beginning and whose power the heretics knew not. Among those who wished to pursue the first end were the Marcionites[a] and Apelles[b] with his followers; with the latter are to be grouped the Montanists and others.[77] As was the case with the group of heretics described earlier, reason did not come to faith or, more properly said, reason did not come to itself. Among the latter group faith did not come to reason or, what amounts to the same, faith did not come to itself. The [latter] separatist mystics rejected all rational thought as applied to faith. They thought of faith in an undetermined or undeterminable infinity and, that as the speculative egoists reduced everything to concepts, the separatists fled every concept and arrived also, like the former group, at a dogmatic indifference or rigidly stuck to the letter

---

a. Irenaeus, *Against the Heresies*, 1:13.

b. Rhodon [Valesius, 96] on Eusebius, *Ecclesiastical History*, 5:13, 2-3: "For Apelles, [. . .] says that the prophecies are from an opposing spirit, being led to this view by the responses of a maiden, Philumene, who was possessed by a demon." Ibid., 5:28, 19: "Some of them have not thought it worthwhile to corrupt the Scriptures but simply deny the law and the prophets, and thus through their lawless and impious teaching, under pretence of grace have sunk to the lowest depths of perdition."

in which no spirit dwelt. Not raising faith to consciousness—they did not uphold the opposite position either—they mixed conscious-ness with faith as did the Montanists, the decisive opponents of all scientific endeavor.[78] Eusebius has preserved for us a nearly complete testimony concerning Apelles, one of the first group mentioned above.[c] On the radical Marcosians, Irenaeus has left a sad and frightening picture.[d/79] Origen expressed himself very well on this false mysticism:[80] "There are many opinions concerning Christ, who, although he is wisdom, does not beget the power of wisdom in all but only in those who devote themselves to wisdom in him. Although he is called a physician, he does not work in all as a physician but only in those who have come to a knowledge of their illness, who flee to his mercy so that they might receive health. I believe it is like this with the Holy Spirit, the root of all gifts. 'To one is given through the Spirit the utterance of wisdom, and to another the utterance of knowledge according to the same Spirit, to another faith by the same Spirit' [1 Cor. 12:8, 9], and thus the Spirit is in all individuals who can grasp it. The Spirit itself enacts and understands what each person needs who is worthy to have a part in it. This sharing and differentiation is not noted by those who hear the Spirit called the Paraclete in the Holy Scripture. They are not aware by what activities and treatments that Spirit is so named. Therefore, they compare the Spirit, I know not why, with some kind of lower spirit and dare to confuse the Church of Christ, bringing as a result great disunity among the members of the Church. But the gospel ascribes to the Spirit such great might and majesty that it says that the apostles could not have grasped what the Lord wished to teach them had the Holy Spirit not come, had it not poured itself into their souls and enlightened them in regard to faith and the essence of the Trinity. The heretics, however, because of their weak insight, not only are incapable of grasping correct teaching in its fullness, but cannot even grasp what we teach. They thus form for themselves unworthy conceptions of the Spirit's divinity and give themselves over to errors and deceptions, deceived by a spirit *that leads astray*

---

c. Ibid., 5:13,5: "It was not at all necessary to examine one's doctrine, but it was necessary that each should continue to hold what he or she believed. For he asserted that those who trusted in the Crucified One would be saved, if only they were found doing good works."

d. Irenaeus, *Against the Heresies*, 1:13.

rather than being taught by the instruction of the Holy Spirit."[e] The sense of these splendid words that cite 1 Corinthians 12:28 describing the whole economy of the Holy Spirit that gives life to the Church is this: the foundation of the Church on faith in the Trinity was not possible without the communication of the Holy Spirit and could not have continued without the Spirit's preservation of it; this is the Spirit's work and the only thing worthy of its power and majesty. Together all believers form an organic whole. By the different communication of one and the same Spirit according to the different needs and characteristics of each person, all are directed to each other and are, together, members completing one another. The one who has received faith is integrated by the one who has been made worthy with the gift of knowledge. If the first separates, he or she has a blind power; if the second does so, that person possesses a bright weakness. Both in their unity form an efficient whole.[81] Since the same Spirit reveals itself in all true believers and since it is the same at all times, it establishes only peace, joy, and unity. Unworthy opinions concerning the Spirit arise if it is not thought of as penetrating the whole and leading individuals in harmony, if all Christians are not thought of as integrating one another through the Spirit and thus as inseparable, if the Spirit is supposed to bring forth isolated formations that break out at one place suddenly,[82] and the result is the dissolution of organic unity by division and schism. Where such an individual single life develops, disturbing the peace of the whole, it is not the Holy Spirit that is revealed, but human error. Irenaeus says that such people deny the arrival of the Holy Spirit as announced in the Gospel of John and described in Acts.[f]

27

In our description of the concept of heresy we have already accented its egotistical element, but the early Church has expressed itself so specifically on this that its convictions regarding this need not be

e. Origen, *On First Principles*, 2:7, 3.

f. Irenaeus, *Against the Heresies*, 3:11, 9: "That they may set at nought the gift of the Spirit, which in the latter times has been, by the good pleasure of the Father, poured out upon the human race, they do not admit the *aspect* presented by John's Gospel in which the Lord promised that he would send the Paraclete; but set aside at once both the gospel and the prophetic Spirit."

described at length. In this the principle of Catholicism appears in greater clarity and is at the same time illumined more completely in that the Church already had a full consciousness of her characteristic at her origin.[83]

Since she saw the principle that begot faith and that which formed the community as the same principle in the fullest sense, she necessarily deduced, as has been said, that those who did not have the first in a general way, could only have the second in a troubled way, and viceversa. All individual, separated, separatistic essence must therefore be in opposition to the Church at her very foundation. The Church had to look upon such heresy as that in which the living relationship with Christ was already weakened in its beginning, in which true, living Christianity must finally die or, as Cyprian said, which can be understood as life dried out like a twig torn from a tree, a brook separated from its source, a ray torn from the sun.[84] In a word: if the new life arises in us only from the community of believers, it must necessarily be lost with division from that community.[85/a] Ignatius says: "Let no one attempt to wish to be cut off and to think of this action as rational; but there is one prayer, one mind, one hope in love and in holy joy. There is *one* Christ, better than whom there is none."[b] This statement arises from the profound thought that Christ will not be manifest in us in egotistic separation, that in division from the totality of believers one wishes with dark desire something better than Christ whom one does not know since Christ is only born in love (this, as was said earlier, is the basic principle of Ignatius). Therefore, Ignatius says elsewhere that self-seeking is clearly the basis of division.[c/86] He states: where there is individualism, the true God does not dwell. Ignatius calls for a return to unity, conversion to the unity of God.[d/87] For him, however, life in the Church's unity formed[88] by

a. Cyprian, *On the Unity of the Church*, 5: "Separate a ray of the sun from the body, its unity does not allow a division of light; break a branch from a tree,—when broken, it will not be able to bud; cut off the stream from its fountain, and that which is cut off dries up." Ibid., 23: "Unity does not allow itself to be divided. A unified organism cannot, broken into parts, be divided into living pieces, nor a living seed into sections. What is separated from its source cannot live and breathe in separation."

b. Ignatius of Antioch, "Letter to the Magnesians," 7.

c. Ibid., "Letter to the Ephesians," 5: "The one, therefore that does not assemble with the Church, has by this manifested pride, and condemned himself or herself. For it is written, 'God resists the proud'" [James 4:6].

d. Ibid., "Letter to the Philadelphians," 8. He begins in a very beautiful way: "I

love is such a firm proof of a living relationship with God, that the consciousness of immortality was given to him in this, and it was impossible for him to see how one could ever be resurrected without this love. Therefore, he said with resulting pain, "In their strife they will die; *it is necessary for them to have love so as to be raised*."[e/89]

Clement of Rome, who had to deal with a church division in his letter to the Corinthians,[90] interweaves throughout the whole letter observations on basic Christian doctrines. He was clearly led by the feeling or clear consciousness that love could not be present anywhere in its total strength where individualism and division were possible.[f] Therefore, he expresses the great thought: "The firmer the faith, the greater the holiness; the deeper the wisdom of the Christian, the less the Christian wished to separate in a self-seeking way from the common life."[91/g] Irenaeus also expressed himself in this way when he said: "We[92] put to shame those who in some way establish groups beside the Church through vain praise or blindness

---

therefore did what belonged to me, as one devoted to unity" [text translated in German]. Cf. ibid., 7, where he says that some wished to draw him away, but he called out in the midst of the congregation: "Love unity; avoid divisions"[text translated in German], for "where there is diversity of judgment and wrath and hatred, God does not dwell. To all them that repent the Lord grants forgiveness, if they turn in penitence to the *unity of God*." Ibid., 8. This is an important thought among the Fathers.

e. Ibid., "Letter to the Smyrnaeans," 7. With Cotelerius one can translate *agapein* as "to celebrate the Lord's Supper." The sense is the same, because for him the celebration of the Lord's Supper is an expression of the union of the Church and the stability of love.

f. Clement of Rome, "Letter to the Corinthians," 3. The statement "Everyone . . . is become blind in his faith" expresses this clearly when he praises their earlier life, stating that they *once* had a beautiful faith.

g. Ibid., 48: "Let one be faithful: let one be powerful in the utterance of knowledge; let one be wise in judging words; let one be pure in all deeds; yet the more one seems to be superior to others [in these respects], the more humble-minded ought one to be, and to seek the common good of all, and not merely his or her own advantage." Cf. the beautiful description of love in ibid., 49. Cyprian, *On the Unity of the Church*, 9, says that only those among whom Christianity is not living, separate themselves: "Let none think that good can depart from the Church. The wind does not carry away the wheat, nor does the hurricane uproot the tree that is based on a solid root. The light straws are tossed about by the tempest; the feeble trees are overthrown by the onset of the whirlwind. The apostle John execrates and severely assails these, when he says: "They went forth from us, but they were not of us; for if they had been of us, surely they would have continued with us" [1 John 2:19].

or evil inclinations."[h] Therefore, he also says: "The true disciples of Christ will flee from those who[93] cause divisions because they are empty of the love of God, and look only to themselves and not to the totality of the Church. For small and insignificant reasons they tear and divide the great and venerable body of Christ and, insofar as they are able, destroy it. They speak of peace but work war. *They are in truth flies, but swallow camels.* They are not able to set right the shame of division by good deeds."[i] Clement of Alexandria also expressed himself in this same way.[j] But no one was firmer on the point than Cyprian:[94] "Many heresies arose from this and still arise because a twisted spirit has no peace, and divisive faithlessness does not preserve unity."[k/95] From this he concludes that the common life in the Church is only possible through the uniting power given through the redemption of Christ alone (Eph. 2:15-6; 3:18-9; Col. 1:20-3),[96] and only through the continuing activity of Christ and the Holy Spirit is it continued. Thus, for him, division is a battle against Christ,[l] an alienation from love and as a result from Christ and God which martyrdom itself is not able to set right.[m/97]

h. Irenaeus, *Against the Heresies*, 3:3, 2.

i. Ibid., 4:33, 7.

j. Clement of Alexandria, *Miscellanies*, 7:15: "Questions arise from which spring the heresies, savoring of self-love and vanity."

k. Cyprian, *On the Unity of the Church*, 10 and elsewhere.

l. Ibid., Letter 72.2: "But what can be greater iniquity, or what stain can be more odious than to have stood in opposition to Christ, than to have scattered *his Church, which he purchased and founded with his blood,* than, unmindful of evangelical peace and love, to have fought with the madness of hostile discord against the unanimous and accordant people of God?"

m. Ibid., *On the Unity of the Church*, 14: "Even if such persons were slain in confession of the Name, that stain is not washed away by blood: the inexpiable and grave fault of discord is not purged by suffering. One cannot be a martyr who is not in the Church; one cannot attain unto the kingdom who forsakes that which shall reign there. Christ gave us peace; he bade us be in agreement and of one mind; he charged the bonds of love and charity to be kept uncorrupted and inviolate; one cannot show oneself a martyr who has not maintained fraternal love. . . . Anyone who has not charity, has not God. The word of the blessed apostle John is: 'God,' he says, 'is love, and he that dwells in love dwells in God, and God dwells in him' [1 John 4:16]. They cannot dwell with God who would not be of one mind in God's Church, even if they burn, given up to flames and fires." Chrysostom, "Sermon on Ephesians," 11:4, refers to this passage of Cyprian: "A certain holy man once said what might seem to be a bold thing. . . . What then is this? He said that not even the blood of martyrdom can wash out this sin."

Accordingly, he cites 1 Corinthians 13:2-3.[98] Therefore, if anyone
seeks to defend departure from the Church because there is much
evil in her, he argues: "Although there are weeds in the Church they
cannot smother our faith and love so that, fearing this to occur, we
leave the Church. (See Addendum 8.) *We only have to endeavor to be
wheat* so that when the Lord comes to gather the harvest, we will be
gathered into his granary."[n/99]

28

Just as the Church community and true knowledge are rooted in one
another, so too conceptions of self-seeking division and error outside
of the Church flow into one another and the first is the cause of the
second.[a] One ought not immediately to think that the Fathers always
were of the opinion that an individual separated [from the Church]
by conscious self-seeking; rather they thought that in such a person
love and the characteristic of Christianity was not yet completely
living and that from this the error and separation flowed.[100] If we go
further, we can reconcile the seemingly contradictory assertions of
Origen. Origen answered the charge of Celsus that the differences of
opinion among Christians testified against their religion by stating
that even this spoke for Christianity's excellence in that there was
always a struggle for the best, just as in philosophy. He then added:
"The sects did not directly arise because of disagreement and
controversy but because many learned individuals endeavored to
penetrate the depths of Christianity. As a result it appeared that sects
developed because individuals conceived of these doctrines, which
all finally believed to be divine, differently, but were led by certain
probable reasons to differing views." Later he states: "In medicine
practitioners are considered noteworthy if they make themselves
knowledgeable in different systems, test them with study, and
choose the best. One can hope to become a good philosopher after
one has entrusted oneself to many schools and has practiced in them,
agreeing with the one best grounded. In a similar way, I say, a

n. Cyprian, Letter 54, 3.
a. Ibid., 54, 3: "And while they insolently extol themselves, blinded by their own
swelling they lose the light of truth." Origen, *Commentary on Romans*, 2:6: "Contention
is to be understood as one of the illnesses of the soul, indeed, the worst, and by it
everything is poisoned."

person who has looked over the differing Jewish and Christian parties with care becomes the wisest Christian."[b] One could in some ways suggest that Origen only sought in this way to rid himself of the pagan charges insofar as it was feasible[101] without expressing his own conviction. He repeated this in his work *On First Principles.*[c/102] In other passages against Celsus, however, he asks that heretics not be confused with true Christians,[d/103] and in his commentaries on Romans he asks why *heresies were numbered by Paul among the works of the flesh.* He answers: Because *their source is fleshly, (self-seeking)[104] sense.*[e/105] In a homily on Ezekiel he writes, "Woe unto those who despise the Church community and trust the pride and the pompous works of the heretics."[f/106] He expresses himself in more detail in the following passages:[107] "Where there is sin, there is multitude, divisions, schisms, disunity, but where virtue is, there is unity, union, and the believers are there one heart and soul (Acts 4:32).[108] And that I might express myself more clearly: the principle of all evil is multitude, the principle of all good is unity, that is, the return to unity from confusion; all of us, if we wish to be holy, must unite ourselves so that we might come to be perfect in the same sense and basic principles so as to be one body and spirit (Eph. 4:4, 13).[109]

---

b. Ibid., *Against Celsus*, 3:13.

c. Ibid., *On First Principles*, 3:3, 3: "As princes of this world (a remarkable change in the Pauline passage) esteem such opinions to be true, they desire to impart to others what they themselves believe to be the truth." Augustine speaks in the same way to the Manichaeans: "They will overcome you if you do not know how laboriously the truth was achieved." In Augustine, who himself experienced the power of evil for so long, one finds the most extensive judgment on those who turn away from the teaching of the Church. Augustine, *On the Usefulness of Believing*, 1: "For one, in my opinion, is a heretic, who, for the sake of some temporal advantage and chiefly for the sake of personal glory and preeminence, either gives birth to, or follows, false and new opinions; but anyone who trusts people of this kind is deceived by a certain imagination of truth and piety." Augustine knows this from his own experience. For the sake of truth he joined the Manichaeans. In his *Confessions*, 4:1, he says, speaking of their errors: "Let the arrogant and such as have not been yet cast down and stricken by thee, O my God, laugh at me." Cf. ibid., 3:12, 21.

d. Origen, *Against Celsus*, 5:59-62.

e. Ibid., *Commentary on Romans*, 6:1: "You will find that these arise from their own carnal senses (1 Cor. 3:3)." Ibid., 2:6: "Thus, arise heresies, divisions, and scandals, because those who are wise and intelligent in their own eyes raise up as a law what seems good to them."

f. Ibid., "Homily on Ezekiel," 9:1. Cf. ibid., *On First Principles*, 2:9, 6: "We, however, although but human, not to nourish the insolence of the heretics by our silence will return to their objections."

However, if unity does not embrace us, but it can be said of us "I am of Paul, I am of Apollos, I am of Cephas" [1 Cor. 1:12], if we are divided and splintered by evil sense, we will not find ourselves in unity where the others are. As the Father and the Son are one, so are those who have one Spirit brought to unity. The Savior said, *'I and the Father are one' (John 10:70), and 'Holy Father, keep them in your name, which you have given me, that they may be one, even as we are one'* (John 17:11, 21). And in the apostle's works one reads: *'Until we all attain to the unity of the faith and of the knowledge of the Son of God, to maturity, to the measure of the stature of the fullness of Christ'* (Eph. 4:13). And again: *'Until we all come to the unity of the body and Spirit of Christ'* [Cf. Eph. 4:13]. From this it is clear that virtue binds many in unity so that we must become one through it and flee the manifold."[g] In another place Origen expresses himself as follows: "They were never in agreement on earth who said *'I belong to Paul or I belong to Apollos or I belong to Cephas or I belong to Christ'* [1 Cor. 1:12], but there was division among them. After this ceased, they were united by the power of the Lord Jesus Christ with the Spirit working in Paul. Therefore, they no longer fought with one another or lay waste to one another to such an extent that they were driven out by themselves."[110/h] (See Addendum 9.)[111]

29

If the source of heresy is seen as the more or less developed, or unconscious[112] yet present self-seeking, and if this idea arises out of the essence of the Catholic Church which is unity and love, neither of which can be separated from holiness,[113] the Fathers must have still more firmly believed in the Church when they heard the judgments of the heretics concerning members of the Catholic Church.[114] The heretics called Catholics "the simple ones," those who believed in authority,[a] and themselves they called "the knowers,"[115]

g. Ibid., "Homily on Ezekiel," 9:1.

h. Ibid., *Commentary on Matthew*, 14:1.

a. Clement of Alexandria, *Miscellanies*, 2:3: "The followers of Valentinus assign faith to us, the simple, but will have it that knowledge springs up in their own selves." Cf. ibid., 7:16, and passim. Cf. Tertullian, *Against the Valentinians*, 2:3.

the free and noble.[b/116] The Catholics they designated sensually and carnally inclined,[c] themselves spiritual; the Catholics ignorant, idiots, common churchgoers who could not follow the height of heretical speculation, and themselves the seed of the elect, the perfect;[d] the Catholics those who worked for salvation, who needed works for holiness, themselves those who could be holy through faith alone, not only without works but in spite of evil works.[e/117] The Catholics were, for them, the impure, they the pure who must rebaptize all Catholics who converted to heresy so as to make them worthy members of their pure society.[f] This is the sectarian spirit.[118] These charges did not in any way cause Catholics pain since they were accustomed to them from the beginning of the Church, and they had been described in the same epithets by the pagans, as every page of Origen's splendid work against Celsus teaches. But the possibility of such pride, which the heretical teachers sought to secure by their theory, must have struck deep into the breast of every Catholic. What is more painful than the feelings stirred up by the descriptions of Irenaeus concerning the pompous behavior of these people? The disciple of Mark writes as follows:[119] "They call themselves perfect and state that no one is to be compared with them in greatness of knowledge,[120] not even Paul, Peter, or any other apostle. They alone have drunk the greatness of knowledge of unspeakable power. They see themselves above every authority and they act freely in all things, fearing no one."[g] In another place he writes: "If someone who hears them (the Valentinians) contradicts them, they assert that such

b. Clement of Alexandria, *Miscellanies*, 3:4: "Having a superior authority to them, they are able to supersede them in morals."

c. Ibid., 3:4: "the people of this cosmos." Ibid., 4:13: "Let not the above mentioned people, then, call us by way of reproach, 'natural persons.'"

d. Irenaeus, *Against the Heresies*, 1:6, 4: "They run us down . . . as utterly contempt-ible, *as fools and ignorant persons, while they highly exalt themselves, and claim to be perfect and the elect seed.*" Cf. ibid., 3:15, 2: "Those who are from the church they call common churchgoers."

e. Ibid., 1:6, 2: "Animal individuals, again, are instructed in animal things; such individuals, namely, are established by their works and by a mere faith, while they have no perfect knowledge. We of the Church, they say, are these persons. Wherefore also they maintain that good works are necessary to us, for otherwise it is impossible we should be saved. But as to themselves, they hold that they shall be entirely and undoubtedly saved not by means of conduct, but because they are spiritual by nature."

f. Eusebius, *Ecclesiastical History*, 6:43. Concerning the Novatians, see ibid., 7:8; Cyprian, Letter 74, and elsewhere.

g. Irenaeus, *Against the Heresies*, 1:13, 6.

a person does not understand the truth and has received no seed from their mother. They say nothing to such a person because they view that person as carnally minded. But if someone offers himself or herself to them as a small sheep, that individual becomes, immediately on being initiated, pompous, and believes that nothing more can be discovered in heaven or earth since the initiated has entered the pleroma [fullness], has embraced a personal angel, and goes forth proud as an Indian, arrogant, and full of darkness."[h] This powerful darkness leads to the assertion that an extensive, careful, and penetrating study into the subject need not be done. But the Fathers often assure us that the heretics never took the trouble to learn to know in all earnestness the Catholic truths against which they fought, but satisfied themselves with superficial knowledge.[i] This is related to the character trait ascribed to them by Irenaeus: "None were considered great unless they discovered a new lie."[j] Tertullian described them as "vaunting themselves as wise and wishing to be teachers rather than disciples."[k] And Clement of Alexandria says: "They took more care *to seem wise than to be wise.*"[l] For these reasons he says elsewhere that they did not have the courage freely to look truth squarely in the face, to carry it in its total strength. They feared every specific issue and, with superficial light-mindedness, they turned away from weighty matters.[m]/[121]

h. Ibid., 3:15, 2.

i. Tertullian, *On the Resurrection of the Flesh*, 3, speaks well against superficiality: "Divine reason, on the contrary, lies in the very pith and marrow of things, not on the surface, and very often is at variance with appearances." In a powerful way, Clement of Alexandria, *Miscellanies*, 7:16, writes: "In consequence of not learning the mysteries of ecclesiastical knowledge and not having the capacity for the grandeur of the truth, too indolent to descend to the bottom of things, reading superficially, they have dismissed the Scriptures."

j. Irenaeus, *Against the Heresies*, 1:18, 1: "No one is deemed 'perfect' who does not develop among them some mighty fictions."

k. Tertullian, *On the Prescription of Heretics*, 41: "All offer you knowledge. Their catechumens are perfect before they are fully taught."

l. Clement of Alexandria, *Miscellanies*, 7:16.

m. Ibid.: "If one is curable, able to bear like fire or steel the outspokenness of truth which cuts away and burns their false opinions, let that person lend his or her ears of the soul. And this will be the case, unless, through the propensity to sloth, they push truth away, or through the desire of fame, they endeavor to invent novelties."

30

The narrow, loveless judgment against the Catholics as noted in section 27 gives occasion for the following observations.

The depth of truth spoken by the Church fathers is seen in their definition of the return to the unity of believers as conversion to the unity of God. Paul had already demanded unity of faith because we have *one* God and *one* Jesus Christ. Every sect creates a god according to its own character, and because egoism lies at its root, it can thus lift itself up only to a constrained, narrow-hearted God and Christ who create a little enlightened group abandoning those who lived earlier or are outside of it.[122] It is completely self-seeking, however, if theory must support this narrowness of heart. There is no doubt that the Gnostic system concerning the highest god and the imperfect demiurge, which traces its descent to the first [the highest god] and the Catholic descent to the second [the demiurge], arose out of its self-seeking and that its narrow insights did not arise out of Catholic theory. Every Catholic who joined them [the Gnostics] was immediately a seed of the elect, and if all had joined them, that is, had they been able to be the ruling party, their theory would have immediately disappeared. These points of view lie at the basis of the small Western sects, and there is need only of a glowing, Oriental fantasy to bring suddenly among us again all the Gnostic Demiurges and Jaldabaoths as the creators of spiritual individuals.[123] Only the coldness of imaginative power restrained Gnostic ideas from arising[124] among the separatists in the Middle Ages among whom such ideas had already established themselves.

Moreover, in the Catholic system or, to speak more properly, in Christianity, a community of all believers is founded by the redemption in Christ, and consciousness of Christ and his divinity comes only in his community. In a thoroughly developed ecclesiastical egoism or a perfected heresy, in which it is supposed that one can find Christ for oneself, true redemption must be denied and Christ along with Christianity in its characteristic majesty is removed from our spirit. We see this in Gnosticism and its principles, and in modern times in Protestantism in which, after the egotistical principle was consistently carried through and the ecclesiastical unity, opposed as foolishness by the dull reformers,[125] was cast out. At the same time Christ was reduced to a human being, redemption fell away, in short, Christianity died among such so-called thinkers.[126] However, after Christianity is once more brought to a place of honor and Christ is acknowledged in his characteristic majesty once again, the desire for union raises itself again and it does so *most among the most profound Protestant theologians.*[127]

31

If we seek to delve into the matter more deeply, we might perhaps meet with success by a comparative use of generally acknowledged truth and an extension of our view over our total subject.

A human being is set in a great whole to act and to view himself or herself as a *member* in it. One must acknowledge this relationship and dare neither oppose oneself to the whole nor set oneself above it. This is what the schools call oneness with the *universal whole*, the harmony of individual and universal lives. (See Seber, *Über Religion und Theologie*, 8-16.) This oneness with the *universal whole* is at the same time true existence in God, the source of true knowledge of God, of the Creator of the *universal whole*, because the *universal whole* as such is grounded in God and is his total revelation. Thus, just as each individual in the whole is grounded in God, God can be known by the individual only in the whole. As only the All of his revelation reveals him completely, one can truly know him only in the All,[128] living in him, embracing the All with a full heart. This is the mystery of our knowledge of God: only in the whole can he who created the whole be known because he reveals himself completely only in the whole. How is the single individual to know him? Only because the individual, although not the whole, can yet *embrace it with great mind, with love.* Thus, although the individual *is* not the whole, the whole is yet in the individual and the individual knows what the whole is. We, as individual essences, expand ourselves to the whole in love. Love grasps God. The *universal whole* is represented for us in humanity. To set oneself above one's position in pride is to set aside the whole, a member of which we are designated to be. We do not thus lift ourselves to the All, but narrow-heartedly draw it down to us and see of God only as much as we are, the many parts of the whole. Although we thus wish *to be* the whole, we know only what a part knows. With the detraction of the whole, God too is detracted, that is, our consciousness of God is darkened, and the fall from God is effected. When sin, which this is, separates itself from God and egotistically places itself as the center of everything, and instead of seeing the whole only in itself, sees itself in the whole, God is set aside, is detracted until, as history teaches us, he is equated with humanity or humanity with him. This is the necessary consequence of the position taken on by humanity. Therefore, there can no longer be *one God and Creator* of all human beings, and as many gods as there are human beings must be made if they are not already formed by other needs of individual groups who had their common world of divinities. A multiplicity of gods arises in the multiplicity of nations. The one Creator, who is known only in oneness with his whole creation, with the loss of this great oneness, must be reduced once again according to the character of the narrow position taken up by human beings. However, viewed from the perspective of a national union, the Creator appears more respected and much more illustrious than in consistently developed egoism. Totally separated, a human being would have no god at all because the god would be like the human being, as was said above, that is, God would in no way be a god. In that each individual can at least see himself or herself in a nationality, there is the possibility of always having a god, albeit a very restricted and human god.

Now to Christianity: Christ, the Son of God, *the new Creator*, can be understood only in the totality of his believers (see section 7), only if the individual sees himself or herself as a member of the whole, *the new Creation*, and God the Father, the Creator of the All, can only be known in the oneness of single individuals with the All. Separated from the totality of believers who are united to a whole through and in Christ, our position is too minuscule for the greatness of Christ. The uniting of all is *his* great work, *his* revelation. In and through revelation he will be known. In complete, fully effected division Christ necessarily sinks to a mere human being. In the early Church, therefore, division from the community of believers was often called a falling away from Christ, a denial of Christ, a battle against Christ, just as the dissolution of the harmony of the individual and universal lives is at the same time a falling away from God. It cannot be strange, although viewing the matter superficially it may so occur at times, that anyone who only knows himself or herself as redeemed should not be aware of this new creation within, the creating power of Christ, Christ's mediation between God and the human person, and thus the uniting of the divine with the human. With the reconciliation and the union reestablished with God by Christ, reconciliation and union with all the reconciled is given, and thus the community of all. In this unity of our life with all the redeemed we are first conscious of true union with Christ, just as we

are of unity with God in the harmony of our individual life with the
universal life. Thus our own true reconciliation through Christ is
actually and essentially linked with our community with him in
community with the totality of the redeemed. The former is identical
with the latter and dare not be separated from it, and therefore faith
in the divinity of Christ cannot remain in division.[a] In other words:
self-seeking, be it ever so refined, is not the measure by which we
measure Christ. By such self-seeking we discover only one thing,
namely, that Christ is like us since we do not discover anything
properly and truly great, truly divinely realized in us. This [discov-
ery of God realized in us] is the consciousness of having been
accepted, of life, of ability to live, and of the need to live in and with
his precious congregation purchased by his blood.[129] Without this
necessity he is like us, because we are with him what we are without
him. Finally, although redemption is so closely tied to the community of believers, it is not said that the person who does not know and
understand the community in the way described—indeed this is the
case with many in the Church—is not redeemed. We often *live* the
truth without being conscious of it and are thus often better off than
with our twisted concepts. I only emphasize here the union between
the two that St. Paul and the early Church with him expressed in the
most specific way.

Nor would one wish to say that it is enough if an individual only
knows that many are redeemed in Christ and that the individual
stands with them in a spiritual, ideal community. Everything that is
truly ideal is real at the same time. The truest spiritual community
is to be understood as it was by Paul and those after him, as always
energetic, expressing and forming itself. The truest spiritual,
spiritually living, and not merely conceptual community is only one
in which we truly find ourselves in community and not merely *think*
we are in community—if we see and acknowledge ourselves as
members of the whole body, live and are in it with all as Paul said
in 1 Corinthians 12:13. The community of believers[130] is thus only

---

a. Augustine,[?] *Letter to Catholics against the Donatists*, 6-7: "Despite what they wish
to bring into the argument and the points they wish to make when they shout 'Behold,
here is Christ; Behold, there is Christ' [Matt. 24:23], we who are truly his sheep, wish
to listen to the voice of our shepherd who says: *Do not believe them.* . . . *The head and
body together are Christ, the head of the only begotten Son of God and his body, the Church,
bridegroom and bride, two in one flesh*" [Eph. 5:23, 30, 32]. Note especially Augustine, *On
the Psalms*, 30:3, 4.

ideal in the proper sense insofar as it is real, just as it is also able to be real because it is ideal.[131]

With the removal of that eternal relationship of the individual to the whole, which is the source of true knowledge of God, each nation modifies in a special way and holds in its own way a limited world of deities. In like manner the heresies in Christianity corresponded to pagan national religions, and as Original Sin in humanity resulted in polytheism, so heresy resulted in a certain "poly-Christism." It would be very striking to study completely the laws by which the conception concerning Christ had characteristically formed itself according to the inner character of the individual heresy.

In pagan national religions the gods are greater than they might have appeared to a completely isolated person. Likewise it is certain that if one lives even in a limited community of faith, one will have greater concepts of Christ than if one wishes to stand fully alone. It is the same with the endeavor of all who wish to see even a little divinity in Christ: they do not stand by themselves but are always driven to form a sect. In addition to the different heretical conceptions already noted about Christ and God, another conception arose by which Christ was still acknowledged as God but in which the indispensable necessity of a community, as in the Catholic Church, was not expressed in the most specific way. This group's view of redemption was that our justification was only *declared*, that God *viewed* us as justified in him. In the Catholic Church, however, it was always affirmed that God *justifies* us essentially and *internally*, that is, that he actually gives holiness, which is one with love and which therefore will not be separated in any way from faith. This is based on the fact that the one who has true faith in Christ the Redeemer is at the same time assumed to be necessarily taken up into community with all believers, a community formed through love. A justification merely declared is related to the egotistic point of view of the believer. Therefore, in section 30 it was noted that Catholics in the second century were already called "holy works."

From all this one sees, I believe, that a return to the Church may rightly be called a return to the unity of Christ, indeed, a return to the unity of God, for "who has seen me (Christ) has seen the Father" (John 14:9) and knowledge of the Son is knowledge of the Father.[b]

---

b. Optatus, *Against the Donatists*, 1.21: "The divine will forbade, among other matters, three things: you are not to kill, you are not to follow foreign gods, you are not to cause division in the chief commandments. . . . In a certain way they declared war on

In paganism[132] from Celsus to Julian the declaration was made against Christianity: to want *one* God for all people is madness; it is to tear humanity forcibly from its natural relationship, and therefore Christianity must be destroyed as unnatural. At the very beginning heresy spoke as follows against the Church: to want one Christ is not suitable; each person must be able to have his or her own Christ. But these comparisons we now leave aside.[133]

32

The early Church thus understood heresy as something evil; it saw it as evil in its very root.[a/134] (It is self-evident that the individual heretic is not being referred to here, but rather the inner essence of heresy that flowed from the spirit of this world. An individual could well have received a faithful mind from the Church, but the Church's rays broke off in a twisted way in that person's under-standing, or such a person always found himself or herself in disharmony with self. The one who condemns heresy does not condemn heretics; the Spirit of Christianity is the source of the first, the spirit of this world the source of the second).[135] We can add what is yet to be said of the way heresy was presented in the early Church.[136]

In fact, an ideal view of heresy, as Clement and Origen, for example, gave of the Church,[b] is completely impossible. If we proceed from the beginning of the Church, seeing as her original image the uniting of the divine with the human in Jesus or the community of the disciples with Christ and among themselves as was presented as a pattern for believers in John, if we look upon the *one* Spirit giving life to believers, the *one* doctrine in all biblical

---

God, as if there were another God who received another sacrifice." Aubespiné [note 61, p. 20] notes in addition: "Those who cause a division and divide the Church seem to introduce a multitude of gods; in that they divide themselves from the community of the Church, they necessarily divide themselves from God with whom the Church is united in covenant through Christ." The holy fathers often noted the text: "Is Christ divided?" and one does not need to be reminded how significantly they considered Ephesians 4:5-6.

a. Justin Martyr, *First Apology*, 26; Tertullian, *On the Prescription of Heretics*, 40; Origen, *Commentary on Romans*, 10:5; *On Titus*, 4; Eusebius, *Ecclesiastical History*, 4:7.

b. Clement of Alexandria, *Miscellanies*, 7:17; Origen, *On First Principles*, 1:6, 2.

writings,[137] we proceed from unity. If we look at the only perfection of the Church, if everything is to be placed under Christ, we see unity over against everything else. According to its essence heresy is divisive and its principles are not capable of establishing unity. Heresy, therefore, falls completely outside of the Kingdom of God;[138] in this lies the evil. One can truly say: so exalted is the Church, the totality of believers was never Christian *enough* to portray the idea of the Catholic Church purely in life. Moreover, believers would never be unchristian enough to make the essence of heresy a thing of value, so lowly is heresy!

What institution is there whose reality is necessarily better than its ideal and what institution is to be praised if it falls below its ideal?

Indeed, one can say: if the idea of the Catholic Church is realized, then the Holy Spirit has conquered the world. If heresy is victorious, the world is triumphant. Heresy, therefore, lying outside of the Kingdom of God,[139] has no proper being.[140] Not established by the divine Spirit but only present in and through humanity, heresy falls in with the world[141] in its development and in its battle against the Church.[142] Therefore, like evil, it is a mere negation, only present so as to bring true beings to an ever clearer consciousness, to lift up the will of the Church against it (heresy), and to establish that will more firmly. Since the divine principle of life is only communicated to believers and is not original with them, they always need to posit an antithesis by which the development of all that is finite is caused. As good first comes to our consciousness through evil, the finite, so the early Church also by a negative determination pointed to heresy in relation to the Church. Tertullian had already expressed himself very clearly on this.[c/143] And Origen said: "If, for example, I oppose the teachings of Marcion or of Basilides or some other heretic with the word of truth and the testimonies of Holy Scripture or with the fire of the divine altar (the Church),[144] is not their weakness clearer by this opposition? If Church doctrine were established only for itself and not surrounded by the assertions of heretics, our faith could not appear so bright, so proven. Because of this, Catholic doctrine is besieged by its contradiction so that our faith might not grow stiff in

---

c. Tertullian, *On the Prescription of Heretics*, 1 and 30. Some scholars consider the "oportet esse haereses" ["It is necessary that there be heresies" (1 Cor. 11:19)] on which Tertullian is basing his argument, to mean that he *wished* to have them. He is opposed to this.

peace but, moved by practice, become pure. Therefore, the Apostle said that there must be heresies [1 Cor. 11:19], so that the proven might be known, that is, the altar must be surrounded by the incense of the heretics so that the difference between believers and unbelievers might be clear to all. Had the faith of the Church shone forth as gold from the beginning, had her word shone through the fire as purified silver, the words of the heretics would have had greater mockery and shame as a common dark ore. Do you wish to know how[145] the good as such is to be known only by the antithesis of the inferior? Who of us can know that a light is something good, if we have never discovered the darkness of night? Who would find honey sweet without ever having the sensation of bitterness? If you take away the devil himself and the powers who attack and oppose us, the virtues of our Spirit will not develop without battle."[d] (See Addendum 10.) These profound comments of the great Alexandrian arise fully out of a view of the developing history of Christianity. Between the opposition of the idealistic Gnostics, on the one hand, and the carnal Chiliasts and materialistic Montanists, on the other, Catholic doctrine moved brightly. The Docetists attacked Christ's humanity; the Ebionites, Theodotians, Paulinians, and others attacked his divinity. How gloriously did the necessity of both natures of his person in the redemption come to consciousness because of this: how well formed and developed did everything become! If any doctrine is present among a significant number of believers in the Church more in a dark sense than in clear consciousness, if its impact on life is not noted, if it is upheld by many only as a dead mass[146] or is stretched out beyond its determined limits, there always arise those who, uneasy with the situation, form an antithesis in the Church itself,[147] as the Alexandrians and the Romans did against the Chiliasts and the Judaizers. If it happens, however, that any Christian characteristic is misunderstood by anyone and upheld in this misunderstood way and is cast aside by those who also misunderstood and misconceived it,[148] and if these then by their own power think up something in place of this according to the previously outlined principles and believe that they must find truth outside the Church and against it and immediately[149] begin an egotistic development, an open battle arises which is first properly enjoined by casting the egoists out of the common community.

d. Origen, *Homilies on Numbers*, 9:1.

One can explain what has been said in the following way: heresy is only possible in the Church because of evil, because every darkening of truth is caused by sin, and before heresy was outside the Church, it was in her. Thus one can say: the battle of division will last longer, the more sin and error flowing from sin is found in the Church. The result is always like its cause: the more error there is among a greater number inside the Church, the more numerous will be the opposing errors in the separated parties and the longer will be the battle. But[150] truth proceeds from this, developed and shining. If truth is so acknowledged, so that it is known as it beams forth, the egotistic development goes the way of all flesh. It disappears because it has reached its determined goal, that is, it helped to portray the truth.[e/151] Thus all sects that were in the Church in her first century disappeared, and all parties that separated from her later have destroyed themselves. Since the sixteenth century they are only written and spoken about. But if the Church needs this battle and her members stand together so that they may be completed and raised up by heresies,[152] she still cannot look upon herself as one initially seeking.[153] She leaves error to others and holds to herself the truth developed through it.[154] No one can call this evil. She is not to be sorrowful that new error always arises so as to elevate her truth.[155] Without sorrowing for the fact, we must admit that evil will always be sufficiently present. Those church groups, however, who always fight against the unchangeable Church positions are like teachers who always endeavor to leave something evil in their children so that they might always look good: surging evil will never stay away, and the teacher must only hold fast to the good.

33

It cannot be determined *from*[156] heresy *itself*[157] what its content is properly to be, because according to its (heresy's) character it expresses itself merely as a denial and in its principles nothing Christian whatever is to be found since what is Christian is always given only by the divine Spirit and is thus always in the Church.[158] But what heretics arrive at themselves in heresy is always found

---

e. Error must then be stopped by proper preaching, but not by might. By power the development and progress of truth will be hemmed in, and hypocrisy, the destroyer of all religious sense and truth, raised up.

outside of Christianity in the wide kingdom of nothingness. The heretics borrowed partly from a philosophy that arose unrelated to Christianity and partly from one-sided constructions within the Church which themselves were very different according to the character of the time. As a result, the heretics were as different as the philosophers and as numerous as possible. (Even accepting these two factors, however, the source of a doctrine of a particular school can be fairly well determined.) Therefore, the fathers of the Church, also following here the analogy of evil, said that heresy is always related to the Catholic truth and cannot be thought of aside from it,[a] and that the developed forms of heresy are infinitely divided among themselves, are opposed to each other, and are full of contradictions, disharmonies, and complications.[b] One finds, in fact, that their own productions are continually taken up in solving these contradictions,[159] and that the individual forms of heresy, although all arise from the same principles, arrive at contradictory results. In fact, nothing self-evident is found in heresy, no inner unity of life, no identity and firmness of consciousness; everything flows.[160] It is only an infinite multiplicity, not a unity, and each one among many, each individual heresy, already bears the seeds of destruction in itself. *It wishes to build a common life on the foundation of egoism*; this cannot be done:[161] because it arose by separation, no community can arise from it; it must then be able to[162] beget a cause, an action opposed to the Church.[c/163] Therefore, there can be no proper history of heresy just

a. Tertullian, *On the Prescription of Heretics*, 29: "Were heresies before true doctrine? Not so; for in all cases truth precedes its copy, the likeness succeeds the reality. Absurd enough, however, is it, that heresy should be deemed to have preceded its own prior doctrine."

b. Irenaeus, *Against the Heresies*, 5:20, 1: "These heretics, mentioned earlier, since they are blind to the truth, and deviate from the way, will walk in various paths; and therefore the footsteps of their doctrine are scattered here and there without agreement or connection." Ibid., 3:24, 2: "Alienated thus from the truth, they deservedly wallow in all error, tossed to and fro by it, thinking differently in regard to the same things at different times and never attaining to a well-grounded knowledge." Clement of Alexandria, *Miscellanies*, 7:16: "They accordingly despise and laugh at one another. And it happens that the same thought is held in the highest estimation by some and by others condemned for insanity."

c. Tertullian, *On the Prescription of Heretics*, 42: "I am greatly in error if they do not among themselves swerve even from their own regulations, for as much as every person, just as it suits his or her own temper, modifies the traditions received after the same fashion as the one who handed them down did, when that person molded them according to his or her own will. The progress of the matter is an acknowledgment

as there can be none of evil or of error. Indeed, we know nothing of its existence to the sixteenth century[164] except through the Catholic Church and her history, the memory of which was preserved.[d/165]

Therefore, the Church fathers remarked that the different structures of heresy, as of evil, although not united among themselves and opposed in continual battle to each other, nevertheless agree in their fight against the Church.[e] The drive to preserve themselves gave them *this* point of unity, and the result did not put their anticipations to shame.[166]

34

It was said above that nothing Christian will be found by heretical principles. This does not mean that heresy does not have anything Christian in it. If this were so, heresy would fall completely outside of Christianity and would not in any way be able to be discussed in a Christian Church history. Rather, it means, as was said, that what makes heresy heresy and what it finds by *its* principles, is unchristian, for it always looks to one individual thing alone that it wishes to destroy by its principles. Since it does not relate[167] this one principle to the rest of its content which it sets forth as uncontested,[168] it forms within itself what was Christian and what still bound it to the Church.[169] The individual heresy is thus one that has preserved and established itself by its principles, that is, by the egotistic and purely human elements in itself.[170] Because its decrees were by human activity and human beings, the followers of these heretical teachers were also called prisoners, those who were made servants of human beings and of evil,[a/171] who had given up their freedom

---

at once of its character and of the manner of its birth. *That was allowable to the Valentinians which had been allowed to Valentinus; that was also fair for the Marcionites which had been done by Marcion—even to innovate on the faith, as was agreeable to their own pleasure."*

d. Cf. the addendum in [A. Gratz,] *Der Apologet des Katholicismus: Zeitschrift für Freunde der Wahrheit und der Brüderliebe; Zur Berichtigung mannigfaltiger Entstellungen des Katholicismus*, section 5, on the Church which alone can make one holy. Note pp. 62ff. by Professor von Drey.

e. Tertullian, *On the Prescriptions of Heretics*, 41: "For it matters not to them, however different be their treatment of subjects, provided only they can conspire together to storm the citadel of the one only truth."

a. Irenaeus, *Against the Heresies*, preface, 1: "By means of their craftily constructed

under the divine Spirit that ruled in the Church. They had accepted the principles as well as the name of human beings although Christians ought to allow themselves to be taught only by Christ.[b/172] The society to which one of these individuals had given a personal name they did not call a church (there could only be one Church as there is only one Christ), but a gathering, a school, a diatribe, or whatever.[c/173] Since they were not established by Christ, as desired in the Christian Church, they thus held it a great shame to be named after the founder of a school. Clement of Alexandria wrote: "The majesty of the Church, like the principle of her construction, is given by her unity. It is superior to everything; nothing is similar to it. Some of the followers of the heretics, however, are named after the names (of their founders), as the Valentinians, the Marcionites, the Basilidianites, even if they cite Matthew, for as the teaching of all the apostles is one and the same, so is their transmis-

---

plausibilities they draw away the minds of the inexperienced and take them captive." Cyprian, Letter 60, 3: "The foe and enemy of the Church despises and passes by those whom he has alienated from the Church, and led out of her as captives and conquered." Therefore, for Ignatius, being found outside of the Church's unity is the same as being "in bonds." See his "Letter to the Philadelphians," 8, and "Letter to the Ephesians," 17: "Be not anointed with the bad odor of the doctrine of the prince of this world; let him not lead you away captive from the life which is set before you." Eusebius, *Ecclesiastical History*, 4:7, 10: "so pitiably led astray by them to their own destruction."

b. Origen, *Against Celsus*, 3:75: "Although we give instruction, we never say, 'Give heed to me,' but 'Give heed to the God of all things, and to Jesus, the giver of instruction concerning him'." Ibid., 5:51: "We have found the better part; and in showing that the truth which is contained in the teaching of Jesus Christ is pure and unmixed with error, we are not commending ourselves, but our teacher, to whom testimony was borne through many witnesses by the supreme God." Against this Irenaeus writes, *Against the Heresies*, 3:2, 1: "Every one of these . . . is not ashamed to preach oneself."

c. Clement of Alexandria, *Miscellanies*, 7:15: "They glory rather in being at the head of a school than presiding over the Church." As they are here defined as a diatribe so in Eusebius, *Ecclesiastical History*, 4:29, 3 they are called a school: "[with the opinion] that he was superior to others he established a peculiar type of doctrine of his own." Cyprian, *On the Unity of the Church*, 12: "and since heresies and schisms have risen subsequently, from their establishment for themselves of diverse places of worship." Clement of Alexandria, *Miscellanies*, 7:17, also uses the word "groups." The expressions "diatribe" and "school" were particularly fittingly sought because, for them, Christianity has a purely scientific character and must therefore first be sought. Since Christianity is to protect this character, it must always be like its source, that is, given over to it.

sion. Some are named after peoples, as are the Phrygians; some after their activities, as the Encratites; some after their chief dogmas, as the Docetists and Hamatites; some after the basic principles and subjects they venerate, as the Canaanites and Ophites; some after their evil endeavors as the Simonists and the Eutychians."[d] Origen says: "Because I am a member of the Church and am named not after the founder of a school, but after Christ whose name I wish to bear and who is hallowed over the whole earth, I desire to be called and to be a Christian in deed and in name."[e]

This is clearly also the meaning of Christ's words: "But you are not to be called rabbi" [Matt. 23:8]. Christ here had the separated and special schools of the Jews in mind in which many revealed what *seemed to them* the wisdom of the law. In Christianity everything must be directed back to *one* beginning. So that this is possible Christian doctrine itself will never fall away, and therefore it needs no restorer, no self-corrupted and self-authorized teacher, whose view rests on special personal insights and discoveries, who first wishes to discover the Christian law, to interpret it according to personal wisdom, and then to teach what it is.[174] Each is to be simple and no one a special teacher. All are to be disciples of only one teacher, so that, as Irenaeus says: Christ always teaches and human beings learn. It is therefore also said of the heresiarchs that they strove for the reputation of one *teacher.*[f] Therefore, the Church fathers moved against heresy, the center of which they saw as purely egotistical and as that around which everything rotated, extending light forward and backward, drawing upon ancient error, and pointing out first to the future the unchangeable way which they had to follow. In and for itself it is the same thing whether Montanus's

---

d. Ibid., 7:17.

e. Origen, *Homily on Luke*, 16 (Cf. Justin Martyr, *Dialogue with Trypho*, 36): "They are among us according to the designations of the people from whom their *doctrine and conviction* earlier arose. . . . Thus, one is called a Marcionite, another a Valentinian, another a Basilidianite, some this, some that, in that all describe themselves according to the inventor of their wisdom just as philosophers do." Compare Gregory of Nyssa, *Against Apollonius*, 3: "The great and worthy name of Christian is not named; the Church was torn into human groups." Chrysostom, *Homily on Acts*, 32: "We do not describe ourselves according to human beings, for we have no human leader such as Marcion, etc." There is nothing more significant than such passages. Especially to be noted is Ephraem of Syria's poem against Bardesanes, Marcion, and Mani.

f. Eusebius, *Ecclesiastical History*, 4:29, 3: "Becoming exalted with the thought of being a teacher." Cf. ibid., 6:43; Clement of Alexandria, *Miscellanies* 7:16; Origen, *Commentary on Romans*, 4.

reformation is to complete Christianity or if Marcion wishes to draw from the dust that which with his appearance had already disappeared.[175] Likewise, it is the same thing if the egotistically motivated spirit is called Glaucias or the Paraclete by the glowing fantasy of the Oriental or if the cold Occidentals give the matter a cooler designation.[176] Such a spirit supposes it must make an *epoch* since there is none in Christianity except that which began with Christ and the descent of the Holy Spirit and every other is only a period, that is, a development of the one given and ever remaining power.[g] The character of heresy, however, is that it separates past and future and places itself between them.[177]

How very clear this basic insight concerning heresy and its antithesis[178] which the Catholic Church forms became can be seen in a beautiful passage from Tertullian: "What follows if a bishop, . . . teacher, or martyr is unfaithful to the *doctrine* of the Church? Do the heresies then come to truth? *Do we test our faith according to persons, or persons according to the faith?*"[h/179]

---

g. Tertullian, *On the Prescription of Heretics*, 29: "In whatever manner error came, it reigned of course only as long as there was an absence of heresies. Truth had to wait for certain Marcionites and Valentinians to set it free. During the interval the gospel was wrongly preached."

h. Ibid., 13. Cyprian, Letter 55, 24: "Anyone who is not in the Church of Christ is not a Christian. Although such a person may boast, and announce his or her philosophy or eloquence with lofty words, yet that person who has not maintained brotherly love or ecclesiastical unity has lost even what he or she previously had been."

4. Unity in Diversity[1]

Although all believers form a unity, each preserves his or her own individuality. No knowledge of God comes through reason left to itself; knowledge of God rests on the basis of revealed faith, which *all* have alike despite the different forms in which they possess the same thing. The greatest diversity in Christian customs exists in the Church. The true nature of disagreement in the Church. Freedom in worship.

35

Although the Catholic principle binds all believers into one unity, the individuality of each is not suspended, for each individual is to continue as a *living* member in the whole body of the Church. The life of the individual as such has its source in his or her characteristic, which will never die in the whole. Indeed, the whole itself would cease to be a living [organism] if the characteristic life of each individual, out of which alone it exists, should be lost. Through the manifold characteristics of single individuals directly, through their free development and unhindered movement, it becomes a living organism, gloriously flourishing and blossoming. If all human members became eyes, the body would cease to be. If the characteristic activity of different members were constrained and their contribution to the whole life despised, the body would be disturbed in its many activities, the flow of surging powers cut off, and as the activity, especially that of important members, would be constrained, the whole life process would cease. However, if all individual members were active without the special activity of each individual being determined by *one* moving principle, they would be involved in a wild activity destroying every single member and the whole in the same way. The constant law for the common organism[2] is the image for the Church body: an unconstrained unfolding of the characteristics of single individuals that is enlivened by the Spirit so that, although there are different gifts, there is only one Spirit.

The different characteristics of single individuals reveal themselves, however, in general, at times in relationship to Christian
theory, at times in relationship to Christian life in the narrow sense,[3]
at times in matters of external worship. The purpose of this chapter
is to describe how the Catholic principle in the period under
discussion expressed itself on these matters and how the free
development of single individuals was brought into harmony with
the existence of the whole.

Christ and his apostles presented the gospel with great simplicity
and depth. It was to be grasped in faith as the power of God without
the proofs, without any of the arts, by which individuals seek to
offer and direct their words to others. It was necessary that Christianity had to be considered as the subject of speculation, because
some had more opportunity and direction for speculation, others
less. The use of speculation on the part of unbelievers, Jews as well
as pagans, and their distortions in the heretical schools immediately
provided an opportunity and a demand for those capable of it to
make use of their abilities for the best defense of Christianity. They
did this so as to portray it to some through their reason, and to
disarm others who had rejected it through the analysis of the essence
of Christianity by reference to the Christian consciousness,[4] which
remained ever the same, or to the tradition.[a] To the individual drive
of some to speculate, what was sufficient to meet its needs was
provided; to the same drive in others, a saving remedy was given.

Already among the apostles we see these different directions of
the Spirit arise. As has often already been noted, speculation and
dialectic arose to the fore in Paul, and he used his spiritual individuality against Jews and pagans and against Jewish and pagan
Christians. In John's work, on the other hand, there was depth and
fire of mind.[5] In Ignatius we meet the Johannine interiority and life
of a believing soul, a noble mysticism.[6] In Clement of Rome a
Pauline character develops, but Ignatius stands closer to his teacher

---

a. Tertullian, *Against Marcion*, 1:1: "Now as far as any controversy is to be admitted
lest our compendious principle of novelty . . . should be imputed to want of confidence." Ibid.,
Against Praxeas, 2: "But keeping this prescriptive rule inviolate, still some opportunity
must be given for reviewing the statements of heretics, with a view to the instruction
and protection of divers persons; were it only that, it may not seem that each
perversion of the truth is condemned without examination, and simply prejudged."
Descriptions and developments of Catholic doctrine can be found among all the
Church fathers and almost always in opposition to heretical intentions.

John than Clement does to Paul: depth of mind is more closely
related to Christianity and reaches it more easily than does speculation. The same parallel as that between Ignatius and Clement can be
drawn between Irenaeus, who is of the Johannine School, and Justin.
Irenaeus, glowing throughout directly with faith, pierces[7] far more
deeply into Christianity than does the philosophical Justin. With
Justin, a Christian philosophy of religion proper first appears. In the
Alexandrian School this philosophy reached its greatest heights in
the period under discussion.

One may easily note that we are here dealing with the relationship between faith and knowledge, and it is possible that those who
find themselves at the heights of the most sophisticated speculation
are in community with those who always remain in faith, a faith that
always ought to remain *the same*. If it does not, however, it seems that
speculation must be chained in its activity. Or must the community
be broken and the faith changed?[8]

36

It was argued earlier that *no knowledge of God can be arrived at* without
a special revelation.[9] Clement of Alexandria who, next to Origen,
offered the most comprehensive and deepest studies in this matter,
expressed himself on our knowledge of God as follows: "The basis
for each individual thing is difficult to discover, but to study the
original basis of all things offers the greatest difficulty. How is the
divine to be grasped since it is not a genus or a difference, a method,
a single being, or a number, an accident, nor anything in which it
can be discovered? It is not even the All, for the All belongs under
the concept of the Greatest and it is the Father of the universal
whole.[10] Even less can a part be distinguished in it, because unity is
indivisible. Therefore, it is also infinite, not because it cannot be gone
beyond, but because all special and spatial relations find no
application in it. Therefore, it is also without form and nameless. If
at times we do name it, these names are not proper to it. If we say
it is the One, the Good, Intelligence, the Absolute, Father, God,
Creator, or Lord, we give it these names in our thirst *so that our spirit
can hold to something, and guard against false directions*. One of these
alone does not point to God, but all together point to the power of
the Almighty because adjectives are directed either to inner differences[11] between things or express relationships to some other things

standing beside them. All this, however, may not be considered in regard to God. Nor is God grasped by demonstration, for this establishes something earlier and better known. There is nothing before the begotten. *It must thus be left to the divine grace and its Logos to teach us to know the Unknown.*[a] Thus Clement asks: "Is there, then, no other kind of pious[12] knowledge than that which is taught by the Logos?" He answers, "I do not believe so."[b] In another place in agreement with the passage quoted, he answers the charge that was made against the evidence and reliability of faith that a purely rational knowledge would be of more certainty yet: "All deductive knowledge is mediated, and if one is to arrive at it, all the intermediate steps to it must be directed back in and for themselves to something undeduced. At that point faith enters again, namely, revealed at this undeduced point, and this the philosophers did not discover."[c] The charge of Celsus that the concept of God could be formed by the human activity of enunciating the good human characteristics above and removing the evil, Origen answered in the following way: "When the Logos says 'No one knows the Father except the Son and he whom the Son has revealed' [Matt. 11:27], he is declaring that God is to be known by God's grace which does not come into the human soul without God and thus by the unmediated inner action of the divinity. It is understandable that knowledge of God is too great for human nature. By human nature great errors have crept into this knowledge, that the goodness and loving kindness of God toward human beings comes to them by his miraculous grace with the gift of knowledge (*phthanein tēn tou theou gnōsin*). He knew beforehand that those people would live worthy of the One known and would not distort pious dispositions against him, particularly not if they are led to death or laughed at by those who do not know what piety is and imagine everything else below them."[d/13] "That essence can be thought about but is at the same

a. Clement of Alexandria, *Miscellanies*, 5:12.

b. Ibid., 2:2 [source quoted].

c. Ibid., 2:4: "Should one say that knowledge is founded on demonstration by a process of reasoning, let that person hear that first principles are incapable of demonstration, for they are known neither by art nor by sagacity. . . . The first cause of the universe can be apprehended by faith alone. For all knowledge, capable of being taught is founded on what is known before. . . . For knowledge is a state of mind that results from demonstration, but faith is a grace."

d. Origen, *Against Celsus*, 7:44. Cf. ibid., *On the First Principles*, 1:1, 1: "For what other

time so infinite it cannot be grasped because as the highest it reaches out beyond human beings and is infinitely superior to confined nature. It is possible for human beings to attain the essence through the great immeasurable grace of God in Jesus Christ, the bringer of superabundant grace, and in the Holy Spirit, his helper. Although human nature is incapable of reaching this wisdom that created everything, the impossible is made possible through our Lord Jesus Christ, who has become righteousness, wisdom, holiness, and redemption for us (1 Cor. 1:30). If no one knows what God is other than the Spirit of God, a knowledge of God is impossible for us (1 Cor. 2:11-12). But behold how possible it is: "Now we have received not the spirit of the world, but the Spirit that is from God, that we might understand the gifts bestowed on us by God'" [Ibid.].[e]

37

For this reason Clement with all the Fathers of the early Church who expressed themselves on the matter taught that there was a power of faith in human beings,[14] a desire for the divine, an anticipation, a need for it, the foundation and inner capability to receive the true knowledge of God, but if this was left to itself, it only erred in darkness, did not come to clear consciousness, and fell into continual misconceptions and contradictions.[a] Thus, Athenagoras says that the Greek poets and philosophers were led to the divine by a natural inclination, and that they reached it in anticipation, but that the power of this inclination in itself was not far-reaching enough to gain a correct empirical knowledge of God. However, since they wished to be taught by themselves and not by God, they were counseled in their inanity and contradiction by each other.[b] According to Justin, this inclination is the seed of the Logos spread among all people.[15] According to this principle, the Fathers taught that the

---

light of God can be named, 'in which anyone sees light,' save a power of God, by which a person, being enlightened, either thoroughly sees the truth of all things, or comes to know God himself, who is called the truth? Such is the meaning of the expression, 'In your light we shall see light' [Ps. 36:9], that is, in your word and wisdom, which is your Son in himself, we shall see you, the Father."

e. Ibid., 1.

a. Clement of Alexandria, Miscellanies, 5:1: "faith is" for him "the ear of the soul."

b. Athenagoras, A Plea for the Christians, 7. Much more striking is the passage in Tertullian, On the Soul, 2.

Greeks and other pagan peoples[16] had single truths concerning God and divine things but not the truth itself, and that these single truths were communicated only to specially chosen men by the Logos itself, which never abandoned the pagans;[c] the truths have their source in an original revelation. This was the basic thought at the root of the repeated assertions by the Fathers that the Greeks borrowed their wisdom from the Hebrews.[d] These intermittent,[17] separate rays of divine wisdom never had a significant result, partly because they could not bring forth holy plants in unholy poisoned ground,[e] and partly because they lacked objectivity. Therefore, those who found themselves in possession of truths were uncertain whether those truths corresponded to something outside of themselves or whether they were merely subjective products or some erroneous impressions or assumptions. In Jesus, however, separation came to unity, need to fullness, unconsciousness to clarity. Truth became objective, appeared in Jesus Christ, the Son of God, the truth in itself.[18/f] Therefore, there is no certain and true[19] knowledge of God aside from revelation through the Logos which is received in faith, without faith in his personal appearance in the fullness of time.

Nor was there given a knowing of God by faith, not tied to revealed faith. In summation, we can say that rational knowledge rests finally on faith; the faith of reason, however, needs the faith of revelation. As a result (pure human)[20] philosophy is seen as far lower than the faith of revelation, as something that must first prepare for

---

c. Justin Martyr, *First Apology*, 5; Irenaeus, *Against the Heresies*, 2:6, 2; Clement of Alexandria, *Miscellanies*, 1:6; 5:10; 6:6.

d. Justin Martyr, *First Apology*, 44; Theophilus, *To Autolycus*, 3:16; Clement of Alexandria, *Miscellanies*, 1:6 and *passim*; Origen, *Against Celsus*, 6:78; *Prologue to Commentary on Song of Songs*.

e. Tatian, *Against the Greeks*, 13, 15, 20, in strong expressions.

f. Justin Martyr, *Second Apology*, 8: "It is not surprising if the devils are proved to cause those to be much worse hated who live not according to a part only of the word diffused [among humanity], but by the knowledge and contemplation of the whole Word, which is Christ." Note especially Clement of Alexandria, *Miscellanies*, 6:15: "The proof of the truth being with us is the fact of the Son of God himself having taught us." Ibid., 1.20: "Hellenic truth is distinct from that held by us—although it has the same name—both in respect of extent of knowledge, certainty of demonstration, divine power, and the like. For we are taught of God, being instructed in the truly 'sacred letters' by the Son of God. Because of this, those, to whom we refer, influence souls not in the way we do but by different teaching." Ibid., 1:7: "*One speaks in one way of the truth, in another way the truth interprets itself. . . . Resemblance is one thing, the thing itself is another.*"

the full appearance of truth, as a preparatory school for the Greeks in the same way as the law was for the Hebrews.[g]

38

If we look at the character of the apologies composed by the Church fathers from the beginning of the second century ("Letter to Diognetus") to the end of the third, we notice nowhere that they take the form of mediating Christianity by reason, by something separated from it: Christianity is set *directly* against all that is not Christianity.[21] The apologies proceed from the principle that Christianity answers the highest human needs completely and conclusively. It therefore can be presented only under the principle of the ethical disposition belonging to it so as to stimulate such a disposition, that it can be put on and grasped as the thing promised, as the fulfilled desire, that one can be raised to a clear consciousness of one's higher nature, and that reason come to fullness itself.[a] Therefore, Clement also says expressly that as human beings we are not fitted to take up freely the power of God offered to us and that this attentiveness to take it up will always be rewarded with ever more inner community with God.[b] Here again they were convinced that they need only portray the characteristic of Christianity and to draw upon paganism so that by inner necessity it would appear in its nothingness. It was never considered that reason left to itself *could* order[22] Christianity. Indeed, the opposite was stated: Christianity was in a position to test all the productions of reason.[c] The higher needs of human beings and reason conscious of itself were seen as one and the same as Christianity, and the latter as the former. To possess Christianity and to come to a higher self-consciousness were one and the same. In fact, if we consider more closely what that which is called a critique of

g. Ibid., 6:6.

a. Clement of Alexandria, *Miscellanies*, 3:5.

b. Ibid., 5:13: "Wisdom which is God-given, as being the power of the Father, rouses our free will, and admits faith, and repays the application of the elect with its crowning fellowship."

c. Ibid., 2:4: After a long explanation he concludes: "Faith is something superior to knowledge, and is its criterion." Irenaeus, *Against the Heresies*, 4:32, 1. Clement sees Christianity chiefly as the center through the light of which everything is illuminated and even the Mosaic revelation is understood. Clement of Alexandria, *Miscellanies*, 4:21. Cf. Justin and Origen, *On First Principles*, 4:6.

revelation properly is, we establish the characteristic of Christianity, the way in which it came into the world of appearance as a rule for all revelations, and then subsume the Christian once again under that rule. We thus also establish those truths concerning God and human beings, which became so much our own with the appearance of Christianity that without them we could no longer think of ourselves, as the inner criteria by which the divine dignity of any given religion that calls itself revealed must be accepted although what is worthy of God first came to consciousness through Christianity.[23] In other words, we compare Christianity with itself and naturally find, if it fits well, an agreement, but we then assert that we have proven Christianity to our reason.[24] One was not saved from such deceptions, now often raised in our own day,[25] in the early Christian centuries. It was acknowledged that one can *know* the divine (through God) but cannot *judge* it.[26] Christians themselves were for the greater part pagans and as such saw paganism (that is, the non-Christian as reason left to itself) around them on all sides. They thus knew from experience what this might lead to and gave themselves over to the vain endeavor to judge[27] that by which they had found themselves judged[28] as nothing.[29] Finally, it may be stated that the early Church acknowledged no mere rational knowledge of God[30] and the like. In the confessions of faith it did not omit certain general truths understood as self-evident and by reason alone,[31] but they viewed true knowledge of God in general as the characteristic Christian doctrine. The profoundest reason for all this, however, lies in the basic perception of the Church according to which it desires a pure, holy soul for a pure knowledge of God. This soul only God can give; it does not exist outside the Christian Church. For this reason no pure knowledge of God is possible without it. Without its saving power we would immediately carry idols in ourselves again and the *external* would then not be absent for long.[32]

39

From all that has been said to this point it is clear that we are in no way discussing a knowing in the Christian Church unrelated to Christian faith, nor is there any thought that the Christian received some religious truths by himself or herself and other truths by Christian revelation. Such a division was alien to the early Church. Even that which was known earlier appeared to the early Church in

Christianity in an entirely different light and in a deeper, more joyous meaning. Because of this there was no threat of restricting individuality or disturbing unity, since all were convinced that they could not begin deeper than with Christ, and therefore did not wish to begin deeper.[33] Anyone who did so wish was seen as unchristian. In the Christian Church one can only speak of the free development of a Christian individuality.[34] We have yet to speak of *Christian* knowing and to consider if the unity of believers is not disturbed by it or if by the knowing that one receives in Christianity one does not strive to be free of faith, namely, the faith of the Church,[35] and thus wishes to rise above faith and be of the opinion that in this way one can do without the Church community.[36] Clement of Alexandria and Origen carefully describe the way Christian knowing is made firm. Clement writes: "The essence of knowing consists in the relationship of our spiritual activity to the object of perception. The result of this relationship is evident. What is given[37] is thus the basis of knowing. Faith, however, is the given."[a/38] In another place he writes: "As soon as faith becomes the object of reflection,[39] knowing that rests on a firm basis arises."[b] The given, the positive, if it is taken up in us,[40] thus presents the material that spiritual activities seize upon to produce a scientific structure of knowledge. A Christian philosophy of religion distinguishes itself from simple faith not by the content of its knowing but only by the form that has taken the two together.[41] The relationships of all single components of faith among themselves and to the whole are first clear to a Christian philosophy of religion. At least it endeavors to make them clear. As a philosopher the believer makes himself or herself the object of his or her own reflection and the faith which to that point has been unconscious becomes conscious.[c] Therefore, Clement designates *gnosis*, "a becoming conscious of truth, an understanding of truth *through itself*."[d] To understand this and the aforementioned fully, and to understand completely the essence of a Christian philosophy of religion as described by Clement, it is necessary to refer to the

---

a. Clement of Alexandria, *Miscellanies*, 2:4.

b. Ibid., 2:2.

c. Origen, *Against Celsus*, 7:46: "who accepts the faith which the lowliest persons place in him [Christ], as well as the more refined and intelligent piety of the learned."

d. Clement of Alexandria, *Miscellanies*, 5:1: "Knowledge of the Son and the Father, which is according to the gnostic rule—is that which in reality is gnostic—the attainment and comprehension of the truth by the truth."

definitions of faith that Clement established partly by himself and partly, as he says, with the help of others. He first rejects those who hold that faith is a mere assent[42] to something as true. Rather, he defines it as a "spiritual grasp," as "an insight through grace," as "a direct knowledge," as "an agreement of the inner disposition" (to something given historically [*historisch*]), as "a *uniting* with the supernatural," as "the certainty of the thing hoped for in us," as "a wisdom working through itself."[e/43] What is given historically [*historisch*], the external faith, thus becomes by the power of the Holy Spirit an individual life in the human person. It carries an unmediated certainty in itself and testifies of itself how the discoveries proceeding from the association of spirit and body come to consciousness directly from the inner sense. The believer now makes this Christian truth living in himself or herself an object of[44] perception, and *gnosis* is the result of this self-perception which is an acceptance of truth by truth. Faith is not here seen as something existing outside of us which is in us by concepts alone,[45] but as something united with us, rooted in us, living, and expanding life.[46] *Gnosis* is thus a reconstruction of the faith of the Church,[47] a scientific development of the content of a believing mind. However, faith here steps forth from the mind[48] as a living unity, as a self-conscious whole, because everything appears in the most living union and in its interrelatedness, and there are no breaks noticeable, which is not the case in simple Church doctrine that contains only foundations. The Christian philosopher of religion thus appears greater than a simple believer who holds exclusively to the philosopher for knowledge. But this only appears to be so, for in the Christian philosopher there is merely a full development of what in the

---

e. Ibid., 2:4.2; 5:1 *pistis* [faith] is not *opinion* [*hypolēpsin*] but *contemplation* [*theōrētikē*]; saying "yes" in the fear of God, the basis of the promise, unity working acceptance." Theodoret defines faith as "a seeing of the supersensual," *aphanos, pragmatos, theōria*, standing, rootedness in God, *hē peri to on enstasis*, "an immediate inferiority of the unseeable, something not given over to doubt, the soul of the inner rooted character of the believer" *diathesis anamphibolos tais psychais tōn kektēmenōn enidrumenē*. Other definitions are in Potter on Clement, *Miscellanies*, 2:2. [Potter refers to Philo's use of *epistēmē*, to Stobaeus who referred to the Stoic definition of faith as "firm knowledge," and to Theodoret who, taking up the definition of faith from Clement, understood it as "a primary base and foundation of knowledge . . . a voluntary assent of the soul"] and in Lumper 4:440 [Lumper's lengthy definition of faith extends from 440-447]. Basil, *On True Faith*, 2: "Faith is firm acceptance of that taken up *in the fullness of truth* and revealed by the grace of God."

believer is undeveloped faith (and in the believer faith is more often stronger, as Origen says,[49] since the power of faith gives fruit to life without breaking of its rays by concepts).[f] Therefore Irenaeus says:[50] "The fact that some know more, others less, according to their spirit's capacity, is not because they change the basic principles but because they rework [*proserazesthai*] what is less clear according to those principles and bring them into agreement."[g] Elsewhere he writes: "Neither the most learned nor the most eloquent among the leaders of the Church says anything other than this (the doctrine of the Church),[51] for no one is above the teacher nor does weakness lessen the transmission; *since faith is one and the same*, one person does not add to it nor does another take away from it."[h] Origen points out in the following way how this *gnosis* is also grounded in the method of Christian transmission: "One must know that the holy apostles preached faith in Christ in regard to each and every object that they held as necessary. They were, therefore, incapable of carrying on study concerning divine science and left this to the more enlightened. They left the search for a proof of their doctrine to those who had more noteworthy gifts from the Holy Spirit, in particular the gifts of understanding, wisdom, and knowledge. They spoke of the existence of other gifts, but were silent as to how and whence they existed. They did this certainly so that those eager friends of wisdom who came after them and who had made themselves worthy and capable of taking up wisdom, might have opportunity to manifest the fruits of the Spirit."[i] In almost the same manner Irenaeus also expressed himself before Origen. He also designated the subjects that

---

f. Origen, *Against Celsus*, 7:49: "Even in regard to those who, either from deficiency of knowledge or want of inclination, or from not having Jesus to lead them to a rational view of religion, have not gone into these deep questions, we find they believe in the most high God, and in his only begotten Son, the Word of God, and that they often exhibit in their character a high degree of gravity, purity, and integrity."

g. Irenaeus, *Against the Heresies*, 1:10,3. *proserazesthai* means "to rework" as is clear in this and the section that follows. Neither the ancient nor the Bill translation catch the point. [Both suggest that the heretics *add* to Catholic truth.] Irenaeus is speaking against the heretics who have changed their inherited faith by scientific endeavors. Their *gnosis* is also distinguished essentially from that of Catholics. Thus he says (1:3, 6): "According to the breakdown, their whole position must fall since they accepted deceptive descriptions of the Scriptures *and formed their own foundation*." According to the translations indicated it must read "as they formed." Irenaeus wishes to say that they established their own foundation before they came to the Scriptures.

h. Ibid., 1:10, 2.

i. Origen, *On First Principles*, preface, 3.

could be material for Christian speculation.ʲ What the Church fathers put forth here as a basic proposition presents itself for our study in their extant writings. They generally set forth their Catholic consciousness in a short confession.ᵏ Therefore, Clement characteristically says that *gnosis* is built in the common faith, and that faith lies under *gnosis* as the latter's foundation. As the reflex of a believing individuality *gnosis* did not wish and could not raise itself above the faith of the Church, the eternal, the all-embracing, and the divine, but it looked upon faith as its source as well[52] as its criterion. In his introduction to his work *On First Principles*, Origen therefore remarked: "Those who confess Christ differ not only in small matters but also in important ones, namely, in the doctrine of God, Jesus Christ, and the Holy Spirit. It therefore appears necessary in this and in every single matter to draw a sure line and to establish a firm rule and *then* to begin study of these. Many Greeks and barbarians promised wisdom but we no longer seek it among them. We now believe in the Son of God and are convinced that they are to learn from him. Likewise, there are many who believe they understand Christian doctrine but some of these have turned from the leaders who were to preserve the doctrine of the Church, who in succession received the tradition of the apostles, and who remained until now in the Church. Only that which has never turned away from the Church and the apostolic doctrine is to be held as truth."ˡ/[53] Thus it is true that the Christian must not wish to perfect Christianity, but to perfect himself or herself through Christianity. Anyone who wishes the first renounces the second as well.[54]

40

Since faith penetrates a person's whole being and essence, philosophy unrelated to faith cannot be found in anyone. Philosophy too must be penetrated by faith. If *gnosis* is the reflection of the whole believing mind, the philosophic formation of a Christian, if the Christian has received it, cannot be set aside from faith. The ideas of

---

j. Irenaeus, *Against the Heresies*, 1:10, 3, Clement of Alexandria, *Miscellanies*, 5:1, states that the point of faith must lie at the basis of gnosis.

k. Irenaeus, *Against the Heresies*, 1:9, 1ff.; Tertullian, *On the Prescription of Heretics*, 12,13; Origen, *On First Principles*, preface, 4.

l. Ibid., preface, 2.

reason must be wedded to faith, and the penetration of these two by one another, by which as is self-evident faith appears as in control, will in this case also be *gnosis*.[55] As is clear from what was said earlier, there is in the early Church's concept of *gnosis*[56] no suggestion at all that it must be bound to a specific philosophy; rather, it itself is the highest philosophy. In the early Church it was chiefly Platonic philosophy[57] that had the distinguished honor of being related with Christianity. Moreover, it was an eclectic philosophy that was then used in all the schools and could free itself of their errors. In these speculations, because one drew the divine into the circle of the earthly and the individual and sought to contain the unbounded within finite limitations, it was unavoidable that at times too little was said, at times too much, and often nothing at all. At the least, one could avoid misconceptions on the part of those who first sought to test their strength in this. (See Katerkamp, *Kirchengeschichte*, 1:267ff.)[58] Thus within the Church an opposition was formed by the more mystical theologians who placed the plain apprehension of Christianity in faith before speculation and chastized the latter at times as *vain* and presumptuous. At the end of the second century the moderate Irenaeus stood at the head of this group. The Church herself, however, stood with admirable peace in the center. The Spirit that gave life to her nourished her, penetrated, and united all. In it individual antitheses were overcome.[59] In the consciousness of her power the Church allowed all her children to follow their own individual characteristics freely,[a] as long as they did not take any *conscious* direction against the acknowledged *common* [teaching] that had always existed. (They did not seek to discover this by traces of innocent, harmless expressions—cf. Addendum 11—for in this case all the Church fathers would have been outside the Church, a position, as we have shown, opposed by all their intentions.) In this case it would not have been an *individual* but an *egotistic* activity; there is a great distinction between the two. By this Christian character itself and true freedom would have been lost and, insofar as individuals were desirous of upholding this egotistic activity, they found themselves outside the Christian Church. The knower was thus not unfaithful by his or her *gnosis* or because such a knower

---

a. Tertullian, *On the Prescription of Heretics*, 14: "So long, however, as its form exists in its proper order, you may seek and discuss as much as you please, and give full reign to your curiosity, in whatever seems to you to hang in doubt or to be shrouded in obscurity."

sought to change faith into knowledge. As Clement said, it was a believing knowledge, because such a person possessed the *same* scientific faith although in a different form.[b/60] The unity and difference of both remarkable points of view of Christianity described here are grounded in the Church. Both present a different position and as a result indication is given how in all their differences they are nevertheless not different and moreover not distinguished and how they can and must present themselves.[61] The Church sees itself as a direct divine power, as a life in and through the Holy Spirit, and she *never* moves to a sharper, external description of her inner life without at the same time fearing that it will be profaned here in the earthly and temporal realm. Never does she wish to express it in a stronger conceptual form than when she is forced to, than when distortions develop and a false, unchristian life wishes to manifest itself in doctrinal form. As a result, she always turned aside from such forms of doctrine without positively expressing herself on them until she could no longer simply avoid the matter. Church history from the second to the sixth century expresses this most clearly in regard to the doctrine of Jesus Christ.[62] The speculation of each individual believer, however, is the image of the Church when it saw itself pressed to give a more precise expression to its confession. One can see this confession of the Church as the *total and original speculation* of believers, as the unmediated portrayal of their inner, total faith.[63] The individual believer must find this original speculation in himself or herself. However, since the Church only set forth its unmediated consciousness in individual cases and only set it forth as consciousness, the believer seeks to discover the construction of this according to consciousness itself, to make the common consciousness fully individual in the manner already described. Mystical and speculative theologians are related similarly. If music is to be heard, it can only be received by individuals in its total impression, in the blending of the different tones of instruments and voices. Individuals can, after they have heard the music, break it down into its individual parts and note closely what association of individual elements beget a particular sound, according to what laws it operated, and what can yet be heard from these. The mystic rejoices in the glorious harmonic play that Christianity brings forth in its

b. Clement of Alexandria, *Miscellanies*, 2:4: "Knowledge, accordingly, is characterized by faith and faith by a kind of divine order."

inner life in its totality. The mystic lives in intuition in unmediated, spiritual tasting, and considers it a disturbance of this, a weakening and removal of it, if one proposes to analyze it. The speculative theologian takes up analysis. *But the speculative theologian must have heard the harmony and received it* for himself or herself or such a theologian is speaking of something foreign and does not know of what he or she is speaking. In this is their unity, and the two together form the different situations of the Church. and find their justification in the Church's life, as they find in it, too, the necessity of their method and activity. If the speculative theologian treats what is to be a mere description of the reflective understanding as something that stands on its own, and tears it off from life, the mystic is enraged and like Irenaeus speaks against those who wish to explain the mystery of the begetting of the Son by the Father.[64] "If the Son of God was not ashamed to leave the knowledge of the last day to the Father alone, but said what was true, neither are we to be ashamed to give those questions that are too great for us to God. No one is above our Lord. If someone therefore tells us how the Son was brought forth from the Father, we are to tell that person that bringing forth is to be called a testimony, name, or revelation, or that no one knows how one is to describe it, since it is beyond study . . . neither Valentinus nor Marcion, neither angel nor archangel. . . . Only the Father who begot and the Son who was begotten know. Since the begetting is beyond explanation, it is not with those who try to explain it. They are not in their right mind since they promise to uncover what cannot be uncovered. Truly all know that the Word was brought forth by the spiritual activity of a human being. Those who discuss this matter by referring everything that can be grasped to the only begotten Son of God have discovered nothing great by their speculation, nor have they brought any hidden secret to light. The same is true of those who, as if they were the midwives (*quasi obstetricaverint*) at the first begetting, name him the unsearchable and unspeakable, comparing him to spoken human words." He explains himself immediately in what follows: "It is far better and more significant to know little in simplicity and to become like God through love than to blame God in the supposition that one has known much and understood much. For this reason Paul said 'knowledge puffs up, but love builds up' [1 Cor. 8:1]. He was not here finding fault with true science of God or he would have had to lay charges against himself. He knew that individuals through their knowing become proud and lose love. It is, therefore, far better, as has been said, to know nothing and not to understand any single cause for created things other than to believe in God and to cling to his love, than to be puffed up by science and to lose his love that gives human beings life. It is better to wish to know nothing other than Jesus Christ the crucified than to become godless through subtleties and insignificant study. . . . If we can thus explain anything in the physical world and leave other things to God, what is wrong with learning much *by God's grace* in the Holy Scriptures which are heard supernaturally, *and leave the rest* to him not only now, but in the next world so that God might always teach and the individual always learn."[c] However, if the mystic is disturbed and considers empty fantasies as true spiritual life and high enlightenment, speculation will set that individual right, as Origen in the passage cited earlier [in section 25] did with separatistic mysticism, and as Irenaeus did when he saw himself forced to step forth and defend his faith against foolishness.[65]

41

Written speculations and constructions were allowed to follow their own paths, but if they went to excess they were not allowed to do so without fraternal admonitions. The results of such speculations, insofar as they contained purely individual and local matters, were not taken up into public confessions, which held fast to what was common, historical [*historisch*], and transmitted. Nevertheless, the Church did draw[66] from such speculations the most unmistakable benefits. After the formation of this Catholic[67] *gnosis* we find the so-called false *gnosis* of the heretics so constrained, so attacked on all sides, and so caught up in its own essence that, powerless and exhausted, it soon withered away.[a/68] In that the Church's speculative theologians held fast to the faith and acknowledged and defended all the rights belonging to faith with deep self-knowledge and humility,[69] they pointed to the firm foundations of the Christian Church. However, because they endeavored to bring faith to self-

---

c. Irenaeus, *Against the Heresies*, 2:28, 6; 2:26, 1; 2:28, 3. Although it is specifically directed against Valentinus and other teachers, it is against speculation, as are the words of Justin, Theophilus, Athenagoras, and others.

a. Eusebius, *Ecclesiastical History*, 6:18. From Origen (cf. de la Rue edition, Letter Fragment, fol. 4). See Pamphilius, *Apology for Origen*, preface.

consciousness and to describe its individual parts that had been expressed in the Church's apostolic transmission in regard to the essence of Christian faith and known Christian interests, they closed the way to human teachings and opinions. To a mind that is in fact faithful but in which faith is found as an unstructured and unconscious[70] mass, any doctrine can be taught as a true and pure portrayal of faith,[71] even if it contradicts the earlier faithful conceptions of the believer and destroys faith itself as a consequence. The extensive growth of heretical parties in this period is to be ascribed in great part to this fact. The element of mere self-seeking in them does not explain everything, but when one is of the opinion that the true faith, which no one may leave, is united to the elevation of oneself above others, such an opinion flourishes. Because of this the Church fathers continually complained that ignorant and simple people were deceived.[b] Clement of Alexandria remarked that one could indeed be a believer without enlightening faith, but that without it one could not understand[72] one's faith, and therefore was incapable of distinguishing right from wrong. One could so distinguish only if one were raised to a clear consciousness of faith.[c] From this one may note that Catholic *gnosis* was clearly conscious of its beneficent active relationship on[73] the Church. Clement expressed himself yet more precisely on this.[74] He called *gnosis* "a perfect work of faith" and an "unshakable construction" of faith.[d] As a result, the study of philosophy was insistently called for, so as to establish faith more firmly in itself. Clement of Alexandria rightly held that if individuals had sought in vain the way of demonstration and deduction unrelated to faith, they would hold consciously to faith by which

b. Irenaeus, *Against the Heresies*, preface, 2: "the inexperienced." Origen, *Against Celsus*, 5:64: "The expression 'stumbling-block' is, indeed, of frequent occurrence in these writings—an appellation that we are accustomed to apply to those who turn away simple persons, and those who are easily deceived, from sound doctrine." Often referred to in Tertullian.

c. Clement of Alexandria, *Miscellanies*, 1:6. After he has noted that the ideas of the good and the true are only gained through nurture of consciousness, he continues: "One can be a believer without learning; so also we assert that it is impossible for an individual without learning to comprehend the things which are declared in the faith. But to adapt what is well said, and not adopt the reverse, is not simply caused by faith but by faith combined with knowledge."

d. Ibid., 2:2: "Unmoved certainly in faith." Ibid., 1:2: "by the use of an ampler circuit, obtains a common exercise demonstrative of the faith."

alone many had already been won.[e] But only those who knew human struggle from experience and spoke from experience could properly speak of the insufficiency of human knowing and point to faith as the only thing necessary. Experience gave their words weight and credibility. In addition, Clement called for philosophical studies because of their formal value, which they demonstrated by the sharpening of the mind and the preservation of a clear, precise view, so necessary for the presentation of doctrine and the logical refutation of opponents.[f/75] Origen paid little attention to the charge of his pagan opponents that only gross ignorant men were and ought to be in the Church. He stated that all believers were to penetrate more deeply into their faith in and for themselves and to possess a higher formation. Yet, since this was not possible for the greater number because of their daily responsibilities and incapability, simple faith was enough for them and scientific knowledge of faith was always only the possession of a few.[g] But to those who have grasped the dogmas of faith in their deep relationship and in their various ties and foundations, Origen assigns the greatest responsibility to share with others what they have. He emphasizes this particularly since otherwise errors will find easier access because of the lack of healthy nourishment:[76] "False teachers raise themselves up against the

e. Ibid., 1:2: "Even if philosophy were useless, if the demonstration of its uselessness does good, it is yet useful." Gregory Thaumaturgus requires philosophy; see his *Panegyric*, 7:13 et al.

f. Clement of Alexandria, *Miscellanies*, 1:20: "Perspicuity accordingly aids in the communication of truth and logic in preventing us from falling under the heresies by which we are assailed." Basil, *On Isaiah*, 2.92: "The power of dialectic is a firm protection for the truths of faith. It makes it capable of withstanding its enemies." Note the beautiful passage in Hilary, *On the Trinity*, 12:20: "The Apostle did not leave us a faith that was bare and devoid of reason; for although a bare faith may be most mighty to salvation, nevertheless, unless it is trained by teaching, while it will have indeed a secure retreat to withdraw to in the midst of foes, it will yet be unable to maintain a safe and strong position for resistance. Its position will be like that which a camp affords to a weak force after a flight; not like the undismayed courage of those who have a camp to hold. Therefore, we must beat down the insolent arguments that are raised against God, destroy the fastness of fallacious reasoning, and crush cunning intellects that lift themselves up to impiety with weapons not carnal but spiritual, not with earthly learning but with heavenly wisdom." The point of Petavius, *Opus de theologicis dogmatibus* [*De trinitate*, prolegomena,] 3 [on the use of philosophy and logic in theology], is well taken. It treats the relation of faith and *gnosis* according to the basic ideas of the ancient church. Cf. Neander, *De gnosis fideique*, Heidelberg, 1811.

g. Origen, *Against Celsus*, 1:9 [source quoted].

Church of God on the pretext of knowledge, circulate a mass of writings, and promise a clarification of the evangelical and apostolic doctrines. If we remain silent and do not oppose them with healthy and true doctrine, because of the lack of saving nourishment for parched souls, they will gain power over those who rush to their advertised, but in fact impure, food. It is therefore necessary that each person who can defend the doctrine of the Church purely and without falsehood, and is in a position to oppose the false *gnosis*, should rise up against the heretical form and speak the depth of the evangelical word against it."[h] In this way a deeper insight into faith, a Christian *gnosis* but one not in the language of the learned and by their intelligence, was to be extended throughout the whole Church, that is, anyone who had higher insights was to help others to self-understanding and to teach those who had just received the divine life[77] to gain clarity. In this sense Clement says that as true *gnosis* cannot be without faith, so faith cannot be without *gnosis*.[i/78] *Gnosis* in this, its final relationship to the Church, goes immediately over into the other person whom, in that it protects, it purifies at the same time. The Catholic Church, as is necessary, allows nothing to work upon her from outside so as to first find truth, but she desires that always according to the foundation of her whole history, a comparison of her truth with itself will cast out the foreign element as such. In this matter, as well, it is necessary to raise faith to self-consciousness. As has been said, encroachment upon the Church, especially by heretical parties, made it possible that some took up into themselves an opposing element without noting it as such. Thus also within the Church many opposing elements stood beside one another; these needed to be separated so that truth as such was *known* and error as negation disappeared by itself. How much Catholic *gnosis* helped in this matter in the early Church in specific ways is in part demonstrated elsewhere. In no case can it be completely described here.

42

If individuals through their special gifts and their conscientious formation of them fulfilled these for the whole,[79] the whole preserved

---

h. Origen, *Commentary on John*, 5:4.

i. Clement of Alexandria, *Miscellanies*, 5:1: "Neither is knowledge without faith, nor faith without knowledge."

infinitely much more, indeed everything, for them. In that she [the whole, the Church], having begotten them in her womb, nourished them, communicated to them the life-giving Spirit, and already formed a Christian life in them before they came to a developed Christian consciousness, their depth of contemplation was possible and their height of speculation was reached. Clement and Origen said that this contemplation filled those who possessed it with great pleasure, unspeakable joy, and heavenly consolation.[a/80] According to the idea of the Catholic Church, Christian life precedes speculation; speculation creates out of the rich treasure of inner experience, out of the uncreated fullness of holy life.[81] As unfathomable as this life is, even so deep and rich is reflection on it, the spiritual characteristic of which gives it thought and capability. Anyone who begins with unsteady concepts loses himself or herself in a shallow breadth because such a person wishes to have fruit before sowing seed and begetting a plant from which the fruit grows. The character and mind of such an individual is deprived of all firmness and strength by its hollow speculation, indicating that such a person is incapable of great matters. (See Addendum 12.) Catholic gnostics, on the other hand, grow in all these matters to an ever higher virtuousness, for as their contemplation only arose from this, so it was a movement of this again and a new strengthening of it.[82] As the Church establishes a pure and holy life as the source of the knowledge of God and true faith, so also especially does *gnosis*. *Gnosis* works back again to the purification of life, and strengthens the depth of reflection. The more this [contemplation] flows forth into the whole Church's life, the richer does this life's blessing stream back upon contemplation.[b] This truly holy scientific knowledge is, therefore, also seen as a gift of the Holy Spirit,[c/83] and the Church expresses herself on this

a. Clement of Alexandria, *Miscellanies*, 7:16. Origen, *On First Principles*, 2:7.

b. Clement of Alexandria, *Miscellanies*, 5:1: "The apostle, then, manifestly announces a twofold faith or, rather, one that admits of growth and perfection. . . . That which is excellently built upon is consummated in the believer, and is again perfected by the faith that results from instruction and the word."

c. Origen, *Against Celsus*, 6:13: "Divine wisdom accordingly, being different from faith, is the 'first' of the so-called charismatia of God; and the 'second' after it—in the estimation of those who know how to distinguish such things accurately—what is called 'knowledge' is *gnosis*; and the 'third'—seeing that even the more simple class of persons who adhere to the service of God, so far as they can, must be saved—is 'faith.' He then refers to 1 Cor. 12:8-9 and goes on: "It is no ordinary individuals whom you will find to have participated in the 'divine' wisdom, but the more

decisively in that she honors as saints the greatest defenders of her truth.[84]

Thus, since the Church can have in it members of differing individualities, the needs of all can be satisfied.[d] She gives nourishment to all, all move freely and happily, working in each other and for each other, one member supporting the other. Faith and knowledge share themselves and flow into one another.[85] All together form a great organic whole enlivened by one Spirit. Single individuals grow and the whole flourishes.[86]

No constraint of individuality comes from *the Spirit* of the Catholic Church. Rather, she forms individualities in virtue and power. This can be seen in the character of Catholic writers. No Church has brought forth so many great and influential persons as the Catholic [Church] has throughout the years of her existence. Great, weighty duties awaken the Spirit. There is no greater or more significant duty than to defend the truth and to make its kingdom firm. This is the duty of the Church. Setting her members in a great community, she extends her power as far as she herself exists. The leaders of heretical congregations wished to squeeze the external truths of Christianity into the confines of their time and individuality. As a result their work perished with their time, which they sought to give the character of eternity. The period following them did not take the pains to transmit their opinions to the future, or even to stir itself to indicate that it bewailed the loss of things related to this spirit. It had a proper sense that the time that complained of the loss possessed the ability to pass on similar products but had no reason to trouble itself to do so. Those who were the works of our eternal Father, on the other hand, defended the things of Christ, of

---

excellent and distinguished among those who have given in their adherence to Christianity; for it is not to the most ignorant or servile, or most uninstructed of humankind, that one would discourse upon the topics relating to the divine wisdom." Clement of Alexandria, *Miscellanies*, 7:10, and particularly Origen, *On the Song of Songs*, prologue.

d. Origen, *Against Celsus*, 7:41: ". . . who has given light and taught the way of piety to the whole race, so that no one can reproach him if anyone remains without a share in the knowledge of his mysteries. Such, indeed, was the abounding love that he had for human beings, that he gave to the more learned a theology capable of raising the soul far above all earthly things, while with no less consideration he comes down to the weaker capacities of ignorant men, of simple women, of slaves, and, in short, of all those who from Jesus alone could have received that help for the better regulation of their lives."

the Church, of the salvation and consolation of humanity, and were many times willing to suffer and to die for them. To this day, outside the confines of time, they have worked a thousand blessings. They shone in the twilight of dark centuries and are now the one present source of a renewed deep Christian life. They will work until we no longer need letters. The love and truth that bind us with them require that they remain present to us in their writings until, in the Spirit who created the community, we no longer need any mediation.[87]

43

A historical review of the relationship in the early Church between the principle of unity and of individuality in regard to Christian life in the narrow sense can be briefly presented. Christian ethics are to be seen as the portrayal and unfolding of the inner, holy principle in life. What they were or in what specific manner the holy disposition expressed itself was transferred by the apostles to the congregations and was passed on again by these congregations.[88] But the same battle that the Church had to wage for the protection of pure faith was repeated for the proper preservation of Christian ethics. As happened in the case of the defense of doctrine, so in the cause of ethics what is truly Christian must first be firmly held in life. We now find everything in order and designated and can in no way think that it was ever different. We are of the opinion that everything is self-evident.[89] Because of this captivity that exists only in the present, the Church does not value her Spirit, her struggles, and the necessity of the community of all people.[90]

It is in this case as if an individual, to specify the content of faith, called in a freedom unworthy of a Christian. One can give analogies—history supports them—to demonstrate that the Holy Scriptures and their words must be passed on. Thus some said they were lords of the Sabbath, of a royal race, and that for sons of kings there was no law. "Such a position is established by the followers of Prodicus," says Clement of Alexandria. "They falsely call themselves Gnostics in that they assert they are by nature sons of the first God. But misusing their high birth and their freedom, they live as they wish. However, they wish to live in lust.[91] For them, as lords of the Sabbath, there is no law. As such they are above every race, distinguished by birth, the sons of kings. For kings, no laws are written."[a] The followers of Valentinus are similar (Clement said that Valentinus himself was free of ethical excesses, but he raised up his *gnosis* in a one-sided way just as others did faith. Faith is as little to be divided from works as is the inner from its external revelation. It is totally different with Catholics. Holiness of life came first for them and always went alongside knowledge. Valentinus, however, like many other heretics, divided science and life, faith and works, inner and outer). Valentinus's followers taught that "the animal individuals[92] have an animal formation. They are strengthened by works and mere faith, but they do not possess perfect *gnosis*. But these are those in the Church. Therefore, it is necessary for us (Catholics) to perform good deeds, since we cannot be saved in any other way. They, however, are saved in every way, not by works but because they are so by nature in a spiritual way."[b] Quite consistently they add, "As gold is not sullied in dirt, neither are they by desires." It is said of the followers of Basilides that they lived more unchastely than the pagans, and of the Carpocratians that they asserted that right and wrong are founded only on human opinions.[c] Thus far could they separate concept from life. These and many other sects calling themselves Christian despised virtue and all law. Against them stood others who tied human beings in a constraint as unnatural as the licentiousness of the first group. Among these were the Marcionites. Clement of Alexandria rightly said that one could divide heretics into two classes: they either teach that one may live as one wills or insist on a godless and inhuman sternness.[d/93] In most cases now, as was said, the pattern is determined so that the Christian disposition in it can only express itself in a specific way, and those who offer opposing norms are seen as bearing an opposing disposition in themselves, as finding themselves outside the Church. However, there are also points where the expression of a holy disposition is fully given over to the individuality of each individual. In the early Church marriage must especially have been viewed in this way, as the use of personal possessions and the practice of eating and drinking must have been. Christianity came into a completely corrupted world in which the body held complete power over the spirit and held it imprisoned, in which ethical excesses in sexual and

a. Clement of Alexandria, *Miscellanies*, 3:4.
b. Irenaeus, *Against the Heresies*, 1:6, 2. Cf. the terrible things in ibid., 4.
c. Clement of Alexandria, *Miscellanies*, 3:3.
d. Ibid., 3:5.

sensual desires and the covetousness tied to them had reached the highest point. It was thus natural that Christians, forming an opposition and despising sensual lusts, held themselves distant from what was for the world the highest and only thing. As a result many sold their goods, divided the proceeds among the poor, and supported themselves by the works of their hands. When they saved much, they gave it away again. They ate very little and only the poorest food. Some never married and preserved their virginity throughout their life. Others married but made a vow of sexual abstinence. Still others determined not to take a second spouse after the death of the first, and others did other things. By this firmness they made a good impression on the world, which had fallen into feebleness. Their earnest ethics contained a more weighty rebuke than any words. But this was only to be an expression of a pure disposition, above the carnal, a means by which they convinced themselves of the existence of such a pure disposition, and thus came to a self-consciousness in which they trained themselves (therefore *askēsis* [training]), strengthened themselves, and then worked in their own way in their surroundings. They did not, therefore, raise *their* practice to a general law and they allowed others to establish, express, and form the same pure disposition according to their characteristics.

They thus saw marriage as a divine institution, goods and belongings as blessings of God, food and drink as his gifts.[e/94] Those outside the Church were not so thorough. Some believed that the freedom and independence of the spirit from the body could not be demonstrated unless they destroyed the body and gave themselves over to all desires, or to make the spirit's lordship complete[95] had women in common. Others rejected all marriage, as did Marcion, or all second marriages, as did Montanus, and introduced one *legal* and complete abstinence from certain foods, as well as stern, long, and

---

e. *Apostolic Canons*, 4:3: "Anyone who holds that marriage and the drinking of wine—aside from proper ascetic practice—is wrong and forgets that ali is good and that God made human beings as man and woman and by doing so despises the creation is to be cast out of the Church." This command is often noted in the *Apostolic Constitution* 6:10, 11, 14, 26. Note this as well as Eusebius, *Ecclesiastical History*, 4:23, where Dionysius of Corinth ordered a bishop not to lay the yoke of virginity on *all*. One can see how much trouble it cost the Church to uphold its basic principles. Through Christianity an immense excitement for life and great power arose and because of this the greatest activity was needed for its regulation.

often repeated fasts, that is, they made their individual preferences into general laws. This appeared as egotistical, and therefore as unchristian, and this unchristian character was also cast out of the Church.[f]

44

Individuality is somewhat limited in its nature; it is not the spiritual but only [directed] toward the spiritual and a form of it. It is therefore localized, temporary, purely contingent, and to this degree founded in the temporal and the sensual.[96] Anyone who gives it universality confuses the sensual with the spiritual, the cause with the result. That the two are not so simply related is easily understood. For this reason Marcion sought to find individuality's source in higher laws. He formed his own view of the world, or rather borrowed it from Cerdon. He took up two or three absolute principles and taught that matter arose fully from evil. From this he deduced that marriage which concerned itself with the material arose from evil, cast aside the Old Testament as arising from the same principle, and did the same with the first three Gospels after he had abridged the fourth. What a frightful display! But this is the essence of egoism, which must construct everything according to itself and impress its essence on everything so that the total order of the world and of salvation[97] becomes a reflection of its limitation. This is the essence of every heresy and the basis of its nothingness: it wishes to raise the limited individuality of its master to generality. Therefore, what was only its own small like-minded characteristic must in changed circumstances disappear since it is not spiritual, true, or permanent. Other characteristics are proper to Christian humility: to take up Christianity completely into oneself, to cast out as of no use that which opposes the gospel in its own sight, and to clarify and form by the Spirit that which is to be with it. Therefore, although Marcion had a profound insight concerning Christianity, and although he possessed great religiosity, his insight was not profound enough and his religiosity was not pure enough to suppress the selfishness in him completely. It seems to me that above all a certain

---

f. Apollonius in Eusebius, *Ecclesiastical History*, 5:18, 2: "His actions and his teaching show who this new teacher is. This is the one who taught the dissolution of marriage; who made laws for fasting."

one-sidedness prevails in the derivation of the Gnostic heresy. We seek anxiously to discover the Oriental theosophy from which Gnosticism might have been created and that is good, but this endeavor ought to be designated more as a search for a likeness of errors than for its source. Its source is always in human beings and therefore is always the same. Human beings repeat themselves and discover themselves everywhere again. Two eternally opposing substances are supposed; it is a reflection of the situation of one's own mind, which torn and divided by sin finds no unity and instead of seeking the cause of this in its own evil direction of will, raises it to an eternally existing, independent essence, a part of which is allowed to flow from itself to human beings. Sin is thus explained, so as not to need to negate it, as if one could not, or the whole person would be negated with it. The revelations of God in the Old Testament are divided from those in the New Testament because a coherence, unity, and organized development of One wisdom is never found in the limitations arising out of sin, because human beings and their point of view are made a law for the world, by which action division necessarily follows. In a like manner according to the judgment of so many concerning the Christian Church and its history, a part will be given over to Satan until the second redemption of the world![98] It was no different with Montanus than with Marcion. To give universality to his individual spirit's direction and to a strengthened image of his Phrygian nationality, his opinion of himself was raised to that of the Paraclete or to the one who had sent the Paraclete so that his egotism might find a general acknowledgment.[99] Clement of Alexandria therefore strikingly designated the Montanists as those who emphasized physical purity, who laid emphasis on work which in and for itself was dead and nothing, as those who confused the virtue of the Spirit with the body,[a/100] whereas without the Spirit the body is only dust and ashes. Tertullian said, after he had joined the Montanists: "The Catholics cast us

---

a. Clement of Alexandria, *Miscellanies*, 3:6: "The mass which knows no temperance is with the body, not with the Spirit in the Kingdom of Heaven. Without the Spirit, however, the body is dust and earth." Compare the beautiful definition of purity (ibid., 5:1): "Purity is 'to think holy thoughts.' Against this a Montanist, according to Origen, says "Do not come near me; I am pure for I have not touched a woman and my mouth is not an open sepulchre, but I am a Nazarene of God and I drink no wine as they do."

out merely because we teach fasting more than marriage."[b] But how much more noble and Christian are Clement of Alexandria's words: "We happily praise virginity and those to whom it is given. We marvel also at monogamy and its value. But we believe that one must have empathy and that we must help carry one another's burdens so that none believing themselves to stand, fall."[c] In this Clement can be cited alone before all because he expressed himself so clearly. He stated the intentions of his Church.[d] However, Tertullian, too, splendidly declared the intentions of the Catholic Church in that he stated the reasons that Catholics opposed to the egotistical novelties of the Montanists. From apostolic times the Catholic Church with general agreement had kept the practice of fasting partly on particular days of the week for reasons indicated earlier, partly to give an expression of the inner sorrow of Christians because of the suffering of Jesus on those days.[e] It was so in the forty-day fast. After noting this Tertullian adds: "Except for this Catholics, or the bestial ones, said that each person could fast as he thought best and according to external situations, but not according to the *new legal* determinations. In such a way the apostles observed it without introducing another more specific and general yoke to the observed feasts. . . . Our (the Montanists) Xerophagiens are an imitated law coming very near to heathen superstitions in which by mortifications and fasting at certain mealtimes Apis, Isis, and the Great Mother are honored. But faith is free in Christ, and one does not need to keep the fasts initiated under the Jewish law because the apostles allowed everything and cast out those who forbade marriage and who denied the taste of certain food created by God. We (the Montanists) are, therefore, noted as those who fell away from the faith in recent times, who also listen to spirits deluding the world, to lying teachers, as those who possess a scorched conscience. Thus, we are associated with the Galatians as those who observe certain days, months, and years. They charge us with the words of Isaiah, who said *the Lord desires no such fasts* [cf. Is. 1:14], that is, not

---

b. Tertullian, *On Fasting*, 1: "These strive against the Spirit for they plainly teach more frequent fasting than marrying."

c. Clement of Alexandria, *Miscellanies*, 3:1: Compare the beautiful treatment of the ascetic and martyr, Alcibiades, in Eusebius, *Ecclesiastical History*, 5:3.

d. Ibid., 3:1: "What our viewpoint is must be expressed."

e. Tertullian, *On Fasting*, 2: "At all events, in the Gospel they think that those days in which 'the Bridegroom was taken away' were definitely appointed for fasts."

refraining from food, but doing works of righteousness. In the gospel the Lord succinctly set aside all anxious concerns in regard to food, saying that one was not made unclean by what one took into one's mouth but by what went out of it [Matt. 15:11]. . . . Thus, the Apostle taught that God did not require food so that we could get something if we ate or lose something if we did not eat it (1 Cor. 8:8). *'That alone helps if we believe with our whole heart and love God and neighbor'.*[f] These enlightened principles of the bestially designated Catholics, Tertullian sets against his egotistic sophists.

Thus an infinite mass of individualities develop freely and untroubled beside one another in this matter. The Church looks upon all externality as given by the Spirit so as to form and act in the Spirit and to reveal the Spirit. All these differences, however, are enlivened by one Spirit which binds all in joy and peace.[101]

45

If anyone opposed an acknowledged Christian custom that merely expressed the Christian disposition through itself and not also through its opposite, two results could occur: Such a person either denied the Christianity of the custom or acknowledged it, but [in the latter case] the non-Christian had so much power over the individual that there was no victory possible in the battle. In the first case the person was completely unworthy of Christian community and was excommunicated, as was anyone who opposed a Christian doctrine in full consciousness. Of this we spoke earlier. In the second case the individual was looked upon as one who initially had the concept of becoming a Christian and was sent back again into the preparatory classes with the catechumens. The more evil the deed that betrayed that person's distance from a Christian disposition, the further back in the class was the individual sent. In neither case could the person be said to have destroyed Christian freedom, because the first had stated something unchristian, whereas the other had still not raised himself or herself up to the Christian. The latter had first also to acquire a higher concept of the dignity and excellence of the Christian Church and to learn to know the value lying in her to be her companion. The Church indicated how high a conception she had of herself by partially or completely shutting such persons off

f. Ibid.; cf. ibid., 13.

from community with herself. The one punished indicated that he or she was not a stranger to a sense of the value of being in the Church because such a person did not separate from her, although free to do so. In that the individual held this freedom to be no freedom, he or she indicated the capability for freedom which the Church offered. The Church distanced such a person from herself in the confidence of bringing that individual near to her, and in taking away the individual's (lower) freedom she gave the person a higher one.

Here, as well, the heretical communities held to extremes. Either they had no penitential system and persons of non-Christian theory, as well as persons of unchristian practice,[a] could call themselves members, or by a pride near to that which initially brought them into existence, no sorrow on the part of an individual could bring about reconciliation with the whole. This latter practice was carried out by Montanists, Novatians, and Donatists. Among the Marcionites the married formed the penitential class. If external practice counted for nothing among some, among others it was too highly valued. Among some freedom was understood as wanton capriciousness; among others, a stern willfulness was understood as freedom.

46[102]

Our reflections on the material treated in this and earlier chapters lead us to treat the true nature of the antitheses in the Church's domain as well as the danger of a repetition of these. In this way charges that have been made against the Church of the first three centuries can be more specifically met.

It is said that the mystery of all true life consists in its ability to penetrate all that is opposed to it. One may say that "Every opposition exists truly and in a real way only in that it is established in one and the same thing." A choir is formed from the voices of different persons, men and women, boys and girls, each in their own way joined in one harmony. Without this manifold number and variety a grating, wearying monotone results, an antagonistic discord, without a unified sound. The art of the choirmaster, in whom the harmony must have penetrated deeply in a living form, [is main-

---

a. Tertullian, *On the Prescription of Heretics*, 41: "I must not omit an account of the conduct of the heretics—how frivolous it is, how worldly, how merely human, without seriousness, without authority, without discipline, as suits their creed."

tained] so that he would always point out to everyone as the image-maker of others, what harmony is, and be that harmony, and, as a result, avoid cacophony. The conductor's wisdom by which he sought to form the choir upholds the voices that please him so that an essential constancy of the whole is not removed from the whole. Disharmony can arise. If he gives somewhat more direction to the male bass voices, he does not intend to indicate that the male essence consists in strong depths and that the deeper the sound the better it is, but he does so that this firmness might be harmonized with the charm and mildness of the other voices. If the male is itself incapable of a disharmonious loudness and does not accept the admonition of the conductor, or if it thinks that *it* is uniting everything in itself, it has to withdraw from the whole as unsuited for forming it, as opposing the full structure, and as destroying the harmony. In such a case it is not forming an *antithesis*—for true antithesis can be found in unity—but a *contradiction*. Valentinus said something similar in a beautiful myth. Disturbances arose in the spirit world because, despising its completeness, an Aeon [age] wished to establish its pleroma [fullness] separate from the All-Father. Since the Holy Spirit taught these fools that only by holding fast to the community could Bythos [depth] be known, they all united themselves in him. Thus, each Aeon ceaselessly became what the other was without ceasing to be what it itself was. One became Nous, another Logos, another Anthropos and so on. Each fulfilled itself and formed a marvellous harmony. Each received what it lacked from the other and thus they all came to true knowledge and praised the All-Father. (Valentinus took this from the Catholic Church and carried whatever suited his principles into the spirit world. In his own school he could find no such notions. Likewise, in his emanations he has Ecclesiasticos [Church] and Macariotes [Blessed] arise from the Abyss, blessedness in the Church community! If only he had taken the most glorious matters of the Church and carried them into his spirit world. If he had only wished for that in the Church, which did not exist in his spirit world! Then he would have experienced in the former what he fabricated in the latter.)

Because of what has been said everything that is truly and purely opposed to the *Christian domain* must be established in unity: it must move freely and easily in that domain. The same must be true of the most general antitheses, the realistic beside the idealistic apprehension of Christianity, and likewise true mysticism, be it contemplative or practical, alongside true Christian speculation in its various directions. It is true that religion begets various views of the world according to various periods, cultures, races, peoples, families, individuals, indeed according to its various stages of development. In fact, religion can make itself known completely only in an infinity of such variations. As a result this infinity in unity is possible insofar as it expresses itself in true antitheses, since unity is also in infinity. If it were not so it would not be the infinite unfolding of the One and the Same.

Since these true antitheses are possible, they must become actual, because true life consists only in the penetration of that which opposes it. Therefore, as we said earlier, true Christian life is not possible in any heresy because there are no antitheses in heresy, and there are no antitheses because there is no unity. Had they brought unity with them in their division, they would not have arisen. Likewise, no true antitheses could have formed in them since a true antithesis exists only in relation to another against which it is set in one and the same, and thus unity is necessary in both. What in the Church has the true nature of an antithesis, appears outside the Church not as an antithesis but as standing by itself alone, because it cannot reach its completion, but destroys itself out of sorrow and anger, and dies. It is just as Origen said in a passage cited earlier regarding the mystical sects. [See above, section 26.] When antitheses as life forces arose in that which wished to live by itself, they were not genuine antitheses, but contradictions, since they set aside unity. Therefore, there could be no genuine, common life since no true life is possible in contradiction. Tertullian, therefore, said that heresies were all mixed together and for them no virtuous unified life was possible. If the contradictions changed into true antitheses, they had to bear unity within themselves; that is, that which wished to live solely for itself ceased to be as soon as it came to self-understanding and sense. It no longer desired to live by itself and entered into community.

Someone might say that this is of no consequence since heresies were earlier viewed in this work as antitheses to the Church, since they were described as that which is not in unity with her, and true antitheses are only possible in unity. Such a person could say that it is contradictory to posit, on the one hand, that all antitheses must be established only within unity and thus that the possibility of self-life is ascribed to the Church, and, on the other, that heresies are necessary to awaken and complete the Church. To this we must answer freely that we should not have designated heresies as antitheses to the Church but always as contradictions. The second point has, however, more weight, and other positions of the early Church seem to support it. Heresies were cast out from the unity of the Church. If they necessarily belonged to the life of the Church, how are they to exist outside the Church? Must they not much more expand the unity that shut them out and change it into a higher unity in which the Church, which shut them out, was itself but a part? How can heresies be called evil if they are *necessary* appearances?

I do not see how the Church could form a higher unity with those heresies that separated themselves, those of Marcion, Mani, Paul [of Samosata], Artemon's school, and others. Where is unity if Artemon says that Christ is not true God and the Church says he is? If Mani posits an evil substance existing from eternity and claims that the Paraclete came with it? In this case the Church would not take up into herself an antithesis, but a contradiction. Even if one said that here a unity, *one life*, was formed, such would not in fact have been the case. If we move from variations in individual matters and look at the differences between the Church and the heresies in general, the two distinguish themselves, to put it briefly, as love and egoism. Where, then, is unity? Love and egoism are not antitheses. If we wish to understand the antitheses between Church and heresies as quiet and movement, even this would be false, for there are heresies that are quiet and others that are always in a state of movement. In the Church, however, the quiet was moved and the movement quieted, that is, antitheses penetrated each other toward unity. It could be said that on the one hand, the Gnostics, baiting and attacking everything, represent the ideal, and on the other that the Montanists, grasping everything in the crudest way, represent the real, that the two are differentiated and this All is brought into unity by the Catholic Church.

Since the Church in her unity contains all antitheses and is all-embracing, she is freely acquainted with all. Both the contradictory parties mentioned could thus arise from her. Once they had separated, they could no longer live. They found points of contention in themselves and could not reconcile their differences. Reconciliation was possible only in the Church. To put it another way: their contradictions changed to antitheses; thereby unity was given, and their reconciliation to one another was thus a return to the Church. It is clear thus that the Church embraces in itself all Christian truth of both contradictory schools. Each took a part of the Church with itself; the part made each a heresy. In this regard unity within the Church was not found. Otherwise there would have been no reason for separation and a conscious unity after the division. The Church thus formed the unconscious unity of all heresies before the division. Only during the division was she with all, whereas all were in contradiction with each other. What was characteristically Montanist and Gnostic was not Christian as content or as form. No Christian antithesis was formed as a result and no Christian unity of life could begin. In regard to the possibility of the self-existence of the Church without heretical contradiction, one must note, as was earlier said, that evil as the source of error ever remains in the Church. Through evil, however, that which, according to its nature, is called to be an antithesis becomes a contradiction. Thus it is possible and always necessary that believers, always holding fast to the true nature of the antithesis, reflect the infinity of the possible developments in the Christian religion, and thus preserve and activate life through the free play of many individuals moving in harmony. Since these antitheses that give rise to life so often become contradictions, the Church accepts her responsibility for a faulty antithesis to her life without acknowledging it as in itself necessary and thus good. Evil does not become good although it bestirs the good. It must always be accepted that the good in and for itself can be described without evil.

47

We must still discuss the relationship of the principle of unity to the free formation of individual aspects of external worship.[103] Worship, as here treated, is the expression of religious ideas, movements, and acts through forms in space, through physical symbols and symbolic acts, interspersed with speech or accompanied by it. Just as doctrine is the inner faith of the Church grasped in concepts, so worship in its most significant aspect is faith reflecting on itself in significant signs. From this inner identity of worship with doctrine one can explain why as early as the second century Christians were as concerned with the unity of doctrine as with that of worship and why they never lost this concern. As a result the Palestinian bishops argued over the celebration of Easter: "Take care that copies of our works are received by the churches *so that we do not bear the guilt of those who light-mindedly lead their souls into error.*"[a] According to this Pope Victor's behavior must be judged—not according to the common search for power, but also not on the basis of sovereignty.[104] The question concerned not so much the day of the feast as the intention to draw closer to Judaism, the expression of which seemed to collapse the Easter feast with that of the Jews. The early Church offers many examples of the relationship between worship and doctrine. Many Gnostic schools did not celebrate Christ's birth. This expressed their belief that Christ was a mere man whose birth could not be the basis for special joy. On the other hand, they celebrated the feast of his baptism because, as they believed, only at this time did the divine first bind itself to him by the dove. Others did not celebrate Good Friday because they believed that Christ only had the appearance of a body and thus could not suffer, or because the divine withdrew itself from him in the suffering. Others did not celebrate Easter because they denied the Resurrection. Cyprian insisted on the rebaptism of those baptized by heretics because he did not believe that the forgiveness of sins was possible in heretical communities. Pope Stephen did not want such rebaptism; he considered the forgiveness of sins and holiness through their disposition and individual faith to be possible in their communities.[105]

Since external worship is an expression of inner faith, it was necessary that worship, broadly conceived, develop throughout the whole Church alongside unity of faith. The question as to whether or not it is correct to use physical symbols in Christianity, a spiritual religion, does not belong here, but a word might be said regarding it. It depends on an impulse of nature. There is a powerful religiosity in us. We are compelled to develop this reflex until our whole religious characteristic has revealed itself in it as in doctrine. We believe that such religiosity is not truly alive in us if we do not find it fully expressed again externally. It is good that this is so. If we meet our productions again, the religious power that produces the symbol is awakened and reproduced. The strongest races extend their inner life to future generations who, perhaps powerless, are not able to form new life but only to receive it. However, if they possess the capability to understand what earlier generations created, they beget in themselves again the same life that was earlier expressed.

a. Eusebius, *Ecclesiastical History*, 5:25.

(Weak times and individuals can create no worship forms nor any doctrinal concepts; indeed, they are dissatisfied with such. For them everything is weak that can be specifically designated as something or can enter happily and cheerfully into *appearance*. Therefore, they desire everything to be as hazy and nonspecific as possible. Everything possible is to be thought and discovered along with it and thus is nothing at all. Everything must be conceived of in the widest possible way so that everything can move freely and not be cast aside as unchristian; the narrow image, the inner lack of strength, the inner division, and faithlessness related to it.) Christian religiosity is necessarily a common religiosity. We do not know of an unmediated activity of finite spirit. Symbols, like the word, mediate inner movement. They are not only the unifying point of all but are also the organ through which the interiority of the one flows out into totality and back from it again. This holy symbolism is an expression of unspeakable discovery. Words are not capable of defining what overflows their domain; this task is often given to the role of signifying. Great thoughts grasp individuals at one time, work upon them with penetrating and shattering power, and place them in a higher region. Symbolic designations in particular have a close tie to religious matters. They are mysterious and yet expressive.[b/106] Christianity greatly rejoices in symbols. This is already evident in that Christ offered the highest to believers in the form of a symbol, namely, *himself.* Acceptance into the congregation takes place in a symbolic manner. When Christ gives his believers the Holy Spirit, he breathes upon them. When he wishes to teach them humility in his school, he washes their feet. Nature and art are thus consecrated together for his Church. It is fitting that what he left behind for the continual use of his believers be highly valued: symbol and context, signifier and signified, belong together as sacrament. The bread does not merely signify him; it is him. We do not merely remember him; he is present, he is in us, and we in him. Baptism does not merely signify purification; true baptism is purification itself. Even if the symbols, which the Church begets out of inner need, do not possess this power, they nevertheless gather believers together around them, are together an organ and expression of love, and "where two or three are gathered in my name (Christ), there am I in the midst of them" [Matt. 18:20]. Ignatius noted this; he ascribes to the gatherings

b. See Creuzer, "Ideen zu einer Physik des Symbols," in his *Symbolik und Myth,* 1:52.

of Christians a sanctifying power and a power to forgive sins because they are the expression of love.

This is also present in the essence of the symbols of worship; in its most significant parts it always develops in the same way and thus always expresses spiritual unity. It would be absurd to say, however, that one must insist on the external so that the internal may be expressed. This would be a fabrication and would go too far. Here is no compulsion. Here is free, natural development, and therefore unity with inner necessity within the *designated boundaries*.

48

Whatever the progression of symbols and symbolic activities are to be, their union and variation with speech and poetry, which may be linked with that which was commended by Jesus, remains ever bequeathed to his Church and its separate parts.[107] Herein the great wisdom of the apostles presents itself clearly to the observer. In this matter little was required by them, and their requirements were not at all times the same. Little was directly prescribed. Everything was to be an externally free expression of the religious. In time this expression *had to develop in itself according to need* and only that was to be considered as a proper goal which was not brought in from the external but was the result of the inner working in the external. The apostles were employed in building up inner Christianity. They could not be concerned with expressing this in confessions and liturgical forms because the *inner* which is to reflect itself in these had first to be engendered. Because of this the person who wishes to establish the apostolic period as the permanent guide is clearly unacquainted with the essence of external worship. Such individuals already indicate their imprisonment to the external since they look upon worship as something external which can be accepted or rejected. They think that one is celebrating the Lord's Supper as Jesus and his disciples did since one has no external form. But one only does as they did if one has the inner form and not if one avoids this or that external form. And what does such a person do other than declare the form of one time to be that of all times, and thus in fact forces all into one form?[108] The early Christians were persecuted and thus had great cause for sorrow, but the liturgical elements in their symbols and poetry declare their joy and happiness. In the third century, after long periods of peace, we find a great desire to express the inner movement in a glorious, external worship. The Christian temple in Nicomedia that was greater than the imperial palace gives us a sense of this, as do the many gold and silver vessels that were confiscated by the pagans during the Diocletian persecution. How can we explain the rich forms of worship that suddenly developed with the Constantinian support of the Church if we do not suppose that the inner, in a powerful way constrained until that period, had always wished to break forth but was not able to? With Constantine it flowed out joyously and full of life because a powerful Spirit drove it, and nothing stood in its way any longer. The community, the essence of the Catholic Church, is an inexplicable feeling; concepts cannot reach it. The more this essence develops and can freely come forth, the more must the symbolic be taken up. Sects, on the other hand, egotistic in their essence, are unfriendly, and therefore necessarily opposed, to the beautiful. In battles with the pagans who did not seek to express the inner externally but believed that religion was created in its externals, all ceremonies, it must not be forgotten, were to be used as carefully as possible.[109]

We must concede that, on the one hand, there is a drive toward an evolution of symbols and, on the other, a restriction, but on the whole a progressive expansion. We must also note that no fetters were placed by the Church on what was needed and that unity did not exist because the first and second centuries determined the third or the third held rights over future centuries or attached itself to the earlier ones.

Looking back on these centuries we find the freest development. Momentary needs were not all similar. In one area bishops were required to set up a Christian feast against a pagan one so that Christians might be concerned with Christian matters and not turn to paganism[110] or paganism by analogy offer inducement to a Christian feast.[111] In other places one had to endeavor to provide Christian Spirit for an individual pagan symbol or practice because the people did not take it up for itself or because it appeared necessary. The Church dealt very freely with this. Pagan, like Jewish practice and anything external, is not in itself evil, but the disposition tied to it may be evil. The Christian Church could thus accept pagan symbols (indeed, prayer formulae such as the Kyrie) if they were exceptional and a Christian idea could be bound with them. To attack the Church because of this is the result of both Gnostic and Pharisaic narrowness. Did the Church not accept in the ancient languages many words that had other meanings? Is the external in itself pure or impure?[112]

All the external worship practices that he handed down, the Supper, Baptism, and so on, Christ took from Jewish practices already in use. Even the Lord's Prayer he formed according to a prayer formula of his day. The apostles borrowed such things as the laying on of hands from the synagogue. They borrowed no pagan practices because originally they did not live among pagans. Judaism did not obtrude on paganism. Both were united in Christianity. As a result Christianity, as it expanded among the pagans, could borrow much from paganism. It was pointed out that neither circumcision nor uncircumcision, but only faith in Christ and the new spirit counts for anything [cf. Col. 3:11].

Finally, the differing characters of the East and the West can be noted as found in their liturgies. Although they were different, they were still bound closely together by something other and higher.[113] The principle of unity stood above forms, and in all its movements it resulted in nothing other than expressing *one* spirit in the many forms.

Let us move from these general remarks to individual examples. In a letter to Cyprian, Firmilian said: "The Romans did not accept everything as originally handed down. This is already clear in that there are differing practices in regard to the Easter celebration and *many other holy practices.* Everything was not practiced in the same way as it was in Jerusalem. In many other lands there were also differences in external matters, but nevertheless the peace and unity of the Catholic Church was not disturbed because of them."[a] If, in addition to unity given *by itself* as already noted, one desires another unity, this desire testifies to a mind not grandly grasping the essence of unity, to an unclear conception concerning the one Spirit giving life to believers, to a love for small and paltry things, an inclination to the external. Indeed, such minds wished to place spiritual unity in chains, narrow its general recognition with *contingent* external limits, constraining it with many stipulations and, wherever they found spiritual unity, endangered it whether by replacing it with another or curtailing it. If for the sake of exterior unity anyone destroyed or did not further internal unity, such acts would not only be laughable but unanswerable. Victor first threatened to do *this* and

---

a. [Firmilian to] Cyprian, Letter 75, 6

as a result justifiably was attacked by Irenaeus. One can ever keep Easter with Jews without being judaically disposed. Although we cannot find in Victor's behavior any search for power, there is evident a constrained, although easily explained, view of the matter.[114] "The controversy," said Irenaeus, "not only concerned the time but also the form of the fast itself. For some think they should fast one day, others two, others more, and yet others forty; and they count the hours of the day and night together as their day. This variety in its observance did not originate first in our time but long before in that of our ancestors. It is likely that they did not hold to strict accuracy and thus formed the continuing custom in simplicity and ignorance. Yet they maintained community with us and we with them *and the unity of faith stands before variations in fasting.* . . . The priests who presided before Soter in the Church which you now rule—I mean Anicetus, Pius, Hyginus, Telesphorus, and Sixtus-—neither held Easter like them nor allowed those under them to do so. And yet they kept community with those who came from churches in which it was observed, although opposition was more generally increased. But none were ever cast out because of this form. The priests, who did not observe it, sent the Eucharist to those churches who did. And when the blessed Polycarp came to Rome to Anicetus and they disagreed about certain other matters, they immediately made peace without quarreling over this point. Anicetus could not persuade Polycarp to observe these things since he had always observed them in the way he did with John, the disciple of the Lord, and the other apostles with whom he had lived. Nor could Polycarp persuade Anicetus to observe them according to his way. Anicetus said he had to follow and remain true to the customs of the priests who had gone before him. Under such circumstances unity was not disturbed. And in the church Anicetus gave Polycarp the right to celebrate the Eucharist so as to honor him, and they parted in peace so that in whatever way they celebrated, they enjoyed peace with the whole Church."[b] There is a remarkable ancient fragment which is likewise ascribed to Irenaeus. It reads as follows: "The apostles ordered that we judge no one regarding food and drink, feasts, new moons, and sabbaths. Where, then, arise controversies and divisions? We celebrate feasts, but we do so in the leaven of evil and baseness in that we tear apart the Church of God

---

b. Eusebius, *Ecclesiastical History*, 5:24, 12-17.

and hold fast to externals *so that we can cast out the better, faith and love.*"ᶜ Every desire for unity in external worship that did not thus freely develop from this same Spirit itself or was not established by this same inner need by necessity or by acknowledged appropriateness, was turned aside as inadmissible and unenlightened. Yet the greatest freedom existed in unity.

We can close the whole discussion to this point with a passage from Eusebius the truth of which will be enlightening. After he has spoken of the many heresies disturbing the Church, he concludes: "The truth commended itself and shone in the course of time in an ever greater light. Immediately the inventions of the enemies conquered by themselves were extinguished. The novelties of heresies increased, the former passed away and appearing in new forms and in different ways ever varying, disappeared. But the common and only true Church grew in glory and ever more expanded. Her worth, her purity, her free grand sense, her noble, pure life, and her divine philosophy shone over the whole race of the Greeks and barbarians. At the same time the accusations that had been brought against her characteristic disappeared. Our doctrine remained alone glorious among all. Unopposed, it presented itself, so that it marked itself out before all by its nobility and health, by its divine and truly wise content. As a result no one until now presumes to mock our faith and slander it as our enemies once did."ᵈ/[115]

---

c. Fragment from Eusebius, in Lumper, 3:243, where one can see the critical discussion which as is clear Lumper treats one-sidedly.

d. Eusebius, *Ecclesiastical History*, 4:7, 12-14.

Part II

Unity of the Body of the Church[1]

1. Unity in the Bishop

The Church is the external, visible structure of a holy, living power, of love, the body of the spirit of believers forming itself from the interior externally. The hypothesis of an invisible Church occurs only in a conceptual religion.—The diocese: its center is the bishop, the likeness in human form of the congregation's love. There are clerics and lay persons; that is, different gifts are distributed and there must be points of connection among believers. The nonobservance of this divine economy results in slavery. The general priesthood of Christians.

49

The concept of the Church is defined in a one-sided manner if she is designated as a construction or an association, founded for the preservation and perpetuation of the Christian faith. Rather, she is much more an offspring of this faith, an action of love living in believers through the Holy Spirit.[2] If we consider a Christian deed, we must always *presuppose* a Christian disposition, of which every deed is a revelation. We must do so at least insofar as we speculate concerning it, since a Christian disposition will not be found even momentarily idle in any person without productively working on all sides. If we say merely that the Church is a so-called construction, we leave the impression that Christ had, so to speak, *ordered* his disciples *together* without arousing in them an *inner* need that brought and holds them together, that the Church existed before believers, since they first became believers in it, that the Church was above all something different from believers, something aside from them. As the divine principle, communicated to believers, is one in itself, and thus begets unity of faith in those in whom it is placed, so it also reveals itself as distant from self-love and therefore as drawing together, binding together, and uniting all in whom it is found into a great social unity, that is, as establishing them as a Church, the bond of which is love, since love alone gathers and unites and forms.[a/3] If love was given by the divine Spirit, the Church was established at the same time by it. This Church must be fully visible according to a model penetrating all orders of its being and life.[4] The body of a person is a revelation of the spirit manifests its presence and develops in the person. The political state is a necessary phenomenon, a formation and structure of the *koinōnion* [community] given by God. Every human transaction is a revelation of a person's moral power. Where powers of a certain kind are always found, they present themselves visibly, expressing their character.[5] Thus, with the entrance of the divine Spirit into humanity, with the establishment of this new power, a new external manifestation must be given, one expressing that power, and one previously not anticipated.[6] (See [K. L. von Haller, "Kräftige, gute Gedanken über die sichtbare und unsichtbare Kirche," *Wiener Jahrbücher*, vol. 25, pp. 87, 90, et al.) If this structure of the divine Spirit would cease, if there would no longer be any Church, the Spirit itself would no

---

a. The formation of the visible Church is, therefore, the greatest act of believers. A Christian merely *appears* to be passive when entering the great common life and is then being immediately determined by the totality of believers. In this passivity, the greatest activity is contained, the greatest possible independence and freedom. The opposing point of view rests on a one-sided determination of what independence is; it holds that we are capable of giving and begetting but not that we receive and take. The power required in *independent* reception must in many cases be greater than that which occurs in giving. The latter is almost always egotistic and without the former is always so. If one always wants to give and to determine and to be active in this way, one *suffers* (under one's lowly endeavors), and in that one believes oneself to be free, one is often a slave. In the independent power of receiving, self-denial and love rule, and in that one allows things to be done to oneself, one does things oneself. However, everyone who wishes to give in a *truly independent manner* must *first* have received, and *by this* all human unions are begotten and preserved. To give without having received, and to receive, is only possible for God. All goodness is in the power of the believer which binds one with the Church, if the power is present in its full, pure activity. In addition, a great spiritual power is given so that one can remain in the community of believers. This is reflected in the history of the early Church in the battle that Cyprian along with many confessors and martyrs had to endure. They could allow themselves to be scorched and burned by the pagans, but not conquer their own egoism or give up their one-sided, determined, willing independence. Therefore, Cyprian said "The Church makes the martyrs." (Cf. Cyprian, Letter 27, 3 [German translation] and *On the Unity of the Church*, 14. Note also Origen, [*Commentary on Romans*, 1:1,3]: "If the grace of the Spirit is lacking, they cannot be members of the body of Christ.")

longer be present, or it would only be understood conceptually as drawing itself away. With the Church's annihilation there would no longer be any Christianity, no longer an objective and true Christianity.[7]

The thought of an invisible Church founded on earth by Christ is so completely opposed to Christianity, however, that only the visible Church was assumed by Jesus Christ, by his apostles, and by the early Church. This Church was always present as a fact as far back in time as we go. Christ anticipated a visible Church in that he directed those who believed in him to enter it by visible baptism, established the Lord's Supper, said to Peter "I will give you the keys of the Kingdom of Heaven, and whatever you bind on earth will be bound in heaven, and whatever you loose on earth will be loosed in heaven" [Matt. 16:18-20], and repeated these words to the other apostles. Since these words may be understood as referring to acceptance into the Church or to the actual forgiveness of sins, a visible association is presupposed. The case is the same in the apostolic writings. When Paul admonishes the Ephesians to preserve unity of faith (Eph. 4:5), his words would be robbed of all true meaning if he were speaking of an invisible Church in which it would be unnecessary as well as impossible to protect such unity, and therefore also peculiar to require it. The visible Church is also assumed as a fact in that Paul and John teach that heretics are to be avoided. In this case believers are seen as a visible association with a specific religious point of view so that those who oppose this point of view can be separated from it; without a visible community no such separation is possible. The same fact can be established if believers are seen as members of a body determined to help one another, who are to be bound closely with one another, and are built on the apostles and teachers (Eph. 4:11-13). Thus all are to be as one *spirit*, as one *body* (Eph. 4:4). As an inner being gives life to all, so all are to exhibit themselves externally as a unity. Even in the period immediately after that of the apostles, a visible Church was always presupposed, as is clear from everything previously written in this book.

If, then, the Church is to be viewed as the external production of an inner forming power, as the body of a spirit creating itself, it is by all means necessarily this institution through which and in which true faith and true love are preserved and perpetuated. *One* common, true *life* forms itself through the totality of believers as a result of two factors: a spiritual power and its external organic manifestation. Because of this, as has been said, the Christian Spirit and the Church are related as are spirit and body in the human person.[8] The spirit of a human being is, above all, the enlivening, animating principle. The Spirit comes to self-consciousness and manifests this in that it shapes a bodily organism. By the destruction of the body the human spirit itself looses its earthly being. It is the same with the Christian Spirit: [if it had no body,] it would only wander about erringly in dubious, uncertain appearances, if I may so express myself, without acknowledging itself as the Christian Spirit or making itself known to others since it would have no true being. For this reason Paul calls the Church (1 Tim. 3:15) "The pillar and bulwark of truth," the bearer of these, since she is the substratum of the Spirit. However, since the divine Spirit, through which the Christian Spirit is communicated to the believer, can never and dare never disappear, it cannot ever leave the body by which it is borne even to the end of the world.[9] In the body, faith exclusively perpetuates itself. The human spirit works and is further active through the orders, organs, and functions of the body. In a like manner the Spirit ruling in the Church begets organs for its activity.[10] The Church and the Spirit living in believers belong completely together, were established at the same time, and are indivisible to such a degree that, if it was said above that the communal life of the believers consisted of two factors, it must be understood that the two can be separated only by [intellectual] reflection but can never be separated in life. It must also be said that the active power given to believers by the Holy Spirit forms the visible body of the Church, and that the visible Church preserves and bears the higher power granted to it and communicates it. For this reason it is of course no mere institution which always relates to the matter to be promoted by it as means and end. The relationship is as the member to the whole body.[11] The analogous notion of mechanism cannot be separated from the concept of an institution. The Church, however, is a living organism. We have yet to show, in the period under discussion, what the orders, organs, and functions are by which the Church body expresses itself as such, preserves an inner unity of life, and binds together everything internally and works externally.

Of the heresies, we have only to say that according to all their principles they could present no visible Church: a concept begets no life, no communal concept, and therefore no communal life, even though some such life did exist in them. What was said earlier must be repeated: egoism can never be the basis of community. It can be the basis of an invisible one, that is, of one that is not seen because it does not exist, but never of a visible and existent one. (See Addendum 12.)[12]

50

Christ chose the Twelve Apostles from the multitude of his disciples. They were to proclaim his teaching throughout the whole world and to have general oversight over his believers. In the same way the apostles set special individuals over the congregations founded by them. These took the apostles' place so that the apostolic office should never cease to exist. Christ did not leave to chance the proclamation of his teaching or the manner of the proclamation. Nor did his apostles. Without this orderly and regular proclamation of the gospel, one or two, or perhaps many, might have grasped something of the gospel and brought it to others, but without a doubt such a gospel would have remained indistinct, weak, and powerless. Uncertain, wavering tones of the gospel would have quite definitely been lost on the earth. By the order already indicated, the preaching of the word attained a consistency, certainty, emphasis, and determinateness. Around this one center gathered many adherents and associates. They formed a mass that with concentrated power opposed all that was non-Christian. By this power they continually received the Word among themselves and *lived* love, fighting paganism with a united, firm, and determined drive. Suppose that each Christian lived separately and somehow took on the name of Christian: in such a case Christian teaching would have reflected thousands of forms, modifications, and confusions. Among whom were the pagans to experience what Christianity was, if Christians themselves did not properly know it? Among whom were those needy individuals to seek further teaching? To whom among so many opposing parties were they to turn? Where were they to see and experience what love was, which no words or writing can teach, if it was not preserved in the life of Christians? But how could Christians exhibit love in life without community if they were themselves divided and disunited like the pagans? The pagans knew only the Christian community.[a] Because the congregations immedi-

---

a. Eusebius, *Ecclesiastical History*, 5:1, 20, on the martyr Sanctus, writes: "He girded himself against them with such firmness that he would not even tell his name, or the

ately formed themselves under the episcopal office, Christianity
attained a firm establishment, an objectivity in which the individual
could rightly discover and know how to live (that is, love) and to
view God and the world so as to be a Christian. Thus a unity and a
demonstration of unity of doctrine was possible, and because of this,
the unconquerable authority of this unity was possible, an authority
which, as Augustine very beautifully and rightly said, was a miracle
for all future times, established by Christ and the first leaders of
congregations so that they might draw to themselves persons who
had not experienced the truth of Christianity in itself and could not
do so.[13] And in this fact the Christian community is an abiding
miracle of the divine Spirit, a demonstration of its continual, direct
inner activity, and the most impressive activity for all who are
capable of receiving this greatest and most exalted [gift]. As, I hope,
has been made clear above, there was at this point no thought given
to teaching by the Holy Scriptures and certainly no suggestion that
the Scriptures fulfilled everything in themselves. The faithful
transmission of the Scriptures had, of course, already occurred
through congregations; the majority of the apostles' Epistles were
written to such *congregations*. Without a determined, ordered, and
continual teaching office one could not in any way think of a
continuing tradition, which, as we heard, is fully necessary to
demonstrate the identity of the higher consciousness of the Church
throughout all moments of its existence. Had it been left to chance
as to who was to proclaim the gospel and how it was to be proclaimed, there would have been great differences, no unity of
doctrine, and a chaos of conceptions would have arisen but not what
we have now to reflect on under tradition. It could hardly have been
in fact as some so-called histories of dogma describe it. What could
be more pitiable? At the best there would have been a proliferation
of sects or schools, but no Church, no Christian unity of life, and we
would have known as little of what Christianity is as anyone would
have known in any postapostolic period. We would all be *seeking*
after Christianity as after a truly lost thing if one was even so much
as inclined to seek it. What is primary is not the person of the bishop

---

nation or city to which he belonged, or whether he was bond or free, but answered
in the Roman tongue to all their questions, 'I am a Christian.' He confessed this
instead of name and city and race and everything besides." Cf. Chrysostom, "Homily
on Acts," 46.

as such, even if considered as having the greatest doctrinal capability, but the bishop's quality as the center of the unity of all.

From this it can once again be made clear in what essential union the unity of believers with Christianity consists and how Christianity is understood as taken away and believers as such destroyed if unity is not established in the community. As we saw, a true battle on the part of Christian parties would never once have been possible without a visible Church. One can only battle against something standing, living, unchanging, and constant. Otherwise the battle would have been like that of the philosophers, that is, Christianity would have been completely removed from the people and from life. However, after a visible Church had formed itself by a union of all, one experienced Christianity, and whoever wished to do so could attack it. A battle was then beneficent.[14] One cannot imagine what would have come out of Christianity without that apostolic institution, or rather one can easily imagine that it would not have conquered the world. What is of God is God. What God has joined, human beings are not to put asunder.[15]

51

The fact that the apostles appointed leaders, bishops, and priests everywhere and installed them in their positions is undeniably proven by the history of the early Church. (See section 9.)[16] Clement of Rome, who was himself a disciple of the apostles and must have known their institutions very well, said: "The apostles proclaimed the gospel for us from the Lord Jesus Christ, and Jesus Christ from God. Christ was thus sent by God and the apostles by Christ. They took over the task. Convinced by the Resurrection of our Lord Jesus Christ and strengthened in the doctrine of God with the fullness of the Holy Spirit, they went out and preached the coming of the Kingdom of God. They preached in the cities and in the country and testing the first believers by the Spirit, placed them in positions as bishops and deacons for the future."[a] This passage is particularly noteworthy: because Clement wished to make the seditious Corinthians aware of the full weight of the office of Church leadership, he described so expressively the apostles, who had been sent by Christ

---

a. Clement of Rome, "Letter to the Corinthians," 42.

and equipped with the fullness of the Holy Spirit, as the founders of this office. There is no need to demonstrate how determinedly and repeatedly Ignatius expressed himself on the foundation of the episcopal office by the apostles, since all his letters discuss this. The clearest testimonies are also provided in that in the congregations in which there were presbyters, one was set above the others as a bishop.[b/17] This is indicated clearly in the Scriptures, namely, in the Epistles to Timothy and Titus; further proof is available in the Revelation of John. How could Clement[c/18] and Ignatius[d] have expressed themselves more often on the matter? It is self-evident that nothing follows from a similar use of different terms, and every objection based on the remark that bishops were still called presbyters at the end of the second century by Irenaeus and by Church fathers who lived later has no real weight. In Irenaeus there is no doubt whatever that a distinction is made. Moreover, Irenaeus and Tertullian believe they can demonstrate as certain an episcopal succession from the apostles in the churches established by them.[e/19]

b. Irenaeus, *Against the Heresies*, 3:3, 1.

c. Clement of Rome, "Letter to the Corinthians," 40: "His own peculiar services are assigned to the high priest, and their own proper place is prescribed to the priests, and their own special ministrations devolve on the Levites."[Along with Cotelerius in his note to this section] I am not impressed by the reasons that are given for understanding this passage as referring solely to the Jewish priesthood.

d. Ignatius of Antioch, "Letter to the Magnesians," 6: "Your bishop presides in the place of God, and your presbyters in the place of the assembly of the apostles"; "Letter to the Philadelphians," 7: "Give heed to the bishop, and to the presbytery and deacons"; "Letter to the Smyrnaeans," 8: "See that you follow the bishop, even as Christ Jesus does the Father, and the presbytery as you would the apostles."

e. Irenaeus, *Against the Heresies*, 3:3, 1: "We are in a position to list those who were installed by the apostles as bishops in the churches and [to demonstrate] the succession of these men to our own times."[Ibid., 3:3, 1] Salmasius, *Dissertatio [Librorum de primatu papae]*, 11, 22, 205, says that the apostles installed *nullos singulares episcopos* [no singular bishops], but this is certainly unhistorical [*unhistorisch*]. Irenaeus [*Against the Heresies*, 3:3.4] says of Polycarp: "installed by the apostles in Asia, appointed bishop of the Church in Smyrna, *whom I also saw* in my early youth." Tertullian, *On Prescription against Heretics*, 32: "Let them produce the original records of their churches . . . in such a manner that their first bishop shall be able to show for his ordainer and predecessor some one of the apostles or of apostolic individuals—one, moreover, who continued steadfast with the apostles. For this is the manner in which the apostolic churches transmit their registers: as the church of Smyrna, which records that Polycarp was placed therein by John; as the church of Rome, which makes Clement to have been ordained in a like manner by Peter. In exactly the same way the other churches likewise exhibit those who were appointed to their episcopal places by apostles." See the original research of Petavius, *Opus de theologicis dogmatibus*, 4:9ff. [*De*

They trace back individual churches to the time of the apostles, and Eusebius does the same with great precision for many other churches. As a result, from apostolic times there must have been *one* leader who was a rank above the rest and was properly called a bishop in each church.[f] It is clear that the statements by Jerome cannot be used against this argument; to cite only one of so many later writers against the earlier authors demonstrates nothing, even assuming that it must be interpreted literally and aside from Jerome's polemical standpoint. Although Jerome says that only later one of the presbyters was chosen as a common leader so as to avoid divisions, no such period can be properly pointed to. It is much more likely that he is merely advancing a possibility, and wishes to point out what would have happened had there been no bishop rather than what did indeed occur historically,[g/20] so as to express the definition and the idea of the bishop.[h]

52

The idea of a bishop according to the clear conception of the period here under discussion and as it proceeds from the essence of the Catholic Church must be thus specified: *All believers, as soon as the forming, holy principle was active in them, felt themselves so drawn to one*

---

ecclesiastica hierarchia, 5:7, 1]. In 4:6 [*De ecclesiastica hierarchia*, 1:2], he refutes the notion that no "singular bishops" were installed [and notes that bishop and presbyter are not parallel terms. In the *De ecclesiastica hierarchia*, 1:5, Petavius refers directly to Salmasius's position on "singular bishops."] His argument in its general outline must be accepted. See also Bingham, *The Antiquities of the Christian Church*, book 2 [which treats the subject of bishops generally. Ibid., 2:1, 3, maintains the distinction between bishops and presbyters and discusses installation of bishops by the apostles].

f. Eusebius, *Ecclesiastical History*, 2:24; 3:4, 11, 13-15; 4:1, 19-20; 5:6.

g. Jerome, *Commentary on Titus*, 1: "The presbyter is the same [*idem est*] and he who is the bishop, and before the influence of Satan entered the Church, the Church was ruled by a general council [*communi consilio*] of presbyters." If taken literally, the statement of Jerome arises out of the interpretation of the biblical passage, and the interpretation may be false; it does not arise out of the historical situation that casts light on it. What is upheld here above all is the *communi consilio* [general council] of the Church, which our interpretation does not reject. What the *idem esse* of the bishop and presbyter can and does signify is not here at issue. We wish only to say that at the beginning one of many presbyters was raised up as the center of all.

h. Note Clement of Rome, "Letter to the Corinthians," 44: "Our apostles also knew, through our Lord Jesus Christ, that there would be strife on account of the office of the episcopate."

another and so striving for union that this inner movement was not satisfied until it saw itself formed in an image. The bishop is thus the uniting of believers made visible in a specific place, the love of believers for one another made personal,[21] the manifestation and living center point of the Christian disposition striving toward unity. Because the perception of this union is continually given in the bishop, he is the love of the Christians themselves coming to consciousness and the means to make this firm. This thought, that the union around a bishop is an expression of[22] the mutual love of all, lies at the basis of the work of Clement of Rome who had to console a congregation, of Ignatius who feared divisions, of Cyprian who fought against proud self-seeking individuals.[a] Therefore, the community of believers with one another is measured according to its union with the bishop, and the love of believers for Christ is the original image of that union as well as the expression and impression of it.[b] In this union of ideas, according to the work of Ignatius, the bishop himself is the type of Christ, and bishops are called Christ's deputies.[c] Since the bishop is the personified love of the congregation and the center of all, the person who is bound to him is in community with all, and anyone who is separated from him has withdrawn from the Christian community of all and is separated from the Church.[d] The Church is thus in the bishop and the bishop in the Church.[e] This center is therefore so necessary that without it congregational union is unthinkable, and the concept of a Church is so determined that a united people is one in one bishop.[f] Two bishops in a congregation are as impossible as two

a. Clement of Rome, "Letter to the Corinthians," 42-49; Ignatius of Antioch, "Letter to the Magnesians," 6, 2: "*Continually* love each other in Jesus Christ. Let nothing exist among you that may divide you; but be united with your bishop." "Letter to Ephesians," 2: "*In every way* glorify Jesus Christ, who glorified you, that by a unanimous obedience, you may be perfectly joined together in the same mind and in the same judgment . . . and that being subject to the bishop . . . you may *in all respects* be sanctified."

b. Ignatius of Antioch, "Letter to the Magnesians," 7: "There is one Jesus Christ than whom nothing is more excellent. Therefore, all run together as into one temple of God, *as to one altar*, as to one Jesus Christ, who came forth from one Father."

c. Cyprian, Letter 63, 14: "That priest truly discharges the office of Christ, who imitates that which Christ did." Cf. Letter 59.

d. Ignatius of Antioch, "Letter to the Ephesians," 5; "Letter to the Philadelphians," 7, 8; Cyprian, Letters 40 and 69.

e. Cyprian, Letter 66, 8: "You ought to know that the bishop is in the Church, and the Church in the bishop."

f. Ibid.: "The Church is a people united to a priest, a flock that adheres to its pastor."

centers in a circle; one of the two cannot be the center.[g] In that the Christian [essence] of all is united in him as the center of all, he expresses it and is its organ. A communal religious act without him is, therefore, impossible.[h] He is the public and regular teacher (Here the foundational description of the Church is beautifully seen once more. Who is better able to proclaim *the truth* than the image of *love*?), for the apostolic doctrine handed over to the congregation is at its fullest in him.[23] He expresses the religious movement of all. His prayer to God before the congregation is the prayer of all. Because the congregation is in him and he in it,[24] it may be said that the keys of authoritative power are given to the congregation and to the bishop; they are the authoritative power given to the Church by God and used by the bishop.[i] However, this is the same as saying that sins are forgiven by love. Sin separates; a union extending from the heart includes forgiveness of sin. In the bishop, the image of the love of all, the reconciliation with all occurs, and Christ calls that good and blesses what so occurs just as he also brings it about.[25] As the image of the love of the congregation, as the most beautiful offspring of it, he is the first image of all Christian virtues (1 Peter 5:1-3).[j] To him, the ideal, the pattern for the congregation, its finest flower, all are to look, and anyone who contemplates his life is to be inspired to turn back to Christ. His speech is a stream of inner life. His deeds

g. "Epistle of Cornetius to Fabius," in Eusebius, *Ecclesiastical History*, 6:43, 11: "He did not know that there should be one bishop in a Catholic church." Cyprian, Letter 55, 8: "And as after the first there cannot be a second, whoever is made after one who ought to be alone, is not second, but is in fact none at all." Cf. Letter 59.

h. Ignatius of Antioch, "Letter to the Philadelphians," 7: "Do nothing without the bishop"; "Letter to the Smyrnaeans," 9: "The one who does anything without the knowledge of the bishop serves the devil" because of his express egoism.

i. Tertullian, *Scorpiace*, 10: "Remember that the Lord here left the keys of the Church to Peter and through him to the Church." Augustine often notes this. Cf. du Pin, *De antiqua ecclesia disciplina*, 3:1 [which treats excommunication and refers to Augustine on the keys].

j. Augustine, *Questions on the Old and New Testaments*, 127: "The chief priest of God must be purer than the others. . . . *He is his vicar.*" The vicar of Christ is thus not merely to sit in authority. Cyprian, Letter 67, 2: "We ought in the ordination of priests to choose none but unstained and upright ministers, who, *in a holy and worthy manner*, offering sacrifices to God, may be heard," etc. Indeed, he says [ibid., 67,3], "Nor let people flatter themselves that they can be free from the contagion of sin while receiving communion with a priest who is a sinner." Origen, *Commentary on Matthew*, 12:14. The bishop had the power of the keys only if he like Peter lived in a holy manner. *Apostolic Constitutions*, 8:55.

reveal an uncreated wealth of divine grace.[k] He is, therefore, the Father, and also the bridegroom of the Church, the organ of Christ vitalizing and fructifying all.[l/26] The person who has committed a serious fault after baptism is unfit to receive this high vocation. He cannot thus be a servant of the altar and, if he does commit such a sin, he cannot so remain. Because the bishop is to exhibit the love of all in a living image, all must be active in his selection.[m] Each must give witness that he is above all of them in love for Christ and in the power to proclaim him. All must see in him a person who unites all and who must possess the love of all as he exhibits the love of all. He is not holier than others because he is a priest, but he is a priest because he was holier.[n/27] He who is eager for episcopal dignity is unfitted for it, and he who is fit for it is not zealous for it. The former does not feel its burden and laboriousness, and anyone who feels these does not wish to undertake them.[o] He gives himself over to a higher call, not to his own (that is, not to the voice of his pride, his love of power, and so on.).

Because of all this, it is best said not that the bishop has this or that right, but that there comes to him *concern, responsibility* for the

k. Origen, *Commentary on Romans*, 9:2; *Against Celsus*, 8:75.

l. Ambrose, *Commentary on Luke*, 8:13: "You, who passed on the priesthood to me, are my elders; you are my sons, I say, or my elders, sons as individuals, elders as totality." The lovely images of *sponsus, sponsa* [bridegroom, bride] which are often used of Christ are here used of the bishops.

m. Origen, *Homily on Luke*, 6: "The presence of the people is required in the ordination of a priest, so that all know and are certain that one *who is from and a rank above the people, who is more learned, more holy, more eminent in all learning*, has been chosen for the priesthood. This is to be done in the presence of the people lest, later, opposition arises or anyone has scruples." Cyprian, Letter 67,4: "In the presence of the people either the crimes of the wicked may be disclosed or the merits of the good may be declared." Tertullian already noted in his *Apology*, 39: "Tested individuals, elders, preside over us, obtaining that honor not by purchase, but *through a demonstration of their worth*."

n. Clement of Alexandria, *Miscellanies*, 6.13: "not righteous as a presbyter, but a presbyter as righteous."

o. Origen, *Against Celsus*, 8:75; Cyprian, Letter 55, 8, also praises Cornelius, bishop of Rome: "He did not either ask for the episcopate itself, nor did he wish it; nor as others do when the swelling of their arrogance and pride inflates them, did he seize upon it, but otherwise quiet and meek, and such as those are accustomed to be who are chosen of God to this office. . . . He did not, as some do, use force to be made a bishop, but he suffered compulsion, and was forced to receive the episcopal office." This is the subject of the glorious book of St. Chrysostom, *On the Priesthood.*

whole congregation,[p] and that his office is called a service,[q] and he, a servant of all.

52a[28]

Although the bishop is, in the way described, an offspring of the congregation who chose him, he does not act on the orders of the people. His office is not an arbitrary one, arising out of human agreement. It is positive [that is, historically existent] and of divine origin. (It might be said that love and faith come from the interior and must be a free offspring of the human spirit;[29] in spite of that they are positive.) We have noted that the apostles themselves installed bishops everywhere, and therefore it is a divine law by which the office of bishop is founded. In Acts 20:28 Paul admonishes the elders called to Miletus to "take heed to yourselves and to all the flock, in which the *Holy Spirit* has made you overseers, to care for the Church of God." If, as was said above, the bishop is an offspring of the congregation, the inner disposition, the higher need, according to which it acts here to make itself a center of the congregation's love, is not human since a human being is in no way capable of begetting this love. It is a work of the Holy Spirit, and is therefore the episcopal office itself.[30] Because of this the apostles could install a bishop before a larger congregation was present and, without having to await a congregation's verdict, anticipating the future disposition yet to come fully among Christians. Therefore, there could be no further doubt that these centers were the proper expression of love. Among imperfect Christians the episcopal office appeared as *law,* and the presence of the bishop was to tell them what they were and toward what they were to strive. In the bishop they saw the ideal perfection of the congregation. Among perfect Christians and those near to perfection, those who had completely suppressed egoism, the office was seen first as a free production of a person who became *spontaneous[ly active]* through the Holy Spirit.

---

p. Origen, *Against Celsus*, 8:75: "We constrain those who, through excess of modesty, are not easily induced to take a public charge in the Church of God." *Apostolic Canons,* 37: "All circumstances of the Church, the concern of the bishops embraced."

q. From this came the expressions *leitourgia, diakonia*—"work, service." See Clement of Rome, "Letter to the Corinthians," 44; *Apostolic Canons,* 28; Eusebius, *Ecclesiastical History,* 6:29; 4:7; 3:34; Origen, *Against Celsus,* 8:75.

In the choice of a bishop the congregation thus went beyond itself in the proper sense. In that its members begot him as their mutual love in a person, the congregation appeared as perfected, but in that the bishop was still to be a pattern for the congregation and the Kingdom of God was to be built in it, the congregation appeared first as striving for perfection through him. Yet neither the perfection nor the desire for it is a human work. The bishop's function, however, is necessary in both cases. Because in both he is the most perfect expression of the Christian need for union and instruction and because the bishop was already established by the apostles, human capriciousness can in no way change this organ of the body of Christ.[31]

53

On the one hand, the need for a bishop is brought about by the Holy Spirit and, on the other, this need is satisfied by the same Holy Spirit. This is the Spirit who imparts different gifts. Whereas in one person the need to receive is raised, another possesses a fullness of faith and love to satisfy that need. One has received the ability to give, the other to receive, one to build up, the other to be built up. To one was given the power, strength, and wisdom to lead (*to hēgemonikon*); others need to be led.[a/32] After Paul clarified this in 1 Corinthians 12:1-27, he continued in verses 28 and 29: "And God has appointed in the Church first apostles, second prophets, third teachers, then workers of miracles, then healers, helpers, administrators, speakers in various kinds of tongues. Are all apostles? Are all

---

a. Basil the Great, *On the Spirit*, 26, 61: "The Spirit is understood, in relation to the distribution of gifts, as a whole in parts. *For* [as Paul states in 1 Corinthians, 12:12ff.] *we are all 'members one of another, having gifts differing according to the grace that is given us.'* Wherefore, 'the eye cannot say to the hand, I have no need of you; nor, again the head to the feet, I have no need of you,' but all together complete the body of Christ in the unity of the Spirit and render to one another the needful aid that comes of the gifts. 'But God has set the members in the body, every one of them, as it has pleased him.' But 'the members have the same care for one another,' according to the inborn spiritual communion of their sympathy. Wherefore, 'where one member suffers, all members suffer.'" A great many writers note such profound, true biblical views of the organic relationship of the unity of all believers. In particular Augustine does so. See his *Commentaries on the Psalms*, 2:21, on Ps. 10, Sec. 7. The homilies of Chrysostom on 1 Corinthians 30-33 discuss them extensively.

prophets? Are all teachers? Do all work miracles?" And in Ephesians
4:11 he says: "And his gifts were that some should be apostles, some
prophets, some evangelists, some pastors and teachers." If we look
at the practice of Christ in the choice of his apostles, it is impossible
for us to accept the opinion that he took those nearest to him as the
best without being directed by higher motives. The apostles were
certainly the best prepared and most receptive among all the Jews.
Peter, the first of the believers,[33] had the most receptivity among
them, and therefore he was marked out by Christ above all the
others, since he was admonished to strengthen the others and we
later meet him at the head of all. In a passage already cited, Clement
of Rome said that the apostles installed as leaders of the others the
"first" believers in the places in which they taught. Since they first
grasped the proclamation of the Kingdom of God, they were, for
certain, the most mature, and therefore they were the best suited[34] to
win over others.[35] The Church, like St. Paul, looked on the powers
and gifts of those who were given for the needs of others as the
work of the Holy Spirit, and the episcopal office was therefore seen
in the same way.[b/36] They are, therefore, necessary organs of the
Spirit, to "equip the saints for the work of ministry, for building up
of the body of Christ" [Eph. 4:12], as St. Paul stated after he had
noted that the Spirit gave to the Church apostles, teachers, and
pastors. The preservation of doctrine, love, and all of Christianity
depends on these organs in the body of Christ, as is clearly seen
from these remarks on the divine economy. As all believers are led
together by the holy unitive power communicated to them, so the

b. Irenaeus, *Against the Heresies*, 3:24, 1 after he designated the Church as the source
of divine gifts: "'For in the Church,' it is said, '*God has set apostles, prophets, teachers,"
and all the other through which the Spirit works.*'" Origen, *Commentary on Romans*, 9:2 (to
Rom. 12:3-5): "*Therefore, in a specific way, ordering the whole organism of the Church*, as
each of the members of the body has its individual functions and follows its offices
and can do nothing other than give itself over to the other by mutual consent, so in
the Church, in the body of Christ, each of us has a specific function. Some individuals
direct their whole energy to divine wisdom and the doctrine of the Word and persist
in meditation on the divine law day and night and are thus the eyes of this one great
body." Note particularly *On First Principles*, 2:7, 3, and the passages noted in section
21. See Origen, *Commentary on Romans*, 1:3, 2: "So that one might become this or that
member in the body of Christ by the grace received." Writing to the Corinthians he
says: 'To each the manifestation of the Spirit is given as each requires it' (1 Cor. 12:7),
and shortly after he adds 'One and the same spirit does all, giving to each as it wills.'"
Here he also answers the charge that one could make against this view of the matter.

power promises the various distribution of gifts, by which all need one another and constitute an organic *whole*.[c/37]

54

Nevertheless, there is a priestly dignity in all Christians. What is meant by this is indicated in the following passage from Origen which we select from the many that could be cited.[38] After he explained the Jewish custom, according to which only the priests dare enter a separate place in the Temple, he said that this had mystical significance: "Do not marvel that only priests could enter this compartment, for all who were anointed with the holy oil became priests,[a/39] as Peter in 1 Peter 2:9 said to the whole Church: 'You are a chosen race, a royal priesthood, a holy nation.' You are a priestly race and because of this you draw near to holiness. But each of us has our own sacrifice in ourself and light our own sacrificial altar so that we might always burn. If I give up all that I have and take up my cross and follow Christ, I bring a sacrifice to the altar of God; if I give up my body, burning with love, and gain the praise of martyrdom, I bring a sacrifice to the altar of God. If I love my fellow believers so that I give up my life for them, if I fight to the death for righteousness and truth, I bring a sacrifice to the altar of God. If I purify myself from evil desires, if the world is crucified to me and I am crucified to the world, I bring a sacrifice to the altar of God and

c. Ibid., 1:2: "We do not say that one must be enough; as the eye has a special function, namely, to see, and *yet is only one of all members and in all members* and does everything in all members and the individuals all work with it. Thus those who have received any *one* specific gift by the grace of faith do their special work, but in all their acts remain bound to the other members and participate in them." See Addendum 13. For this reason in excommunication there is the expression "to lock no one *out of the Church, which would complete* that person." Chrysostom, *On the Priesthood*, 4:18; 3:97.

a. What is expressed in the proposition is explained in the Creed; in the Old Testament only priests were anointed but in the New Testament all Christians were by baptism. *Apostolic Constitutions*, 3:2, 1: "Priests and kings were formerly anointed, not because those who are now baptized are ordained priests, but as being Christians, or anointed, from Christ the Anointed (*unctiones cognomine, hos apo tou Christou Christianos*—clearly a false derivation) a royal priesthood, and a holy nation, the Church of God, the pillar and ground of the marriage chamber, who formerly were not a people, but now are beloved and chosen." Cf. de Marca, *De discriminatione*, 2:5 [who makes the same point with reference to Origen, "Homily 9 on Leviticus, 16" and *Apostolic Constitutions*, 3:15.]

am a priest at that altar. . . . Blessed are those whose sacrifice the
Lord and true High Priest finds so living and burning that he holds
them worthy to lay it on the altar. Blessed are those in whose hearts
he finds such soft, pure, and spiritual a sense, such a multitude of
virtues, that he rejoices in them and brings them to the Father as a
sacrifice. *But unhappy is the soul whose fire of faith is extinguished, whose
love is grown cold.* . . . Such are all those who draw back from the
word of God so that they are not ignited for faith, burned for love,
and blaze for mercy. Ought I to point out to you how a fire proceeds
from the words of the Holy Spirit that ignites the hearts of believers?"[b/40] The early Church maintained concepts such as these
concerning the general priesthood of Christians and concerning the
similarity of believers and priests. All were to be bound with God in
the same way by living faith and purity of heart. However, the
dignity of Christians was in no way so established that the eternal
orders of God in the Church were destroyed, the organs of the
community brought to nothing, or each believer given over to self-
seeking so that union in Christ itself and proper Christian dignity
was lost.[41]

The distinction between clerics and laity, when closely considered
and determined precisely according to its innermost essence, was
seen as nothing other than a distinction of gifts in the Church upheld
by the Holy Spirit. It is necessary for a union of believers which can
only be reached through the organs and united members by which
every distinction in gifts is closely related. Only in the association of
all in the community and in the preservation of this organ is true
Christian dignity preserved.[42] The maintenance of this organ, because
it occurs through love, is the freest act of the Christian. By it as the
offspring of the highest independence of believers (because there is
no self-seeking here), the purest freedom is necessary, and the
continuation of the Church is the living exhibition of the freedom of
the children of God reigning in her.

---

b. Origen, *Homily on Leviticus*, 9:9. Cf. Tertullian, *On Prayer*, 28, and *Apostolic
Constitutions*, 3:15, where the antithesis with the pagans is particularly noted. In a
church that does not follow the Catholic pattern a distinction necessarily arises
between esoteric and exoteric as has become manifest in our day. Against this Clement
of Alexandria, *Instructor*, 1:6, speaks in particular.

55

Moreover, the bishop led the congregation for the most part in a communal manner.[43] The apostles made decisions on the most significant questions in the active presence of the whole congregation (Acts 15) (although they did not decide *according to* the will of the majority, for if this were the case, we would still all have to be circumcised). This apostolic practice was continued after their deaths.[a] The apostles did not send their Epistles to the bishops of congregations, but to the congregations directly. The same is true in the later period, as is indicated by the letters of Ignatius, the letter of Polycarp to the Philippians, the catholic letters of Dionysius of Corinth, the open letters of the congregation at Smyrna to the Philomelians and all Catholic Churches, the letters of the Gallican churches in Vienne and Lyons to the Asiatic churches and the answers to these. The bishop was considered part of the whole congregation, although the most active part, as the letter of the Romans to the Corinthians, which was written by Clement, the Roman bishop, indicates. The bishop was thus not raised above the others, since he was understood as one with the congregation, and it was not considered aside from him nor he aside from it. He was still the pure product of its love, and the congregation proceeded purely out of the power of his doctrine and holy love. However, the presbytery or rather the total number of presbyters of one Church, who like him were chosen for spiritual preeminence, formed the narrower and second counsel of the bishop. Without the presbyters as his senate, the bishop did nothing, indeed, dare never do anything of consequence.[b]

a. Cyprian, Letter 55, 5: "thus with the advice of all the bishops, presbyters, deacons, and confessors, as well as with the laity who stand fast." "Stand" here does not mean a physical *standing* but indicates those who did not fall during the persecution, the lapsi. Ibid., Letter 69, 15, to Cornelius: "Scarcely as I persuade the people; nay, I extort it from them that they should suffer such as to be admitted." Letter 19, 2: "For this is suitable to modesty and discipline, and even the life of all of us. The chief officers meet together with the clergy in the presence also of the people who stand fast. To the people, moreover, honor is to be shown for their faith and fear. Thus we may order all things with the religiousness of a common consultation."

Many Catholic writers believe that the divine institution of the bishop cannot be properly established unless the people are suppressed, and Protestants believe they cannot assert the dignity of the people other than by denying the unifying significance of the bishops. Both are extremes; only the Catholic *Church* is right.

b. Cyprian, Letters 5 and 13, and regularly in the *Apostolic Constitutions*.

This original relationship of the bishop to the congregation had to be significantly changed when the character of congregational members itself changed. Had the early Christians turned to Christianity out of the deepest felt needs for salvation itself, this would have been quite different. Almost immediately, however, there were Christians by birth who were still fully strangers to Christianity and among whom the need for salvation had to be awakened after they had been made members of the Church. Many also came to the Church out of impure motives. Some grasped Christianity more with the understanding than with the mind. Still others took it up more out of feeling, on a momentary emotion, than by an acceptance, accompanied by a new creation of the whole person. There were long periods of peace in which Christians slept and sensual pleasures took control.[c] When, after the lengthy enjoyment of an undisturbed peace, persecution broke out again, the condition of most Christians became clear. Cyprian painted the behavior of his congregation as follows: "They did not wait to leave the Church or to deny her until they had been captured or questioned. Many were conquered before the battle, overcome without a fight. Nor did they let it be said that they had only sacrificed to the idols under compulsion. They went freely into the forum and eagerly hastened to (spiritual) death as if they had long wished for it, as if they only had an opportunity which they long desired. How many, who were not dispatched by the authority as evening came on, prayed for a quick end to their destruction?"[d] Considering the character of such Christians nothing more can be said. "They were one heart and one sense," for where sensuality reigns, there is division and corruption. The bishop now was no longer chosen out of the highest unitive activity of love working in *all* Christians. Rather, he always related more to the congregation as the law does to a person in whom disposition is weak and unholy. The law now indicated what the individual opposed. The bishop now evermore entered a position in which he must indicate and fulfill what is and should be, rather than what his presence had earlier expressed. Congregation and bishop were increasingly opposed to one another and seemed as if they wished

---

c. Cyprian, *On the Lapsed*, 8. Eusebius, *Ecclesiastical History*, 8:12, concerning the persecution under Diocletian.

d. Cyprian, *On the Lapsed*, 8. Cf. Eusebius, *Ecclesiastical History*, 4:41, where Dionysius of Alexandria states that those called were in particular so faithless and weak.

completely different things. In the bishop Christianity had to speak
to those who first wished to be Christians. Earlier, holier times had
presented him as the communal image of all. Now he had to speak
again to all and present himself as an image to them so that he
might be the express image of first love that had been abandoned,
so that he might not allow this disposition to fall away,[44] but beget
anew what had begotten him. Or can we only wish that the bishop
was now the image of his congregation, that his will and its were
identical? He, therefore, seemed to act often *without* and *against* the
will of the majority of the congregation. Only a few of the best were
on his side, and he had to act in such a way if Christian manners,
order, and propriety were not to suffer, indeed not to die. One has
only to note the relationship of Cyprian to his congregation in the
dispute over the lapsed and in his struggle with the pride of
confessors. World history points to no period and no nation whose
constitution was earlier than its express folk custom. The former
always proceeded from the latter. How can a poor historical
[*historisch*] judgment now conclude that it was the pride and search
for power on the part of the bishops that changed their relationship
to the people? It was not characteristically the bishops who raised
themselves up, but the people who sank, and as a result the bishops
obviously appeared higher and more powerful than earlier. But
because, abandoning every higher law, self-seeking in its various
forms has been made the leading idea in Church history, it must
obviously be discussed here again.

One of two possibilities could now freely become more and more
obvious. In the first place, the spiritual superiority of the bishop,
bound together with his reputation which came to him through the
apostolic institution, could be misused in the tyrannization of the
people. This resulted from the dignity, which was asserted in the
Catholic Church and surrendered to human presumption like
members of heretical congregations. In the second place, the higher
freedom having been dispossessed by the lower, the people could
come to chose bishops as the image of their lower activities, as the
expression of their self-love. Since the choice was their own, through
anarchy, they became their own despot,[e] controlling the will-less

---

e. Cyprian, *On the Lapsed*, 6: "Not a few bishops, who ought to furnish both
exhortation and example to others, despising their divine charge, became agents in
secular business, forsook their thrones, deserted their people, wandered about over
foreign provinces, hunted the markets for gainful merchandise, while fellow believers

and powerless bishop. The course of the discussion will prove
instances of attempts of both kinds. Only the character of the
Catholic Church guarded against this. Since situations could be
changed as noted, orders were formed that would not allow such
changes. We now move to a discussion of this by which a quality of
the bishop can be discussed that has to this point only been touched
on.

---

were starving in the Church. They sought to hoard money; they increased their gains
by multiplying usuries." In these cases the presbyters were of little use since they
acted very much like the bishops. Ibid: "Among the priests there was no devotedness
of religion, among the ministers there was no sound faith: in their works there was
no mercy, in their manners there was no discipline."

2. Unity in the Metropolitan

Neighboring congregations unite, and their bishops form a homogeneous whole, which begets an organ and center for itself in the metropolitan. Without the metropolitan, an individual bishop dare undertake nothing of significance. The Synod.

56

What follows from what has been said is this: in each more significant Christian congregation the bishop, according to the apostolic institution, formed the center. The bishop along with the presbytery was entrusted with the regular teaching and leadership responsibility in the congregation so that the whole congregation took an interest in deliberations concerning ideas and their earliest history. To such a city congregation belonged many or a few village congregations. These usually received the Christian religion from the larger congregation, and therefore attended its communal religious gatherings or took a presbyter from the city congregation. The presbyter, who in some cases returned to the city congregation following the worship service and who in other cases remained permanently with the smaller congregation, formed the village congregation's center. These groupings of Christian associations, however, were completely fortuitous. The Holy Spirit, which here formed a common life, is the same in all Christians, and as it prepared an organ in these congregations through which it expressed itself as the forming and uniting principle, it therefore had to combine those believing congregations that lay near one another, viewing the former boundaries as nothing in themselves. This union that resulted from an inner impulse produced an organ by which it came to clear consciousness of itself, and through the functions and activities of which its own life in turn was nourished and promoted. As geographically united believers stood in union with their Christian neighbors, it was natural that neighboring diocesan unions should also be established in a closer relationship. Christianity's inner forming impulse, which knows nothing of any isolation or separation, is thus the true basis for the union of the metropolitanate. The Church body forms itself organically from the interior outward as the structure of an inner, active power, not from the exterior inward in the manner of stones and all inorganic materials. According to such an essence, abandoned by life, spirit, and power, those who know how to discover nothing except external contingent causes by which to explain their formation degrade the Church of God. It may not thus be asserted that the ecclesiastical relationship of the metropolitan province was grounded in its essence on the extensive commerce carried on between the residents of the smaller and larger cities, that the larger cities were commonly the metropolitan province, and that Christianity usually spread into the provincial cities from these. *All these relationships merely determined the point of uniting, but in no way the uniting itself.*

57

In regard to the antiquity of the union under a metropolitan, there are no doubts that in its essence and first elements it arose after the broadly.[a/1] The interdependence of neighboring bishops and their union as a whole, the essence of a metropolitan union, is already spoken of in Clement of Rome. "Through the Lord Jesus Christ," he

---

a. De Marca, *Dissertationum de concordia*, 6:1 [the whole of Chapter 1 refers to the metropolitan; Chapter 8 treats the apostolic source of the office]; 3:5ff. A critique of this viewpoint is to be found in du Pin, *De antiqua ecclesia*, 1:6 [who states that some hold that the metropolitan position began with the apostles and others that it began with Christ; du Pin accepts neither position—for him it arose out of the secular structures of the time, the imperial metropoles]. De Marca bases his view that the union under a metropolitan had an apostolic tradition behind it on the facts that Peter (1 Peter 1:1) sent Epistles to specific provinces, Pontus, Galatia, and so on, and that Paul sent an Epistle to all the churches of Galatia and directed the letter for the Corinthians to all the brothers in Achaia at the same time as well as to those whom Titus left behind in Crete. The apostles thus understood the political provinces in an ecclesiastical relationship.

In the expansion of Christianity, generally from the capital cities of a province outward, the union under a metropolitan was openly introduced and gave direction to the inner power and need. Those cities in which the apostles themselves dwelt were looked upon instinctually as centers for others. The reasons that I introduced for the antiquity of a union of neighboring churches signify yet more than this.

said, "our apostles knew that there would be strife because of the episcopal dignity. They therefore set down extensive regulations as precautions, installed bishops, and established the rule that *when the leader of a church died, the leaders of the neighboring churches should bear the care of the orphaned church,* so that proven men could follow in the service of those who fell asleep. We believe, then, that one cannot lawfully cast out of their service those who were appointed by them (the apostles themselves), or who after the apostles' death were appointed by others as responsible for such an institution with the agreement of the whole church, and who blamelessly, with humility, peace, and dignity, humbly served Christ's flock and received a good witness from all over a long period."[b] The closer union that is here

---

b. Clement of Rome, "Letter to the Corinthians," 44: "Our apostles also knew, through our Lord Jesus Christ, that there would be strife on account of the office of the episcopate. For this reason, therefore, in as much as they had obtained a perfect foreknowledge of this, they appointed those already mentioned and afterward gave instructions that when these should fall asleep, other approved men should succeed them in their ministry." The presentation of this passage in the text [as edited in J.B. Cotelerius, S.S., *Patrum qui temporibus apostolicis floruerunt* . . ., vol. 1, 172-173, from whom all the alternate readings discussed below are taken] is based on a translation of the phrase *kai metaxu epinomēn dedōkasi* [and afterward gave instructions]. The explanations of the passage, known to me, do not catch the sense of this passage. Junius translates *epinomē* with *praescriptae officiorum cives* [prescribed citizens of offices], Salmasius with *praeceptum* [prescription], Ussher with *ordo praescriptus* [prescribed order], de Marca with *forma* [form], Hammond with *series* [series] or *modus successiones* [mode of succession]. Others believe the text is corrupted and wish to substitute either *aponomē* or *epilogē* for *epinomē*, but Cotelerius rightly opposes this. Nowhere does *epinomē* have these senses. It means properly the *epinomia* (pasture), resting on treaties or legal determinations, on the right of pasturage of another people, or rather, a right of pasturage agreed upon between two peoples, as *epergasia*, an acre, *epigamia*, a mutually agreed upon marriage. The Church's use of the word *pasture* is known, but there is no fitting noun from *poimainō*; therefore *epinomē* indicate "the right mutually agreed upon by church pastors to care for the flock in certain cases in other dioceses," and thus here, in the vacation of an episcopal seat, it designated the concern that it be properly filled. That the influence of other bishops was active in this is clear from the antithetical phrases "other approved men" and "all churches"; if the "approved men" were from this, it must be "the other churches falling asleep."

Clement, however, wishes to make it conceivable that a bishop approved of by *others* and accepted *by the congregation* itself could not be cast out without reason. Cotelerius also accepts this antithesis between the neighboring bishops and the congregation, as the citation noted indicates. That this is of apostolic origin, Cyprian indicates in Letter 67, 5: "*For this reason you must diligently observe and keep the practice delivered from divine tradition and apostolic observance, which is also maintained among us, and almost throughout all the provinces; and for the proper celebration of ordinations all the neighboring bishops of the same province should assemble with that people for which a prelate*

noted between neighboring episcopal churches continued for a long time without form, structure, or specific boundaries. Already in the second half of the second century, however, we find it self-deter-mined, fairly well described, and fully conscious of itself.[c/2] What had been an instinctual association became clear with the fixing of a common center. The higher Christian consciousness, as soon as it is awakened in us and grows to clarity, works on all sides, pene-trates all individual functions of the Spirit, and forms them harmoni-ously. Likewise, as soon as the uniting of a number of episcopal churches had clearly developed and expressed itself by begetting a specific organ as such, this higher whole of all individual parts strengthened itself and created an outward form of itself in the most like manner possible. The individual churches lived a true common life and viewed themselves as members of one body.[3]

58

The bishop, the center of a single diocese, was the most appropriate organ for contact with another diocese. In a wide-embracing corporation direct union between single individuals was not possible. The one who united his church with the others dared not undertake anything significant in his congregation without this union.[a] He must hold council with the common center and this center in turn was responsible to all individual members of the union.[b] "Thus,"

---

is ordained."

c. Bingham, [2,] 16, [sections 3-4], cites the only situation in which the existence of this in the period can be deduced.

But I must add a more significant passage, which Bingham overlooked, in which Ignatius of Antioch, "Letter to the Romans," concludes by saying: "Who had priority in the region of Rome?" Rome is thus already in Ignatius the *prokathēmenē* of the greater part of Italy. This sheds light on Ignatius's designation of the church of Antioch as the *church of Syria* ("Letter to the Magnesians," 14.15). Thus, here, in the middle of Italy and Syria, a center of a number of dioceses very quickly fixed itself clearly, and this casts a certain happy light on de Marca's penetrating statements [see note above]. That in Gaul, for example, the union under a metropolitan developed only at a later date (see Plank, *Geschichte*, 1:84) is easily explained.

a. *Apostolic Canons*, 35 [See *Apostolic Constitutions*, 8:5.47].

b. Ibid., 28: "We command that a bishop, or presbyter, or deacon who strikes the faithful that offend or the unbelievers who act wickedly, and thinks to terrify them by such means, be deprived, for our Lord has nowhere taught us such things. On the contrary, 'when he was stricken, he did not strike again'" [1 Peter 2:23]. Canon 46.

according to the *Apostolic Canons*, "there will be unanimity, and God
will be glorified through Christ in the Holy Spirit (who brings about
union)."[c] It is the nature of the weak to seek protection from the
strong, and it is just as natural for the strong to serve arbitrarily in
their superiority. Arbitrary, indeed unchristian, activities on the part
of bishops, which had occurred very early, and neglect of the
congregation[d] were now eliminated. An individual bishop had a
counterweight in the other bishops as a group. The healthy members
of the body came to the aid of the suffering member. Often individual episcopal congregations were in danger of giving themselves to a
most unsuitable bishop. The weaker part of the congregation allowed
itself to be somewhat determined in its choice by lower passions[e]
and the nobler and more thoughtful part was not able to control it.
However, as members of a greater body, the latter group did not
stand alone. All the congregations forming this body had a voice in
their bishops. They had purity of faith, holiness of morals, and
doctrinal capability to test the chosen bishop, and only if they were
convinced of the presence of these qualities did they agree to the
choice. Such agreement was called confirmation. *Therefore*, there were
a number of bishops active in the consecration of a bishop, and there
was a law that without the metropolitan the ordination had no
ecclesiastical validity. The possibility of such an active influence of
neighboring churches arose out of the observation that all formed a
unity and all parts had to develop mutually: the emphasis that these
churches could give by their unified activity rested fully on the
conviction that arose out of the innermost depths of Christianity that
the individual part was nothing without the whole. If the individual
church or an ignoble part of it stood on its own ground, the other
churches drew back from it as from an egotistical member. According to the ecclesiastical use of language, they broke off community
(which the egotistical member had already given up because it
proceeded without consideration for the common life),[4] whereby the
egotistical member was set outside the community, that is, it was

c. [Ibid., 35.]

d. Ibid., 30: "If any bishop has gained that dignity by money." Ibid., 31: "If a bishop
makes use of the rulers of this world to be a bishop of the church." I accept
Beveridge's position [reprinted in Cotelerius, 455ff.] that the *Apostolic Constitutions*
were published at the end of the second and the beginning of the third century and
the phrase "rulers of this world" does not hinder me in this.

e. Clement of Rome, "Letter to the Corinthians," 44. Xenophon, *Cyropaedia*, 41, 52, 55.
Eusebius, *Ecclesiastical History*, 6:11.

excommunicated. The excommunicated church, however, which in its isolation had not been convinced it should preserve the Christian character, gave in and, overcoming egoism, it conquered its own foolishness with which it was in danger of counseling itself in the worst possible way. The same was the case if an individual bishop lost the spirit of the whole. Feeling that alone he was nothing because he had become what he was through the whole, he joined with the whole and so joining he maintained the determining character of a bishop who cared for his congregation and was not to oppress or leave it. From all this it is clear once again that the whole union could not arise externally. Because its continuation also rested only upon innermost grounds, the mode and possibility of its continuation clarified its beginning. But it is also clear that, as this external union proceeded from inner living needs, the external union worked back on it as well and remained the greatest need. Each manifestation of a moral power becomes a strengthening of itself.

59

The relationship of the whole's activity to the individual part, however, made necessary the personal association of the leaders of all individual congregations. It called synods into existence. If we look at all that has been said to this point, we notice how the apostles had already discussed the weightiest matters together in common when it was possible (Acts 15), how because of the way in which Christianity expanded from certain mother churches, those who were extended together from such a center were immediately directed to their coherence as has already been demonstrated, and how by the apostolic order that neighboring episcopal churches were to work together when a seat of one of them was vacated, that coherence was more closely determined. In this we have discovered the seed of the synod's essence. In the gatherings to ordain a new bishop, without doubt, they held counsel regarding other broader ecclesiastical matters as well, and when bishops came together for such purposes, their gatherings were expressly called synods.[a] This seed grew with the outward formation of the metropolitan union to so great a degree that with the full growth of the metropolitan

---

a. *Synod of Antioch*, canon 19.

province the bishops' gatherings were also fully formed outwardly, and the inner laws of formation that applied to the former applied also to the latter. Both were completely identical and maintained themselves as the geographical union of many groups who were scattered. It was, therefore, to be expected that the explanation of a synod should be sought where the bases of the metropolitan union were sought. Thus it is understandable that Greek amphictions were used as patterns and that no synods would have appeared in the Church had there been no amphictions. But one ought rather to say that in humanity's common experience there was already present a weak prototype of the need for a communal life, a shadow of the future Christian life. In fact, we can find no basis for not acknowledging the gathering of the apostles in Jerusalem as a prototype of the synod.[5] Although Tertullian mentions only Greek synods, it must clearly be understood that this is because synods first received and had a full outward formation and regular form there. Before Tertullian wrote, many synods were held—in particular, all those that the controversy over the celebration of Easter necessitated, and also those that were called earlier in regard to the Montanists. If we ask more closely who attended the synods, we must answer that it was the bishops above all. But in the bishop the whole congregation appeared. If the bishop is the unity of believers, he is not thinkable without them. In him the whole congregation appeared or in him the congregation was present at the synod.[b] Yet it was not impossible for priests or deacons to attend. Because the bishop did not lead his own diocese alone, aside from his relationship to the metropolitan union, but was at the peak of the presbytery, he could be accompanied by a part of the presbytery at the synod. Often the people were also present.[c] At a synod in Antioch against Paul of Samosata, it was a presbyter, Malchion, who rose up against him[6] and saw through Paul's arts of sophistry.[d] Moreover, the synodal conclusions of a province were not merely communicated to the bishops of other provinces but also to the priests and the whole Catholic Church.[e]

b. Tertullian, *On Fasting*, 13: "Besides, throughout the provinces of Greece there are held in definite localities those councils gathered out of the universal churches, by whose means not only all the deeper questions are handled for the common benefit, but the actual *representation* of the whole Christian name is celebrated with great veneration."

c. Council of Carthage, 256 (Pearson edition of Cyprian, 158).

d. Eusebius, *Ecclesiastical History*, 7:29.2.

e. Ibid., 30:1.

Just as the fully formed union under the metropolitan is in general the counterpart of the diocesan union, so was the government of the metropolitan's area. As everything occurred with common consent in the diocese, so did it here. Just as the bishop acted in the center of the priestly *corona* (as it is said) and was surrounded by the people, so did the metropolitan act in the counsel of bishops, surrounded by the presbyters. The greater the circle of united churches was, however, the more necessary was it that the people be more in the background, and in the provincial synods it was no longer *orderly* for them to be present except, so to say, for the sake of making it public, since only the people in the city in which the synod was held could be present. Because all believers were gathered in their bishops, one would certainly find it spectacular if a complaint was raised over the neglect of the people—as if the bishop was something separated from the people with an isolated interest, something unrelated to their existence or thinkable without them, as if the bishop was not in the people nor the people in him. The wisdom of these conclusions best overcomes the folly of the complaint, and the active, true Christian results guarantee the Christian basis out of which the institution arose. With communal power heretical novelty was opposed, and only because the whole *adelphotēs* [fraternity] expressed itself, did the weak gain firmness to stand against temptation,[7] was the Christian people fed with fraternal wisdom, and the ecclesiastical life and love increased and developed.

3. Unity of the Total Episcopate

Unity and union of the total Church. While the immediate followers of the apostles still lived and formed a center of unity, a regular union of all churches developed in their bishops so that the inner spiritual unity of all believers fully expressed the external; union under the metropolitan was the step by which this was possible. The total conception of the Church is the love of believers manifesting itself in a specific form. The independent development of particular churches aside from the unity of all.

60

But this manner of ecclesiastical community, the metropolitan union, was only a step upon which the union with all believers and with it a communal life of all Christians[1] was possible. The boundaries of the Church community by the union of the diocese with the bishop as the center came into being in the same way only to produce the organ by which further union was introduced and could be brought about. It was in fact a divine work, for what was nobler, an organ of love or the offspring of love? Thus the metropolitan union structured itself likewise only as a resting point so as to preserve the desired end with new-formed, stronger power in the struggle for an orderly union of all believers. But what appeared to be accepted by us in our description of a succession was not so in history. As the seed of the union of neighboring churches was planted with the foundation of a church, so was that of the linking of neighboring churches. It is love's need to reveal its activity as far as receptivity for love is present. And as far as receptivity for love is present, love's power must be capable of stretching out. The qualities of love to receive and to give are thus as infinite as love itself and are given at the same time as love. In the true Christian Church the possibility to work in an orderly way on the totality of believers must thus have been given and this possibility must have been given at the beginning.[2] It is for history to demonstrate the development and to discover the order in which it occurred. During their lives the apostles formed the point of union of all Christians together. They presented themselves as this in their Epistles that they sent to small or large groups of Christians. They brought these Christians together externally through their disciples, through mutual representatives of the remotest congregations, just as they had taught by their sermons, lives, and writings the inner union revealing itself externally. They thus taught Christians to regard themselves as a great visible whole, in which all belonged together, and shared a common fate. But the individual churches were first in the development, were caught up in a great inner ferment, and as the union of believers here first had the concept of achieving a firm, certain structure, it was impossible for such a development to be completed under all the churches together. It lay in the essence of a true, organic nature forming itself externally from within, that through various developmental instances it neared its perfection. The thought of a free union of all believers in the world, the necessity of this union and of a whole life, was too great to be understood by all with full clarity. Even less understandable to most was the manner in which it might continue. The souls of many Christians were yet too small to grasp such ideas even after this marvellous appearance has been present in the world for centuries, and they explained the fact in a way not much different from the way in which the Macedonians and the Romans bound the world into a kingdom and the Mohammedans and the Mongols attempted to bind it.[3] But the power, and the beginnings of the forms in which this power was to manifest itself, was nonetheless given. Demands were immediately made that the power develop and reveal all its wealth. These demands were none other than activities that assumed that the power did not exist. In Corinth an attempt was made during the life of the apostle John, who lived the longest of the apostles, to destroy the congregation founded by the apostle Paul and to break the unity. The result was that the congregation not only grounded itself more firmly, but the general union of all Christian churches was brought more clearly to consciousness. The Roman congregation was sought to mediate in the matter.[a] It did this through a letter written by its bishop Clement and through five

a. Clement of Rome, "Letter to the Corinthians," 1.

representatives.[b] Because opportunity was given to the Roman congregation to renew the unity and love of another congregation, it strengthened its own [unity and love] so that the influencing as well as the receptive congregation attained a clearer consciousness of the uniting power.[c] We find the same in the case of Ignatius. Because a still unconscious unity was threatened to be disturbed by the heretics, the Church was led to self-reflection, and because love was given opportunity to act, she was awakened and strengthened. Throughout all his epistles one finds the thought that Christians are to bind themselves together through the bishop to form an impenetrable union. Thus all the congregations to whom he wrote from Antioch to Rome were described as a unity of many from the motion extended from *one*. All rotated around Ignatius as the planets around the sun. As unity of faith and community of Spirit lie at the basis of the Ignatian epistles,[4] so unity expresses itself as an appearance in external life. Ignatius points out very beautifully in the same letters how the external visible union of all Christians is a necessary expression of an inner disposition and how in it an inescapable need to satisfy this results: "My fellow believers," he says in one place, "I am completely filled with love for you, and *I strengthen you in overflowing joy*."[d] In another place he writes: "I speak to you as to those who are also my fellow disciples. By you I am to be strengthened in faith, in exhortation, in endurance, in long-suffering. *But love for you does not let me be silent*. Therefore, I encourage you in the first place that you are unanimous in faith in God."[e] But he expresses the union of all Christians not only in letters. Like the apostles, Ignatius too ties individual churches together through representatives, as he explicitly notes, to express participation in mutual circumstances.[f/5] We find the same in Polycarp after Ignatius's death. He too forms a group of churches around a common center and his letters prove this[g] in that individual congregations turned to him as they did to Clement.[h]

---

b. Ibid., 59.

c. Ibid., 7: "These things, beloved, we write to you, not merely to admonish you of your duty, but also to remind ourselves. For we are struggling in the same arena, and the same conflict is assigned to both of us."

d. Ignatius of Antioch, "Letter to the Philadelphians," 5 [source quoted].

e. Ibid., "Letter to the Ephesians," 3.

f. Ibid., "Letter to the Philadelphians," 10, 2.

g. See Eusebius, *Ecclesiastical History*, 5:20, 8.

h. Polycarp, "Letter to the Philippians, 13: "Both you and Ignatius wrote to me."

61

Although the immediate disciples of the apostles still firmly formed the higher points of the uniting of all the churches by their personal dignity, an *orderly* association of these churches among themselves had already developed in a remarkable manner. The bishops who were furthest away from one another established direct contact *by writing*. Doing this they informed each other of the most significant occurrences in their churches. Between A.D. 140 and A.D. 150 Marcion, who had been excommunicated by his father, a bishop in Sinope, came to Rome (at exactly the same time Polycarp was there concerned with *communal matters*) seeking acceptance into the Church community. But through his father, the Roman Christians already knew of his excommunication, and he was told: "We cannot do this without the approval of your revered father, for we have one faith and one disposition; we cannot act against your father, our good colleague."[a] A few years later (A.D. 157) the Montanists were in contact with the Roman bishop Anicetus so as to gain though him an acknowledgment of their existence within the Church. Tertullian expressly states that through the assent (later withdrawn) of the churches of Asia and of Phrygia, Montanus was accepted into the community again.[b] For this purpose Asiatic churches entered into a union with the Gallic church. They immediately expressed their opinion and endeavored to bring about peace between the churches.[c] If Victor later threatened the church of Asia Minor with excommunication (A.D. 196), he must have earlier stood in communion with them, as Irenaeus expressly says of the bishops of Rome from Anicetus to Victor.[d] This is also proven by those synods called by Victor and held from Gaul to Asia Minor. Their decrees were transmitted to all the churches, as Eusebius expressly notes regarding the bishops who gathered in Palestine; he preserves an excerpt from the synodal writings.[e] Already in the *Shepherd* of Hermas, written in the first half of the second century, bishops were described in the ideal building of the Church as those who, alongside the other

a. Epiphanius, *Heresies*, 42 [suorce quoted].
b. Tertullian, *Against Praxeas*, 1.
c. Eusebius, *Ecclesiastical History*, 5:3, 4. Note the comment of Valesius [on this section who emphasizes the relationship of all churches with Rome].
d. Ibid., 5:24.
e. Ibid., 5:24-25.

clerics, bore the other believers and were linked and joined to one another in the closest way possible.[f] From the middle of the second century there was a very close orderly union between all churches through the bishops and no especially important development arose in any one part of the Church that was not looked upon as a matter of the whole Church, the totality of believers, and decided by it.

62

If we look once again at the grounds of which the early Church was conscious and out of which the influence of the individual on the whole and of the whole on the individual parts or the union of all among themselves proceeded, we see matters exactly as Ignatius saw them. The churches of Lyons and Vienne expressed themselves clearly on this matter in their letter to the Asiatic and Phrygian Christians. It is addressed: "The servants of God in Vienne and Lyons wish peace, grace, and salvation to their fellow believers in Asia and Phrygia, *who have the same faith in the redemption and the same hope.*"[a] From the custom already noted in Irenaeus that the bishops mutually shared the Eucharist as a sign of community, the union of all as well as the deep reasons for this union in the essence of Christianity is made clear.[b] And after Tertullian pointed out the unity of the faith of the Church, he said: "We maintain community, we call ourselves fellow believers, we practice hospitality; we do all this *because one holiness has been transmitted to us.*"[c] Clement of Alexandria wrote: "The power binding the Church together is faith."[d/6] Aside from this close union of all churches we still discover that particularly important personalities worked everywhere and became a point of union for many churches in their own way. Thus, Dionysius of Corinth in his Catholic epistles (A.D. 164) to the

---

f. *Shepherd* of Hermas, Vis. 3:5, 1.

a. Eusebius, *Ecclesiastical History*, 5:1, 3. Cf. Valesius [who in his note on the opening addresses suggests that the churches of Vienne and Lyons were under the jurisdiction of one leader].

b. Eusebius, *Ecclesiastical History*, 5:24, 15. Cf. Valesius [on this section].

c. Tertullian, *On the Prescription of Heretics*, 20: "Their peaceful communion and title of brotherhood and bond of hospitality—privileges that no other rule directs than the one tradition of the selfsame mystery." Ibid., 21: "We hold communion with the apostolic churches because our doctrine is in no respect different from theirs."

d. Clement of Alexandria, *Miscellanies*, 2:12 [source quoted].

Spartans, Athenians, Romans, Nicodemians, and the Christians in Pontus and Crete, and so on, among whom he fought heresy, admonished these communities to unity, explained Catholic doctrine, and commanded that they preserve the faith[e] or praise the faithfulness in it. Moreover, individual churches still informed the total Catholic Church of their special circumstances and of those whom they had excommunicated. Thus the Church of Smyrna told of the martyrdom of her bishop Polycarp, and the Gallic Church wrote to the congregations at Rome and in Asia concerning the victory of its heroes of the faith.[f] Dionysius worked as did Irenaeus.[g]

In so rich, living, and extensive a composition is the union of the Church portrayed, and all this still occurred in the second century.

63

In the middle of the third century, however, a great new danger arose threatening to tear the Church apart, yet because of it she drew more firmly together, developed her basic principles more clearly than earlier, and described the method and manner of her union more sharply. It was the Novatian schism that had this and other results. The schism arose because of two completely antithetical groups, one that refused to accept into the Church those who had fallen away in the Decian persecution, another that wished to accept them once again without an act of penance on their part. Both groups finally united against the Church. They expanded from Rome and Carthage throughout a great part of the whole Church. As a result the affair took on an external stubbornness of character and both opposing sides were supported by martyrs and confessors. Among these were many who in shameful pride believed they could take care of the needs of others, by their own, as they believed, superfluous merits. These were strongly supported by those who had fallen away in the persecution. There were others, who because they had suffered, were much more strenuously opposed to the lapsed and treated them with unchristian harshness. The first group

---

e. Eusebius, *Ecclesiastical History*, 4:23, 1-6: "I write because the brothers admonished me to write."
f. Ibid., 4:15.
g. Ibid., 4:23.

threatened to take all dignity and power from the Church, and the second to lend support to the charge of cruelty and to cast many into doubt. As a result, the closest coherence was required of all bishops and all well-minded persons. Therefore, Cyprian said: "This is a matter not merely of a few churches, or of one church or of one province, but of the whole Church."[a] In a letter to the Roman priesthood he wrote: "I have not stated a law in this; I have presented myself as a discoverer. . . . I believed I must remain standing by your basic principles, so that our actions, which are communal and ought to agree in every way, do not contradict each other."[b] Dionysius, bishop of Alexandria, wrote to Novatian and to Fabius, bishop of Antioch, who was inclined to Novatian's opinion. His letter reads as follows: "If you have been forced, as you say you have been, against your will, demonstrate it by freely recanting. You must endure all so as not to split the Church of God. It would be as praiseworthy to be a martyr for the preservation of unity as to be a witness to the true faith. Indeed, I believe it would be more praiseworthy. In the latter case one gives testimony for one's own soul, but only in the former for the whole Church. And if by conviction the fellowship returns to unanimity, your uplifting will be greater than your fall. Your fall will not be taken into account, but your rise will be praised. If you are not capable of succeeding with them, save, save your own soul. Live well and preserve the community in the Lord."[c] Cornelius, bishop of Rome, also wrote to Fabius.[d] The Roman presbytery answered Cyprian with these words: "It is fitting that we all be watchful for the body of the whole Church, whose members are scattered throughout different provinces."[e] To Bishop Stephen of Rome Cyprian wrote: "Because of this, dearest brother, the numerous body of bishops is unified by a closely tied unanimity and bond of unity so that if one of your colleagues initiates a heresy and begins to tear apart or destroy Christ's flock, the others come to its aid. . . . For although we are many pastors, we feed but one flock and all the sheep together which Christ purchased by his suffering and death."[f] "There is one episcopate," Cyprian

a. Cyprian, Letter 19, 2.
b. Ibid., 20, 3.
c. Eusebius, *Ecclesiastical History*, 6:45.
d. Eusebius, *Ecclesiastical History*, 6:43, 3-4.
e. Cyprian, Letter 36, 4 [source quoted].
f. Ibid. 68,3

writes in his book on the unity of the Church, "from which the individual bishops have a part, but they have it with a responsibility for the whole."[g/7] Thus what had long been present in the Church was clearly and methodically expressed. Who would still be able to assert against the whole development that a new doctrine or a new phenomenon had now risen up in the Church or that Cyprian and his book on the unity of the Church had alone introduced this? As the Church formed her deepest, innermost foundations according to one unity, this unity must express itself externally as one. To call such an external portrayal of an inner unity, however, the "empirical concept" of the Church in place of which the "ideal" must be established is to establish an abstraction, a shallow concept, death, in the place of *life*.[8]

Each bishop is an offspring, resting on a divine institution, of a specific group of believers contingent in and for itself, and by this the totality of bishops is a total product of all believers, completely indivisible and one, as the believers themselves are, whose unity the bishops present.[9] Everything that has been cited proves that this homogeneity was felt at the time. Note the following passages. "St. Paul taught this," wrote Cyprian, "and pointed to the holiness of unity when he wrote (Eph. 4:4-6) 'There is one body and one Spirit, just as you were called to the one hope that belongs to our call, one Lord, one faith, one baptism, one God.' *This unity we must maintain and defend. Above all, we bishops must do so, we who have leadership positions in the Church, so that we present the episcopate itself as one and indivisible.*"[h] And elsewhere he writes: "A Church came forth from

g. Ibid., *On the Unity of the Church*, 5: "the episcopate itself to be one and undivided [*in solidum teneri*]." "Undivided" is properly used as a legal term to describe the circumstance by which many are so allied in a matter that each individual is responsible for the whole and not merely for a part coming to the individual's care according to the number of participants. In the case that one or another of the participants is insolvent, that individual's responsibilities fall to the others. Salmasius, *De primatu papae*, 80, determines the meaning thus: each bishop has to rule his diocese so that no other bishop dare say anything to him regarding it. But in such a case Cyprian instead of proving the unity of the Church would divide it. De Marca, *De concordia*, explains the passage better in 6:1-2 [where he states: "The unity of the Church is one although divided in many members throughout the whole earth; there is therefore one episcopate in her which is diffused everywhere in a concord of many bishops"] than in 1:2, 4 [where he speaks of unity as arising out of the Roman see]. See also Pearson's edition of Cyprian, 78.

h. Cyprian, *On the Unity of the Church*, 4-5.

Christ throughout the whole word, divided into many members; *moreover*, one episcopate expanded through the unanimous group of many bishops."[i] Because of this the expressions "unity of the episcopate" and "unity of the Church" were used interchangeably. For example, Cyprian noted that "he [Novatian] had separated himself from 'the bond of the Church' and the 'college of bishops.'"[j] In this one will note the analogy that is here once again presented between the relationship of an individual bishop to his Church and that of the episcopate to the totality of the Church.

Let us again contemplate the greatness to which the Church drew her members. How did she come to this position? She was filled and impelled by the Spirit which tore down the boundaries established by the flesh. This greatness she shared with her members, so that fully freed of the weight of the power of this world's spirit, they freely bound themselves together in Christ the Lord into one whole, a scandal inconceivable to the children of this world. The work is also not of this world. So internally did they unite themselves that they expressed their union visibly in a powerful way. They experienced and saw what to this point they had not so clearly and purely seen: Christ was true God from eternity, of a like essence with the Father. For the construction of the phenomena was such that, immediately after the time of Cyprian, when the sense of the unity of the Church came to the forefront in the most living manner, the divinity of Christ was most fully expressed at Nicea, where for the first time all believers were gathered in the images of its love. Now that they themselves had become great enough, they were capable of acknowledging Christ in his total greatness. Oh, let us ever, ever be great and free, let us ever wish to love and keep the unity of the Spirit through the bond of peace. Then the greatness of Christ will not speed away, for our eye will be pure and will be able to see him in his purity.[10]

64

The whole constitution of the Church is, therefore, nothing other than embodied love, the type of the individual bishop in his

---

i. Ibid., Letter 55, 24 [source quoted]. Ibid., 73, 26: *"Charity of spirit, . . . the bond of faith, and priestly concord*, are maintained by us with patience and gentleness."

j. Ibid., 55.

diocese:[11] on the one hand, the expression of the inner movement of the believers striving for active union and, on the other, a movement back toward them to fix and protect them in their purity and power. The Church itself is the real, realized reconciliation of human beings with God through Christ. Because of this, individuals are reconciled with one another through Christ and through love in him as a unity with him. Thus they are and manifest a unity among themselves; this is the inner essence of the Catholic Church. The episcopate, the constitution of the Church, is only the external expression of its essence, not the essence itself. This distinction must always be maintained. External unity in the episcopate flows out from the internal. As morality has often been expressed in terms of law, so the episcopate has customarily been, but it cannot be conceived of in this way.[12]

The constitution of the Church, it follows, is also the concentration of love that is to act in its total strength on the individual members of the great body, bound by love against the spirit of the world. Thus in her essential activity she is completely penetrated by the great words of Paul: "Not that we lord it over your faith; we work with you for your joy" [2 Cor. 1:24]. A great many of those misled in the Novatian controversy shared in this joy. After the whole Church had acted in regard to the lapsed, namely, those in Rome where they had accepted a schismatic bishop as an expression of the spirit of division, the following resulted: "They begged for pardon," said Cornelius, bishop of Rome, in a letter to Cyprian. "They wanted to present before God a pure guiltless heart, following the Gospel which said, 'Blessed are the pure in heart, for they will see God'" [Matt. 5:8]. (Note here how the cause of division is judged. It arises out of sin, because they sought pardon, and out of an impure heart, because they wished thereafter to keep a pure one).[13] "This was made known to the people," the letter further states, "so that those who had seen it for so long a time outside of the Church in error and pain could now see it again within the Church. There was a great flowing together of fellow believers. There was one voice of thanks on the part of all toward God. The heart's joy brought forth tears. They embraced one another as if they had just been freed from prison. 'We know,' they said, 'that Cornelius, bishop of the Holy Catholic Church, was given to us by God the Almighty and Christ our Lord. We acknowledge our error. We were deceived. We went astray through deceptive, faithless counsel. Although we seemed to have community with schismatics and heretics, our heart was always upright in the Church. We know that there is one God, one Christ whom we confess, and one Holy Spirit, that there must be *one* bishop (as the portrayal of inner unity) in the Catholic Church."[a] This joy in the Roman Church was followed immediately by one throughout all parts of the whole Church. "Know now, fellow believers," wrote Dionysius of Alexandria to Stephen in Rome, "that all earlier separated churches in the East and beyond have united. All Church leaders have the same disposition and rejoice without bounds because of the unexpected peace which has come." (He then names the Syrian, Palestinian, and Phoenician churches and those of Asia Minor as well as others and continues:) "On all sides, in one word, all are delighted and praise God because of unity and fraternal love."[b]

Behold, these are Catholic feasts. Christians did not rejoice in and because of division; division caused pains. But when unity embraced hearts and spirits again, joy resounded throughout the whole Church. To rejoice in division would be sin against the Holy Spirit, not an acknowledgment of the presence of the Spirit in the Church. We must repeat here again: the union of the erring members with the others directed them to the right way: they could not stand against love working in union. In the flame of love the light of understanding ignited itself, and error disappeared with sin.[14]

The sense of the passage of St. Paul in Ephesians 4:11-16 is now clarified, I believe. "And his gifts were that some should be apostles, some prophets, some evangelists, some pastors and teachers, to equip the saints for the work of ministry, for building up the body of Christ, until we all attain to the unity of the faith and of the knowledge of the Son of God, to mature manhood, to the measure of the stature of the fullness of Christ, so that we may no longer be children, tossed to and fro and carried about with every wind of doctrine, by the cunning of men, by their craftiness in deceitful wiles. Rather, speaking the truth in love, we are to grow up in every way into him who is the head, into Christ; from him the whole body, joined and knit together by every joint with which it is supplied, when each part is working properly, makes bodily growth and upbuilds itself in love." We here return to the point with which we began. We find Christ and remain in truth, if we remain in love,

a. Cornelius to Cyprian, Letter 49, 2. Compare Cyprian's beautiful answer in ibid., 51.

b. Eusebius, *Ecclesiastical History*, 7:5, 1-2 [source quoted].

unity, and community. Paul and the Church formed by him according to the spirit taught by Christ teach that true constancy comes only in the Church as imparted to believers of this great congregation. In this Paul says we are *adult* outside of it and in division we are *children*, accepting every wind of human doctrine of one's own and others' foolishness.

We have demonstrated and will continue to point out what the orders and distinctions are by which unity is possible. We will come to know in which each of us is to belong, if we ask God about it. He gives to each the measure of his power.

All who have to this point fought against living unanimity between the maintenance of Catholic doctrine and ecclesiastical organization have had a sense of it. (They always grasp one or another of these aspects and make the members of the Church, the organs of love and unity, suspect. They are like the king who promised to give peace to a town that fought him on condition that it give up those who were most opposed to him. One of these spoke out in the people's assembly: "Wolves promise peace to the sheep on condition that the dogs be sent away."[c]

65

We must now describe more closely *how* the bishops' unity expressed itself in an ordered and legal way. It did so, as we have already noted, through the metropolitan union. The activity of the bishops of one province was only a mediating one in the choice of a bishop. They stood in place of the whole Church. After the metropolitan at the head of his bishops was convinced of the orthodoxy, pure life, and other required qualities of a chosen bishop, and had ordained him, he informed the whole Church. The candidate himself began community with the Church by his letters which he sent to the bishops. Customarily they also contained a confession of faith (*epistolai koinōnikai*, pacificae, communicatoriae). The acceptance of and reply to this letter of peace was known as the confirmation of the newly chosen bishop throughout the whole

c. [On the fable, see Walter Wienert, *Die Typen der Griechisch-Römischen Fabel* (Helsinki: Suomalainen Tiediakatemia Academia Scientiarum Fennica, 1925), 50]

Church.[a] When the choice of Cornelius as bishop of Rome, made in conformity to the law, was contested, Cyprian pointed out that "he was made bishop by very many of our colleagues who were then in Rome, who sent us very honorable, praiseworthy letters, full of the most beautiful testimonies on the ordination. . . . Since he was legally installed in the bishop's chair according to God's will and was confirmed by the agreement of us all, anyone who wishes to be bishop in his place must certainly be outside the Church. *He does not have ecclesiastical consecration, if he does not have the unity of the Church.*"[b] This right of confirmation was possessed by even the smallest church as a member of the whole.[c] If anyone threatened to gain power through the most powerful party in the episcopal cathedral, he could not in any way achieve firm possession of the seat. The unity was so firm (and at the same time so necessary for the health of individuals and the whole) that he could not remain in his position without being generally acknowledged. Because of this such impetuous persons had to seek union with the whole Church in every way, but in this attempt they generally floundered.[d] If such a bishop developed principles that he earlier did not have or had not made known, his attempt was opposed, but in the opposite way. The neighboring bishops investigated the matter, withdrew from community with him, and through them the whole Church withdrew from community. As union with one bishop contained his confirma-

---

a. Cyprian, Letter 59, 9: "It was decided by the advice of all of us to write to you, that there might be found a short method of destroying error and discovering truth, *that you and our colleagues might know to whom to write, and reciprocally, from whom it behoved you to receive letters.*"

b. Ibid., 51, 8 [source quoted].

c. Ibid., 48, 1, in which the Adrumentine colony appears to confirm Cornelius and its seeming aversion to him is understood. The Roman bishops had for centuries chosen to send letters of communication and their confessions of faith to the bishops of the Church after their election. Thus Gelasius I [in Letter 13 (shorter form)] says "It is customary for the new bishop of Rome to send his confession of faith to the holy Church." Cyprian's Letters 1 and 2 contain confessions of faith to the Dardanian bishops. Cf. ibid., 9. The biographer of Gregory the Great, John the Deacon [in his *Life of Gregory the Great*, 1:39ff.], says that this pope did the same.

d. Cyprian, Letter 36, 4: "For previously, when from the company of that very wickedness a certain Futurus came, a standard-bearer of Privatus, and was desirous of fraudulently obtaining letters from us, we knew who he was *and he did not get the letters that he wanted.*" Novatian, who wished to be bishop of Rome, had to allow himself to be consecrated by a number of bishops whom he found by some means. Now his situation was certain, but the *whole Church* did not confirm him and his endeavor failed. Eusebius, *Ecclesiastical History*, 6:45.

tion, so his deposition was actualized by the withdrawal of this union. For as little as one could be a bishop without being made a member of the whole body, so little could he remain a bishop if he was robbed of this association. In Antioch, Bishop Paul of Samosata, a proud and completely contrary bishop, suppressed the hymns to Jesus Christ in which Christ was praised as God. Some neighboring bishops agreed with his principles. The presbytery of the Antiochian church lived in deep moral depravity, and the bishop allowed this so that his own depravity would be overlooked. A part of the congregation was won over and authorized by the poorest means to approve his speeches loudly in the church, and the better part of the congregation, which was in deep sorrow and was held down by tyrannical measures, dared not offer resistance.[e] Had the Antiochian church been isolated, had it not been a member of the great body that experienced the sufferings of each individual member and offered its whole power to it to reestablish it in its original relationship and to give it health and power again, had the organic union of the Church body been of such a kind that its action could have given no impression, the suffering part would have lost its true faith, its freedom, its Christian dignity. Because of this great synods immediately gathered in Antioch, the last of which shared its conclusion with the whole Catholic Church: it had withdrawn from communion with Paul, that is, it had excommunicated him and had placed a worthy man in his position. The synod then stated: "We make this known to you so that you write *to him* [the new bishop] and receive from him the letters of peace. Paul, however, ought to send letters to Artemon (whose heresy he appeared to renew) which contained Artemas's principles and ought to take up communion with him."[f] From the standpoint we have now taken, we can explain a remark on the essence of ecclesiastical ordination, the necessary source for proper church service which penetrates all orders. As the apostles received from Christ the charge of preaching the gospel which they could not nor did not give to themselves, no one can ever in the future give it by himself or herself. One's mission must be given. The whole Church gives this in the ordainer because she alone can worthily stand in the place of Christ.[g] Moreover, each part in which

---

e. Ibid., 7:20.

f. Ibid., 7:30, 17.

g. From this arose the expression that God installs bishops which is seen in the

the ordinand, the chosen person, is active, is a part of a greater whole. The well-being of this part is internally joined to the whole in its relationship to the whole—therefore all through whom the ordinand receives his *capability* have the right of confirmation and the authorization to withdraw consent if the one made capable proves himself unworthy.[h] According to its external appearance the ordination is nothing other than the acknowledgment of the whole Church that her Spirit is in a specific believer and that this Spirit makes that believer worthy to represent the love of a specific number of believers and to join them with the whole Church. In the ordination, the Holy Spirit is not so much first communicated as it is acknowledged that specific gifts have been *earlier* communicated to the one who is to be ordained. The Spirit moves where it will and human beings are to direct themselves toward the Spirit, not the Spirit toward them, although certainly the Spirit will give itself in a stronger measure to the pastors of flocks on petitions from the congregations (1 Tim. 4:14; 2 Tim. 1:6).[15] However, because the ordinand has his mission and confirmation through the whole, he takes on responsibility to proclaim not his doctrine but that of the whole, that is, the doctrine of the Church that is received through the Holy Spirit. In this way light is shed on the rebuke that is brought against the Church because only those ordained in the prescribed

---

testimony of the whole Church. Cyprian, Letter 55,8: "I come now, dearest brother, to the character of Cornelius our colleague, that with us you may more justly know Cornelius, not from the lies of malignants and detractors, *but from the judgment of the Lord God, who made him a bishop,* and from the testimony of his fellow bishops, the whole number of whom has agreed with an absolute unanimity. . . . *He cannot have the ordination of the Church who does not hold the unity of the Church.*" Letter 55,24: "Although there is one Church divided by Christ throughout the whole world into many members, and also one episcopate diffused through a harmonious multitude of many bishops, in spite of God's tradition, in spite of the combined unity of the Catholic Church, compacted everywhere, he is endeavouring to make a human church." Ibid., 69.3: "*Nor can one be reckoned as a bishop who, succeeding to no one, and despising the evangelical and apostolic tradition, sprang from himself. For he who has not been ordained in the Church cannot have nor hold to the Church in any way.*" Now the whole association, in which the continuation of the Church is established in regard to the unbroken episcopal succession, is also made clear, as is the reason why she in no way acknowledges a teaching office, which does not stand in this succession.

h. Ibid., 55, 24: "He then who neither maintains the unity of the Spirit nor the bond of peace or separates from the bond of the Church and from the assembly of priests, can neither have the power nor the honor of a bishop, since he has refused to maintain either the unity or the peace of the episcopate."

manner can have power over the ordained teaching office. A communal life cannot be thought of without this ordinance.[16]

66

In this unity and coherence that the episcopate saw as necessary as soon as it attained self-consciousness, the characteristic of the individual greater members of the whole Church that were earlier thought to be permanent could suffer or seemed necessarily to diminish. But on a closer view of episcopal unity this concern was set aside. The totality of the episcopate was considered the highest and most spiritual product of believers, distinguished above all merely geographical relationships through which the individual church had its characteristic. If geography had been a factor in the production of unity, a contradiction would have existed in this unity, that is, unity could never have come into being, because each particular is in its essence a plurality and never gained its union through itself but always through something different from it. In the unity of the Church, whose expression and organ the episcopate is, the aforementioned external relationships were also seen as contingent, and as soon as the episcopate stepped beyond these and above every finite bond, unity came into being. The unity of the episcopate as such did not in any way know these characteristics which could not as a result be the object of its activity. Only because the Church is placed in time and space is there a multitude of bishops. If these are removed, there is no longer a Church. Thus the many individual bishops are there as a result of the particular needs and characteristics that have arisen through the aforementioned finite and limited forms which they therefore satisfy according to the orders established for the governance of the individual churches and insofar as those churches are independent of the other churches. The spirit of unity is in each individual church, but the unity is not that which forms the special character of the individual part. Cyprian, who held fast to unity, expressed himself on this very specifically.[a] So also

a. Cyprian, *On the Council of Carthage*: "Neither does any of us set himself up as a bishop of bishops nor by tyrannical terror does any compel his colleague to the necessity of obedience; since every bishop, according to the allowance of his liberty and power, has his own proper right of judgment, and can no more be judged by another than he himself can judge another." Cyprian, Letter 73, 26: "I have briefly

finally each diocese and the embodiment of a number of those who constitute a metropolitan union by legislation and particular occurrences is directed for itself as long as it suffices for itself.[b]

Finally, the activity of eminent bishops and specially gifted believers is in no way limited by the full outward formation of the association and the relation of all individual members, but is more impressive and extensive because of this. In the first formative period of the Church the apostles and their most remarkable disciples held closely together and the latter had to live in such a way until the orderly Church union had more closely developed. They did this so as to guide by their personal presence what could not be given in the, as yet, irregular order. Thus the Church designated such men [sic] as a circle, not containing the Church, but always expressing her powers.[17] Those who had accepted the whole Christian truth from the Church with a depth of mind and were gifted with necessary intellectual capacities, worked with reverence and love as wide as the name of Christ was heard. Customarily the bishop ruled his diocese and was firm in union with the whole Church, but he disappeared in the multitude as did the most insignificant of believers. Of Cyprian, Gregory of Nyssa says: "He is not only the head of the church of Carthage or of Africa, which since his time and because of him is made famous, but also of the whole West and almost to the eastern, southern, and northern boundaries."[c/18] His letters still testify to us how he could warm the Christian world by the sun of his mind. Where did Origen not work, and who can determine the boundaries of Dionysius of Alexandria's activity?[d/19]

---

written to you, according to my abilities, prescribing to none, and prejudging none, so as to prevent anyone of the bishops doing what he thinks well, and having the free exercise of his judgment." This Cyprian states on a weighty matter.

b. Ibid., 55 and 36.

c. Gregory of Nazianzus, *In Praise of Cyprian*, 18, 129 [source quoted]. Compare *Oration*, 21, concerning Athanasius: "Oversight of the whole Church is entrusted to him." And note Basil, Letter 52: "In addition to the special cases of our common Lord for the church entrusted to him, he has great care for the totality of the churches."

d. Eusebius, *Ecclesiastical History*, 6:45, 46; 7:20, 22, 26.

4. Unity in the Primate

The visible Church lacks the keystone if it remains in the pattern described above; the unity of the episcopate and of all believers in it must represent itself in one Church and one bishop: he is the living center of the living unity of the whole Church. The Primacy. Steps in the development of this office.

67

For a long time I doubted[1] if the primacy of a church belonged to the characteristic of the Catholic Church. Indeed, I had decided to deny it, because the organic union of all parts in a whole, which the idea of the Catholic Church completely required and which is the Catholic Church, seemed fully achieved in the unity of the episcopate as it has been here described. In addition, it is evident that there is little material in the history of the Church in the first three centuries that resolves all doubts regarding this matter.[2] But a freer, deeper view of the biblical Peter and of history,[3] a living penetration into the organism of the Church, convinced me of the necessity of the idea. The historical construction of it came later, however.[4]

From what has been said to this point, one can see immediately that the developments toward unity could not be complete. In the succession described a member is lacking, the keystone of the whole. In a complete organism, as in the universal whole, individual parts are organic so that each member is seen as a type of the whole, and the power forming the whole repeats its basic form within individual parts. Likewise, if we must view the whole as complete according to the above description, we discover that the succession in the ecclesiastical organism is suddenly broken off and the forming power weakened. As a result it cannot complete the whole work according to its established types. In the diocese we discover the bishop as the center in which the rays of love concentrate themselves,[5] and in further union the metropolitan is the center as the head of a number of gathered bishops.[6] We have now discovered the

unity of all bishops—but still no representation of their unity in a
living image. We see in the totality of these bishops the unity of all
individual members of the Church, and we seek, because we are
impelled to do so, to see the whole presenting once more the type of
individual formations, the personally existing reflection of this unity.[7]
We would have had to see the bishops as a merely human product
if their institution was not apostolic or, much more, if it did not stem
from Christ himself out of whose mandate and in whose Spirit the
apostles acted. Likewise, we would be inclined to view the center of
the whole, even if one was found in history, as a human work, if this
basic principle did not also arise chiefly in the history of Jesus and
the apostles. It may not, however, be contested and has seldom been
contested that Peter filled the primacy among the apostles, but one
needs to deduce this finally from the individuality of the Apostle.[8]
It is correctly stated in this regard that if he was not capable of this,
it would have been sufficient if he had only received such capability
and practiced it.[a] It is necessary to introduce additional references[b/9]

a. [Johann Sebastian von Drey, *Das Suchen nach Wahrheit, oder Vergleichung der
katholischen und protestantischen Kirche mit der apostolischen der ersten Jahrhunderte*. Von
J.G. Rätze. Leipzig, 1803 . . .,"] *Theologische Quartalschrift* 3 (1823): 478ff.

b. To found or build a church is nothing other than to gather the first person or the
first believers, upon which others are built, into one place. This Irenaeus states in
Against the Heresies, 3:3-4: "The apostles, Peter and Paul, having laid and built the
foundations of the Roman Church, committed the episcopate to Linus" [German
translation with Greek text; note use of *themeliōsantes*, "laying the foundations," here
and in following quotations]. "The church of Ephesus founded by Paul" [German
translation with Greek text]. Cf. ibid., 1:10, where the word *hidruō* (to seat) [is used.]
Origen, *Against Celsus*, 1:10, regarding Paul, says: "He did not wish to build where the
foundations had already been laid, but he went where the gospel had not yet been
preached" [German translation with Greek text]. Ibid., 3:28: "God desired to commend
the doctrine of Jesus, a doctrine which was to save mankind, and make firm through
the apostles the foundations of the rising edifice of Christianity, which was to increase
in the succeeding ages" [German translation with Greek text]. Cf. Eusebius,
Ecclesiastical History. 5, 6: "The blessed apostles having founded and established the
Church" [German translation with Greek text]. All the apostles were, therefore,
designated as the foundation of the building of the Church upon which the rest of the
Christians were built, as is seen in the letter of Paul to the Ephesians 2:20,22. The
phrase "upon Peter will I build my Church" [Matt. 16:18], designates Peter in
ecclesiastical language as the first believer. Cyprian understood it in this way in Letter
71, 3: "The Lord chose him first" and set him over against the "the early and the late,"
among whom he meant Paul. Therefore, Augustine could say interpreting Matthew
16:18 [in his *Tracts on John*] that the Church was built on the confession of Peter, on
his faith, and in another place that it was built "upon Christ," because the Church
stands only by faith, the founder and giver of which is Christ. Origen, Ambrose, and

in establishing the primacy, however, because of deviations from the context and spirit of patristic passages regarding the matter. Peter factually documents his position.[10]

68

When the apostles were scattered, Peter could not carry out acts as primate, nor will anyone believe that it was necessary even if he was authorized to do so. During the period in which Christianity was first established in individual congregations and in which the unity of all individual churches was understood in its first formation, the primacy of one church and its bishop could not manifest itself absolutely. If we wish to grasp the primacy in its idea, we must, as has been said, present it as the personalized reflection of the unity of the total Church.[11] It was not possible, however, for the unity of the whole Church to make itself an object by self-perception and to present a personal likeness as the offspring of this before it had completely penetrated itself. Before the period that we earlier described in which the unity of the Church stepped forward with full consciousness (in Cyprian's time), those who desired irrefutable historical [*historische*] evidence for a primacy were desiring something excessive and had to be repelled because it was not possible according to the law of true development.[12] In a like manner, the endeavors of those who decided so fully to discover that law or were of the opinion they had discovered it, had to appear fruitless and untenable. The primacy, as every characteristic of Christianity, is not to be viewed as a dead concept but as life and proceeding from life. (For the feeling and reason of every Christian will oppose the view that either Polycarp and Anicetus or Clement of Rome agreed on a

---

others call true believers, the rocks on which the Church is built. Obviously John 21:15-17 cannot be used to support the primacy of Peter. There Jesus says: "Do you love me *more* than these?" How could Peter know that? He could know how much he loved Christ, but in no way could he know if he *loved him more* than others. Thus Christ could not ask this. It is almost a reproach against the words of Peter [in Matt. 26:33]. If the primacy cannot be established directly by these passages, they still express characteristics about Peter and have a special importance with other similar passages. What has been said does not set aside the profound comment of Augustine in *Tracts on John*, 118 [which speaks of "the power of the keys" given to Peter "on behalf of all"].

primacy[a/13] in the same way as they did on the unity of the Church and similar matters, and will hold it as appearing not only as unprovable but as outrageous and detracting from the dignity of the Christian Church in the greatest way.[14]) Needs had to be established. These manifested themselves in history as facts and from these the concept was first developed. Church history is, as I have repeatedly said, nothing other than a development of Christian life. What good is the dead statement[15] "You must have a center of unity," even if proclaimed by Christ, if no needs in the inner depths of the believers are present to express it? For all that, this would never have had any effect in life. Everything favors this assertion. Christ did not enter Judea with the statement: "I am the Son of the living God." Such a statement would not have had the least effect. He waited until the reception of his life was made living in the great insights of his disciples, the natural expression of which arose by itself on the first opportunity: "You are Christ, the Son of the living God" [Matt. 16:16].[16] To make the point in a similar way, Christ never said, so far as we know, "You are to venerate the saints," a statement no one would have understood. There were still no saints; no believer had yet died. Only after this occurred did the need develop from the interior by itself. The same need formed us by the Holy Spirit living in us so that we view all believers who were alive as an individual whole in Christ. It was also the need that formed a community of the living with the dead (because Spirit, not death, unites us) and taught us to continue to love those who had lived with Christ and his Spirit and through him had become holy.[17] Thus, before a personalized image of the unity of believers could truly manifest itself, this unity on which further development followed had to be present.[18]

---

a. Schmidt, *Bibliothek*, 2:1ff., has, as is known, the agreement being reached by Anicetus and Polycarp and more firmly established by Hegesippus. Münscher, *Elements of Dogmatic History*, 2:81 [sic; but cf. sections 35-36], calls this an ingenious combination. Kästner in his *Agape*, 18, says: "Clement first knew how to bend the different Christian apostolic sects into a body and to discipline and regulate in the same way all the compliant congregations according to his so-called apostolic covenant constitution. To accomplish this he made use of many writings *forged* for the spirit of the time according to the names of imagined and commonly honored Christians, the introduction of a newly *discovered exposition of the genuine* apostolic and prophetic books, as well as faithful, crafty, and powerful help in many localities." Henke, *Kirchengeschichte*, 1:175, accepts the statement. Such historical [*historisch*] impieties necessarily proceeded from the doctrine of the invisible Church.

69

We wish also to reject the opinion of those who on this basis acknowledge no primacy, because they see the Church as a lifeless mass, think of everything as a dead concept always having been finished, and for them the thought of a true spiritual life is strange.[19]

It is notable, however, that from the time we see the Church body fairly much formed as such, we can discover no occurrences to which we can trace this formation in which the Roman Church, especially designated and marked out in time, was not interlocked and involved. This is the case in the Montanist movement and the controversy over the celebration of Easter. The hypothesis that Rome's political greatness established the influence of the Roman church, since the primacy of the Church was often traced to its political preeminence so as to insist upon an outward formation in all its forms, was already markedly opposed by Irenaeus in the famous passage: "It would take too long to explain the succession of all churches in this work. It is therefore enough to embarrass all who form false churches to cite the tradition set down by the apostles of the greatest, oldest, and best known church founded by the glorious apostles Peter and Paul. . . . With this church because of its greater preeminence [potiorem principalitatem] all churches necessarily [necesse est] agreed [convenire], that is, all believers everywhere, for the apostolic tradition is maintained [conservata est] in it [in qua] always by those who are everywhere."[a/20] Here the reputation of the Roman

---

a. Irenaeus, *Against the Heresies*, 3:3,2 [source quoted]. That *convenire* can mean *symbainein* [come together] cannot be doubted; *potior*, or *potentior*, as it is often read, is not "more powerful" but is equivalent to *hikanōteros* [most competent]; for this word earlier translators often used *potens*. Thus the letter of Clement to the Corinthians is called *potentissimas litteras*, whereas the original text preserved by Eusebius, *Ecclesiastical History*, 5:6 reads *hikanōtatēn graphēn* that is, "a preeminent, remarkable letter." *Principalitas* is not merely *archē*, origin (as in Gieseler [section 51, 150-151] and Böhmer in de Marca, 1: 1, section 9), which the translator would not have mistaken since he renders it properly elsewhere. Nor can it properly be linked with *in qua* [in which], in which the basis of the principality is to be contained. It is equivalent to *kyros* [authority] which gains precedence in ecclesiastical language (Canon 4, Nicea on the metropolitan) and may easily be translated with *principalitas*. *Necesse est* is clearly *anankē* [constraint] not *dei* [it is to be], but *conservata est* [it is maintained] is not to be rendered with *sōzesthai* [to save] but with *diaphyllattesthai, thesaurizesthai* [to conserve, accumulate]; it is customary to render it with both together, indeed, with *aoristos* [indefinitely]. This accumulation of doctrine in Rome I understand from the letters of peace which were sent by bishops on their election to many others but especially and

Church as founded by Peter and Paul is as specifically stated as it can be. It is also, in fact, remarkable that the authority that the Roman Church ought to have in evidence of the apostolic tradition was linked with the political greatness of the city of Rome. That Peter came directly to Rome and did not die in Eugubium is clear from the fact that he never lived in Eugubium.[21] But direct proof for the primacy does not rest in this, nor in the other facts noted. In the Montanist affair the Roman Church and others, especially the Gallic, had a share. Nor is anything said of the Roman Church as the church of the primacy, but only as one that acted with the others, and was looked upon as eminent because of its apostolic foundation. In regard to Victor's behavior in the controversy over Easter, the statement of the synod of Palestinian bishops cited above suggests that his motives arose out of a sense of duty, which because of the direct share of each individual church in the good of the whole in and for itself, each one in similar circumstances could command. If in the end the passage cited from Irenaeus speaks in favor of the greater preeminence of the Roman church, this eminence cannot be traced back to Peter with as much certainty as we would wish since the Church fathers see it as founded at the same time by Paul. If it is not feasible to draw definite conclusions from the aforementioned

---

always to the bishop of Rome so that it expresses what Optatus of Milevus said of the Roman church: "with whom the whole commerce of forms of the earth are concordant in one society of communication" [De schismate donatistarum, 2:3]. This statement is particularly strengthened by a passage in Augustine in which he says that the African church *never* communicated with the East other than through the Roman church. The Roman church, as the whole Western church to which Africa belonged, shared in the institution of Eastern bishops. On this direct union followed. The passage is found in Augustine, *Against Cresconius*, 3:38: "This is above all believable because an Eastern church never wrote to the bishop of Carthage passing over the Roman bishop." It is not necessary to prove that this custom did not first arise in Optatus's time. The facts given earlier document its common use already in the middle of the third century. Because of its general use it could not then have been at an early stage of growth. From all that has been said it is evident that the beginning of this custom must be placed at least in the middle of the second century.

For the interpretation that the tradition of all churches was maintained in Rome by *others* coming there by chance, one can, Irenaeus wishes to say, make an analogy: in Eusebius, *Ecclesiastical History*, 5:24, 7, Polycrates of Ephesus is quoted as saying: "having met with the brethren from everywhere." But even with this the *potior principalitas* was not *principalitas* if everything Irenaeus wished to say of Rome was found in each major city. For this reason the translation of *principalitas* with *archē* must be set aside. How can one explain *potior*? Was the church of Rome's *archē potior* [beginning stronger] than that of the Antioch or Ephesian church?

material for a primacy consciously established by Peter, one
nevertheless can see that, to the extent the unity of the church
developed ever more fully as an external association, individuals felt
drawn with partially conscious necessity to *one* point, and in this
regard the primacy is highly significant. It must thus be accepted
and seen in the whole course of the development of ecclesiastical
unity. However, we have already shown why there could still be no
indubitable facts demonstrating the primacy of a church.[22]

70

However, with the beginning[23] of the phenomena, in which the unity
of the Church and of the episcopate manifested themselves[24] most
fully in life and[25] developed in theory, the Roman church and her
bishop appeared as the personalized center of the episcopate. *An
inner union of the fact forces us to this conclusion.*[26] Cyprian says of the
Roman church in a letter: *"They set sail to the seat of Peter, to the first
church [ecclesiam principalem], from which the unity of bishops [unitas
sacerdotales] has arisen [exorta est]."*[a] Here the eminence of the Roman
church is traced back to Peter. We could hardly understand this
passage, however, if another composition of Cyprian, *On the Unity
of the Church*, was not preserved. In it he finds the prototype of the
unity of the Church in the fact that Christ gave St. Peter, as *one*, the
power of the keys.[b/27] As the prototypical unity of the Church is in

a. Cyprian, Letter 59, 14 [Latin text quoted]. Compare the *principalitas* of Irenaeus.
The *exorta est* in the perfect tense is notable and leads to our editing of the text cited.

b. Ibid., *On the Unity of the Church*, 4: "That he might set forth unity, he arranged by
his authority the origin of that unity, as beginning from one." Even if the expression
"et primatus Petro datus" [and the primacy given to Peter] is interpolated in this
passage—see what is said in [my review of Katerkamp in] *Theologische Quartalschrift*
(1823), 510ff.—it is still evident in Cyprian, Letter 71, 3: "For neither did Peter, whom
first the Lord chose, . . . claim anything to himself insolently, nor arrogantly assume
anything so as to say that he held the primacy, and that he ought rather to be obeyed
by novices and those lately come." Cyprian also said [ibid.]: "Peter indeed had
primacy, but when Paul cast before him his Judaizing, he made no use of it and did
not say, 'I have the primacy; all must listen to me,' but acknowledging his errors, he
gave an example of humility [text in German]. Nor did he despise Paul . . . furnishing
thus an illustration to us both of concord and of patience." This is also found in a
passage in Tertullian, *On Chastity*, 1.

Peter, so in him is inherited the Roman Church, the seat of Peter, the continuing living image of the episcopal unity.

The further development and outward formation of the primacy belongs to the later period. It is not my intention to gather all the less important facts from which the presence of a visible center of the visible Church could be proven.[c] I only wish to center on the chief periods of development and to establish a proper position.

Two extremes are possible in ecclesiastical life, and both are called egoism. They arise if *each as an individual* or *one individual* wishes to be all. In the latter case the bond of unity is so narrow and love so warm that one cannot free oneself of its strangling hold. In the first case everything falls apart, and love grows so cold that one freezes. One egoism begets the other. Neither one nor another must wish to be all. Only all can be all and the unity of all can only be a whole. This is the idea of the Catholic Church.[28]

---

c. Planck, *Geschichte*, 1:123, judged for the most part correctly [in stating that in the third century bishops took even greater preeminence over the other churches, but he goes on to comment that this does not support the Roman claim. See also ibid., 7, 111-124, where he discusses the matter]. Note especially du Pin, *De antiqua ecclesia*, 2:2.

Conclusion

General Review. Overview of the whole history of the condition of the Church. Her law.

71

From the previous discussion it can be seen that the primacy did not begin to manifest itself other than in preliminary ways during the first three centuries. Even near the end of that period, it still moved without definite form. Although there are specific indications how and where it manifested itself in fact, one must still point out that it never appeared alone but was only active with other bishops and churches. Nevertheless, it began to take on its own stamp and at the same time only waited for a call to manifest itself. We move forward, however, on three formations of unity in the explication of the evolution of the Church's life: the bishops, the metropolitans, and the primate. In the early Church the bishop was, as it were, hidden among the rest of the believers. Unconsciously all united with the bishop. The apostles established the bishop, and believers did not know that they had one. It was a relationship like that of a child to a parent which is accepted instinctually, an unconscious unity of the believers' life. Before it was acknowledged, this paradisiacal life was broken. Egoism threatened to tear the bond. Individuals drew closer together and held fast with conscious necessity to what had earlier directed a living yet unknown impulse to itself. An inner necessity for the maintenance of Christian character formed the bishop as the consciously acknowledged center of all. This same character could not now have been maintained if the circle of united believers had not expanded itself still further until, throughout the episcopate,[29] all had united themselves in a visible living unity, clear to itself, to a true communal life. Against egoism there had to be opposed an infinite love, revealing itself with all power. All parts were now consciously determined by the whole, the one lived in all and through all, and all in it. On the way to this ruling evolution which could only be reached by supernatural, divine power, the same phenomena reappeared as had in the begetting of the first formation of unity. As the bishop was originally hardly *noticed* as such among all the believers, but only *was* the one around whom they gathered, so was the metropolitan initially in the wider unity of bishops and the primate in the totality of all bishops. In all, however, the further miraculous phenomenon is to be noted: the more the inner living unity of all Christians was attacked, the more powerfully did it express itself. The greater the egoism, the greater the love. The more disturbing the circumstances, the more centralizing and stirring was the power. We discover a great wealth, a great flexibility of forms of unity. According to need, one or the other of these took priority. The more the situation of the Church flourished, the more the earliest bond of the Church was expressed through the episcopate, and the others, the metropolitan and the primate, fell into the background. In times less conducive to growth, the metropolitan union was greatly active. It created itself as the center according to the measure of the need. Likewise, in later periods we see the formation of primacies, exarchates, and patriarchates. In the saddest and most complicated circumstances for the Church, the primacy appeared in the most pronounced way; *the whole power of the Church, otherwise divided, was concentrated in one* so as to be able more energetically to oppose all who attacked her prosperity. If we sum up everything that was expressed as the historical law of the constitution of the Church, we see how all formations of unity necessarily must be in seed in the divine order (this can also be said of the metropolitans) so that the Church herself may not be without counsel or help in any situation. Let every party separated from the Church look through its association and declare if it has in itself the counsel of all levels of culture, *if it developed outwardly from its own being*. It is immediately seen that no bending of these forms so as to present general unity has an absolute merit, except insofar as it answers a certain need. All must work so that the forms be filled with the life out of which they poured, so that we might consciously retain the original unity of Christian life, the love of which we were not previously conscious, just as we all must be zealous so that the doctrinal concepts of the Church sink back once again into the mind of each believer and here are seen and held to firmly with the clearest consciousness as a unity from which they developed. The unfounded assertion that "earlier there were no such forms; we want to return to the old ways" is unclear. Is it that this assertion only wishes to go back part-way or all the way to the very beginning of the Church? If we are to have the old life again, we will *necessarily* have the old forms again. We must, therefore, it seems, rise above these antitheses. Medieval reformers from the twelfth century on always viewed the existing condition of the Church as the cause of the Church's wretchedness and thought that if they could only do away with it all, salvation would come. But that condition was the *result* of wretchedness, not the *cause*. Since they confused the two, they accomplished nothing. They placed all their activity on the results and the phenomena in the external Church which related solely to that time. Had they directed their activity together with all power and wisdom to the inner foundation of Christian life as many, indeed very many, in the Church did—even those whom they cursed—the condition would *necessarily* have changed again, and thus with the cause gone, the results would have disappeared. One always feels that self-seeking with its character of moral coarseness and ignorance greatly darkened the Middle Ages. But instead of positing that the hierarchy necessarily had to form itself differently than it had to do earlier, one found in it the source, whereas it was what arose out of the source. This twisting of the causal relationship was the most significant reason for the misdirected, thoughtless reformation of that time. During our own time it is the reason for the saddest depiction of history, for misunderstanding the greatest men, and for the most distressing detraction of the dignity of the Church and her spirit. Under and by the protection of the hierarchy thus formed, Christian life and all science prospered and flourished and brought forth at that time what was always glorious and greatly noteworthy. And it did bring forth a great deal. But to establish her relationship to the time and not to understand it as contingent, the hierarchy traced it back to general, and therefore completely necessary, acknowledged grounds. She developed her form that had been shaped by circumstances into a system, easily deluding individuals, but not by deceit. What was necessary for one time immediately appeared as generally good and dependent on no overriding temporal situation. When the beautiful seeds planted in the constitution of the Church at the time ripened, the stiff form of the hierarchy should have changed with the circumstances that had been changed *by it*, and those forms of unity that had fallen away should have again stepped into the foreground. However, since human beings attempted by principles to give generality and necessity to a form, limited by the individuality of [a specific] time, life disappeared from the principles and the school. The hierarchy did not understand itself. By her use of culture the hierarchy made the position accepted earlier unnecessary; she did not see this. Thus it came into conflict with life. This contradiction was the more glaring, the more excessively the hierarchy used her might. When the divine Spirit leading the Church wished to indicate that the circumstances had passed when all power of the Church had united itself in one person, the Spirit no longer provided such a bearer the total power to control it with dignity. Extraordinary times, like extraordinary men such as [the Popes] Gregory VII [d. 1085], Alexander III [d. 1181], and Innocent III [d. 1216], had passed by. Common men received the papal dignity, a sign that this dignity no longer needed to be the old one in all its greatness. The reformations that were undertaken or wished to be undertaken in the first half of the fifteenth century within the Church were ridiculed. Reformation was carried on externally, that is, to establish a desired change in the Church, reformers took their position outside the Church, tore apart the life of the Church, made principles that were opposed to all communal life and, in their results, necessarily to all Christianity. They proceeded in this direction by going back to principles that the circumstances seemed to demand. They separated and thus set up separating and destructive principles. While these were being firmly held, others *for the greater part* stuck to the views that had been developed in the Middle Ages in and under completely different circumstances. The forming principle, the inner character of the constitution of the Church, was unclear to both parties, although much more *greatly* in the separated group than in the stiffly medieval group, which of course in Germany has now hardly any followers who think that that earlier condition is necessary for all times.

Addenda

Addendum 1

The Holy Spirit in Believers
According to the Doctrine of the Fathers

By the Holy Spirit, insofar as it is in the Church, is meant not only a power maintaining itself as it were outside of human beings that merely brings forth certain results in them—not *energeia* only present to believers, but one finding itself *ousiōdōs essentially* in them, and thus giving salvation and making children of God as follows (according to Rom. 8:15-16)[1] from it. Aside from the particular cases of Christians, this doctrine has its common ground in the principle that God can certainly not be thought to be working according to the ways of human and finite beings, which are always outside of that on which they work and of that which they do. With God this is not so; where he works, there he necessarily is, and what is has being insofar as it is grounded in God.[2] Thus Augustine says in a very beautiful passage on the creation of the world: "He did not create and leave [the world]; but things are of him and in him" (*Confessions*, 4:12).[3] If we must accept this, how much more must we assert that *the life of the saints* does not have its innermost being and essence beside God and outside of him, but rather that it is from God and in God, and that God is thus its *ground*.[4] The Holy Spirit is *in us; it dwells* in believers. Such expressions have their source throughout the Holy Scripture, although not always in the same sense. This does not mean anything other than that every true good is an outflowing of the original good and is grounded in it.[5] We say that the Holy Spirit is in the Church. What is the Church, however, other than the totality of believers? We say that the Spirit guides the Church, but we do not think that it guides as a driver guides horse and wagon; certainly it does not do so mechanically. Christ is our life. He is in us and we in him.[6] This does not merely mean that we have his *doctrinal concept*, but he binds himself to us in a living, real, and substantial way.[7] As has been said, this is particularly expressed in the eucharistic doctrine of our Church.

From the beginning Catholic mysticism knew and expressed the deepest possible speculation regarding our relation with and established being in God. Indeed, this mysticism is the basis of the Catholic Church. This is not to deny that there was a time among Catholics[8] when declaring someone a mystic was stating something questionable about that person, but one always had to add an adjective if one wished to indicate something significantly bad by the term.

Origen speaks quite accurately concerning this approach (which, however, the Church never stated in a canon; she only said that the Holy Spirit was always in her).[9] Origen protects himself against the possible conception that the Holy Spirit might by this mysticism be compared to a physical body:[10] "And since many saints participate in the Holy Spirit, the Spirit cannot therefore be understood to be a body, which being divided into corporeal parts, is partaken of by each one of the saints" (*On First Principles*, 1:1, 3). He adds that this is like the art of healing which many have, but which is nevertheless not *divided* among them. However, this analogy is not to be pressed, since every science consists merely of *concepts*, and this is not the case with the Holy Spirit.[11] "But these are not to be deemed altogether parallel instances in a comparison of medicine to the Holy Spirit, *as they have been adduced only to establish that that is not necessarily to be considered a body, a share in which is possessed by many individuals.* For the Holy Spirit differs widely from the method or science of medicine, in that the Holy Spirit is an intellectual existence and subsists and exists in a peculiar manner, whereas medicine is not of that nature" (Ibid.).[12] From this communication of essence from the Holy Spirit, Didymus [the Blind] of Alexandria proves divinity itself in that no finite essence can penetrate another and communicate itself essentially with it. He says: "It is therefore evident that the Holy Spirit has nothing in common either with physical or with nonphysical creatures. Other substances receive this substance of sanctification from the Spirit, but it is, above all, their giver and creator. Those who enjoy communion with it are called partakers of the Holy Spirit and are sanctified by it. If they are sanctified by communion with the Holy Spirit, it is clear that such persons have a part of it, but that the Holy Spirit gives the sanctification" (*On the Holy Spirit*, 4). Likewise, Athanasius cites 1 Corinthians 3:16, 'Do you not know that you are God's temple and that God's Spirit dwells in you,' and continues: "If the Holy Spirit were a creature, we would not have part in it with God. . . . But since we have said that we partake of Christ and God, it is clear that the purification and the seal in us (1 John 2:28) is not of a finite nature, but of the nature of the Son through the Spirit in him who binds us with the Father. John teaches this when he writes in 1 John 4:13 'By this we know that we abide in him and he in us, because he has given us of his own Spirit.' However, if by communion with the Holy Spirit we are also partakers of the divine life, is it not madness to say that the Holy Spirit is created?" ("First Letter to Serapion," 24).[13] Likewise Cyril of Alexandria says: "The Spirit does not come to us through divinity as a stranger, but, as I may say, as a divine character, and dwells in the saints and always remains in them if they purify the eyes of their spirit by pious intentions and preserve the grace by untiring acts of virtue" (*Commentary on John*, 9:14).[14] He cites John 14:15, "If you love me, you will keep my commandments. And I will pray to the Father, and he will give you another counselor to be with you forever, even the Spirit of truth, whom the world cannot receive, because it neither sees him nor knows him; you will know him, for he dwells with you, and will be in you."[15] Gregory of Nazianzus suggests that in the pre-Christian period the Spirit was only active in individuals and noted in mere results, but now it is present in essence: "Now the Spirit is come in a perfect way, no longer as before when it came only in single acts, but essentially as one might say, *being with and living with people. The Son bound us bodily with himself; he also promised that the Spirit would come bodily*" ("Oration" 41:11). In a remarkable passage Basil says that one does not have to think of the communication of the Holy Spirit simply as an active conceptual union:[16] "If it is not possible for people to impress their image upon any material except by sharing their form with it, how is the creature to raise itself to equality with God if it is not a partaker of the divine image? *The divine image, however, is not like the image of a person, a dead form, but is living. It is an essential image that makes [one] to an image,* through which all who are partakers of it become images of God" (*Against Eunomius*, 5).[17] The Fathers understood that this being of the Holy Spirit was in believers, parallel in a certain way with the being of the divinity in Christ, and, as has been noted above, they held that believers are children of God, just as the whole Christ was called and is the Son of God because of the uniting of the divinity with the human Jesus. This uniting the Fathers understood as the prototype of the union of God with individuals, with the distinction, however, that in Christ the divinity belonged to the person of Jesus. This is not the case in believers because in Jesus the union was *hypostatikē* [hypostatic], in believers it is called *sxetekē* or *kata sxesin* [situational]. "Not once have we indicated that union with the Holy Spirit is neither *physikē* [natural] nor *hypostatikē* [hypostatic], that is, neither natural nor personal, as if one person or nature resulted from both. For Augustine says they are children of God by the grace of adoption, and therefore each is an only begotten" (Petavius, *Opus de theologicis dogmatibus, De trinitate*, 8:7 [which treats *ousiōdōs*]).[18] This essential union with the Holy Spirit that it communicates to all believers is thus their inner unifying principle.[19] In addition to the passages already cited in the discussion we add the following.[20] Basil, in his work *On the Holy Spirit* in which he describes in various ways the indwelling of the Holy Spirit, says that the Spirit is in us *as the whole in the parts*, according to the distribution of its gifts,[21] and we are in the Spirit as parts in the whole since we form a community in it: "As parts in the whole, the Holy Spirit works according to the distribution of its gifts . . . and we as members in a whole are a unity in the Spirit because we are all baptized in one body by one Spirit (1 Cor. 12:13)" (*On the Holy Spirit* 26:61). Chrysostom writes: "We have all known this same Spirit, and have all tasted this same grace, says Paul. Now one spirit formed us *and gathered us all together into one body*—for this is the meaning of 'we were baptized into one body': and vouchsafed us one table, and gave us all the same watering, for this is the meaning of 'we were made to drink of one spirit'—and united persons so *widely separated*; and many things then became a body when they are made one" ("Homily 30 on 1 Corinthians," 12:12). Augustine says: "The one God has created us, the one Christ has redeemed us, *the one Spirit has united us*" (*Against the Donatists*, 35, 58).[22] This is the sense of the blessing so often used in Catholic prayer, "The communion of the Holy Spirit be with you all." The greatest particularity and closest specificity[23] of doctrine is united with this mysticism, however. This is not the case in any separatistic-mystical sects, which commonly lose clear consciousness before great depths and end in a hopeless pantheism. The reason for this not occurring in the Catholic Church lies in her essence. Already at the time of Origen and through him the Church fought against those who allowed a theology of the Holy Spirit in believers, separated from its communication and nothing more than a Christian community spirit,[24] no special divine hypostasis. (For further historical discussion, see Petavius, *Opus de theologicis dogmatibus, De trinitate*, 7:4ff.)[25]

Addendum 2

[Definitions of the Holy Spirit]

According to the Holy Scriptures, the[26] Holy Spirit is also called at times the Spirit of truth, at times the saving Spirit, at times that which begets love in us. Irenaeus says: "The Spirit is *Truth*" (*Against the Heresies*, 3:24, 1). The *dilectio* [love] is a *charisma* [gift], and indeed *omnibus charismatibus supereminentius* [supereminent above all gifts] (Ibid., 4:32,8). Origen writes: "Out of its fullness, *the fullness of charity* as the apostle Peter taught, the Holy Spirit is poured into the hearts of *the saints* so that they participate in the divine nature, so that through the Holy Spirit the word of the Lord might be fulfilled: 'As you, Father, are in me and I in you, may they be one in us' [John 17:21]—namely, effective participants of the divine nature in the fullness *of love* through the ministration of the Holy Spirit" (*Commentary on Romans*, 4:9). Later, the sanctifying Spirit is almost always called the Spirit of love by the Latins or love itself. However, the Greek Fathers call it more often the sanctifying, perfecting[27] power, *dynamin, hagiastikēn, teleiōtikēn*. Augustine writes: "And therefore most rightly is the Holy Spirit, although God, also called the gift of God. And by that gift what else can properly be understood except love, which leads to God, and without which any other gift of God whatsoever does not lead to God?" (*On the Trinity*, 15:18, 32). "If there be among the gifts of God none greater than love, and there is no greater gift of God than the Holy Spirit, what follows more naturally than that the Spirit is itself love, who is called both God and of God?" (Ibid., 15:19, 37). In the passage cited earlier from Augustine in Addendum 1 [*Against the Donatists*, 58] he adds to the office commonly ascribed to the Holy Spirit, namely, to save us, the office of binding us together.[28] Caesar of Arles [actually, Augustine] writes: "Only because of love is the Spirit characteristically called a gift" [Augustine, *On the Trinity*, 15:18, 32]. Basil and Cyril, however, write: "That saving power, which goes out essentially from the Father and gives perfection to the imperfect, we say is the Holy Spirit." Cf. Basil the Great, *On the Holy Spirit*, 26:61-62, and Cyril of Alexandria, *Thesaurus*, 34. John of Damascus writes: "God is also the Spirit, the Holy Spirit, a saving power" (*On the Orthodox Faith*, 18).

Addendum 3

Fuller Discussion of the Various Meanings
of the Word *paradosis*

Paradosis, "transmission," is used in many ways by the Greeks. Here
we are only treating the meaning that is parallel with *patroparadota*,
"transmitted by the Fathers," and used by Dionysius of Halicarnassus
[*Roman Antiquities*, 1:5, 48] and others. By it they mean *sayings* of an
earlier period in a twofold sense: "They either contain the earlier
belief and the earlier doctrine, or historical [*historische*] events"
(Creuzer, *Symbolik*, 1:87).[29] The traditions of the Jews are well known.
Elsewhere they are called *deuterōseis* and their teachers *deuterōtai*.
Origen often had them in mind and described them fittingly in his
Commentary on Matthew [13:15-17 on Matt. 17:28].[30] In the language
of the Christian Church *traditio* also has various meanings. In
Eusebius (*Ecclesiastical History*, 3:1) there is a historical [*historische*]
statement: "Thomas, according to tradition, was sent to Parthia." The
sayings of Papias, who gathered together accounts from Jesus' life,
his parables, and teachings, which are neither found in the Gospels
nor were otherwise generally known, are also called *traditiones*
(Eusebius, *Ecclesiastical History* 3:39, 11). Eusebius also associates
agraphos [unwritten] with *paradosis* to specify more fully the character
of the letters. He calls Papias a man of weak insight since he
believed all sayings. Customs, practices, and usages in the life of the
Church are also called *traditiones*. Thus Stephen, bishop of Rome,
expresses himself on the baptism of heretics which he declared valid:
"Nothing is introduced except *what is transmitted*" (Cyprian, Letter,
74, 2). On the other hand, a bishop in an African synod calls this
tradition a *custom* which he wishes to show is to be abolished.
"'Christ says,'" the bishop states, "'I am the Truth,' not 'I am a
custom.'" Where a truth is clear, a custom regarding truth ceases"
(Libosus of Vaga, Council of Carthage, 256, *Statements of Bishops*, 87,
30). However, Cyprian on this same matter says: "Where is this
tradition from? Does it come from the authority of the Gospels or the
authority of the Lord?" and he refers to his practice of rebaptizing
heretics as *divinae et sanctam traditionem*, "a divine and holy tradition," because he believes it can be demonstrated from the Holy
Scriptures[31] (Cyprian, Letter 74, 2). Tertullian calls on unwritten
disciplinary traditions to support his contention that a Christian is
not allowed to receive a soldier's crown: "It ought not to be admit-

ted, if no cases of other practices that, without any written instrument, we maintain on the ground of tradition alone and the countenance thereafter of custom, afford us any precedent. To deal with this matter briefly, I shall begin with baptism. Just before we are going to enter the water in the presence of the congregation and under the hand of the president, we solemnly profess that we disown the devil, his pomp, and his angels. On this confession we are thrice immersed, making a somewhat fuller pledge than the Lord has appointed in the Gospel. Then, when we are taken up (as newborn children), we taste first of all a mixture of milk and honey, and from that day we refrain from the daily bath for a whole week"[32] (*On the Crown*, 3). The doctrines of the heretics are also called *traditiones*. Thus Cyprian writes: "Despising God's tradition, they seek strange doctrines, and introduce teachings of human appointment, whom the Lord rebukes and reproves in his Gospel, saying, 'You reject the commandment of God, that you may keep your own tradition'" [*On the Unity of the Church*, 19]. In Eusebius's *Ecclesiastical History*, 7:1, Dionysius of Alexandria speaks of this same doctrine: "They fall into the systems and transmissions of the heretics." The heretics themselves call their characteristic doctrines a tradition (Irenaeus, *Against the Heresies*, 3:2, 1).

In this work we have nothing to do with these traditions here nor with the true disciplinary traditions. In the treatise itself I sought to develop only the concept of the dogmatic tradition as it appeared in the total impression of the history of the first centuries. At this point I want to indicate more closely the *individual* passages in which is described what was introduced in section 12 as the meaning of *paradosis*, as the *original doctrine*.[33] Tradition is the total transmitted doctrine of the Church independent of Scripture.[34] Irenaeus writes: "For how should it be if the apostles themselves had not left us writings? Would it not be necessary to follow the course of the tradition that they handed down to those to whom they committed churches? To which course many nations of those barbarians who believe in Christ assent, having salvation written in their hearts by the Spirit, without paper and ink, and carefully preserving the ancient tradition" (*Against the Heresies*, 3:4, 1-2).[35] One sees here how tradition was received over the generations by which it was directly passed on, if I may so express myself, and was not separated from the gospel *living* in the believers, but "was written *in the hearts* of individuals by the *Holy* Spirit" [Heb. 8:10]. The description of those who see tradition as something standing independent of the holy life of the Church and continuing from the past and into the future, cannot be justified either by the language or by an enlightened view of the matter itself. They see tradition as something external, not even as something flowing forth again from an inspired mind, one knows not how, as something at the same time preserved magically by the Holy Spirit. The first proclamation of Christian doctrine through Christ and its preservation are related in almost the same way as the creation and preservation of the world are. God did not withdraw after the creation, but the creation retained its foundational being in him; its preservation is, as one is accustomed to say, a continuing creation.[36] What use would it be if in the whole Church it were said "Christ is God," but if this statement did not come out of the inspired mind[37] of believers, that is, if the mind did not rest in the statement, did not have peace and joy in God, did not truly find itself redeemed because Christ the Saviour is God, and if because of this it did not out of inner necessity once again proclaim "Christ is God"? Without this we plant a word without understanding it. As a result it would have been laid down in the confessions and would be of no use for our true understanding—we would only have a dead letter once again.[38]

The total, proclaimed doctrine of the Church, as the interacting activity of all that Christ and the apostles gave for the perpetuation of the doctrine of the Church, whether written or oral, is called tradition in the following passage: "Since such great proofs are, therefore, present, truth must not be sought elsewhere among others, since one can easily receive it in the Church in which the apostles have set down everything that is truth as in a precious treasure so that everyone who will may take the drink of life. For this is the entrance to life; all others are thieves and robbers. One must, therefore, shun them, love the doctrine of the Church above all, and hold to the transmission of truth" (Irenaeus, *Against the Heresies*, 3:4, 1).[39] The transmission, perpetuated in the Church in unbroken succession from the apostles in which we compare the present tradition or doctrine of the Church with the doctrines of the Church in all previous centuries, "this is the same power of transmission" (Irenaeus, *Against the Heresies*, 1:10, 1-2).[40] Here this same tradition is also always called preaching and faith: "If it is demonstrated to be [based] on the apostolic tradition which will be continued in the Church through the succession of bishops" (Ibid., 3:2, 2),[41] insofar as this continuing tradition is embodied and originally preserved to transmit such a demonstration. Eusebius speaking of Ignatius said:

"He admonished them to hold fast to the apostolic tradition, the certainty of which he testified to in his writings and which he held necessary to embody" (*Ecclesiastical History*, 3:36, 4).[42] "At that time Hegesippus, Dionysius of Corinth, Pinytus, Philippus, Apollinaris, Melito, Musanus, and Modestus and, above all, Irenaeus lived. From these to our own time the written true faith of the apostolic transmission and the pure doctrine came" (Ibid., 4:21).[43] To this written tradition the written gospel[44] belongs and makes one point with it. Origen says: "By transmission I have discovered what the four Gospels are which are undisputed in the whole Church of God" (Origen, *Commentary on Matthew*, preface;[45] cf. Eusebius, *Ecclesiastical History*, 6:25, 4, 3:3, 3).[46]

Addendum 4

[Definitions of "Heresy"]

Hairesis, like the Latin *secta*, has many meanings. In Origen's works the different Greek philosophical and medical schools are very often called this, as are the Jewish religio-ecclesiastical parties: "Because of this there are many schools in philosophy" (Origen, *Against Celsus*, 3:12). Cf. ibid., 3:38, 5:63; Eusebius, *Ecclesiastical History*, 6:18, 3. Sextus Empiricus calls Zeno, the leader of the Stoic school, a *hairesiarchēs* (Zeno, *Contra Mattem* [Sextus Empiricus, *Outlines of Pyrrhonianism*, 3:245]). Clement of Alexandria also calls the Catholic Church a party, a school: "The ancient Church which is the truest *gnosis* and in fact the best heresy" (*Miscellanies*, 7:15). In Tertullian and Cyprian the Christian religion is called a sect (Tertullian, *Apology*, 46); Cyprian, *Three Books of Testimonies against the Jews*, preface: "Certain chapters on the religious doctrines of our schools."

Addendum 5

[Definitions of "Catholic"]

As Clement of Alexandria had already noted, the adjective *catholicus* was given to the Church in opposition, *pros diastolēn* to the heresies (*Miscellanies* 7:17). As the term "heresy" describes a separation from unity, so *ekklēsia katholikē* [Catholic Church] describes unity in diversity in such a way that it cannot be dissolved without the parts that make up the whole being destroyed by such dissolution. The meaning of *katholikos* [catholic] is defined by its etymology. *holos* [whole] is used of things whose parts cannot be thought of outside of the whole, where everything stands in an organic coherence, be this coherence physical or spiritually alive or merely intellectual, and also where a part is the image of the whole in opposition to a whole composed out of various things. In Greek one says of a mass of water that it is a *holon*, but one does not say this of a house. The Latins translate it with *totus* and *universus* (as the Commentator on Epictetus's *Enchiridion*, 31, says indicating the difference between *holos* and *hapas*: "The first is distinguished from the second in that it is used for something simple, for example, fire, water. The second is used for something that is made out of many, for example, a whole house, since the house is made of stone, wood and other things."). Aristotle writes: "[The first signifies] a whole that is lacking no part" [*Metaphysics*, 4:23, 26]. Both definitions are distinguished from one another and are not close). Therefore: *to holon*, the *universal whole*, *holon to soma*, the whole body; and Ignatius says, "The whole is faith and love to which nothing is to be preferred"; *pistis* [faith] and *agapē* [love] form a *holon* [whole] ["Letter to the Smyrnaeans," 6, 1; "Letter to the Magnesians," 1, 2] which embrace a mass of parts, or many specifics, organically bound and contained in this *holon*. Clement of Alexandria uses *katholikos* in almost the same way (*Miscellanies*, 4:9). The confession of Christ by faith and life he calls *homologion katholikēn* [catholic confession], in opposition to that which occurs *merikē* [partially], merely *dia phonēs* [through speech]. Diogenes Laertius calls the generic concepts that have formed themselves through what is common as regularly appearing specifics, the *prolēpseis, katholikē noēseis* [catholic, general concepts]: "They speak of them, I believe, as a concept, a correct idea, a thought, or a catholic idea, that is, one fully drawing itself together in the memory as a concept of the manifold appearances. One of this kind is 'human being' in that when one says 'human being,' one immediately sets forth the human form conceptually" [*On the Lives of the Philosophers*, 10:33].

    Catholicus is already used in the aforementioned sense of an organic coherence of all believers according to Ignatius: "Where Jesus Christ is, there is the Catholic Church" ["Letter of the Smyrnaeans," 8], "Where Jesus Christ truly is, there the uniting of all Christians is a unity." Immediately before this he states: "Where the bishop is, there the full congregation [*plēthos*] is to be, just as the catholic Church is where Christ is."[47] *Plēthos* is designated in the first statement and *ekklēsia katholikē* [Catholic Church] in the second. The first designates the believers united to a unity in a specific place, the second designates the unity of all believers together. If one reverses the passage it reads: Where Jesus Christ is, there the believers all together form a unity, just as through the bishop the believers of a specific church are to be united. He thus proves the unity of a specific church by the unity of the whole Church. If we look at the two other ideas expressed here in the two statements, they are "bishop" and "Christ." Here the comparison is not retained. There was no personage known to Ignatius who was physically related to the whole Church in the way the bishop was to the individual church. He thus took Christ as the inner, unitive, and life-giving principle of *all* believers, the unseen ground of unity and the head of all. But because of this we do not wish to say that it follows that the *ekklēsia katholikē* [Catholic Church] must signify the unseen Church, since this would not express what Ignatius wishes. The separatists could then oppose him by stating that they wished such an invisible unity also, but not a visible one as was portrayed by a bishop. In the same way, Augustine writes: "There is a debate between us over the question: Where is the Church—with us or with them? In whichever case it is only one, and our predecessors called it 'catholic,' to indicate by this designation that the Church is 'through all' since this is what the Greek words *kath' holon* mean. But this Church is the body of Christ as the Apostle said, 'According to his body which is the Church' [Col 1:18, 24]. From this it clearly follows that one who is not a member of Christ cannot participate in redemption through Christ. *The members of Christ are bound together by this bond of love, and only by this are they joined with their head, which is Jesus Christ.* Thus, the whole, which is Christ, is head and body. The head is Jesus Christ himself, the Son of the living God. God himself is the Redeemer of the body of Christ who died because of our sins and was raised for our salvation. His body is the Church of whom it is said: 'He shall create for himself a glorious Church without spot or blemish . . .' [Eph. 5:27]" (*Against the Donatists on the Unity of the Church*, 2:2). Here I must note how superficially and poorly is the concept of the Catholic Church of those who always have in sight the external description, the appearance, the external union, and who cannot raise themselves to inner being and life. If they do not first find in the earliest period a form of external union as it expressed itself in a later period, they deny the being of the later Catholic Church itself in the earliest period and wish to discover a *completely and essentially other one*. I must further note in this Augustine passage what I developed in section 31 and support with other passages from Augustine: the established being in the community of believers is linked with the bond with Christ; love forms the unity and through this we are joined to Christ. "The members of Christ are bound together with the bond of love and by this are joined to their head."[48] *Katholikos* is used in Eusebius as in Ignatius in the superscript to "Letter to the Smyrnaeans" on Polycarp's death (Eusebius, *Ecclesiastical History* 4:15, 3). This unity in diversity, the characteristic *katholikē*, is joined with commonality. Therefore, *ekklēsia katholikē* can also signify the character of the Church not narrowed by temporal and spatial events. Unity in diversity is the begetting of *divine power*[49] which cannot be understood in narrow margins. Thus it and only it must expand beyond all times and places and have existence according to its capacity. This meaning of *katholikos* is already noted in the Augustine passages. Therefore, Cyril of Alexandria writes: "She is called 'catholic' because of her expansion over the whole earth from one end to the other" [*Catechism*, 28, 23]. From this, as well, there is an antithesis in that heresy arises if one does not allow oneself to be determined by the whole, the body of Christ, or to be ruled by the Spirit of Christ. Thus one necessarily takes upon oneself the restrictions that lie at the base of what is human. One's work is thus restricted to a specific time and place. Therefore, Clement of Alexandria points out:[50] "It is clear from the earliest and truest Church, that later heresies and those that first arose after this time were introduced by novelties and were false. From this it is clear that the true Church is only one—for there is only one God and one Lord. Therefore, the one chiefly to be honored is praised according to its quality as unity since it is a pattern of one principle. The Church thus participates in the nature of the one, which the heresies wish forcefully to tear into many parts (in the *biazesthai* [to tear] is designated the unnatural, the taste for struggle). According to her basic conception, according to her ideas, according to her origin, according to her excellence, we assert that the ancient Catholic Church is one. But also according to her excellence the Church like her forming principle *kathaper hē archē tēs sustaseōs* is only one. It surpasses everything else. There is nothing that is like it or similar to it" (*Miscellanies*, 7:17).[51]

Therefore, the Catholic Church is also called "that which stands over all" and "that which spans the heavens and embraces the earth." The first designation is quoted by Eusebius from a writer of the second century (*Ecclesiastical History*, 5:16, 9); the second is added to *katholikē* in the letter written by the congregation at Smyrna to the Philomelians. "Thinking of all those who have bound themselves to him as well as the whole Catholic Church extended over the earth" (Ibid., 4:15, 15). From this addendum on *katholikos* it appears that the original meaning of the word was not "that which extends itself from one end to the other."[52]

Since the Spirit of the whole is in every part of the great whole because it will be the same in each part, it is called Catholic (Eusebius, *Ecclesiastical History*, 4:15, 4:43, 11; Cyprian, Letter 48, 3; Letter 52). All this can also be said of the doctrine of the Church; it is Catholic and each individual part of it is (Eusebius, *Ecclesiastical History*, 4:7, 18), On the introduction of the word *katholikos* in the Apostles' Creed, see Johann Georg Walch, *Introductio in libros ecclesiae Lutheranae symbolicos* (1732), 107.[53] Finally, I make one clear attack on the opposing definition: that it cannot be held and that it is disproved by history each person will be able to judge from the material given. See also Breitschneider, *Dogmatik*, vol. 2 [section 126 which treats the term "catholic"] and Augusti, *Archaeologie*, 6:36[54] [who insists that the terms "heretics" and "schismatics" continued to be used to designate Christians who separated themselves from the Catholic Church], and elsewhere.[55]

Addendum 6

Augustine's Answer to the Statement of the Heretics that in the Catholic Church There Is Only a Faith in Authority and a Constrained Faith

Augustine in *On the Profit of Believing* expresses himself with great depth on this matter. He writes against the Manichaeans who also attacked the Catholic Church as a constrained faith, a blind faith in authority. To vindicate his own freedom of faith, which allowed itself to be determined completely only by previous inner testimony, Augustine wrote: "You know, Honoratus, that we fall into the hands of these people for no other reason than that they promise that those who listen to them they will free from all error and lead to God by pure and simple self-conviction, casting off their frightful constraint of authority. Why did I despise for some nine years the religion that was given to me as a child by my parents to follow those individuals and to listen earnestly to them, other than that they said that we were frightened by superstition and that faith was *demanded* of us before self-realization, whereas they constrained no one to believe unless the truth was first established and developed." He continues: "Who could not be attracted by such promises, particularly the soul of a disciple who thirsts for truth, which imagines itself as being of importance after instruction into the schools of many scholars and knows how to talk a great deal? So was I then. I despised the so-called old wives' tales and endeavored to hold fast to and sip the unlocked, pure truth as promised by them. What reasons called me back again? . . . I discovered among the heretics a greater accomplishment and eloquence in refuting others rather than a firm and certain proof of their position. But what should I say of myself in that I was soon a Catholic Christian? Almost dried out and dead by such great thirst, I once again grasped at the breasts of the Church with great yearning. I moved myself closer and pulled at them so that what could preserve me and reach me as new life and hope for renewal of life and salvation might flow out to me in my situation. What should I say of myself? You, who were not yet a Christian, had little ability to oppose my rush forward to hear and to prove that which you set aside. Tell me, I ask, recall what gave you joy with them other than a certain great ostentation and a promise of self-evident insight? Only too late did I see that it is very easy for an average scholar to speak much and for long and with great gravity of the errors of the ignorant. If they bring us something of their own characteristic, we think it must necessarily be accepted *since something else with which we could satisfy ourselves would not be offered.* They treat us like the deceptive bird catchers are accustomed to do; with birdlime on branches beside water they trick the thirsty birds. *They remove and hide in every way the water that is found everywhere, or they frighten the birds back from it with treacherous arts so that they are handed over to their treachery not through free will but of necessity.*

But why did I not answer myself as follows? Such fine and crafty comparisons and similar reproofs can be spread out sharply and bitingly against all who learn something from their opponents. Because of this I believed that I must demand that they stand back from such things, leave ragged positions, set material against material, content against content, ground against ground" (*On the Profit of Believing*, 1:1-2).[56] In another place he writes: "They attracted others because they promised to make the darkest matter clear, and by this chiefly to find the Catholic Church at fault because she prescribed faith for those who came to her, whereas they laid no yoke of faith (*jugum credendi*) upon anyone. But they prided themselves on opening the source of doctrine. What, you say, could be more praiseworthy? No, it is not so. They did not do this in the consciousness of their power, but to create for themselves a great following under the pretext of independent insight. The human soul naturally rejoices in such a promise" (Ibid., 21).[57]

In his *Confessions* Augustine often notes that he never knew the simplest doctrine of the Church and yet was the strongest Manichaean proselytizer. The characteristics of the Church had been presented to him as almost absurd, and the less one seemed to need to take pains to consider these characteristics, the more certain was Augustine that they could be cast aside. Only after he had frequently heard Ambrose in Milan did the significance of the Church's characteristics first strike him. "For first, these things also had begun to appear to me *to be* defensible; and the Catholic faith, for which I fancied nothing could be said against the attacks of the Manichaeans, I now conceived might be maintained without presumption; especially after I heard one of two parts of the Old Testament explained, and often allegorically—which when I accepted literally, I was 'killed' spiritually. . . . Yet I did not then see that for that reason the Catholic way was to be held because its learned advocates, who at length, and not irrationally, answer objections; nor that what I held ought therefore be condemned because both sides were equally defensible " (*Confessions*, 5:14, 24). "Rejoicing, I blushed that for so many years I had barked not against the Catholic faith, but against the fables of carnal imaginations" (Ibid., 6:3-4). "The more shame I felt that, having been so long deluded and deceived by the promise of certainties, I had, with *puerile error and petulance*, prated of so many uncertainties as if they were certainties" (Ibid., 6:4-5).

With precise logic he develops the following statements in *On the Profit of Believing*: It is certainly a basic principle of the Church to demand in the first place faith in her authority, but one is to consider that everything human proceeds from faith. The disciple believes the teacher, the child its parents. Jesus worked miracles in the first place to give an external example and to establish belief in his doctrine, the truth of which all persons were to make their own internally. His friend, Honoratus, to whom Augustine wrote, might now see how things were. Hundreds of sects promised the truth, but all, especially those that boasted they were able to give an internal insight right at the beginning, first demanded faith in their authority, at least insofar as one acknowledged on their word that their system of proof was valuable until one proved it for oneself. One must now ask with whom among all these parties requiring faith one is to begin. A step above all the rest is the Catholic Church, worthy of honor by her greatness, her age, her direct descent from the apostles. To her one should first turn. Now Augustine proceeds: One must accept that a Church that has all authority for itself will continue forever. In her one can rely since all things proceed from authority. "When therefore we see so great help of God, so great progress and fruit, shall we doubt to hide ourselves in the bosom of the Church, which even unto the confession of a human race from *the* apostolic chair through successions of bishops (heretics in vain lurking around her and being condemned partly by the judgment of the very people, partly also by the weight of councils, partly also by the majesty of miracles) has held the summit of authority? To be unwilling to grant her the first place is either surely the height of impiety or headlong arrogance. For, if there be no sure way into wisdom and health of souls unless where faith prepares them for reason (the self-evident inner conviction),[58] what else is it to be ungrateful for the Divine help and aid, than to wish to resist authority furnished with so great labor?" (*On the Profit of Believing*, 35). One may compare with this Augustine's statement in *On True Religion*: "Another thing that must be considered is the dissension that has arisen among individuals concerning the worship of the one God. We have heard that our predecessors, at a stage in faith on the way from temporal things up to eternal things, followed visible miracles. They could do nothing else. And they did so in such a way that it should not be necessary for those who came after them. When the Catholic Church had been founded and diffused throughout the whole world, on the one hand, miracles were not allowed to continue till our time, lest the mind should always seek visible things, and the human race should grow cold by becoming accustomed to things that when they were novelties kindled its faith. On the other hand, we must not doubt that those are to be believed who proclaimed miracles, which only a few had actually seen, and yet were able to persuade whole peoples to follow them. At that time the problem was to get people to believe before anyone was fit to reason about divine and invisible things. No human authority is set over the reason of a purified soul, for it is able to arrive at a clear truth. If there were no pride, there would be no heretics, no schismatics, no circumcised, no worshippers of creatures or of images" (25:47).

These final thoughts, for the most part taken from *On the Profit of Believing,* prove that the Catholic Church's practice of first requiring belief necessarily proceeds from the characteristic of religious truth. Inner conviction, inner faith, unmediated spiritual insight is first a result of life in the Church, the continual purification of all evil in the soul. "But do you not think that the person who does this first believes that the goal set forth can be reached, and who purifies his or her life in obedience to certain great and necessary precepts will not reach pure truth? You certainly think so. . . . *Which path can be holier than that by which one first prepares oneself to accept the truth,* in that one ascribes to faith what was ordained by God for the preparation and preparatory exercise of the soul" (*On the Profit of Believing,* 24).[59] "I do not hold it as the holiest thing before inner insight, if one is not yet prepared to reach that insight, to form the soul by faith for the reception of the seed of truth, but chiefly that it is necessary that sick souls might not otherwise come to health again."[60] After he has mentioned the virtues that are found among Christians, he speaks of the unmediated impression on them: "People always complain of their weakness, that they are not able to do anything because of it, without coming closer to God, without lifting up a holy disposition. This occurred by divine foresight in the prophets, by the Incarnation and teaching of Christ, by the journeys of the apostles, by the suffering of the martyrs, by their crucifixion, their blood, their death, *the preaching life of the saints*" (Ibid., 35).[61] Thereafter, he says that one begins with external faith in the authority of the Church, although one does so for good reasons, but that one ends with the inner freest act of the Spirit, out of which can be seen the falsity of the schools who begin with what is to be at the conclusion: "*Not all of that* (which determines external belief—in the early period miracles and later the appearance of the Church) *is necessary* for the wise. Who would deny it?" (The concept of the wise person he gives in 33: "The wise person is so bound with God in the Spirit that nothing comes between the two and divides them; for God is truth and no one is wise who does not grasp truth in the Spirit."[62]) *But it concerns itself with this in that we can be wise, that is, grasp the truth,* which a spotted soul cannot do. These spots of the soul are, to put it briefly, the love of anything except God and the soul. *The purer anyone is of these spots, the easier it is for that person to see truth. Thus, to wish to see the truth so as to purify the soul, since one thus purifies it to see, is certainly false and misdirected*" (Ibid., 35).[63] Augustine has thus victoriously proven what he wished to prove. "It is my intention, if I am able to accomplish it, to set forth that the Manichaeans thoughtlessly and with unholy dispositions attack those who follow the authority of the Catholic faith before they can grasp the truth which can only be seen with a pure spirit and who are by faith prepared and made ready for God who enlightens them" (Ibid., 2).[64]

With great depth he answers the one-sided use of the Holy Scriptures by the Manichaeans by which they promise to give an independent testimony. Indeed, he states that their defense does not preserve an inner insight, but establishes only an external faith, a prior acceptance based *on the view* of someone else by which an individual establishes that he or she made a correct interpretation. It is only an independent faith if one perceives for oneself that one has received an unmediated certainty by experience gained from the Bible through interpretation. From this one again sees the externality of the faith of the schools, their literal and conceptual orientation, and how deeply the essence of faith is understood through the Spirit of the Catholic Church. "Believe the Scriptures," he says. "But every composition, if it be brought forward new and unheard of, or commended by a few with no reason (self-insight)[65] to confirm it, it is not the piece of writing that is believed, but those who bring it forward. . . . Curb, I pray you, your obstinacy and that untamed lust, I know not what, of spreading your name: and advise me rather to seek the chief of this multitude and to seek with care and pains to learn *something concerning these writings from these (the Church),*[66] *but for whose existence I should not know what I had to learn at all*. But return into your dens, and lay not any snares under the name of truth that you do not endeavor to take from those to whom you yourself grant authority"(Ibid., 31). The central point of this whole book is the statement: "*Unless those things be believed, which each one, if he shall conduct himself well and shall be worthy, attains unto and understands, and altogether without a certain weighty power of authority, true religion can in no way be rightly entered upon*" (Ibid., 21). Augustine often comes upon the charges of the schools that the Catholic Church compels individuals to faith, wishes and brings forth only a faith in authority, and shrinks back from a free independent insight.

Thus, in Letter 118, 5 after he has noted that error in regard to God and divine things is caused by sin ("Wherefore, seeing that the minds of human beings are, through the pollution of sin and the lust of the flesh so blinded that even these monstrous errors could waste in discussion concerning them the leisure of learned individuals"), he comes to the point that Christ, by the total impression that his earthly appearance made, required prior external faith in himself and by this a holy life, the sources of the knowledge of his doctrine: "Will you, Dioscorus, or will any individual of an observant mind, hesitate to affirm that in no way could better provision have been made for the pursuit of truth by humankind than that a man, assumed into ineffable and miraculous union by Truth himself and being the manifestation of his person on earth, should *by perfect teaching and divine acts move individuals to saving faith* in that which could not as yet be intellectually apprehended?" He continues: "Those who do not find themselves in the unity of the Catholic community but pride themselves with the name Christian, see themselves constrained to be opposed to faith and dare to deceive the inexperienced under the pretext of protecting independent insight (*et audent imperitos quasi ratione traducere*), although the Lord himself came chiefly as a means for salvation and required faith of the people. But they are also constrained, as I said, because they stand far back if their authority is set beside that of the Catholics. They attempt to conquer the authority of the firmly established Church with the words and promises of self-sufficient reason (*conantur ergo auctoritatem stabilissimam fundatissimae ecclesiae quasi rationis nomine superare*), *for this is the same regular judgment of all heretics.* But that ruler of faith (*fidei imperator*), who gives joy to all, surrounded the Church with a fortress and foresight by the most famous churches of peoples and nations, by the apostolic sees, and armed her by a few, pious, learned, and truly spiritual individuals with the full richness of invincible grounds (*invinctissimae rationes*), and this is the most fitting discipline that takes the weak above all into the citadel of faith where they are made safe and are protected by the most powerful means."[67]

Augustine distinguishes faith (still resting only in the authority of the Church which always walks in the place of Christ), the knowledge of reflection, and finally unmediated certainty, spiritual sight. Heresy begins from the point of reflection where the individual, not bound to the whole in love and thus not held by it, cannot be finished with reflection in a mediated knowledge of the Christian religion by concepts of the understanding, but believes it has discovered contradictions and the like, and therefore frees itself. For Augustine the true standpoint occurs if one, regardless of such movements that arise among many[68] over time, remains in the community which takes up a holy life streaming from the Church, allows oneself to be formed throughout by this, and so begets, in oneself independently, the faith of the Church. Augustine does not mean that having come to this point, one *grasps* all individual points of faith. Rather, he says more often, they do not allow themselves to be adequately conceptualized, and one must always seek to raise oneself above concepts. One must *live* in the truth which is in fact much greater than to know by concepts. Here the *living conscious* unity, which was earlier only unconscious and hoping, enters the Church. *Love*, the mysterious and hidden work of the Holy Spirit, is first unconsciously bound to the Church; *holiness*, which streams out of this into the life of single individuals filling it with divine power, and *truth* have passed over into a living unity. It is unnecessary to note that Augustine completely agrees with the Fathers of the first three centuries, whose testimonies were introduced in the earlier chapters.[69]

If we look at the beginning of heresy, we note that it arises at the same time as Gnosticism, whereas the Church was only preaching and requiring faith. The character and the difference of both reflect themselves very well in this. Heresy *knows directly*, but the Church *first believes*; after that knowledge concerning faith is added. It is, therefore, necessary that the greatest shallowness and superficiality must appear among the heretics. Preserving her original character, the Church can never establish freedom in thought as her first principle and foundation, but rather life, love, and faith in the community out of which freedom forms itself. Fully developed heresy must always first establish freedom and can never be that without being unfaithful to its origin and contradicting itself. It cannot be free of its nothingness without abolishing itself. Finally, this relationship between faith and knowing was held at all times, as Anselm of Canterbury, for example, proves. His oft-quoted statement, "I do not understand that I might believe, but I believe that I might understand," would have been less challenged by scholars had the latter clearly understood the relation of this truth to the essence of Christianity. (See Schrökh, *Kirchengeschichte*, 28:397[70] [who holds that Anselm was not a Christian and that the adage "faith seeking understanding" is unphilosophical and leads to persecution].)

Addendum 7

Comments on the Allegorical-Mystical Interpretation, Chiefly that of Origen

The observations on the allegorical-mystical interpretations of the Church fathers in the first centuries, their origin and true meaning, their relationship to the expansion and defense of Christianity, and the period of their decline is one of the most miraculous phenomena in the ancient Church. To this point it has in no way been as properly evaluated as it ought. Huet in his *Origeniana* as well as the learned Benedictine de la Rue, the latter better than the former (in his preface), have certainly described the matter very well, especially as it was understood by Origen, but, it seems to me, they have not treated it comprehensively enough.[71] The allegorical method of interpretation was certainly based on the allegorical exegesis of the writings of Homer, Hesiod, and all of ancient mythology as carried out for a long time earlier. Moreover, the Idealistic School of the Alexandrians and that of the Palestinian Jews had done the same with the Old Testament. It is also known that Origen supported his practice by reference to passages in the New Testament (Gal. 4:21; 1 Cor. 10:4; 2 Cor. 3:6; Gal. 2:16, 17; etc.). In addition the whole Jewish people must have appeared to Christians as a prophetic and mystical nation in which lay a great invitation to the allegorical method of exegesis, an invitation far greater for Christians than for Jews. But, as one might expect, many of these inducements had the opposite effect. Since individual Greek philosophic schools interpreted writers allegorically, should not the Christians be led to treat their authors in a different way? How could a Christian compare in the same way the Greek myths and the Holy Scriptures that had been given by the apostles? And if one had reason to interpret the Old Testament in an allegorical-mystical manner, this method was not fitting for the New Testament. With Christ the fullness of time came.[72] *All evidence indicates that the allegorical-mystical interpretation as practiced in the ancient Church and regulated by Origen was intended to explain things in the Scriptures that were in themselves unclear and that were not understood. One was particularly induced to use the method because of pagan seizure of the Holy Scriptures and because of heretical teachers. How extensively allegorical interpretation served in the expansion of Christianity among Jews and pagans cannot be reckoned. It stands together in an essential union with the begetting of a pure apprehension of Christianity, and all this in sum is the most living proof that the high value placed on the Holy Scriptures proceeded from nurture in the Christian Church and that the possibility of maintaining pure Christianity must be sought far more deeply than in the simple assertion that we have a Holy Scripture. It was on the same basis that we first came to believe that truth was set down undistorted in the Holy Scriptures.*

Passages of Origen such as the following concerning the Mosaic law should be noted. "If, according to this understanding (the allegorical),[73] we say that the Supreme God has proclaimed the laws to human beings, I think that the legislation will seem worthy of the divine majesty. But if we stand by the letter and we accept what is written according to this or what the Jews believe or what it appears to be according to the multitude, I would be ashamed to say and to confess that God gave such laws. For human laws, for instance, either of the Romans, or the Athenians, or the Spartans, seem more elegant and reasonable. But if the Law of God is received according to this understanding as the Church teaches, then clearly it surpasses all human laws and is believed to be truly the Law of God. And so, with these first fruits for spiritual understanding, as we reminded you, let us speak briefly about clean and unclean animals" (Origen, "Homily 7 on Leviticus," 5). "If we come to the laws of Moses many are absurd and impossible in their plain sense" (Origen, "On First Principles," 4:17). "Now who is there, pray, possessed of understanding, that will regard the statement as appropriate, that the first day, and the second, and the third, in which both evening and morning are mentioned, existed without sun, moon, and stars—the first day even without a sky? And who is found so ignorant to suppose that God, as if he had been a husbandman, planted trees in paradise, in Eden toward the East." And regarding the New Testament he says similar things: "The same style of scriptural narrative occurs abundantly in the Gospels, as when the devil is said to have placed Jesus on a lofty mountain to show him all the kingdoms of the world and their glory. How could it literally come to pass either that Jesus should be led up by the devil into a high mountain or that the latter should show him all the kingdoms of the world (as if they were lying beneath his bodily eyes, and adjacent to one mountain), that is, the kingdoms of the Persians and the Scythians and the Indians? Or how could he show in what manner the kings of these kingdoms are glorified by human beings? And many other instances similar to this will be found in the Gospels by anyone who will read them with attention, and will observe that in those narratives that appear to be literally recorded, there are inserted and interwoven things that cannot be admitted historically, but that may be accepted in a spiritual signification" (Ibid., 16). Many other difficult matters in the New Testament he treats in ibid., 28. There are in the Holy Scripture impossibilities, contradictions, and other such things. What results are to follow from this? It is clear that it is not a divine writing since the first necessity for such a piece is that it be free of such things. The pagans came to such a conclusion, as did many heretical teachers, partly in regard to all, partly to a number of biblical books. What did Origen conclude? Clear contradictions, *obvious* foolishness, must be at times present in the Holy Scriptures so that one will not evade penetrating deeper than the literal sense, and so that one will seek there a hidden, higher, spiritual sense on all sides and continue to seek this where there is no obvious impossibility, where the historical-grammatical interpretation can be accepted without further study. If everything were clear, understandable, and obvious at first sight, one would never have been inclined to seek an anagogical level. "But as if, in all the instances of this covering, the logical connection and order of the law had been preserved, we would not certainly believe, when thus possessing the meaning of Scripture in a continuous series, that anything else was contained in it save what was indicated on the surface; so for that reason divine wisdom took care that certain stumbling blocks or interruptions to the historical meaning should take place, by the introduction into the midst of certain impossibilities and incongruities" (Origen, *On First Principles*, 4:15). "Nor was it only with regard to those Scriptures that were composed before the advent of Christ that the Holy Spirit thus dealt" (Ibid., 4:16). One wonders if all this is something other than the thought that one does not understand the Holy Scriptures correctly? As if Origen only sought to help himself from this possibility insofar as he could?[74] The comment is certainly neither false nor insignificant that the Holy Scriptures were highly venerated not so much because of the correct and clear insight that what they contained was divine but because what was introduced by heretics contained the opposite. Likewise, the reasons by which our contemporaries wish to demonstrate the Scripture's authenticity as one demonstrates the authenticity of secular literature are useless. The third century could assent to no *such external* reasons for accepting the Scriptures as uncorrupted if they were convinced that evident contradictions and things unworthy of God were found in them. It was the nurture in these, the nurture in the Church, that was considered to be so completely

under a special direction of God that what was generally accepted
by the Church as enlivened by the Spirit of God could not be
considered a human work. One came to the Holy Scriptures with the
highest veneration and respect for them, *presupposing* that even if it
appeared so, nevertheless there *was* nothing in them unworthy of God,
however one explained them (and what do we do but this?). To put it
another way, one did not have to know and penetrate everything in
the Scriptures. This Irenaeus clearly said and it is inherent in
Origen's insight. But what is required for one to gain possession of
a holy writing? Are these comments more striking if one notes why
Origen and the other allegorists found no contradictions in the *actual*
and *characteristic* doctrine of the Holy Scriptures and only in special
and unnoteworthy places? Why were such not found in the doctrine
of God in the form of a servant, in a suffering God? These doctrines
seemed obviously contradictory, as pagans, Jews, and many so-called
Christians stated. Why not in the doctrine of *one* God who is
threefold? This also appeared to many as a contradiction. Why does
Origen declare that Sabellianism which seems to be far from
contradictory is nothing other than superstition? (*On First Principles*,
preface). Why like so many heretics does one find no contradiction
between the Jewish and Christian revelations which are said to come
from one God when they have so distinct a character? That one does
not find contradictions in these and other matters is not because the
Holy Scriptures as such are not able to contain even obvious
contradictions. It would not have been difficult for Origen following
his rules of interpretation to find a loophole and explanation for the
contradictions. But those doctrines were so rooted in him and stood
so firmly in his Christian being and life that he could not and would
not count them among the points to be treated allegorically or
mystically. The Holy Scriptures as such were not able to provide him
with a critique that could be used in relation to the aforementioned
and other basic doctrines as well as for those matters that appeared
to him as contradictory. This critique flowed from elsewhere, from
the Church and its nurture (see section 4, near the end). Origen
speaks clearly on this in *On First Principles*, 4:9. Before he explains
his insight concerning allegorical-mystical interpretation he says: "To
those who are convinced that the Holy Scriptures are not the work
of human beings, but were written and came to us through the gift
of the Holy Spirit according to the will of the Father and Jesus
Christ, we dare point out how one is to read them according to our
judgment *so that they will hold fast to the rule of the heavenly Church*

(ekklēsia ouranios) of Jesus Christ as it came to us through apostolic succession."[75] The "heavenly church" is not to be interpreted according to any "law of allegory" where the natural and supernatural world correspond and are separated from one another as do the "carnal" and "spiritual Jerusalem." Rather by the phrase "through apostolic succession" it is proven that what is meant is the ever visible, unbroken, continuing Church of Jesus Christ who came down from heaven. When it is noted further that the allegorical-mystical rules of interpretation must be ordered to the Canon of the Church, this is not to say that the Church gave the allegorical-mystical rules of interpretation or established interpretations since these are first to be sought. Shortly after the section quoted he writes: "Now, that there are certain mystical economies made known by the Holy Scriptures all, and the most simple of those who hold to the word, have believed. But what these are, candid and modest individuals confess that they do not know"[Ibid., 4]. The sense of the passage, if we reflect on the beginning of the section, must be: the false, unchristian, so-called conceptions (section 8) that are taken from the Holy Scriptures come from interpretations according to the dead letter ("not understanding the Scripture according to its spiritual meaning, but the interpretation of it according to the letter" [Ibid.]). The Scripture must be spiritually interpreted because it is given by the Holy Spirit, the Spirit is given by the Church, and the Church was founded by Jesus and has come to us through an unbroken succession. What contradicts the Church must be rejected as false. Compare [Origen] "Homily 7 on Leviticus," 5: "If *what the Church teaches* is received as the law of God according to this understanding, it exists above all human beings." Note as well the preface to *On First Principles*, 8: "Then, finally, the Scriptures were written by the Spirit of God and have a meaning not only as is apparent at first sight, but also another, which escapes the notice of most. For those words that are written are the forms of certain mysteries, and the images of divine things. Respecting these there is one opinion of the whole Church, that the whole law is indeed spiritual; but that the spiritual meaning that the law conveys is not known to all, but only to those on whom the grace of the Holy Spirit is bestowed in the word of wisdom and knowledge." This is nothing other than to say that the Holy Scripture must be spiritually interpreted, that is, it can and must never be found in contradiction with the testimony of the Church. How this is to be done is dependent on the insight of her members. One sees from this that it is not a restriction of the exegete

if the exegete interprets the Holy Scripture according to the doctrine of the Church, and that it is not freedom if one explains the Scripture in whatever way it strikes one to do so.[76] One also sees that the explication of the Scripture from the life of the Church did not begin first in the fifth or sixth centuries or only in the Latin Church. One sees further what is the case when the Catholic asserts that the Church explains the Holy Scriptures: interpretation is related to the totality, to the spirit of the whole, not to single passages that Origen interpreted according to this exegetical method. There is something uncommonly significant, inspired, and truly divine in the way a Catholic reads the Scriptures. The Catholic reads them with the totality of believers, which without distinction in time is bound together through one Spirit. It is as if they were all together united in one holy temple where the Spirit stirs and moves through all, as if all were one soul, as if one family read the same letter of a loving and beloved father. All are there flooded over by the same feeling, *but as the thought of one or the other child goes deeper, the child finds it more lively, powerful, and encompassing.* This is what is meant by the Council of Trent's *unanimis consensus* [unanimous consent], the image of unity in all freedom.[77]

From this point it is clear how in the early Church where a capricious allegorical-mystical interpretation ruled so greatly from the time of the letter of Barnabas to Origen, not only did the teaching of Christ and the apostles not fall away, but, as all assert, it was most purely preached and all false opinions, as manifold and strong as they might be, were victoriously suppressed. In this we are directed to a higher, unconquerable power penetrating the Church, and we learn to grasp Christ and his word: *I am with you to the end of the world* [Matt. 28:20]. If our age had the courage to penetrate into the depths of the history of Christianity, how many of its words of power would seem expressions of weakness! But since they wish to teach themselves and rise above all times, they understand neither earlier times nor themselves. The allegorical-mystical interpretation saves for many the esteem of the Holy Scriptures and the teaching of the gospel. Origen turned all his intellect and all possible intelligence to its foundation. Most of what he says on this topic has, in spite of his sincerity, little use, but the attacks of the heretics were overcome in the eyes of his contemporaries, their conclusions against the characteristic of the gospel lost their power, and as de la Rue rightfully notes, believers in the Church were confirmed and the pagans won over.

The truths of the gospel are true and remain so, beyond the passing conclusions that confirmed them. We need a bridge to cross the water to firm land. Examples are that bridge, but once we reach truth, it roots itself in us and created examples are not so greatly needed. Each age has its own, and many bridges, moving and standing, wood and stone,[78] leading over the stream. Origen and others saved the esteem of the Holy Scriptures, but the manner of the rescue counts for nothing.[79] How such uses were still necessary in the fourth century to explain the Holy Scriptures, many passages in Augustine indicate. He heard the Scripture explained mystically by Ambrose in Milan, and this was for him the first incentive to doubt the Manichaean errors: "Many places of those books having been expounded to me, I now blamed my despair on having believed that no reply could be made to those who hated and derided the law" (Augustine, *Confessions*, 5.14. 24). "I rejoiced also that the old Scriptures of the law and the prophets were laid before me to be perused not now with the eye by which they seemed absurd when I attacked your holy ones for so thinking, whereas in truth they did not so think. Happily I heard Ambrose in his sermons to the people often most diligently recommend this rule: 'The letter kills, but the spirit gives life' [2 Cor. 3:6]. Opening the mystic veil he spiritually explained what seemed to teach perversity according to the letter, teaching nothing that offended me although he taught such things that I did not as yet know were true" (Ibid., 6:4, 6). How significant and deep were the remarks he later made over the law and its relationship to Christianity! The history of his formation in this is certainly the form of the early and later Christian Church. An unaided small mystical explanation of single Old Testament passages led him to the truth until, possessing it, a great conception was possible. The spirit "of the Church according to the apostolic succession" taught the early Fathers so that they could and dared find nothing in the Holy Scripture unworthy of God or contradicting general faith. They helped themselves through intelligent, wise, and spiritual insights. Thus they rescued the Holy Scriptures for their descendants who were gifted with richer formation, greater experience, and filled with more opportunity for deeper insights.

Finally, through the basely carnal explication of the Holy Scriptures that had arisen so externally in the Church and of which there were many examples evident in the following periods, one was necessarily led to the other extremity. From this the following results can be seen. These explain all that has been said to this point. After paganism had almost been conquered and the sects that attacked the Catholic Church had been rendered harmless (allegory had been called in as a help against them), after the Chiliast, Montanist, and other base notions of Christianity had been for the most part overcome, the allegorical-mystical exegetical method of Origen began to be set aside and the Antiochine School arose specifically in antithesis to it. The allegorical-mystical method did not in any way cease thereafter nor had the grammatical method not been present earlier; the letter was a principle in Origen's mystical method. What is noteworthy, however, from all this and for all times is, as we have already said, this: if the Church were grounded on changeable hermeneutical principles, she would not be served with the name "Church," nor would she designate commonly and firmly what Christianity is. She must continually distinguish her faith from a changing hermeneutic, and a higher law, a deeper ground by which Christianity will be carried, must be acknowledged. The suggestion, so prized in modern times, that one must explain the Christian Holy Scriptures as one does pagan writers, is not new. Already in ancient times, the Holy Scriptures were interpreted like Homer, Hesiod, and others. Using this principle according to changed circumstances will do no less damage to Christianity now than it did then.[80]

Addendum 8

Augustine on the Behavior of a Person
Persecuted by a Party in the Church

In *On True Religion*, 11, he writes: "Often Divine Providence allows even pious people to be locked out from the community of Christians by the stormy unrest of carnally minded individuals. If they patiently endure insult and injury for the sake of the peace of the Church and do not attempt to bring in schismatic or heretical novelties, they will teach people the type of disposition and upright love with which one is to serve God. Such individuals intend, after the storms have calmed, to return. If this does not occur because the storm continues or because a wilder one would be stirred up by their return, they maintain their will to help even those who were responsible for the storms and unrest and they do not form new congregations. They defend to the death and support by their testimony the faith so that it continues to be proclaimed in the

Catholic Church. These the Father, who sees secretly, crowns in secret. Such people are rare but there are examples. Indeed, there are more than one might suppose."[81] Compare Augustine, *On Baptism*, 1:17. What infinite love does the mind which can thus speak bear within itself.[82]

Addendum 9

[Origen on Unity]

In the most manifold changes Origen requires unity. Thus he somewhere notes the characteristic of the Holy Scripture in which singular and plural are often switched. He writes as follows: "When God gives Adam a commandment in Genesis 2:16-17, he says, 'From every tree in Paradise you [singular] may eat, but from the tree of the knowledge of good and evil you [plural] are not to eat; on the day in which you [plural] eat of it, you [plural] will die.'[a/83] He begins with the singular and moves to the plural. If he gives a commandment by which he wishes to protect their lives, he uses the singular, for those who follow God and hold firmly to his will form, although they are many, a unity through their agreement. As a result he uses the singular when he speaks of receiving a good (eat [you singular]). Since, however, division occurs in disobedience, he no longer speaks in the singular but in the plural. Thus he also uses the plural when he describes Adam and Eve as mourning and crying to God. After they have found God, however, the text no longer reads: 'He spoke to *them*,' but 'to *him*,' because the many were one in that they had found God and heard his teaching. One person becomes many in sin; because the individual is divided from God, divided from and falls from unity. But many, in obedience to God are one,

---

a. [Greek text of biblical passage cited.] Origen used the Greek translation. The Hebrew does not read in accordance with it. That such contrasts arise is true; that there are none here does not affect my argument since I am concerned with describing the disposition of the period, not its linguistic knowledge. The reason Origen came to this conclusion is notable for a further characteristic of this period. He says [just prior to the section quoted]: "Since the words of Scripture have the form of a solecism, they confuse the reader by their language, with the result that the reader incorrectly suspects (it is not what they in fact show) that the writings are not divine letters *and thus some dare to change the Scriptures on the pretext of emendation*" [*Commentaries on Hosea*]. His criticism also has an apologetic intention. Cf. Addendum 7.

as the Apostle says 'We many are one bread and body' (1 Cor. 10:17), and elsewhere 'We, though many, are one body in Christ' (Rom. 12:5), and again 'one God, one Christ, one faith, one baptism' (Eph. 4:5). That those who please the Lord are one is seen in Christ's prayer to God for his disciples: 'Holy Father,' he says, 'I pray that as we are one so they may be one in us' [John 17:21]. If the saints are called completing members, what are they other than one body? In the *Shepherd* of Hermas the one tower built of many stones is seen as if it was built from *one* stone. What does this work indicate other than that the tower is of the same disposition and unity?" ("Fragments on Hosea"). He also discusses the singular and the plural in his *Commentary on Romans* where he explains his view of the restitution of all things. There he describes the Church as the form of that holy state.[84] In *On First Principles*, 1:6, 2, he writes: "And in keeping with this is the declaration of the same apostle when he exhorts us who even in the present life are placed in the Church, in which is the form of that kingdom which is to come, to the same similitude of unity saying: 'That you all speak the same thing and that you not be divided among yourselves, but that you be perfectly joined together in the same mind and in the same judgment' [1 Cor. 1:10-11]."[85] Thus Origen writes against heresies and splinters; they cannot arise without contradicting themselves. But he does not simply speak in an apologetic, polemical manner of the unity and community of all. At every opportunity he endeavors to bring this characteristic of the Church to consciousness. Nothing works more significantly for the formation of a truly Christian mind than making the idea of community truly active in believers.

Addendum 10

Augustine on the Heresies, as Instigations
to a Clearer Development of Christian Doctrine

In *On True Religion*, 8:15, Augustine writes: "It is truly written, 'There must be heresies so that they which are approved may be revealed among you' [1 Cor. 11:19]. Thus let us make use of this gift of Divine Providence. From among such people come heretics who even if they are in the Church, are in error. If they were outside the Church they would be of great use not because they would teach the truth (because they do not know it), but because they could stir up *those who had a sensual faith to seek the truth and the spiritual Catholics to explicate it.* There are many approved by God in the holy Church, but these are not revealed among us *as long as we rejoice in the darkness of our ignorance and would rather sleep than look upon the light of truth.* In this way many *are awakened from their sleep by heretics so that they may see and enjoy the day of God.* Let us therefore use the heretics not so as to approve their errors but so as to assert Catholic teaching against their pretenses and to become *more vigilant and cautious,* even if we are not able to recall them to the doctrine of salvation."[86] Compare his *Enarrations on Psalms,* 67, n39, where he translates verse 31 from the Hebrew, *mithrappes b'ratsê keseph* [a crux text, translated "humbled with bars of silver"], incorrectly as "those who are tested with silver *are excluded.*" By this translation he comes to the correct conclusion that Christian consciousness arises more clearly and develops more greatly, the more specific the battle with the heretics becomes. "Among the silver smiths are those called *exclusores* who make vessels in a certain shop from a formless mass (*qui de confusione massae noverunt forma vasis exprimere*). Much contained in the Holy Scripture is hidden and known only in slightly deeper insights. It will not be explained more clearly and better except if one is required to answer heretics. In such a case those who are not driven to study by themselves are awakened from their slumber and made aware that the opposition can be refuted."[87]

Very often he comes back to these ideas and seems eager to correct the unconcern and laziness that so often through its lack of the deep penetration and free movement of the Spirit falls into error, begets error, provides opportunity for justifiable attack, and is not in a position to convince others of their evil. *Enarrations on the Psalms,* 54, n2, serves this image: "Moreover because of heretics the Catholic faith is asserted and because of those who think evilly, those who think well are tested. Many things lie hidden in the Scriptures and the heretics are clever; they stir up the Church of God with questions. . . . Because of this they are named according to the art of silversmithing *exclusores,* that is, the expressers of form from a certain confused mass. As a result many who are able to investigate and study the Scriptures will lie hidden among the people of God and do not set out the solution to difficult questions since no attacker has raised any. Would a perfect discussion of the Trinity have arisen before the Arians railed against it, would a perfect treatise of penance have been written before Novatian stood against it, would a perfect treatment of baptism have been written before the rebaptizers publicly contradicted it? Those things that were central to the unity of Christ (of the Church)[88] would not have been said except after separation began to trouble the weak, and those persons who were able to discuss and solve these questions, opposing the questions of the impious, publicly explained by their sermons and disputations the obscurities in the law so that the weak not perish." Cf. ibid., Ps. 7, n15, and Ps. 9, n20. Note also *On True Religion*, 25.47: "At that time the problem was to get people to believe before anyone was fit to reason about divine and invisible things. No human authority is set over the reason of a purified soul. But pride does not lead to perception of truth. If there were no pride, there would be no heretics, no schismatics, no circumcised. . . . *If there had not been such opponents before the people was made perfect as promised, truth would be sought much less eagerly.*"

Addendum 11

Augustine's Defense of St. Cyprian: St. Pamphilius's Apology for Origen and Complaints against His Adversary[89]

Nothing is holier for a believer than faith. It is the believer's and humanity's salvation. Every attempt to describe faith rationally must be based on the purest and holiest disposition and be continually accompanied by it. The *individual* believer has[90] seldom, perhaps never, so taken up Christianity into life that *all* life's seeds and branches arose, achieved a characteristic being, and rooted themselves in the believer. If this were the case, which holiness, always able to be aspired to by human beings, presupposes, then the greatest possible gift of knowledge (the greatest scholarly talent that is so bound with it that the researcher brings together all paths, and can grasp all points where *one* life will pour itself out in a new branch) or the knowledge of the inner life, the life development and presentation, must itself create life; this is not possible for us.[91] If the richest inner experience is present, knowledge cannot correspond to its greatness, or vice versa. The greater the misunderstanding, however, the more we are open to errors. The Christian philosopher of religion and every scholarly theologian must acknowledge this and with it, accept the necessity of the common life that completes them. Such a theologian or philosopher must eagerly allow himself or herself to be improved and directed correctly by the Church in which all gifts of the Holy Spirit are communicated to all, not to one individual alone.

What Augustine said so elegantly regarding this is notable for all times.[92] In his *On Baptism against the Donatists*, 2:8, 13, he defended Cyprian's action on rebaptism. He courageously and regularly expressed his individual conviction on this and defended it logically. He noted how one is to look to the whole and to be prepared to give up a position if the opposing reasons are better than one's own. He wished to introduce and further a study of the matter. *However, since he was opposed only by a custom and there was none that was portrayed in its inner relation as significant,* he remained faithful to his conviction, especially *since he had not broken off community with those who held fast to the transmission without being conscious of its inner reasons, but he always expressed himself most energetically on behalf of unity.* The passage reads as follows: "I believe that Cyprian freely expressed himself against the custom (*quid sentisset liberius expromisse*) because of this, and first spoke out against it *on the basis that if there were another who had a better revelation, he would follow it.* He did so also to point out that one must imitate not only diligence in teaching but modesty in learning. But if there was no one who put forward a position so excellent that all probable reasons set against it could be refuted, he would remain faithful to his conviction in trusting consciousness, not giving up what he held as true, and holding to the unity that he loved. Since at the time there were no others than those who opposed him with custom and did not support their position with a defense that could move his great soul (*quibus illa talis anima moveretur*), this firm man would not give up his position, which though untrue (as later seen) was not disproved by the true but not supported custom."[93]

There are many other examples in history that can be added to his in which traditional points of faith were attacked in the strongest and clearest manner. Nor was there any one in the Church who knew how to integrate an attacked opinion so fully into the whole and to present Christianity and its value in concepts so that the attack was weakened. But if one was not capable of a solid conceptual defense, one still held firmly to the life expressing itself in the Church,[94] convinced that this would not be deceptive. And the future guaranteed and still guarantees the victorious dialectic upholding the defense.[95] In general human history there is a fitting analogy. There are certain ideas[96] expressing themselves as facts of consciousness whose presence are testified to as far back as history reaches. And humanity continues, by tradition, to pass them on from one generation to the next, although individuals and even whole schools opposed them. Nevertheless, individuals continued to speak of such ideas and believed in the voice of God revealing itself in the interiority of human persons.[97] How evil in these earlier cases it would have been if the traditional life had allowed itself to be overcome by a concept! (Those who oppose the early Church's belief in tradition and say that Cyprian cast aside tradition and wished only to allow himself to be taught by the Holy Scriptures make themselves laughable.[98] All the passages of Scripture that Cyprian cited in defense of the Scriptures prove nothing. These people honor Cyprian because he cast aside tradition, yet at the same time they must admit that in the very points that he cast out[99] he was in great error.) With Christian truths the case is very special. Because they are grounded in a holy mind and develop from it, one can say with the greatest certainty that what was held firmly from the earliest time by all believers, in spite of all attacks, was not lost, rested on an irrefutable need of Christians, flowed out from the Christian spirit into its elements, and that *Christ himself was its initiator.* Seen from the point of view of history, Augustine's statement in *On Baptism*, 4:24, 32, has great weight: "What is held by the universal Church, and that not as instituted by councils, but as a matter of invariable custom to have been handed down by apostolic authority, is rightly believed."[100] Such a Christian characteristic can in the movement of time be greatly distorted, and it can be defended with poor reasons, but the reasons brought against it will always have an inner nothingness in them or only be effective against distortions.

What Augustine says in *On Baptism*, 3:4, 6, has much truth in it:[101] "I have read Cyprian's letters and would have been convinced by him if I had not been brought to careful observation by the great insights of others. These were equal to him and perhaps beyond him in the grace of insight, an insight begotten throughout the whole world by so many Latin, Greek, and barbarian peoples spread through the Church, the Church that bore Cyprian himself. I cannot believe that they did not agree with him without good reason. I am not of the opinion that on a difficult question it is impossible that one or two see better than many, but one must not lightly, without full consideration and investigation of the matter, decide for oneself or a few against uncountable numbers who hold the same belief, who are of the same community and who are distinguished by great

spirit and rich learning."[102] In the same work, 1:18, 28, he convincing-
ly expressed the idea of catholic unity toward which all Christians
are directed for their fulfillment in a unified whole in love:[103] "For
this reason God did not disclose his error to so great a man, so that
his pious humility and love in the maintenance of the Church
community might be revealed and maintained not only for Christians of his day but for the holy knowledge of all ages. For although
a bishop of such great merit, so great a church, such great power,
rhetoric, and virtue had a different opinion about baptism than is
confirmed by the more closely grasped truth (and even many of his
colleagues, although not with clear consciousness, held what was
held by the earlier custom of the Church and later the whole
Catholic world), nevertheless he did not separate himself from those
who thought otherwise by forming his own congregation, and he did
not cease to counsel the others that they 'forebore one another in
love, eager to maintain the unity of the Spirit in the bond of peace'
(Eph. 4:2-3). *For the bond of the body is to remain so that if there is illness
in any of the members, it might be overcome through the health of the
group rather than result in death by an amputation and no longer offer
caring help.* If he had separated, how many others would have
followed? What kind of name would he have gained for himself?
How much more widely would the Cyprianists have spread than the
Donatists? But he was no son of perdition but of the peace of the
Church. *Endowed with so great an illumination of Spirit he failed to see
one thing and as a result a far greater was seen through him.* And yet the
Apostle writes 'I will show you a still more excellent way: if I speak
with the tongues of mortals and of angels, but have not love, I am
a noisy gong or a clanging cymbal'[104] (1 Cor. 12:31-13:1). Had he
penetrated imperfectly the secrets of the sacraments, known all
mysteries, and lacked love, he would have been nothing. Yet,
although he imperfectly penetrated this mystery, he was honorable,
faithful, and courageous, and thus he achieved a martyr's crown so
that even if his clear spirit as it seemed to human eyes was wrapped
round by a cloud, it might be overcome by the worthy clarity of his
glorious blood. Not in vain did the Lord Jesus call himself a vine
and those who belonged to him grapes on the vine, and say that if
they were cut off from the vine they would be as useless branches
bringing forth no fruit [John 15:1-5]. What is this fruit other than the
new offspring of which he says, 'A new commandment I give to

you, that you love one another' (John 13:34).[b/105] This is the love without which other things are useless. The Apostle says: 'The fruits of the Spirit are love, joy, peace, patience, kindness, goodness, faithfulness, gentleness, self-control' [Gal. 5:22-23]. Love is the source and beginning of these. 'Every branch that does bear fruit he prunes, that it may bear more fruit' [John 15:2]. Those who have the fruit of love in great abundance can still make use of purification of other things. Even these the farmer does not leave untended. Although that holy man thought something different concerning baptism than truth required, and although this was later strengthened by careful research, nevertheless he remained in the Catholic community and his error was outweighed by the riches of his love."[106]

In the same book, 2:5, 6, Augustine writes: "And so it is that often something is imperfectly revealed to the more learned that their patient and humble charity from which proceeds the greater fruit may be proved, either in the way in which they preserve unity when they hold different opinions on matters of comparative obscurity, or in the way in which they receive the truth when they learn that it has been declared to be contrary to what they thought." The charge of the Donatists that Cyprian did not defend rebaptism alone but that many of his contemporaries did so as well is not possible, as Augustine indicates: "If he had been the only one holding that opinion with no one to agree with him, he might have been thought, in remaining, to have shrunk from the sin of schism because he found no companions in his error. But when so many agreed with him, he showed, by remaining in unity with the rest who thought differently from him, that he served the most sacred bond of universal catholicity, not from any fear of isolation but from the love of peace"[107] (*On Baptism*, 6:5, 8. Also significant is ibid., 5:17-22, 23).

But to return to the topic here under consideration. There were those, on the other side, who defended the errors and one-sided views of a Church member, viewing such a person as not distant

---

b. Among the biblical passages with which Augustine supported his conviction, we note those concerning love which today one does not relate to love as identical with the Church community and characteristically arises from it. It is not an arbitrary action, as it seemed to Augustine, to so interpret the passages quoted in an opposite way. This interpretation like so many others in the Church can only be understood and made useful in the life in the Church. That 1 Cor. 13:1 is related to 1 Cor. 12 is indisputable; Galatians 5:32 has a true light compared with v. 20, as has John 13:34 compared with 17:21, 22. The connection of these passages are often noted in Irenaeus, Origen, and Cyprian.

from the disposition of the Church (a thing very easily done), by the power of their gifts, expanding these one-sided views and struggling *in love* to justify the errors. The history of the Church gives us many examples of this and particularly the history of the first three centuries. These indicate that the aforementioned demand arising out of the essence of common life was not always observed. If one wishes to be just, one must concede that the one group failed by too simply forgiving error (through the reflective understanding), the other did so by too rapidly condemning it. *Insofar as they arise out of an innocent heart*, their failures are honorable. They arise from the religious interest of Christians. Many never made an open substantial development of doctrines of faith. Faith itself lived in them but they always knew it as their own and as true only under a certain accepted exterior form, and not capable of finding one form of faith in identity with theirs[108] in open development,[109] they saw it as a deviation. Others did not understand the relationship and the union of the individual with the whole, or they did not know that at times there is no such union to be found. This group was adverse to those who could discover and express nothing. Thus we can always wish that believers bear each other's burdens and see themselves as members of one body.

In the following passage by a martyr, St. Pamphilius, we see strikingly described the carriage of one of the noblest and greatest disciples of his time, of Origen, the behavior of his opponent, and Pamphilius's own noble disposition. The passage is from Pamphilius, *Apology for Origen*, preface: "We note," says Pamphilius, "that Origen carried out his studies with a great fear of God and deep humility, requesting that he be excused what he missed in his all too narrow studies of the text. Often he set such studies aside and stated that he saw the correctness of his explications not as stated (he did not wish to establish anything as final), but that he wrote according to his powers; he states that he searched for the sense of the Holy Scriptures, but in no way was he suggesting that he had purely and perfectly grasped it. In many things he expressed a sure feeling but this did not mean that he always reached perfection. At times we find him stating that he had great doubt concerning many matters. At times he noted that he hesitated in the case of many texts and pointed out the difficulties in them but did not offer a solution. Rather, in all humility and love of truth he was not ashamed to admit that he did not know the answer. He often said (a fact not noted clearly enough by his contemporary ignorant attackers) that if anyone said or wrote something more significant than he did, to such a one attention should be given. Many times he gave many interpretations of one and the same passage since he wrote down what came to him. He did so with great fear, however, as one who knew that he was writing about the *Holy* Scriptures, and he commanded those who were reading his work to test the details of his explanations if there were several of them and to hold to the one that seemed best to the sensible reader. Certainly he knew that not everything that he propounded was likely or certain since the Holy Scriptures contained too many mysteries and hidden truths. To know his full intention one need only note in how pure and catholic a manner he speaks concerning all discussions in his preface to Genesis: '*If they had not been so lazy and weary that they were not able even once to enter into study even though our Lord and Saviour had commanded them to*, I would certainly have been silent in my consciousness of how far I am from that light of spiritual insight that is required in the study of such illustrious subjects.' A little later he says, 'If anyone in study comes upon a difficult passage, that person can comment on it but not by setting aside all other explanations. Only two persons can do so: an insolent person who had lost all feeling of human weakness and is not in control, or perfect persons and those who faithfully know that they are taught by the Lord Jesus himself, that is, those who have a knowledge of the word of truth and its wisdom through which all things were made. I, however, trust only in my average powers, but believe in him and rejoice in the honor of being his disciple. I am not saying that I have received the understanding of his Holy Scriptures face to face. The whole world in its strength and majesty could not attain to such. Therefore, I cannot speak as the apostles, but I thank God that although there are many who do not know their own limitations and who acknowledge worthless and disordered, indeed half-baked and fictional, insights with great power as incontrovertible statements, I am not unknown in my ignorance in such important matters that are beyond my powers of comprehension!'"

Pamphilius continues: "How much better would Origen's disparagers have acted had they acknowledged without preconceptions and with all the uprightness and love of truth that we owe all our colleagues in love that Origen is our neighbor whom we owe love according to the commandment of the Lord, and had they read his books with the mild indulgence that he takes up in his prefaces, they would truly have found something worthy of an insightful judgment.[110] But they now mock and attack without consideration those who according to the commandment of the Lord busy themselves with the Holy Scriptures, frighten others away from reading Origen's books, and assert that one should read anything, even that in bad taste, other than his commentaries. In this they make themselves laughable. In their contentious pride, or to express myself better, to reveal more easily their prejudicial madness, his attackers read a work of his under the name of another, whether mistakenly or deliberately omitted. Such works please and are praised and considered in every way marvellous so long as the author is not known. But as soon as it is known that Origen was the author, what was considered highly pleasing immediately mispleases and is considered heretical, and what had earlier been lifted to heaven is by the same mouth and tongue dragged into hell. It is also the case that at times his attackers do not understand Greek. Some have no learning and others, although they seem to have some knowledge, do not possess enough to read his works. If they have read them, they do not have enough learning to reach and hold the depth of his thoughts by which he has spoken in many consider-ations and connections. There are also many who, if one asks them where in what book or place a certain conception of Origen that they attack is to be found, say that they have no knowledge of it, have not read it, but have their information on hearsay. Their statements are thus laughable since they make judgments on and condemn things that they have never learned and could not understand. Although Origen wrote many books that preserve valuable and instructive material and seldom contain anything that is offensive to the ignorant or envious, others go so far in their rage as to leave aside and pass by everything in this which in their own understand-ing is catholic and serves the upbuilding of the Spirit and training in scientific knowledge. They make no judgments regarding this as they could and should, but zealously learn only that which can be used to attack."[111]

Addendum 12

On the Weakening of the Spiritual Power of Life
through the Skeptical Character of Heresy

If Christianity is accepted in and from life, the first thing that is
grasped is the mind, the seat of power, the strength of the will, and
the continuing source of life. If the dead concept, however, comes
first, which possesses no fruitful power for the mind, the result is a
crippling of religious character and an incapacity to do any truly
great things.[112] This incapacity must be understood as the result of
heresy, as a mere formalism, when one considers that heresy's
confessors came to their conclusions by their studies of those things
that opposed the position of the Church fathers.[113] (It is fortunate that
within its domain, heresy did not continue in its skeptical character
but, maintaining contradictions within itself, preached its doctrines
as entirely certain.) Clement of Alexandria described the characteristic of heretics as[114] a continual battle among themselves and with
others, the unrest springing from this battle against the Catholics
concerning whom[115] he said, "The desire that pleases the pagans, the
strife, the characteristics of heretics, is something other than the joy
that the Church possesses" (*Miscellanies*, 7:16).[116] And in the *Miscellanies*, 2:11, Clement says: "Faith and the knowledge of truth give the
soul a constancy and firmness. Error is inconstancy and change. The
gnostic (according to Clement's use of the term, the perfect Christian)
has rest, peace, and joy."[117] The weakness of the heretics he treats in
a different way, describing the three parties already noted: "There
are three states[118] of the soul: ignorance, self-assurance, and certainty.
The pagans are in ignorance, the heretics possess self-assurance, but
certainty belongs only to the Church" [*Miscellanies*, 7:16].[119] This is
most clearly revealed from the expansion of the Christian religion.
Christianity could gain no proper life among heretics; the swaying,
moving, torn mind could not bring itself under the concern,
suffering, and life experience of preaching the gospel among
pagans.[120]

(Likewise no pagan could be converted by the proclamation of
the gospel according to the principles of heresy. If the heretic wished
to be consistent with the principles of a heretical school in missionary work he or she must begin by saying: freedom of faith is your
basic principle; the highest maxim of your church is the untroubled,
free interpretation of the Holy Scripture; what you believe you must

not leave as a law to your descendants who must be allowed to find something completely different through a free interpretation of Holy Scripture; just as I have found something completely different than many others who wish to be Christians, that is, the heretic must first say nothing to them so as through negations not to make a position concrete or to form authority of faith.[121] I would like to see a pagan who would believe someone coming with the base principle of seeking and standing alone. In this we see the nothingness of heresy correctly. It cannot present its contents without belying its form, and only the person who does not acknowledge this or covers it up is suitable to be a missionary for them)."[122]

Tertullian also complains about this, namely, that they do not endeavor to convert pagans as much as they endeavor to conquer Catholics (*On the Prescription of Heretics*, 42): "But what shall I say concerning the ministry of the Word, since they make it their business not to convert pagans, but to subvert us? This is rather the glory that they catch at, to compass the fall of those who stand, not the raising up of those who are down."[123] The battle among Christians and the belief that Christians do not know what Christianity is has caused Christians infinite trouble. Celsus often cast this charge. I believe that one can understand this by considering a passage in John 17: "I do not pray for these only, but also for those who believe in me through their word that they may all be one . . . and *so that the world may believe that you sent me*" (John 17:20-21). A yet greater result threatens Christianity because of this in that during the persecution the heretics manifested not merely a weakness of character but a lack of character.[124] They avoided persecution by the belief that if Christ was a mere man, one had no need to acknowledge a man.[125] Among the idealistic Gnostics pure conceptual religion took preeminence: true martyrdom was their principle, true knowledge of God. To acknowledge Christianity to the point of death they considered to be suicide (Irenaeus, *Against the Heresies*, 2:32, 9; Eusebius, *Ecclesiastical History*, 5:18). (In Eusebius, *Ecclesiastical History*, 4:15, 46, we find described among the martyrs a Marcionite, Metrodor, and light is cast on this by the passage in Irenaeus already cited that "here and there one" had the courage to confess. Kastner in his *Agape* is to be corrected in that he denies this completely, namely, that it was in the system of some of the heretics to confess).[126] Clement calls this the sophism of their cowardice (*Miscellanies*, 4:4: *theilias sophismata*).[127]

In a more careful manner, Tertullian describes for us the behavior of heretics in persecution. From this we see that they were not ashamed to use the Catholic principle, according to which one could not deny Christ without losing communion with the Church, to increase their numbers during the persecutions.[128] He says: "When faith glowed, when the Church burned, the Gnostics came forward, the Valentinians came forward, and all the attackers of martyrdom came forward[129] to confirm their position. They knew that many simple, ignorant, and weak people existed and they believed that they could not bring these to themselves more quickly than if fear would open an entrance to the soul. This was especially so if terror had crowned the faith of a martyr.[130] At the beginning they walked alongside with a friendly appearance and carefully, almost as if they were saying, without a special disposition, 'Must innocent persons so suffer?' They did so in such a way that it seemed as if they were fellow believers or good pagans. 'A party that has not been despicable would never be so handled![131] Note well: they are lost and for no reason.' Proposition one. Then another is added: 'These simple souls do not know what is written and how it is written concerning what, where, and before whom one must confess the Lord. Much more, one cannot call oneself simple but rather vain; indeed, it is madness to die for God. Who will save me, if the one who is to save me kills me? Christ died for me once; he was killed for me once, so that we do not need to be killed. If he desires this of us, is he also awaiting his salvation by our deaths? Does God desire one's blood, if he casts aside the blood of animals and sheep? Certainly he would rather have the confession of a sinner than his death'"[132] (*Scorpiace*, 1).

From other passages in Tertullian one sees that the heretics narrowed Christ's requirement that one must confess him before others to mean that one must confess him only before the apostles (Ibid., 9), and "before others" meant that they only had to make a confession in heaven (Ibid., 10).[133] In this one sees their whole manner of viewing Christianity.[134] Where is heaven? Is it not where Christ is? And is Christ not in believers? In this one sees the complete division of the present and the future, the opinion that we now only possess a concept of Christ, not Christ himself, and that the Holy Ghost was only given to the apostles.[135] As a result, the later Church is an essentially different Church from the apostolic Church, and every believer is directed to the latter. It also suggests that if *God* is only confessed in faith, it is enough. At this point one can see clearly the concept of the invisible Church which the confessors of Christ are to form, as well as the conceptual union between Christ and his believers and between the believers among themselves. As a result there is a sharp division between the inner and the outer.[136] The Catholic Church teaches an essential living union with Christ. The believer is to have taken this up in his or her whole being.[137] *Being* and *thinking* become a unity in the believer, and, therefore, if the believer is not able to be what he or she thinks, the believer gives up temporal being in which an opposition between being and thinking is demanded and thus maintains his or her eternal being. Moreover, the union among believers is a visible and living union; it is inner love that as an inner union must express itself externally. As a result, the person who cannot maintain this visible community cannot live.[138] As a result, one dies, and, dying, indicates to all and to oneself that one lives in Christ. On the other hand, the person who gives up the living visible union with believers and only wishes to save the invisible one, denies Christ. Such a conceptual and intellectual union with the Church is then looked upon as none at all, and the heretic as a result finds himself or herself outside the Church. Only through repentance and renewal of life can such a one again be taken up into the Church. Here again one meets the connection between the stability and life of the Christian witness and the Church community[139] which we have likewise seen given preeminence by Cyprian.

Tertullian, in *Scorpiace*, 9, clearly penetrates the innermost reasons for the behavior of the heretics. He says that Christ was not understood by them as living but as a mere concept. Unfortunately, his reflection on Luke 12:8 is mistaken because he does not understand Hebrew and bases his interpretation on the Greek words *en emoi* (in me) whereas it is said that those who deny him, deny "me," since the construction of the Hebrew word *hûdhâ* [to declare allegiance to] with *b^e* [in], *l^e* [to], and *eth* [accusative indicator] means the same [to acknowledge me]. But what follows from this is correct: "One who confesses oneself a Christian, bears witness that one is Christ's; one who is Christ's must be in Christ. If one is in Christ, one certainly confesses in Christ, when one confesses oneself to be a Christian. . . . Therefore, it is vain to say that if I deny I am a Christian, I am not denied by Christ since I have not denied him."[140] The necessity of confessing Christ is particularly well pointed out in Ignatius of Antioch's "Letter to the Romans," 6: "If one has Christ within oneself, let such a one consider what I desire and have sympathy with me, as knowing how I am straitened." What kind of understanding must the pagans have had concerning Christianity if they had experienced at every moment the Christians as not existing?[141] The Romans also noted this since they took to the sword to do away with Christianity. It seems vaguely to have crossed their minds[142] that one need only cease to view Christianity as a matter of life and common life[143] so as to destroy it and to render paganism innocuous.[144]

Justin says expressly that the heretics were not in the least persecuted *because of their basic principle* (*First Apology*, 26:7): "They are neither persecuted nor put to death by you, at least on account of their opinions."[145] Cyprian, in Letter 61, 3, says[146] that all the secular power was raised and directed against the Church, and then says that this occurred so that "the Lord might show which was the Church, . . . which is *the united and true people of Christ linked together in the love of the Lord's flock*, whom the enemy would harass, whom the devil would not spare as being his own. . . ."[147] Heretics, once prostrated and made his own, he despises and passes by. He seeks to cast down those whom he sees as standing"[148] (cf. Cyprian, Letter 60, [149]). The Catholic bishops, however, very much[150] felt the need of the connection between martyrdom and the confirmation of Christianity. Just as there was a single proof of the constancy of Christian conviction given with [Christian] life, so the death of a single person was often able to awaken the life of hundreds; no concept or speculation was able to do this. In how great an antithesis did Ignatius of Antioch stand to the Gnostics when he conceived of[151] his coming martyrdom chiefly *as to bring himself to a clear consciousness that for him Christianity was more important than everything, and therefore he understood his death for Christianity as the living expression of his love for Christ* ("Letter to the Romans," 3)! In his "Letter to the Romans," 7, he says to the Roman congregation, which wished to turn to the secular authority so that he be spared,[152] admonishing them: "Still living I write to you, but I do so looking forward to my death. My desire is to be crucified; in me there is no fire that needs to be cooled, but inwardly it calls to[153] me, 'Come to the Father.'" How great a love must he have begotten for Christianity?[154] (The most living penetration of being and form, the inner and the outer we here hold together.)[155] When the Christian community at Carthage shouted out at the heroic and joyous death of their bishop, Cyprian, full of spirit,[156] "Come let us die with him," he probably did as much for the foundation of Christianity in his hour of death as in his whole life. This is the visible Church.[157] [Cf. Pontius the Deacon, *The Life and Passion of Cyprian*, 18.]

Addendum 13

Concerning the Participation of All Christians
in the Priestly Vocation

In the passage in which Origen describes the activity of individual members of the body of Christ, he says that all must be integrated and that the eye of the spiritual body, the priests, must extend their power over the whole body. However, in that the priests communicate their power, the need necessarily arises for them to use the power properly. It will only truly blossom if all possess the most living interest in the good of the whole, and if that good is seen not only as the concern of the priests. The priestly vocation is then to be looked upon as ordained and public, but not as exclusive. If it were exclusive, it would result in the paralysis and death of the whole since it would not only indicate that externally, at least, a living participation in the spread and foundation of Christian piety is to be found only among the priests, but also that they themselves possess no power since they have no ability to develop any. Therefore, in the first century it was emphasized, and we wish to expand upon this in some single points, how the total activity was considered and existed. I say "total activity," that is, an activity of all in unity. In the case where there was such activity of all but no unity, there was no love. We must look first at[158] the expression of *the construction* of the Church, arising as it does in the basic principles of Christ as expressed by the apostles and maintained by the whole history of the Church. According to this image, the totality of believers is considered to be a *house* (1 Tim. 5:14). On the one hand, this describes an external community and a union of individual parts (the *oikon pneumatikon*, 1 Peter 2:5), but at the same time a mutual apprehension and mutual working of *all* of those who make up the *oikeioi tēs pisteos* [the community of the faith] (Gal. 6:10). On the use of the concept of building to describe the establishment of the Christian Church, see Matthew 16:18 and 1 Corinthians 3:10. Thus, *oikodomein* [the act of building] (1 Cor. 10:23), is understood as the separate parts working for fellow Christians and in other cases as the totality of mutual Christian activity (1 Cor. 8:1; Rom. 14:19).[159] When we look into the Holy Scriptures we find the communal aspect expressed.[160] In Polycarp's, "Letter to the Philippians," 13, 2 the word "to build" is used as the embodiment of all Christian virtues, as the stimulation and awakening of them: "by them (the letters of Ignatius) you may be greatly profited, for they treat of faith and patience and of all things that tend to edification in our Lord." This is an expression that can only be formed through the obscure sense that all is nothing without community but that the community is only something through the activity of all.[161] ([Xenophon,] *Cyropaedia*, 8:7, 15, vol. 2, p. 278, edited by Weiske, uses *oikodomein* in the figurative sense. What is here said of *adelphoi* [brothers], namely, those individuals who live in an *oikon* [house], is valid for Christian *adelphoi* who are *pneumatikoi*).[162]

The fact that *all* believers were active in the building of the Church explains the spread of Christianity (Acts 8:1-4, 11:19-21). This fact is testified to by Justin in his *Dialogue with Trypho*, 3, and especially by Celsus in Origen, *Against Celsus*, 3:55, where Celsus attacks Christians for their great industriousness, particularly on the part of laborers, to spread Christianity. Christianity came into Georgia through a slave, through a Tyrian youth. Through Aedesius and Frumentius it came to Abyssinia, and through captives to many German groups. Frumentius expressed his communal concern in that he allowed himself to be consecrated by Athanasius, that is, he acknowledged Athanasius. He did not wish to found any separated community.[163] In fact, how could Christianity in so short a time have overcome paganism without the restless activity of all its adherents? It is quite clear in the Holy Scriptures that each Christian could publicly teach at the beginning, just as it is also clear that disturbances arose and that because of them the practice was discontinued.[164]

Moreover, it was often the case that specially gifted laypersons gave public lectures and the bishops themselves were not ashamed to listen to them. This was the case with Origen (Eusebius, *Ecclesiastical History*, 6:19, 16): "In Palestine he was asked by the bishops to teach publicly in the Church and to explicate the Holy Scriptures although he was not yet a priest."[165] Light is cast on the matter by the fact that Alexander, bishop of Jerusalem, and Theoktistus of Caesarea wrote to Demetrius of Alexandria, defending this fact: "You say in your writings that this was never heard of and that the laity preached in the presence of bishops. This is false. Wherever useful persons were found who could help their fellow believers they were commanded to instruct the people by the holy bishop. This occurred in the case of Euelpis of Neon in Larandi and Paul of Celsus in Iconium" [Ibid.].[166]

One sees from this passage that the practice occurred only very seldom and always under the command and oversight of the bishops. Just as a layman touched upon the priestly office in the proclamation of Christian doctrine, particularly in the case of private conversation, every true Christian had the power to forgive sins. Thus, Origen, in his *Commentary on Matthew* 13, n31, states that all believers are bound together in the closest way through mutual communication and exchange of work, through encouragement, prayers, and activities of all sorts, to awaken the sleeping powers among others, to give newness, and thus to establish in the place of sins more living zeal for a holier disposition. Some, Origen says, have forgiven sins and through spiritual influences have brought it about that in the place of sins, holiness in Christ has been established, and what they loosed, heaven also loosed, just as heaven binds what through the pious activity of such believers cannot be loosed. This is the sense of the passage as it seems to me.[167] The whole life of a priest is then the practice of the power of forgiving sins, and through the priest in particular, as the most active, it flows out over the rest of the Christians who also participate in his calling. The special forgiveness of sins through the priest is not set aside by Origen, but one can say that priests truly, in the place of God, *express, along with the inner working of the totality of believers* with the help of the Holy Spirit, what earlier worked upon them through their life, the power of the sacrament, their doctrine, and from this arises everything of importance. Origen has been falsely charged as improperly linking the power of the forgiveness of sins of the priest to the priest's ethical purity, as did the Donatists and others.[168] That he did speak correctly of the need of pure piety on the part of priests, and how far he did so, is clear from the following.[169]

In defending Origen Bishop Huet (*Origeniana* II, qu. 14, n1) already quite correctly pointed to the passage of Jerome in the third book of the *Commentary on Matthew*, 16:19: "Not understanding the place of the bishop and the presbyter, they assumed something from the Pharisees so that they thought they could damn the innocent or forgive the guilty, but what is heard before God is not the opinion of the priests but life." Huet, however, did not understand the matter deeply enough. Origen discusses it further in his *Commentary on Matthew*, 12, n14, where he says: a bishop can forgive sins as Peter did, if he has the firmness of Peter's faith so that the Church is built upon him. But if he believes that he is able to do it without these qualities, it is clearly an arrogant assumption to suppose that by the *upbuilding* power of the holy life of priests which awakens the sinner, a striving for renewal of life under the Holy Spirit's inner help is established in the place of sinfulness *before* the word of the forgiveness of sins is expressed, and that thus a priest, "bound by the bonds of his own sins," throughout his whole life retains the sins of others rather than forgiving them; that as a result the Church is not built upon him, that he does not build up the Church and certainly should be no priest and that he does it through presumption, and that he does it falsely. Since the forgiveness of sins is tied to improvement of life, it can be furthered more through life than through word.

Thus Origen quite correctly intends that the life of the priest and the endeavors of the whole community must particularly be taken into account. Augustine speaks in very much the same way in his *On Baptism against the Donatists*, 3, 23, where he explains how a priest is able to have the power of forgiving sins even if he is at the same time a sinner.[170] The power to forgive sins was given to the Church, the true untarnished Church, the true, pure, single root of the visible Church.[c] Through the Church's faith, love, and prayer, it forgives, and God thus forgives sins through it. The sins of those who are truly *united* with the Church are forgiven. The matter of the *personal* purity of the bishop who is found in sin does not, therefore, arise. In him, indeed, is the whole community. He expresses the love of the community, and this community forgives sins (in other places, he says "Christ directly"; it is thus to be understood that Christ forgives sins through the Church).[171] It is not the bishop, bound by his sins, who forgives sins. *Such a person* cannot forgive them. The passage reads as follows: "If the apostles represented the Church (*si personam gerebant ecclesiae*) and John 20:22 was said to them as to the Church itself, then the community of the Church forgives sins, and

---

c. Augustine distinguishes an invisible Church in the visible Catholic Church. In the invisible Church he understands that the truly good and those who are living with Christ are bound. It is invisible because no one can say: "I, this person, and that person, belong to it." It is, however, always present; *On Baptism*, 7:51: "Of this house it is said, 'Lord, I have loved the habitation of your house and the place where your honor dwells' (Psalm 26:8) and 'He makes those of one mind in a house that house' [Ps. 68:6]. . . . To this house it is said, 'Forbearing one another in love, endeavoring to keep the unity of the spirit in the bond of peace;' (Eph. 4:2), and 'For the temple of God is holy *which temple you are*' [1 Cor. 3:17]. *For this house is composed of those who are good and faithful, and of the holy servants dispersed throughout the world, and bound together in the unity of the Spirit, whether they know each other personally or not.*'" Those who form true unity in the visible Church and those who make it to continue are set forth in the priests in whom and to whom Christ works all the good that he wishes to work.

excommunication from that community is not according to the capriciousness of human beings but according to the will of God and the prayers of the saints who live in the Spirit who judges all things but who itself is not judged by anyone. The rock (the believers firmly grounded on Jesus Christ) retains, the rock forgives. The dove (the image always used of true believers and of those bound in love with themselves and with Christ) retains, the dove forgives. The unity retains, the unity forgives. Unity, however, is in the good alone, in the priests, or in those who strive in mutual obedience for the spiritual. It is not in evil persons. They can make noises outside or be endured with sorrow in the Church; they may baptize or be baptized. They are tolerated with sorrow in the Church although they do not belong to the true Church community, to the glorious Church that has no spot and no failure or anything like these, yet if they improve and confess that they came to the Church laden with sin, they are not baptized again, but may begin to belong to the true Church bound in love, *through whose activity sins are forgiven (per cujus gemitus peccata solvuntur)*. So also it is for those who were clearly not in the Church, if they received the same sacraments and came correctly directed to the unity of the Church, and were not tied down by the repetition of baptism but by the law and the bond of love. . . .[172] But they (the evil bishops) do not give forgiveness of sins. This is given through the prayers of the saints, that is, through the activity of the true Church, which is always the baptizer if those who receive baptism belong to its community. For the Lord would not have said to robbers and usurers 'Whosoever's sins you bind . . .' [Matt. 16:19]. The one who is in community with love is loosed and the one who has no community with it is bound, whether such a one is clearly outside the Church or seems to be bound in it."[173]

Augustine, in *On Baptism*, 7:99, says: "Taking all these things therefore into consideration, I think that I am not rash in saying that there are some in the house of God after such a fashion as not to be themselves the very house of God, which is said to be built upon a rock, which is called the one dove . . . *which has received the keys and the power of binding and loosing. If anyone shall neglect this house when it arrests and condemns him [. . .] let that person be unto you as a heathen and a publican.*"

The Church fathers agree on this, that wherever the unity of the Church in its innermost, deepest essence and being is grasped and is present as a living form in a mind, sin is destroyed in its roots. Every sin was understood as a disturbance of the community and

through sin every community would finally be destroyed. As a result
the forgiveness of sin was understood as the work of the community
of believers: through the believers and through the community, the
love of the Holy Spirit flowed into hearts, united believers with one
another, and in this true union sin could no longer exist; it was
forgiven. From this it came about that all mortal sin had to be
confessed to the bishop and the whole congregation. Because of sin
the community was broken. The sinner separated himself or herself
from everyone. The reacceptance of a sinner into the community
was, as a result, a reconciliation with all, a forgiveness on the part of
the congregation, a renewal of love and unity.

Later, when confession before the whole community was set
aside, one only had to make one's sin known to the bishop *in whom
the whole community was found.* This seems to me to be the *essential*
relationship between confession and the forgiveness of sins and
repentance in our Church. On the one hand, it is clear that as love
binds believers together, sin separates them. The sinner sees himself
or herself, according to the Spirit of the Church, as fallen from the
community and thinks of separating from it. If a sinner *feels urged,*
however, if such a person indicates that he or she has understood
the essence of Church community, and if the living feeling of
unworthiness reflects that such a person is beginning to be worthy
to become a member of the body of Christ, that is, in one's heart-felt
admissions that one is a sinner, then one's sins will be forgiven. On
the other hand, confession is the most complete expression from the
innermost community of all. An individual can keep nothing hidden;
he or she will be urged to communicate it. All form together one
family. The Catholic Church would have to be something completely
different if confession had not been formed in her. It seems that
there would be a great change in her character if she ceased to
practice confession, and certainly she would, as a result, come very
close to an egotistical view of believers.[174]

If one sees that the totality of believers working in the case of
forgiveness of sins is centered in the bishop, much more so is it in
the case of baptism as indicated in what has been said earlier. The
Donatists rebaptized impure Catholics and charged that they had
declared their baptism in a heretical community as valid, since
sinners cannot baptize properly. But Augustine asks if proud self-
seeking bishops baptizing in the Church are not sinners? He refers
to what I have explained in the first chapter and what lies at the
basis of this work, namely, that Christians are taught directly to live

and love in a Christian manner in the community so that those who form in the Church her characteristic invisible bond, who stand truly with Christ in community, are communicated to by the Holy Spirit in such a way that it is through their prayer that a baptisand becomes a child of God, but the baptism's efficacy does not depend immediately upon the baptizer. See Augustine, *On Baptism*, 3, 16: "But it is understood that invisibly and imperceptibly on account of the bond of peace (the Church community)[175] divine love is breathed into their hearts so that they may be able to say that it is 'because the love of God is shed abroad in their hearts by the Holy Spirit which is given unto them,'" [Rom. 5:5], and in ibid., 17, Augustine says: "How did they baptize those who used to plunder estates by treacherous deceit and increase their profits by usury, if baptism is only given by that indivisible, chaste, and perfect dove, that unity which can only be understood as existing among the good? Is it possible perhaps that by the prayers of the *saints who are spiritual* within the Church, as though by the frequent lamentations of the dove, *a great sacrament* is dispensed with secret administration of the mercy of God, so that their sins are loosed who are baptized, not by the dove, but by the hawk, if they come to that sacrament in the peace of Catholic unity?"[176]

Thus a baptism is not a separated act, but is given *before* the gathered community and communicated by it.[177] Moreover, it is by the whole Church and thus by the totality of the believers that the Church offers Christ in the Holy Sacrament to God the Father. In the place of other Augustinian passages, I will quote de Marca, *De discriminatio*, 2.8: "It would not be wrong to add that out of the dignity of the mystic and spiritual priesthood (of all believers)[178] the important sacrament of mediation which indeed is from the priests alone, is properly speaking, consecrated by the Church, that is, by the universal union of the faithful and the bride of Christ, which does not have spot or blemish. It is thus said to be offered to God. Therefore, Augustine observes that the connection of the things marvellously arises from the unity of the Spirit, so that Christ offers through the Church as it offers through him, because as individuals who are each day present in their own way at the mysteries, they are able to be there as they teach what they recite in the Mass." Thus the whole congregation offers in the priest because he is its unity, or all practice a spiritual activity[179] that expresses itself and is consecrated in the priest. Thus the vocation of the priest is certainly understood as common.[180] Likewise, finally, the quality of the bishops, insofar as it finds itself in a preeminent sense[181] the fundament of the Church, is given over to all true believers.

Along with the passage already cited from Augustine in which this is said, compare Origen, [*Commentary on Matthew,* 12:10]: "If we understand the words of Peter, 'You are Christ, the Son of the living God,' not as being said by flesh and blood but by the light sent forth into our hearts by the Heavenly Father, we will be what Peter was. We will also be, as he was, pronounced blessed, because the cause of his blessedness will also be given to us. It was not revealed to us through flesh and blood that Jesus was the Christ, the Son of the living God, but through the Father who is in heaven. The Father gave it from heaven so that we might live there, and he gave us such a revelation, which lifts those who receive it to heaven, if they remove the covers of their souls and receive the Spirit of the wisdom of God. Every disciple of Christ is a rock, and on such rocks is the whole doctrine of the Church built and the holy pattern of life promised to it. In every perfect person who possesses the totality of the activities, dispositions, and doctrines bringing about holiness is the Church, built by God. If you hold that on Peter alone the whole Church is built, what do you say about John and the other apostles? Might we dare say that against Peter alone the gates of hell are weak, or have no power; have they power against the other apostles and the perfect ones?"[182]

Throughout the learned bishop Huet's *Origeniana,* II, qu. 14, there are other parallel passages from Ambrose. See Origen's *Commentary on Luke,* 9: "Those who conquer the flesh are the foundation of the Church and if they are not able to be equal to Peter, they are able to imitate him."[183] In Gregory of Nyssa, *On Perfection,* there is the passage: "In this and in similar ways we are a rock if we strive according to our powers to reach in changeable nature, the unchangeable and perfect."[184] This is thus the relationship of the laity and their participation in the vocation of the priests according to a Catholic viewpoint.[185] I do not know how else, according to the spirit of the Church, the dignity and the power of the individual with the idea and the direction of the whole would be united, and how one can in the firmest manner reproach her, that is, her Spirit, with the charge of giving up single individuals so as to preserve the whole. But if the idea appears disturbed when she wishes to step out from her pure, heavenly clarity and to make herself active in time and place, let me strive and battle against these impediments, not against the Church itself.

A closer discussion concerning the historical [*historische*] truth of my description of an idea of a bishop can be given, namely, that he is the unity of believers made actual in one person.[186]

I have said that in the early Church a general priesthood of all Christians was acknowledged. One must marvel at the meanings that were found in this concept and now arise again. Many believe that if one speaks of a general priesthood of all believers, this indicates a general ecclesiastical egoism and that all Christians are priests. All must then be egoists. One could hold, although one would not mean, that the union of believers would be a capricious and accidental one and that it would bring each to separatism in spite of the person's Christian character. According to the essence of the egoistic view, each person is his or her own priest, that is, unmediated through the community of believers, a person can hold true doctrine and all grace. If this supposition were true, the Catholic Church would carry in itself an inner nothingness. This point of view is, in fact, the base and beginning of all separatism and once having accepted it, nothing can be opposed to it, although the writers who defend the priesthood of all Christians in this sense still express themselves, albeit ineffectively, against separatism. What is to be said if one finds in the early Church something that supports this? If it is simple to find passages of this type in the writers of that period—as one can in Irenaeus who says: "Every just person has the rank of priest," and in Origen ["Homily 9 on Leviticus," 16] as well—nevertheless, in all their writings do they not make the opposite point, as I have, I hope, pointed out?

Are the first three hundred years and their inner characteristic essence thereby brought to nothing? One can achieve nothing by this other than to bring different words together without the characteristic spirit. The passages of the Church fathers in which they speak of the general priesthood are praised. Others, however, in which they declare themselves against all division in the strictest way, are set aside or considered as external and Jewish even though those passages cannot be read as contradicting the former passages. This view of the general priesthood as meaning the same thing as a general ecclesiastical egoism is tied in the closest way to the concept of an invisible Church. But can one find in the Church fathers the slightest trace of such a concept? The well-known passage of Tertullian [*On Chastity,* 7] is often brought in at this point. In it, so as to point out that all Christians, laypersons and clerics, can be made to follow the same demands, Tertullian states that all Christians could once judge what is now only established in a rule through a *law of the Church* by the priests in the narrow sense, and that where there is one believer alone, such a believer could individually still offer a sacrifice and be his own priest. Ignatius does say in many places that the isolated celebration of the Eucharist is considered separatistic and egotistic and this, it appears, can be considered as contradicting what Tertullian says occurred regularly in the earliest periods.

But one must realize that the enlightened disciple of John is speaking of this action as unchristian—*diabolō latreuei* [he worships the devil; cf. Pseudo-Ignatius, "Letter to the Philadelphians," 9], he states—if it is done with a consciousness of separation. One also sees that the idea of the Supper was not clear for every person, and that therefore it needed ecclesiastical teaching and clarification. If one concludes from Tertullian that each believer could celebrate the Supper for himself, since only such a conclusion makes sense of the controversy, one only indicates that one has not yet grasped the concept of the Supper. If it is always celebrated among Christians as the actualization of the union of Christians with Christ, how can one, separated from the others, go to the Supper and be for oneself, one's own priest? If one does not wish to separate oneself, how can one celebrate alone and against him in whom the whole community is seen as united? In such a person the members of the Church are not only portrayed as a unity among themselves, but also as a unity with the totality of the Church. What could a person intend to establish through personal celebration in thus wishing to unite with Christ but separating from the community even though Christ and his community are one? The early Church already correctly asserted that such a person does not receive the body of the Lord, but only common bread, and that such a person's consecration is no consecration. In this sense no one can be his own priest. Therefore, the earliest Christians, who very often celebrated the Eucharist in their own homes, did not bless a separated celebration of it, but only one in which the bread that was received was consecrated in the community of all through the ordained point of the union of all. Moreover, the individual priest dare not celebrate the Eucharist if and where he wished, but he could do so only in the orderly gathering of all who joined for the celebration of the Eucharist, later called the Mass, and only if he remained in the community. Outside of the community he lost his power since in egoism nothing can be accomplished.

As a result it is charged that already in the first three centuries the concept of a Judaic priesthood had established itself in the Church. This was concluded particularly from the general association of those who in the Old Covenant declared themselves against the ordained Levitic priesthood with those who under the New Covenant stood against the episcopate. It is difficult to understand how one can go wrong on this subject if one *studies* the sources themselves. A simple review of that relationship in the striking Cyprian texts in his *On the Unity of the Church* already noted indicates that all speak against separatism and for unity and community, the representative of which is the bishop. Separation from the bishop was a dissolution of the community. One must then turn the Old Testament into something completely different, into a deeper and purely Christian sense, just as the New Testament priesthood is something completely different from the Judaic.

There is a further charge laid against the early Church, namely, that in it the priests were already seen as mediators between believers and God, and that because of this the mediating role of our only Mediator was taken away. Everything that has been said will indicate that this charge arises out of an egoistic view of believers. If the Church fathers had used any fuller expressions, they would have suggested nothing better than that the Church community mediates Christ to us or that he is bound far more indivisibly with it and is established with it at the same time. He gives himself to us only through his own, thereby to demonstrate that they belong together and are one in him. He thus leads us to the Church community and in it to himself and to the Father. He is thus the All, working in the All. He is the single and true Mediator and only through him do we have trust in the Father. He unites us with the Father. But in this role he uses his believers, and all true believers have a part in his office through him. *The priest, however, is the synecdoche of all believers because he expresses their unity.* The two can be separated from one another only where mediation through Christ with God is understood as a purely external one-sided faith, as a faith that is conceived of as only supposed to stand, according to which one stands together with him but not necessarily at the same time with the whole Church in a living union.

Here again the type of the universal whole arises. Every individual is related with every other in this universal whole inwardly and in a living manner, and mediates mutual present being and life. But it is God who bears all in all and in whom all stand. No creature dare puff itself up to believe that it mediates even if it does mediate. As in the second case there is a community of nature, in the first there is one of male and female saints. Finally, I wish to say that many of the Fathers have not expressed themselves clearly at times on this matter. We must, therefore, read everything as it relates together.

Appendices

Appendix 1

Pragmatic Glimpses
[Autumn 1823 or Spring 1824]

1. The Relationship between Dependence on the Bible Alone and the Spirit of Heresy

Heresy understands the Christian as isolated and knows no common Spirit; the spirit of the individual holds to the spirit of the Bible. Bible in hand (the Bible always appears as heresy's only basis for knowledge), it always puts forward as certain the position that Christianity can never be found more than in the individual. This is the case whether an individual considers the Bible as the only source and wants to be taught only by it *before or after* he or she has separated. Before the letter was the Spirit. Christianity lived first in the mind of our Lord and his apostles, and thereafter was set down in letters. The person who possesses the living Spirit will understand the letters. The same Spirit that the apostles possessed is the one that the Church will possess eternally. The person who has this Spirit will acknowledge it in the form of the Church. Here the Spirit meets itself once again.[a] Every true Christian who possesses the living Spirit must be able to bring forth a Bible. The structural form of the Spirit as it was in Jesus, however, obviously far outdistances all others as the prototype and these are only able to approximate the first, which is the same in each true Christian.

One cannot rightly say that the individual must learn from the Holy Scriptures; this is only a rediscovery, a coming to understand and conceptually grasp oneself—a clear self-consciousness of the Christian Spirit in the individual Christian.[b] Forms in the realm of the Spirit bring its mathematical predispositions to consciousness,

---

a. Before the letter . . . again] Cf. T (with A1 variants), section 8: If Christianity . . itself again.

b. Every true Christian . . . Christian] See T (with A1 variants), section 8, final note.

and thereby the Spirit only discovers itself in them and becomes conscious of them again. In the same way, anyone who does not have the Christian Spirit will not find *which* form contradicts the Spirit, but will find nothing contradictory in and for self. Therefore heresy finds *everything* in the Bible, whereas the Catholic only and always finds the Spirit because the Spirit does not contradict itself. The purest and noblest structural form of the Spirit is that described in the Bible; it is there found unfolded and expressed, related to individual life tasks in which the ways of viewing the Spirit are provided. Therefore, Catholics say that this Spirit dare not first be sought; it is always present. And the Church explains the Bible, that is, one does not find the Spirit by the letters, but the letters are only externalities, the revelation of the Spirit. As the universe and history are revelations of God but as such do not allow that person to know the true God who does not already carry God-consciousness in himself or herself, so the biblical words are revelations of the Holy Spirit but are not clear to the person who does not carry them within. Only Spirit begets Spirit and life life; the letter never gives birth to the spirit or what is dead, life.[c] Heresy separates itself from every analogy. One could not understand a human product if it did not express the human spirit in itself. Likewise one cannot understand the Bible, the external manifestation of the Christian Spirit, if one does not possess the Spirit. The Christian Spirit, however, is different from a merely human one. Where will the Christian Spirit be necessarily preserved except in the Church, where it always moves and lives and brings life about and always begets itself again? The person who approaches the Bible aside from this Spirit as it *always* was in the Church merely brings his or her own *human aspect* to it and takes only the human from it. That person's spirit and the biblical Spirit do not know one another, and therefore the person thinks that he or she must draw forth from the Bible in externalities and in concepts what is in it. Above all that person attempts to bring understanding to the Bible and believes that understanding has been achieved if word is compared with word, form with form, so that it naturally begets again only word and form, reducing like to like, whereas the Bible can only be understood if Spirit meets Spirit.

c. And the Church . . . living] Cf. T (with A1 variants), section 8: As a result the principles . . . is living.

Words never have life, nor does a constitution ever beget nationality. Life must bring forth words and the life of a people the constitution. The Christian Spirit begets the Bible. (If one brought the ancient Roman constitution into present-day Rome as Arnold of Bresica and [Cola di] Rienzo wished to do, what would the result be?— As if forms were able to create a Spirit. We do not understand Rome's constitution if we do not explain it from life.) [Marginalia: (What is the exegetical basic proposition that one is not to explain the Bible on the basis of doctrine?) It was born of the Protestant period.]

If the two are divided, neither can be understood. How could one, then, as in the sixteenth century, decide to understand the Bible alone, if the Christian Spirit was not first brought along from the ancient Church? Rather, such a person will fade and die, the further one is distanced from the trunk, and one can only bring life to such individuals now, insofar as they return to primitive Christianity.

Thus, if Christianity could be begotten in individuals from the Bible alone, full egoism would arise, but not a commonality. Heresy is egoism; it returns in all its manifestations to the basic proposition, which makes the Bible the single ecclesiastical foundation.

If the heretic asserts "Religious freedom must be the basic proposition of a church; each person can and dare follow his or her own viewpoint as before," the Catholic agrees with the first proposition, but denies the second. For the Catholic this is the same thing as saying: "True Christianity cannot be specified; it can have no being aside from the individual." This is to make indifferentism the basic proposition of the Christian Church. Because the Catholic values Christianity as something objective, truly existing, guided and maintained through the divine Spirit aside from the individual, the Catholic establishes freedom in the hypothesis of this objectivity in itself. Thus the Catholic does not follow his or her own *individual* conviction, torn off from life, but the revelation of the divine Spirit throughout all of Christian history that encounters the individual in the ever enduring total faith of the whole. A Catholic thus understands himself or herself as free, if the whole lives in the individual and the individual in the whole. As the activity of divine grace points to itself in the whole, so also it points to itself in the individual. One can thus see that the Catholic establishes a higher freedom as the foundation of the Church, the freedom of the children of God who are led by the divine Spirit (Romans), whereas the heretic holds fast to a lesser freedom as a basic proposition, always acknowledging freedom as something and thus makes freedom to err: *but in error a person is never one.* Such a position is simplistic and understands freedom as servility to error.[d]

The heretic establishes freedom of study as the condition of a dignified and noble life. This freedom of study is for the heretic, however, the same thing as the complete power always to bring something forth as the results of study. The Catholic holds firm to the first proposition, but turns aside from the second.[e] The heretic proceeds from the notion that one can think of oneself as empty or as not a Christian. The Catholic, on the other hand, begins to study with his Christian consciousness, because the Catholic can neither cease to be a Christian nor is able to cease to be because the Catholic's Christian consciousness has grown so much with his or her essence that the Catholic would cease to be what he or she is or is thought to be; however, we think of such a person as a Catholic. Therefore, the Catholic always premises study on a description of Christian consciousness or confession of faith. Tertullian, Origen, Irenaeus, and others [*sic*]. The heretic views Christianity with the mind, merely as thought, that is, as an unknown (and it always is such to the heretic) greatness and charges that the Catholic does not know Christianity. But the Catholic was always a Catholic first. He or she could only study as a Catholic, not as a non-Catholic. The Catholic always begins with the result that the heretic wishes to have.[f] The Catholic views things as a Christian, the heretic as a nonChristian. As a Christian one is thus convinced that one can be truly free to study, that is, one may no longer dare choose between truth and falsehood which a lower view of freedom of study sees as non-freedom, which the heretic has fortunately risen above. The Catholic never considers making a decision about error or carrying out a critique of it (and, therefore, it is simple for a Catholic to rise above error and to be enlightened by the Holy Spirit). Because the heretic has the aforementioned concept of freedom of study, he or she must rightly declare: One does not have freedom but first becomes free in concept and one's life is thus conceptually first because the heretic always first seeks what is true, and thus only the

d. One can thus . . . error] Cf. A1 addition as noted in T, section 19, final endnote.

e. The heretic establishes . . . second] Cf. T (with A1 variants), section 19: It now also follows . . . doing it.

f. The heretic proceeds . . . to have] Cf. T (with A1 variants), section 19: The heretic thus . . . position of the heretic.

truth, that is, the possession of truth, not the seeking, makes one free. The heretic must thus equally acknowledge that he or she conceptually becomes unfree because such a person can just as easily be grasped by error and then lose freedom for certain. The heretic thus always finds himself or herself initially at a point of indifference. If the heretic thinks that he or she is no longer seeking, but has found—as was always the case (Tertullian)—the heretic would be able to propose from a personal standpoint that he or she no longer has freedom of study itself; however, if the heretic holds that one has the right to reject what has been found, it is clear that the heretic is not yet beyond the concept of being free to choose—thus freedom is first and because it always must be first, it never is.[g] The heretic sets freedom in seeking, the Catholic in finding. If we consider the two as established, as believers who have found what was sought, both would hold their principles against one another, and the Catholic would reconstruct his or her system. The Catholic would demonstrate whether he or she would have to be an ecclesiastical egoist or not. The Catholic would always and everywhere call upon the principle of unity because that is the Catholic foundation whereas the heretic would cite division, which is the heretical principle.

The Church will always be determined in a one-sided way if one defines it as an institution or an association, founded for the preservation and enlivenment of the Christian religious disposition. It is much more a begetting of love living in the believer through the Holy Spirit.[h] If the Spirit is given, the Church is established since the Spirit necessarily forms a body, but the body never forms the Spirit. The purpose of the Church is thus not to preserve and extend Christianity. If this were the case one would always need to suppose that there was a time when Christianity was without a Church or likewise that the Spirit had lived without a body and had established for itself the distant purpose of preserving itself. [Marginalia: In a completely harmonious way the Catholic views Christianity not as a concept but as life and thus does not view the Church as a concept but as a life. As a result the union is no conceptual union (if such were possible) but a real one in actuality.] It is much more the

g. As a Christian . . . never is] Cf. T (with A1 variants), section 19: The Catholic was thus truly convinced . . . never is.

h. The Church will always . . . Spirit] Cf. T, section 49: The concept of the Church . . . through the Holy Spirit.

necessary externalization of the internal, a product of the same, and therefore in every way as old as Christianity itself since the living Spirit of the Church could have no moment in which it did not reveal itself in which its forming, uniting power did not display what it itself gave to Christianity as a proof of its life and presence. If this structure of the divine Spirit would cease to be a visible form, if there were no longer a Church, the Spirit itself would no longer be present or would be reduced to a concept which would give the appearance that the Church were a structure to preserve Christianity or a replacement of the external for the internal.[i]

Because Christianity according to the Catholic principle is taken up from life and out of it, and not through speculation, it is active and first grasps the mind, the seat of power, and the will and after this the individual experiences and becomes aware that Christianity is from God according to John, as something given, whereas speculation seeks to take up what it finds in *life* and to describe this through knowledge so as to comprehend and restructure the harmony of life as an intellectual unity. Thus the power of the will and the depth of speculation are united. Thought and life, the ideal and the real, appear to it as a unity, but as in life the real first appears and the ideal comes thereafter, so also here.

Because the heretic proceeds from speculation, and nourishment comes to him or her for this, the fullness of the religious Christian life, Christianity merely as an object of speculation or much more of dialectic, is viewed as something communicated conceptually and through concepts. Thus true strength and power of character is injured and never develops. Pure concept never fructifies the mind even if someone beginning as a skeptic achieves the perfection of his or her conceptual system (which cannot be seen as possible). Heresy is thus a true injuring of the will's power without begetting a deep speculation.[j] The fire is heresy in contradiction with itself. The Church is never what she is as an object of research, but is something completely different, as something given, brought to her adherents. In this the inner spirit of Christianity is active. *This same* premise is present in the hypothesis of an invisible Church that Christ is supposed to have founded. On this matter heresy openly

---

i. If the Spirit . . . internal] Cf. T , section 49: If love was given . . . true Christianity.

j. Because Christianity according to . . . speculation] Cf. T (with A1 variants), Addendum 12: If Christianity is accepted . . . truly great things.

expresses her essence. The power to draw is given by God to the spirit and life, not to the concept. Only spirit and life can truly beget an external structure because wherever they are, their power is present; it cannot remain invisible but presses forward into visibility, overcoming everything. Heresy proves itself powerless in this matter, as incapable of stepping forth into the world of phenomena. It therefore externalizes itself with convulsive movements against everything in which the religious Spirit reveals itself and points to itself as alive. How were the martyrs attacked and their motives explained? The gifts to churches, cloisters, hospitals, universities, the crusades? The missions? and missionaries? The miracles, and finally the whole external Church? Because they were not capable of acknowledging a Spirit where an external work appeared, but supposed that there was only a spirit where none appeared. For the heretics that was the true Church alone which one never protected, which never pointed to itself and was thus in all places as a *ghost* . . . [sic] as if God had not revealed himself in the universal whole. Therefore, heresy and the denial of God are so close. It would have been very peculiar if true unity had proceeded from egoism.

Because heresy established freedom of study as a principle, it refused to give to this basic proposition some true sense and meaning. Philosophic study concerning the essence of our spirit is not possible without positing an established being of spirit. Our consciousness is, in fact, twofold: the being and productive aspect and the reflecting aspect which makes the former an object. The actually being and productive consciousness gives material for the merely thinking consciousness. The reflecting aspect does not then beget life, but life is its source, its foundation. It is the same with Christian consciousness. It is living and reflecting. The Christian must have already long *lived* as a Christian and thus have material at hand before he or she is able to move the reflecting Christian consciousness, that is, before study can begin. If free study is presupposed, what is to be studied? Where is the material? How can a Christian result appear since nothing Christian is reflected upon since it was presupposed that no Christian material was present?[k] Or is the Christian life of others to be studied? That cannot be done because it does not have any independence.

k. Because heresy established . . . present?] Cf. T (with A1 variants), section 19: The principle concerning freedom . . . first be studied.

2. Pragmatic Glimpses

The Catholic Church presents to her confessors what is given in history to change it into their interior, to internalize it. She does not believe that one can come to truth first through error. Such an approach she gives over to the heretics and considers it, as it in fact is, a false path. When a Protestant believes that one must first begin by studying the historical Jesus, the Protestant desires to arrive, if things go well, *in the end* where the Catholic begins. What exists in history, received through external witnesses, must first have had life through the inner witness; this is true. From this standpoint the *church* proceeds; she gives another form of research to the *individual*.

3. The Sixth Century and Thereafter

It is always good if the individual, during the time that is a stranger to spiritual power, has a feeling of the time's weakness and turns again to the place where the power was so as to strengthen himself or herself there. Those who are conscious of their ignorance will [turn] to where all the treasures of wisdom are gathered—Gregory of Tours [(538-594)], the ambassadors of Pope Agatho [(678-681)], in [Claude] Fleury [*Ecclesiastical History*], where one clings to the ancients because on one's own one can produce nothing better. Where one is thus incapable of producing something striking, something original, except by taking up from others what is striking in the ancient world and in which one swells up with a wisdom that gives no thought to the future, all the miseries come to the fore which the spectators of our time declare as foolishness. Thus the praise of foresight at this time. See the close of the second period of the Church history. Where one is not wise in one's own power, one is wise in accepting the wisdom of others. Therefore, the Catenas of Nicetas [of Heracleios] and Theophylact and Oecumenius.

The idea of the Catholic Church can be understood as coming into reality in *two* or, if one wishes, *three* periods, cultural stages of religious faith, points of religious development. At the highest point religious inwardness, where faith is taken up as a living unity, grasps spirit and mind, and this inner life rules among the majority as it did in the first period, the external and contingent are nothing, and no division is allowed. This situation develops in two different ways: in the first case, one moves out from the circumstances as they were in the first period or returns to that period at a future time; in the second, as was the case with the battle with the northern barbarians, faith was conceived by the majority as something purely external that did not require any energy to accept but, if not accepted, resulted in the loss of salvation. In the first case, one *wills* not to divide and the mind finds an inexpressible joy in this union. In the second case one *can*not bring about division; the single individual cannot break through the *external* bond. The interim period of a religious half-culture is the most unfortunate period for Catholicism—the understanding knows no unity, egoism only separation. We are in such a time. Catholics do not allow the unity of the essential to exist alongside the nonessential. Sects do not accept the essential and necessary before the nonessential.

Since religious faith disintegrates in concept (concepts may be clearly dissected), few divisions can exist (since divisions can exist only in concept), and few concepts have come into being in the Church. However, the more such concepts are taken from the unity of faith and become accepted as laid down in the Church, the more one has opportunity to understand and explore individual concepts, and the more divisions arise. There are no *single* doctrines and for this reason no splinters can occur.

If egoism is the inner ground of all division, it must find itself again in all sects in an external form. This is most clearly seen in the designations of Catholics that we find among all heresies. For the Gnostics, Catholics are the "physical ones," they the pneumatics. It is the same with the Montanists. For the Novatians, Catholics are the impure and they the Cathars [pure]. The Donatists will not even sit with Catholics without becoming impure (to join the Donatists is to further separate oneself because among them heretical egoism is expressed in its sharpest form). Where is gnosis (*gnōsis*) purity (*katharsis*)? If egoism is once to become the basic principle of the Church of God, will such wisdom and purity continue? [Marginalia: (The weak who have the first beginnings, who still have *soicheia* [the rudiments of knowledge], are the perfect *teleioi* who give perfection to Christianity through their own spirit) follow human tradition]

It is the fate of these heretics that the apostles, too, must commonly share the fate of Catholics, that they too are called *physikoi* and the Catholics thus accept this charge brought against them.

At the end of this period we find the apostles' doctrine established. They overcome everything that initiates a single individual life. Obviously. If life in the great unity is the correct evangelical

Christian life, the Catholic principle flowed out from God and has an objective foundation; it rests *outside* of the human person. It is a divine idea. The heretical principle, on the other hand, is egotistic and lives only in the individual; it *is* above all therefore nothing, has no *true being*, comes into being only in and through the individual, disappears once more with the individual, and can appear once again only in such a way. But because it has no *being*, the heretical principle cannot agree with itself and therefore the phenomenon arises that all later heresies consider earlier ones as nothing. It is pure negation as is evil which does not exist in any way, is not positive, and because it is not established, it has no objective principle, is in eternal conflict with itself, and works toward an ever continuing dissolution of itself. This was the case with Basilides or Valentinus who allowed evil to fight with themselves before the good touched either. Only when we are all transfigured in Christ where there will be one full single vision will all negation disappear and all conflict cease, that is, there will be no heresy. [Marginalia: That which does not *exist* in the invisible Church is understood as *becoming* in the visible. If it is always considered as *being* in the first case, in the second it will always be *firmly understood* as becoming that will be made real, but never that which is *nothing*. The means must therefore be given.] But therefore the idea that will be one in eternity must certainly be given as the idea of the Church. Other-wise, how shall what is completely *nothing*, what is merely possible through contemporary limitations and will therefore not even at the end of time come into manifestation, how can that be the principle of the Church? A pure negation. All analogies lead to this—the good that will finally be *victorious* will always be troubled by conflict and appears here as im*pure*. Is one then not to establish it as an eternal principle?

Faith in Jesus' divinity cannot be demonstrated. Only the person who does what Jesus commands can be inwardly certain that Jesus' teaching is from God and that he himself is God. In the believer, Jesus' divinity comes to be a need, so inwardly moving with the believer's essence and so alive, spreading throughout his or her soul, that now for the first time this innermost aspect comes to complete consciousness. Faith in Jesus is the highest level of human self-consciousness. In Jesus the believer comes to know God and, for the first time in a true fashion, self. Self-consciousness is life, and therefore faith in Jesus is the highest life: who sees me sees the Father [cf. John 6:46] and who does not know him, does not know the Father or self. I am the life [cf. John 14:6], and this higher life is itself taken away from an individual who does not have this faith. From the time of the apostles the Church was grasped by this faith. The witnesses to this faith among the Church fathers are their expression of it. The faith of the Church expresses itself in them. Thus from the earliest period a Catholic sees his or her Church as living in this faith, in such an unbroken manner, indeed, that those who share this faith as they hold to the inner root of their life, view it as what they wish to take as their own life and higher self-consciousness, and for this reason the corrupt, dead, or deadening aspects are cut off or fall away as desiccated twigs and useless scions. The life of the whole is like that of the individual. Without this faith the individual never sees his or her Church, the whole. (Nothing else lasts from the beginning, nothing else joins itself in an unmediated fashion to the life of Christ and his apostles, takes that life up in itself, extends it, and plants it.) Faith is ever expressed in the Church's whole length and breadth, is the source of her life, was her self-consciousness. (The Church never had a consciousness of herself without faith.) The traditional demonstration of the truth of this faith is the life of the Church, for which it needs no critical or exegetical apparatus, which no doubt can destroy, no so-called philosophy undermine. Everyone who wishes truth and certitude orients or can orient himself or herself to the Church. Such a person cannot even consider the Church of Christ without this faith because the Church never was without it. Those who conceive of themselves without it, conceive something totally other, and for one to imagine such a Church, that is, to set *one's thoughts* in the place of objectivity, is to be heretical; this is also the equivalent of following oneself.

The heretical Church that wishes to divide itself from this life and to live separated from it, is, therefore, necessarily in continual hesitation, in seeking, because it has lost the true center; it sweeps here and there between life and death as a *church* life. The *single individual* can lift himself or herself to truth if he or she creates a self only unconsciously from the *new* source. Because in this the individual expresses his or her self as a single individual, he or she cannot come to a necessary and infallible commonality, that is, can establish no true, and therefore continuing Church. Because the heretic steps away from the unbroken stream of Church life and begins an *individual, new,* (so-called) *independent* development, there is the possibility and necessity of such an *individual,* ever *new* development, and, therefore, there is also the avowal of the possibility of a contradiction with the development already begun and with this (for who will draw a boundary to novelty's ever renewing itself?) an abolishment of oneself. Each heresy, therefore, stands in contradiction with itself (it establishes nothing; it is always only a minus). Because it establishes itself, it establishes at the same time its own contradiction, contradictio (in the modern period expressly called "protestant"). Heresy is, therefore, a non ens [nonbeing]; it has no characteristic sense. And Catholicism is, insofar, the eternal affirmation, the position, truth. The Catholic does not trust self but grasps the ever present essence and only that, sets it firmly in self, expresses self in it with one word, the life that flowed out from Christ, was given to the apostles, flowed out only in him, participates in those who are his, was there before the individual and will remain after the individual, that is, the present is *one* with the past and the future. (Unity is thus not simply one being with things contemporary.) The heretic will make predications, find as if it were an ever present essence, that is, the impossibility of his or her permanence, in contradiction to the Kingdom of God which from the time of Christ could never cease, and therefore the heretic has no permanence with self, the equivalent thus of not being.

(Even Neander is not free from this when he states each person must first discover [truth. See the introduction to his *Antignostikus*].)

This from the side of truth. From the side of love, egoism is also nothing.

The heretical principle makes improvements from itself because it establishes *itself* as the judge of truth. Completely false. Truth has no other criterion than itself; the heretic wishes to designate the objective through the subjective, and therefore never finds what is objective but changes everything into the subjective. That falsehood, which slips into the Church life that existed first, has no being, and therefore cannot be judged. What becomes and became is, therefore, compared with *what is*, namely, Church life is compared with itself and thereby what is a human image is decided on; the objective with itself. The heretic does somewhat the same in that he or she compares the earlier, that is, the Holy Scripture, in some fashion. As a result the Holy Scripture is equivalent to X for the heretic who must then seek what it should be; the heretic thus wishes to seek an X through an X, an unknown greatness through another unknown; the heretic has no criterion of truth. Therefore, no heretic ever agrees with another and no heresy with itself, nor an earlier time with a later. According to the Catholic principle of Catholicity, every *new* plant that the heavenly Father through his Son did not plant will be rooted out, and the person who plants such a plant claims the ever enduring church life for himself or herself.

The heretic, if clinging to the Bible, *now* gives meaning to the letter and is, therefore, uncertain if his meaning agrees with the object. The Catholic grasps the meaning of the letter which was itself there with the Catholic before the letter, was there at the same time the Catholic first existed. The Catholic holds to this life, and therefore has certainty. A Catholic does not lift himself or herself above his or her meaning.

[Translated from Johann Adam Möhler, *Nachgelassene Schriften Nach den stereographischen Copien von Stefan Lösch (1881-1966)*, Herausgegeben von Rudolf Reinhardt. *Band I. Vorlesungen, Entwürfe, Fragmente*, Übertragen, bearbeitet und eingeleitet von Reinhold Rieger (Paderborn: Bonifatius Druck, 1989), 36-53.]

Appendix 2

Selections from Lectures on Church History [1823]

1. Purpose of the Study of Church History

In and for itself no particular purpose can be designated for Church history. Outside of itself Church history as the redemption and salvation history of the human race has nothing that it wishes to attain. Therefore the study of this history in itself cannot be used as a means to something else. We reiterate the events of this history ideally so as to tell of the temporal works of Christ and his Spirit with pure joy and to have an overview of these and to learn to know how he is the one in whom human beings are awakened; we do so also to point out in the general history of humanity the greatest participation aside from any special purpose, and how we ourselves have experienced it, and by this to become conscious of the community and unity in which we are set. In addition special goals that can be followed by this study are not set aside. On this matter there is no doubt, and there can be no doubt, that Church history like all history has the finest influence on the spirit's formation, and in all ways it preserves a firm character formation and practical excellence.

Both form themselves through life and observation as history steps before us in life. [Marginalia: And the parts that it preserves, the needs that proceed from it, and the applications that can be made from it are manifold.] (2) It teaches us not so much to grasp the divinity of Christianity as if we view its actions, the formations of whole nations, the divine and heavenly sense, which we see step forward in so many individual cases. (3) Church history is a school of piety and virtue. For the theologian (4), however, it has a particular value in providing a historical consciousness of the basis and consciousness of the Church whose spiritual potential the theologian particularly represents, as well as fitting such a theologian directly for the care of souls. [Marginalia: The present rooted in the past, goals not. No historical sense, the present. No direct interest.] Its impact on other profane as well as theological sciences is extensive.

[Translated from Johann Adam Möhler, *Vorlesungen über die Kirchengeschichte*, ed. Reinhold Rieger, 2 vols. (Munich: Erich Wewel, 1992), 1:10-11]

2. Concept of Church History

In general, a Church is a union of human beings who acknowledge the same religion so as to broaden and maintain among themselves a specific religiosity and ethic of this religion. Since this institution unites itself on the basis of a sure doctrine of faith, a history of the Church must tell the character and fate of the Church. Since this doctrine must necessarily externalize itself to a lesser or greater degree upon the customs and all relationships between human beings, the history of its actions will have to be delineated. As a religious union it has religious practices directed to the external adoration of God; history treats these and their changes. As an institution the union of these individuals has a constitution which history treats in its various changes. As an external union it comes into contact with other similar external unions, with other churches, with the state, and history separates out the friendly or inimical changing actions of these unions. In general, this is the content of Church history: in a word, it is the narration of the events in and with a religio-moral union.

Since it follows from the concept of a Church that there must be as many churches as there are religions, there are thus as many different church histories: Jewish, Mohammedan, Christian. We treat only the Christian. Christian Church history is thus a narration of the events in and with the religio-moral union that Christ founded.

3. Universal and Special History

[Marginalia: Universal history treats all the miraculous events in the Christian Church that have been drawn together as one from the origins of Christianity to the present time.] Church history is either a universal or a special history. Universal history treats the whole of Church history as one systematic whole, ordered partly according to time, partly according to matter. Special history, on the other hand, looks at single states and narrates the events of the Christian Church in these. In this sense there are histories of the Italian, the French, and the German Church. One could thus think that universal Church history arose out of special histories which received such a universal character that they told the history of a single state in its ecclesiastical relationship by stages from the beginning on.

4. Principle of Church History

The basic philosophical, scientific struggles that began at the end of the previous century raises one of the most difficult questions in relationship to Church history. Through this what had always been sensed darkly since the writing of Church history came to clear consciousness: Namely, questions were raised concerning the principle of Church history. But to avoid immediate misunderstandings, it must be noted that one does not understand by the principle of Church history some sort of idea out of which, as in a pure rational science, history is to be deduced and construed a priori. This would not give any history, which is an *experiential* science. The questions concerning the principle of Church history are nothing other than: What forms unity in the endless diversity of things which drew themselves together in the course of the Christian centuries? What is the direction of the chaos of events? What is the goal of the swirl of phenomena? History begins its path according to the eternal plans of Providence and follows, in spite of many obvious disturbances, one given direction. The point toward which this direction moves must be the principle of Church history. What is the direction of the Church? Or rather, what should the Church be? The idea of the Church herself is the realization of the Kingdom of God on earth. Therefore the history of the Church in the objective sense can be nothing other than the history of the realization of the Kingdom of God on earth. The principle of Church history is thus the Kingdom of God or that which under the special leading of the providence of the Holy Spirit in faith in Jesus brings into realization the Kingdom of love. This is the principle that preserves unity in diversity for us. This is the point toward which the course of events takes its direction, toward which the historian must thus continually look and never be in error. The historian will thus determine the character of a specific period or a specific party in a period according to its proximity or distance from this idea, that is, the historian must review chiefly and fully the relationship in which each period of Church history stands to Christian religiosity and morality. It is obvious that the preparation of Church history according to one principle first raises truly rational interest. If the mere narration of events, of the continuing changes of phenomena generally, produces and maintains fantasy, this higher conception of unity seeking reason on the other hand gives peace. Because nothing more individual remains, the manifold phenomena have a deeper relationship, those things that are scattered and clearly unrelated appear in a miraculous search for a single point. This speaks to our higher nature and preserves us from all one-sided emphases in history. Lacking this higher viewpoint many historians have lost themselves in particulars and establish as their foundation the human that in all sides externalizes its might. They do not raise themselves up to contemplate the working of the Holy Spirit in the history of the Christian Church and discover in this profane view nothing but sorrows, horror, and all things hateful.

5. Purpose of the Study of Church History

It is the plan of Providence that the human being is to be formed by, in, and through a human institution. Past generations lived for future generations (against egoism). But the past thus is the source of the present (or the present is the product of the past). All previous eras thus establish themselves as steps of formation upon which one is raised up to the present. History is the organ through which past eras speak to us and transmit the result of their having been. However, if the general result of all Church-historical phenomena (as was clarified in the previous section) is that the divine Kingdom make itself real, if we note that everything moves in this direction, if not quickly, at least slowly and with certainty, each of us must draw himself or herself to that which reflection over the whole of the past has presented, that is, the realization of the Kingdom of God in each of us, or formation in the religiosity or morality founded on faith in Jesus is the highest purpose of Church history for each of us, and thus all for the whole institution, since through it, gentlemen, are the goals (which it reaches through this weighty study which it here for the formation of its spirit, for the formation of authentic Christian religiosity and morality has achieved), given to all classes of human beings in whose union we live and work. We must learn to achieve the Christian religion lovingly from the heart, be inspired for it, if we see its great world-forming actions, the fortunate influences that it manifests on all things human. This is the chief purpose of Church history if we grasp it in its totality, if we look upon the large mass. How this relates to the furtherance of religiosity and morality will be discussed in the next section. We are speaking of the special needs and uses of Church history.

[6. Practical and Theoretical Use of Church History]

For easier discussion we wish to treat the parts and uses that Church history preserves under the topics: theory and practice.

a. Practice:

If we wish to note in particular the parts that Church history preserves, nothing more is to be encouraged than religiosity and virtue. We may remark that Jesus and his apostles appeared in Church history, that the first Christians above all, as well as many others who raised Christianity as an example for human beings are brought before our sight, that we meet enough individuals who gave themselves to truth, knowing they would die for it, that we meet individuals who were prepared to offer everything for the good of their fellow human beings and the advancement of the things of God. We often see, find the opportunity, in that which evil itself stirs up. Church history preserves for us above all a treasure of practical wisdom. A chance event can seldom arise in life that had not arisen earlier. Others find themselves in the same situation. Thus their wise or foolish bearing is a model for us. [Marginalia: If it is certain that only through external stirring of experiences the inner person achieves development and consciousness, history provides an endless number of examples for such formation. It is nothing other than a broadened experience. Our circle of experience is narrowed through time and space. Through history the experiences of all generations and times, insofar as their transmission is possible, are ours and they work upon us in an instructive and formative manner. The shortness of our life is at the same time lengthened through the study of history to the extent that this study itself is widened. As life works on life, so history makes it possible for us to form present possibilities for our activity, to gain for us a practical ability, and a wide-ranging conception of subjects for our use. A mere speculative processing hinders strength of character in that it acts solely with concepts. With it come bound at the same time unity and clarity of thought with practical life skills in us.] We see manifold superstition arising before us; we see how it violates human beings, and the waste it brings about. All this teaches us to hate it. But in that we observe what provides a cause for its rise, what circumstances are favorable to it, if we note that ignorance is its mother, the means are given us at the same time to distance ourselves from it and what follows from it.

History teaches us how there press upon the Christian Church many malformations that later as chief matters whose source is not longer known we seek to raise defenses against. History points them out to us in their true form, and taught by history our judgment cannot be false.

History teaches us the essence over against appearance, distinguishes the necessary from the contingent, content from the form. It allows everything nonessential to stand before our eyes. Under changed circumstances some of these pass, others last. The person who knows history knows its value and knows how to judge according to relationships. Above all, Church history leads us into the most manifold places, into relationships with wise persons and fools, with fanatics and illuminated individuals, with those who think differently and those who think the same. Through this it teaches us temperance, discretion, and wisdom. History in general is our leader and teacher in life; Church history follows this direction and in many cases is even better. [Marginalia: If we look at this more specifically we can distinguish in the study of history a formal and a material part. In the formal judgment of the value of Church historical study its influence can be observed on the stimulation, formation, and structuring of the highest powers of the human person. Just as the purely speculative sciences stir and shape chiefly human powers of thought, so history works above all on practical potentials and powers, influencing them by forming and structuring the life of the human person. Only life is made to work upon life. In history, however, only life stands before us. It broadens, in this way, the narrowness of our own experience and lengthens our life. The experiences of all times and places, insofar as their transmission is possible, become our experience, our possession. Should our era or the place in which we live be lacking great examples of piety or sure virtue to stir our pious and ethical situation, to awaken our slumber, to direct our spirit once again on a new path and structure one of its characteristics, the past completes the present and holds before us its great characters and models, and brings our own spirit to a development and clear consciousness of itself.

A practical virtue, versatility, and practical life skills are gained through the views and wide range that history preserves. But the strength of character through speculative study, if treated in a one sided fashion, is harmed. If we look back over the material part that Church history preserves, its relationship to the individual science comes into view and here its significance is greater than [sic]

In relationship to the sciences, however, the influence of church history is wider than has been believed. Leaving aside the theological sciences

(1) political history without church history is completely uncomprehensible. As soon as Christianity was victorious over paganism, the Church began to influence the states and to bring about the most manifold changes. Because of disturbances in the Church the Eastern Empire was greatly shaken and its decline hastened. In the West the Church was the real teacher of the states, the Church and the states were completely enmeshed in one another. When revolutions occurred in the state, the Church was always involved. Indeed, she finally directed external might over the state, thwarted or encouraged the plans of the strongest princes, and the later political construction of Europe arose out of causes in which the relationship of the Church to the state must be sought. On the well-known Peace of Westphalia that ended the wars of religion, established the

relationship between states, and brought forth a new order, see (c) below.

(b) *Concerning Civil Right.* How much light Christianity spread in this regard is clear from the single remark that by the new religious-moral principles, ethnic, state, and private legal principles, if they did not need to be restructured in new relationships, had to be modified. This influence externalized itself as soon as Christianity was established as the state religion in the Roman Empire. Many earlier laws were repealed and new ones established. Many edicts in Roman law touch the Church aside from this. The influence of Christianity on the formation of law in the northern states is clearer. From this one sees that Church history is inseparable from a history of civil law. A part of state law, however, the relationship between Church and State is best clarified by Church history. See below (d).

(c) *On Philosophy and Art.* The close relationship between philosophy and religion is illuminated as well in a superficial overview. A religion, which has such significant information on the essence of God and the human person, God's relationship to the universal whole and the human person, must have the weightiest influence on all practical sciences. What these influences were and how they remain only Church history can explain. The history of philosophy for a long period of the Christian Church is so close to it that it is a part of the history of religion. Art, however, carries the character of religion into the most important of its branches, painting, sculpture, music, architecture, and their specific forms. Out of the character of religion the chief parts of church historical study arise for the scientific artist, aside from that material that the artist takes from Church history. Above all Church history is important for every type of science since with the rise and fall of enlightened religious principles science itself at each point rises and falls.

(d) Without Church history canon law is not understandable at all nor, even more so, is any basic knowledge of it thinkable. How canon law was the constitution of the Church, how the constitution continually changed, and how another form was put in its place, how individuals ever more enmeshed themselves in the new order of things, how attempts were made to once again turn back to the old constitution, Church history can fully teach. It alone is the source for protecting the true, disarming opponents, speaking sensibly concerning matters, and judging the Church constitution of a particular period from a fitting standpoint and evaluating it.

Regarding the specific theological sciences Church history is the only source from which (a) the authenticity and the integrity of the books of the New Testament can be demonstrated and the history of the canon created. It is indispensable for understanding this latter issue, not only because the historic [*Historische*] is demanded for understanding each ancient writing, but also on grounds which we can yet further discuss. Moreover, Christian apologetics draws the most beautiful examples for the history of Christianity from Church history. (b) Without Church history it would be impossible to understand the dogmatic teachings of Christianity with certainty and completeness. In itself it makes clear that in the study of the written sources of a particular individual's doctrinal concepts, when case doubts over the true sense of this arise, the relations of the individual's contemporaries must be given preeminent weight. If it is proven that a teacher expressed his or her central principles only orally and that the system was also continued for a period orally, that later sources are merely occasional writings, indeed if it is expressed clearly (John 21:28) that they do not contain everything, that they presuppose oral instruction, and cite the teacher, it is certain beyond all doubt in the determination of all these sources as to what is authentically and truly the doctrine of this individual, history is the decisive factor, if the question needs to be determined. This is also what distinguishes Catholicism essentially from other religious parties; it acknowledges on the fore-mentioned grounds divine tradition alongside the Holy Scripture as the chief source for the knowledge of Christian doctrine. Since divine tradition can only be created out of history the great value this has for the dogmatician must be clear.

But because one wishes to reflect on revealed doctrines and to place them in relation to other wide-ranging areas of knowledge many kinds of explanations and opinions arise. Because no one wished to bring the divine doctrine, which came from Christ and was not systematized by the apostles, into a system, numerous connecting links were necessary that had to be discovered because they were not originally transmitted. These conceptions and connections grew and in time were held as revealed doctrines. Church history now teaches the dogmatician when and under what circumstances such things arose and protects the dogmatician from confusing the human with the divine or giving the human too great a value.

Similar reflections make Church history particularly important for morality.

Polemic, the *theological art of war*, which defends religion, the Church, against attacks, takes its most useful weapons from Church history.

Without Church history pastoral theology is a science of experience. Church history protects those concerned with practical pastoral care from great misconceptions in that it provides them with manifold situations. It encourages them to continual activity in that it offers them the finest human examples, allows them to see the invaluably best influence in life, to practice enlightened knowledge and tireless cautious zeal, and, on the other hand, to overcome the most troublesome results that arise from priests' ignorance and inability. In so far as the person involved with pastoral care finds opportunity in this review, he will be inspired in his office and will have tireless ability to carry it out. One needs only to recall that Christ and the apostles and individuals like the apostles appeared earlier in pastors' lives and in their pastoral roles, and the truth of what has been said will not appear dubious. More concerning this will be said at the beginning of the next section.

Finally, it should be noted that aside from a specific use of Church history we are led to its study through the same mysterious drive that leads us into the most distant past or antiquity. Everything that is human, that human beings suffered and did, is of interest to us. We see ourselves in our fellow human beings. How much more, then, will religious history and particularly the history of the religion that we acknowledge have an interest to us? Finally, we do not understand the present without the past. What is, one learns first properly to know by reflection on what was. Thus, to understand our present religious-ecclesiastical position in all its relations so as to orient ourselves, history is in every way necessary. This last value one often wishes to see as the chief purpose of Church history, but even if this is not the case, the use of Church history is nevertheless of great importance.

7. Selection of Material

For Church history to achieve its end, to be useful and valuable, it can be no simple register of names and dates, but, at the same time it cannot treat all events. This is particularly true of Church history that is offered only as a small section of the academic timetable. For this reason those matters must be chosen that have the greatest universality, that reflect great internal value, or had significant results. The needs of the theologian must be particularly considered and the selection must lead to a view of the idea and highest purpose of Church history.

8. Division of Church History

Church history can be divided in very different ways according to the differences of place and time or the content of these. If it is done according to spacial relations the whole breadth of the Christian Church can be the subject of its discussion, or it can be treated according to specific areas, the borders of which form the different national states, and in so far as it treats *all* these individual separated parts, it transmits the history of the whole Church. But the Church forms its essence according to an undivided whole, it so eagerly grasps everything together that such a treatment would not be possible without the greatest difficulty. Universal Church history thus dare not be handled as an inner concept of special history, but it must cast its glance over the whole expanse of the Christian Church at the same time. If the temporal aspect in particular is looked at, content will have priority, the stuff of history will be singled out, and similar and previously separated things brought together and presented from the beginning of the Christian Church to our own time. The history of dogmas, the external constitution of the Church, Church practices, the effects of Christendom on the life and fortunes of people, and so on. will be especially treated and all this together will provide a universal history. But all the manifestations of Christianity and the Church are formed together so that one of these material matters cannot be understood without the others that occurred at the same time. If Church history is divided according to the different character of the times, it is best to view all the parts of the Christian Church together, to gather together what is similar in matter. This is fitting for the nature of the matter in which nothing is divided but everything forms a unity: as much as possible must be brought together. An actual pragmatic treatment is possible, a clear conception is made simpler and a thought is supported. As far as the periods or eras are concerned they are . . . [sic]. The same material is given. But one must not be pedantic on this matter, holding that in each period the same rubric must be treated, since the character of eras differ. Two ways can be taken, both of which have been followed. One can narrate everything merely in a chronological order, that is, according to time, and what happened. By this means, however, the events come together in no other union and no other relation than that which occurs in time and a truly pragmatic view of history is because of this too wide reaching and numerous matters cannot be treated. Nor is the thought of the period supported by this means, but is confused.

Another way is to divide the whole of Church history temporally in larger sections. But there are many different views regarding this. . . . [Here follows a brief review of how other historians have done this.]

[Translated from Johann Adam Möhler, *Vorlesungen über die Kirchengeschichte*, ed. Reinhold Rieger, 2 vols. (Munich: Erich Wewel, 1992), 1: 29-42]

Appendix 3

Selections from the Lectures on Canon Law [1823]

1. Tradition as the Source of Canon Law

Tradition is "the faith of the Church of the first Christian era insofar as through it a regulation is viewed as the expression of Christ or of the apostles and as such is passed on through oral doctrine."[a]

The Catholic continues to reflect on this as follows: since Christ himself did not write down his teaching nor commanded his disciples to do so and since they composed their first works fifteen years after the death of their divine teacher and their other works much later, there was for certain a period during which the whole Christian doctrine was continued only traditionally. One can, therefore, say that the Holy Scriptures themselves are only a part of this tradition that the apostles received and passed on from Christ.

---

a. The quotations here and in most of the second paragraph are taken directly from Ferdinand Walter, *Lehrbuch des Kirchenrechts*, 17-19

They are only a part (although by far the weightiest part) since the apostles nowhere declared that they wrote down everything and in fact stated the opposite (John 21:25). Therefore, from the time of the apostles the same view was taken of oral transmission as the Holy Scriptures indicate. 2 Thessalonians 2:14: Hold firm to the doctrine that I taught you in writing and orally. Irenaeus, *Against the Heresies*, 3:4: Therefore, we keep one tradition that reaches back to the time of the apostles, that is, one that always and everywhere was held firm in the Church, of divine origins. Even the Protestants can base the doctrine of the inspiration of the writers of Holy Scripture on tradition, indeed, the authenticity and integrity of the Holy Scriptures themselves, not to mention such Church practices as worship on Sunday and infant baptism. In general, therefore, nothing opposes tradition as a source. Whether this or that individual tradition is of divine origin must naturally first be demonstrated in an historical critical manner.

These are the grounds why we also count the original tradition among the divine sources for canon law.

2. Divine Tradition

From what has been said so far it is evident that the indefectibility of the Church relates only to that which is actually a revealed doctrine from Jesus; it is not the case that through infallibility new, previously nonexistent truths are communicated to the Church. All the seeds of the Holy Spirit were given at the same time as the Spirit communicated itself and undertook formation. These seeds could be more clearly brought to consciousness as they developed, but all was already given at the beginning with the Spirit's essence and inner ground. Through the seeds would come forth only what was present. The doctrine that was in the Church was to be passed on without falsification. The Church is, therefore, not a revealer of new teaching, but only a bearer of truth as Paul calls her in 1 Timothy 3:15. She only speaks out of that which she has been given to know in and through transmission, that is, divine aid is concerned only with preservation. From this the following can be said:

1. If freedom from error concerns only doctrine, be it theoretical or practical, it is not related to matters of discipline, certainly to nothing nonessential or contingent.

2. If Christian doctrines are revealed by Jesus, their freedom from error cannot be based on philosophical concerns, facts, and so on.

3. If, when controversies arise, the Church only declares what revealed doctrine is, what the original, ever-present doctrine is, it is necessary when upholding infallibility that there be no new revelation through the Holy Spirit but only preservation of what is already given. In this respect the activity of the Holy Spirit and its influence on the Church is established. On this basis

4. the significance of the divine tradition or transmission for the whole Church system is illuminated.

The acceptance of this rests on the following propositions: the teaching of Christ was presented orally by Christ himself and his disciples. Later the Gospels, which offer us unquestionable details regarding the teachings and deeds of Jesus, were composed by Jesus' disciples and the disciples of the apostles, even though none of them were intended to present a complete outline of Jesus' doctrine (John 21:25). Numerous apostles wrote letters, but they did so always calling on the oral instruction that they had received (2 Thess. 2:15, 3:6, 2 Tim. 1:13-14; 2:2). It took some time, however, before the Gospels and Epistles, which had for the most part been directed to single congregations, circulated universally. But even then most rooted themselves in the oral instruction that was the more carefully preserved, the more one became aware of its significance. Attention was given to the apostolic doctrine in all the congregations in which the apostles or their followers were found. It was considered not as something past that must first be transmitted through historical critical methods, but as always present in living word. When controversies arose, reference was made to the general teaching of the Church, in particular of the chief apostolic churches, and the unity that arose in this manner was correctly set over against novel ideas and was viewed as the doctrine that had always been present in the Church. Irenaeus, Tertullian and others argued in this way (Irenaeus, *Against the Heresies*, 3:3; Tertullian, *On the Prescription of Heretics*, 32; Origen, *Commentary on Matthew*, tr. 29, no. 46). It was even less possible to establish a full proof from the Holy Scriptures since the heretics had set parts of the Scriptures against other parts, had mutilated the authentic works, and had by preconceptions twisted the interpretation of those on the authority of which agreement had been reached. As a result it was necessary once again to demonstrate the authenticity of the Scriptures and this cannot be done by the Scriptures themselves but only out of the tradition and with the view of the Church. Therefore, Augustine said: "I would not myself have accepted the Scriptures if the view of the Church had not made this possible."[1] And any questionable, difficult passages that appear to contradict one another and from which a variant doctrine could be deduced are judged by the tradition.

Divine tradition is not related merely to this or that individual doctrine, but to the totality of the Christian-apostolic teaching, although individual doctrines can be quite definitely demonstrated from this. For us tradition is no longer merely oral transmission but the common faith of the Church set down in the Creeds. The writers who lived at that time, above all the Church fathers, are only examples of what is believed, how any one fact testifies to each qualified witness. On these foundations rest the well-known proposition of Vincent of Lerins that what is Catholic is what was always, everywhere, and at all times believed in the Church. [See] Vincent of Lerins, *Commonitorium*, 3: "We hold that which was passed down everywhere, always, and among all. We acknowledge this to be the one true faith that the Church confessed throughout the whole earth." In all other cases what is authentically Christian is quite properly tied to the teaching office of the Catholic Church.

Because of misunderstandings and misinterpretations of this principle many have charged the Catholic Church with opposing freedom of conscience, introducing human premises as divine commands in the place of the gospel, hindering the fulfillment of the human race, and establishing as a norm for all time what individuals from an earlier period have decided. One sees that earlier propositions are purely evangelical. By submitting to them the Catholic is using free acts of will and is following inner conviction. In this way Christ is concerned for the Church and it can be demonstrated that no church is possible in any other way. If the Church generally in any particular period expressed its faith over a contentious doctrine, this cannot be changed in the future because it is an expression concerning a fact, concerning the inherited general faith of the Church that can in no way be contradicted at a later time. How could a later period know better what was inherited, what the transmitted apostolic doctrine was, than an earlier period? The doctrine of Jesus Christ would appear as problematic if the contradiction between a later period and an earlier one were upheld in such a way that no certainty can be established concerning a particular situation. The doctrine also appears as problematic because the Holy Spirit, thought of in this matter as protecting the doctrine of Christ in a written form, cannot contradict itself. Therefore, it is not faith in human propositions because in this case only that is communicated under the direction of the divine Spirit that was always the doctrine of the Church and thus is of apostolic and truly Christian origin. The statements of the Church such as that of the Council of Nicea, for example, is not the subjective judgment of the Fathers who gathered there, but a testimony to the faith inherited from the apostles. The person who accepts their statement, accepts not a human judgment but the inherited apostolic doctrine. One is also justified in turning the argument around and pointing out that anyone who studies what the doctrine of Christ is, who believes that he or she has bracketed all the past and the present, destroys the life of the Church, acts in an unevangelical manner, opposes the order of Christ, and is in fact following human concepts, namely, one's own. True freedom is to follow the commands of Christ with freedom.

The ground of misunderstandings arises if at any particular period a doctrine is expressed in a general synod, and one looks upon this confirmation as a discovery, a novelty, whereas in fact an already long-standing doctrine was thus only made firm in the face of new insights and errors as they arose, so as to give greater certainty. Because each individual church expresses the inherited doctrine through its bishop (the opposing interpretation has newly arisen and is not grounded in the apostolic transmission), the individual congregation, which can be taken by surprise, is made firm through the public exposition of the whole body. As has been said in matters of faith the Church has no legislative, productive power which preserves the truth, but only one which fends off error.

As a result the true progress of the human race is in no way destroyed. According to the established propositions of the Catholic Church, only that is protected that is the doctrine of Christ. The progress of human culture cannot be established in its rejection of the doctrine of Christ in any way. Such an action would be a step backward. In the Christian sense (to penetrate this sense more deeply), to make progress is to understand the relationships within the doctrine of Christ in itself and between the doctrine and other matters, to be grasped and penetrated by the doctrine, and in this manner to change faith into understanding, if one may so state the matter. True progress would be hindered if the style of presentation of a particular period, the manner of conceiving a doctrine according to a particular age according to that age's explanation and foundations, would be viewed as one and the same thing as the doctrine of Christ itself. Such a view is in no way in the spirit of the Catholic system.

Vincent of Lerins expresses himself strikingly on this matter: "What did the Church in its conciliar decisions do other than grasp the earlier simple faith more carefully, preach in a more penetrating fashion what had earlier been preached indifferently, and form with greater care what had earlier been despised with all too great certainty" (*Commonitorium*, 32). The Church did this through its conciliar decrees because of heretical novelties, so that she could pass on markedly in a written manner to her followers what she had received from her ancestors through a purely oral transmission. She thus brought together a great sum of doctrines in a few words and for the most part in a form easily understood, marked not with a new sense but with a new terminology.

[Translated from Möhler's 1823-1825 Lectures on Canon Law as published in Joseph Rupert Geiselmann, ed., *Geist des Christenthums und des Katholizismus* (Mainz: Matthias-Grünewald, 1940), 399-403]

Appendix 4

On the Salvation of the Pagans [1825]

It has always been accepted by all and must indeed be accepted by all Christians that no one can save himself or herself, but that all need the Saviour and Redeemer. In the early Church Jesus was viewed with clearest consciousness as the individual from whom all truth that was found in the pagan world came. Likewise, it was taught that he was the origin of all true good that could be found in that world: the search to know the truth and to know the good were one in their roots. Justin says that in Socrates the Logos opposed the pagan gods through the daimon. Must not this be understood as the Logos through Socrates opposing error, sinfulness in polytheism through which idolatry was possible? [Justin, *First Apology*, 15; *Second Apology*, 10]. The relationship in which the Redeemer stands to the whole pre-Christian world is clearer yet in Irenaeus. He had to deal with individuals who broke the relationship of later Christianity with the earlier period and understood the earlier period as being under the direction of an evil spirit or at the least one of a lesser good god. Irenaeus says that from the beginning of the world Christ worked among all human beings, that he directed them to a sense of their sinfulness, awoke in them the need and in it the yearning for redemption, and thus prepared everything for his coming; all those who lived rightly bore in themselves a desire for the Redeemer and eagerly accepted his voice. All these individuals belonged to the Church and were saved. They formed images of the future, and the present embraced them in its idea. These great ideas placed Christ as the center of human history, to which everything was drawn, that directed all things, that penetrated all things, that communicated life and power wherever it was found, and therefore gave salvation to all those that followed it. Irenaeus, *Against the Heresies*, 4:22, 2: "For *all individuals all together who from the beginning according to capacity, in their generation have both feared and loved God* and practiced justice and piety toward their neighbors, *and have earnestly desired to see Christ and to hear his voice. . . .* [sic] For it is truly one God who directed the patriarchs toward his dispensations, and has justified the circumcision by faith and the uncircumcision through faith [Rom. 3:30]. For as in the first we were prefigured, so are they represented in us, that is, the Church, and receive the recompense for those things which they accomplished" (Cf. ibid., 2:6,2).

Christ's descent into hell is, as is well known, related to this topic. On it Irenaeus says: "It was for this reason too that the Lord descended into the regions beneath the earth, preaching his advent there also, and declaring the remission of sins to those who believe in him, . . . [sic] those who proclaimed his advent and submitted to his dispensations, *the just*, prophets, and patriarchs, to whom he remitted sins in the same way as he did to us, which sins we should not lay to their charge, if we would not despise the grace of God. For as these individuals did not impute to us our transgressions that we wrought before Christ was manifested among us, so also it is not right that we should lay blame on those who sinned before Christ's coming. For all come short of the glory of God [Rom. 3:23] and are justified not by themselves, but by the advent of the Lord—they who earnestly direct their eyes toward the advent of his light" (Ibid., 4:27, 2).

These ideas are made particularly clear in Clement of Alexandria, and in his work there appears a particularly close union between the rays of truth given through the Logos and the justifying power offered to the pagans. He depicts the truth itself as appearing in

Christ, the center of all earlier individual rays of light which nevertheless all arise in him. Likewise he describes the pre-Christian world as standing under Christ's direction in moral matters, and thus often calls the Logos the educator of the human race. In *Miscellanies*, 1:7, he states that philosophy (he means truth as it arises in all systems since what is false in it is of human source) came to the Greeks according to a divine plan like rain to the land that enriches it. He continues: "The one who from the beginning of the world sowed the enriching seed and has ruled in every age as the Lord Logos, created the land which is in the human person, but the different character of times and places that received him begot diversity."[2] Therefore, he says in *Miscellanies*, 6:17, that if one does not ascribe philosophy to God, one sets aside Providence, the concern of the divinity for every individual being. Reason begets the good, but the incitement to it is given by God. "Now then many things in life take their rise from some exercise of human reason, having received the kindling spark from God." This kindling power reveals itself chiefly in the good. Clement then continues: "Indeed the intentions of virtuous individuals find their base in the inner working of divine activity, in that the soul is directed in a certain manner and the divine will communicates itself to the human spirit. Servants of the divinity aid in this service. . . . The Shepherd is concerned for each individual sheep. A marked concern, however, is directed to each one that possesses particular abilities and is particularly able to be of use to the whole. Among these are those who have the ability to lead and teach. Through them the power of providential concern in particular reveals itself, if God wishes to demonstrate his good deeds toward humankind through the teaching and leadership of such a person, and he always so wishes. Therefore, he raises up individuals who have the qualities for saving acts, for pious intentions, for peace and good deeds. However, wherever good manifests itself, it arises out of a good intention and is redirected back to such an intention. . . . How absurd is it then that those who ascribe to Satan disorder and unrighteousness, make him the founder of good institutions and philosophy! Satan must then have been closer to the Greeks than the divinity. Each must give what it in itself is: to fire warmth is ascribed, to light, illumination. Nothing good comes from evil and light cannot bring forth darkness. Philosophy does not arise from evil since it makes human beings virtuous. It is of divine origin since God can only do good deeds."[3]

Therefore, he ascribes to philosophy a justifying power (*Miscellanies*, 1:4, 5 and 1:5), but at the same time interprets this as a power that begets and is directed to the appearance of the Lord himself (Ibid., 6:6). "Just as in the fullness of time preaching came, so foundations, the law, and the prophets were given to the barbarians and philosophy to the Greeks so that they could receive the preaching of the gospel."[4] And just as Irenaeus says that Christ announced redemption to the just who had earlier died, so Clement ascribes the same to the pagans as well as to the Jews (Ibid., 6). Thus, all beginnings of salvation arise in Jesus Christ and reach their full end in him. (See also Lumper, 4:462, although a certain constraint leads him otherwise somewhat astray.)

[Translated from edition by Emil Joseph Vierneisel, "Aus Möhlers handschriftlichem Nachlass," *Theologische Quartelschrift* 119 (1938): 109-117. According to Vierneisel, the manuscript was included with the corrections to Möhler's *Unity of the Church*.]

Appendix 5

Introduction to the Lectures on Church History 1826-1827

1. On History, Its Concept, and Its Laws in General

Objectively considered history is the spiritual life of humanity developing and establishing itself in time under the direction of Providence. Subjectively it is the ideal reconstruction, the knowledge concerning the development of that spiritual life of humanity. The human person, therefore, established under its relationship to the directing Divinity, appears to us here in its becoming and in its continuing formation. The two aforementioned spiritual natures, God and the human person, are thus the factors, and history is their common product. We must now view the essence of the human person to penetrate deeper into the nature of history. Acting with freedom, the human person's spirit is the producing power in all its movements and endeavors, and although the human person, as one essence established in a complete relation and limited with finitude, requires external stimulations and activities to attain independence for itself and to become free to work, nevertheless something cannot be or be called truly human in which the spirit of the human person, stimulating and working upon it, taken up and active in it, has not determined its thoughts, wishes, and acts accordingly. All of history must accordingly be understood as an evolution of the human spirit, as the actions of its power. The totality of phenomena in the area of humanity is the material of history. However, the human spirit itself is that which, hidden in it, appears there. In history the law that all phenomena must relate to the active spirit and so must be established under the law of causality presents itself as the ideal reconstruction of the spiritual life of humanity unfolding in time. For us there is nothing comprehensible that cannot be conceived in the aforementioned form, in its initial beginning. That is the pragmatism of history. As in actual life everything occurs necessarily according to the aforementioned law, so it must be described and understood according to the same. What does not fit into this form is historical contingency, which history is not able to take up into itself. (This treatment of history is possible in that the historian is a human person and can therefore understand all things human.)

The expressed treatment of history, however, comes under the law of the *understanding* of causality. This law is, however, nothing other than a reflection of a higher law of the reason. Reason seeks the absolute, a source that has no source, but itself is the source of all things, that is the supersensual and eternal. Thus this higher rational reflects the understanding, which therefore also in the same way seeks the base of everything given in time, that is, the ground of all phenomena. The understanding in and for itself moves forward in its general view of the world in an infinite regression and never finds that which has no source in the observation of the source of the universal whole, that is, never satisfies the higher human person. In the same way mere pragmatic description in history never offers satisfaction. The laws of reason here always desire, even here, an eternal, which stands above the temporal, a coherence of the whole sensual world with the suprasensual, a grasp of the former in the latter. The human person also acts according to eternal laws, is the establisher of a series of phenomena, and in a like manner according to the type of the individual is the whole of humanity. The divinity binds humanity to a whole, leads it to a final end, without disturbing human freedom. . . .

2. Christian Church History

Until now history has been conceived as a large whole as it forms itself through the development of all spiritual powers of the human person, through the coming-forth of all its needs and the institutions that express these needs, through the inner mutual activities of all peoples forming a great total life under God's supreme guidance. This all-embracing history can, however, like the human person itself according to its differing spiritual powers and needs, be divided into two large parts, the one of which contains the development of its fully highest, its religious, powers, the other of which contains the unfolding of its other powers. In both parts two great institutions arise: the Church and the State. Thus there is a church history and a state history, a division that was first possible and necessarily arose through Christianity, but which can be applied to the pre-Christian period, a division between religion and nation. And thus the history of states must be viewed from a religious point of view. All history, particularly the Church history before Christ, is the introduction and preparation for Christ, the center of the whole of world history. Church history is concerned with Christ's foundation and work. Christian Church history is therefore in the objective sense Christian life developing and unfolding in time. In the subjective sense it is the description of this development, knowledge concerning it. A completely new life of the greater part of humanity entered with Christianity. The subject of Christian Church history is the one who planted this new seed of life, how the initiator so planted it, what means he established for its nourishment and preservation, how it expanded and worked, how it was threatened to be narrowed and suppressed.

3. The Idea of Christian Church History

Anyone who wishes to write true history must, since one history of humanity can be divided into many parts, begin from a unity, from a basic thought penetrating the whole that carries and allows everything to be grasped within itself, toward which everything relates itself, which binds every individual into a true organism and through this leads to an actual work of art, a free creation of human beings. Every history is indeed a writing of a life, and this specific inner life power, this specific characteristic is that which unfolds itself organically. Because of this all phenomena stand in a specific history in a dynamic relationship to the individual life principle. This is also the case in national history. The inner principle of a history must thus be specifically conceived, so as to understand the individual part as well as the whole. To describe this in concepts is to express its idea. In Church history as well as in history generally, the search for this idea is the more necessary, the more the freedom of the human person can be thought to be denied, because when this is done the concept of history itself is negated. Therefore all movements even in the area of Church history are given which are possible through the possibility of a twisted use of freedom. Evil and good appear beside one another and it often appears as if the mass of the first conquers and the higher and divine is pressed down. If we are not certain of the higher idea, which bears the whole, we enter into danger, lose ourselves in a wasted chaos of events, and do not arrive at a true understanding of Church history. We have many examples of this. Most contemporary writings on Church history offer such. On the other hand, the continuing change of events will create a fantasy, the understanding can be satisfied by a common pragmatism, although the demands of reason cannot be. To find the idea of Church history we must have grasped the Christian Church herself and her essence. The Church is the unity of the life of all Christian believers founded through the redemption in Christ and the communication of the divine Spirit, which manifests the reconciliation of human beings with God through Christ in the reconciliation and uniting of human beings among themselves. Without divine love and a holy sense this community cannot stand, and only through these does it stand. If this is now the true concept of the Church, Church history can have no other leading idea except this, the unity of Christian life, and no higher unity. We see all this and gravitate to it. Everything comes together here in a true organic way, and organically proceeds from here, the soul of the whole. At the same time we can designate by this the value of the great periods in history and all individual periods of Church history. The more this unity and community stands forth with freedom and conscious-ness, the more value it has for us. Great disturbances constrain and break in upon these, but unwearied we find again the divine power to renew true life in unity. The true understanding of whole periods is the more possible for us the more we discover the key in this idea, so as to distinguish and grasp the different times according to their basic character and to orient ourselves to our own times, and thus to dare to cast a prophetic glance onto the future.

Others view the Church herself in an undetermined way as a structure established to reach religious-moral ends, and for this reason establish the achievement of such ends as the leading idea. Without piety and ethics the whole is nothing at all. But Christian piety without community is unthinkable and is only formed and preserved in community. . . .

[Translated from Johann Adam Möhler, *Vorlesungen über die Kirchengeschichte*, ed. Reinhold Rieger (Munich: Erich Wewel, 1992), 1: 3-8; cf. Joseph Rupert Geiselmann, ed., *Geist des Christenthums und des Katholizismus* (Mainz: Matthias-Grünewald, 1940), 391-96]

4. Particular Characteristics of the Church Historian

If Church history is a development of Christian life, no one will be able to understand it except the person in whom that Christian life is awakened, at least in whom it is beginning to be awakened. [Marginalia: Just as the aesthetic sense is an inner source for evaluating beautiful objects presented externally, so the Christian sense, the inner source, consecrates us to the manifestations of the Christian life outside of us, to discover its meaning in participation and love, to grasp the essence that it expresses in itself, and to discover its source.] Life can only be grasped by life, just as only life begets life. The actions of the Christian sense that are begotten through the higher divine activity in the Christian, meet us here. Who is able to evaluate this other than the person in whom that activity has formed itself and in whom a divine life is planted? Such a person takes up the charges that are directed against himself or herself from the outside and answers them. We also understand the general history of humanity because we feel and discover the human itself. In the same way the presence of special Christian thought and feeling is the source of the influences in Christian history. Above all, nothing external can be known by us in a living way unless a receptivity that stands with it internally and homogeneously is present. One must thus live in the Church with spirit and mind to understand its history. The Church must have already sought to have visited its formation on us successfully to understand the totality of its forms and developments. As a result of the lack of this characteristic, history is so often disfigured. One could say that because of this history must necessarily be partisan and one-sided. [Marginalia: Basic Principle: No religion, no native country? Charge. One must be history to write the history of the Jews. Pagan, Turkish? A higher human culture is necessary to understand a lower one, not the converse.]

[Translated by Johann Adam Möhler, *Vorlesungen über die Kirchengeschichte*, ed. Reinhold Rieger (Munich: Erich Wewel, 1992), 1:9-10]

5. The Principle of Tradition

Heresy can be compared with the Fall. In the original Fall of the human race the unity of humanity's spiritual power was ruined. In each of the many peoples in whom the one race had fallen one spiritual power, repressing all others, maintained a high one-sided counterbalance. The first fall repeated itself: the great community of Christians, the one Church, divided itself into sects, each of which allowed itself to be determined in its view of Christianity by only *one* certain spiritual capacity without preserving the other parts that were fitted for it. [Marginalia: As a result ever more monstrous structures and distortions arose. It was as if all members of the body wished to be the tongue.] As a result each grasped only that side of the one Christianity that expressed its capacity, the direction of which they finally transmitted. Thus the Gnostics took up the gospel with only an overwealming feeling and with a fantasy full of desire and directed toward the infinite and supernatural. They, therefore, only valued the divine in Christ. On the other hand, those who opposed the doctrine of the divinity of Christ sought to grasp Christianity with the understanding alone. They held fast to the human in Christ, expressed to the understanding as the finite, and the divine nature of Christ escaped them. [Marginalia: "Which conception of Christianity does my feeling best relate to?" asked the one. "Which does my understanding best relate to?" asked the second. And a third asked: "Which does my fantasy best relate to?" This is egoism, the drive to let oneself be set off over against God and Christ.]

Other sects moved between these two extremes, without being able to achieve the unity and harmony of the spiritual power, and for this reason they could not grasp the one and whole and true gospel. In this manner the division of one spiritual power from the others resulted in a separation of a part of the gospel from the whole, and with this the splintering of one member of the Church from the whole body of the Church. However, the principle of the unity of the Church returned here again. In this new fall the phenomena repeated itself in that a diversity of created principles was initiated. The original Fall into sin was accompanied by polytheism. Each nation had its particular divinity. In the second fall the result was that the creator of a new life, Christ, was presented differently in each sect and a type of poly-Christism arose. Finally, the history of sects in themselves suggests that characteristically a Babylonian confusion of tongues was formed as a result of the confusion of thoughts and splintering of souls that infinitely weighed down upon those who did not belong to a specific sect and often made it impossible for them to consider their essence closely. [Marginalia: Subjectivity of Christianity among all]

In the Catholic Church the true ground of all these phenomena was correctly grasped. One viewed the sects in fact as a continuing development of the original fall into sin, and thus properly noted that among those who founded sects no full new birth was in evidence and the old self-seeking ruled continually. As a result, the external separation from community arose with the Church and its doctrines, as did the separation of the spiritual capacity from a not yet completely active inner union. From this one concluded that spiritual reunion with God in Christ had to be known in the remaining unity with the totality of believers. [Marginalia: See Paul, Romans, 16:17; Col. 1:6; 2:6; 2 Thess. 2:15.]

In the further pursuit of this basic proposition against the heretics, however, the Church first came to a full consciousness of herself in the whole and in her individual parts and gained the opportunity to express this. That she was led to this is the single remaining benefit that came from heresy. . . . Heresy was confronted so as to overcome its false teaching: [5] From the beginning of the existence of the Church through all the following periods Christ and his Spirit worked in the Church in the whole as in each true believer individually. The continuation of the Church is an eternal repetition of her beginning, an eternally new creation of Christ. The Church does not change. The spirit of Christ is always the same in her, the same, that is, as understood as the divinity, its activity, the new Holy Spirit of believers in the Church. In the same way faith, through which the spirit of Christ is received, is the same from the beginning through all time. . . . Races and individual human beings change, but Christ and the Holy Spirit in the Church remain eternal and with them so does the word of Christ. Christ retains consistency between himself, his word, his teaching and true understanding; Or, the inner and outer spirit, the spirit of the tradition and its teaching (*tradux spiritus* [Tertullian, *Scorpiace*, 9] and *traditio, paradosis*) are never overcome.

If the same Spirit is active in individual believers as is in the whole, the individual can then only agree with the whole if he or she has not taken up a foreign spirit. Anyone who wishes to be always in possession of the original doctrine of Christ and the apostles must take only the general doctrine of the Catholic Church, *the* Church, which was there from the beginning and in which the same doctrine in an unbroken continuum, in a continual spiritual generation with the Spirit of Christ, was passed on. [Marginalia: One does not come to possess the true apostolic doctrine through the use of the Scriptures alone. The oral transmission, the *living* word, was earlier than the Scripture. Before the apostles and their followers wrote, they preached and passed on their writings only to those who had continually taken up the living preaching in the Church and into whom the Spirit of Christ had already been breathed.] The Holy Scripture dare not, therefore, be separated from the Church, its inner and outer tradition. Originally the individual books of the Scriptures were passed on physically to those who were already Christians and had thus been raised in the Church. Thus, Scripture and tradition belonged together for all times, and the sense of the Scriptures is truly contained in tradition for those of us in the Church.

The demonstration from tradition can be outlined in the following form which is most accessible to a merely human point of view. The apostles founded the various churches, Antioch, Ephesus, Philippi, Corinth, Rome, and so on. All these were in agreement with one another. How is it now possible that the original truth should be forsaken and that a unity of error be reached? Anyone who wishes to know the Christian-apostolic truth should seek it in the apostolic churches, which are the Catholic churches.

These basic propositions the Catholic Church developed against heresy. She founded herself on these so that the believers would form from the time of Christ throughout all ages a unity, a moral person, which insofar as it is moral must have a higher self-consciousness. This is the one faith insofar as we consider it as a spiritual possession of believers. In this way the individual was

bound to the whole and its holy transmission which, with all the
objective specificity and unchangeable necessity of history, opposes
subjective arbitrariness. At the same time the doctrines of faith were
set under divine protection for all times as their divine origin alone
would indicate. Moreover, since the Holy Scriptures were indivisibly
bound to the Church and her doctrine, in the spirit of which alone
were the Scriptures to be explained, a twofold approach resulted. If
any reader cultivated merely one or the other spiritual power and as
a result accepted only that aspect of the Holy Scriptures that the
dominating spiritual power presented, the other side reviewed the
matter, pointed to the unchangeable common tradition and set the
matter straight. Thus the Holy Scripture was mediated by the
tradition in the whole and saved in its individual parts. We have
seen that almost all the sects rejected or mutilated the Holy Scriptures in whole or in part according to their own one-sided interpretations of Christianity and thus composed completely new Holy
Scriptures.

By means of tradition, however, which not only contained all the
ideas of the Holy Scripture but expressed many more specific and
clearer ideas than these, the Scriptures were firmly held, pure and
unfalsified. Indeed, those Scriptures that were holy were the direct
object of the tradition and at no time could be considered other than
by means of it. Finally, the best path to inner purification and
cleansing from sin and the renewal of a holy and divine life is bound
in the closest fashion with the system of Church and tradition as it
has been presented. Through the activity of the Holy Spirit bound
with individuals' own human power the unity of the human person
with God and the harmony of the human race in itself was reestablished. Thus the individual was made more accessible to the
knowledge of the Christian doctrines of faith as the disposition itself
was made ready and proper in a purer, holier, and more divine way.
As a result the greatest value was placed on the Church. St. Irenaeus
therefore expressly demanded that the customary education in the
Church be directed to an understanding of the Holy Scripture and
tradition; Clement of Alexandria remarked that only the holy sense
was directed to holy doctrine; and Origen stated that Christ was
grasped only in the community, that is, in inner living formation
with the Church, which is not possible without pure love. The deep
wisdom of the Church can be first fully known if it desires that the
Holy Scriptures be read only with the Church, and therefore the
comment is often made that outside the Church the Scriptures cannot

be understood. If the sense for the Gospel is taken up on the way to spiritual rebirth and through the Church's education, then it can also be first understood. In opposition to the heretics who believed they had grasped the whole after they had considered one side of Christianity and handled the Holy Scriptures accordingly this was made quite clear. (3) It is obvious that the Holy Scripture was first saved in its totality through the system of the tradition of the Church. Holy Scripture, part of tradition. On all sides, all parts of the Scripture. Hermeneutic rules defend the Scripture well even though they are not the only things taken up by the Church. (4) Development can only occur according to rules. "Development" is "becoming." All becoming, however, establishes a being, firm and specific. This is formed through tradition. Becoming is the Church and being, she will become. In this antithesis the high earnestness of the Church stands, her deep wisdom over against the simplicity of the heretics who express their next best opinions as the true gospel and thereby deny everything that they cannot grasp because of their sinful limitations.

The clearest discussion of the doctrine of tradition occurs in Irenaeus, bishop of Lyons (d. A.D. 202), in his composition *Against the Heresies* (1:10; 3:3), and in Tertullian, who has already been made mention of in the history of the Montanists. His work on prescription in which he treats tradition in particular was written when he was a Catholic. But even as a Montanist, in contradiction to his newly formed principles, he held firmly to tradition. Perhaps Tertullian does not develop his thoughts on this matter as deeply as does Irenaeus, but he does so with greater precision and style.

6. The Catholic Confession of Faith

Viewed in the abstract and externally, tradition is nothing other than the totality of the inherited Church doctrine. The tradition that in its essence was written and opposed to the heretics as the general inherited doctrine of the Church is not mere word; it was written, and therefore held for the future so that the identity of the consciousness of believers of a later time could be externally associated with the earlier period. This occurred in the public liturgy, in the hymns and the prayers of believers, which are indeed the expression of the faith, as well as in the writings of the Fathers of the Church which are connected in an unbroken descent from the apostles. Thus

Eusebius, a writer who opposed the Theodotians, cited ([*Ecclesiastical History*,] 5:28) the Church's hymns and earlier Catholic writings. Paul of Samosata also sought to suppress hymns that glorified Christ as God to set aside the express direction of earlier belief. In particular, the confessions of faith were noted which at particular times were distinguished and set forth against the heretics as the Church's faith. But not all confessions of faith arose in opposition to the heretics. Among these were the Apostolic Creed which was not named because the apostles wrote it in its present form but because it contained the apostolic faith and reached back to their day. It has been asserted that it was written against the Gnostics on the basis of a baptismal formula and that the closer treatments of the Church's faith on the Father, the Son, and the Holy Spirit were added as and insofar as the Gnostics took up these issues. [Marginalia: It is not indicated what an antithesis means.] The need was earlier felt as alone reliable to express the basis of the Christian faith in few sentences as the Gnostics attacked these. Finally, the so-called Oriental, Roman, and Aquilian Creeds, themselves in the form of the Apostolic Creed generally, developed from it, are only other editions of it and point to its antiquity. [Marginalia quotation from Augustine, Sermon 212, On the Creed]

In its very simple structure and obvious plainness the Creed conceals an inexhaustible richness in itself with the unfolding of which the spiritual powers of the centuries have busied themselves. It was truly understood only in the Church. The clearest evidence of this is the misunderstandings of the sects who knew it but understood its simplicity and consciousness as poverty, as it was used at the time. [Marginalia: bibliographic references.] The more often this happened the Church explained it more closely and brought what was hidden to light. Thus, for example, the Church expressed its faith in the divinity of Christ in words, stating that he was the only begotten Son of the Father. This doctrine the Ebionites, Theodotians, and Atremonites also knew, but they understood by the expression "only-begotten son" a mere human being whom God designated as his beloved above all other human beings. [Marginalia: Therefore, the later Creeds expressed themselves more specifically and took up all particular developments that arose in the battles with the Gnostics, opponents of the divinity of Christ, and the anti-Trinitarians.] In this manner the doctrine of the Church developed and a comparison of the so-called private creeds which we find in Irenaeus (*Against the Heresies*, 1:10), Tertullian (*On Prescription against Heretics*,

13), Origen (*On First Principles*, preface), and Gregory Thaumaturgus leads to a brief overview of the interesting comments on the manner in which the development generally proceeded. Continually closer specifications of which the Apostolic Creed contained because of the battles with the heretics were carefully taken up. Thus Irenaeus called Christ "God" instead of merely "the only begotten Son of God," and Tertullian in his Creed against Praxeas (*Against Praxeas*, 2) specified the matter more closely by saying that the Son was to be distinguished in person from the Father. In spite of this, both commented, and properly, that the faith that each expressed had been there from the beginning; it was, of course, the undeveloped faith that was first taken up into clear consciousness because of the attack on the faith by the heretics.

This development of faith, whose necessity is clear and whose reality is undeniable, the Church fathers of this period already grasped. [Marginalia: Therefore, in fact, the Church reached that development and ripened in the fullness of time in a slow but certain way against the Gnostics and the Montanists who swirled in darkness. The first saw the continual higher development of faith as (Here the text breaks off).]

[Translated from Johann Adam Möhler, *Vorlesungen über die Kirchengeschichte*, ed. Reinhold Rieger (Munich: Erich Wewel, 1992), 2:553-563; cf. Joseph Rupert Geiselmann, ed., *Geist des Christenthums und des Katholizismus* (Mainz: Matthias-Grünewald, 1940), 403-9]

Appendix 6

Outline of the Lectures on Church History:
[Pre Nicene Period 1823, 1826, 1827]

What follows is a list of the extant sections of Möhler's 1823, 1826, and 1827 Lectures on Church History as established by Reinhold Rieger.

Introduction
    On History, Its Concept and Laws in General (1823, 1827)
    The Idea of Christian Church History (1826)
    Special Characteristics of the Historian (1826)

Purpose of Church History (1823, 1826)
Concept of Church History (1823)
Universal and Special History (1823)
Principle of Church History (1823)
Purpose of the Study of Church History (1823, 1826)
Practical and Theoretical Use of Church History (1823)
Selection of Material (1823)
Division of Church History (1823)
Sources of Church History (1823, 1826)
Guides to Church History (1823, 1826)
Use of Sources (1823, 1827?)
The Leading Idea of Church History (1827)
Periods of Church History (1827)

First Period: From Christ to Constantine the Great

Founding of the Community (1826?, 1827?)
The Resurrection, Ascension, and Sending of the Holy Spirit
    (1826?, 1827?)
Miracles of the Apostles, Martyrdom of Stephen, Conversion of
    Paul (1826)
Proclamation of the Gospel among the Pagans. Paul (1826)
Inner Activity of Paul; His Ideas (1826?, 1827?)
Political Situation of the Roman Empire at the Beginning of this
    Period (1823?)
Political Situation of the Jewish People (1823?)
Religion and Morality among the Jews (1823)
Jewish Sects (1823)
Jesus' Disciples (1823)
External Worship and Church Discipline (1827)
Expansion of Christianity in the Apostolic Period (1827?)
Persecutors of Christ (1827?)
Primary Doctrines (1823?)
Divisions over the Meaning of Doctrine (1823?)
Valentinus (1827)
Marcion (1827)
Simon Magus (1823)
Ebionites and Nazareans. Cerinthus (1823)
Deviations from Church Doctrines on Christ and the Trinity
    (1823)
Christian Feasts (1823)

Patterns of Assembly (1823?)
Baptism and Baptismal Practices (1823?)
Excommunication, Penance (1823?)
African and Roman Schisms. Novatians (1823?)
Christian Customs (1823?)
Ascetics and Anchorites (1823?)
Montanists (1823?)

[Parts 2 and 3 treat the periods from Constantine to Charlemagne and from Charlemagne to Gregory VII]

[Translated by Johann Adam Möhler, *Vorlesungen über die Kirchengeschichte*, ed., Reinhold Rieger (2 Bde.; Munich: Erich Wewel, 1992), 1: xxi-xxiv]

Endnotes

Endnotes

Abbreviations:

A1: "Faith and Love": Möhler's initial draft for the *Unity*.
A2: Möhler's reformulated draft of the *Unity*.
K: Calligraphic copy of the *Unity*.
A3: Möhler's annotations to K.
T: 1825 published form of the *Unity*.
+: indicates an addition made by the particular version noted.
Angle brackets <> indicate the placement of a footnote by Möhler in a passage not take up in the final version; the text of Möhler's footnote follows the Endnote extract and is marked with <<>>.

Preface and Part I, Chapter 1

1. For contents of A1, see Introduction. A2 reads:
Part I: Unity of the Spirit of the Church
    Chapter 1: The Mystical Unity of the Church
    Chapter 2: The Unity of Doctrine
    Chapter 3: The Attempt to Destroy Unity
    Chapter 4: Relation of the Unity of Believers to the Individuality of Each Person
Part II: The Visible Church
    Chapter 1: The Bishop and the Diocese
    Chapter 2: The Metropolitan and His Area
    Chapter 3: The Visible Unity of All Individual Churches
    Chapter 4: The Primate

2. Friedrich, *Johann Adam Möhler, der Symboliker*, 3-7, prints another outline of a preface by Möhler. It reads:

It is the custom in a preface to state how one was induced to write the work that accompanies it. The following motivated me: the material that I treat has to this point received the most contradictory explanations. I had, therefore, given up hope of achieving a result that could make a claim to be anything more than a purely subjective view of the matter. What must follow from such a pessimistic approach is obvious. I immediately began work on a part of medieval Church history, but a historical [*historische*] construction was impossible for me. Disconnected from and bereft of every higher idea that would contain and penetrate the whole history, and lacking such a firm historical center, I still had to deal with my subject even if I could not discover a necessary link to an earlier era, nor, above all, perceive a steady development from the earlier to the later period. But how could I do this since the earliest history of the Church appeared to me at the most important points as unarranged and unarrangeable matter? If inner necessity directed me to establish a necessary deep connection in the whole history, I had to know to what the later periods were connected. Even if I had not wished to know anything of the whole of history or to believe in a continual inner historical development, it was still necessary to know that out of which everything developed and what was firm and enduring. But I did not reach this because of my aforementioned indecision with regard to the early history of the Church. Indeed, I had not studied the sources myself, but had simply read them and believed what others were supposed to have found although they too, for the most part, had made no study of the primary sources. The best and only help that appeared to offer itself was, here as in all cases, that I examine and study the materials for myself. I immediately stopped the work on which I was engaged and read the writings of the early Church fathers. What I gained from that I share here with the public since a learned scholar to whom I submitted the manuscript for judgment counseled me to do so.

Perhaps someone, having learned to know the whole method by which I treated the material, will say to me with the poet [Goethe]: "What you call the spirit of the times / Is fundamentally the individual's own spirit / In which the times mirror themselves" [*Faust*, Part 1, ll. 577-79]. To this I only answer that I have not only studiously cited the sources, but have quoted them verbatim so that all readers may reach their own conclusions as to whether my judgments are true or false. I had intended to omit many citations but the thoughtful judge of my manuscript wisely counseled me against this. Moreover, I add, the times or persons treated by a historian must reflect themselves in that historian. How else is a historian to outline an image of them? With Christian Church history there is, in addition, something particularly special. We must not only have a clear image of the subject in ourselves in the same way as the historian of the Greeks must have, but we must live in the Christianity of the time and it in us, since Christianity is chiefly a matter of life and Church history is a development of life. The person who holds the view that Christianity could have perished or did so at any time, or that the Church could ever be anything other than it is or was, cannot write history. In every era, from that in which Christ founded the Church to the present, Christianity and the Church were always the same, and they always will be the same because he *was* and always *is* and *will be* the same. The person who now lives in the Church and truly lives in her will also live in her earliest era and understand her, and the person who does not live in the Church of the present will not live in the earliest Church and will not understand her, because both are one and the same. Above all, it must be one's own spirit in which the times not only mirror themselves but live. But will we not thus carry ourselves into the history of the Church? The person who has come from the Church carries nothing foreign back into her. The Church has nursed such a person and placed an image of her being and essence in that person. She first set herself in the individual, and it is this which the individual sets forth again. Thus the true image of the Church must be given again. It is she who writes about herself, who describes her essence. Who can know it better than she? The person, on the other hand, who believes that one must take a position outside the Church or who holds that the Church can or must be something other than she was, and who thus writes the Church's history outside the Church or in a church that has become something else, must truly carry into her a foreign element or not understand her characteristic nature. The Church must truly have given herself to such a person, if that person wishes to present her truly once more in a faithful image. To do this, however, the person must be in her and not outside of her or in another. Thus, if one assumes that the Church can be anything other than she was, one declares the impossibility of writing a true Church history. One can easily see that I do not think much of the proposition that to write a history one must be without religion, native land, and the like. Insofar as this means that a historian must be unbiased, I agree, but one can be unbiased only if one has religion, and this must be a specific religion since there are no unspecific ones. A Catholic will thus write history as a Catholic and a Protestant as a Protestant. The Protestant will everywhere discover self, that is, the party that arose in the sixteenth century, or will cast aside everything that is not of this party. Anyone who argues that the study of the early Church was useless for my purpose, that what I first was to clarify I must have already clarified so as to write what I wrote, is correct in a certain sense. But through this history I first brought to consciousness what I already carried in me without clear consciousness—therefore, the indecision and the possibility of self-contradiction.

Someone may note that I began with the Holy Spirit whereas I should have begun with Christ. I could well have first said that Christ came as the divine emissary and taught and did other things, but I thought I could presuppose this. The deeper reasons for beginning as I did will present themselves in the material. The Father sent the Son, and the Son the Spirit. However, we come through the Spirit to the Son and through the Son to the Father. Therefore, I begin with the Holy Spirit.

Preface to A1 reads: The Church as a moral person presents herself in a twofold mode after the analogy of the physical being in its reflective and productive powers—the first, which contains the characteristic of her contemplation, or faith; the second, which expresses her productive activities, the foundation of which is love. The principle of a Church will, therefore, need to penetrate both its modes. These are characteristically only different structures of one and the same thing, if there is to be *one* principle, and reflection only divides what in its life and essence is indivisible into apprehension and description. If the principle of the Church in her productive and contemplative activities as in her unfoldings is one thing, these two aspects are often not separated when they are described, and the one demands light from the other and crosses over into the other's territory.

Our work is thus divided into the following sections: (1) into the history of the Catholic principle in relation to faith and (2) into the history of the Catholic principle in relation to love.

The basis for the division of our subject as well as the justification of the formulae in which it is conceived devolves on the description of this subject itself.

3. Chapter headings throughout T are A2 additions.

4. human spirit] A1: nature

5. but he saw it . . . influence] A1: but he ascribed it to divine actions that influenced him [him; *sic* A2] as cause

6. the activity] A1: an activity

7. A1 adds: But as the Spirit is only one, so are the results of its activities considered in all cases as one; they beget faith where they are able to express themselves purely and are not in any way hemmed in.

9,13] In the footnote following "Similitudes," 9, 13, A1 adds: "'What is this tower then? It is,' he says, 'the Church.' 'And what are the virgins, Lord?' And he said to me: 'These are of the Holy Spirit [*Spiritus sancti*].'" *Spiritus sancti* is not as in the Oxford edition [of Barnabas and Hermas (1685)] to be explained as in the plural, but the term is *hagiou pneumatos eisi*, "they are the workings of the Holy Spirit." These *virgines* [virgins], or *potestates filii Dei* [powers of the son of God], are according to c. 15 the Christian virtues, the list of which is opened by faith and closed by love. Moreover, here the Holy Spirit and Christ are not separated in their churchly activities as they often are. "For a person is not otherwise able to enter into the Kingdom of God, unless these cover [the person] as clothing."

8. essentially] A2 replaces with German word "reel" and then overscores the term.

9. These activities of the Holy Spirit . . . Eucharist] A2+

10. are] A1: should be

11. A2: Leib] A1: Körper

12. its image . . . expression] A2+

13. The same conviction . . . as the receptive] A2+

14. All believers . . . same] A1 reads: All believers thus form the body of Christ, consequently in itself an indivisible unity since its division would no longer be the revelation of one and the same Spirit establishing itself in them and through them.

15. all parts] A1: integrating parts

16. A1 adds: even if they already hold a position

17. In the footnote A2 combines two notes in A1. A1 closes the Hermas' passage: ". . . and one body and one color of their garments." The *vestes* [garments] are the holy disposition revealing itself in virtues. This disposition is understood as identical with the Holy Spirit itself, as the images here are not always held together by exact logic. If one wishes to oppose the application of this passage, and teach that in it an ideal perfection of the Church is described that will never be fulfilled at any moment in its earthly existence, I would reply that no temporal point in the earthly existence of the Church can be pointed to at which her construction will be completed in the specified manner and at which all her members keep all the commandments made by Hermas. What is given in this passage is, however, a description of a true believer as it occurs in the present life. The book contains, of course, rules for living.

A2 adds after "one body": If one wishes to oppose this interpretation of the passage by insisting that it indicates an ideal fulfillment of the Church that will never be reached at any moment in time, it can be said that there is no one period in the earthly existence of the Church in which its building is completed in the aforesaid way. But Hermas portrays the tower first as conceived in its building and hastening towards its perfection and states how the believers are to work; moral adages are given.

18. According to the Geiselmann edition, 333-35, A1 here includes a passage that Geiselmann indicates should be compared with section 32 in A1 and A2 and with section 34 in A3. The passage with notes reads as follows:

The Church fathers here cited express in this material in didactic form the faith of the Church in their time. Thus, Justin the philosopher describes the believers as forming a unified spiritual whole. Just as those, he says, who believe in Christ have a single name taken from him, so they have become one soul, one community, and one Church through him.<1> Justin does not here mean merely unspecific feelings that bring Christians together, but that the same faith lies at the base of unity. This is demonstrated by many passages in the *First Apology* as well as in the *Dialogue with Trypho*. In these he refuses to accept the association of the Church with sects and insists that there is no community between the two, that even if sectarians call themselves Christians, they are not such, any more than all are philosophers who call themselves by that name, since they do not share Christianity's basic presuppositions.<2>

Clement of Alexandria speaks about the unity of the Church as follows: "From what has been said, it is clear that the true Church is one, namely, that which is truly old and that in it those are taken up who are righteous according to the predestination of God: God is one and one is the Lord. For this reason that which is preeminently venerated is praised according to the character of its unity since it is an imitation of the one principle. The Church participates in the nature of the one since it is a unity that the heresies tear by force into many pieces. According to her foundation, her conceivability, her origin, and her preeminence, we assert that the ancient, the Catholic Church is one, which leads those who have been predestined by God to unity of faith . . . through the Lord. But the preeminence of the Church is, like the principle of her foundation, determined according to unity, rising above all others. There is nothing that is like or similar to her."<3> Cyprian expresses himself briefly and clearly, saying: "Since one and the same Lord lives in us, he binds and unites all his own with the bond of unity."<4>

So closely do the early believers unite faith and love that both are completely tied to one another by them: where faith has developed itself through the communication of the Holy Spirit, there the same uniting divine power reveals itself, and where this union is found, there the same faith is given.

Ignatius, the worthy companion of the apostles, quite clearly grasped this when, in his "Letter to the Philadelphians," he shared the consecration of Christianity with them with the words: "All things together are good if you believe *in love*."<5>

<<1>>[Justin,] *Dialogue with Trypho*, 63: "Moreover, that the word of God speaks to those who believe in him as being one soul, and one synagogue, and one Church, as to a daughter; that it thus addresses the Church that has sprung from his name and partakes of his name." And 42: "Such a thing as you may witness in the body: although the members are enumerated as many, all are called one and are a body. For, indeed, a commonwealth and a Church, although many in number, are in fact as one, called and addressed by one name." See also ibid., 116.

<<2>>Justin, *First Apology*, 26,6: "All who take their opinions from these individuals are, as we said before, called Christians, just as those, who do not agree with the philosophers in their doctrines, have yet in common with them, the names of philosophers given to them." See especially the *Dialogue with Trypho*, 36.

<<3>>[Greek text] *Miscellanies*, 7, 17.

<<4>>[Note as in T, note 8.]

<<5>>[Greek text]. It is as Paul says in Ephesians 4:16: *alētheuontes en agapē*, "hold the truth firmly with love." If one wishes to agree with Grotius ["Annotationes in epistolam ad Ephesios," in *Operum theologicorum*, 2:2, p.897] and translate the passage, "Be righteous in love," the text must read *en tē agapē*. But the full context supports our reading.

19. so that the *one* spirit . . . divine Spirit] A2+

20. And Origen writes . . . Spirit] A2+

21. An early draft reads: The Church is the mother and is related to Christ as a bride to a bridegroom, as the receptive to the begetting principle, *pudica virgo incorrupta* [a virgin pure and incorrupt], which acknowledges no other begetting power than that of the Holy Spirit, *unius viri amorem casto pudere servat* ["she guards with chaste modesty the love of one man" (Cyprian, *On the Unity of the Church*, 6)]

22. of our faith] A2+

23. A1 adds: for in the Church, Paul says, God established apostles, prophets, teachers, and the totality of the remaining activities of the Holy Spirit. None can participate in these who do not give themselves to the Church; rather they rob themselves by evil inclinations of life. Since where

24. Therefore . . . Church] A2 continues the quotation as follows: They dig for themselves perforated fountains of earthly excavations, drink filthy water, fleeing the faith of the Church so that they cannot be drawn over, they cast aside the Spirit so as not to be taught.

25. The same conception . . . world] A2+

26. A1 adds: begot a new spiritual life in them

27. individuals . . . did] A1: individuals could no longer take possession of it directly as the apostles did

28. sent out by the Lord] A2+

29. *communal life*] A1: total life

30. A1 adds footnote: Irenaeus, *Against the Heresies*, 1:10, 2: "Although the languages of the world are dissimilar, the import of the tradition is one and the same." Following the footnote A1 adds: If they appeared to draw themselves only to the side of the Christian life principle mediated by faith, the other side of this (relating to love) is still expressed in deed, and the existence of their future inheritance is recognized with clear consciousness.

31. No merely self-taught . . . herself] A2+

32. self-baptized] A1: self-ordained

33. source] A1: means

34. and without knowing . . . believers] A2+

35. conviction] A1: belief

36. as was believed] A1: as the belief was. A1 footnotes this: Cyprian, Letter, 69, 3: "Nor can he . . . who has not been ordained in the Church be reckoned as a bishop. He can neither have nor hold to the Church in any way."

37. Footnote is an addition of A2. A1 adds: "Irenaeus describes both as bound together." A1 footnotes this addition: Irenaeus, *Against the Heresies*, 5:20, 1: "The Church gives unto us to see that the faith of all is one and the same . . . and preserves the same form of ecclesiastical constitution."

38. According to the teaching . . . discover] A2+

39. *Each individual . . . the Church*] A2+; by a direct imprint in himself or herself] A3+; *Each . . . imprint*] A1 reads: How this is to occur the Church fathers note. They discuss the following in detail. Thus Christianity, held as whole only in the life of the Church and extended only by the Church, is first to be taken up in the life of the individual so as to achieve true Christian knowledge by a direct imprint] A2 reads: by a direct insight

40. After demanding a holy life of them] A2+

41. A2 adds to the beginning of the Clement quotation: Let us therefore do battle to be found among the number of those who trust him, so that we might participate in his promised gifts. But how will this happen? If our spirit is firmly grounded in faith in God; if we seek that which is pleasing and agreeable to him; if we follow the way of truth, giving up all evil. A1 footnotes the passage: Clement, "To the Corinthians," 35.

42. A1 adds: the high priest of our sacrifice, the helper and supporter of our weakness

43. reject] A1: condemn

44. The writer of the splendid letter . . . death] in A1 occurs after the following section: No one is more impressed . . . live in us and we in them.

Footnote] This letter . . . earlier] A2+

45. No one . . . than] A2+

46. Ignatius . . . Christianity] A1: With deep insight the holy Ignatius, this great disciple and pattern of the apostle John, conceived of the life of the Church

47. light-filled] A1: love-filled

48. arising out . . . teaches] A1: germinating in the womb of the Church, glowing through the Christian, teaches

49. One . . . *Christ*] A2: The content of all his letters one can express as follows: love, and by loving you will find Christ; One can . . . love] A3+

50. In the Church . . . her] A1: In this love Christ is praised and spoken of and portrayed; in this love one can enter into Christ himself and come to understanding of him; in this communal life the heavenly Father himself discovers who the true disciple of his Son is, as well as this, that the disciple has become a partaker of God. Again he writes that therein all unholiness will be completely destroyed.

51. only in it] A3+; A2: through it

52. and "Faith and love . . . them] A2+

53. Christian] A1: spiritual

54. Clement . . . clear] A1: Clement of Alexandria makes use of an image similar to that of Theophilus to make this clear

55. A1 adds: and the enlightened one

56. A1 adds: (Error)

57. A1 adds: (true knowledge)

58. A1 adds: who shake off sleep as they are inwardly awakened or better like those

59. *of God*] A1: of the Spirit

60. *the holy . . . holy*] A1: the source of the holy can, however ["however" corrected to "thus"] find joy only in the holy. (As a result the exchange between different persons, *oikos, oikodomeis*; Ignatius, 'holiness in love'). A1 adds full Greek source of translated section in note; A2 adds: (The formation of holiness is only possible in community with Christians and in looking upon their life.)

61. This great thought . . . *believers*] A2+.

Footnote] K adds: Schleiermacher thus indicated the essence of Catholicism in his dogmatics very well and agrees almost word for word with this passage from Origen [See Schleiermacher, *The Christian Faith*, 28].

62. In other places . . . divinity] A3+

63. Christianity's characteristic existence . . . sense] A2+; A2 originally had the following introduction: We come to the same result, that faith was founded by the direct communication of life from the Church, by a direct view of life, if we observe the way in which Christianity reached out to the pagan world. Only life begets life. If Christianity must and should be conceived of as a matter of life, we will understand what Justin says.

64. A1 adds: The pagan philosopher, Celsus, charged Christianity as follows: Jesus appointed eleven or twelve notorious individuals for himself. They were base tax collectors and fishermen who fled here and there with him, supporting themselves in a scandalous and miserable way [Origen, *Against Celsus*, 1:62]. Origen opposed this as follows:

65. A1 adds: and yielded to the word of God

66. A1 adds: To this glorious thought he adds this as well: "Each person will be enlightened as to how great the power of the gospel is which, even without a teacher, conquers such persons who trust in its convicting might that is active through divine power [*theia dynamis*]." [Origen, *Against Celsus*, 1:62]

67. The manner . . . beings] A2+; A1: This basic principle of Christianity revealed itself in the reception of pagans into the Christian Church

68. that *this* activity preserved . . . God] A2+

69. The Church expressed . . . *philosophy*] A2+; The final sentence in A1 reads: These principles also form the Church's language usage according to which those who so took up Christianity in their life that all things were shaped by it, were called "philosophers" and their life was called "the true and godly philosophy."

Footnote] Cf. ibid., 6:3] A1 adds: Concerning Heracles, the disciple of Origen, Eusebius writes: "After he had given abundant evidence of a philosophic and ascetic life, he was esteemed worthy to succeed to the bishopric of Alexandria." And when Eusebius finishes speaking of the life of Origen he concludes, "presenting examples of the philosophic life" (cf. ibid., 4:7). This form of language is first seen in Cl[ement of Alexandria], *Miscellanies*, 1:20, and continued for some time. Cf. Chrysostom, *On the Priesthood*, 1:4; Justin Martyr . . . *Priesthood*, 1.1] A2+; Eusebius's reference to Heracles's is in Eusebius 6:3, possibly misplaced by Möhler.

70. of the Church] A2+

71. that the individual's . . . source] A1: that the individual's understanding is grounded in and has its source

72. of the Church community] A1: of the whole life of the Church

73. An early draft reads: To place true Christian knowledge before true Christian life is to dispense with all true sense because it is the result of a separation of willing and knowing, and lies at the base of the corruption of human nature (Schleiermacher[, *The Christian Faith*, section 8; trans., section 3]). Just as sin caused a darkening of the power of knowledge, so true Christian virtue, as well as life and nurture in the Church, begets true Christian knowledge. Over against the Christian point of view there is a Pelagianism in this to which none who wish to have harmony in their whole spiritual life can ascribe. How could one consider that our good actions are throughout caused by the influence of grace, but our point of view is not? In the first case the mere letter of the law cannot beget an action in us according to the sense of the law but needs a continued union with God. How then, in the second, is the mere letter to beget a genuine Christian point of view without the continual communication of God? If one accepts this, how can one avoid being pressed to what is a *common* point of view. In pre-Christian times, the sinfulness (and with it false knowledge, polytheism) of each individual was seen as the common guilt of the whole according to Christian ideas, and each generation and each individual *inherited* full ethical incapacity from the preceding generation back to the first human being. In a like manner the grace and Christian perfection of each individual is tied to the individual's life in the whole so that life in the Spirit results from the union and heritage (which was physical in the first case and is spiritual in this) of all previous Christian generations back to Christ. Just as earlier there was no true knowledge through life, now true knowledge proceeds from the life of the Church. Just as earlier no one inherited by a physical heritage from earlier generations anything but spiritual confusion, so the one who is not now united spiritually with the whole life of Christians, with the unbroken Church, has consciously or unconsciously no spiritual rebirth, no adoption by God. I do not see how, in the earlier case, in sin, one can find a tie between the corruption of the individual and the corruption of the whole, and in the second, in the Christian life, not maintain the express union of the individual and the whole, and yet consider that there is consistency or that the inconsistency is of no significance.

74. the practical moral fall] A1: the sin

75. As a result . . . gods] A1: As a result the Divinity could no longer be mirrored in the individual and could no longer be taken up. Thereafter the human person only directed sight toward the earth and made only earthly gods (personified powers of nature, etc.); A1 adds note: Theophilus, *To Autolycus*, 1:2: "For all have eyes, but in some they are covered and do not see the light of the sun. But it does not follow that because the blind do not see, the light of the sun does not shine. . . . So you have the

eyes of your soul overspread by your sins and evil deeds. One ought to have a pure soul like a polished mirror."

76. for understanding Christianity] A1: so as to find Christian teaching acceptable

77. In paganism . . . before] A1: According to the ideas of the early Church the analogy of the Christian life with the pre-Christian is then obvious. In paganism the sinfulness of each individual and with it false knowledge was seen as the common guilt of the whole, and each generation as each individual *inherited* its full moral incapacity, its moral death, from the generations immediately preceding it.

78. has its source . . . root] A1: is tied to the individual's life in the whole, so that the individual's spiritual life has its source in its link to and root

79. A1 adds: no true knowledge of God was possible in the sensual life; true knowledge arose out of life in the Church. The person. . . .

80. An early draft adds: As in the first case there was a common guilt, in the second there was common grace; in the first the general division of sin, in the second the general union of grace; in the first the separating spirit in all, in the second the uniting Spirit; in the first one is nothing but a sinner, in the second one has true stability (*hypostasis, substantia*). In the first case one shared nonbeing in sin and this penetrated everything; in the second that which was poor and groundless moved to absolute being, divinity, in which all must now share.

81. The chief result . . . through] A1: If we gather together from our study to this point what results we have for the Catholic principle, the following should be said: Christianity is founded on; Christianity is founded on] A1, A2; A3: The Church exists through

82. A1 adds: not in a concept (Schleiermacher is correct)

83. Specifically, the following points . . . particular] A2+; A1: However, if we applied this principle to Christ, partly to indicate its opposite in this example, partly because what we have received from him lies mostly in the heart, we would express ourselves as follows: With Christianity which we have received in and out of the living unity of the Church, Christ is completely given as the creative power of the new life, and therefore as God. With this unity the living divinity of Christ disappears; to divide ecclesiastical unity is the same as to take away living faith in the characteristic value of Christ. Christ is given directly from life to believers and therefore also becomes their life and is not divisible from it. Their Christian life, however, is one with the life of the Church and indivisible from it. This faith<1> conceived as life, becomes for them a need, is so inwardly meshed with their essence, and lives so broadly throughout their soul and life<2> that their innermost being first comes to clear consciousness in him. Faith in Jesus is for them the highest point of self-consciousness. In him the Christian has [text reads: have] first learned to know God and therefore also himself or herself. Self-consciousness is life and therefore the highest life is faith in Jesus. Therefore Ignatius says: "In the life of the Lord our life is taken up, through him, through his death, and yet some deny him. But how would we be able to live without him?"<3> Likewise Clement of Alexandria.<4>

<<1>> Christ spoke to Peter after he had made his statement of faith: "On you I shall build my Church and the gates of Hell shall not conquer it" [Matt. 16:18]. This is the true living faith: the Church is built on a God-inspired life.

<<2>> Clement of Alexandria, *Miscellanies*, 3:5: "A tree is known by its fruits, not by its flowers and leaves and branches. Knowledge is therefore from the fruit and structures of life, not from word and flower. For we do not say that the word by itself is knowledge, but a certain divine knowledge, and that light which is innate in the soul by obedience to the laws makes manifest all things that arise through generation,

and instructs the individual to know himself or herself. As the eye is to the body, so is knowledge to the mind."

<<3>> Ignatius of Antioch, "Letter to the Magnesians," 9, cited in original as note in T.

<<4>>Clement of Alexandria, *Miscellanies*, 4, 7: "Does not the one who denies the Lord deny oneself? Does not one who deprives oneself of his or her relation to the master, rob the master of authority? Anyone, then, who denies the Savior, denies life for the light was life" [John 1:14].

A2 reworking this section of A1 reads: In particular, *in and out of the living unity of the Church Christ is fully given* to the consciousness of the Christian [K: Christians] as the creative power of the new life in them ["therefore as God" overscored]; *with this unity, therefore,* the living Christ merges; *to divide the unity of the Church is the same as to take away living belief in* ["*the characteristic value of*" overscored] Christ. We know of no Christ whom we, isolated, have formed; we receive him only from the Church. Moreover, *Christ was given directly from life to believers and therefore also to their life and is not divisible from this. Their Christian life, however, is one with the life of the Church* from which it flowed out to them and is therefore indivisible from it.

K agrees with A2 but the singular uses of "Christian" are plural and A1 "the creation . . . life" reads in K: the all-grounding power of God, giving holiness and with this the community.

84. just as we experience nothing . . . *work*] A3+

85. Moreover, as Christ . . . holiness] A2+

86. A2 reads: Love and holiness are the sources of truth that were preached by the apostles and out of which arises completing universality; "that were preached . . . universality" overscored.

87. Love is the source . . . holiness] A3+; A2 reads: All this is also the gift of the Holy Spirit;

88. thus it can be said . . . true] A2+

Part I, Chapter 2

1. conceptual expression] A3+; A2: expressed word

2. A1 adds: After we have described the basic premises of heresy and its activity against the Catholic Church (insofar as it seems to belong here), it is fitting to expand on the principle of the Catholic Church more closely.

3. As . . . Christian] A1: After we have described the basic premises of heresy and its activity against the Catholic Church (insofar as it seems to belong here), it is fitting to expand on the principle of the Catholic Church more closely. As soon as it was present in a living way, inner faith; A1 formulated "inner faith" first as "the Holy Spirit communicated to the Church and giving her life" and second as "the religious activities in the minds of believers."

4. must seek expression] A2+

5. just as . . . Rom. 10:17] A1: just as in fact it is chiefly communicated by the living word of faith that has been manifested outwardly.

6. The internal . . . was] A1: This inner essence of the Catholic principle was

7. partly because, properly . . . doctrine] A1: partly because it was understood historically [*historisch*] and was given externally.

Footnote] Geiselmann (412) indicates note 1 as an A3 addition but in textual notes he indicates two alternate readings: "we only participate in his divine life" as an A2 reading for A1: "we only participate in his divinity"; and "the truth as something *given* to us" as an A2 reading for A1: "as it (the divinity) given to us."

8. his doctrine] A1: the divine

9. even . . . time] A2+

10. A1 adds: We dare not disturb this order and should prove the teaching that by the Catholic principle external faith is considered as nothing without inner

11. Like the apostles . . . itself] A3+

12. Without any . . . Scriptures] A1: Out of this arises the relationship of the Catholic principle to the Holy Scriptures, on which [the Scripture] the Catholic Church is not grounded

13. filled the apostles] A1: the apostles possessed

14. fill] A1:possess

15. from the Church] A2+

16. If Christianity . . . again] See Appendix 1, "Pragmatic Glimpses."

17. that is . . . itself] A1: that is, one does not receive the Spirit through the letter

18. only] A2+

19. The apostles themselves . . . them] A2+

20. As a result the principle . . . living] See Appendix 1, "Pragmatic Glimpses."

21. and poets] A2+; A1 adds: and he found in our times many similar to him

22. A1 adds: In *Against Celsus* Origen says: "He cites much, particularly from Plato, so that he can describe that which an intelligent person can also approve of from the Holy Scriptures as commonplace. Thus he says: 'This was stated better by the Greeks, and it was done by them without threatenings and promises from God and his Son'."<1> In another place Origen writes: "As he says, he points us to divinely inspired poets, sages, and philosophers . . . and promises to offer guidance for us in them."<2> Origen points to the power of the Gospel to change life and among other matters remarks: only those who have a pure heart can see God. . . .<3> True piety is not given either through the truths grasped by Plato concerning the highest good or by his readers.<[4]> But the simple language of the Holy Spirit inspired those who came to the Scriptures with a simple sense and who renewed their light with the oil spoken of in the Holy Scriptures.<5> "Our decision cannot achieve a complete purification of the heart: we need God who created the heart."<6> "The convincing power that was given to Jesus' apostles by God came from the Spirit and a higher power, and therefore expanded itself or, rather, the words of God quickly changed many who were born and brought up in sin and whom no punishment would have changed. But the word changed, shaped, and formed them according to its sense."<7>

<<1>>Origen, *Against Celsus*, 6:1 [source quoted].

<<2>>Ibid., 7:4 [source quoted].

<<3>>Ibid., 6:4 [source quoted].

<<[4]>>The text at this point originally read: I do not want to attack what was well said by the Greeks, but only say what was given by Plato. . . .

<<5>>Ibid., 6:5 [source quoted].

<<6>>Ibid., 7:3 [source quoted].

<<7>>Ibid., 3:68 [source quoted].

23. on the lofty . . . believers] A1: on the high vision that they have from Christ

24. A1 adds: Every true believer, one can say, must characteristically be able to beget a holy scripture, but only in Christ did the continually creative divine principle speak; in Christ only is it communicated. Because of the divine principle the believer is always stirred to accomplish what is bidden. Among the apostles there was a completely extraordinary inner working of God. One cannot actually say that a

newborn person must first learn in the Scripture what he or she does not yet possess. What is involved is a learning to grasp and understand what one is in oneself, a becoming conscious in oneself of an already received Christian spirit. In the Holy Scripture this Spirit most nobly and clearly developed itself, related itself to individual life activities, etc. [See also Appendix 1, "Pragmatic Glimpses."]

25. we have . . . Church] A2+

26. living] A1: such

27. is not possible] A1: was not possible; the inner tradition always runs parallel with the outer

28. first . . . original] singular in A2; plural in A1

29. this doctrine] A1: the essence of Christianity

30. formation] A1: developing

31. the doctrine] A1: consciousness

32. special] A1 immediate

33. special] A1: very special

34. Yet . . . life] A1: No one viewed oneself as forming a separated life, but looked upon the organic whole.

35. sought an explanation] A3+; A1: sought his full understanding and completion in the Christian spirit; A2: sought his completion, to discuss it in the language of a renowned theologian [Schleiermacher].

36. with that of the whole] A1: with that of the spirit of the whole

37. By nature . . . say?"] A2+

38. A1 adds: or to the apostolic church established nearest to him or her

39. A1 [Geiselmann not clear on source] adds: This is the fullest demonstration that such a teaching could only come from the apostles. How could a doctrine penetrate all churches, where individuals watched so closely, if the churches did not come from the apostles?

Finally, there is no evidence whatsoever that only African and Gallic writers supported themselves by tradition. Cajus, or whoever the writer of the *Little Labyrinths* was, demonstrated that Eusebius supported the divinity of Christ against the Artemonides by tradition and that Hegesippus traveled everywhere, searching for tradition, and found it everywhere. The Alexandrians' pattern is the same.

40. which again only . . . apostles] A2+

41. What resulted from . . . person] A3+

42. If Christian doctrine is . . . love] A2+

43. If anyone . . . development] A1: If anyone began with an egotistical development (working from the previously mentioned principles) that was offered as a true Christianity, there was no other way to refute such a person but by tradition. As follows from what has been said earlier, it would not have been possible to do so by the Holy Scripture, for some had completely different Holy Scriptures, some a few, but not all of the Catholic Scriptures. If they had the Catholic Scriptures, these were greatly mutilated; if they had them at all and in their entirety, the hermeneutical principles of exegesis used made Christianity as a characteristic doctrine laughable and completely robbed it of its positive character.<1> The refutation by tradition was, however, identical with the agreement of the Church's abiding faith, that is, the demonstration of the novelty of such an egotistical discussion.<2>

<<1>>Tertullian, *Against the Heresies* [sic; *On the Prescription of Heretics*], 17, 18: "Though skilled in the Scriptures, how will you progress, when what you maintain is denied by the other side, and what you deny is defended? [18:] And you lose nothing except a voice in contention." And then: [17:] "Now this heresy of yours does not

receive certain scriptures, [. . .] and whichever of them it does receive, it does not receive as whole. . . . But even when it does so receive some, it perverts these by the contrivance of diverse interpretations. Truth is just as much opposed by an adulteration of its meaning as it is by a corruption of its text."

<<2>>Ibid., 31.

44. Footnote] the actual order] A1 adds in German: (of the earlier and freer being); later introduced] A1 adds: Tertullian, *On the Prescription of Heretics*, 7: "These are the doctrines of human beings and of demons produced for itching ears of the spirit of the world's wisdom, which the Lord called foolishness and chose the foolish things of this world to confound even philosophy itself. For philosophy is the material of the world's wisdom, the rash interpreter of the nature of divine disposition."

45. A1 adds: At the same place he lists the Roman bishops from the time of Peter and Paul.

46. which, Clement . . . time] A2+

47. A1 adds: A striking impression is certainly made by the passage in Tertullian in which he points the heretics to the apostolic Church where the doctrinal seats of the apostles are still found, where one can still read the letters written to them, hear their voice again, and see their face. "You who wish to indulge a better curiosity in the business of your salvation, go to the apostolic churches, where the thrones of the apostles are still preeminent. In those places their own authentic letters are read, uttering the voice and representing the face *of each of them individually*" [Tertullian, *On the Prescription of Heretics*, 36, 1; source quoted]. The disciples of the apostles who were installed in their positions as church leaders by the apostles continued the growing correspondence with other congregations as they did among themselves. As a result, just as the apostles set forth the unity of doctrine, so their disciples held to this doctrine received from them and confirmed it. These letters were themselves read before the congregations for a long time. Letters such as these were written by Clement of Rome, Ignatius of Antioch, Polycarp of Smyrna, and the author of the letter to Diognetus. From all of these we still have letters, as well as one from the congregation at Smyrna to that at Pontus. Moreover, all the letters of Ignatius and that of Clement to the Corinthians prove that the congregations sent members to one another. Polycarp himself traveled to Rome, and Ignatius went to many places. Thus each congregation learned to know the apostolic transmission of others and found in all places the same transmission.

48. Thus, in the middle . . . congregations] A2+

49. There is . . . sect] A1: May the reader of this small work of mine not be displeased if I cite the letter of Irenaeus to Florinus, a Roman priest who later joined the Valentinian sect—a letter that I have never read without the deepest inner stirring, and

50. to express] A1: so that I might express

51. grace] A1: mercy

52. the confessions of the Church] A3+

53. A2 adds and overscores: It is the present tradition that will be past for future generations, just as the tradition of a former generation is for us a past one.

54. in] A1; A2: with

55. its truth] A1: the truth (its doctrine)

56. transmitted from the apostles] A1: through the Catholic Church

57. as if it were something that did not exist earlier] A2+

58. The proof from tradition . . . faith] A3+

59. A1 adds: by which the Fathers greatly limit their hope to convince the heretics

60. *to demonstrate . . . Church*] A1: to demonstrate the identity of the consciousness of the Church as a moral person with its individual members and thus to make firm and ground it in its Catholic witness.

61. The Church, then, . . . present] A2+; This insertion of A2 is based on a section in A1 that adds immediately after the earlier footnote: To this degree the Catholic Church knows no past in which the Christian religion was given. Past and future here lose their meaning and disappear into an ever-abiding present. Christ is always here, his spirit always gives life to the Church, and likewise his expression, the Word, is always spoken and received in the whole breadth of the Church.

62. Thus the whole Church . . . whole] A1: Thus the individual believer only portrays the antitype of the whole Church, and thus the believer becomes conscious of his or her character as a counterpart and impression.

63. By an inner necessity . . . generations] A3+

64. written] A2+

65. as soon as . . . believer] A1: as soon as the Christian life of the Church has established itself in that believer

66. same . . . unchangeable] A1: faithful and same image of her, who is always itself the same unchangeable person.

A1 then adds the following section: Now the Catholic is fully clear concerning all relations, and this consciousness of personal identity fills that Catholic with unending joy.

This is the direct opposite of heresy and the heretic. If the Catholic compares his or her consciousness with that of the heretic, the heretic is seen to have absolutely no harmony. Throughout its whole history heresy is only confusion, division, contradiction, war—in short, everything that appears always to result from egoism. Along with this must arise all the sorrowful feelings: isolation, singleness, uncertainty.

The proof of tradition on this side occurs through a series of writings, which begins with the immediate disciples of the apostles and goes through all times in an unbroken manner. In these the living word proclaimed at every moment appears embodied, and tradition is rightly named a vessel in which the word is preserved and continued. If we wish to describe the concept of tradition negatively, [we may note that] it is no series of sayings that are preserved in a manner in which God only knows, but the living gospel, ever proclaimed in the Church. It relates not to this or that individual doctrine which through it, through tradition, is to be proven, leaving others, over against it, to find their proof elsewhere. Rather, it stretches forth to the whole spirit of Christianity, to individual doctrines. We would be certain of none of these without it. Just as our Christian consciousness was for us an active, higher power from the Church, so was its unfolding, its relationship to individual doctrines. Only to later, individual apprehensions of tradition did it appear that individual Christian groups cast aside tradition out of which certain teachings alone were to be traced back, over against those which were to be found in the Holy Scriptures. Catholic scholars then narrowed the range of tradition to the first group insofar as a special pressure was placed upon them to do so. The period concerning which we are speaking knew nothing of this division. The whole of Christendom is given in tradition's breadth and only in it. What has been said concerning this relationship between Scripture and tradition must be further developed. We have yet to describe the two more closely and the way their relationship was expressed in the early Christian centuries [Cf. section 16, 5].

67. It is self-evident . . . doctrine] A2+

68. A3 originally reads: From the Christian consciousness that

69. A Catholic of Cyprian's time . . . it] A3+; A1 begins section 13 after T 13,6.

70. A2 originally adds: which one brings to others in a mechanical way

71. Since Christianity is seen . . . synods] A2+

72. A1 reads: We have earlier treated the essence of the Christian Church, why she cannot be grounded on the Scripture, and how heresy always claims it is founded on Scripture.

73. heard from Jesus and proclaimed once again] A2+

74. A1 adds and overscores parenthetical section: and that they raised such (Peter indicates this concerning the Pauline Epistles) is known.

75. doctrine] A1: expression

76. A1 adds: as by a thing that was not given for them.

77. A1 adds: (churchly)

78. do you mutilate the gospel?] A2+

79. Footnote] He states . . . Florinus] A3+

80. Footnote] understand much of them] A2 adds: Cf. Walter, *Kirchenrecht*, 22; against this Augusti, *Archaeologie*; In modern . . . tradition] A3+

81. From . . . Church] A1: According to Catholic principles, true veneration and high evaluation of the Holy Scriptures are only possible insofar as one does not let them say anything unworthy or deceptive. Therefore, these are expressions of a disposition that stands against itself as is indicated in the following passage from Irenaeus.

82. As a result . . . thing] A1: The identity of both in the view of the early Church appears finally in the fact of persecution during which a Catholic considered it a matter of indifference to deny Christ or to give up the Scriptures: both are for the Catholic the denial of Christ.

83. Section 16 is based on an early draft and sketch in A1 and a major reworking of these in A2, additions in A3, and a number of other changes to A2 in T.

A1 reads: If we wish to express the relationship of tradition to Scripture in a formula, it would be as follows: the (external) tradition is the ever-present expression of the Holy Spirit, living in each moment but at the same time embodied, it moves the whole of the Christian life [corrected to: believers]. [In the margin but not overscored: "Tradition is . . . the embodiment of that totality" as in T 16,1.] Scripture is the expression of this same Holy Spirit, embodied at the beginning of Christianity through the apostles [cf. T 16, 2] in such a way that not everything that the disciples taught was contained in it. Without possession of tradition, the higher sense of Scripture is lacking. Without the latter, the purity and specificity of the former is lacking, or: tradition, which is one with the whole Christian life, gives the Spirit; Scripture gives the form. Without the Spirit from tradition we find only ourselves in the Bible. Without the Bible we always grasp the Spirit in ["human" overscored] our own form, the difference between which makes the presence of the Spirit itself dubious. Therefore both are given together and both are preserved in the Catholic Church which, as we saw, firmly opposes every division of this sort. However, this is only the relationship between tradition and Scripture in the narrow sense, since aside from the expression of the Holy Spirit in the Scripture, there are also others given in the Christian life of the early Church which are to be viewed as pure and necessary expressions of the Christian Spirit since their beginning cannot be found anywhere [in history] but as established with the beginning of Christianity itself.

An early draft of section 16 reads:

1. Tradition, insofar as it embodies itself, will be as little understood outside the Church as the Holy Scripture, and we must object to the portrayal, such as that of

Münscher [*Elements of Dogmatic History*, section 16] . . . and others, of an ever-enduring tradition as that of a certain period and to the interpretation of Holy Scripture by [Eberhard Gottlob] Paulus [*Evangelienkommentare*, 1800-1804], and others.

2. Tradition, indeed, completes and determines the Holy Scripture; if [one wishes to hold that] it contains more than Scripture, this must be demonstrated in each individual case and the demonstration must trace the issue [under discussion] back to the earliest times.

3. If it is said that one does not need tradition alongside the Holy Scripture, the position is rejected in a twofold way. If one understands by tradition the living doctrine proclaimed in the Church, and thus understands Scripture without the living gospel or Church nurture as Irenaeus calls it, [we] will understand even as little of the Holy Scriptures as if tradition was given without the same present living gospel [cf. T 16, 4: If it is understood . . . the Scriptures without it]. Tradition, insofar as at each moment it is the ever-present living gospel, communicates the Christian Spirit for every following moment and with the Spirit, the understanding of the ever-enduring expression of the written Gospels [Cf. what follows with section 16:4, 5, and 8]. If the living gospel proclaimed at all times had not also been written down, if tradition had not thus been at the same time embodied so that we had not had the same material from apostolic times until our own, no historical [*historisch*] consciousness would have been possible and we would have lived in sad circumstances, without knowing how we came to be, what we are, and not only what we are but what we are to become. Indeed, if we could not have demonstrated the identity of Christian consciousness with that of all ages, we would have doubted its correctness, and have had no certainty if it was Christian. We would then not have used the possession of the Holy Scriptures since we would, of course, have had to interpret them, and we would have doubted if [our interpretation] was the correct one. Since it can now be shown how the Christian Spirit expressed itself in the same way in all ages, we are certain what the correct conception of Christian doctrine is, namely, that which was throughout all time. If this were, indeed, not correct, we might rightly doubt whether or not it is a Christian Spirit, what Christianity is, and [wonder] if everything would not be lost in an empty deception as is the case with those who cast aside tradition and find themselves in such circumstances. For them everything takes on a mere subjective form and there can be no discussion of an objective, churchly Christianity.

4. Those who think they can demonstrate anything merely from tradition, the veneration of the saints, purgatory, and the like, do not know what they wish. We have everything from tradition, and therefore those who do not accept tradition have already cast aside everything. We do not come to consciousness of God, of Christ, without Church life; and without the possibility of demonstrating this as always consciously present in every single point back to the time of the apostles, we would rightly cast it aside since it would be no necessary belief of the Church, for without the church it could never have been, nor could we have been.

The division arose because the Reformers supposed that the most important doctrines could be grounded by the Bible and they cast aside other things as not biblical that were merely present in tradition, and were therefore human. They took up only that which could be finally demonstrated on the basis of the Bible alone, and insofar as they did this tradition was reduced to very narrow confines. This is not the case: in the early Church each and every point that the Reformers asserted had to be upheld step by step through the tradition since all were opposed by the use of the Bible. All the points that the Reformers allowed to stand were denied on the basis of Holy Scripture and in every case they had to be secured through the tradition of the continuing life of the Church. The doctrine of God in its fullest dimension, of the Son of God in all its points, of the Creation, desire, and sorrow, in short, nothing that is and nothing that might be was denied on the basis of the Bible by those who called themselves Christians. It is striking that this is not acknowledged since it is so clear in history.

When the Reformers say that something is in the Bible, they are correct, but they make the statement because they were raised in doctrine and tradition and came in the Spirit of Christianity to the Bible. We say that without this Spirit they would not have been able to discover what they did. The longer the Church that was formed by the Reformers stood and was rooted in the basic proposition "By Scripture alone," the more distant was it from the directions [of tradition, and] the more did contention arise over what they proposed was found in the Bible, until they finally denied everything and were once again driven to turn back to the tradition of the Church as is the case with [the contemporary Protestant theologians and preachers] Schleiermacher, [Philipp K.] Marheinecke, and [Franz] Theremin. That the Reformers did not understand what tradition is, is quite clear from what is said in the *Augsburg Confession* [Article 26] concerning *traditiones*.

One must not suppose, however, that tradition always remained something unrelated to the Scripture. The Scripture was of course read. Tradition remained as little independent of the Scripture as Scripture of tradition. Without the Holy Scripture Christian doctrine would never have been protected in its purity and simplicity, but without tradition the understanding of Holy Scripture would have been lacking to us and Scripture would have been a riddle for us. Without the Scripture we could not have formed a complete image of the Saviour because dependable material would have been missing and everything would have been made into uncertain fables. Without tradition the Spirit and the interest to develop an image of the Spirit (therefore the Church protected both and continually held fast and firmly to both), indeed, the material to do so, would have been lacking. In fact, as we shall soon see, Holy Scripture itself was only preserved through the Church and her tradition.

Further to No. 3: If it is said that Scripture alone is enough for Christians, one may rightly ask what the meaning of this assertion is. Scripture alone, aside from our conception, is nothing at all; only the product that comes to light through the relation of our spiritual activity on the Scripture is something. And here, says the Christian, tradition according to the twofold meaning given above is necessary. If one understands by it the living gospel proclaimed in the Church which Irenaeus called the Church's nurture, we understand as little without the Holy Scripture, as the Scripture was given to believers without tradition. Our spiritual activity must thus be penetrated by the Christian Spirit, if from its relationship to the Scripture a Christian product is to arise.

If the apostles' students thus had proof for the objectivity of their conception in their direct relationship with the apostles, we too began from the apostles in the same continuing character of apostolic doctrine throughout all the centuries.

4. [sic] One can thus say that the holy books are, going back in time, the earliest steps in the embodied tradition; and the same continuing conception of that which is Christianity from the apostolic time on tells us, along with Christian nurture or the totality of believers from the apostles on, how the oldest embodiment of Catholic doctrine must be conceived.

5. The question if the tradition is coordinate or subordinate to the Scripture, if beside the Scripture a tradition is necessary, is not answerable (since it is established on the principle that the Scripture is something different from tradition): 1. because

according to their source they cannot be separated from one another; 2. if one understands by Scripture the first member in the embodied tradition, the question is, "Is the part over the whole?"; 3. if one understands by tradition the Church's nurture that always arises from the fullness of the Holy Spirit's living proclamation of the Gospel, the Christian Spirit reared up by this Spirit in each individual is seen as the basis for understanding the Holy Scripture and thus stands above other books.

84. From what has been . . . opposite (John 20:30-31, 21:24-25)] A2+

85. Much less can it be . . . letters] A3+

86. A3 adds and overscores: We can express ourselves briefly on this matter: It is the nurturing of individuals' consciousness to the Church and the general consciousness of the Church in different periods of their existence.

87. his or her thought . . . tradition] T. A2: their expression. The possession of the Holy Scripture would be of no use to us (even if we had it without tradition, which, as we will shortly see, is not the case) since we must interpret it, but we would be in doubt as to the correct interpretation.

88. with the totality . . . those] T. A2: with the apostles who had proof for the objectivity of their conception. So too did we

89. A3 adds and overscores: which is necessary for the fixing of doctrine for individuals.

90. If it is said . . . principles] A2+

91. There is no opposition . . . Scripture] A3+

92. The assertion that . . . unclear] A2+; A2 also adds: What is the doctrine of Scripture?

93. This too arises . . . assertion] A3+

94. Those who think . . . it] A2+

95. Does nurture in . . . division] A3+; A2 adds: This division arose because the Reformers taught that everything could with only a few exceptions be established by the Bible, and as a result it seemed that tradition was reduced to those few matters rejected by the Reformers. The early Church knew nothing of this.

96. In the . . . refuted] T. A2: Everything, as the Reformers agreed, was already refuted

97. that is, by their twisted use of them] T+

98. A2 adds: If the Reformers state that their agreement with the Church is biblically founded, they are correct, *but they state this because they were nurtured in the Church and in her tradition,* because they came to the Bible with the Spirit of the Church without which they would not have found it. But the longer the Church founded by the Reformers stood on this principle, the more was characteristic Christianity found in the letters of the Bible, and the farther time separated them from the Church's spirit which had been taken over, the more did arguments arise and the more were matters denied which they met in the Scriptures. Finally everything was denied. As a result one was compelled to flee to the Church tradition. This is now often done by intelligent Protestant theologians. How little the Reformers knew what tradition is, is clear from the fact that the *Augsburg Confession* [Article 26] unites this concept with the word *traditiones.*

99. Of such the earliest Church . . . simplicity] A2+; A2 then adds: The first member in the line would be lacking. Without it, without a characteristic beginning, the line would not be understandable; it would be twisted and chaotic.

100. It is certainly . . . Church] A3+

101. Moreover, without . . . Scripture] A2+

102. Without Scripture . . . lost] A3+

103. In brief, everything . . . grace] A2+

104. And why . . . meanings] A3+

105. The question . . . Church] An early draft of A1 reads: It is most important to ask why Christianity did not expand through the Holy Scripture, why Jesus did not teach his students according to a compendium, why for centuries [Christian] growth was based on the living word.

106. concept] An early draft reads: dead word

107. self-seeking] and early draft reads: self

108. A1 adds: In explanation of our treatment of the question we may note that at all times the church egoists called upon the Scriptures and wished to separate these from life. This was the result of their twisted and, I add, unchristian beginnings. The Bible has many meanings, but only for those who have separated themselves from the Church; those who possess the Spirit that gives life to the Church do not find this.

109. before that nation is acquainted with its content] A3+

110. and are biblically raised] A3+

Part I, Chapter 3

1. A1 has following title: Chapter 2: The Catholic principle in battle with the heretical or with churchly egoism; the external tradition as the expulsion of heretics from the sphere of Christianity.

2. The principle of . . . chapter] A2+; A2 originally read: The Catholic Church principle will become much clearer to us if we set the heretical over against it as we will do now; K replaces "the theoretical principle" in A2 with the "search for expression" and A3 with "the principle of heresy" and then with "the characteristic of heresy."

3. Socrates was a prelude to Christianity] A2+

4. A1 adds: An act of power on their part would have had to overcome this (which could not occur).

5. power] A2: Kraft; A1 Gewalt

6. aside from a continual living relationship with God] A2+

7. take up] A1: receive

8. deeply enough] A3+

9. ideas] A1: concepts; A1 has note that reads: The comparison is often used by Clement of Alexandria, *Miscellanies*, 1:19: "Making a comparison of those addicted to philosophy with those called heretics." Tertullian, *On the Prescription of Heretics*, 8: "they bring forward a Stoic, Platonic, and Christian dialectic."

10. and with] A2+

11. At this section in A1 an unnumbered page is inserted with the annotation: "For Chapter 2 Nr 1 at the end." The page reads as follows:

It did not sufficiently satisfy their curiosity. The Greek and Eastern philosophies of religion and theosophies contained theogonies, cosmogonies, and geogonies, a wide range for pompous fantasies and proud speculation. These seized upon Christianity, but they did so not to learn from it but as if they first needed to know what it was. Suddenly the Christian world was expected to experience that it preserved in its bosom a disclosure of the deepest mysteries—unknown to it, of course—among its treasures. The Christians themselves, it was supposed, were those who had to this point believed that to know such things was for the Father alone. In this the theosophers had not the slightest sense that they appropriated for themselves transcendence, considering themselves natural sons of God. They thus moved conceptually in their observations beyond their natural Father and his immanent works and they were so convinced of this [cf. section 29] that they called themselves "Knowers" and their system "Knowledge," and charged Catholics with being "simple people" and mere "trusters in authority." According to older methods, treating everything in poetry, allegories, images, and myths, they found myths as well in the most significant characteristic of Christian doctrine. The hidden kernel of these myths they freed from clumsy biblical hulls[, as they put it,] and they wrapped it again in their own system of images. In this sense they were different than the modern Gnostics who pretend to see the presumed kernel (the so-called rational truth) according to the Western characteristic without any images. It is perhaps not unfitting (in opposition to these speculative theologians, before describing the Catholic refutation of this position) to listen to a Catholic Church father [Irenaeus,] who particularly concerned himself with opposing them [cf. section 40]: "It is far better and more significant to know little in simplicity, and to become like God through love than to have known much and understood much and to blame God. For this reason Paul said 'knowledge puffs up but love builds up' [1 Cor. 8:1]. He was not finding fault here with true knowledge of God or he would have had to lay charges against himself. He knew that individuals through their knowledge become proud and lose love. It is, therefore, far better, as has been said,<1> to know nothing and not to understand any single cause for created things other than to believe in God and to cling to his love, than to be puffed up by knowledge and to lose his love that gives human beings life. It is better to wish to know nothing other than Jesus Christ the crucified than to become godless through subtleties and insignificant study.

If, then, in regard to created things, some things are left to God and others are given to us to know, what is wrong with learning by God's grace much of what is in the Holy Scriptures since the whole of the Scriptures belong to what is supernatural, and leave the rest to him not only now, but in the next world so that God might always teach and the individual learn."<2>

The inserted section ends here and A1 continues: Number 2. By heresy one understands in general the studied endeavor to communicate Christianity<3> by mere thought without consideration for Christian life, and thus to do so with a doctrine that develops and calls itself Christian but is separated from the ever-enduring, common Church life.<4> Since heresy believes that it is able to communicate Christianity egotistically for itself alone, it establishes intelligibility, autonomy, and intellectual freedom as chief principles.<5> Moreover, heretics insist that one must live in a quiet and conciliatory manner and that in this true unity exists, not in unity of belief. Religious freedom and intellectual freedom were the moving ideas of heresies.<6>

<<1>>That he does not reject science, as Gieseler says [*Compendium*, 4th ed., section 52], we shall see below. He says this merely in opposition to those who wish to know everything. He wishes merely to say that *Love* in simplicity is better than *to pretend* to believe in Christ and to know everything in pride.

<<2>>Irenaeus, *Against the Heresies*, 2:26, 1-2. [See section 40.]

<<3>>Tertullian, *On the Prescription of Heretics*, 6: "In almost every letter, enjoining us to flee adulterous doctrines, he condemns heresies, the works of which are *adulterous doctrines*. The following. [Möhler here is seemingly referring to note 1 in section 18, which quotes the section following].

<<4>>Tertullian, *On the Prescription of Heretics*, 6. [See section 18, note 2.]

<<5>>Clement of Alexandria, *Miscellanies*, 1:19. [See section 18, note 4.]

<<6>>Tertullian, *On the Prescription of Heretics*, 5. He opposes this position: "Moreover, when he blames dissensions and schisms that are undoubtedly evil, he immediately adds heresies. Now that which he subjoins to evil things he, of course, confesses to be itself an evil. . . . In short, since the whole passage points to the maintenance of unity and the checking of divisions (in as much as heresies sever individuals from unity no less than schisms and dissensions), no doubt he classes heresies under the same head of censure as he does schisms and dissensions, and by so doing he does not approve those who have fallen into heresies; more especially does he do this when he exhorts individuals to turn away from such heresies, teaching them that they should 'all speak and think the selfsame thing,' the very object that heresies do not permit." [Cf. section 18, note 6.]

12. based on Oriental theosophy and Greek philosophy] A3+

13. we are speaking here especially of the mystical separatists] A3+

14. and that which arises from it] A3+

15. A2 adds: and Polycarp

16. a contemporary disciple of the apostles themselves] A3+

17. or that in time it could pass away] A3+

18. saw their duty] A3+; A2: viewed their vocation

19. The heretical masters . . . Pelagian.] A2+; A2 adds: If one holds both as the work of the Holy Spirit, it is clear why one must separate. The Church unites; it does not separate. If the Church, which always was, were in the heretic, the heretic could not act in a separatistic way.

20. Heresy can therefore . . . understanding] A3+

21. Footnote] A3+

22. as a result of their principle that Christianity could be lost] A3+

23. even if . . . millennium] A2+

24. It is as . . . likewise] A3; A2: It is as if one had as a child already lost consciousness and later asserted that one understood oneself as the subject, whereas in fact the person would have no knowledge, not even of earlier existence. Others who had not lost their consciousness would attempt to orient this person, but the person could not orient anyone.

25. *Those who had preserved . . . way*] A3+

26. By this return . . . paganism] A2+

27. and Judaism. We now . . . matters] A3+

28. The principle . . . principle] A1: If the heretic establishes freedom of study as a Christian church principle, the Catholic must state that this beginning appears to be opposed to all true sense and meaning.

29. Our consciousness . . . begin] A1: The philosophic study of the essence of our spirit is not possible before the spirit is established in the philosopher. Our consciousness is, namely, double: the living, acting consciousness and the reflecting consciousness. The first gives material to the second. The reflecting consciousness does not beget the living consciousness but is the cause and base of it. It is the same with the Christian. The Christian's consciousness is divided into a living and a reflecting consciousness. The Christian must *live* as a Christian. There must also be a Christian material present. This must master the reflecting consciousness, that is, before study can begin.

30. that must first be studied.] A3+; The principle concerning freedom of study . . . . studied] See Appendix 1, "Pragmatic Glimpses."

31. An early draft reads: The heretic can only conceive of Christianity as a mere thought, as a dead concept, if he or she wishes to act consistently, and all the heretics'

operations begin with that which reason uses at each preferred instance. Just as the Christianity of the heretic here appears as a mere thought, so is the Christianity of heresy. It remains a thought, it does not come near any other church, as a mere thought, not embodied, truly invisible. Christianity spreads *pneumati kai dynami* [by spirit and power]. It is thus always portrayed by Paul and the early Fathers as a power of God in the whole and in individuals, not arising through reflection, [but] through direct consciousness, through the change it brings about in a person. Thus it comes to reflection, which is not its basis.

32. The heretic . . . Christianity] Although there is no clear indication in Geiselmann, this section appears to be an A2 addition.

33. and yet wishes to be called a Christian] A3+

34. given by the Church] A3+

35. The heretic thus thinks . . . heretic] A1: The Christian Church, however, is like Christianity itself, a direct power of God (see above). As such she can establish or be established [later addition by A2: And Christianity cannot be seen as seeking something, for in such a case it would see itself as not yet existing]. She is completely positive and can have no mediating and skeptical academy. The heretic begins with the principle that believing oneself to be without Christianity, that is, as a non-Christian,<1> one can best judge what Christianity is. The heretic views Christianity as an unknown greatness and charges Catholics that they do not know Christianity. The heretic bases himself or herself on this principle alone before he or she becomes Christian. As a Christian the heretic cannot study as a non-Christian. The Catholic begins at the point the heretic wishes to find. [See Appendix 1, "Pragmatic Glimpses."]

[All of T note a plus the following:] *On the Prescription of Heretics*, 8: "It is written, they say, 'Seek and you shall find.' [Matt. 7:7]. Let us remember at what time the Lord said this. I think it was at the outset of his teaching when there was still a doubt felt by all whether he was the Christ, and when even Peter had not yet declared him to be the Son of God, when John had ceased to feel assurance about him. With good reason therefore was it then said, 'Seek, and you shall find,' when inquiry was still to be made of him who was not yet known. Besides, this was said in respect of the Jews. For it is to them that the whole matter of this reproof pertains since they had [a revelation] where they might seek Christ. . . . 'You search the Scriptures,' he says, 'in which you hope for salvation; but they testify of me' [John 5:39]. . . . Not yet had he cast to the dogs the children's bread [Matt. 15:26]; not yet had he charged them to go into the way of the Gentiles [Matt. 10:5]; only at the last he instructed them to go and to teach all nations and to baptize them [Matt. 28:19] when they were soon to receive the Holy Spirit, the Comforter, who would guide them into all truth [John 16:13]. And this therefore stands. If the apostles, who were ordained to be teachers of the Gentiles, were themselves to have the Comforter for their teacher, far more needless was it to say to us 'Seek and you shall find' [Matt. 7:7] to whom was to come, without study, our instruction through the apostles and to the apostles themselves by the Holy Spirit." It is quite proper to insist that one who first wishes to establish what a Christian is demonstrates that he or she is not a Christian.

36. The Catholic was thus truly convinced . . . is] See Appendix 1, "Pragmatic Glimpses."

37. The opinion that . . . be] A2+

38. The freedom of . . . forever] A3+

39. has . . . character] A1: is . . . institution

40. previously given] A2+

41. the schools] A1: the systems of such who wish to belong to it on the path of study, of those who call themselves Christians.

42. with certainty] A3+

43. A1 adds: "Origen, *Against Celsus*, 8:2: "In which state everyone, by greater exercise of power, will chose what he or she desires and will not obtain what has been chosen."

44. A1 adds: They assert that by this the character of the Christian Church is lost and Christianity itself which is always something existent, present, and not first to be sought, that by such an action the individual submits to pride and, without the divine Spirit, is not able to discover what the Spirit is. Such an individual thus places true freedom in the acceptance of what is given and allows that freedom to work in what is accepted. The heretic thus takes the higher freedom as his or her own, the freedom of the children of God directed by the divine Spirit and believes erroneously that freedom is what heretical freedom itself is, enslavement to error.

A1 footnotes this section: Clement of Alexandria, *Miscellanies*, 3:5: "As the eye in the body so knowledge to the mind. Nor do they speak of liberty by which one is enslaved to pleasures as those who drink sweet bile. But we learn liberty, by which our Lord freed us from pleasures, desires, and disturbances."

For A1 addition and T "It now also . . . it" see Appendix 1, "Pragmatic Glimpses."

45. In regard . . . disagreement] A1: If the Catholic principle established the divine Spirit as the basis of the Christian Church, the heretical principle made the letter its basis, the letter, namely, of Holy Scripture.<1> A great controversy arose as a result and it clearly indicated that nothing can be done with the letter alone, that a spirit must speak from it, and that if the divine Spirit does not, the human will.

<<1>>Tertullian, *On the Prescription of Heretics*, 14: "But they treat the Scriptures and recommend their opinions from them. Indeed, from what other source could they derive arguments concerning the things of faith except from the records of faith." Irenaeus, *Against the Heresies*, 3:11, 7: "So firm is the ground upon which these Gospels rest, that the heretics themselves bear witness to them, and starting from them, each heretic endeavors to establish his or her own peculiar doctrine."

46. On this . . . them] A1: This first question, then, necessarily arises: "What are the divine Scriptures?" And herein is indicated the greatest difference of opinions. The evangelical and apostolic Scriptures, namely, which we still possess, were in no way given directly by their writers to all Christians. But most of these, as mere occasional pieces, were originally only in the hands of those for whom they were directly intended or in the hands of their friends. Only at the end of the second century (can one say) were they circulated throughout the Church, so that each individual church had more or less all of the Holy Scriptures in its possession.

47. Footnote] A1 adds text in Greek and the following, all of which is then overscored: If one attacks the Catholic Church by charging that in its use of tradition, it argues in a circle because it corroborates it in the Holy Scriptures, the Church trusts itself. Whom should it rather trust? The heretics? This is not to ignore that those do find rest who do not accept the basic principles of the Catholic Church and consider them as lies.

48. A1 adds: Directed by all this the Catholic could not approve the forged compositions. But those who had first forged them cast them aside since they did not find it useful to promulgate new compositions in contentious cases. If the heretics wanted to demonstrate against the Catholics that Catholic doctrine was unchristian, they could not demonstrate this from contested books.

Footnote] A1 adds: The canonicity was not in such a case the same as authority [overscored by A3]

49. Footnote] A1 adds: "For the Ebionites who use Matthew's Gospel only are refuted by it, making false suppositions with regard to the Lord. But Marcion, mutilating the Gospel of Luke, is proved to be a blasphemer of the only existing God, from the passages that he still retains. Those who separate Jesus from Christ, alleging that Christ remained impassable, but that it was Jesus who suffered, preferred the Gospel by Mark. . . . Those, moreover, who follow Valentinus, make copious use of the Gospel of John to illustrate their conjunctions. . . ." Of course, the Valentinians used another gospel in addition to that of John, namely, the "Gospel of Truth." Cf. ibid., 9. This gospel was different from all others.

50. Footnote] A1 adds: "The fourth . . . like a flying eagle pointing out the gift of the Spirit hovering over the Church. . . . For the Gospel of John relates his generations from the Father. . . . Matthew again relates his generations as a man. . . . Because of this a humble and meek man is kept up through the whole Gospel."

51. Footnote] A1 adds: "The doctrine of divinity that had, as it were, been reserved for him as their superior, by the divine Spirit." Like the completely different situations and relationships in which Jesus appears in the same Gospel to give opportunity for doubts.

52. The Epistles of the apostles had the same fate] A3+.

Footnote] A1: For aesthetic reasons Tatian found Paul's Epistles and the Acts of the Apostles not in harmony with the others. Eusebius, *Ecclesiastical History*, 4:29.

53. as he or she said] A3+; A1 and K: As they said

54. which he still accepted as genuine] A3+

55. A1 and K add: and cast out everything else.

Footnote] A1 adds: Cf. Gratz, *Kritische Untersuchungen über Marcions Evangel* (Tübingen, 1818); Hahn, *Das Evangelium Marcions*, (1823.)

56. Footnote] A1 begins the citation: "By means of their craftily constructed plausibilities, they draw away many."

57. Footnote] A1 adds: To correct Gieseler. They do not cite the tradition as a whole but the *secret* tradition.

58. Thus . . . protector] A3; A1 and K add: Valentinus who rejoiced greatly in images did not without reason choose Glaucias as the man with the bright shimmering eye for his protection; Footnote] A1 adds: If one wishes to translate the Homeric *glaukōsis* ('the one with shining eyes') with this Glaucias would be a parallel.

Footnote] Clementine writings] A1 adds: Neander, *Gnostic System*, "Anhang."

59. Footnote] As a result . . . error] A3+

60. See section 12, n4] A3+

61. or those that arose . . . consciousness] A3+

62. and its practice] A3+

63. false interpretations] A3; A2 and K; rational principle of interpretation

64. alone] A3+

65. What purpose . . . wisdom] A3+

66. the Spirit . . . Church] A3; A1 and K: the Spirit promised to the Church

67. From these facts . . . spirit] A2+

68. hermeneutics . . . rules] A2; A1: No church, we insist, can be built on the Scriptures as explained according to the proper hermeneutical propositions. Hermeneutics is nothing other than a kind of reversed logic. Logic presents a formal process of thought and looks upon thinking as such a process unless a heuristic use can be made from it. Hermeneutics sets forth something already thought, indicating

how the laws of thought are turned so as to teach how one can find what was thought in a particular case; it does this without containing in itself a criterion of the truth of that which is found in it.

69. It transmits only . . . reason] A2; A1: The principles of reason (that is, reason here on earth) communicate a certain content of a composition to our spiritual essence. Because hermeneutics was once considered to be the art by which one discovers the sense of a work, in our time it is held that one can interpret the Holy Scripture in the same way as a pagan work and reshape it by hermeneutic rules, indicating that the keystone of this hermeneutic is lacking, since human beings had not yet grasped the sense of the Holy Scriptures but only an aggregate of doctrines relating to God. The key that was used was a moral interpretation and what resulted was a religion within the limits of reason, within its principles. The heretics, with whose Church principles we are here concerned, at a very early period desired the same, as we indicated above—the necessary fate of each individual church that founded itself on the Scripture if it developed consistently. Among the heretics of the early Church that would only have been conceivable according to such premises alone (as they endeavored to turn to a fantastic exegesis), had their system not had the same Oriental character, and their interpretation therefore resulted in one parallel to this.<1>

<<1>>Hermeneutics (I am here speaking of biblical hermeneutics) most properly (but how marvellously?) directed unites a totality of concepts with the knowledge of Near Eastern languages and all other exegetical tools; what comes to us is the human, the national, and the individual aspects of the writer, not the divine. To be able to grasp the divine and to be able to mediate it to our spirit, there must be a divine principle in us that the Church communicates to us, as is fitting for the divine.

How can one so generally express the principle that Holy Scripture must be interpreted in the same way as all other profane literature? As a result one finds in it everywhere only the profane.

How could one establish the rule that dogmatics cannot be introduced into interpretation? Can any sensible person think that Christianity conceived of as a dead human concept can be set aside as one wishes? That one can find the Christian without the Christian spirit? If one wished, however, to seek one's dogmatics in the next best way, the [dogmatic] expression would be extremely unmeasured and superfluous because of a mass of other rules. Even the system of accommodation has, as I sense it, something unspeakably contrary; one can and indeed must say that Christ used the language of his people and that therefore the simple concepts of Christ and his apostles must be explained by philology. But if one wishes to call this accommodation, one must also call accommodation the fact that Christ spoke a human language consistently.

From all this it is clear that hermeneutics is only of true value for the one who acknowledges a higher principle than that which turns itself over to human rules. [Geiselmann does not indicate whether or not the remaining section in the text ('the acts . . . reason') is an addition of A2 or not, but since no parallel section is noted, it is likely that it is.]

70. as it were] A3+

71. soon] A3+

72. and place] A3+

73. A1 adds: (The followers of Artemon are properly to be counted among this number since, according to Eusebius, their biblical criticism was not historical; as a result they had no fear of the loss of transcendence since they considered themselves to be the natural sons of the highest God).

74. a form for] A3+

75. primarily] A3+

76. enlightening individuals] A3+

77. A1 adds: who began the reformation in the Church and wished to support it. This is characteristic of egoism in that it considers itself as the enlightened center looking forward and backward. It draws the earlier world of error and weakness after it, astonishing the present and directing the future accordingly. In Christianity, however, there is only one center the same today and in eternity. The spirit that ruled in the sects was thus a human spirit. Since the beginning of the sixteenth century, it was possible to doubt this. Those sects followed their own dark radical fantasies instead of divine illumination.

78. or rigidly stuck . . . endeavor] A3+; K adds: It is well known how the Montanists were the opponents of every scientific endeavor yet remained literalists.

79. One of the first group . . . picture] Geiselmann indicates on 442 that the section is inserted by K, but on 441 that it is A2.

80. false mysticism] A3+

81. The one who has . . . whole] A2+

82. that break out at one place suddenly] K+

83. In our . . . origin] A2; A1: We have outlined above the principles of heresy as they are expressed in history without indicating their innermost essence according to the basic principles of the early Church although this essence could, in no way, be fully treated in the description to this point. The Fathers, however, expressly understood self-seeking as the deepest form of heresy, just as they saw division from the common life (which does not always arise from difference of doctrine) arise from this source [self-seeking], as we noted above, and error in understanding was seen more as rooted in self-seeking than was error or division described at its source; "than . . . source" overscored in A1.

84. All individual . . . sun] A1: Since the early Church could only think of herself as true, living Christianity in terms of her common life because life can be only received from and through life, all individual, separated, and egotistic essence was for her a horror in which true Christianity itself had to fail; or rather, such essence appeared to the early Church as that in which a living union with Christ would be weakened. Since the Church was seen as having her life's source and fullness through the Holy Spirit, she understood that pieces torn off from pieces with life would dry out as a twig, torn from the tree, as a stem that separated itself from a source and as a sunbeam torn off from the sun are unthinkable.

85. In a word: if . . . community] A3+.

Footnote] Unity . . . separation] A3+

86. Footnote] A1 adds: "Let no one be deceived: unless one be within the sanctuary, one lacks the bread of God."

87. Footnote] unity of God] A2; A1 originally had "unity" and corrected it to "common life."

A1 adds: Minds in which he saw division, he presents as wrapped with bands that hinder the development and expression of love.<1>

<<1>>Ignatius, "Letter to the Philadelphians," 8. He begins very gloriously: "I have worked according to my character as a human being for the communal life [German translation]. (Cf. ibid., 7, where he says that some wished to draw him away, but he called out in the midst of the congregation: "Love unity, flee division.") [8:] "I then did my best as one who is set on unity. Where there is division and anger, God does not dwell, but the Lord forgives all who repent if they turn to the unity of God [henotēta

theou] and the counsel of the bishop." It can be easily demonstrated that the *henotēs theou* is not related to either polytheistic or Gnostic error. It is important to note that he calls a return to the common church life a return to the unity of God. It can be demonstrated throughout all of Christian history that the ideas of each party concerning God are fully related to that party's common church life. The small separatistic commonalities generally view God in as narrow terms as they themselves are. They see themselves, a few hundred people, as the elect, chosen, God-illumined remnant. From this it follows that God has hardened and cast off the rest and given them over to darkness of heart.

In the modern Protestant church, however, in which the churchly egoism that one can choose Christianity for oneself is fulfilled, the characteristic of Christianity is completely denied, namely, that God appeared in Christ and that we are truly redeemed through him. First through Christ and in him are human beings united; thus, without him, they are divided once again. Both follow logically.

88. formed] A1: penetrated

89. Footnote] Lord's Supper] A1 in both places: Agape

90. A1 adds: Clement is completely penetrated by the thought that true Christianity cannot be drawn down by division.

91. Therefore, he expresses . . . life] A2+; life.] A3+

92. We] A1:By the apostolic succession we

93. flee from those who] A3+; A2 and K: direct those who

94. Clement . . . Cyprian] A1: Clement answers the pagans by stating that their charge concerning the truth of Christian disunity over doctrine is serious but can be documented only with difficulty. As a result there has been so much study concerning this. As a result, as well, the heresies with their love of praise and self-seeking without having learned or fittingly grasped the truth fall into the madness of knowledge. In the same manner Cyprian expresses himself.

95. A1 adds: And Eusebius says of Tatian: "Haughty and proud, wishing to be a teacher, and pompous as one of many others, he established his own school."<1>

<<1>> Eusebius, *Ecclesiastical History*, 4: 71; cf. 6:43.

96. Eph. 2:15 . . . 3] A3+

97. Footnote] A1 opens the Cyprian passage as follows: [13:] "What peace, then, do the enemies of the brothers promise themselves? What sacrifices do those who think that they are rivals of the priests think that they celebrate? Do they think that they have Christ with them when they are collected together, who are gathered together outside of the Church of Christ?"

98. From this . . . Corinthians 13:1-3] A1: Cyprian also proceeds from the principle that the common life in the Church is possible only through the uniting power in Christ and can be continued only through the abiding inner work of Christ and the Holy Spirit. He sees egoism as the final basis for division<1> and it is for him, therefore, a battle against Christ, an alienation from love and, because of this from Christ and God which even martyrdom cannot overcome and therefore he quotes Paul in 1 Corinthians 13:2-3 [quoted in full].

<<1>> Cyprian, *On the Unity of the Church*, 8: "Who then is so wicked and faithless, who is so irsane with the madness of discord, that either he or she should believe that the unity of God can be divided, or should dare to rend it?"

99. Therefore, if anyone . . . granary] A2+

100. Just as the Church . . . flowed] A3+; the error and separation flowed.] A2 and K: the error in the research flowed

101. insofar as it was feasible] A3+

102. One could in some . . . *Principles.*] A2+.

Footnote] In Augustine . . . ibid., 3:12, 21] A3+

103. In other . . . Christians] A1: Although Origen here knew how to explain the rise of the different Christian sects, in his defense against Celsus, as we have indicated, he still protected himself in another place against confusing heretics with true Christians and agreed generally with the passages already noted from the rest of the Church fathers.

104. *self-seeking*] A3+

105. A1 adds:, the pride of the heart.

Footnote] "You . . . 1 Cor.3:3)"] A1: "If you ask how heresies are counted among the works of the flesh, you will find that they arise from their own carnal sense. For thus the Apostle speaks of them: Vainly puffed up by a carnal mind and not holding to the head" [Col. 2:18-19].

Footnote] Thus] A1 adds: "One of these and indeed the worst is languor of the soul. It is to be understood as contention and by it every work is impoverished. Thus. . . ."

106. A1 adds: Consequently, the general conviction of the early Church might be understood as holding that egoism was the root of heresy. This is already clear from the most superficial reflection on earlier mistaken judgments by the heretics on the Catholics. By such judgments the heretics scarcely allowed themselves to be seen as children of one and the same heavenly Father or scarcely expressed themselves in the characteristic sense of the word in that they clearly demonstrated that they held to a more limited god as their creator. How this conviction is tied to the essence of Catholicism can be readily enough seen in the earlier discussions. Because Catholicism views the principle that begets faith with that which grounds the community, with that, namely, which brings forth love, as one thing completely that can only be divided in reflective thought, it necessarily holds that the person who does not hold the first in common can only possess the second in a troubled manner.

Over against this, heresy believes that one can possess love without having the same faith described above; heresy thus arises in a division from the original unity and views both together as one. Catholicism thus holds heresy, arising from division and leading to division, as evil, indeed as evil itself.

107. He expresses . . . passages] A1: It would be surprising if we did not find in so great a writer as Origen, so significant a defender of Christianity, the same ideas concerning the Christian Church in opposition to separatism.

108. Acts 4:32] A3+

109. Eph. 4:4, 13] A3+

110. K adds: Disunity destroys just as unity forms, and unity grasps the Son of God who is in the middle of the united ones.

111. See Addendum 9] A3+

112. unconscious] A3+

113. neither of which can be separated from holiness] A3+

114. A1 adds: Thus the heretical principles (one cannot really say: the heretical principle) were formed. How interminably troubling they were to the Catholic Church can hardly be described. Such sects sprang forth in all places, and the basic propositions of none of them were so surprising or astonishing that they did not find followers; indeed, the more surprising and astonishing they were, the more were individuals devoted to them. Along with Christianity, a fermentation, a movement as never before seen, entered the whole moral world, but the more disturbing the powers were, the wilder and more confused were their activities. Greek, Jewish, Egyptian, and

Persian elements fought with Christian elements or sought to be considered as Christian. However strongly the Catholic Church was taken up among the pagans and however long a catechumenate it insisted on, many came to the Catholic church who had no sense of the need for redemption, and among these the Christian formation did not penetrate. They soon turned against that which they themselves had taken up in a friendly manner in their bosom. They were all the more dangerous insofar as they bore along with their basic propositions the common speech of the Christians from which they extracted something completely other than what Christianity willed. In secret they sought to stir up various doubts through various questions and they soon promised the solution to these problems through their wisdom. But since they always publicly used the common speech, they went so far in their boldness to complain if they were shut out of the Catholic community after their secret activities were finally discovered.<1> If they were confronted, they gave elusive answers, explained themselves ambiguously, or completely denied their teaching.<2> They made a great impression since they pretended to demonstrate their positions only from the Holy Scripture.<3>

<<1>>Irenaeus, *Against the Heresies*, 3:15.2

<<2>>Clement of Alexandria, *Miscellanies*, 7:16: "And sometimes they deny their own doctrines when they are refuted, being ashamed openly to own what in private they glory in teaching." Tertullian, *Against the Valentinians*, 1: "If you propose to them inquiries sincere and honest, they answer you with stern look and contracted brow and say, 'The subject is profound.' If you try them with subtle questions, with the ambiguities of their double tongue, they affirm a community of faith."

<<3>>Tertullian, *On the Prescription of Heretics*, 15: "They put forward the Scriptures and by this insolence of theirs they at once influence some. In the encounter themselves, however, they weary the strong, they catch the weak, and dismiss waverers with a doubt."

115. The heretics . . . knowers] A1: so that they called themselves "the knowers" and their system "knowledge" and charged the Catholics as being simple people and mere trusters in authority. [See section 18, endnote 22.]

116. and noble.] A2+.

Footnote] A1 inserts beginning of Clement quotation: "How are they, who do these things, better than the people of this cosmos, or are they similar to the worst people of this cosmos?"

117. not only without works but in spite of evil works] A2+

118. This is the sectarian spirit] A3+

119. But the possibility . . . follows] A1: But the confidence with which they give themselves these names, the unspeakable pride that they direct against the Catholic Church, the lightness with which they promise the deepest wisdom, powerfully stirs up self-seeking in all classes, and many were happy to raise themselves up above common conceptions and to set themselves without struggle into the class of such noble natures. The statements of the Church fathers concerning the pompous activity of these people and the aggressive drive of their pride are intended to strike us in the innermost parts of our souls and to fill them with pride. Thus Irenaeus speaks of the students of Mark.

120. They call . . . knowledge] A1: They travel in this manner throughout the towns, deceiving women whom they lead astray by calling themselves the perfect ones, suggesting that no one can be compared with them in greatness of knowledge.

121. For these reasons . . . matters] A2+

122. who . . . it] A3; K, A2: who lived before its enlightenment

123. Demiurges . . . individuals] A3; Geiselmann indicates that there was a variant reading in A1 and K but is unclear as to what it is.

124. Demiurges . . . arising] A3; Geiselmann indicates that there was a variant reading in A1 and K but is unclear as to what it is.

125. by the dull reformers] A3+

126. among such so-called thinkers] A3+

127. The narrow, loveless . . . *theologians*] A2+

128. A3 originally adds: by which one becomes ideally like the All.

129. This [discovery of God] is . . . blood] A3 originally: This is the ability to live and live actually in the Church which has been purchased through him.

130. The . . . believers] A3 originally: The community of the saints

131. A3 originally adds: There is more said of this in other places. Zimmer, in his book on the law and the concept of history, says, "Since all people on the earth are only *one* whole and only *one* people and live only *one* life as an organic whole [even though every individual people like every individual part has its own life, it follows that the history of every individual people can and must be seen as a part of the general history of humanity." See P.B. Zimmer, *Untersuchung über den Begriff und die Gesetze der Geschichte* 77, sec. 66.]

132. In paganism] A3 originally introduces this section: In an erroneous way one designates the hostile opposition of the individual life toward the universal as freedom and self-sufficiency. The same is the case here. In paganism

133. If we seek . . . aside] A3+; we now leave aside] A3 originally: no longer belong here. As has been often said this is indicated by the passage in Ephesians 4:5-6: *one* Lord, *one* God, etc; the passage has far greater depth than is often realized.

134. The early . . . root] A2; A1: The early Church thus held heresy as something evil, arising from division ["arising from division" overscored]; it saw it as evil in its very root, and as a result one thus then ["and . . . then" overscored].

Footnote] A3+

135. It is self-evident . . . second] A3+

136. We can add . . . Church] A2+

137. if we look . . . writings] A3+

138. A3 adds and overscores: and is against the innermost essence of Christianity; A3 then adds: It is clear that even the heretics belong to this in the wider sense.

A1 adds: If one supposes that in this case the Kingdom of God or the invisible church is confused with the visible, I answer that I am not confusing the two, but that I have set the two side by side. When or where is the Kingdom of God to be if it is not the Church in which believers are to stand in innermost community with Christ and through him among themselves? But one must add that not all those who are in the Church are also in the Kingdom of God. Otherwise how could Augustine's position on the Donatists be accepted as correct? One must distinguish a double aspect of the Church— a completely pure aspect outside of this temporal life and an aspect in which good and bad dwell together. But no one belongs to the invisible church or the Kingdom of God who is not in the visible one.

139. One can truly . . . God] A3+

140. At this point in the text Geiselmann notes the close of the previously added A3 section but in his notes he indicates the end at "God."

141. with the world] A3+

142. and in its battle against the Church] A3+

143. Footnote] Some scholars . . . this] A3+; 30] A1 adds: "The character of the times in which we live is such as to call forth from us even this admonition, that we

ought not to be astonished at those heresies, neither ought their existence to surprise us, for it was foretold that they should come to pass, nor the fact that they subvert the faith of some, for their final cause is, by affording a trial to faith, to give it also the opportunity of being approved. . . ." c. 30 [sic]: "We marvel at his churches. If they are deserted by individuals they thereby prove by that act that we who suffer in the example of Christ are Christians."

144. the Church] A3+

145. how] K; A1:that

146. if it is upheld by many only as a dead mass] A3+

147. in the Church itself] A3+

148. A1 adds and overscores: and the will rises to divide from the Church, to begin an individual life, and as a result they do not view this as originally received from the apostles.

149. believe that . . . immediately] A3+

150. One can explain . . . But] A3+

151. Footnote] the development . . . up] A3+; by might] K; A1: by physical might; destroyer] A3 originally: threat

152. so that they may be completed . . . heresies] A3+

153. She still cannot . . . seeking] A1 reads: as a result she cannot see herself as studying, first seeking, and thereby views herself in fact as *not existing.*

154. developed through it] A3+

155. so as to elevate her truth] A3+

156. *from*] A3+

157. *itself*] A3+

158. and is thus always in the Church] A3+

159. that their own . . . contradictions] A2+

160. A1 adds: just as no proper *history* of heresy can be given (as no history of evil) except through its battle with the Church, it appears in an ever-changing different form. Indeed, we know nothing of its essence through sixteen centuries.

161. this cannot be done] A3+

162. be able to] A3+

163. It is only . . . Church] A2+

164. See note 160 above.

165. Footnote] A3+

166. A2 adds: The doctrine of the Church as the only thing that makes one holy is linked to what has been said in the earlier paragraphs. According to the principles of the early Church the rise of this doctrine dare not be from an improper source. The Church has two relationships, namely, toward the different heretical parties and toward the whole non-Christian world.

Ignatius had already spoken very clearly stating that the person who did not remain in the community of the Church and who began egotistic developments had, through pride, brought judgment upon himself or herself.<1> Theophilus expressed himself in the same way<2> and Irenaeus said that heretics robbed themselves of life.<3> Clement of Alexandria charged that not only did heretics not enter the Kingdom of Heaven, but also that they hindered others from doing so by holding back the truth. Not only did they lack the keys to open the door, but as, one says, they had a counter key that instead of opening it, locked it more tightly.<4> Tertullian<5> and Cyprian expressed themselves precisely on this. Everywhere in Cyprian passages like the following are found: "Anyone who separates from the Church and binds himself or herself to another loses the promises of the Church, and does not gain the merits of Christ, which Christ left to the Church. The person who does not have the Church as mother cannot have God as Father."<6>

Hermas in the *Shepherd* expresses himself mildly, designating heresy more as weak-minded vanity: heretics, indeed, believe, but they are hard-headed, bold, and conceited. They wish to appear to know everything when in fact they know nothing. Because of their boldness they lost their senses, and feeble-minded pride became their master. They float in heights and act as if they were wise, whereas in fact they were fools. They wish to appear to be teachers. Pompous in their foolishness, many fell into emptiness. Boldness and vain self-trust is a great demon. Many were cast out because of it. Some acknowledged their error, did penance, and gave themselves over to the intelligent. But the others too could do penance because they were not evil but foolish and stupid.<7>

On the other hand, in the battle concerning the baptism of heretics, it was stated that those baptized in the name of the Trinity were not to be baptized again.<[8]> The Church thus acknowledged a union between herself and heretical communities, for would she not have had to cast aside their baptism, had she condemned those who had been baptized by them? The Roman bishop, Stephen, who fought against the rebaptism of heretics, pointed out the reasons why he held the earlier position. He asserted: The forgiveness of sins and new birth could follow through baptism in the heretical communities because it came not to the baptizers but to the baptisands who through their faith in the Trinity could receive divine grace.<9>

<<1>> [Ignatius of Antioch,] "To the Ephesians," 5: "Let no one deceive oneself. If one is not within the altar, one is deprived of the bread of God. . . . Anyone therefore who does not assemble with the Church has already manifested pride and condemned oneself." In 16 he emphasizes the impurity of faith for which Christ died: "Such a person, becoming defiled, shall go away into everlasting fire, and so shall everyone that listens to that person."

<<2>> [Theophilus of Antioch,] *To Autolycus*, 2:14.

<<3>> [Irenaeus,] *Against the Heresies* 3:24, 1 [source quoted].

<<4>> [Clement of Alexandria,] *Miscellanies*, 7:17.

<<5>> [Tertullian,] *On Baptism*, 8

<<6>> [Cyprian,] *On the Unity of the Church*, [6]. Cf. *Apostolic Constitution*, 6. Lactantius, *Institutes*, 4:30.

<<7>> [Hermas, *The Shepherd*,] 3:12.

<<[8]>> Cf. an early draft: Community lies so deeply in the essence of the Catholic Church that it acknowledges union whenever one is baptized in the names of the Trinity.

<<9>> ["Letter of] Firmilian to Cyprian," 75 [source quoted].

167. A1 has the following note: To discuss a later and well-known appearance, I refer to the Reformation. The Reformers accepted the doctrines of the Trinity, redemption, grace, and so on, that is, the nurture that they had received in the Church had embodied these truths so deeply in their consciousness that they viewed them as completely undeniable. However, because of later consequences of Reformation principles, the Reformers discovered that the truths must fall and that many of their churches must also fall. The Church's principle of unity was not cast aside by the Reformation but only turned and made laughable, and Protestantism appeared as the completed and fulfilled heresy.

168. A1 adds: (This followed from their principles and was consequently opposed—see sections 16 and 17—just as the whole of heresy in all its individual

appearances necessarily opposed the whole of Christianity and therefore it was with its principles unchristian.)

169. A2 (according to Geiselmann 392, although the Textual Notes indicate A1) adds: Heresy *as such* is always outside the Church although the schools [of heresy] or the individual leaders (of schools) can be in her.

170. K adds: for if one takes this away, unity is reestablished.

171. the followers . . . evil] A1: The heretics, in analogy to sin, were also slaves, namely, slaves of themselves, and their followers were made servants, namely, of their masters.

Footnote] A1 adds text of "Letter to the Philippians," 8: "To all who repent the Lord grants forgiveness if they turn in penitence to the unity of God and to communion with the bishop. I trust in the grace of Jesus Christ who shall free you from every bond."

172. Footnote] of them] A1: of them, perverse in every way, destroying the rule of faith

173. Footnote] They glory] A1: And we know that it is necessary that the appellation of the heresies should be expressed in contradistinction to the truth; from which Sophists, drawing things for the destruction of individuals, and burying them in human arts invented by themselves, glory

doctrine of his own] A1 adds: The basis of this was that they were to learn through concepts, not life. The Greek *hairēsis, secta* is unknown except for this; Clement . . . uses the word . . . it] A3+

174. then to teach what it is] A3+

175. A1 adds: Both agree that the divine Spirit of the Church does not give life, and therefore that Christianity first appears with them.

176. or if the cold Occidentals . . . designation] A3+

177. It is therefore also . . . them] A2+

The character . . . them] A2 originally: In Christianity there are no epochs; all are periods, a development of life given through Christ. However, the character of heresy that casts out the past and first wishes to point its secure direction into the future, separates both and places itself between them as if they proceeded first from its light. Such epochs brought in by the heated Oriental fantasy of a Valentinus through a Glaucias or a Montanus through a paraclete are unchristian. The colder Occidental fantasy results in the Reformation.

The section in A1 originally read: This was in contrast to heresy, every form of which was of the opinion that Christianity never was and that they were called to discover it. In fact, a great lack of honor for God. They looked upon themselves most egotistically as a center, the light spreading forward and backward, drawing the error of the past and pointing an unchangeable way into the future that they had to follow. In and for itself it is the same thing if Montanus's reformation wishes to complete Christianity or Valentinus and Marcion wish with their appearance to lift up from the dust that which disappeared. Both agree that the divine Spirit does not give life to the Church and therefore Christianity first appears with them. The East with its glowing fantasy marks the power which moves it egotistically as Montanus by the spirit or Valentinus by Glaucias, or immediately denies the descent of the Holy Spirit on the early Church as indicated in Acts, so as to concentrate this whole power in itself and like the Manichaeans to begin a clearly marked epoch with itself. The cold Occident calls itself in such cases merely a reformer. In Christianity there are no epochs but *one*. It is given with the appearance of Christ and the descent of the Holy Spirit, and everything else is only a period, an expiration or a development. Since the ecclesiastical egoist believes himself or herself to be called to initiate a new epoch, that individual's appearance can only be accompanied by division among fellow believers, separation of past and future, and the destruction of what is given.

178. concerning heresy and its antithesis] A3+

179. Cyprian quotation missing in A1 and replaced with quotation from Tertullian: "What if a bishop, a doctor, a martyr have fallen from the rule? Will heresies on that account appear to possess the truth? Do we prove the faith by persons or the persons by faith?"[*On Prescription of Heretics*, 3].

Part I, Chapter 4

1. Unity in Diversity] T; A1: Chapter 3. [A2:2] Relation of Catholic Principle to the Individuality of Believers

2. K adds: that each individual member preserve his or her characteristic, but to all of them together is given the direction of an activity through a principle.

3. to Christian . . . sense] A3; A1, K: to Christian custom

4. K and A1 read: the temporal and spatial Catholic doctrine

5. A1 adds: that was directly inflamed by faith.

6. a noble mysticism] A3+

7. glowing throughout with faith, pierces] A2; A1: feeling inwardly, grasped

8. One may . . . changed] A2; A1: We have only to concern ourselves characteristically with the relationship between faith and knowledge, insofar as both are Christian. This is not the place, however, to discuss the relationship between revealed faith and rational knowledge as it was understood in the early Church, but of the link because of the one.

9. It was argued . . . revelation] A2+

10. It is not . . . universal whole] A1 reads "whole" for A2 "All"

11. differences] A3; A1, K: distinctions

12. kind of pious] A3; A1, K: scientific

13. A2 originally added and overscored: But because God saw their pomposity and pride against others, because they imagined themselves to be great in their knowledge of God and in their philosophically created teachings concerning divine things, because they quickly led the unlearned to the worship of idols, to their temples and famous mysteries, he used what was foolish in the world, the simplest of spirits who in fact lived more wisely and purely than many philosophers, to shame the wise who had without shame turned to lifeless objects as if they were God or his image. What intelligent person would not laugh at such an individual who after such extensive and great studies still looked to idols, or viewed them as symbols that could raise one up to some imagined god? Each Christian, however, even a layperson, knows that each spot in the world is a place of the universal whole, of the temple of God

14. a power . . . beings] A3; K, A1: the power of belief among people in reason.

15. According to . . . people] A3+

16. and other pagan peoples] A3+

17. A1 adds: and at the same time lost

18. appeared . . . itself] A3; A1: the personified truth in Jesus; A2: appeared in Jesus, the Son of God, personified truth

19. and true] A3; A1, K omits

20. pure human] A3; A1, K omits

21. A2 adds and K overscores: just as the light of darkness itself disappears when the light appears

22. order] A3; A1: receive the right to prove; A2: prove

23. A1 adds: (Non-Christians then use what has become clear in Christianity so as to cast aside that which is not clear to them, and thus that they have the right to do so.)

24. A1 adds and K overscores: This is natural and proper. The highest is only its own weight. We, therefore, remain firm that Christianity can only be measured through itself, and the aforementioned endeavors only to bring us to clear consciousness.

In the margin A1 notes: It is striking that against the pagans reason is tested through Christianity, but against Christians Christianity is tested through reason.

25. often . . . day] A3; A1, K omits

26. It was acknowledged . . . it] A3+

27. judge] A3; A1, K: test

28. judged] A3; A1, K: tested

29. A1 and K add: If the charge had been laid against our Fathers that if reason could not test Christianity, every error could have arisen as a revelation, they would have considered this strange. They would have done so in the first place because the one who is in possession of Christianity must view everything opposed to it as in contradiction to its highest, living, and actual needs, whereas what is Christian asserts itself against everything that is foreign to it. If we are no longer in possession of it, we in fact acknowledge that every error and reason that is no longer Christian would be as little able to protect us from error as that which never had been Christian.<1>

<<1>> Justin, *Dialogue with Trypho*, 7:8. Origen, *Against Celsus*, 7:44, indicates in the same way as did common Christians against philosophers how many enlightened concepts each had. One must read the early Apologists and Origen in particular to see this properly.

30. of God] A3+

31. alone] A3; A1, K omits

32. not be absent for long] A3; A1, K: follow

A1 and K add: The pagan Celsus already attacked the Christians because they always said, "Believe, if you wish to be saved or leave," and he then added, "as if one were to decide on which god to follow with the throw of the dice." Their philosophers, he believed, could explain everything and would not be hindered even if they wished to say what nothing was.<1> Origen opposed this by noting that Christians had external and internal grounds for their religion. If they wished to make someone aware of this religion, the person's formation was considered. Those who were capable of grasping this they sought to win through a development of their characteristic.<2> Those who were not capable were instructed in the faith with all the reasons already outlined.

<<1>>Origen, *Against Celsus*, 7:11 [source quoted], in relation to the different groups among the Christians.

<<2>>Ibid., 10: "Accordingly, we do not say to each of our hearers, 'Believe, first of all, that he whom I introduce you to is the Son of God'; but we put the Gospel before each one, as character and disposition may fit the person to receive it, inasmuch as we have learned to know 'how we ought to answer each person' [Col. 6:6]. And there are some who are capable of receiving nothing more than an exhortation to believe, and to these we address that alone, while we approach others again, as far as

possible, in the way of demonstration, by means of question-answer." Other examples can be found in Justin, *Dialogue against Trypho*, 2, Theophilus of Antioch, and others.

33. Because of . . . deeper] K+

34. Anyone who . . . individuality] A3+

35. namely, . . . Church] A3+

36. or if by . . . community] K+

37. What is given] A3; K: The perception of the given

38. A2 adds and A3 overscores: This is to say that no certitude arises through mere concepts, through pure speculation, separated from all historical matter [*Historischen*], if the spiritual activity is master of an historical [*geschichtlichen*], positive matter. Therefore. . . .

39. object of reflection] T; A1: object of reflection; K: object of inner observation

40. if it is taken up in us] A3+

41. A1, K adds: The first is itself also the inner, [A3 adds: itself lying in faith] knows the grounds of its faith, and thus as well the grounds of its faith in general as all individual components of the same.

42. mere assent] A3; A1, K: mere assertion

43. Footnote] Other definitions . . . God] A3; A2: For other definitions, see Lumper on Clement of Alexandria. The *pistis* [faith] of Basilides is essentially distinguished from that of the Catholics, for as Clement has expressly noted this is *physikē* [matter] and the believer *heuriskē autēn* [seeks this].

44. object of] A3; A2, K om

45. K adds: as, for example, medicine, chemistry, geography

46. A2, K adds: The faith of the Church that allows everything to be living in us and can preserve this life-giving power complies with this faith that is found in us as expressed doctrine.

47. of the Church] T; A2, K: characteristically

48. faith here steps forth from the mind] A3; A2, K: everything develops from one point

49. as Origen says] A3+

50. Therefore, Clement designates . . . says] A2; A1 reads and overscores: Therefore Clement designates gnosis as a grasping of truth through itself; because through faith the whole human person is grasped, lives a new life in faith, and thus becomes the object of gnostic contemplation, it is characteristically created from the innermost essence of the human person.<1>

<<1>>Clement of Alexandria, *Miscellanies*, 5 [as in T, note 4].

51. the doctrine of the Church] A3+

52. as its source as well] A3+

53. Therefore, Clement characteristically . . . truth] A2+; A2 originally adds: One does not wish through knowledge to lift oneself up to the faith of the Church that carries its certitude in itself, but merely wishes to lift up the faith [A3 adds: which is nothing other than that of the Church] to the consciousness of believers. [A3 adds: The Catholic gnosis does not wish to perfect Christianity but believers in their manner of knowing Christianity.] The faith, however, was none other than that of the Church so that one can say that outside of Christianity there is no true knowledge of God. What Christianity is, the Church alone always teaches us.

54. Thus, it is true . . . well] A3+

55. A2, K add: One may call this the demonstration of faith through philosophy, a less than proper expression since the divine cannot be expressed through the human but must and can be set forth by means of something human.

56. of *gnosis*] A3; A2, K omits

57. Since faith . . . philosophy] A2; A1: For the help of this speculative theology some philosophical system was called in. The doctrines of Christianity were set together with the principles of this system and explained, clarified, and made evident by it, even though the tie between the two did not belong to the (Catholic) gnosis. At that time it was chiefly the Platonic philosophy

58. See Katerkamp, *Kirchengeschichte*, 1:267ff] A3+; A1 adds: which is to be noted in the use of the history of dogma in that what is to be clarified dare not be confused with the clarification itself [A2 corrects: the portrayal with the thing to be portrayed] as so often happens.

59. In it . . . overcome] A3+

60. A1 adds: Unity in essence united all in spite of the differences of their individualities.

K adds: If errors on the part of speculative theologians are to be noted, but must be tolerated, so is it the case with mystical theologians where the same tolerance is to be granted. Because mysticism conceives of faith as a closed, unbroken unity of an inner life witnessed by divine power, sight is its essence, an unmediated, inner union of God and Christ in the Holy Spirit, or as mysticism often expresses itself, a life in God, a sinking in God, the life of Christ in us, and so on. What the mystic here sees, he or she may not or cannot express or explain [matters] in firm and precise concepts—indeed, such concepts are opposed by the mystic. The mystic does not wish to speculate, and if a mystic begins to do so and describes what has been experienced in his or her inner [being], the mystic wishes to be free of such forms, to be tied to none that are available for use and thus appears to be opposed to the content of these forms. The opposition to mysticism has not been proper since these people imitate the essence of the Church.

61. The unity and difference . . . themselves] A3+, but according to Geiselmann's introduction to section A2+

62. K adds: If, therefore, one cannot blame mystics directly for their opposition, nevertheless, mystics should take care not to oppose doctrinal concepts as such; the greatest mystics throughout all time have not done so. A great part of the Church has the need to make its inner religious life as clear as possible, *and members of this part too imitate the Church*, as is evident in their dogmas. One makes a great error if one looks upon many doctrines, for example, on the Holy Trinity, as pure speculation. Such doctrines are an expression of the inner life of the Christian. The whole of Church history demonstrates this. The one who has grasped the whole of the apostolic doctrine lovingly in his or her mind, and wishes to express what Jesus Christ and the Holy Spirit have become for oneself, comes of necessity to Church doctrine and such a person's inner consciousness bears witness to the truth of Church doctrine. *Therefore. . . .*

63. A3 adds: as it historically expressed itself and must express itself

64. The speculation of each . . . Father] A3+

65. However, if the mystic . . . foolishness] A3+

66. Written speculations . . . draw] A3; A2 and K: The Church, therefore, allows this speculation and construction to have its way but does not accept anything it says into her confession insofar as it is individual, human, or constrained, always holding fast to the historical [*Historischen*] and what has been transmitted. Nevertheless, the Church does take from such speculation the unmistakably best parts.

67. Catholic] A2; A1:Christian

68. Footnote] See Pamphilius . . . Origen] A3+

69. acknowledged . . . humility] A2; A1: assert that this possesses a power working through itself, which is lacking to knowledge since knowledge always has its value because of its union with the former.

70. unconscious] A2; A1: pliant

71. pure portrayal of faith] A3+; K om: of faith

72. understand] A3; A1, K: be conscious of

73. beneficent active relationship on] A2; A1: relationship to

74. A2 adds: The relationship of the principles of reason to Christian doctrine begets self-conscious truth [A1 reads: The union of dogmas through comparison begets truth from which understanding follows]; from this follows gnosis. We do not thus need philosophy alongside faith particularly, but because of the advantage that *gnosis* preserves for us, in that by this we come to the firm conviction regarding what we have grasped in faith, because what was earlier merely present in feeling has raised itself<1> to scientific certainty and otherwise calls itself gnosis.

<<1>>*Miscellanies*, 1:2. In my translation of the striking passage I have used, I believe properly, the Latin text and have depended on the comments of Sylburg and Lowth.

75. Footnote] Basil, *On Isaiah* . . . 1811] A3+

76. because of the lack of healthy nourishment] A2+

77. who had just received the divine life] A3; A1, K omits

78. A2 adds: a faith, namely, that is present as mere doctrine, mere concept present in human beings without being rooted in a human being's whole life, is dead.

79. If some . . . whole] A1 originally: If the Catholic philosophers of religion in the Church fulfilled these

80. unspeakable joy and heavenly consolation] A2+

Footnote] 7:16] A1 adds: In the passage cited above in which ignorance is ascribed to the pagans and joyous certainty to believers, he ascribes pleasure to the gnostics.

K adds: He ascribes ignorance to the pagans, uncertainty to the heretics, and certainty to believers, but to the gnostics (according to his use of the term) he ascribes joy.

81. of holy life] A3; A1: of life; A2: of holy life and pure mind

82. as their . . . it] A3; A1 and K read: Contemplation proceeded from the mind but was only a movement and, therefore, a new strengthening.

83. A1 adds and A2 overscores: communicates the manifold gifts but the same in all who gave it.

84. and the church . . . truth] A3; A2: so as to continue the building of his Church, and the Church speaks of this so decisively that she properly venerates the greatest defenders of her truth as saints.

85. Faith and knowledge . . . another] A3+

86. K [Geiselmann also indicates the reading as A2 in later note] adds: The two extremes, however, that we meet outside of the Church were always avoided. On the one hand, a proud speculation arose that disturbed faith, and its adherents valued a proud superficiality and weakness. On the other hand, with the casting out of all knowledge sad confusion arose. Through the Holy Spirit history and knowledge were in marvellous and complete harmony.

87. No constraint . . . mediation] T. The section exists in four forms. Vierneisel places the first of these at the end of section 66.

1. text of the original draft (see Vierneisel, 339-40): <[1]>No Church has brought forth so many great and influential persons as the Catholic has throughout the years. Truth alone is not curtailed in its activity. Great, weighty duties awaken great spirits.

There is no greater or more significant duty than to defend the truth and to make its kingdom firm.<[2]> Setting her members in a great community, she extends her power as far as she herself exists. Further, the leaders of heretical congregations wished to squeeze Christianity's external truths into the confines of their time and individuality. As a result their work perished with their time which they sought to give the character of eternity. The period that followed did not take the pains to transmit their opinions to the future, or even to indicate to the future that it bewailed the loss of things related to this spirit. It had a proper anticipation that the time that complained of the loss possessed the ability to pass on similar products but had no reason to trouble itself to do so. Those who were the works of our eternal Father, on the other hand, defended the things of Christ, of the Church, of the salvation and consolation of humanity, and were many times willing to suffer<[3]> and to die for them. To this day, outside the confines of time, they have worked a thousand blessings. They shone in the twilight of dark centuries and are now the one present source of a renewed deep Christian life. They will work until we no longer need letters, and turn fully with the Spirit who spoke in them through Christ who already unites all.

Who can still assert that through the constricted bonds of the Church the power of the individual is crippled?<[4]>

2. Text of A2 has the following changes in addition to some slight stylistic variations.

<[1]> A2 adds: I must still make some comments on the written works of the Church fathers; A3 omits and adds: No constraint of individuality comes from the Spirit of the Catholic Church. Rather, she forms individualities in virtue and power. This can be seen in the character of Catholic writers.

<[2]> A2 adds: This is the duty of the Church.

<[3]> A2 adds: in the early period; A3 omits

<[4]> and turn fully . . . crippled?] A2: The love and truth that bind us with them require that they remain present to us in their writings until in the Spirit who created the community, we no longer need any mediation.

3. K agrees with A2.

4. A3 as in T with slight stylistic variations; additional addenda and omissions noted in form 2 above.

88. Christian ethics . . . congregations] A2; A1: Individual doctrines of the faith are the unfolding and the expression of Christian theory. In a like manner, one and the same ethical doctrine develops itself in Christian ethics. The apostles transmitted to *the congregations* what the ethical doctrines were and thus what specific virtues and duties were [to arise from] a holy disposition as the portrayal of this holy principle.

89. As happened . . . self-evident] A2+

90. the Church . . . people] A3; A2, K: the Church does not value her struggles and necessity

91. they wish to live in lust] A3+

92. A1 ends with "animal"

93. K adds: Only the Gnostics belong to this group.

94. Footnote] Through Christianity . . . regulation] A3+

95. K adds: unconstrained by earthly matters

96. It is therefore localized . . . sensual] A3; K: It is for the most part and in many cases local, temporary, contingent, and thus grounded in the sensual.

97. order of the world and of salvation] A3; K: heavenly order

98. It seems to me . . . world] Possible addition of A3 according to Geiselmann's system of notation; from this point on he italicizes some sections, not italicized in T to indicate them as A3 additions.

99. K adds: (In our day we find the opposite extreme where one raises one's individuality to a general law and is thus incapable of achieving a free foundation so that everyone is lovelessly declared and explained as superstitious, as a *work*, as *external*, who is not married *as the heretic* was, did not draw out the same from the body *as* did *the heretic*, did not destroy his or her own powers *as* did *the heretic*.) Against those confined principles Clement noted in a beautiful way that even the pagans and their priests who worshipped idols confirmed the wine and the flesh and marriage. The Kingdom of God does not consist in food and drink (Rom. 14:17); and just as humility and mercy are not harsh against the body, so temperance is a holy disposition of the spirit and is to be sought in the internal, not in the external (*Miscellanies*, 3:6).

100. Footnote] Against this a Montanist . . . do] A3+

101. K adds: The contradiction is not "to apprehend Christianity according to its individuality," but "to reform Christianity according to its individuality," not "to allow oneself to be taught by it," but "to wish to teach it."

102. Geiselmann italicizes all of sections 46 and 47, indicating that they are A3 additions.

103. We must still discuss . . . worship] K: The Catholic principle of unity suppresses individuality neither in a theoretical nor ethical way. It requires only the purely Christian of everything that possesses universality according to its nature and does not carry itself in accordance with every individuality, but the universal must penetrate the individual if the individual is to be Christian. If, thus, the Catholic principle only presses toward unity in spiritual matters, it cannot wish to bring about meaning in matters of external worship. Because everything external is constricted according to its nature, the Catholic principle would contradict its own nature and hinder its general knowledge if it created an entrance for the constrained and external in every place where it thought to establish itself. External worship (we are not here speaking of the sermon) is the religiosity that becomes visible in confessions and confessional matters. Where there is inner religiosity, there must be an external, because if the internal is living, it presses out externally to establish itself and to make itself clear and conscious. Christian religiosity is, moreover, a communal religiosity. However, since we know of no unmediated spiritual union between people, the religious movements that are to be participated in always find themselves in something external.

The external communicates the inner experiences of one person with the other and thus becomes not only the unifying point of all but also the organ through which the inner being of one person streams out to the totality and once more flows back from this to that person. It thus brings about activity and life, because it is itself made active and given life in that it expresses itself and allows the dispositions of others to flow back onto itself through its expression. External worship is not, therefore, merely for sensual, lowly people and times; the person in whom a higher grade of inner life has developed will feel driven to communicate it, and the one who does not possess it needs to allow himself or herself to be stirred up. The one who does not do so is like a tree without leaves and branches. These leaves and branches are witness to an inner power, striving outwardly toward development, and through these the related power communicates itself to them at the same time. If the tree no longer blossoms, the inner power is extinguished and is considered to be dead. It is marvellous that Christ, in the life-giving communal acts of worship that *he* instituted, communicates himself in Holy Communion in the most living way to his believers. This is the highest grade of divine life-communication of which we are capable; in the activities of worship that he established as life-giving, occurs worship.

104. An early draft adds: which are established in modern times as the highest law of Church history.

105. An early draft adds: To give an example from a later period: A succession of confessional activities that are associated in the Catholic Church with the Lord's Supper indicate its ideals and pure conception concerning the Eucharist. The presence of Christ in the Eucharist is not dependent on the physical act of the drinking—this would be superstition; it does not depend on the external, but as soon as the faith of the Church and its trust has expressed itself in a living way, Christ is present.

106. An early draft reads: The symbolic has a close union with the religious. The bases of the religious can reach no concept, no thought can grasp it, and if we seek it, we do not raise ourselves above what is an image and signifier. The symbol as the sensual idea is thus so mysterious and so expressive that it lays claim to the whole person, demands all his or her thinking powers, and yet its content is never reached through thinking.

107. K adds: The character of the individual languages, their appearances and wealth of images, the characters of the images themselves, the brevity of the languages, and so on, offer in general the basis of the form that the external symbolic worship of a people wishes to have. The glowing fantasy of the Orient creates a boldness, an exuberance, and a mass of images and is not wearied in the smallest detail. The Oriental is, therefore, broad, sweeping, and its liturgy, like its preaching, has this character. If the cold Occidental always feels its inner power stirred up and expressed in a wide-ranging expression of symbolic activities, it is weakened. Its weak fantasy cannot follow the audacious images. It does not discover their meaning at all, or it does so too late and loses coherence. It presents rather only a few thoughts and, concerned only with these, sinks in the depths. The Oriental, seemingly drawn out on the surface through its manifoldness, is always attempting to establish deep roots. The formed taste desires only high ideas, great experiential content of a symbolic description. The unformed taste does not bind itself through such a law. Where in the case of the first the border for the comic and the meaningless begins, the material for significant earnestness is found in the case of the second. Brevity, clarity, simplicity, meaningfullness, love of symbol, or the succession of symbolic activities as the expression of a basic thought are relative, and if the formed taste can also be greatly distinguished in this, the chief cause is the penetrating, stirring, and *active* [force]. This is linked to external distinctions, however. Everything must be given over to national individualities in this. Moreover, the character of times change. In the first periods, when Christians were the suppressed, persecuted parties, free external developments were hampered. The total religious power was taken up and occupied by the persecutions.

Only striving to press toward the high spiritual unity, which penetrated the one multiplicity and variation of forms, and to press into external unity was important, and although the unity ruling over all forms manifests itself through these distinctions in greater strength, as Irenaeus says, yet it seems natural to discover a certain misunderstanding in this, and therefore to insist that in the meaningful forms at least, the type of a spiritual unity would again be found. The Roman bishop, Victor, therefore, already attempted in the second century to establish agreement on the time of spiritual celebration and by doing so he allowed himself to be led, as can be easily seen, by the most significant reasons of his own time. Only because no constrictions are established and none can be established completely through the Catholic principle were his endeavors fruitless.

108. K adds: And this is truly a clinging to forms and an essence of forms; insofar as one assents and supposes one stands over the form.

109. K adds: And because of this the earliest period cannot be presented as an example in this relationship.

110. so that Christians . . . paganism] A3+

111. K adds: as in the Orient (the muttering of the Mithra feast) one sets the feast of the rising sun along side that of the birth of Christ, or the beginning of the spiritual, but never more the changing sun.

112. K adds: To present the ancient Church in relationship to the external forms of worship as an ever-continuing type is to be imprisoned in the external and in the forms themselves in that one protests against the essence of forms. What is one doing other than establishing the form of one time for all times? And if one does this, is one not saying that one is celebrating the Lord's Supper as did Jesus and his disciples? Because like them one has no forms? If you have love as did the apostles, then you celebrate the Lord's Supper as they did, not if you have the forms which they had.

113. because the people did . . . higher] A3+

114. If, in addition . . . matter] A3+

115. Every desire . . . did] A3+

Part II, Chapter 1

1. An early draft reads: Historic genetic development of the Church as an external visible association. Her organism.

2. The concept of the Church . . . Spirit] See Appendix 1, "Pragmatic Glimpses."

3. [Footnote] What a great spiritual power . . . Christ] A3+

4. K adds: The visible world itself is a revelation of the invisible creating power of the divinity; the individual levels of development in inorganic nature and revelations are differently constituted powers of life, the plant world only the external unfolding of a specific living power.

5. K adds: and for us no power, on the whole, exists that does not make itself known to us in a visible form.

6. An early draft reads: The one divine power communicated to believers must beget one living unity of believers, a visible uniting of all, one Church, and do away with all the categories that have earlier distinguished peoples and nations. Nothing other than this manifestation disturbed the pagan world in its position. See *Wiener Jahrbücher*. Examples to citations from Eusebius, [*Ecclesiastical History*,] 5:1, on the martyr Sanctus.

This cannot be applied to the heretical parties, for during the persecutions they did not in any way confess themselves as Christians. The kind of unity that the martyrs spoke of is demonstrated by the words of the martyr Pionius: "Then Polemo said, 'Are you a Christian?' Pionius replied, 'I am.' 'Of what church?' asked Polemo. Pionius relied, 'Of the Catholic. There is no other among Christians'." Heretical principles cannot in any way beget answers such as that of this martyr. ["Alia acta [Pionii] ex Simeone Metaphraste," 2, 9, in Johannes Bollandus, ed., *Acta Sanctorum. . .*, Feb. 1-6, p. 44]

7. If love was given . . . Christianity] See Appendix 1, "Pragmatic Glimpses."

8. K adds: (I do not want to replace spirit with religion since religion is often considered only as a concept, which is not acceptable here.)

9. K adds: as the body never needs an awakening from the dead because the life-giving spirit continually lives in it.

10. The human spirit. . . activity] A3; K reads: The human spirit works and acts upon the world and accepts its laws through the orders, organs, and functions of the body; in a like manner the Spirit ruling in the Church begets its organ and the organ's functions to work on it and to penetrate the world.

11. For this reason . . . body] A3+

12. K adds: First, however, we must make some comments concerning the rise of the thought of an invisible Church, which was taken up by the teachers.

Section 38 [intended as an addendum in A3 and as a section of the text proper in K]: To my knowledge, they generally never say with clear and precise words that Christ only wished to have an invisible Church, nor do Catholics say that a visible Church was established by him, although they do assume this. According to the description of their basic principles that have been given and according to their whole manner of viewing Christianity, which they see merely as a pattern of thought, a system of concepts, it is necessary that the heretics hold to an invisible Church. As a result the union of believers can be among them nothing other than a conceptual union, a combination of thoughts, that is, an invisible Church, or in other words, as has already often been said, a church that does not exist in any way. What is merely present in concept has no (real) being. According to the Catholic viewpoint, the union with Christ through the Holy Spirit is real, standing not in a mere concept but in a sure doctrine. Therefore, the union among believers, revelation, and its type is itself real and visible.<1> Just as a concept cannot beget life, so a general concept (even that which has been indicated) cannot beget a common life. Moreover, because heresy arose only by breaking off from an earlier, common, and visible union, it cannot accept the necessary *base* of that union. Because heresy itself was called forth by individuals, and without them had no foundation and thus once again disappeared with them or else was each time once again begotten by individuals who thought similarly, it can have no objective, permanent, visible basis, and therefore denies a visible Church itself.<[2]>

If heresy accepts a visible Church founded by Jesus, it has denied for itself the right to exist. It is clear that the visible Church could not first have arisen with Marcion or Valentinus in the second century or with others in the fourth and fifth centuries, but must always have been present. Heresy must then accept that the Church founded by the apostles, which it is not, was always supported with all the elements necessary for her continuing existence and with all required physical and spiritual powers, that is, that heresy had no ground to begin its own development. Thus heresy must accept that Christ and Christianity were not given to us through egoism and separatism but in and through the Church community. How can the chief principle of heresy that Christianity is a matter of *seeking* be supported if it must be accepted that Christianity was characteristically never lost? Or indeed, that it could not once have been lost? That it always lay in a visible Church before one's eyes and stood open to view? How then could so many innumerable *discoveries* be called Christian if it is accepted that Christianity is one and one specific thing and is always to be found in the visible Church founded by the apostles? To establish such a fiction, an invisible Church is formulated—in which everything, even the greatest contradiction, can be upheld, particularly since one sees nothing in it, and therefore sees no contradiction, no distinction between true and false. Moreover, each individual heretical teacher always strove to have a visible Church and to unite all the students in one whole, in contradiction to that heretic's own statements. It seems that here the forming might of Christianity and its opposite should have made the defenders of the invisible Church aware of the emptiness and unchristian nature of their concept. An invisible Church on earth is opposed to history, Christian feeling, and all reasonable conceptions of Christianity. It does not arise from a Christian interest, but from an egotistic one that attempts to add support to its assertions just as one error always supports another. The acceptance of an invisible Church is also founded, all things considered, on completely false conceptions of Christianity's essence, considering it a concept, and on inappropriate concepts concerning the Holy Spirit and the Spirit's relationship to the Church. This development we find in no heretical dogmatic system other than in an early stage.

For very good thoughts concerning the visible and the invisible Church, see *Wiener Jahrbücher*, vol. 25, 87ff., and Haller, in his *Theorie der geistlichen Staaten*.

<<1>>In the doctrine of the Lord's Supper, the whole spirit of the Catholic Church is expressed. Christ shares himself *in a living way* with his believers and founds a living community. If we give up this conception of the Lord's Supper, we give up the characteristic of our Church. Likewise, the characteristic of the Catholic Church necessarily implies belief in the Supper. In the Lutheran Church the doctrine of the real presence of Christ is inconsistently retained, the spirit of the doctrine itself demanding another description. The longer it continues, the clearer must the spirit of the system communicate this to the individual so that it can now be said that it is fairly generally held (among the learned) that in the Supper only *the remembering* of Christ is celebrated (that is, we go together with him merely in concept. Schleiermacher, who has a different conception of the Lord's Supper, must construe the Church in another way, or because he construes the Church in another way, he must establish another kind of life), that is, it is accepted that Christ is not *present in a living way* in his believers, but he only left a remembrance for them in the Supper, that he was *once* here present and is now so merely in remembering, in a dead concept, and that they are bound with him in the doctrine [see Friedrich Schleiermacher, *Der Christliche Glaube* (1821-1822), sections 156-60]. This conceptual union with Christ must also make the union of believers among themselves into a thought union, that is, an invisible Church.

<<[2]>>Moreover, because heresy arises . . . itself] This section is based closely on an earlier draft that adds an initial sentence: The invisible Church of heresy is established with the essence of this in that heresy arises only by breaking off from an earlier common union. . . . and therefore, it becomes a Church that has such a basis, like itself, established on human origin.

13. not located

14. What is primary . . . beneficent] A3+

15. What God has joined . . . asunder] A3+

16. K adds: Already in Acts it is said of Paul and Barnabas that they were concerned for the establishment of this in their missionary journeys [cf. Acts 15]. Note as well 1 Tim. 1:3 and Titus 1:5.

17. In T the note is affixed to the previous sentence on Ignatius, but appears to be referring to the topic in this sentence.

18. Footnote] I am not impressed . . . priesthood] A3+

19. Möhler appears to have confused his Petavius citations in the original footnote; there is also reference to "singular bishops" in 4:5, a chapter that begins on fol. 15 (a folio number cited in T).

20. Footnote] What is upheld . . . all] A3+

21. K adds: *agapē morphōtheisa*

22. an expression of] A3+; K: a work of

23. Here the foundational . . . him] A3+

24. Because the congregation is in him and he in it] A3+

25. However, this is the same . . . about] A3+

26. K adds: After his death the Church is therefore a sorrowing orphan

27. He is not holier . . . holier] A3+

28. Section misnumbered as 52 in T

29. and must be a free offspring of the human spirit] A3+

30. A2 adds: The apostles, however, installed the bishop because they foresaw the need and the inner drive of the believers, and, in that they provided the central point for it, there was to be no doubt in the future that the correct direction of the Christian disposition was in that point.

31. K adds the following note: Basil, *On the Holy Spirit*, 5:26. Many cite this significant conception of organic unity.

32. Footnote] A great many writers . . . extensively] A3+

33. A2 adds: for he is the one who before all the other apostles said: 'You are the Son of the living God' [Matt. 16:16]. Without this conviction, no one is a believer in the characteristic sense, and therefore the apostles were not believers until that point.

34. they were the best suited] A3+

35. K adds: Paul, as well, in his letters to Timothy and Titus, makes significant statements regarding bishops. See 1 Tim. 3:2 and Titus 1:5.

36. Footnote] Note particularly . . . matter] A3+

37. K adds: And on this rests the necessity that all form one unity,<1> just as the unfounded significance of the divisive propositions of heresy. In this the episcopate coalesces with the earlier developed necessary distinctions of individuals standing quietly beside one another. In agreement with this is the fact that it was chiefly the clergy that always formed and defended the Christian religion and the Church in a scholarly manner. The episcopate in the Church was thus absolutely necessary and of an immediate divine source in both its external appearance and its internal powers. Just as there was no congregation before Christian teachers arose in it, there would be no congregation if the teacher disappeared. Just as in such places there is no need to communicate, so there is no need to receive and vice versa. As there is no point of union, so there is no need to be united, that is, no Christian spirit.

Finally, it is Christ's doctrine that the teacher proclaims, it is Christ's name on which one baptizes, Christ's power with which one forgives sins, Christ's flock that one feeds. No human being has given Christian doctrine; how could one proclaim with human words? If one does not baptize in a human name, how can one receive one's power to baptize from a human being? If no human being has the power to forgive sins, how can the office held be called a human one? If one's office is a divine institution, how can it rest on a contract? There is no contract that Christianity continues; it is established through an organ. There is no contract offered to believers to be silent or to proclaim the gospel. Nor is there any contract that it be proclaimed generally. If Christians are driven from one area, they go to another and say with Paul (2 Cor. 5:20): "As those sent in the place of Christ, we beseech you to be reconciled with God," and their preaching will be blessed again. One can then ask the question only as follows: Will the gospel no longer be proclaimed if *human beings* no longer wish to transmit it? It will still be transmitted. As the continuation of the gospel cannot be made dependent upon human beings, neither is the preservation of the teaching office to which its continuation is tied. To call the teaching office a human office is to make the gospel itself a human work, suggesting that further preaching is dependent on human beings.<[2]>

According to the view of the Church, the community of believers is an unmediated divine work. In a like manner members that bind together believers are also a divine institution, and as true doctrine is proclaimed only in this divinely formed unity, so the teaching office itself has a divine source. According to the egoistic conception of believers by which each fundamentally believes himself or herself to be able to be a Christian in separation, members who are bound together in a union are not necessarily seen as a divine institution because this would do away with egoism. Following this argument, if individuals believe that they can communicate the truth separately for themselves, no teaching office can be acknowledged as a divine institution, whose holders are at once the center of love, a beautiful symbol that truth and love are one.

There is a closer union than one can see at first glance between the view of the teaching office as a divine institution and the preservation of doctrine itself as divine. Because the Catholic Church firmly holds that the episcopate was directly founded by Christ and that the continuation of the divine Church is dependent on the divinely ordered episcopate, she holds fast to the doctrine entrusted to her at the same time by Christ. Because the episcopate did not arise from itself or through itself and is in no way human in its source, it dare in no way by itself set down or set aside anything of human origin as Christian doctrine. Outside the Catholic Church we find a view of doctrine as something to be discovered through a human agency, as something that is able to be other than it is, and a view of the teaching office as an office discovered through human beings, arbitrary, as something that can be changed and not something that is to be as it is.<3> Such leaders allow the people to thank them for their existence and for the doctrine that they [the leaders] give to them.<[4]> A further reason lies in the fact that heresy establishes an ecclesiastical egoism as its basic principle and holds that a common life is not necessary but arbitrary. As a result the organ that proceeds from the inner living unity and communicates it must be from a human source and arbitrary. Since each person thinks that he or she is able to discover the true doctrine by himself or herself, that person considers the community and even its organ to be necessarily a human matter.

However, it is necessary that the conception of the episcopate as a divine institution is tied to the true freedom and independence of all believers because it is a divine institution. Only history and the principles of the early Church remove all doubt.

<<1>>In many lands princes stand in the place of the people; this can be striking in very different circumstances, but the idea must be preserved.

<<[2]>>A2 adds: The spiritual ability to preach is seen in certain communities as a gift of God; nevertheless, after an individual is selected for the office, the person is held as in need of yet greater gifts. So as to describe the chosen one publicly as the one equipped for the office and to request God's grace, installation into the office is accompanied with celebrative activities, and the individual is consecrated with prayer, fasting, and the laying on of hands, so that this person is the proper teacher and *only* this one. Acts 14:23; 1 Tim. 4:14;5:22.

<<3>>Tertullian, *On the Prescription of Heretics*, 40, 41.

<<[4]>>A2 adds: In modern times outside of the Catholic Church it is asserted that the people were formerly held in servility to priests and that by the distinction between the clergy and the laity the freedom and value of the laity was set aside. It

is striking to note the basic premises of the Catholic Church as expressed in the early Church in this regard. We have here an opportunity to marvel at the height of the concept of the priesthood of all Christians and the true freedom they have in this.

Footnote] For this reason . . . 3.97] A3+

38. in the following . . . cited] K: from the following: at one time the general Christian priesthood was set over against the Judaic priesthood. Jewish priests alone brought sacrifices, indeed only external ones; all tribes except the Levitic were refused entrance to it; of the high priest only external purity was required to appear before God. Thus according to the Fathers, each Christian as a true priest brings a heart filled with faith, pure, holy, and consecrated, before God, as an inner sacrifice. Justin Martyr says: "We, who earlier lived in impurity and debasement, have by the grace of Christ, removed all the filth with which we had covered ourselves. . . . Jesus was called a priest by the prophets. In like manner we are a true, priestly race of God, since we are as one person believing in God the Creator of all things after we have been freed from our sins by the power of God's firstborn and have been inflamed by the call of his word. God himself bears witness to this when he says that a pleasing sacrifice is brought before him in every place among the heathen. God receives a sacrifice from no one other than his priests."<1>

Irenaeus describes the characteristic of the one making the sacrifice as follows: "Christ desires that the sacrifice be brought in all simplicity and innocence, and therefore says: 'When you bring your gift to the altar and remember that your brother has something against you, leave your offering at the door and reconcile yourself first with your brother; then return and present your sacrifice' [Matt. 5:23-24]. . . . And if someone seeks to present a sacrifice pure and properly only in an external sense, but in his soul does not stand in community with his brother and has no fear of God, God will not forgive the inner sin through the external sacrifice. . . . The sacrifice does not make a person holy since God does not require a sacrifice, but the pure consciousness of the person makes the sacrifice holy." For this reason he says that it is not the material of the sacrifice that distinguished Judaic from Christian sacrifice but that it was no longer brought by slaves but by free persons.<2> Now one can understand the phrase "all the justified are priests." Origen has some beautiful passages on the priesthood of Christians.

<<1>> Justin Martyr, *Dialogue with Trypho*, 116. Cf. Tertullian, *Against the Jews*, 5, 6, and passim, where he raises this distinction in particular: "When God commands sacrifices *with a pure prayer*, offer the best and highest sacrifice to him, which he demands, a prayer from a chaste flesh, an innocent soul, a holy spirit . . . a pure sacrifice in every place, namely, a simple prayer from the conscience."

<<2>> Irenaeus, *Against the Heresies*, 4:28, 1-4.

39. K adds to footnote: Ambrose, *On the Sacraments*, 4.1; Augustine, *The City of God*, 20:10; Leo, "Sermon 3," 32.

40. Footnote] In a church . . . particular] A3+

41. K adds: The [doctrine of the] general priesthood of Christians also indicates that all classes are fitted for it. Unlike Judaism more than one tribe is specified. Rather, it is for all those who have received inner capability and specification through the Holy Spirit, and this is further the reason why the Catholic Church protects the dignity of all Christians. Thus, since among the heretics Christianity is first to be discovered through speculation, they necessarily form among themselves essential differences since some have gained more knowledge than others through talent or circumstance. These have higher knowledge, which they allow to flow out to others as opportunity arises or, as they are accustomed to say, as they are responsible to bear

to them. It is well known that the Gnostics not only distinguished themselves from the rest of the Christians as those standing beneath them, but they also made distinctions among themselves as in the pagan mysteries, in which some experienced more, others less. Thus, the so-called unworthy ones were led around by the reins of human deceit and condemned to double servility, to themselves because in their pride they were convinced of a marvellous sense of greatness believing that the individual is something without the whole, and to others who misused them so vilely. (This situation can be noted from the earliest times to the present which stands in second place to none in this regard.) We have shown, however, how in the Catholic Church *one* inherited faith of all, of the wisest, as well as those who greatly need insight, of the bishops as well as the laity, is held firmly, and how a distinction between esoterics and exoterics is rejected. The innermost aspect of the soul is shocked to think that after God became the teacher of human beings, some should arise who consider their fellows as empty husks and ascribe to themselves a higher knowledge. Since these deceived individuals have cast off the association and union of Christians that was given to them by Christ, they must necessarily lose the characteristic and true worth of believers, delude themselves with the empty appearance of independence, and value every kind of error. The eternal laws of nature must be changed if the Church, which arises through an act of the highest freedom, does not also assure the highest freedom. Clement of Alexandria, a priest, defended the dignity of all Christians very beautifully against this heretical position in his *Instructor*, 1:6: "Have you not heard that we no longer live under that law that was bound with fear, but under the Logos, the instructor toward freedom?...." Paul says: 'You are all sons of God in Jesus Christ through faith.... For you have all taken on Christ, who were baptized in him. In this case it does not merit to be a Jew, a Greek, a slave, free, a man, or a woman; you are *all, one* in Jesus Christ' [Gal. 3:26-28]. Through this same Logos some are not *knowers* and others *seers*, but all who have set aside carnal lusts have the *same, spiritual* value before the Lord." Cf. Irenaeus, *Against the Heresies*, 1:3.

42. true Christian dignity preserved] K: true freedom assured. To take away the members of union is to destroy the community and to give value to human circumstances.

43. K adds: (From this, however, it does not follow that he must do what these people wish.)

A2 originally had the following introduction to 55: Moreover, the bishop was not only not independent in presenting the faith, but he was not independent in the rest of the administration of the Church. Just as he was bound to the divine and the divinely transmitted in the first case, in the second, where his duties touched on human insights, he was bound to the counsel of human beings.

44. K adds: 4a. It is to be regretted and it disturbs the clear conception of the matter greatly that many *Catholic* writers can do nothing more important than describe the bishops as the *monarchs* of the Church and confuse what the bishop became in time and through unfortunate circumstances with the ideal conception of the bishop.

Part II, Chapter 2

1. K adds: Unconsciously they honour as their common mother the branches that come forth from the one root-church and they thus unite themselves around the episcopal metropolitan so that the manner of expanding Christianity gives direction to inner power and the inner need. Here we have complete the presentation of the

relationship of the bishop to his community and diocese. Only the metropolitan as such does not, as does the bishop, owe his central office to the divine and apostolic institution.

Footnote] De Marca bases . . . this] A3+

2. Footnote] Thus, here, . . . statements] A3+

3. The individual churches . . . body] A3+

4. which . . . life] A3+

5. and that no synods . . . synod] A3+

6. K adds: as the deacon Athanasius at Nicea.

7. and only because . . . temptation] A3+

Part II, Chapter 3

1. and with it a communal life of all Christians] A3+

2. K adds: The literary activity of our times, by which members and defenders of the invisible church wish to set it in the place of its living union and thus to satisfy all requirements, is something totally different. The invisible Church is concerned with the individual as individual, the living union with the individual as a member of a whole. In the first case union is optional, in the second necessary. In the first case it is considered that it is possible not to be, in the second it appears as an unbroken inner need. In the first the writer works, in the second the believer and *all* believers. The first is concerned with individual insight, the second with common life. The second is thus power, impact, and liveliness which cannot be overcome. In the first case everything receives the appearance of a scientific understanding, in the second everything is an expression of unchanging, common consciousness. In the first the opportunity for religion is private, in the second public. How could the Christian faith have ever established itself or made its presence known, if it expressed itself through its literary activity.

3. K adds: The method by which they grasped these appearances, the similarities of the basis of explication with pre-Christian situations already mentioned, as well as those found outside of Christianity, demonstrate that these explanations are found outside of Christianity. The fact that the spiritual is only explained sensually, egotistically, and in a pagan way indicates that the explanation itself is only egotistic and pagan and that the explanation is not yet able to belong worthily to the new spirit, just as there is no worthy consecutive treatment of Church history and no construction of it possible on the basis of the principles of the invisible church. It clearly indicates that in no way can a history of the Church as invisible be given.

4. K adds: because otherwise no one would have been able to write so much in dogmatic ecclesiastical situations

5. K adds and overscores: Indeed, the idea of the invisible union of all Christians was so clearly developed by him that he called the totality of this union love, really begotten

Indeed . . . developed] K adds: Indeed so clearly had the idea of a *catholic* Church already arisen.

6. Clement of Alexandria . . . faith] A3+

7. Footnote] Undivided . . . 78] A3+

8. To call . . . *life*] A3+

9. A3 adds: How could one speak of a true total life of all believers, of a unity of spirit and doctrine and preservation of the same, if it did not manifest itself externally and reveal itself through specific organs?

10. Let us again contemplate . . . purity] A3+

11. K adds: According to the idea the totality of the episcopate was thus infallible. The totality of believers (section 41) and the fullness of the Holy Spirit (section 42) was in it. But, nevertheless, since the reality of developed ordination (discussed in section 52) still does not always express the reality of the idea, the totality of bishops is not unerring. If Christian truth and holiness according to their essence are one, and both are one work of the Holy Spirit, active in us, but if the Holy Spirit is not active in an unholy person, that person cannot find the truth. Therefore, in the Middle Ages it was said that when there was a superabundance of pious and enlightened bishops, true doctrine could not fall away in the Church, but by whom it was preserved could not be specified. During the Passion of Christ, for example, when all the disciples left, Mary still preserved Christianity faithfully, and thus all priests could be unfaithful and yet Christianity would be preserved.

12. The Church itself . . . way] A3+

13. Note here . . . one] A3+

14. K adds: Those who left the community of love and did not see themselves as members of love with all believers lived for long according to their pride. They extended the perpetual excommunication of those who fell away in persecution to all those who committed mortal sin after their baptism and they called themselves the *pure ones* in a community of error.

15. In the ordination . . . (1 Tim. 4:14; 2 Tim. 1:6)] A3+

16. K adds: Each person can inherit the ability if he is in possession of the true doctrine, has the ability to teach, and has ethical dignity. If one does not have the doctrine of the Church, one cannot attack the Church because she will not allow the individual's doctrine to be proclaimed rather than her own. If one does not possess this last characteristic and wishes to become a member of the priesthood, no less than all the concepts of ecclesiastical leadership will oppose this action.

17. K adds: while the heretical masters with great intellectual ability were limited by the small area in which their narrow view of Christianity found entrance.

18. K adds to footnote: This obviously belongs in a later time.

19. A2 adds at this point a draft that originally formed the closing paragraph of section 42 (For text see section 42: No constraint . . . mediation).

Part II, Chapter 4

1. I doubted] originally: I doubted on historical [historische] grounds

2. that resolves . . . matter] originally: that could lead us with ease and by necessity to the primacy

3. deeper . . . history] originally: deeper view of history [*Historie*]

4. For a long time . . . however] A3+

5. the bishop . . . themselves] originally: the bishop as the center, as the head of the presbyterium and this as a free senate.

6. An early draft adds: and this as a free senate

7. We see . . . unity] A2; A2 in an earlier draft reads: We await in the totality of these bishops the senate of the whole Church and we seek, because we are compelled

to do so, to see the whole presenting once more the type of individual formations, the head of them

The personally existing reflection] K: the hypostatized reflection

8. A3 adds: We have noted earlier that and why, among all the apostles, indeed among all the other followers of Christ, Peter was placed first, and why among the three who formed the tightest circle (Peter, James, and John) Peter took the chief position. If we do not leave aside the basic insight through which the whole community of believers is preserved, so that some are given the power to give, others to receive, but that all through the same spirit are prepared, we must view the preeminent characteristics of Peter as a gift of the Holy Spirit given to him so that he could fulfill the specific task for which he was responsible. As a result he was first among the believers, and therefore the Church was built on him (Matt. 16:18), and, as later occurrences indicate, he was first among the apostles not only in time but also in order because his individuality gave him the call. From this point of view Luke 22:32 has its characteristic importance, and if this passage was always cited to demonstrate the primacy of Peter, it was done with the proper feeling, although one did not allow oneself to be misled into a twisted use of the passage. The Evangelists, therefore, expressly called Peter "first" among the apostles, but one is not accordingly led to say that the apostles must have made their beginning with some person. If this were the case, every addition would have been useless. Finally, the facts in Acts agree very closely with this, for in that book Peter always appears first in word and deed and leads the whole community. Paul himself goes to Jerusalem to see Peter (Gal. 2:18ff.).

9. Textual additions to footnote as follows: true believers, the rocks on which the Church is built] A2 adds: Therefore, the following pattern of speech arose in the Church from the earliest times. *To build up* someone means nothing other than to communicate to that person the power of faith. As a result the whole Church is called a house of God and the expansion and preservation of the kingdom of God is the building of the Church. As a result the letter of Peter speaks of believers with the image of living stones [1 Peter 2:4-5]. Nothing is more opposed to a separatistic conception of Christianity than the pattern of speech by which all Christians are designated and considered as making up a completion in their various manifestations. This pattern of speech is firmly rooted. Christ is called the *oikodespotēs* [house-builder], the believers *oikeioi tēs pisteōs* [houses of faith] . . . therefore the keys of the kingdom. See Addendum 12.

Obviously, John . . . similar passages] A3+

a special importance with other similar passages] A3 adds: a statement that allows itself more to be felt than to be expressed. In the whole of salvation history Peter takes up a highly significant position in his carrying out of the apostolic office.

What has... 118] missing in the manuscript; taken up only in the final printed version.

10. It may not, however . . . position] A3+

11. as the personalized . . . Church] A3, which originally read: as the concentrated and hypostatized form of the whole church.

12. because it was . . . development] A3+

13. Footnote] A3+

14. and detracting . . . greatest way] A3+

15. According to Geiselmann K adds: also written with emphasis in every particular church founded by Peter and Paul and all the apostles.

16. K adds: Since justification was defended by Jewish Christians through the law, Paul took the opportunity to praise grace in Christ. John, the last of the apostles, gave the highest conception of Jesus since a lower view began to be manifest. The more often the doctrine of Christ was attacked, the deeper did the consciousness of his divinity develop from the inner life of the believers, and at the Council of Nicea this consciousness came forth clearer and more specifically than ever before. Only *insofar* as one considers Christianity as a mechanical and dead concept can a return to primitive Christianity be considered. The kernels that have been given must develop to perfect ripeness and they have so developed through the Spirit given to the Church. The dead concept is always complete and finished; life, however, is endless.

17. K adds: a doctrine which, in fact, was consequently cast out by those who did not wish to consider love among themselves, the living believers, as the basis of the Church, and thought they were able to live a Christian life separated from the foundation. [What follows is illegible in K. According to A2 it reads:] We, we do not wish to live if we are not able to love those who died in Christ as much as living Christians, and we wish to give an expression to this love. [K continues:] Imprisonment in externals is the essence of each conceptual religion. This is always noted. Life, however, is unending. If one has such a concept, one does not trust one's own living spirit if the dead letter does not speak. [The last lines from K replace the original formulation from A2 which reads: The dead concept, external dead faith, which comes from knowledge, can always be taken up in the understanding and Christianity is thus done away with, and the more imprisoned understanding is externally determined. It therefore denies the primacy even if that primacy is clearly expressed in Sacred Scripture. It would cast out veneration of the saints and other things even if its feeling was opposed to such a casting out, or it would change a doctrine, it would deny that it was taught by the *whole* Church during its whole history, because it had such a feeling.]

18. Thus, before . . . present] A3+

19. think . . . strange] K: However, we will demonstrate the necessity of a centre of unity which they cannot do who have no inner need for Church community and for unity itself and consider separation as a basic principle even if Peter was designated more specifically than first among the apostles.

20. Footnote] This statement . . . bishop] A3+

21. That Peter . . . Eugubium] A3; K: No city other than Rome saw itself as becoming first in the church. Anyone reviewing history will uncover the undoubtable leading of the Holy Spirit in the choice of this city.

As far as the interpretation of the last passage from Irenaeus is concerned, the two chief explanations of the passage recently taken up again in controversy are, on an unbiased view of the matter, not recommended. The first holds that Irenaeus contends that the true tradition was preserved in Rome since (if one does not wish to bring anything Mosaic into the Church) Christians from all parts of the Church came there, and as a result one could easily come to a knowledge of the general tradition. The second holds that Irenaeus makes it a requirement for all believers to agree with the Roman tradition. We can understand both explanations as follows: the first wants true doctrine to be in Rome only through those who came there from other churches; the second wishes it to be preserved in the other churches only through the Roman church; in other words, the first supports the true proclamation of doctrine in the Roman church, the second in the other churches. Both oppose Irenaeus since he wishes to direct the Valentinian to the tradition set down and preserved in the same manner in *all* the churches founded by the *apostles*, and he cites instead of the others, the Roman Church with her continual apostolic succession. One can thus say that Irenaeus intends that the transmission was either preserved in Rome through the other churches or in the other churches through Rome, and thus one has him say the opposite of what he wishes to say. (A better way of saying it would be that the true doctrine was preserved neither in Rome alone nor in the other churches alone, but in the relationship between all of the churches—if one does not wish to bring anything Mosaic into the Church. There is no discussion regarding this.) One must distinguish two points here: (1) the Church in Rome is parallel to all others and this is the same tradition in all; (2) the Roman congregation is marked out above all others and this justifies Irenaeus's position in raising her above all others and this is the "greater preeminence" which is explained in the addition "because the apostolic tradition is always preserved in her by the believers." If we mean that this occurred through the chance arrival of believers in Rome, it would not be preeminent and all history would speak against it since one cannot establish a tradition in any church according to chance arrivals of people in a certain city, but the latter must be established by the former, and if the two do not agree, the tradition must be set aside. Preservation is protection, that is, one can see in Rome the tradition of all the churches through the regular correspondence, the letters of peace, that all churches through their bishops wrote to Rome (to which, as has already been noted, confessions of faith were added). In this the "greater preeminence" of Rome was manifested. Therefore, Irenaeus could consider Rome to be above all the churches and its eminence is based on its foundation by Peter and Paul (the apostles of the circumcision and the noncircumcision) who came there because of the political significance of the city.

22. But direct proof for the primacy . . . church] A3+

23. K originally had the following introduction: Impartial research leaves no doubt that according to the passage of Irenaeus, the Roman Church had the highest eminence at the end of the second century.

24. manifested themselves] A3+

25. in life and] A3+

26. K adds: Life, however, preceded concept or concept developed from life.

27. K adds to footnote: He here mocked the Roman bishop who rejected the Montanists but in the mockery itself he acknowledged him as the one upon whom the greatest eminence rested.

28. the idea . . . Church] K: The Catholic Church.

29. Manuscript ends here; remainder from T.

Addenda

1. according to Rom. 8:15-16] A3+

2. being . . . God] A3+; K: being insofar as it participates in the being of God and is grounded in him

3. Thus, Augustine says . . . *Confessions*, 4, 12] A3+

4. If we must . . . *ground*] A3+; K: If we cannot then say that God is found *along side* the universal whole, how much less can we be of the opinion that the life of the saints, their innermost being and essence, has its foundation beside him and aside from him, that God, their source, is not their cause.

5. than that . . . . it] A3+; K: than that there is a dynamic binding of both that every true good is an outflowing of the original good, arises in it, and is grounded in it.

6. He is in us and we in him] A3+

7. but he binds . . . way] A3+; K: but he is living

8. among Catholics] A3+

9. which, however . . . her] A3+

10. A3 adds and overscores: It might be suggested that Origen was here wishing to answer Demetrius [Cydones; on the issue, see Petavius, *Opus de theologicis dogmatibus, De trinitate*, 7:4, 15-16], who believed that if one traced back this Catholic doctrine of the Holy Spirit in believers, a kind of delicate matter of Christ would then be posited as flowing into them, and he thus thought he could prove the doctrine to be an absurdity for if one held it, he said, one could hold that a kind of fine material is understood by the Holy Spirit which Christ poured out upon those who belonged to him. Compare [ibid.,] 2:130, where surprisingly he opposes this.

11. *concepts* . . . Spirit] A3+; K: concepts, but here one must consider life

12. But . . . Ibid] A3+

13. Likewise Athanasius . . . Serapion," 24] A3+; German translation with "by communion . . . created' in Greek.

14. German translation with Greek

15. He cites John 14:15 . . . you] A3+

16. the communication union] A3+; as simply . . . union] K: as simply active, but as a characteristic communication of divine essence

17. A3 adds: Cyril says according to 34 Thes[aurus]: "The Spirit works with us, making us truly holy and uniting us with itself." [German translation with Greek.]

18. The Fathers understood . . . *trinitate*, 8, 7)] A3+

19. K adds: It is not only doctrine that binds us with Christ and the believers. Those who love each other are bound not by their word but by their inner life which the words only point toward and allow one to think about.

20. In addition . . . following] A3+

21. according to . . . gifts] A3+; K: since we are members through the Holy Spirit

22. Chrysostom writes, "We . . . *Donatists*, 35, 58] A3+

23. The greatest . . . specificity] A3+; closest] K omits

24. nothing more . . . spirit] A3+; K: and viewed it as the Christian community spirit

25. A3 adds: Nothing is more opposed to the history of the Church than to say that the Holy Spirit is only the Christian common spirit or (with Demetrius [Cydones]) the common feeling of Christians (Theodor. D. 27 and 130 are together opposed to this). If one understands it as a common feeling, one enters into open opposition with oneself. The Christian common feeling opposed nothing so fiercely as the teaching that the Holy Spirit was only this. What is earlier or was retained more firmly than Christian prayer to the Holy Spirit? Who would wish to pray to a common feeling? The common feeling thus certainly rejects the suggestion that the Holy Spirit is only this common feeling. This is the voice of a separatistic feeling against the common feeling.

An early draft reads: Nothing is so completely opposed to the history of the Church as to say with Schleiermacher that the Holy Spirit is merely the Christian common feeling [*The Christian Faith*, section 131; trans., section 123], or with [Wilhelm Martin] de Wette [1780-1849] that it is the common feeling of Christians. If one understands it as a common feeling, one enters into open opposition with oneself. The Christian common feeling opposed nothing so fiercely as the teaching that the Holy Spirit was only this. What is earlier or was retained more firmly than Christian prayer to the Holy Spirit? Who would wish to pray to a common feeling? The common feeling thus certainly rejects the suggestion that the Holy Spirit is only this common feeling. This is the voice of a separatistic feeling against the common feeling.

26. According to the Holy Scripture, the] K+

27. perfecting] K: perfected

28. In the passage . . . together] T+

29. By it they mean . . . events" (Creuzer, *Symbolik*, 1:87)] A3+; K: They understand "sayings" of the earlier period in a twofold sense: "They either preserve the old faith and the old doctrine, or historical [*historische*] events" (Creuzer, *Symbolik*, 1:87). Diodorus, Strabo, and others make use of this and understand the *sayings* of the earlier period in a twofold sense: they either preserve an old doctrine, a religious conception, or they point to historical events, which may or may not have conformed to the doctrine.

30. K adds: They arise and are confirmed by external observations and notations, and so on. They often contain sayings and fill many volumes with their observations. They were passed on with the Holy Scriptures and observed carefully.

31. because he believes . . . Scriptures] A3+

32. K adds: We pray for the dead, for the newborn, for days of the year, and so on

33. In the treatise . . . *doctrine*] A3+

34. K adds: as the understood expression of the inner, holy disposition, begotten by the divine Spirit.

35. K adds: It is passed on to later generations as an unmediated expression of inner faith by an unmediated impression that makes the whole life of believers or by the Church's nurture of those who live thereafter.

36. The first proclamation . . . creation] A3+; A3 also adds: This does not contradict section 7. No more does it contradict the noted insight concerning the preservation of the world that everything now standing was mediated through what has already stood and the statement of the wise person ["concerning the living God" overscored] made so beautifully concerning this can be applied as well: "Where did the eternal beginning of creation begin?"

37. of the inspired mind] A3; K omits

38. As a result . . . again] A3+

39. Translation in German

40. Translation in German

41. Translation in German with Greek text

42. Translation in German

43. Translation in German with last sentence in Greek

44. K adds: and its truth

45. Translation in German with Greek text

46. A3 adds: From this one can see that the whole gospel is called tradition, and likewise the whole tradition of the Church is called the true gospel. Examples are given in this treatise. The studies on tradition by the learned Chemnitz in his *Examination of the Council of Trent*, topic 2, are not free of his own point of view. He continually works from the principle that tradition may not hold anything opposed to Holy Scripture, and the Church has never denied this. But one must ask not only what that is which is against Scripture, but also what is in agreement with it. "When then traditions are put forward that do not agree with the Scripture and cannot be proven or shown to come from Scripture, it is certain that they are not apostolic" [section 4, 6; trans., 1:248]. Later [section 3; trans., 1:231ff.] he asks whether the traditions that Tertullian, Irenaeus, and others defend are not merely doctrines that

cannot be demonstrated through the Scriptures. The Apostolic, Nicean, and Athanasian creeds cannot be grounded in the Bible. The tradition that is treated in the early Church is consistent with Scripture. He feels, faithful as he is, that the content of the creeds can be found in the Scriptures. He does this because the tradition that he casts aside speaks unconsciously through him, and as a result he believes that the Scripture is enough for him because he has already believed. If he had only lived a few centuries later. He says quite rightly that "the Arians caused great confusion throughout the world" because they did not accept the *homoousios* as scriptural since it belonged to those dogmas that "have a firm and certain testimony in Scripture, although not expressed literally therein" [section 5, 7; trans., 1:254]. But the Arians did not believe that the doctrine of the Trinity was consistent with Scripture, and in a similar fashion he, Chemnitz, also attacks other doctrines held by Catholics. The most learned cannot justify themselves if Tertullian, Irenaeus, Clement, Origen, and others judge all contentious doctrines as able to be grounded in the Scriptures, and they do not know what they should think if those Fathers at the same time speak of tradition. In regard to Augustine on this point even Richard Simon [1638-1712] is somewhat in error. As a result Neander insists that one can only assign those doctrines to tradition that the Scripture could not use. But if Chemnitz means that everything that Tertullian and others teach is contained in the Scripture and that there is no need for tradition ("which cannot be proven and demonstrated from Scripture") he errs greatly. Cf. Tertullian, *On the Crown*, 2-4, and elsewhere.

It was very difficult, however, to come to a clear concept of tradition as held at the time of the Reformation. At that time many theologians supported things from tradition that in part were *opposed* to Scripture or that in part did not for certain come from the apostolic period. As a result it is not surprising that an endeavor was made to bring everything into consistency with the Scripture and that many pure Christian truths were cast out. "An infinite number of other things pertain to the enumeration of Peter à Soto: the sacrifice of the Lord's Supper, celibacy of priests, reservation of the host, the selling of indulgences, the cult of images, legends of the saints and, in sum, that is to be believed whatever the Roman Church believes, holds, and observes, even if it was not contained in the Scriptures, that it was handed down from the Apostles" [cf. Chemnitz, topic 2, section 8,3; trans., 1:273].

47. Translation in German with Greek text

48. In the same way, Augustine writes . . . head] A3+

49. K adds: this power is her inner life according to a unity in and through Christ.

50. Unity in diversity . . . out] A3+

51. Translation in German; K adds: Unity and commonality fall together in this passage. Therefore, Cyril's statement: "She is called catholic because of her expansion over the whole earth from one end to the other." However, it seems that this meaning of the *catholic* Church was not the original, but necessarily came from it. The Church's great character, universal over time and space, arises because the divine power producing the Church must necessarily come to universality.

52. From this addendum . . . other] A3+

53. K adds: The issue is specified by this writer with great conceptual care and closeness.

54. K adds: who states "The source of the Catholic Church and the beginning of the Canon occur at the same time and arise together." We do not know when the Canon arose, but we do know that it arose *in the Church*. Before the sacred books were gathered as a whole, individual churches that possessed them must have seen them in a unity with other books or they would not have passed the books on, believed in

them, or been able to believe. If they had not already formed a unity but taught varying doctrines, on what basis could they have been accepted as sacred books? If the Holy Scriptures were separate and the believers also divided, what impulse would there have been for unity? The Scriptures did not unite themselves. Nor can we say that one learned from them to know that Christians must form a unity. It occurred through united believers. To arrive at a canon, that is, one that acknowledged the totality of believers, something catholic from which the catholicity of certain scriptures flowed must have been present. One of two things must have occurred. Either the Holy Scriptures must have been gathered by each believer or at least in each church so that the need for unity developed from them and they thus united what had been divided, or the unity must have been given by something else. Otherwise one would not know how one could have come to the thought of unity. Augustine opposed the first position since it insisted that a Canon was not present at the very beginning. Unity could not have developed from the Canon if we accept that the union of believers had no characteristic basis or that the act existed before the basis, that is, before the commonly used Holy Scriptures. Thus union had to arise from something else if we wish to explain this. If it is a Christian and clear principle that the apostles did not preach anything other than what they wrote, we are correct in acknowledging their Gospels as the characteristic basis. What could then lead us to ascribe that action to the written, but not living, Gospels? But if we hold that the Scriptures arose from a unity already formed, that is from the Catholic Church, we can explain the rise of the Canon as *supporting* the unity. Finally, I refer to what has been said from which it can be grasped without doubt that without a previously established unity no unity could ever have been brought about through the Scriptures.

But if the meaning of the *Catholic* Church is, as according to Augusti, based on a union of Jewish and Gentile Christians, there is no historical proof. In Ignatius, where *ekklēsia katholikē*, is first noted (at this time the Canon had not yet arisen), the term is not only set against Jewish Christians but also against Donatists and many other classes of heretics.

55. On the introduction . . . elsewhere] A3+
56. Translation in German
57. Translation in German
58. (the . . . conviction)] Parenthetical phrase in German
59. Translation in German
60. Translation in German
61. Translation in German
62. Translation in German
63. Translation in German with Latin text
64. Translation in German
65. (self-insight)] Parenthetical phrase in German
66. (the Church)] Parenthetical phrase in German
67. Translation in German
68. K: the most
69. K adds: To my knowledge the learned Widmer first translated Augustine's *On the Profit of Believing* into German.
70. Augustine distinguishes faith . . . 28:379)] A3+
71. Huetius . . . enough] A3+
72. With Christ the fullness of time came] A3+
73. (the allegorical)] Parenthetical phrase in German

74. K adds: This is clear from the passage collected by de la Rue in the preface to the second part of his edition of Origen, fol. XIV, as it is from the introduction to Pamphilius's *Apology for Origen.*

75. Translation in German with Greek text

76. K adds: if one could say that nothing of the divinity of the Lord, of redemption through his death, stood in her

77. Note, as well, the preface . . . freedom] A3+; K adds: the possibility of the establishment of the basic character in all continuing individual expositions.

78. moving and standing, wood and stone] A3+

79. Origen and others . . . nothing] A3+

80. According to Geiselmann and Vierneisel the manuscript continues: What I have said in section 16 can be explained and our own time can learn from it that one does not bring Christianity into a land if one unloads boxes of Bibles on the ports, but that one must be prepared to die for it, making it known by *word and deed,* but never sending Bibles in place of oneself. How can one be so misled? Is it not because of a time that does not know how Jesus and the apostles preached the gospel and how paganism fell? It may be noted in addition that many who disparaged what Dubois wrote concerning the spread of Bibles throughout India saw that they were not called and therefore used malicious words. [Then follows a sentence which is overscored: However I wish to add that I am not inclined to speak of everything that I said regarding the relationship of the Bible to the Church; this they wish to take from the Christian people.] I do not wish to direct attention to the division of the Holy Scriptures from the Church, but to point to the close tie between them. I do not wish to separate the Bible from believers and far less the believers from the Church.

The experience that great errors are perpetuated even when the people read the Bible is a result of the fact that the gospel was not properly proclaimed in these congregations where this occurred. The cause of this was not the Bible, but poor nurturing by the priests. From this error another arose. Instead of viewing a matter that history clearly pointed to, some sought its source in the reading of the Scriptures—certainly a twisted view.

81. Translation in German

82. K adds: Paganism also has such images: Sparta honored a Damarat, Athens an Aristides, Rome a Camillus. But what did the Roman citizen think of Coriolanus? All this indicates is that the truth in the Church will never disappear, that it can be misunderstood by one or many, but that it will be raised up powerfully and that the Church itself must not be charged with error. If this is to be held firmly as an idea, the circumstances must be considered that arise when someone freely sets the truth aside, an occurrence that is not possible without a disturbance of love. This can occur when one becomes angry in one's faith against the Church to such a degree that one's true base weakens, and the individual dares to take a position outside the Church. If there is such an unholy circumstance within the Church that makes such actions possible, those who brought the difficulties about must find themselves, in fact, outside the spirit of the Church, and if they mock us, why should we not also be opposed to them, the ones who have caused disturbances that are only evil activities?

83. Footnote] A3+

84. not located

85. K adds: This great man, in whom Christianity was so alive, insisted in every way upon the unity to be built by love. He saw this clearly.

86. Translation in German

87. Translation in German

88. (of the Church)] Parenthetical phrase in German

89. Augustine's . . . adversary] A3+

90. A3; K: dare

91. A3 adds and overscores: cf. Seber, *Religion und Theologie*, 70ff.

K adds: All human consciousness, which is not possible without contrasts, is limited, but life is immeasurable. Being and knowledge never achieve identity with us, and since the inner life expresses itself in constrained forms, it appears in a succession and thus is troubled in a twofold way. Life can, therefore, characteristically only be portrayed and grasped in life, which, as has often been said, forms the base of the Church. [A3: the basic outlook of the Church.]

92. K adds: and especially for ours, whose self-seeking knows no boundaries.

93. Translation in German

94. expressing itself in the Church] A3; K omits

95. And the future . . . defense] A3; K: and the future directs what is still lacking

96. K adds: divinity, freedom, immortality

97. In general . . . person] A3+

98. Those who oppose . . . laughable] A3; K: those who say that Cyprian cast out tradition make themselves laughable.

99. in the very points that he cast out] A3; K omits with slight stylistic variations in remainder of sentence

100. Seen from the point . . . believed] A3+

101. has much truth in it] A3; K: therefore

102. Translation in German

103. unity toward . . . love] A3+

104. A2 adds: This passage is often directed by Cyprian to the Church community. This is indeed its meaning as its link to chapter 12 indicates.

105. K adds: Christian love is not merely that which we call general human love. It is much more; it is deeper and higher. It is that divine power in us according to which we raise ourselves so far beyond ourselves that we are able to unite with the community of one spiritual life of all believers in Jesus Christ, and we have the need to so unite ourselves. That community is established through the Redemption and if it becomes part of us in its essence, it first teaches us to know Christ in his characteristic dignity because that community is both itself and his characteristic work. Concerning this community Augustine often says that "it overcomes a multitude of sins" because these are already put to nothing if they enter into us. It is that community of the Holy Spirit that is the essence of the Catholic Church and it is that community through which [the Church] conquers. Out of that community general human love first flows, and without it that love has no firm foundation. Therefore, we see that the Church Fathers often return to this theme in their homilies and that they make demands so often regarding it. In each case it is the demand and the portrayal of the spirit of the Catholic Church. It is the love that can be demanded by no other church without proclaiming with certainty the end of its own position.

106. Translation in German

107. the charge . . . peace] A3+

108. K adds: that is to raise itself beyond the original forms.

109. development] A3; K: formation

110. with the mild . . . judgment] K: with the indulgence that he takes up at the same time, fearing that it will be profaned here in earthly time, although they do not find anything worthy of indulgence.

111. All Pamphilius quotations in German translation

112. If Christianity . . . things] See Appendix 1, "Pragmatic Glimpses."

113. If Christianity . . . fathers] A1 reads: We still need to develop the relationship of the Catholic principle to the heretical in relationship to the spread of the Christian spirit, to the victory of Christianity in the world, and to its external activity.

Since according to the Catholic principle Christianity is accepted not through speculation but in, out of, and according to the life that is taken up in the Catholic Church, the first thing that is grasped is the mind, the seat of power and strength of will and preserving spirit. However, since heretics do not proceed from the fullness of religious life, their system is only a matter of concepts. Mere concept never fructifies the mind, and a crippling of character follows from heresy as a result. This must be fully accepted if one also accepts that heresy's confessors came to their conclusion by their studies of those things that the Church fathers rejected.

114. A1 adds: struggling and

115. whom] A1: whom he acknowledges as those happy in the firm possession of truth.

116. Möhler gives a German translation followed by Greek text. A1 enters the Greek text as a footnote and adds: and elsewhere: "Elated by their vain opinion they are incessantly wrangling and care more to seem than to be philosophers."

117. Translation in German; A1 cites the passage in Greek.

118. states] A1: qualities

119. Translation in German; A1 adds text in Greek.

120. This is most clearly . . . pagans] A1: In ignorance, however, of what Christianity characteristically is and, above all, that it is not found in the Catholic Church, they work to gain victory not only against the pagans but also against the Catholics.

A2 corrects: [Among the heretics] Christianity cannot secure a unifying life, and the twisting, weaving, torn mind among the pagans cannot bring itself under the work and suffering of the preaching of the gospel. But heresy is so certain that there is no truth in the Catholic Church, its battle against the Church is similarly not pursued against the pagans.

121. Likewise . . . faith] A2+; A2 adds and A3 overscores: Whoever preaches boldly the one crucified, the God man who is always the same, preaches the Catholic message regardless of whom he or she is. Who can build a church on negation? Therefore, one should note that she will not continue through negation.

122. I would like . . . them] A3+

123. Tertullian text in Latin in T; A1 cites location and in place of Latin text reads: Therefore, they endeavor to defeat the pagans as well as the Catholics.

124. A yet greater result . . . character] Bblical citation added by A2; A1 reads: If the heretics in this way care nothing for the things of Christianity and in fact cause much harm in that the division among Christians is judged seriously among the pagans, the greatest result that threatens the Christian religion is that they demonstrate the greatest weakness of character as well as lack of character.

125. A1 adds: Cf. John 17:21.

126. In Eusebius . . . confess] Section appears in A1 as note that reads: Irenaeus, *Against the Heresies*, 4:33, 9: "Wherefore the Church does in every place, because of that love which she cherishes before God, send forward, throughout all time, a multitude of martyrs to the Father; while all others not only have nothing of this kind to point to among themselves, but even maintain that such martyrdom is not at all necessary, that their system of doctrines is the true martyrdom." The passage continues, thus disproving Kastner's position in his *Agape*: with the exception perhaps that one or two

among them, during the whole time that has elapsed since the Lord appeared on the earth, have occasionally along with our martyrs borne the reproach of the name (as if he too had obtained mercy), and have been led forth with them to death, being as it were a sort of retinue granted to them. Cf. Eusebius, *Ecclesiastical History*, 4:15, 46-48, which notes the Marcionite Metrodor.

127. A1 adds as note Clement text in Greek: "Now some of the heretics who have misunderstood the Lord, have at once an impious and cowardly love of life; saying that the true martyrdom is the knowledge of the only true God (which we also admit), and that the person is a self-murderer and suicide who makes confession by death; and adducing other similar sophisms of cowardice" [*Miscellanies*, 4:4].

128. without losing . . . persecutions] A2+

129. A1 adds: zealous to bring about their desires, to cause trouble,

130. They knew that . . . martyr] A1: They understood that there were many simple and ignorant people and that weak Christians, as they always do, would not follow through, if a suitable opportunity, pleasing to them, were offered, as when fear made entrance to the soul, especially if terror had crowned the faith of a martyr.

131. A1 adds: Now they went to them

132. Translation in German; A1 adds: And why does he not desire the death of the sinner? Tertullian, *Scorpiace*, 1.

133. A1 adds: that is, if God only knows their faith, it is clear that outside of this invisible union there is need for no union with any other.

134. In this one sees . . . Christianity] A2+

135. and that the Holy Ghost . . . apostles] A3+

136. It also suggests . . . outer] Cf. A1: We have here come to the point in our study that it is most clear that the heretics hold fast to a belief in the invisible church, but it is also evident how this necessarily arises out of the essence of heresy.

Heresy conceives of Christianity simply as a matter of thought, as a conceptual system, but the dead concept does not beget life. It does not enter as a living power into the visible. Therefore, their union with God is only an understanding of union that does not express itself in the act, in the work. The union with believers is therefore only a thought union, an invisible one; therefore, the sharp division between the inner and the outer exists because a mere thought cannot beget an external. Therefore, in all these differing thoughts and concepts of Christianity there is the possibility of considering among all an invisible union, and, because one has different concepts, to postulate an invisible church.

137. A1 adds: in his or her life. A1 also adds note: Ignatius, "Letter to the Romans," 6, adds the striking passage: "If anyone has been within oneself, let that person consider what I desire and have sympathy with me, as knowing how I am straitened."

138. Moreover, the union . . . live] A2+

139. On the other hand . . . community] A1: Just as the union among believers was a living one communicated through Christ, so the person who denies Christ can no longer be in the Catholic community because a union in thought is held as no union. It is set aside. And those who deny Christ with their lives and have taken up an invisible union with him caused the greatest divisions in the visible church under Cyprian.

140. Tertullian . . . him] Text in Latin in T; A1: Tertullian, *Scorpiace*, 9, emphasizes the words that Christ uses (not being acquainted with Hebrew) as he directs him to confess. Only thought is proper and completely expresses the spirit of the Catholic Church. [The passage from Scorpiace follows.]

141. What kind . . . existing] A1: Clement charges the heretics with hypocrisy.<1> What a conception concerning the Christian religion must have been forced upon the pagans by this activity; [it was a religion] that presented itself at every moment as not existing, and yet the Christians said that because of it they would give up all honors, consider all family ties as secondary, and be prepared to sacrifice all earthly things and life itself.

<<1>>Clement of Alexandria, *Miscellanies*, 4:6: "He did not say that they had little faith, but that they were faithless and hypocrites." He does so improperly, however, since they were what they said and they said what they were (according to Lavatar's adage).

142. A1 adds: only as a shadow

143. and common life] A2+

144. so as . . . innocuous] A1: so that for certain it is not able to damage paganism

145. Justin . . . opinions."] Text in Greek; A1: They, therefore, viewed the heretics and *their principles* as, in Justin's words, minor and they, therefore, were not persecuted. [Greek text included in note in A1.]

146. Cyprian . . . says] A1: Cf. Cyprian . . . . He says

147. A1 adds in Latin: For Christ's adversary does not persecute and attack any except Christ's camp and soldiers

148. Text in Latin in T

149. A1 adds as note with Latin text: "The foe and enemy of the Church despises and passes by those whom he has alienated from the Church, and led without as captives and conquered; he goes on to harness those in whom he sees Christ dwell" [Cyprian Letter 60, 3].

150. very much] A1: clearly, inwardly and outwardly,

151. conceived of] A1: looked upon [with footnote]: "Letter to the Romans"; this is the sense of the delightful passage in 3: "Only request on my behalf both inward and outward strength, that I may not only speak, but will, and that I may not only be called a Christian, but really be found to be one. For if I truly be found a Christian I may also be called one, and be then deemed faithful when I shall no longer appear to the world."

152. to the Roman . . . spared] A1: elsewhere to the Romans who wished to hinder his martyrdom

153. to] A1: in

154. A1 footnotes: on the Romans

155. (The most . . . together)] A3+

156. When the Christian . . . spirit] A1: At the joyous and quiet death of Cyprian all the Christian people of Carthage shouted, full of spirit

157. This is the visible Church] A3+

158. In the passage . . . at] K: If priests are considered to be those in possession of a higher religious-moral power, the other believers are not shut out from this special calling (that is, as must be accepted, that the priest sees himself required to communicate by the impulse of the overwhelming power present in him; so the others, who do not reach him in power but also possess a more or less greater power similarly, are no less pressed to communicate in the same way); or the priestly office has only the specific, ordained, and public calling that must reach through all members of the Church. Origen says very elegantly in the passage quoted that the eye with which he compares the priest extends the power of light over the whole body. This lies in the idea of the Catholic Church, a spiritual whole consisting of *living* members. The more all members strive to become active with one another and the

more the work of the spirit of the whole shines forth in every member, the more qualified and noble is this whole. If the first is lacking and the priestly office alone wishes to take control of everything (or because of earlier arrogance none of the other members has the need to communicate themselves), paralysis and death begin, since power and need mutually express themselves; where there is no need there also power is shut out and the priestly office possesses no power since he is not in a position to stir it up. But if power is missing, love is not known. In the active striving of the individual to work, the uniting spirit of the Church is set aside and division and separations reveal themselves; there is power, indeed, but it is blind and it is commonly only the sharing of the antithetical blindness of the Church leaders if they are not enlightened by the Christian spirit, word, and work. The gospel and the early Church opposed both these diseased situations. Nothing says more concerning working together than the . . . .

159. K adds: If, then, Christ is the one on whom we all are built (1 Cor. 3: 10-11) and we build up one another, what is this other than that Christ builds through us, through the mutual related working in and upon each other (Eph. 2:21)?

160. K adds: and thus I must say that I do not know of anything more unchristian than the principle of division.

161. that all is . . . all] A3+; K: that the external Christian virtue is only a conclusion from the totality of believers in which Christ works.

162. An early draft reads [Cf. Vierneisel, 344-45]: If it is an *oikia* [house] and those who belong to it *oikeioi* [house-members], they must have a relationship not only to the *oikodespotēs* [master of the house] but also among themselves. In the opposition, however, between the carnal Israel and the spiritual, one can see that Israelite family and civil rights were based on necessity, on physical heritage, on generation from Abraham, Isaac, and Jacob, and that the spiritual was based on freedom, on spiritual rebirth—'whoever does the will of my Father, is my father, my mother, my sister, my brother' [Matt. 12:50]. Only as the rights of relationship are attained can they be retained. If there is only an external carnal union with God, and the Israelite union is maintained, it must become spiritual. Viewing it in either way, it is clear that whereas in the first case the family is constricted, in the second it expands endlessly in time and space (Matt 21: 2, 3). The union of spirits is not under compulsion. Insofar as the union of this great family has actual inner coherence and must express itself externally, making known its presence and receiving nourishment and renewed life, all the external forms of union are not its goal; they are what they are for the sake of the hearers, and that form is the best in which the Spirit moves most easily and expresses itself most capably.

163. Frumentius expressed . . . community] a3+

164. K adds: The directions do not belong to the ordained because they, as has expressly been said, were very special charismata.

165. German translation

166. German translation

167. This is the sense of the passage as it seems to me] A3+

168. K adds: since God forgives the sins and not the priests, on whose purity nothing can be made dependent.

169. That he did speak . . . following] A3+

170. where he explains . . . sinner] A3+

171. in other places . . . the Church] A3+

172. K adds: For if, as can be gathered from Cyprian, the only leaders in the Church who dare baptize are those who are established by the correct evangelical law

and the correct ordination, was it of the avaricious bishops and simoniacs that Cyprian complained? I believe that they were properly ordained and founded on the image of the apostles, for he says "no arrogant or quick-tempered person" (Titus 1:7). But such men did baptize in Cyprian's time and he complained that he had such as fellow bishops.

173. German translation
174. This seems to me . . . believers] A3+
175. (the Church community)] Parenthetical phrase in German
176. Text in Latin
177. Thus . . . by it] A3+
178. (of all believers)] Parenthetical phrase in German
179. K adds: (What use is it without all of this?)
180. Thus . . . common] A3+; K: Thus the vocation of the priest in all points that establish a part is certainly understood as flowing and common
181. in a preeminent sense] A3+
182. Translation in German
183. Text in Latin
184. Greek text inserted after German translation
185. This is . . . viewpoint] A3+
186. Manuscript ends here; remainder from T.

Appendixes

1. Translation in German; source not located.
2. Translation in German with Greek text.
3. Translation in German.
4. Translation in German; final phrase added in Greek.
5. Opening quotation, although no indication of close.

Glossary

Abbild: likeness ("Gleichniss" is not used in the text)
Abdruck: impression
Absondern: isolate
Annahme: hypothesis
Anschauung: perception, intuition, view
aufgehoben: invalidated (occurs only once in section 10)
Auffassung: grasp, apprehension, point of view
Aufnahme: acceptance
Ausbild: outward formation
Ausdruck: expression
Aussage: statement, utterance
Ausschau: perspective
Aussprache: utterance
Begriff: concept
bestimmten: decided, determined, appointed, fixed, specific
Bestimmtheit: certainty, determination, determining character
betrachten: reflective (see Reflection)
Betrachtung: view
Betrachtungsweise: point of view
Bewusstsein: consciousness
Bild: image
bilden: form
Bildung: formation
Contemplation: contemplation (occurs only in section 42 and in preface to A1)
Darstellung: description, explanation
Dasein: existence, presence
Eigenschaft: quality
Eigentümliche: characteristic
Eigentümlichkeit: characteristic nature
Einzelne: each individual, single individual
Empfangung: reception
Entfaltung: unfolding
enthalten: preserve
Entwicklung: development
Erkenntniss: knowledge
Erscheinung: appearance, phenomenon, manifestation
Form: form
Ganze: whole
Gebilde: image
Gefühl: feeling
Gegensatz: antithesis, opposition
Gegenstand: subject
Gegentheil: opposite

Geistlichen: spiritual leaders, priests (see also Priester)
Gemeinde: congregation
gemeinsame: common
Gemeinschaft: community
Gemüthe: mind
Gesamte: total, whole
Gesamtheit: totality
Geschichte: history (see also Historie)
Gesellschaft: institution
Gesinnung: disposition, intention (German term "Disposition" used only   once   in section 38)
Gestaltung: structure
gewahren: protect
Gewisses: direct knowledge (occurs only in section 39)
Grundsatz: basic proposition
handel: productive (as adj.)
Handlung: transaction
Historie: history [*Historie*]
Idee: Idea
Interpretation: interpretation
Kenntniss: empirical knowledge
moral: moral
Nachbild: example
Priester: priest (occurs only in sections 48, 54, 59, and in last three paragraphs   of Addendum 13)
Reflection: reflection (occurs only in section 39) (see Reflex)
Reflex: reflection (occurs only in sections 44 and 67)
Satz: proposition
Schüler: disciples
Sein: being
sittlichen: ethical, customary
Spaltung: splinter
Tätigkeit: activity, occupation
Trennung: division
unmittlebar: unmediated, direct, immediate
Veranlassung: occasion, cause
Verband: united group, bond
Verbindung: union, relationship
Verein: association, group
Vereinigung: uniting
Verfassung: constitution, condition
Vernunft: reason
Verstand: understanding
Vorbild: prototype
Vorstellung: conception, opinion, notion
Wesen: essence
Wiederspruch: contradiction
Willkür: capricious
Wirkung: action, result, working

Wissen (n.): knowing
Wissenschaft: science
Wissenschaftliche: scientific knowledge

Bibliography

Abbreviations:

ANF   *The Ante-Nicene Fathers. Translations of the Writings of the Fathers down to A.D. 325.* 10 vols. Edited by J. Roberts and A. Donaldson. New York, 1884-1886.

CSEL   *Corpus scriptorum ecclesiasticorum latinorum.* 100 vols. Vienna: apud C. Geroldi filium, 1866-1913.

GS   *Gesammelte Schriften und Aufsätze.* 2 vols. Edited by Joh. Jos. Ign. Döllinger. Regensburg: G. Josepf Manz, 1839-1840.

NPNF   *A Select Library of the Nicene and Post-Nicene Fathers of the Christian Church.* 28 vols. Edited by Philip Schaff and H. Wace. New York, 1886-1900.

PG   *Patrologia cursus completus: Series graeca.* 161 vols. Edited by Jacques Paul Migne. Paris: Lutetiae, 1857-1866.

PL   *Patrologia cursus completus: Series latina.* 221 vols. Edited by Jacques Paul Migne. Paris: Lutetiae, 1844-1864.

1. Works by Johann Adam Möhler

"Adam Gengler's *Über das Verhältnis der Theologie zu Philosophie* (Landshut, 1826)." *Theologische Quartalschrift* 9 (1827): 498-522.

"Anselm, Erzbishof von Canterbury. Ein Beitrag zur Kenntnisz des religiös-sittlichen, öffentlich-kirchlichen und wissenschaftlichen Lebens im elften und zwölften Jahrhundert." *Theologische Quartalschrift* 9 (1827): 435-97, 585-664 and 10 (1828): 62-130. Reprinted in *GS*, 1:32-176.

"*Antignostikus (.) Geist des Tertullians und Einleitung in dessen Schriften, mit archäologischen und dogmen-historischen Untersuchungen,* von Dr. August Neander. . . . Berlin, bei Ferdinand Dümmler 1825." *Theologische Quartalschrift* 7 (1825): 646-64.

Athanasius der Grosze und die Kirche seiner Zeit, besonders im Kampfe mit dem Arianismus. In sechs Büchern. 2 Theile. Mainz: Florian Kupferberg, 1827.

"Beleuchtung der Denkschrift für die Aufhebung des dem katholischen Geistlichen vorgeschriebenen Cölibates. . . ." *Katholik* 30 (1828): 1-32, 257-97. Reprinted in *GS*, 1:177-267, and in J Möhler, *Vom Geist des Zölibates.* Edited by Dieter Hattrup. Paderborn: Bonifatius, 1992.

"Betrachtungen über den Zustand der Kirche im 15. und zu Anfang des 16. Jahrhunderts, in Bezug auf die behauptete Nothwendigkeit einer die bestehenden Grundlagen der Kirche verletzenden Reformation." *Theologische Quartalschrift* 13 (1831): 589-633. Reprinted in *GS*, 2:1-33.

Commentar zum Briefe and die Römer. Edited by F.X. Reithmayr. Regensburg: G. Joseph Manz, 1845.

"De iuris austriaci et communis canonici circa matrimonii impedimenta discrimine atque hodierna in impedimentorum causis praxi austriaca, dissertatio. Additis duobus ad historiam juris circa matromonia utilibus monumentis. Scripsit Dr. Clem. Aug. de Droste-Hülshoff. Bonnae, prostat apud E. Weber, 1822," *Theologische Quartalschrift* 6 (1824): 280-83.

De eenheid in de kerk of hat principe van het katholicisme in den geest van de kerkvaders uit de eerste drie eeuwen. Translated by A.T.W. Bellemans. Introduction by G[ustave] Thiels. Antwerp: Paul Brand Bussum, 1947.

"Einführung der Berliner Hofkirchenagende, geschichtlich und kirchlich beleuchtet von D. Christoph Friedrich von Ammon, Königl. Sächs. Oberhofprediger und Kirchenrathe. Dresden, 1825. . . ." *Theologische Quartalschrift* 7 (1825): 298-302.

Die Einheit in der Kirche Oder das Prinzip des Katholizismus dargestellt im Geiste der Kirchenväter der ersten drei Jahrhunderte. Tübingen: Heinrich Laupp, 1825.

Die Einheit in der Kirche Oder das Prinzip des Katholizismus dargestellt im Geiste der Kirchenväter der ersten drei Jahrhunderte. Tubingen, Vienna, and Prag: Heinrich Laupp, Braunmüller und Seidel, C. Gerold und Haase Söhne, 1843.

Die Einheit in der Kirche. Edited by E.J. Vierneisel. Mainz: Matthias Grünewald Verlag, 1925 [Vol. 2. *Deutsche Klassiker der Katholischen Theologie aus neuer Zeit.* Edited by Heinrich Getzeny.]

Die Einheit in der Kirche Oder das Prinzip des Katholizismus Dargestellt im Geiste der Kirchenväter der ersten drei Jahrhunderte. Edited by Josef Rupert Geiselmann. Cologne and Olten: Jakob Hegner, 1957.

"Einige Gedanken über die zu unserer Zeit erfolgte Verminderung der Priester, und damit in Verbindung stehender Puncte." *Theologische Quartalschrift* 8 (1826): 414-51.

"Fragemente aus und über Pseudo-Isidor." *Theologische Quartalschrift* 11 (1829): 477-520, and 14 (1832): 3-52. Reprinted in *GS*, 1: 283-347.

Gesammelte Schriften und Aufsätze. Edited by Joh. Jos. Ign. Döllinger. 2 vols. Regensburg: G. Josepf Manz, 1839-1840.

"Geschichte der christlichen Religion und Kirche, von Johann Nepomuk Locherer, Pfarrer zu Jechtingen am Rhein, im Groszherzogthum Baden. Erster Theil, Ravensburg in der Grandmannschen Buchhandlung 1824. . . ." *Theologische Quartalschrift* 7 (1825): 99-108, 665-92.

*"Handbuch des katholischen und protestantischen Kirchenrechts (,) mit geschichtlichen Erläuterungen und steter Rücksicht auf die neusten kirchlichen Verhältnisse in den deutschen Bundesstaaten, und namentlich im Königreich Baiern. Von Dr. Sebald Brendel. . . . Bamberg, 1823. . . ." *Theologische Quartalschrift* 6 (1824): 84-113.

"Harmonie der morgenländischen und abendländischen Kirche. Ein Entwurf zur Vereinigung beider Kirchen. Von Hermann Joseph Schmitt, Kaplan in Lohr bei Aschaffenburg. Nebst einem Anhange über die anerkannten Rechte des Primats in den ersten acht Jahrhunderten. Mit einer Vorrede von Friedrich Schlegel. Wien, im Verlage bei Franz Wimmer. 1824." *Theologische Quartalschrift* 6 (1824): 642-56.

"Der heilige Johannes Chrysostomus und die Kirche, besonders des Orients, in dessen Zeitalter. Von A. Neander, Dr. ordentl. Prof. an der königl. Universität zu Berlin und Consistorialrath. Berlin, bei Ferdinand Dümmler. Erster Band. 1821. Zweiter Band 1822." *Theologische Quartalschrift* 6 (1824): 262-80.

"Hieronymus und Augustinus im Streit über Gal. 2, 14." *Theologische Quartalschrift* 6 (1824): 195-219. Reprinted in *GS*, 1:1-18.

"Ideen zur Beurtheilung der Einführung der preuszischen Hofkirchenagende aus dem sittlichen Standpunckte. . . . Leipzig bey Johann Friedrich Hartknoch, 1824." *Theologische Quartalschrift* 7 (1825): 278-85.

Johann Adam Möhler. Bd. 1: Gesammelte Acktenstücke und Briefe. Edited by Stefan Lösch. Munich: Josef Kösel & Freidrich Pustet, 1928.

"Karl der Grosze und seine Bischöfe. Die Synode von Maynz im Jahre 813." *Theologische Quartalschrift* 6 (1824): 367-427.

"Die Kirchenagenden-Sache in dem preuszischen Staate. Eine geschichtliche Mittheilung zur bessern Einsicht in die stetigen Unstände. Von Ludwig Schaaf. . . . Leipzig, bey C.H.F. Hartmann. 1824." *Theologische Quartalschrift* 7 (1825): 285-92.

"Kurtze Betrachtungen über das historische Verhältnis der Universitäten zum Staate." [1829]. Reprinted in *GS*, 1:268-82.

"Die Lehre vom göttlichen Reiche, dargestellt von Franz Theremin Berlin. Im Verlage von Dunker und Humblot. 1823." *Theologische Quartalschrift* 6 (1824): 622-42.

The Life of St. Anselm, Archbishop of Canterbury; A Contribution to the Knowledge of the Moral, Ecclesiastical, and Literary Life of the Eleventh and Twelfth Centuries. Translated by Henry Rymer. London: T. Jones, 1842.

"Lehrbuch des Kirchenrechts mit Berücksichtigung der neuesten Verhältnisse. Von D. Ferd. Walter, ord. Professor der Recht auf der rheinishcen Universität zu Bonn. (440 S. 8) Bonn, bey Adolph Markus, 1822." *Theologische Quartalschrift* 5 (1823): 263-99.

Nachgelassene Schriften Nach den stereographischen Copien von Stefan Lösch (1881-1966), Edited by Rudolf Reinhardt. *Band I. Vorlesungen, Entwürfe, Fragmente.* Translated, edited, and introduced by Reinhold Rieger. Paderborn: Bonifatius Druck, 1989.

Neue Untersuchungen der Lehrgegensätze zwischen den Katholiken und Protestanten: eine Vertheidigung meiner Symbolik gegen die Kritik des Herrn Professors Dr. Baur in Tübingen. Mainz and Vienna: Florian Kupferberg und Karl Gerold, 1834.

On the Relation of Islam to the Gospel. Translated by J.P. Menge. Calcutta: Ostell and Lepage, Britsh Library, 1847.

Patrologie oder christliche Literärgeschichte. Aus dessen hinterlassenen Handschriften samt Ergänzungen. 1. Band: Die ersten drei Jahrhunderte. Edited by Franz Xavier Reithmayr. Regensburg, Vienna, und Linz: Georg Joseph Manz, Gerold, Mechitaristen, von Mösle und Braunmüller, und F. Eurich und Sohn, von Fink und Q. Haslinger, 1840.

"Sendschreiben an Herrn Bautain, Professor der philosophischen Facultät zu Strassburg." *Theologische Quartalschrift* 17 (1835): 421-53. Reprinted in *GS*, 2:141-164.

Symbolik oder Darstellung der dogmatischen Gegensaetze der Katholiker und Protestanten nach ihren öffentlichen Bekenntnisschriften. eingeleitet und kommentiert von Josef Rupert Geiselmann. Cologne and Olten: Hegner, 1958.

Symbolism; or, Exposition of the Doctrinal Differences between Catholics and Protestants, as Evidenced by Their Symbolical Writings. 2 vols. Translated by James Burton Robertson. London: Charles Dolman, 1843.

"Theologisches Votum für die neuen Hofkirchenagende und deren weitere Einführung, abgesehen von D. Carl Imanuel Nitzsch, ordentl. Prof. der Theol. und Evangel. Universitäts Prediger an der Königl. Preuss. Rheinuniversität. Bonn, bey Eduard Weber 1824." *Theologische Quartalschrift* 7 (1825): 292-98.

Dell'unità della chiesa ossia principio del cattolicismo secondo lo spirito del padri dei primi tre secoli della chiesa. Milan: Pirotta, 1841.

De l'unité de l'église; ou, Du principe du catholicisme d'après l'esprit des pères des trois premiers siècles. Translated by Ph[ilippe] Bernard. Tournai: Castermann, 1835.

L'unité dans l'église; ou, Le principe du Catholicisme d'après l'esprit des Pères des trois premiers siècles de l'Église. Translated by André de Lilienfeld. Introduction by Pierre Chaillet. Paris: Les éditions du Cerf, 1938.

"Über das Verhältnis, in welchem nach dem Koran Jesus Christus zu Mohammed und das Evangelium zu Islam steht. Mit besonderer Berücksichtigun der künftigen Schickdsale des letzteren gegenüber dem Christenthum." *Theologische Quartalschrift* 12 (1830): 3-81. Reprinted in *GS*, 1: 348-402.

"Über den Brief an Diognetus. Die Zeit seiner Herausgabe. Darstellung seines Inhalts." *Theologische Quartalschrift* 7 (1825): 444-61. Reprinted in *GS*, 1:19-31.

"Über Justin Apologie, I c.6. Gegen die Auslegung diesrer Stelle von Neander." *Theologische Quartalschrift* 15 (1833): 49-60.

"Ueber die wahre Stelle des liturgischen Rechts im evangelischen Kirchen-Regiment. Prüfung der Schrift: Ueber das liturgische Recht des evangelsichen Landesfürsten. Von D. Philipp Marheineke. Berlin, 1825. . . ." *Theologische Quartalschrift* 7 (1825): 261-77.

"Ueber das liturgische Recht evangelischer Landesfürsten. Ein theologisches Votum von Pacificus Sincerus. Göttingen bei Vandehoeck und Ruprecht. 1824." *Theologische Quartalschrift* 7 (1825): 244-61.

"Variae doctorum Catholicorum opiniones de iure statuendi impedimenta matrimonii dirimentia. Dissertatio canonica. Scripsit Joannes Antonius Theiner . . . Wratislaviae, apud Jos. Max et Socium, 1825." *Theologische Quartalschrift* 7 (1825): 462-86.

"Vergleichung des gemeinen Kirchenrechts mit dem preuss. Allgem. Landrecht, in Ansehung der Ehehindernisse. Ein notwendiges Hülfsbuch für Rechts-Gelehrte und Pfarr-Geistliche besonders in Provinzen gemischten Glaubens-Bekenntnisses. Von Dr. Daniel. . . . Berlin, 1823. . . ." *Theologische Quartalschrift* 6 (1824): 283-85.

"Versuch über den Ursprung des Gnosticismus." First published in *Beglückwünschung . . . Dr. Gottlieb Jacob Planck.* . . . Tübingen, 1831. Reprinted in *GS*, 1: 403-35.

Vorlesungen über die Kirchengeschichte. Edited by Reinhold Rieger. 2 vols. Munich: Erich Wewel, 1992.

2. Volumes cited in *Unity in the Church*

"Alia Acta [Pionii] ex Simeone Metaphraste," 2, 9. In *Acta Sanctorum.* . . . Edited by Johannes Bollandus. Paris, 1863.

Ambrose. *Commentary on Luke* [PL 15: 1607-1944].

Apostolic Canons. See *Apostolic Constitutions* [ANF 7: 500-505].

Apostolic Constitutions [PG 1: 509-1156; ANF 7: 396-505].

Aristotle. *Metaphysics.* Vol. 8. Edited and translated by W.D. Ross. *The Works of Aristotle.* Oxford: Oxford University Press, 1928.

Athenagoros. *Law of Christ* [PG 6: 890-972].

Athanasius. "First Letter to Serapion" [PG 26: 529-608].

Aubespiné. See Optatus.

Augusti, Johann Christian Wilhelm. *Denkwürdigkeiten aus der christlichen Archäologie; mit beständiger Rücksicht auf die gegenwartigen Bedürfnisse der christlichen Kirche.* Leipzig, 1830.

Augustine. *Against Parmenian* [PL 43: 33-108].

———. *Against Cresconius* [PL 43: 445-594].

———. *Confessions* [PL 32: 659-868; NPNF 1: 33-207].

———. *Letters* [PL 33; NPNF, Series 1, 1: 219-593].

———. *Of True Religion.* Translated by J.H.S. Burleigh. London: SCM, 1953 [PL 34: 121-72].

————. *On the Profit of Believing*. Translated by Josef Witmer. Lucerne, 1824.

————. *On the Profit of Believing* [PL 42: 65-92; NPNF, Series 1, 3: 347-66].

————. *On the Psalms* [PL 36-37; NPNF, Series 1, 8: 1-683].

————. *On the Remission of Sins* [PL 44: 109-200; NPNF Series 1, 5: 11-78].

————. *On the Trinity* [PL 42: 819-1098: NPNF, Series 1, 3: 1-228].

————. *On the Unity of the Church against the Donatists* [PL 43: 391-446; NPNF Series 1, 4: 407-514].

————. *Questions on the Old and New Testaments* [PL 35: 2301-92].

————. *Tracts on John* [PL 35: 1379-1970; NPNF, Series 1, 7: 7-452].

Augustine [?] *Letter to Catholics against the Donatists* [PL 43: 391-446].

Barnabas, Epistle of. . . . *Sancti Barnabae . . . epistola catholica. Acessit S. Hermae . . . Pastor.* Oxford, 1685

————. [ANF 1: 123-49].

Basil. *Against Eunomius* [PG 29: 497-669].

————. *Letters* [PG 32: 220-1112; NPNF, Series 2, 8: 109-327].

————. *On Isaiah* [PG 30: 118-668].

————. *On the Spirit* [PG 32: 67-217; NPNF, Series 2, 8: 2-50].

————. *On True Faith* [PG 31: 678-79].

Beveridge. See Cotelerius.

Bill. See Irenaeus 1596.

Bingham, Joseph, *Origenes Ecclesiastical : or The Antiquities of the Christian Church, and other works*. . . . 8 vols. Edited by Richard Bingham. London : William Straker, 1934.

————. *Origenes sive antiquitates ecclesiasticae. Ex lingua Anglicana in Latinam vertit Io. Henricus Grischovius*. . . . Halle, 1723.

Boehmer. See de Marca.

Breitschneider, Karl Gottlieb. *Systematische Entwicklung aller in der Dogmatick vorkommenden Begriffe*. . . . 3d ed. Leipzig, 1825.

Chemnitz, Martin. *Examination of the Council of Trent.* 4 vols. Translated by Fred Kramer. St. Louis Mo.: Concordia, 1971-1986.

Chemnitz, Martin. *Examen Concilii Tridentini secundum editionem 1578*. . . . Edited by Ed. Preuss. Berlin, 1861.

Chrysostom. *Homilies on Acts* [PG 60: 10-384; NPNF, Series 2, 2: 1-328].

————. *Homilies on I Corinthians* [PG 61: 9-61; NPNF, Series 2, 12: 3-269].

————. *Homilies on Ephesians* [PG 62: 9-176].

————. *On the Priesthood* [PG 48: 623-692; NPNF, Series 2, 9: 33-83].

Clement of Alexandria. . . . *Clementis Alexandrini Opera, quae extant.* Recognita et illustrata per Joannem Potterum. Oxford, 1715.

————. *The Instructor* [PG 8: 247-684; ANF 2: 209-296].

————. *Miscellanies* [PG 8: 685-1382; PG 9: 10-602 (Le Nourry edition with notes by Sylburg and Lowth); ANF 2: 299-567].

Clement of Rome. "Letter to the Corinthians" [PG 1: 204-208; ANF 1: 1-21].

Cornelius to Cyprian. See Cyprian. *Letters.*

Cotelerius, J.B. *S.S. Patrum, Qui Temporibus Apostolicis Floruerunt, Barnabae, Clementis, Hermae, Ignatii, Polycarpi Opera, Vera, Et Suppositicia; Unà cum Clementis, Ignatii, Polycarpi Actis atque Martyriis*. . . . *Recensit . . . adspersit Joannes Clericus*. . . . Amsterdam, 1724.

Creuzer, Georg Friedrich. *Symbolik und Mythologie der alten Völker, besonders der Griechen.* 4 vols. Leipzig, 1810-1812.

Cyprian. *Letters* [PL 4: 193-452; ANF 5: 275-409].

————. *On the Council of Carthage* [CSEL 3.1: 436].

————. *On the Lapsed* [PL 4: 477-510; ANF 5: 437-47].

————. *On the Unity of the Church* [PL 4: 509-36; ANF 5: 421-29].

————. *Opera Recognita et illustr. a Joanne Fello. Accedunt Cyprianici, sive tredecim annorum, quibus S. Cyprianus inter Christianos versatus est, brevis historia chronologicè delineata Joanne Pearsonis. Ed. tertia cui additae sunt dissertationes Cyprianicae Henrici Dodwelli.* Amsterdam, 1700.

————. *Three Books of Testimonies against the Jews* [PL 4: 703-810; ANF 5: 507-57].

Cyril of Alexandria. *Commentary on John* [PG 74: 9-756].

————. *Thesaurus* [PG 75: 9-656].

de la Rue, Carolus Vincentius. See Origen.

de Marca, Peter. *Illustrissimi viri Petri de Marca archepiscopi Parisiensis dissertationum de concordia sacerdotii et imperii seu de libertatibus ecclesiae Gallicanae libri octo. Quibus accesserunt eiusdam auctoris dissertationes ecclesiasticae varii argumente. Iusti Henningii Boehmeri selectae observationes libros de concordia illustrantes. . . .* Bamberg, 1788.

Demetrius Cydones [PG 154, 863ff.].

Didymus the Blind. *On the Holy Spirit* [PG 39, 1031-86].

Diogenes Laertius. *The Lives of Eminent Philosophers.* 2 vols. Translated by R.D. Hicks. Cambridge, Mass.: Harvard University Press, 1925.

Diognetus. See Epistle to Diognetus.

Dionysius of Halicarnassus. *Roman Antiquities.* 7 vols. Translated by Ernest Cary. Cambridge, Mass.: Harvard University Press, 1937-1950.

Dodwell. See Cyprian.

Dubois, Jean Antoine. *Briefe über den Zustand des Christenthums in Indien, in welchen die Bekehrung der Hindus als unausführbar dargestellt wird.* Translated by A.G. Hoffmann. Neustadt an der Orla, 1824.

Du Pin, Ludovico Ellies. *De antiqua eccelsiae disciplina dissertationes historicae. Excerptae ex conciliis oecumenicis & sanctorum patrum et auctorum ecclesiasticorum scriptis.* Paris, 1691.

Epictetus. *Enchiridion.* Edited by Christ Gottl. Heyne. Warschaw, 1787.

Epiphanius. *Heresies* [PG 41-42].

Epistle to Diognetus [PG 2: 1167-86; ANF 1: 25-30].

Eusebius. *Ecclesiastical History* [NPNF, Series 2, 1: 73-403; PG 20: 45-906].

————. *. . . Ecclesiasticae historicae libri decem. Eiusdem de vita Imp. Constantini, Libri IV. . . . Henricus Valesius . . . emendavit, latine vertit, & adnotationibus illustravit.* Paris, 1659. [Reprinted in PG 19-25].

Firmilian of Caesarea. See Cyprian. *Letters.*

Fleury, Claude. *The Ecclesiastical History of M. L'Abbé Fleury.* 3 vols. Translated with Notes. Oxford and London, 1842-1844.

Gaius. *Little Labyrinths.* See Hippolytus.

Gelasius I. *Letters and Decrees* [PL 59: 9-190].

Gieseler, John C.L. *A Compendium of Ecclesiastical History.* 5 vols. Translated by Samuel Davidson. Edinburgh, 1854.

————. *Textbook of Ecclesiastical History.* 3 vols. Translated and edited by F. Cunningham. Philadelphia, 1836.

Goetze. See Irenaeus.

Grabe. See Irenaeus.

Gratz, Al. *Der Apologet des Katholicismus: Zeitschrift für Freunde der Wahrheit und der Brüderliebe; Zur Berichtigung mannigfältiger Entstellungen des Katolizismus.* 9 sections. Mainz, 1820-1824.

————. *Kritische Untersuchungen über Marcions Evangel.* Tübingen, 1818.

Gregory of Nyssa. *On Perfection* [PG 46: 251-86].

Gregory Thaumaturgus. *Panegyric on Origen* [PG 10: 1049-104; ANF 6: 21-39].

Gregory Nazianzus. *Orations* [PG 35 and 36; NPNF, Series 2, 7: 203-44].

———. "In Praise of Cyprian." Oration 24 [PG 35: 1167-94].

Gregory of Nyssa. *Against Apollonius* [PG 45: 1269-78].

Grotius, Hugo. *Opervm theologicorvm. . . . Annotationes in Epistolas Apostolicas*. Tom. 2, vol. 2. Amsterdam, 1679.

Hahn, *Das Evangelium Marcions* (1823; not located).

Haller, Karl Ludwig von, "Kräftige, gute Gedanken über die sichtbare und unsichtbare Kirche." *Wiener Jahrbücher* 25, pp. 87ff.

———. *Restauration der Staats-wissenschft, oder Theorie des natürlich geselligen Zustands der Chimäre des künstlich-bügerlichen entgegensetzt. . . .* 6 vols. Winterthur, 1816-1834.

Hammond. See Cotelerius.

Henke, Heinrich Philipp Konrad. *Allgemeine Geschichte der christlichen Kirche nach der Zeitfolge*. Braunschweig, 1802.

Hermas. *The Shepherd* [PG 2: 892-1012; ANF 2: 9-55] See also Barnabas, Epistle of.

Hippolytus. *Little Labyrinths* [For discussion see Quasten 1:195-96; PG 16; ANF 5: 9-153; 599-604].

Huet, Daniel. *Origeniana*. See Origen [PG 7: 633-1234].

Hug, Joahnn Leonard. *Einleitung in die Schriften des neuen Testaments*. 2 vols. Tübingen, 1808 [2nd. ed., Stuttgart und Tübingen, 1821].

———. *Introduction to the Writings of the New Testament*. 2 vols. Translated by D. G. Wait. London, 1827.

Ignatius of Antioch. *Letters* [PG 5: 643-872; ANF 1: 49-96].

Irenaeus. *. . . adversus Valentini et similium Gnosticorum haereses, libri quinque cum scholiis et annotationibus J. Billii. . . .* Cologne, 1596.

———. *Against the Heresies* [Har. II 42.3-4 I 355 f.; ANF 1: 315-567; PG 7].

———. *. . . . Detectionis et eversionis falso cognominatae agnitiones, seu contra haereses libri quinque. Post Francisci Feuardentii et Joannes Erneste Grabe. . . . Studio & labore Domni Renato Massuet, . . .* Venice, 1734. [Reprinted in PG 7].

Jerome. *Commentary on Titus* [PL 26: 589-636].

John of Damascus. *On the Orthodox Faith* [PG 42: 637].

John the Deacon. *Life of Saint Gregory the Great* [PL 75: 59-242].

Junius. See Cotelerius

Justin Martyr. *Dialogue with Trypho* [PG 6: 471-800; ANF 1: 194-270].

———. *First Apology* [PG 6: 327-442; ANF 1: 163-87].

———. *Second Apology* [PG 6: 441-70; ANF 1: 159-93].

Kastner, *Agape* [not located].

Katerkamp, Theodor. *Des ersten Zeitalters der Kirchengeschichte*. 5 sections. Münster, 1823-1834.

Lactantius. *Institutes* [PL 6; ANF 7: 9-328].

Libosus of Vaga, Council of Carthage, 256; Sententiae episcoporum 87.30 [CSEL 3.1, 448; ANF "Statements of Bishops in the Seventh Council of Carthage," 5: 565-72].

Lowth. See Clement of Alexandria. *Miscellanies*.

Lumper, Gottfried. *. . . . Historia theologico-critica de vita, scriptis, atque doctrina sanctorum patrum aliorumque scriptorum ecclesiasticorum trium primorum saeculorum ex virorum doctissimorum literariis monumentis collecta. . . .* 1783-1799.

Massuet. See Irenaeus.

Münscher, William. *Elements of Dogmatic History*. Translated by James Murdoch. 2nd. ed. New Haven, 1830.

———. *Handbuch der christlichen Dogmengeschichte.* 4 vols. Marburg, 1797-1814.

Neander, Augustus. *Antignostikus; or the Spirit of Tertullian.* In A. Neander, *History of the Planting and Training of the Christian Church by the Apostles.* 2 vols. Translated by J.E. Ryland (London, 1851), 2:191-533.

———. *De gnosis fideique* [not located].

———. *Denkwürdigkeiten aus der Geschichte des Christenthums and des christlichen Lebens.* 3 vols. 2nd. ed. Berlin, 1825-1827. [1. ed. 1822; Section I in both editions by A. Tholuck, "Das Wesen und die sittlichen Einflüsse des Heidenthums"].

———. *Generische Entwicklung der vornehmsten gnostischen Systeme.* Berlin, 1818.

Optatus. *Against the Donatists* [PL 11: 883-1104].

———. . . . *De schismate Donatistarum libri septem* . . . . *Opera et studio M. Lud. Ell. Dupin . . . cum eiusdem notis, ut & Gab. Albaspinaei, Mer. Causauboni, Casp. Bartii. . . .* Antwerp, 1702.

Origen. *Against Celsus* [PG 11: 641-1632; ANF 4: 395-669].

———. *Commentary on Song of Songs* [PG 13: 37-216].

———. *Commentary on Matthew* [PG 13: 855-1800; ANF 4: 409-512].

———. *Commentary on John* [PG 14: 21-830; ANF 10: 297-408].

———. *Commentary on Romans* [PG 14: 837-1298].

———. *Fragments on Hosea* [PG 13: 825-828].

———. *Homilies on Genesis* [PG 12: 45-262].

———. *Homilies on Leviticus* [PG 12: 397-574].

———. *Homilies on Numbers* [PG 12: 575-806].

———. *Homilies on Luke* [PG 13: 1801-1910].

———. . . . *Omnia quae graece vel latine tantum exstant et ejus nomine circumferuntur. . . . Opera & studio Domni Caroli Delarue. . . .* Paris, 1733-1759. [Reprinted in PG 11-17].

———. *On First Principles* [PG 11: 115-414; ANF 4: 237-382].

Pamelius. See Tertullian.

Pamphilius. *Apology for Origen* [PG 17: 521-614].

Paulus, Hr. Eberhard Gottlob. *Evangelienkommentare.* 1800-1804.

Pearson. See Cyprian.

Petau, Denis. *Opus de theologicis dogmatibus, auctius in hac nouissima editione libro de Tridentini Concilii interpretatione, Libris II dissertationum ecclesiasticarum, diatribâ de potestate consecrandi, libris VIII. de poenitentia publica.* Venice, 1721

———. *Opus de theologicis dogmatibus a J.-B. Thomas recognitum et adnotatum.* 8 vols. Barri-Ducis, 1864-1870.

Petavius. See Petau.

Planck, G.J. *Geschichte der christlich-kirchlichen Gesellschafts-Verfassung.* Hanover, 1803.

Pontius the Deacon. *The Life and Passion of Cyprian* [ANF 5:7-74].

Pseudo-Ignatius. "Letter to the Philadelphians" [ANF 1:116-119].

Rhodon. See Eusebius and PG 5:1033-38.

Rigaltus. See Tertullian.

Salmasius, Claudius. See Saumaise.

Saumaise, Cl. de. *Librorum de primatu papae pars prima [et unica] Cum apparatu. Accessere de eodem primatu Nili et Balaami tractatus.* Lyons, 1645.

Schleiermacher, Friedrich Daniel Ernst. *The Christian Faith.* Edited by H.R. Mackintosh and J.S. Stewart. Edinburgh: T. & T. Clark, 1928.

———. *Der Christliche Glaube nach den Grundsätzen der evangelische Kirche im Zusammenhange dargestellt (1821/1822).* Edited by Hermann Peiter. In *Friedrich Schleiermacher, Kritische Gesamtausgabe.* Edited by Hans-Joachim Birkner et al., Erste Abteilung, Vol. 7, 1-3. Berlin: Walter de Gruyter, 1980-1984.

Schmidt, J.E. Ch. *Bibliothek für Kritik und Exegese des neuen Testaments.* 2 vols. Hadamar, 1779-1803.

Schrökh, Johann Matthias. *Christliche Kirchengeschichte seit der Reformation.* Vol 28. *Ausführliche Geschichte des dritten Zeitraums.* Leipzig, 1779.

Seber, Franz Joseph. *Über Religion und Theologie: Eine allgemeine Grundlage der christlichen Theologie.* Cologne, 1823.

Sylburg. see Clement of Alexandria. *Miscellanies.*

Synod of Antioch [NPNF, Series 2, 14: 104-21].

Tatian. *Oration against the Greeks* [PG 6: 803-88; ANF 2: 65-83].

Tertullian. *Against Marcion* [PL 2: 263-556; ANF 3: 269-474].

————. *Against Praxeas* [PL 2: 175-220; ANF 3: 597-627].

————. *Against the Valentinians* [PL 2: 559-632; ANF 3: 503-20].

————. *On Chastity* [PL 2: 963-978; ANF 4: 50-58].

————. *On Fasting* [PL 2: 1003-1030; ANF 4: 102-14].

————. *On Prayer* [PL 1: 1243-1304; ANF 3: 681-91].

————. *On the Prescription of Heretics* [PL 2: 13-92; ANF 3: 243-65].

————. *On the Resurrection of the Flesh* [PL 2: 827-934; ANF 3: 545-94].

————. *On the Soul* [PL 2: 681-798; ANF 3: 181-235].

————. *Opera ad vetustissimorum exemplarium fidem sedulo emendata, diligentia Nic. Rigaltii cum eiusdem annotationibus integris, & variorum commentariis, seorsim antea editis. Ph. Priorius argumenta & notas in libros omnes . . . cum notis, ut editione Pamelij.* Paris, 1664. [Reprinted in PG 1,2].

————. *Scorpiace* [PL 2: 143-76; ANF 3: 633-48].

Theophilus of Antioch. *To Autolycus* [PG 6: 1023-1168; ANF 2: 89-121].

Tholuck. See Neander. *Denkwürdigkeiten.*

Valesius. See Eusebius.

Walch, Johann Georg. *Introductio in libros ecclesiae Lutheranae symbolicos observationis historicis et theologicis illustrata.* Jena, 1732.

Walter, Ferdinand. *Lehrbuch des Kirchenrechts aller Christlichen Confessionen.* Bonn, 1842.

Witmer. See Augustine, *On the Profit of Believing.*

Wienert, Walter. *Die Typen der Griechisch-Römisch Fabel.* Helsinki, 1925.

Xenophon. *Cyropaedia.* Weiske edition [not located].

Xenophon. *Cyropaedia.* 2 vols. Translated by William Millar. Cambridge, Mass.: Harvard University Press, 1914.

Zeno. *Contra Mattem.* Edited by Immanuel Becker (1842) 582, 20.

Zimmer, P.B. *Untersuchung über den Begriff und die Gesetze der Geschichte.* Munich, 1817.

3. Secondary sources

"Ansichten und Beobachtungen über Religion und Kirche in England. Von Karl Heinrich Sack . . . Berlin, 1819. . . ." *Theologische Quartalschrift* 2 (1820): 105ff.

Adam, Karl. *The Spirit of Catholicism.* Translated by J. McCann. New York: Macmillan, 1929.

Altaner, Berthold and Alfred Stuiber. *Patrologie; Leben, Schriften und Lehre der Kirchenväter.* 9th ed. Freiburg: Herder, 1980.

The Ante-Nicene Fathers. Translations of the Writings of the Fathers down to A.D. 325. 10 vols. Edited by J. Roberts and A. Donaldson. New York, 1884-1886.

Aubert, Roger. "Das schwierige Erwachen der Katholischen Theologie im Zeitalter der Restauration." *Theologische Quartalschrift* 148 (1968): 9-62.

————. "Die ekklesiologische Geographie im 19. Jahrhundert." In Jean Daniélou and Herbert Vorgrimler, ed. *Sentire Ecclesiam: Das Bewusstsein von der Kirche als gestaltende Kraft der Frömmigkeit*, 430-73. Freiburg: Herder, 1961.

Aubert, Roger, et. al. *The Church in the Age of Liberalism*. Translated by Peter Becker. New York: Crossroad, 1989.

Aubert, Roger, and Rudolf Lill. "The Awakening of Catholic Vitality." In Roger Aubert et al. *The Church between Revolution and Restoration*, 206-57. Translated by Peter Becker. New York; Crossroad, 1989.

Baur, Ferdinand Christian. *Die christliche Gnosis, oder die Religionsphilosophie in ihrer geschichtlichen Entwicklung*. Tübingen: C.F. Osiander, 1835.

————. "Erwiderung auf Herrn Dr. Möhler's neueste Polemik gegen die portestantische Lehre und Kirche in der Schrift: *Neue Untersuchungen. . . .*" *Tübinger Zeitschrift für Theologie* 8 (1834): 127-248.

————. *Der Gegensatz des Catholicismus und Protestantismusnach den Principien und Hauptdogmen der beiden Lehrbegriffe, mit besonderer Rücksicht auf Herrn Dr. Möhlers Symbolik*. Tübingen: Ludwig Friedrich Fues, 1834.

Bedarida, Renée. "Le pere Pierre Chaillet: de la theologie de Möhler á la résistance." In Pierre Bolle et Jean Godel, eds. *Spiritualité, theologie et resistance: Yves de Montcheuil, theologien au maquis du Vercors: collegue de Biviers*, 49-61. Grenoble: Presses universitaires de Grenoble, 1987.

Benrath, G.A. "Evangelische und Katholische Kirchenhistorie im zeichen der Aufklärung und der Romantik." *Zeitschrift für Kirchengeschichte* 82 (1972): 203-17.

Bilmeyer, K. "J.A. Möhler als Kirchenhistoriker, seine Leistungen und seine Methode." *Theologische Quartalschrift* 100 (1919): 134-98.

Butler, Perry. *Gladstone: Church, State and Tractarianism. A Study of His Religious Ideas and Attitudes*. Oxford: Oxford University Press, 1982.

Bolshakoff, Serge. *The Doctrine of the Unity of the Church in the Works of Khomyakov and Möhler*. London: SPCK, 1946.

Brunner, Heinz, *Der organologische Kirchenbegriff in seiner Bedeutung für das ekklesiologische Denken des 19. Jahrhunderts*. Frankfurt: Lang, 1979.

Casper, Bernhard. "Erkenntnisse aus der kritischen Beschäftigung mit den frühen Aufsätzen und Rezensionen F. A. Staudenmaiers (1828-1834)." *Theologische Quartalschrift* 150 (1970): 262-68.

Chadwick, Owen. *From Bossuet to Newman: The Idea of Doctrinal Development*. Cambridge: Cambridge University Press, 1957.

————. *The Popes and the European Revolution*. Oxford: Clarendon Press, 1981.

————. *The Victorian Church*. 3d ed. London: Adam and Charles Black, 1971.

Chaillot, Pierre, "Hommage a J.-A. Möhler pour le centenaire de sa mort." *Revue des sciences philosophiques et theologiques* 27 (1938): 161-84.

Coker, F.W. *Organismic Theories of the State*. New York: Columbia University Press, 1910.

Congar, Yves M.-J. "Johann Adam Möhler 1796-1838." *Theologische Quartalschrift* 150 (1970): 47-51.

————. "Sur l'evolution et l'interpretation de la pensee de Moehler." *Revue des sciences philosophiques et theologiques* 27 (1938): 204-12.

————. *Tradition and Traditions: A historical and theological survey*. Translated by Michael Naseby and Thomas Rainborough. London: Burns and Oates, 1966.

Corpus scriptorum ecclesiasticorum latinorum. 100 vols. Vienna: apud C. Geroldi filium, 1866-1913.

Corpus Christianorum. Turnhout: Brepols, 1954-.

Danielou, J., and H. Vorgrimler, eds. *Sentire Ecclesiam. Das Bewusstsein von der Kirche als gestaltende Kraft der Frömigkeit.* Freiburg: Herder, 1961.

"*Denkwürdigkeiten aus der Geschichte des Christenthums und des christlichen Lebens.* Herausgegeben von Dr. A. Neander. Erster Band. Berlin, bei Ferdinand Dümmler. 1823. . . ." *Theologische Quartalschrift* 4 (1823): 727ff.

Dietrich, Donald J. "German Historicism and the Changing Image of the Church, 1780-1820." *Theological Studies* 42 (1981): 46-73.

―――. *The Goethezeit and the Metamorpohsis of Catholic Theology in the Age of Idealism.* Bern: Lang, 1979.

Drey, Johann Sebastian von. "*Das Suchen nach Wahrheit, oder Vergleichung der katholischen und protestantischen Kirche mit der apostolischen der ersten Jahrhunderte. Von J.G. Rätze. Leipzig, 1803. . . ." Theologische Quartalschrift* 3 (1823): 450-84.

―――. "Das Wesen der Puseyitischen Doctrin." *Theologische Quartalschrift* 26 (1844): 417-57

Dru, Alexander. *The Church in the 19th Century: Germany, 1800-1918.* London: Burns and Oates, 1963.

―――. *The Contribution of German Catholicism.* New York: Hawthorn Books, 1963.

"*Einleitung in die Schriften des neuen Testament* von Dr. Joh. Leonard Hug, Professor der Theol. and der Universität zu Freiburg in Breisgau. . . . Zweite verbesserte und vermehrte Auflage. i Th. 503 S. Stuttgart und Tübingen . . . 1821." *Theologische Quartalschrift* 4 (1822): 276ff., 461ff.

Erb, Peter C. *Pietists, Protestants, and Mysticism:The Use of Late Medieval Spiritual Texts in the Work of Gottfried Arnold.* Metuchen, N.J.: Scarecrow Press, 1989.

Eschweiler, Karl. *Johann Adam Möhler's Kirchenbegriff. Das Hauptstück der katholischen Auseinandersetzung mit der deutschen Idealismus.* Braunsberg: Herder, 1930.

Faber, George Stanley. *Letters on Tractarian Secession to Popery, with Remarks on Dr. Newman's Principle of Development, Dr. Moehler's Symbolism. . . .* London: W. H. Dalton, 1846.

Fehr, Wayne L. *The Birth of the Catholic Tübingen School: The Dogmatics of Johann Sebastian Drey.* Chico, Calif.: Scholars Press, 1981.

Fitzer, Joseph. *Moehler and Baur in Controversy, 1832-1838: Romantic Idealist Assessment of the Reformation and Counter-Reformation.* Talahasee, Fla.: American Academy of Religion, 1974.

―――. *Romance and the Rock: Nineteenth-Century Catholics on Faith and Reason.* Minneapolis, Minn.: Fortress Press, 1989.

Förch, Gerhard. *Theologie als Darstellung der Geschichte in der Idee: Zum Theologiebegriff Friedrich Brenners, 1784-1848.* Würzburg: Echter Verlag, 1980.

Forstman, Jack. *A Romantic Triangle: Schleiermacher and Early German Romanticism.* Missoula, Mont.: Scholars Press, 1977.

Franklin, R.W. *Nineteenth-Century Churches: The History of a New Catholicism in Württemberg, England, and France.* New York: Garland, 1987.

Friedrich, Johann. *Johann Adam Möhler, der Symboliker.* Munich: Beck, 1894.

Fries, Heinrich und Georg Schwaiger, eds. *Katholische Theologen Deutschlands im 19. Jahrhundert.* 3 vols. Munich: Kösel, 1975.

Funk, Philipp, "Die geistige Gestalt Johann Adam Möhlers." *Hochland* 27 (1929-1930): 97-110.

Geiselmann, Josef Rupert. *Die Einheit der Kirche und die Wiedervereinigung der Konfessionen.* Vienna, 1940.

―――. "Der gefallenen Mensch. Die Wandlungendes Erbsündebegriffs in der Symolik Joh. Adam Möhlers." *Theologische Quartalschrift* 124 (1943): 73-98.

————. *Geist des Christentums und des Katholizismus. Ausgewählte Schriften Katholischer Theologie in Zeitalter des deutschen Idealismus und der Romantik.* Mainz: Matthias Grünewald, 1940.

————. ed. *Johann Adam Möhler: Die Einheit in der Kirche und die Wiedervereinigung der Confessionen. Ein Beitrag zum Gespräch zwischen den Konfessionen.* Vienna: Friedrich Beck (Schöingh & Haindrich), 1940.

————. "Joh. Adam Möhler und die Entwicklung seines Kirchen-begriffs." *Theologische Quartalschrift* 112 (1931): 1-91.

————. *Die Katholische Tübinger Schule: Ihre theologische Eigenart.* Freiburg: Herder, 1964.

————. "Kirche und Frömmigkeit in den geistigen Bewegungen der ersten Hälfte des 19. Jahrhunderts, " In Jean Daniélou and Herbert Vorgrimler, eds. *Sentire Ecclesiam: Das Bewusstsein von der Kirche als gestaltende Kraft der Frömmigkeit,* 474-530. Freiburg: Herder, 1961.

————. *Die Lebendige Überlieferung als Norm des christlichen Glaubens: Die apostolische Tradition in der Form der kirchlichen Verkündigung—der Formalprinzip des Katholizismus dargestellt im Geiste der Traditionslehre von Joh. E. Kuhn.* Freiburg: Herder, 1959

————. *Lebendiger Glaube aus geheiligter Überlieferung: Der Grundgedanke der Theologie Johann Adam Möhlers und der Katholischen Tübinger Schule.* 2. Aufl.; Freiburg: Herder, 1966.

————. *The Meaning of Tradition.* Translated by W.J. O'Hara. New York: Herder and Herder, 1966.

————. *Die theologische Anthropologie Johann Adam Möhlers: Ihr geschichtlicher Wandel.* Freiburg: Herder, 1955.

————. "Der Wandel des Kirchenbewusstseins und der Kirchlichkeit in der Theologie Johann Adam Möhlers." In Jean Daniélou and Herbert Vorgrimler, eds. *Sentire Ecclesiam: Das Bewusstsein von der Kirche als gestaltende Kraft der Frömmigkeit,* 531-675. Freiburg: Herder, 1961.

Geisser, Hans Friedrich. "Die methodischen Prinzipien des Symbolikers Johann Adam Möhler: Ihre brauchbarkeit im ökumenischen Dialog." *Theologische Quartalschrift* 168 (1988): 83-97.

————. *Glaubenseinheit und Lehrentwicklung bei Johann Adam Möhler.* Göttingen: Vandenhoeck & Ruprecht, 1971.

————. "Glück und Unglück eines Theologen mit seiner Kirche—am Beispiel der beiden Tübinger Johann Adam Möhler und David Friedrich Strauss." *Zeitschrift für Theologie und Kirche* 83 (1986): 85-110.

Gollowitzer, Helene. "Drei Bäckerjungen." *Catholica* 23 (1969): 147-53.

Grabmann, Martin. *Die Geschichte der katholischen Theologie seit dem Ausgang der Väterzeit.* Freiburg im Breisgau: Herder, 1933.

Die Griechische christliche Schriftsteller der ersten Jahrhunderte. 41 vols. Berlin: Academie Verlag, 1897-1941

Gritz, Martin. "Kirchengeschichte als Geschichte des Christenthums: Anmerkungen zur Konzeption eines christlichen Geschichtsbildes bei Johann Adam Möhler." *Zeitschrift für Kirchengeschichte* 101 (1990): 249-65.

Gross, Werner. *Der Wilhelmstift Tübingen, 1817-1869.* Tübingen: J.C.B. Mohr, 1978.

Hafen, Johann Baptist. *Möhler und Wessenberg, oder Strengkirchlichkeit und Liberalismus in der katholischen Kirche.* Ulm, 1842.

Hales, E.E.Y. *Revolution and Papacy.* Notre Dame, Ind.: University of Notre Dame Press, 1966.

Hammans, Herbert. *Die neuen Katholischen Erklärungen der Dogmenentwicklung*. Essen: Ludgerus-Verlag Hubert Wingen, 1965.

Hanssler, Bernhard. *Die Kirche in der Gesellschaft. Der Deutsche Katholizismus und seine Organisationen im 19. und 20. Jahrhundert*. Paderborn: Bonifacius, 1961.

————. "Johann Adam Möhler—Theologe der Kirche." *Hochland* 35 (1938): 17-26.

"Herbert Marshs . . . vergleichende Darstellung der protestantisch-englishen under der römisch-katholischen Kirche. . . . Aus dem Englischen übersetzt und mit Anmerkungen und Beylagen versehen, von Dr. Johann Christoph Schreiter. . . . Sulzbach . . . 1821. . . ." *Theologische Quartalschrift* 4 (1822): 60-81.

"Historisch-kritischer Versuch über die Entstehung und die frühesten Schicksale der schriftlichen Evangelien. Von D. Johann Carl Ludwig Gieseler. Leipzig 1818. . . ." *Theologische Quartalschrift* 1 (1819): 579ff.

Himmelfarb, Gertrude. *Lord Acton: A Study in Conscience and Politics*. Chicago: University of Chicago Press, 1962.

Hinze, Bradford E. *Narrating History, Developing Doctrine*. Atlanta, Ga.: Scholars Press, 1993.

Hocedez, Edgar. *Histoire de la théologie au XIXe siècle*. 3 vol. Paris: L'Edition Universelle et Desclée de Brouwer, 1948.

"Irland's Zustände alter und neuer Zeit. Von Daniel O'Connell . . . Aus dem Englischen von Dr. A. Willmann . . . 1843. "*Theologische Quartalschrift* 25 (1843): 667-78.

Kasper, Walter. *Die Lehre von der Tradition in der Römischen Schule*. Freiburg: Herder, 1962.

————. "Verständnis der Theologie damals und heute." In his *Glaube im Wandel der Geschichte*, 9-38. Mainz: Matthias Grünewald, 1973.

Koenig, Hermann. "Die Einheit der Kirche nach Joseph de Maistre und Johann Adam Möhler." *Theologische Quartalschrift* 115 (1938): 83-140.

Köhler, Joachim. "War Johann Adam Möhler (1796-1838) ein Plagiator? Beobachtungen zur Arbeitstechnik und zu den literarischen Abhänigkeiten in der Katholischen 'Tübiner historisch-kritischen Schule' des 19. Jahrhunderts." *Zeitschrift für Kirchengeschichte* 86 (1975): 186-207.

Kuhn, J.E. "Nekrolog Möhler." *Theologische Quartalschrift* 20 (1838): 576-94.

Kustermann, Abraham Peter. "'Katholische Tübinger Schule'. Beobachtungen zur Frühzeit eines theologiegeschichtlichen Begriffs." *Catholica* 36 (1982): 65-82.

————. "Der Name des Autors ist Drey: Eine unvermeidliche Vorbemerkung zum Apologet-Manuskript Johann Adam Möhlers." *Catholica* 43 (1989): 54-76.

————. "Pseudepigraphie und literarische Anleihen in der Tübinger Theologie des 19. Jahrhunderts: Ein Plädoyer für den kritischen Umgang mit Texten." *Zeitschrift für Kirchengeschichte* 101 (1990): 287-300.

Lipps, Michael A. *Dogmengeschichte als Dogmenkritik: Die Anfänge der Dogmensgeschichtsschreibung in der Zeit der Spätaufklärung*. Bern: Peter Lang, 1983.

Lösch, Stefan "J.A. Möhler und die Theologie Englands im 19. Jahrhundert." *Rottenburger Monatschrift für praktische Theologie* 6 (1922-23): 198-202; 221-27.

————. "Möhler und die Lehre von der Entwicklung des Dogmas." *Theologische Quartalschrift* 99 (1917-1918): 28-59, 129-52.

————. *Prof. Dr. Adam Gengler, 1799-1866. Die Beziehungen des Bamberger Theologen zu J.J.I. Döllinger und J.A. Möhler*. Würzburg: Schöningh in Komm, 1963.

Lynch, T. "The Newman-Perrone Paper on Development," *Gregorianum* 16 (1935): 402-47.

Madges, William. *The Core of Christian Faith: D. F. Strauss and His Catholic Critics*. New York: Peter Lang, 1987.

McCool, Gerald. *Catholic Theology in the Nineteenth Century*. New York: Seabury, 1977.

Merkle, Sebastian. "Moehler." *Historisches Jahrbuch des Goerres-Gesellschaft* 58 (1938): 249-467.

Migne, Jacques Paul, ed. *Patrologia cursus completus: Series graeca.* 161 vols. Paris: Lutetiae, 1857-1903.

Migne, Jacques Paul, ed. *Patrologia cursus completus: Series latina.* 221 vols. Paris: Lutetiae, 1844-1865.

Minon, A. "L'attitude de Jean Adam Möhler dans la question du développement du dogma." *Ephemerides Louvanienses* 16 (1939): 328-84.

Müller, Adam. *Die Lehre von Gegensatz . . . Erstes Buch.* Berlin, 1804.

Müller, Gerhard Ludwig. "Vom Leben mit dem Toten zum Leben nach dem Tod. Die Bestimmuning der Communio Sanctorum als Ort christlicher Auferstehungsbotschaft in der "Symbolik" J.A. Möhlers." *Catholica* 36 (1982): 31-48.

Müller, Max. "Die Tübingen katholische-theologische Fakultät und Württembergische Regierung vom Weg J.A. Möhlers (1835) bis zur Pensionierung J.S. Drey (1846)." *Theologische Quartalschrift* 132 (1952): 22-45; 213-33.

Mozley, Anne, ed. *Letters and Correspondence of John Henry Newman during His Life in the English Church.* London: Longmans, Green, and Co., 1898.

Neander, Augustus. *History of the Planting and Training of the Christian Church.* Translated by J.E. Ryland. Edinburgh: T. Clark, 1842.

Neander, Augustus. *The Life of St. Chrysostom.* Translated by J.C. Stapleton. London: R.B. Seely and W. Burnside, 1845.

Newman, John Henry. *An Essay on the Development of Christian Doctrine: The Edition of 1845.* Edited by J.M. Cameron. Harmondsworth: Penguin, 1974.

Newsome, David. *The Convert Cardinals: Newman and Manning.* London: John Murray, 1993.

Nichols, Aidan. *From Newman to Congar: The Idea of Doctrinal Development from the Victorians to the Second Vatican Council.* Edinburgh: T. & T. Clark, 1990.

Nichols, James Hastings, ed. *The Mercersburg Theology.* New York: Oxford University Press, 1966.

Nienaltowski, Henry Raphael. *Johann Adam Möhler's Theory of Doctrinal Development: Its Genesis and Formulation.* S.T.D. diss., The Catholic University of America, 1959 (A lengthy abstract was published in "The Catholic University of America Studies in Sacred Theology" series, no. 113 [Washington: The Catholic University of America Press, 1959]).

Nitzsch, Karl Immanuel. *Eine protestantische Beantwortung der Symbolik Möhler's.* Hamburg: F. Perthes, 1835.

O'Meara, Thomas F. *Romantic Idealism and Roman Catholicism: Schelling and the Theologians.* Notre Dame, Ind.: University of Notre Dame Press, 1982.

Padberg, Rudolf "Johann Adam Möhlers 'Literarische' Reise 1522/23." *Catholica* 42 (1988): 108-18.

Petri, Heinrich. "Katholizität in der Sicht Johann Adam Möhlers und ihre Bedeutung für den ökumenischen Dialog." *Catholica* 42 (1988): 92-107.

Pottmeyer, Hermann Josef. *Unfehlbarkeit und Souveränität: Die päpstliche Unfehlbarkeit im System der ultramontanen Ekklesiologie des 19. Jahrhunderts.* Mainz: Matthias Grünewald, 1975.

Quasten, Johannes. *Patrology.* 4 vols. Westminster, Md.: Christian Classics, 1950-1966.

Reardon, Bernard M.G. *Religion in the Age of Romanticism.* Cambridge: Cambridge University Press, 1985.

Reinhardt, Rudolf. "Bekannte und unbekannte Texte aus dem Nachlass Johann Adam Möhlers. Eine kritische Sichtung." *Catholica* 36 (1982): 49-64.

―――. "Dionysius Petavius (1583-1652) in der Tübinger Schule: Ein Bericht aus dem Nachlasz von Stefan Lösch." *Theologische Quartalschrift* 151 (1971): 160-62.

―――. "Ergänzungen und Bemerkungen zu Johann Adam Möhler Gesammelte Aktenstück und Briefe." *Zeitschrift für Kirchengeschichte* 80 (1969): 382-94.

―――. "Johann Adam Möhler und die Konversion der Malerin Emilie Linder: Ein unbekanter brief aus Möhlers Münchener Zeit." *Theologische Quartalschrift* 151 (1971): 264-68).

―――. "Die katholisch-theologische Fakultät Tübingen im 19. Jahrhundert. Faktoren und Phasen ihrer Entwicklung." In Georg Schwaiger, ed. *Kirche und Theologie im 19. Jahrhundert*, 55-87. Göttingen: Vandenhoeck und Ruprecht, 1975.

―――. "Korrespondenz aus dem nachlass Johann Sebastian von Dreys." *Theologische Quartalschrift* 149 (1969): 389-91.

―――. *Tübinger Theologen und ihre Theologie: Quellen und Forschungen zur Geschichte der Katholisch-theologischen Fakultät Tübingen*. Tübingen: J.C.B. Mohr, 1977.

―――. "Quellen zur Geschichte der Katholisch-Theologischen Fakultät Tübingen." *Theologische Quartalschrift* 149 (1969): 369-91.

―――. *Verzeichniss der gedruckten Arbeiten Johann Adam Möhler's (1796-1838)* Aus dem Nachlass Stephan Lösch (*1966) Unter Mitarbeit von Jochen Köhler und Carola Zimmermann. . . . An addendum to Georg Schwaiger, ed. *Kirche und Theologie im 19. Jahrhundert*. Göttingen: Vandenhoeck und Ruprecht, 1975.

"Reisen eines Irländers, um die whare Religion zu suchen . . . von Thomas Moore . . . übersetzt von Mortiz Lieber . . . 1840." *Theologische Quartalschrift* 23 (1841): 315-16.

Rief, Josef. *Reich Gottes und Gesellschaft nach Johann Sebastian Drey und Johann Baptist Hirscher*. Paderborn: Ferdinand Schöningh, 1965.

Rief, Josef and Max Seckler, "Eine Liste der Tübinger." *Theologische Quartalschrift* 150 (1970): 177-86.

Rieger, Reinhold. "Johann Adam Möhler—Wegbereiter der Ökumene? Ein Topos im Licht neuer Texte." *Zeitschrift für Kirchengeschichte* 101 (1990): 267-86.

―――. "Unbekannte Texte von Johann Adam Möhler: Bericht über eine Edition." *Theologische Quartalschrift* 168 (1988): 153-58.

Riga, Peter. "The Ecclesiology of Johann Adam Möhler." *Theological Studies* 22 (1961): 563-87.

"Romanism and Protestantism in Germany." *English Review* 2 (1844): 1-35.

Rothe, Richard. *Die Anfänge der christlichen Kirche und ihrer Verfassung: Beilage über die Echtheit der Ignatianischen Briefe*. Wittenberg, 1837.

Saegmueller, J.B. "Der Kirchenrechliche Anstoss zu Johann Adam Möhlers theologischer Entwicklung." *Theologische Quartalschrift* 122 (1941): 1-13.

Savon, Herve, *Johann Adam Moehler. The Father of Modern Theology*. Translated by C. McGrath. Glen Rock, N.J.: Paulist Press, 1966.

Schäfer, Philipp. *Kirche und Vernunft: Die Kirche in der katholischen Theologie der Aufklärungszeit*. Munich: Max Hueber, 1974.

Schaff, Philipp. *August Neander*. Gotha: F. A. Perthes, 1886.

―――. *Germany: Its Universities, Theology and Religion with Sketches of Distinguished German Divines of the Age*. Philadelphia: Lindsay andd Blakiston, 1857.

Scheele, Paul-Werner. *Einheit und Glaube: Johann Adam Möhlers Lehre von der Einheit der Kirche und ihre Bedeutung für die Glabensbegründung*. Munich: Ferdinand Schöningh, 1964.

―――. "Glaube und Glaubensbegründung in der Sicht Johann Adam Möhlers." *Catholica* 23 (1969): 91-111.

―――, ed. *Johann Adam Möhler*. Graz: Styria, 1969.

————. "Johann Adam Moehler." In Heinrich Fries und Georg Schwaiger, ed. *Katholische Theologen Deutschlands im 19. Jahrhundert*. Vol. 2: 70-98. 3 vols. Munich: Kösel, 1975,

Scheffczyk, Leo. "Josef Rupert Geiselmann—Weg und Werk." *Theologische Quartalschrift* 150 (1970): 385-95.

Schelling, Friederich Welhelm Joseph von. *Bruno; oder über das göttliche und natürliche Princip der Dinge. Ein Gespräch* In *Schellings Werke*. Edited by Manfred Schröter. Munich: C. H. Beck und R Oldenbourg, 1927, 3: 109-228.

Schleiermacher, Friedrich. *On Religion: Speeches to its Cultured Despisers*. Translated by John Oman. New York: Harper and Row, 1958.

Schmid, Alois von. "Der geistige Entwicklung Johann Adam Möhlers." *Historisches Jahrbuch* 18 (1897): 323-56; 572-99.

Schmitt, Carl. *Political Romanticism*. Translated by Guy Oakes. Cambridge, Mass.: MIT Press, 1986.

Schnabel, Franz. *Deutsche Geschichte im neunzehnten Jahrhundert*. 8 vols. Freiburg im Breiusgau: Herder, 1965.

Schwaiger, Georg, ed. *Kirche und Theologie im 19. Jahrhundert*. Göttingen: Vandenhoeck und Ruprecht, 1975.

A Select Library of the Nicene and Post-Nicene Fathers of the Christian Church. 28 vols. Edited by Philip Schaff and H. Wace. New York, 1886-1900.

Sicouly, Pablo. "Yves Congar und Johann Adam Möhler: Ein theologisches Gespräch zwischen den Zeiten." *Catholica* 45 (1991): 36-43.

Smart, Ninian, ed. *Nineteenth Century Religious Thought in the West*. 3 vols. Cambridge: Cambridge University Press, 1985.

Sperber, Jonathan. *Popular Catholicism in Nineteenth-Century Germany*. Princeton, N. J.: Princeton University Press, 1984.

Starck, Johann August. *Theoduls Gastmahl oder über der Vereinigung der verschiedenen christlichen Religions-Societäten*. Frankfurt am Main: J.C. Hermann, 1810.

Stockmeier, Peter. "Der Kirchenväter in der Theologie der Tübinger Schule." In J. Moeller et al., ed. *Theologie im Wandel: Festschrift zum 150jährigen Bestehung der Katholisch-theologischen Fakultät an der Universität Tübingen, 1817-1967*, 131-54. Munich, 1967.

Swidler, Leonard. *Aufklärung Catholicism, 1780-1850: Liturgical and Other Reforms in the Catholic Aufkärung*. Missoula, Mont.: Scholars Press, 1978.

Theologie in Aufbruch und Widerstreit: Die deutsche katholische Theologie im 19. Jahrhundert. Edited by Leo Scheffczyk. Bremen: Carl Schünemann, 1965.

"Theologische Zeitschrift. Herausgegeben von Dr. Friedr. Schleiermacher, Dr. W.M.L. de Wette, und Dr. Friedr. Lucke. Erstes Heft. Berlin 1819. . . ." *Theologische Quartalschrift* 2 (1820): 278-90.

Tristram, Henry. "J.A. Moehler et J.H. Newman; La pensée allemande et la renaissance catholique en Angleterre." *Revue des sciences philosophiques et théologiques* 27 (1938): 184-204.

Tüchle, Herman, ed. *Die Eine Kirche: Zum Gedenken J.A. Möhlers 1838-1938*. Paderborn: Ferdinand Schöningh, 1939.

Vermeil, Edmond. *Jean-Adam Moehler et l'ecole catholique de Tubingue. 1815-1840*. Paris: Librairie Armand Colin, 1913.

Vierneisel, Joseph. "Aus Möhlers handschriftlichem Nachlass." *Theologische Quartalschrift* 119 (1938): 109-17.

von Ruville, Albert. *Back to Holy Church: Experiences and Knowledge Acquired by a Convert*. Translated by G. Schoetensack. London: Longmans, Green, 1911.

Voss, G. "Johann Adam Möhler and the Development of Dogma." *Theological Studies* 4 (1943): 420-44.

"*Über das Verhältnis der Theologie zu Philosophie* von Adam Gengler (Landshut, 1826)." *Theologische Quartalschrift* 9 (1827): 498-522.

"*Ueber Religion und Theologie*. Eine allgemeine Grundlage der christlichen Theologie von Franz Joseph Seber, Doctor der Philsophie und Theologie, und öffentl. ordentl. Professor der Dogmatik und Moral and der katholisch-theologischen Facultät der Königl. Preussischen Universität Bonn. Köln, 1823. b. M. Du Mont-Schauberg. VIII. und 306 S. in 8." *Theologische Quartalschrift* 6 (1824): 452ff.

"Ueber die Schriften des Lukas ein kritischer Versuch von Dr. Fr. Schleiermacher. . . Erster Theil. Berlin 1817." *Theologische Quartalschrift* 1 (1819), 218-33.

Voegelin, Eric. *Science, Politics and Gnosticism*. Chicago: Henry Regnery, 1968.

"Vorträge über die in der päpstlichen Kapelle übliche Liturgie der stillen Woche; von Dr. Nicolaus Wiseman . . . übersetzt durch Joseph Maria Axinger . . . 1840." *Theologische Quartalschrift* 22 (1840): 667ff.

Wagner, Harald. "Das Amt vor dem Hintergrund der Diskussion um eine evangelisch-katholische Grunddifferenz" with a "Vorbemerkung J.A. Möhlers Darstellung der Ordination in 'Einheit', 65" *Catholica* 40 (1986): 39-58.

———. *Die eine Kirche und die viele Kirchen: Ekklesiologie und Symbolik beim jungen Möhler*. Munich: Ferdinand Schöningh, 1977.

———. "Johann Adam Möhler: Fakten und Überlegungen zu seiner Wirkungsgeschichte." *Catholica* 43 (1989): 195-208.

———. "Die Kirche und ihre Einheit in J.A. Möhlers 'Athanasius.' " In Peter Neuner und Franz Wolfinger, ed. *Auf Wegen der Versöhnung: Beiträge zum ökumenischen Gespräch*. Frankfurt am Main: Josef Knecht, 1982, 81-94.

———. "Möhler auf dem Weg zur 'Symbolik.' " *Catholica* 36 (1982): 15-30.

"Maria Ward's . . . Leben und Wirken. . . . 1840." *Theologische Quartalschrift* 23 (1841): 683-91.

[Ward, William George]. "Arnold's Sermons." *British Critic* 30 (1841): 298-364.

Welch, Claude. *Protestant Thought in the Nineteenth Century*. 2 vols. New Haven, Conn.: Yale University Press, 1972-1985.

Werner, Karl. *Geschichte der katholischen Theologie, seit dem Trienter Concil bis zur Gegenwart*. Munich: J.G. Cotta, 1866.

Wörner, Balthasar. *Johann Adam Möhler. Ein Lebensbild*. Edited by P.B. Gams. Regensburg, 1866.

Index of Holy Scripture

General Index

Abraham, 17, 53, 58, 437
Abstinence, sexual, 189
Abyss, 195
Abyssinia, 314
Acceptance, 81, 94, 96, 175, 200, 211, 227, 241, 249, 286, 352, 396, 418
Achaia, 102, 231
Acland, T.D., 63, 64
Acta Sanctorum, 416
Acton, J.E.E.D., 21, 65, 66
Acts of Andrew, 132
Adam, K., 3
Adoption, 93, 182, 272, 382
Aedesius, 314
Aeon, 195
Africa, 254, 260, 386
Agatho, Pope, 334
Alexander III, Pope, 266
Alexander, Bishop of Jerusalem, 314
Alexandria, 382
Alexandrian School, 159, 168
Alexandrians, 100, 159, 289, 386
All-father, 195
All, the, 153, 154, 168, 177, 195, 323, 384, 404
Allegorical-Mystical Interpretation, 289-96
Allegory, 5, 138, 140, 289, 290, 292-94, 296, 396, 431
Altaner, B., 69
Ambrose, 220, 256, 283, 295, 320, 421; *Commentary on Luke*, 220, 320; *On the Sacraments*, 421
Anagogy, 291
Analogy, 43, 46, 56, 59, 60, 101, 161, 202, 246, 260, 270, 301, 328, 377, 383, 407
Angels, 151, 180, 275, 303
Anglican, 64; High Church, 62, 66
Anicetus, Pope, 204, 241, 257, 258
Anselm, 56, 62, 288

Ante-Nicene, 7, 49, 52, 69
Anthropos, *See* Foreign terms
Antioch, 39, 81, 88, 92, 94, 101, 124, 144, 216, 218, 219, 233, 235, 236, 240, 244, 251, 260, 311, 312, 365, 384, 387, 406, 410
Antithesis, 20, 39, 48, 49, 118, 119, 158, 159, 195-98, 225, 232, 280, 296, 312, 367, 368. *See also* Opposition
Antonines, 105
Apelles, 115, 130, 141, 142
Apis, 192
Apollinaris, 277
Apollonius, 134, 190
Apollos, 149
Apologists, 90, 409
Apostle, 88, 93, 101, 103, 104, 113, 132, 133, 145, 146, 149, 150, 159, 183, 185, 193, 239, 256, 273, 279, 298, 303, 304, 380, 402
Apostles, 10, 13, 41, 44, 45, 54, 55, 60, 63, 81, 84-87, 90, 91, 97-109, 112-18, 120, 124-26, 128, 131, 132, 133, 136-40, 142, 163, 167, 176, 177, 187, 192, 201, 203, 204, 211, 213-17, 221-23, 226, 231, 232, 235, 236, 238-41, 248, 251, 254, 256, 257, 259, 263, 275, 276, 281, 284, 285, 289, 294, 306, 310, 313, 316, 320, 327, 335, 337, 338, 343, 347, 348, 350-52, 354, 365, 367, 368, 370, 379, 380, 384-92, 395, 396, 398, 399, 405, 413, 416, 417, 419, 425-27, 430-32, 438. *See also* Disciples
Apostolic Canons, 189, 221, 233, 234
Apostolic Constitutions, 131, 132, 189, 219, 224-26, 233, 234, 406
Apostolic period, general reference to, 40, 45, 46, 54, 55, 61, 86, 99-101, 104-7, 109, 112, 115, 116,